The 19 papers in this volume — a small sample of George Zodrow's contributions to the theory and practice of taxation in five areas — exhibit the traits we expect to find in his work: comprehensive coverage of topics, thorough knowledge of both prior literature and policy context, penetrating analysis of issues, and innovative thinking. His theoretical investigations are motivated by a desire to solve important practical problems. Conversely, his discussions of practical problems of taxation are informed — indeed, underpinned — by sound theoretical analysis. As a body, these papers show why Zodrow is one of the leading tax policy economists of his generation.

Charles E. McLure, Jr.,
Senior Fellow (Emeritus),
Hoover Institution, Stanford University

These essays by George Zodrow offer deep insight on many of the most challenging and long-standing questions in public finance. They advance our understanding of consumption versus income taxation, of the problem of tax design when jurisdictions compete for revenue, and of the economic effects of property taxation. They are collectively a "how to guide" in using powerful analytical tools to address fundamental problems of tax design, and they deliver important lessons for both practitioners and researchers.

James M. Poterba,
Mitsui Professor, MIT, and
President, National Bureau of Economic Research

George Zodrow's research contributions are many and varied, and are not easily summed up in a few sentences. He has established himself in the front rank of scholars in public economics — and in public policy. His work on optimal tax reform was truly pathbreaking. He has pioneered many real-world applications of tax reform in his work on income tax reforms and consumption tax reforms (including his development of the notion of a "hybrid" consumption tax). He has also made important contributions to state and local tax issues, especially with his analyses of property tax incidence and of tax competition. In all of his work, he has demonstrated exceptional theoretical and empirical skills, along with an uncanny ability to explain complicated issues in a way that is accessible to everyone. George is widely seen as one of the pre-eminent experts on many aspects of public economics, and his published papers — many of which are collected in this volume — are essential readings for anyone working on those issues.

James Alm,
Chair and Professor of Economics,
Tulane University

This book offers a rich set of George Zodrow's works that have dramatically impacted both academic and policy thinking for decades. His work (with Peter Mieszkowski) interpreting the property tax as a capital tax revolutionized how we analyze the property tax and subnational government behavior alike. More broadly, he makes remarkable contributions to appropriate reform across many taxes and for different types of governments. George's insights are worthy reading for everyone with an interest in how to enhance the tax system.

William F. Fox,
Boyd Distinguished Professor of Business, University of Tennessee,
and Director, Boyd Center for Business and Economic Research

TAXATION IN THEORY AND PRACTICE

Selected Essays of George R. Zodrow

Ophelia,

Only two years old and you already have a World Series championship and a book dedicated to you. You must be amazing!

Love you,

Papa 2019

TAXATION IN THEORY AND PRACTICE

Selected Essays of George R. Zodrow

George R. Zodrow
Rice University, USA

World Scientific

NEW JERSEY • LONDON • SINGAPORE • BEIJING • SHANGHAI • HONG KONG • TAIPEI • CHENNAI • TOKYO

Published by

World Scientific Publishing Co. Pte. Ltd.
5 Toh Tuck Link, Singapore 596224
USA office: 27 Warren Street, Suite 401-402, Hackensack, NJ 07601
UK office: 57 Shelton Street, Covent Garden, London WC2H 9HE

Library of Congress Cataloging-in-Publication Data
Names: Zodrow, George R., author.
Title: Taxation in theory and practice : selected essays of George R Zodrow /
George R Zodrow (Rice University, USA).
Description: 1 Edition. | New Jersey : World Scientific, [2020] |
Includes bibliographical references.
Identifiers: LCCN 2019020052 | ISBN 9789811205132
Subjects: LCSH: Taxation. | Property tax. | Capital levy.
Classification: LCC HJ2305 .Z63 2019 | DDC 336--dc23
LC record available at https://lccn.loc.gov/2019020052

British Library Cataloguing-in-Publication Data
A catalogue record for this book is available from the British Library.

For any available supplementary material, please visit
https://www.worldscientific.com/worldscibooks/10.1142/11407#t=suppl

Desk Editors: Shreya Gopi/Ong Shi Min Nicole

Typeset by Stallion Press
Email: enquiries@stallionpress.com

Printed in Singapore

To the dream team of incredible ladies that has guided,
inspired, and loved me over the years:
Ada, Dorey, Katherine, Laura, and now Ophelia

Contents

Foreword

George Zodrow is an excellent applied theorist who has contributed significantly to the basic understanding of tax systems. His research has explored essential questions about the design of tax systems at different levels of government. This valuable book collects 19 of George's most original and influential contributions. The important chapters in this book deal with issues such as the following: Should capital be taxed when this factor is highly mobile between regions? Should the reform of existing tax systems be carried out instantaneously or gradually? What are the advantages and disadvantages of substituting a broad-based consumption tax for an income tax?

George is eclectic and versatile in his research style. He relies both on simple models that yield clear-cut results and on more complicated systems which are simulated with specific parameter values to analyze the effects of various tax policies. In addition, he is the author of several valuable overview papers. Some of these set out arguments for and against various tax reform proposals; others summarize broad theoretical and empirical literatures.

Another aspect of his contributions appears in this book as two joint chapters with Charles McLure. George has consulted extensively on the design of tax policy for several developing countries, and one of these joint chapters concern a new system of taxation they proposed in Bolivia. Similarly, he has worked at the U.S. Treasury, where he contributed to the Treasury proposal that was the foundation for the comprehensive tax reform enacted in 1986. The chapter he and Charlie wrote from this experience is two insiders' intriguing summary of how the original Treasury proposal was conceived and what remained of the proposal after political considerations intervened in shaping the final legislation.

When a tax system is revised and the new taxes are capitalized into different asset classes, the changes induce arbitrary gains and losses. Martin Feldstein, who was among the first to recognize this problem, suggested that one way of reducing such arbitrary gains and losses is to first announce the tax reform and then postpone its enactment. George then studied these issues more systematically, using an analytical framework that allowed the efficiency effects of the reform to be weighed against the arbitrary wealth redistributions. He demonstrated that, contrary to Feldstein's conclusions, in the absence of adjustment costs, the optimal strategy is to introduce the reform immediately but partially. George later extended this work, introducing various types of adjustment costs and analyzing the possible use of grandfathering as a means of transforming losers into winners. Considering a specific tax system revision, he was the first to investigate formally the "carryover problem" associated with the imposition of a consumption tax that would double tax savings initially financed with after-tax dollars under an income tax. He concluded that the optimal reform policy would be to phase in the consumption tax in place of the income tax.

I have had the pleasure of working with George on numerous papers over the years. The most influential of these collaborative efforts is part of this collection. Published in 1986, this paper laid the foundation for a large literature on tax competition among local, state, and national governments, a literature that is growing steadily even now, more than three decades after we wrote our paper. In this paper, of which George is distinctly the senior author, we formalized the intuition that reliance on a local property tax will lead to under-provision of local public goods once policy makers recognize that capital, which is perfectly mobile between communities, will be driven out by the tax. Our formulation has often been described as the standard workhorse model of tax competition, and it has been generalized in a large number of directions.

George and I have also written several papers on the incidence of the local property tax. In one of the chapters in this book, we constructed a model that extended my earlier work on the property tax to include most of the characteristics of the Tiebout model of local governments. As in the earlier paper, our model shows that capital bears the burden of a local property tax system. This result implies that the benefit view of the property tax, which maintains that the tax is paid by the consumers of local public services, is valid only when local zoning is so precise that a resident household or firm must invest a specific amount of capital in a jurisdiction to have their taxes match their benefits. George has insightfully reviewed the debate on property tax incidence in a number of papers, including one in this book. He has also refined this theory by developing a model which shows that the capitalization of intrajurisdictional property tax differentials is consistent with both the "capital tax" and "benefit tax" views, countering the claims of proponents of the benefit view that such capitalization provides compelling evidence in favor of their interpretation of the incidence of the tax.

George has also been a major contributor to the analysis of taxes on consumption. By my count, he has written approximately 40 papers on various aspects of consumption taxation, 6 of which are included in this book. These papers suggest the breadth of his work in this area. One deals with the general case in favor of a broad-based consumption tax. Another argues for the equivalence of two alternative forms of direct consumption taxes in the presence of uncertainty. Others discuss the treatment of financial instruments under consumption taxes, transitional issues related to changes in the price of housing and other assets, and the appropriate excise taxation of electronic commerce.

This book of important papers is a capstone to George Zodrow's distinguished research career. What they reveal is a thinker who works repeatedly on the analysis of practical and concrete applications. The motivating force behind these articles is the conviction that for government to tax appropriately, systems of taxation must be profoundly understood. This book is a giant step in that direction.

Peter Mieszkowski
Professor Emeritus, Rice University

Introduction: Taxation in Theory and Practice — Selected Essays of George R. Zodrow

I have been privileged to spend my entire academic career at my undergraduate alma mater, Rice University, which has provided an ideal environment for me to teach and conduct my research, focusing on issues related to taxation at the national, state and local, and international levels. Like most economists in academia, my early research was primarily theoretical in nature. However, sparked in large part by a year spent at the U.S. Department of the Treasury during the preparation of the two reports that led to the much-celebrated Tax Reform Act of 1986 (TRA86) as well as numerous subsequent tax policy consulting projects, my work took a more applied bent that is reflected in some of the more recent publications included in this book. Finally, I have in recent years worked on computable general equilibrium (CGE) models, both to simulate the macroeconomic and distributional effects of tax reforms in the United States and to simulate theoretical models to gauge the relative importance of various results.

My research on the theory and practice of taxation can be organized into five general areas: (1) optimal tax reform, or an analysis of the best ways to implement tax reforms taking into account the thorny transitional issues they raise, (2) consumption-based taxes, including the economic effects of replacing the current income tax with a progressive consumption tax such as the Bradford X-Tax or a multi-rate expenditure tax, (3) income tax reform, both in the United States and in developing countries, (4) state and local tax policy, including especially the effects of the local property tax, and (5) tax competition, using models of interjurisdictional competition that are applicable at both the state and local and the international levels. The remainder of this introduction to my research is organized around these five general themes.

1. Optimal Tax Reform: Transitional Issues in Implementing Tax Reforms

I was fortunate indeed to have as my dissertation advisers at Princeton two of the most eminent — and most congenial — denizens of the world of public finance, David Bradford and Wally Oates; I could not have completed my graduate work without their expert guidance and wise counsel. My dissertation and some subsequent research built on a seminal paper by Martin Feldstein (1976b) who first developed the theory of optimal tax reform, an important extension of the much more widely known theory of optimal tax design. While the latter constructs optimal tax structures under the implicit assumption that the tax system is being designed on a "clean slate," Feldstein argued that in reality tax reform involves changing an existing tax structure, which results in largely capricious and thus inequitable reform-induced windfall gains and losses, given that individuals and firms have made significant commitments based on the existing tax system. As a result, enacting a tax reform will differentially impact otherwise equally-situated individuals depending on how they responded to the existing tax structure. For example, elimination of the home mortgage interest deduction would differentially impact homeowners and renters living in similar homes, and elimination of the tax exemption for state and local bonds would differentially impact the owners of corporate and subnational government bonds.

Feldstein argues that such reform-induced horizontal inequities are a serious problem. He recommends postponed full enactment — current enactment of the full reform but with a postponed enactment date — as a means of reducing the magnitudes of the windfall gains and losses caused by the reform, although at the cost of delaying the attainment of the gains associated with the reform.

1.1. *Optimal implementation of tax reform*

In my dissertation research, I extended Feldstein's analysis to consider alternative ways of implementing desirable tax reforms. While Feldstein assumed a policy of postponed full enactment, I approached the issue as a government optimization problem — what is the best way to implement a desirable tax reform (e.g., full or partial enactment, immediate or delayed/phased-in implementation)? The resulting "optimal tax reform" problem is formulated as choosing the method of implementing reform to maximize a social welfare function that is an aggregation of the gains and losses caused by the reform. In this formulation, the gains are weighted less than proportionately and the losses are weighted more than proportionately, with the extent of the weighting captured by a parameter that defines the curvature of the social welfare function. The aggregation of gains and losses captures the efficiency gains associated with implementing the reform, while the weighting reflects the government's aversion to the inequities associated with capricious reform-induced redistributions of income.

I applied the analysis to the case where a metropolitan government, facing property tax differentials across two jurisdictions in the metropolitan area while providing a pure public good to all residents of the area, introduces a policy of metropolitan tax base sharing and rate equalization (such as that utilized in the Minneapolis–St. Paul area at the time); such a reform not only results in efficiency gains but also causes large redistributions of income as the property tax changes are capitalized as windfall gains and losses in metropolitan land values.

The main results of the analysis are two-fold. First, the unconstrained optimal policy is "immediate partial enactment" — immediate implementation of less than full enactment of the reform. The intuition underlying this result is that the efficiency losses associated with tax differentials increase more than proportionately with the size of the differential. As a result, it is desirable to implement some reform immediately to capture the efficiency gains from reducing these differentials to some extent as soon as possible. However, full enactment of the reform is not desirable because with continued movement toward equalization of tax rates, the efficiency gains from the reform become smaller while the associated gains and losses, which are subject to the weighting described above, become ever larger; moreover, further delayed partial enactment is not desirable because delay reduces the efficiency gains and reform-induced redistributions proportionately, so that if partial reform is desirable it should be implemented immediately. The second result is that if the government is constrained to eventual full enactment of reform, the optimal phase-in policy is immediate partial enactment.

These results were presented in my Princeton dissertation, which won the 1980 National Tax Association (NTA) Annual Competition for Outstanding Doctoral Dissertations in Government Finance and Taxation (Zodrow, 1980). The results on the optimal implementation of tax reform were published in 1981 in the *National Tax Journal* (Chapter 1 of this book), while related results analyzing the incidence of the reform involving metropolitan tax base sharing and rate equalization were published in the *Journal of Urban Economics* (Zodrow, 1984).

1.2. *Adjustment costs, grandfather rules, and other aspects of optimal tax reform*

I extended my work on optimal tax reform in several ways over the next few years. In an article published in 1985 in the *Journal of Public Economics* (Chapter 2), I added adjustment costs to my model of the optimal implementation of tax reform, an extension that is realistic but significantly complicates the results. These results are summarized as follows. First, if adjustment costs are concave, immediate one-step partial enactment is still the optimal policy, since spreading reform out over several periods only increases the amount of adjustment costs incurred. Second, in the more commonly assumed case of convex adjustment costs, the results depend on the level of adjustment costs, with larger adjustment costs implying longer delays in the enactment of reform in order to delay such costs. Specifically, immediate partial enactment is optimal for modest adjustment costs, phased-in partial enactment is optimal with intermediate adjustment costs, and postponed partial enactment is optimal with sufficiently large adjustment costs. Some numerical simulation results, however, suggest that the gains from phased-in or delayed enactment, relative to the policy of one-step immediate partial enactment, are small.

A second paper examines the role that grandfather rules — which specify exemptions from the effects of reform for existing investments — play in the theory of optimal tax reform (Chapter 3). This paper shows that grandfather rules can in principle be a very effective tax reform implementation tool, redistributing the gains from reform more equitably, and in some cases even converting a reform into a Pareto-improving tax change. However, the analysis also shows that grandfather rules should be used with caution because market adjustments often imply that reform-induced losses are relatively small so that little grandfathering is needed, and because inappropriately structured grandfather rules can cause efficiency losses to be the net result of an otherwise efficiency-enhancing reform.

A third extension shows that phasing-in of reform is likely to be the optimal implementation policy in the case of intergenerational reform-induced redistributions where the implementation of a tax reform, such as the enactment of a cash-flow consumption tax, would result in the taxation of income that had already been taxed under the pre-reform regime (Zodrow, 1986). In Zodrow (1985), I compared my "optimal tax reform" analysis of the desirability of immediate partial enactment of reform to a complementary analysis by Hettich (1979), which evaluates the partial enactment of reform using an "equitable taxation" framework based on the assumption that deviations from an ideal comprehensive income tax base are undesirable but immediate movement to such a tax base is impossible due to political considerations, administrative costs, or other unspecified factors.

1.3. *Simulating the transitional effects of tax reform*

Finally, in recent years I have had the distinct pleasure of working with my former graduate student, John Diamond — now the Kelly Fellow in Public Finance at the Baker Institute for Public Policy at Rice and the director of the Institute's Center for Public Finance — on numerous studies simulating the macroeconomic and distributional effects of implementing tax reforms in the United States. These analyses use a large-scale dynamic overlapping generations CGE model that we have constructed (Zodrow and Diamond, 2013; Diamond and Zodrow, 2015). The model is especially well suited to analyzing the transitional effects of implementing tax reforms, as it tracks the effects of reforms in each year following enactment on all current and future generations, as well as 12 lifetime income groups within each generation, and explicitly calculates the effects of reform on asset values.

For example, in an article from Diamond and Zodrow (2008) (Chapter 4), we use the model to analyze the transitional effects, including changes in the prices of business assets and owner-occupied and rental housing, of a reform involving a move from the current income tax to a consumption-based tax — an issue that I have also examined in Sarkar and Zodrow (1993) and Zodrow (1997a, 2002). John and I have also used our model to investigate a wide variety of other tax policy issues (e.g., Diamond and Zodrow, 2007, 2013, 2014, 2018; Diamond *et al.*, 2014). In addition, various versions of our model have been used by the U.S. Department of the Treasury (President's Advisory Panel on Federal Tax Reform, 2005) and the Joint Committee on Taxation (2005, 2017), and we recently participated in a project examining Social Security reform under the auspices of the Congressional Budget Office (Nelson and Phillips, 2019).

2. Consumption Taxation

My paper with John described above provides a natural segue to the next area of my research, which involves the analysis of various taxes that are based on consumption rather than income. My interest in consumption taxation dates back to my graduate school days at Princeton where David Bradford was my advisor. Dave had just returned from a two-year stint at the U.S. Department of the Treasury where he served as Deputy Assistant Secretary for Tax Policy and directed the preparation of the highly acclaimed *Blueprints for Basic Tax Reform* which was released in 1977 (and later republished as *Bradford and the U.S. Treasury Tax Policy Staff*, 1984). That book carefully and compellingly develops the case for replacing the income tax with one of two options for direct taxation on the basis of consumption: (1) a "tax post-paid" version with a deduction for saving coupled with full taxation of all withdrawals from saving (similar to current traditional IRAs), or (2) a "tax pre-paid" version with no deduction for saving but full exemption of dividends, capital gains and interest income (similar to current Roth IRAs). In both cases, the corporate income tax would be replaced with some form of business-level cash-flow tax that allows expensing of all business-related purchases (rather than the deductions for depreciation allowed under an income tax).

2.1. *Direct consumption-based taxation of capital income*

In addition to my research on the transitional issues raised by a move to a consumption-based tax cited above, I have published numerous papers examining various aspects of consumption taxation. This includes a paper that was part of a Brookings Institution/Urban Institute conference volume on *Taxing Capital Income* (Aaron *et al.*, 2007) in which I examine the arguments for consumption-based taxation of capital income on efficiency grounds, in terms of both horizontal and vertical equity, and with respect to simplicity in compliance and administration (Chapter 5). My general conclusion is that a strong case can be made for a consumption tax reform in all of these dimensions, but that many of these advantages could easily be muted if relatively "pure" proposals for such reforms are modified to accommodate a variety of real-world complications and political pressures, including extensive transition rules and a highly progressive rate structure, and as the details of more fully specified proposals are developed. Other papers that examine issues related to consumption based direct taxation include Zodrow (1990, 1997b, 2002/2003, 2003a).

Another important dimension of the consumption tax debate is whether moving to a direct consumption-based tax would be a suitable reform for a developing country, especially one that already uses an indirect consumption-based tax in the form of a value-added tax (VAT). I have participated in international tax consulting projects in a wide variety of developing countries (from Aruba to Zambia, as I used to tell my daughters[1]) since the late 1980s and many of these explored various consumption tax options.

[1]The tax reform project in Aruba was certainly one of the most pleasant, as my wife and younger daughter Laura accompanied me and we had a wonderful time enjoying the sand and sea as well as "jeeping" the hidden roads of the gorgeous island. Indeed, on our way

Many of these projects were with Charles McLure, my long-time advisor, mentor, and hiking buddy, dating back to my days as an undergraduate mechanical engineering and economics double major at Rice. Charlie introduced me to the world of international tax policy advising through a project in Colombia that he warned me might be the best one of my career; we met almost daily with the Finance Minister and were hired directly by the government of Colombia, which was deeply interested in investigating the possibilities of implementing either a consumption-based direct tax system or fully indexing their income tax system for inflation. Although the Colombians ultimately took the latter approach, our group also developed a detailed consumption tax option (McLure *et al.*, 1990) that they considered seriously as well.

Charlie and I developed the case for a direct consumption-based tax in the context of a developing country in a lengthy article published in the *Tax Law Review* (Zodrow and McLure, 1991). Although many of the arguments were similar to those made in Chapter 5, several factors made the consumption tax option especially appealing for developing countries. For example, because administrative resources are so scarce in developing countries, the simplicity advantages of a direct consumption tax are especially appealing, particularly if the business tax is designed to be similar in structure to an already existing VAT. The properties of a business cash-flow tax — applying a marginal effective tax rate of zero to new investment but taxing economic rents at the statutory rate under the tax — are also appealing to a developing country that wants to encourage new foreign direct investment while also taxing the economic rents earned by investments in any natural resources (Echavarría and Zodrow, 2005). In addition, any concerns about the implications for vertical equity of a consumption-based tax can in many cases be addressed with reforms of an existing wealth tax or estate/inheritance tax.

Charlie and I further explored options for consumption-based tax reform in Bolivia, another fascinating project in which we met often with President Gonzalo Sánchez de Lozada, who had a degree in economics from the University of Chicago and had developed an abiding interest in

---

home Laura let me know that she hoped I had made at least one "big mistake" in my report — so that we would have to return to Aruba and fix it!

direct consumption taxes after reading Hall and Rabushka's classic book *The Flat Tax*, published in 1995. As part of this project, we developed a "hybrid" consumption tax plan, which combined a pre-paid tax at the individual level (which ignores capital income and loans) with a business-level cash-flow tax that included cash-flow treatment of loans (which includes the proceeds of loans in the tax base and allows full deductions for repayments of principal and interest). In an article that appeared in *International Tax and Public Finance* (Chapter 6), we make the case for this particular approach to consumption-based taxation, arguing that it is preferable on administrative and economic grounds to either of the "pure" alternatives (see also McLure and Zodrow, 1996b).

In any case, the Bolivian government ultimately decided (on two separate occasions, first for a corporate tax and later for a tax on investment in their natural resources sector) against implementing a consumption-based direct tax option. Their primary concern — which we always knew would be a troublesome issue — was that the U.S. Internal Revenue Service (IRS) would rule that a business cash-flow tax would not be eligible for foreign tax credits against the domestic tax liability of U.S.-based multinationals. Such treatment would be highly undesirable, as above-normal returns to investment would be subject to double taxation (recall that normal returns are exempt from tax under the business cash-flow tax so that double taxation problems arise only for above-normal returns). Extended discussions with representatives from the IRS and the Treasury Department generally confirmed this fear, and the Bolivians abandoned their attempts to implement any form of cash-flow tax.

2.2. *The creditability of consumption-based business taxes*

Charlie and I discussed this unfortunate result in which U.S. policy effectively precluded reforms that were otherwise deemed desirable in an article published in the *National Tax Journal* (McLure and Zodrow, 1998). That article presented the economic case for allowing creditability for cash-flow taxes, arguing that such treatment was appropriate under current law at that time, under either the fairly general wording of the statute or the mechanical tests applied to implement the regulations (see also McLure and Zodrow, 1996a).

More recently, we revisited this issue in an article with noted public finance expert Jack Mintz that was published in *International Tax and Public Finance* in 2015 (Chapter 7). This article further develops and extends arguments made in an *amici curiae* brief (Altshuler *et al.*, 2012) presented to the Supreme Court of the United States supporting a suit by a U.S. company, PPL and its subsidiaries, against the IRS. The PPL case concerned a one-time retroactive "Windfall Tax" levied by the British government on 32 public utilities that were privatized between 1984 and 1996. The terms of the privatization agreements stipulated that for an "initial period" of typically about four years the privatized firms were not subject to rate regulation other than being precluded from raising prices. The firms were quite effective in improving the efficiency of their operations and earned substantial profits over their "initial periods" even with constant prices, which in turn gave rise to demands for taxation of the "excess profits" that were argued to be attributable to privatized values that were too low. When the Labour government took power in 1997, it introduced a "Windfall Tax" designed to achieve this goal, levied on the difference between two calculated values — the "value in profit-making terms" and a lower "flotation value" which was the privatization value. Fairly straightforward manipulation of the tax formula shows that it is effectively an excess profits tax, which would normally be creditable under IRS regulations.

The IRS, however, ruled that the "Windfall Tax" was not creditable because the original formulation of the tax was not consistent with an excess profits tax, arguing that the mathematical manipulations that converted it to an excess profits tax were "irrelevant and immaterial." The Court ruled unanimously for PPL, concluding that it was the economic substance of the tax and not its form (the difference between the two stated values rather than an explicit definition of excess profits) that determined whether the tax should be creditable.

In our paper, we argue that there are three reasons why the Court's decision in the PPL case — that economic substance rather than legislative form determines creditability — suggests that cash-flow taxes should be creditable. First, although cash-flow taxes typically do not allow the deductions for interest expense commonly associated with a creditable income tax, the fact that they allow expensing (immediate deduction) of purchases of depreciable assets rather than deductions for depreciation more than offsets the lack of interest deductions. Second, cash-flow taxes are economically equivalent to allowance for corporate equity taxes that have been deemed creditable by the IRS. Third, because cash-flow taxes exempt normal returns to investment but tax above-normal returns at the statutory rate, they are equivalent to excess profits taxes — in which case the logic of the PPL case implies they should be creditable. We conclude that cash-flow taxes should be creditable against the domestic tax liability of U.S. multinationals, thus, as discussed previously, removing an obstacle that has precluded numerous countries from adopting such taxes.

2.3. *Uncertainty and the choice of a consumption tax base*

Another issue that has arisen in many discussions of direct consumption tax reforms is the form such taxes should take at the individual level. As discussed previously, the two primary candidates are the "tax post-paid" or "individual cash flow" (ICF) approach under which savings are deductible while withdrawals of both principal and interest are fully taxable, and the "individual tax prepayment" (ITP) approach under which savings are not deductible (hence the tax is "pre-paid") but all returns and return of principal are untaxed.

It is straightforward to show that with certain returns, the two approaches are equivalent in present value terms (e.g., Zodrow and McLure, 1991). However, some observers have argued that the two approaches are quite different in the presence of uncertain returns to investment, as above-normal returns are taxed under the ICF approach but not under the ITP approach (U.S. Department of the Treasury, 1977; Graetz, 1979), arguably implying that the latter approach is fundamentally unfair. In contrast, using numerical examples, other observers have argued that this distinction is largely irrelevant, as investors under the ICF approach will recognize that the government is a silent partner in their investments that shares in both risk and reward and increase the size of their investments so that the after-tax outcomes are identical under both the ICF and ITP approaches.

In an article published in the *Journal of Public Economics* in 1985, I provide a formal proof of the equivalence of the ICF and ITP approaches under uncertainty, responding to two papers by Ahsan (1989, 1990) in which he argues that the ICF and ITP approaches are equivalent only if above-normal returns are included in the ITP tax base, consistent with the Treasury and Graetz positions noted above. Specifically, I show that Ahsan's results are obtained only if one assumes that the government can assume risk costlessly. In contrast, numerous researchers stress that the government cannot absorb the risk associated with uncertain revenue flows costlessly; for example, Gordon (1985, pp. 5–6) concludes that "risk in government tax revenues is as costly to bear as private risks" since the government bears the risks of "random tax rates on other income, random government expenditures, or random government deficits."

Specifically, I show that, within the context of Ahsan's model, if the government discounts future revenues under the ICF tax at the average rate of return to saving in the economy (rather than the riskless rate of return assumed by Ahsan), the ICF and ITP approaches are fully equivalent even in the presence of uncertainty. This result is of considerable practical significance, since proponents of the ITP approach commonly stress its simplicity advantages over the ICF approach, as only the former excludes capital income from the tax base. By comparison, the ITP approach extended to include above-normal returns in the tax base as recommended by Ahsan would be even more complicated than the ICF approach (since above-normal returns would have to be identified), eliminating an important advantage of the ITP approach. My analysis suggests that such a complication is unnecessary.

2.4. *Optimal taxation of electronic commerce*

My final paper under the consumption taxation heading examines a completely different topic: the optimal excise taxation of electronic commerce. The central issue considered is whether optimal commodity taxation considerations might provide a rationale for preferential treatment of electronic commerce — for example, because the individuals who purchase goods over the Internet tend to be highly price responsive (Fox and Murray, 1997; Goolsbee, 2000). I examine this issue in a paper that was published in 2006 in the *National Tax Journal* (Chapter 9).

In this paper, I extend the standard optimal commodity taxation model to consider several factors relevant to the taxation of electronic commerce. These include the following: (1) multiple goods that are close substitutes in their physical attributes, but less than perfect substitutes because they differ in terms of their mode of purchase and other attributes such as ease of shopping, purchase and return, ability to "touch and feel" the good, and delivery costs, times and uncertainties, etc.; (2) distributional concerns; (3) goods that are exempt from commodity taxation for social, political, or administrative reasons; (4) a subgroup of individuals who purchase goods over the Internet, with the demand for such goods exhibiting a relatively high own-price elasticity; and (5) differentially high costs of administering and complying with sales taxation of goods purchased over the Internet.

The paper includes both a theoretical analysis and a broad range of simulations calculating the relative optimal commodity tax rate that should be applied to electronic commerce under various circumstances. Not surprisingly, the results indicate that the optimal tax treatment of traditional and electronic commerce varies considerably depending on key parameter values, implying that electronic commerce should receive preferential tax treatment in some cases and be subject to relatively high tax rates in others. Nevertheless, the results suggest that uniform tax treatment of traditional and electronic commerce is much more likely to be desirable than tax exemption or a significant tax preference for electronic commerce.

In particular, in none of the cases analyzed does the optimal tax rate approach zero, with the largest "optimal" tax preference for electronic commerce on the order of 30 percent, and many much less than that. A key factor leading to prescriptions for moderate preferential treatment of sales over the Internet is relatively high administrative and compliance costs, lending some credence to the argument that uniform taxation is much more likely to be desirable if advances in computer software or simplification efforts are successful in reducing the costs of administering and complying with taxation of Internet sales. Moreover, differentially higher taxation of electronic commerce is also optimal in a variety of cases, with distributional concerns playing an especially large role in prescribing relatively high tax rates on Internet goods, and in some cases resulting in surtaxes in the neighborhood of 35–40 percent.

The simplest characterization of the results presented in this paper is that the optimal tax rates on electronic commerce tend to cluster around the rate applied to traditional commerce. Thus, on balance, it seems clear that tax exemption of Internet goods is very unlikely to be even close to optimal, and the optimal differentials calculated in this analysis suggest that it is unlikely that the traditional prescription of uniform taxation should be over ridden by optimal taxation concerns, especially once the administrative and political difficulties of implementing differential taxation are taken into account.

3. Income Tax Reform

A significant portion of my work, including some related to international tax policy consulting, has focused on reforms of the income tax rather than the more ambitious approach of replacing the income tax with a consumption-based direct tax. Some of the most interesting work was related to the time I spent at the U.S. Department of the Treasury working on "Treasury I" and "Treasury II," the two reports that were the precursors to the TRA86 that is still widely hailed as the best example of tax reform — if not government policy making (Blinder, 2018) — to have been accomplished in the U.S. in recent years.

I was very fortunate to be asked to participate in this momentous project by Charlie McLure, who was the Deputy Assistant Secretary for Tax Analysis at the time. I especially enjoyed the opportunity to interact with the outstanding tax economists in the Treasury Office of Tax Analysis, including (but by no means limited to) Gene Steuerle, George Carlin, Tom Neubig, Jerry Auten, and Paul Wilson, as well as the driving force behind the project, attorney Ronald Pearlman, who was the Assistant Secretary for Tax Policy. It was a truly formative experience to explore the amazingly wide range of topics addressed in the "fundamental tax reform project" with the talented and incredibly hard-working individuals at the Office of Tax Analysis — an experience that shaped my research career for many years to come. My time at the Treasury was not without its ironies, including the time I worked with Treasury economist Susie Nelson until 4:00 a.m. one morning just before Treasury I was released, writing the chapter on why we decided *not* to take the consumption tax route toward fundamental tax reform, as well as the fact that my "boss" at the end of my stay, Secretary of the Treasury James A. Baker III, is now the namesake of the Rice University Baker Institute for Public Policy where I am a Faculty Scholar.

3.1. *Treasury I and the Tax Reform Act of 1986*

One of my favorite papers is Chapter 10 in this book, an article that Charlie and I published in 1987 in the premier issue of the *Journal of Economic Perspectives*, which analyzes the fundamental tax reform project, comparing the recommendations made in Treasury I with the final provisions actually enacted in TRA86.[2] We began this paper by identifying several critical initial decisions made during the formulation of Treasury I, including the decisions to pursue a sweeping fundamental reform of the income tax structure with a focus on promoting investment neutrality and eliminating the opportunities for tax shelters that plagued the existing tax system, while meeting the twin constraints of revenue and distributional neutrality. Indeed, these latter two constraints resulted in a highly disciplined process, as the designers of the tax reform package were forced to make difficult trade-offs to maintain revenue and distributional neutrality (and the absence of similar constraints in the development of the recent Tax Cuts and Jobs Act enacted in 2017 implied that it was a much less successful reform than its storied predecessor).

However, another constraint imposed early in the process was much less felicitous. Specifically, a few months into the tax reform process, in response to pressure from the National Association of Realtors, President Reagan promised that mortgage interest would continue to be fully deductible under any tax reform proposal. This effectively ensured that investment neutrality could not be attained under any fundamental income tax reform package since investment in housing would remain tax preferred relative to other investments. Moreover, the case for imposing full income taxation on non-housing investment under the principle of taxing all real economic income was much weaker if the income from housing was largely untaxed. The architects of Treasury I decided to

[2] See also McLure and Zodrow (1994), which examines the impact of academic tax theory on the "real world" process of tax reform.

continue to pursue the goal of taxing all of the real economic income generated by non-housing investment — but certainly recognized the problems implied by not extending this treatment to investment in owner-occupied housing.[3]

We then turned to a detailed analysis of each of the key provisions of Treasury I and how they were altered under TRA86. Since space considerations preclude a discussion of each of these items, I will simply discuss our two main general conclusions.

First, we concluded that although TRA86 was justly viewed as a "political miracle," it was nevertheless disappointing that many of the provisions of Treasury I that were integral parts of a coherent system painstakingly designed to measure real economic income as accurately as possible (e.g., deductions for economic depreciation that were indexed for inflation) were jettisoned during the process leading up to TRA86 and replaced with various ad hoc provisions (e.g., accelerated depreciation deductions). In particular, the deviations from the accurate measurement of real economic income were sufficiently problematical under TRA86 that it had to maintain the "backstop" individual and corporate alternative minimum taxes — provisions that significantly complicate compliance with and administration of the tax system and indicate fundamental problems with the tax system; these provisions would have been unnecessary under Treasury I. It seems clear that even though an income tax system that reasonably approximates a tax on real economic income is complex, the deviations from such a system that were enacted under TRA86 resulted in even more complexity.

Second, we wondered whether the experience with the development of TRA86 suggests that it is simply too difficult to enact a tax system that is reasonably consistent with the Treasury I goal of imposing a tax on real economic income, and whether one of the consumption-based direct tax options discussed in the previous section might be a preferable approach.[4]

---

[3] Moreover, the problems associated with maintaining the mortgage interest deduction were exacerbated by the subsequent decision to provide for inflation indexing of deductions for interest expense, which had the effect of reducing deductions for interest expense for non-housing investment, while leaving intact full deductions for interest expense on investment in owner-occupied housing.

[4] Charlie elaborated on this point in a provocative paper that inquired whether TRA86 represented the "death throes of the income tax" (McLure, 1988).

Although consumption-based taxes are not without their problems — including the issues related to the treatment of gifts and bequests, the transition from an income tax, and the international complications stressed in Treasury I — we concluded by noting that they were certainly worthy of further consideration as an alternative approach to fundamental tax reform.[5] As suggested in the previous section, the debate regarding the relative merits of income-based and consumption-based taxation continues to this day.

3.2. *The windfall recapture tax*

As is well known, TRA86 provided for dramatic reductions in both the top corporate income tax rate, which was reduced from 48 percent to 34 percent, and the top individual income tax rate (which applies to much of the income earned by businesses that are organized as pass-through entities rather than C-corporations subject to the corporate tax), which was reduced from 50 percent to 28 percent. Although such rate cuts are generally desirable in the sense that they lower the cost of capital and stimulate investment, they also have the undesirable side effect of reducing the rate of taxation applied to the income earned by existing investments. This results in windfall gains to existing investors, which have no positive incentive effects for future investment; indeed, for a given revenue cost, the revenue loss to the government from reducing the tax rate on existing investments implies that the tax rates on future investment must be lower than they otherwise might be, reducing the positive effects of reform on future investment.

One of the provisions I worked on during my tenure at the Treasury was designed to offset some of the windfall gain accruing to the owners of existing investments attributable to corporate rate reduction; I analyzed this provision in an article that appeared in 1987 in *Public Finance Review* (Chapter 11). In particular, I examined a novel proposal contained in Treasury II (the follow-up set of proposals that was designed to be more politically feasible than the original Treasury I report) for a "windfall recapture tax" (WRT) that would have assessed a transitional tax on certain owners of depreciable assets that were in existence prior to the reform.

---

[5] For further discussion along these lines, see McLure and Zodrow (2007).

Specifically, the WRT was designed to equal the product of the proposed rate reduction (13 percentage points in the case of large corporations under Treasury II) and the amount of "excess" depreciation deductions taken by the taxpayer, defined as the difference between the accelerated deductions received under pre-reform law and a more conservative "earnings and profits" measure of the actual economic depreciation of the asset. The basic idea is that accelerated depreciation deductions result in an interest-free loan from the government to the firm that is taken out when accelerated deductions exceed economic depreciation (so that less income is included in the tax base) and repaid subsequently when economic depreciation exceeds accelerated depreciation (which is typically zero at that time since the asset is fully depreciated). In the absence of the WRT, the taxpayer would benefit from "taking out" the implicit loan at the pre-reform tax rate, but "paying back" the loan at the reduced post-reform tax rate (when the initially tax-deferred income is included in the tax base). As suggested by its name, the WRT was a one-time tax (phased in over three years) designed to recapture this revenue loss.

In the chapter, I argue that the WRT was an application of the theory of optimal tax reform discussed in Part 1 of this book. Specifically, if the enactment of a tax reform creates arbitrary windfall gains and losses, concern about such reform-induced redistributions can be offset with compensation. Although the optimal tax reform literature typically focuses on compensating those who suffer reform-induced windfall losses (Feldstein, 1976a), the same principle implies that those who experience windfall gains should be taxed. The WRT was an excellent example of a transitional tax consistent with the application of the compensation principle.

The chapter discusses a variety of design issues raised by the WRT proposed by the Treasury and includes some simulations of the effects of various alternative designs (including one proposed by Aaron (1985)). It points out two key problems with the proposed WRT, as (1) it was highly selective, identifying one windfall gain for (negative) compensation while ignoring other reform-induced windfall gains and losses; and (2) it was unanticipated in that previous reforms involving rate changes were not accompanied by such a provision. At the same time, however, the WRT to a first approximation would have imposed an efficient one-time lump-sum tax on the owners of existing assets that would have offset a relatively arbitrary reform-induced windfall gain and thus could have allowed larger future rate reductions or the introduction of other provisions that could have improved incentives for future investment.

The WRT was one of the most controversial provisions of Treasury II and ultimately was not included in TRA86 (although not before the idea of expanding its scope to address other windfall gains was discussed at some length). Nevertheless, the idea of recapturing some of the windfall gains to old investments associated with rate reductions in order to finance larger future rate reductions has considerable appeal, and the subject was again broached — although again ultimately dismissed — during the debates surrounding the rate reductions enacted under the Tax Cuts and Jobs Act in 2017. It thus remains to be seen whether such a provision will ever be enacted, regardless of its theoretical appeal.

3.3. *Taxing capital income in small open economies*

My experience with income tax reform has not been confined to the United States, and indeed I have spent considerable time on international tax policy projects, often under the auspices of multilateral organizations such as the World Bank, the International Monetary Fund, and the Agency for International Development. As discussed previously, my first such experience came shortly after I returned to Rice from the Treasury, when Charlie McLure asked me to participate in a tax reform project in Colombia, a country that rivals the United States in its seemingly perpetual preoccupation with tax reform. We analyzed both consumption and income tax reforms for the Colombians and ultimately published a lengthy book on our experience in the Duke University series on Fiscal Reform in the Developing World (McLure *et al.*, 1990),[6] excerpts of which were published in the book *Readings on Taxation in Developing*

[6] One incident not described in that book occurred when I arrived in Bogotá and a customs agent found a stuffed doll that my older daughter Katherine, who was three-years old at the time, had inserted in my luggage to keep me company while I was away from home. I was able to prevail upon the agent not to slice the doll open with his handy machete only by convincing him that it was highly unlikely that I would be smuggling contraband *into* Colombia.

Countries edited by Bird and Oldman (1990). I returned to Colombia on several occasions in the future, and Charlie and I reviewed the nation's many efforts at tax reform in two World Bank volumes on tax reform in developing countries (McLure and Zodrow, 1991, 1997). As noted in the previous section, Charlie and I later collaborated on several consumption tax reform projects in Bolivia, and I have also been involved in many other reform efforts in recent years, most recently two fascinating projects in China headed by Ruud de Mooij of the IMF.

Many of these projects, including those in Colombia and Bolivia, focused on dealing with the difficulties faced by developing countries in determining how to structure their systems of corporate income taxation to raise desperately needed revenue, while still attracting foreign direct investment from multinationals based in the United States and other countries. Building on some earlier work (Zodrow, 2006, 2010), I conducted a formal analysis of this issue in a paper with Rice graduate student Margaret McKeehan that was published in 2017 in *International Tax and Public Finance* (Chapter 12). Our paper models the "balancing act" that has to be performed by any small open economy in designing its system of capital income taxation.

Specifically, we construct a model of optimal capital income tax rate determination for a small country that is weighing the relative importance of a wide variety of factors that determine the optimal extent of capital income taxation. These factors include the following: (1) a highly elastic supply of mobile foreign capital, including highly desirable firm-specific mobile capital that earns economic rents; (2) the ability of multinational enterprises (MNEs) to use various techniques, including transfer pricing, the relocation of the ownership of intangibles, and the use of loan reallocations that facilitate interest stripping, to shift income away from high-tax jurisdictions; (3) the desire to tax location-specific rents, especially those earned by foreigners, at relatively high tax rates; (4) a sense that MNEs are likely to shift income to low-tax locations so that a relatively high statutory tax rate does not discourage foreign direct investment as much as it otherwise might; (5) the possibility of a "treasury transfer" effect, under which foreign MNEs based in countries with residence-based tax systems that allow a foreign tax credit are indifferent to local taxes since they only replace taxes that would otherwise be collected by their home countries (an effect that is increasingly less important as more countries switch to territorial tax systems, but still relevant as such countries typically have minimum tax provisions that are subject to foreign tax credit offsets); (6) the desire to maintain a corporate income tax with a rate comparable to the top rate under the personal income tax to provide a "backstop" to that tax that prevents individuals from incorporating to avoid or defer personal income tax on their labor income; (7) limitations on the extent to which the economy is appropriately modeled as "small" due to imperfect capital mobility or imperfect substitutability of imported and domestic consumption goods; and (8) a sense that a corporate income tax that applies similar or identical rates to domestic and foreign investment is indispensable from a political standpoint.

In this paper, Margaret and I first construct a theoretical model of the determination of the optimal capital income tax rate in a small open economy that takes most of these factors into account. We then simulate a more complicated version of the model that includes all of these factors under a wide variety of circumstances. The results of course depend on the model specification and parameter values used. Nevertheless, several general conclusions can be drawn from our analysis.

First, although the opportunity to tax immobile location-specific rents accruing to domestic residents does not provide a significant rationale for capital income taxation in our benchmark case, the optimal capital income tax rate increases approximately linearly as the fraction of location-specific rents that accrue to foreigners increases, in some cases exceeding the tax rate on labor income. Second, an operative treasury transfer effect provides a strong rationale for capital income taxation — an effect that may become more relevant over time as more countries adopt anti-base-erosion provisions such as those enacted by the United States in 2017. Third, the potential for labor income shifting puts upward pressure on capital income tax rates to reduce the labor-capital income tax differential. Fourth, the availability of a separate tax on the income earned by location-specific capital significantly reduces optimal capital income tax rates. Fifth, the optimal capital income tax rate is only moderately sensitive to wide variations in the shares of location-specific and ordinary capital. Sixth, the amount of residual taxation is generally more influential in determining the optimal capital income tax rate than the residual tax rate. Finally, several offsetting effects of international income shifting imply that the optimal capital tax rate is only marginally sensitive to the costs of international income shifting, declining slightly as such costs decrease and the amount of income shifting increases.

4. State and Local Tax Policy

I have also worked a great deal in the area of state and local tax policy, including numerous papers with my esteemed Rice colleague and close friend, Peter Mieszkowski. Indeed, I was delighted when this body of work was recognized by my colleagues at the NTA annual conference in 2009 when they honored me with the Steven D. Gold Award for "significant contributions to state and local fiscal policy and a capacity to cross the boundaries between academic research and public policy making." At the same conference, Peter was awarded the most prestigious prize given by the NTA, the Daniel M. Holland Medal, which recognizes lifetime achievement in the theory and practice of public finance. It was truly a spectacular day for Polish public finance economists from Rice University!

4.1. *Tax reform options in Texas*

The most comprehensive state tax policy project I have worked on culminated in a report that I prepared in 2004 for the Joint Select Committee on School Finance in my home state of Texas.[7] A condensed version of that report was published in the December 20, 2004 issue of *State Tax Notes*, and excerpts from that publication comprise Chapter 13 of this book. In that report, I describe the criteria that public finance economists use to evaluate tax structures, draw some general conclusions for state tax policy, and then evaluate a wide ranging set of proposals for reforms of the tax structure in the state of Texas. My general conclusions are the following:

[7]This report draws on my earlier book evaluating state sales and income taxes (Zodrow, 1999) as well as a paper examining sales taxation of services with my former graduate student Michele Hendrix (Hendrix and Zodrow, 2003). A more recent exposition of my views on state tax policy appears in an interview that was conducted by Billy Hamilton of *State Tax Notes* and appeared in the October 27, 2014 issue of that publication.

(1) state benefit taxes or user charges, on both individuals and businesses, should be used to the maximum extent possible; (2) mobility considerations, coupled with political pressures in the state, imply that any progressivity of the tax system should be limited; (3) non-benefit taxation of mobile state businesses should be minimized; and (4) gross receipts taxes should be avoided.

Some of the specific policy recommendations for potential state tax reforms in Texas made in the report include the following: (1) the state sales tax base should be broadened to include untaxed consumer goods and services (but not business services), with concerns about the distributional effects of such a policy addressed with a targeted means-tested sales tax rebate — ideally coupled with an attempt to exclude all business inputs from the sales tax base; (2) excise tax rates should be increased to levels comparable to those in other states and the scope of the state lottery could be expanded; and (3) the state business franchise tax should be reduced and applied to all businesses, subject to a small firm exemption and the adoption of various measures to reduce opportunities for tax avoidance.

The report also discusses three much more sweeping options for state tax reform. Two are precluded by the Texas constitution but are worthy of further consideration — a personal income tax and a state-wide property tax. The final option is a state-wide consumption tax, such as a consumption-based state VAT or a modified version of the tax that would allow businesses a deduction for wages that would be taxed at the individual level, subject to a standard deduction and personal exemptions to exempt the poor from tax. The report recognizes that all of these VAT-related options would add a new layer of complexity to administration and compliance and would also introduce a variety of new problems not shared by the existing tax system in the state.

4.2. *The "capital tax" view of the incidence of the property tax*

The incidence of the property tax has been a question that has intrigued me for a long time, dating back to my graduate student days at Princeton when I spent countless hours poring over Peter's seminal paper on the topic (Mieszkowski, 1972). That paper adapted the Harberger (1962) model of national tax incidence to analyze the incidence of a local property tax applied by two sets of taxing jurisdictions, those with relatively high tax rates and those with relatively low tax rates. Peter concluded that the incidence of the property tax was captured in two components: a "profits tax" effect that reflected the average burden of the tax and was borne by all capital owners (much like the burden of the corporate income tax tended to be borne by all capital owners in the Harberger model) and "excise tax" effects in each jurisdiction that reflected the effects of taxes that were higher or lower than the average level of tax (e.g., relatively high taxes were reflected in higher consumer prices or lower returns to labor and land).

Peter's view of the property tax was challenged by proponents of an alternative "benefit tax" view which asserts that the property tax, when combined with the appropriate zoning ordinances and analyzed within a model of competing local jurisdictions, such as that envisioned in the seminal paper by Tiebout (1956), was effectively a benefit tax.[8] In this case, the property tax is a non-distortionary user charge for the local public services provided to the residents and businesses within the taxing jurisdiction; the early proponents of this view were Hamilton (1975), Fischel (1975), and White (1975).

In a paper that appeared in 1986 in *Regional Science and Urban Economics* (Chapter 14), Peter and I constructed a "reformulation" of what we now refer to as the "capital tax" view of the property tax.[9] Although our analysis is based on the model used in the original derivation, the key aspect of the model is that it incorporates many of the features of local use of the property tax stressed by proponents of the benefit view.

Specifically, we construct a model that explicitly considers interjurisdictional competition, individual utility functions that include varying tastes for local public services, segregation into differing communities according to individual tastes for local public services, and a simple form

[8] Alternatively, as proposed by Hamilton (1976), local jurisdictions are heterogeneous with respect to housing but are characterized by perfect capitalization of all fiscal differentials into housing prices.

[9] Peter's conclusions regarding the incidence of the property tax (Mieszkowski, 1972) were for a long time referred to as the "new view" of the property tax, and we described our paper as a reformulation of that new view. We subsequently replaced the dated "new view" designation with "capital tax" view.

of land-use zoning — all factors that were ignored in the original Mieszkowski (1972) derivation. We then show that adding all of these "benefit-view-type" features to the capital tax view model does not change its basic results, as long as (1) capital is mobile across jurisdictions in response to interjurisdictional property tax differentials, and (2) capital is fixed in total supply at the national level. Under these circumstances, the incidence of the property tax is still determined by the profits tax and excise tax effects, despite the various benefit view features that characterize the model. Thus, as we argued in an earlier paper (Zodrow and Mieszkowski, 1983), the critical assumption underlying the benefit view is that fiscal zoning is sufficiently precise that households cannot adjust their consumption of housing at all in response to the imposition of the tax on house values. We argued that assumption was implausible — although the issue is still very much a subject of debate. Indeed, Oates and Fischel (2016, p. 415) begin their recent review of the property tax literature by observing that, "Our understanding of the incidence of local property taxes is in a sad state."

4.3. *Alternative views of the incidence of the property tax*

In 2001, I was invited by the *National Tax Journal* to discuss my views on the debate regarding the incidence of the property tax. Drawing on some earlier research (Mieszkowski and Zodrow, 1989; Zodrow, 2001), I did this in a paper entitled "The Property Tax as a Capital Tax: A Room with Three Views" (Chapter 15). The "three views" of property tax incidence in the title are the "traditional view," which uses a partial equilibrium analysis of the residential housing market to argue that the tax is fully shifted forward to consumers as higher housing prices, and the "benefit tax view" and "capital tax view" noted above. The central theme of the article is that each of the three views can — to a considerable but certainly not complete extent — be derived within the context of the model that generates the capital tax view of the property tax.

The paper proceeds in three steps. First, I show that since the traditional view is based on a partial equilibrium analysis, only the excise tax effects of the capital tax view are relevant. Drawing on Wildasin (1986), I show that when the land supply of the taxing jurisdiction is fixed and certain conditions on parameter values obtain, those excise tax effects indicate the full shifting of the tax into housing prices that characterize the traditional view.

Second, beyond the point noted above that adding a large number of benefit-tax-view type features to the original capital tax view model does not change its results, I show, following Zodrow and Mieszkowski (1983) and Mieszkowski and Zodrow (1985) as well as Bradford (1978), that the capital tax view can be derived within the context of a general equilibrium model of a single taxing jurisdiction and the rest of the country. Specifically, in this case, the burden of the tax is borne by the residents of the taxing jurisdiction as either higher housing prices (the traditional view) or lower returns to labor and land. I note that this result is roughly consistent with the benefit tax view, in the sense that in the aggregate local residents pay for the local public services that they receive.

At the same time, however, these local excise tax effects are offset by opposing excise tax effects in all other jurisdictions, where housing prices decline and labor and land returns increase. In addition, a very small reduction in the return to capital due to the imposition of the tax in the local taxing jurisdiction is applied to the entire remainder of the (fixed) national capital stock, with the net result being that the net return to capital declines by the revenue raised in the local taxing jurisdiction — the standard profits tax effect of the capital tax view. Note, however, that although this derivation of the capital tax view has the "flavor" that the property tax is a benefit tax, the mechanism for achieving this result is very different, as the burden of the tax on local factors and consumers under the capital tax view arises due to the outflow of capital in response to the imposition of the tax that is precluded under the benefit tax view.

Third, I review empirical evidence that might distinguish between the capital tax view (which encompasses the traditional view) and the benefit tax view. This evidence is mixed and is subject to different interpretations. For example, Ross and Yinger (2000, p. 2043) argue that, "The evidence against the benefits view is overwhelming," while Oates (1994, p. 142) concludes that, "As things stand, it is impossible to reject either the new view or the benefits view in favor of the other." In any case, the central message of this part of the article is that even though there are fundamental differences between the two views, they are sufficiently similar that it is often difficult to distinguish between them empirically.

4.4. *Intrajurisdictional capitalization and the incidence of the property tax*

I expand on a particular aspect of this final point in an article that appeared in 2014 in *Regional Science and Urban Economics* (Chapter 16).[10] Specifically, the existence of intrajurisdictional capitalization of fiscal differentials into housing prices is an essential element of what is arguably the more plausible derivation of the benefit view — the analysis by Hamilton (1976) of local jurisdictions that are heterogeneous with respect to housing prices. Moreover, Fischel (2001) argues that the empirical evidence supporting intrajurisdictional fiscal capitalization is conclusive and that this provides compelling evidence that the benefit tax view accurately describes the effects of the property tax.

In this paper, I examine that contention. Specifically, I construct a model similar to those used to generate the benefit tax view and show that the model generates the benefit tax view under the assumption that the capital stocks used in housing are fixed in both jurisdictions, but generates the capital tax view if the supply of capital is mobile across jurisdictions. I then calculate the intrajurisdictional capitalization effects that occur with an increase in the property tax in both versions of the model and show that in a benchmark case these capitalization effects are identical, even though they reflect the capitalization of fiscal differentials in the case of the benefit tax view, but tax-induced reallocation of capital across jurisdictions in the case of the capital tax view.

More generally, I simulate the model and show that a broadly similar pattern of intrajurisdictional land value fiscal capitalization occurs under both views. Indeed, I argue that the differences in capitalization effects in the simulations are sufficiently small that it is unlikely that intrajurisdictional capitalization effects can be used to distinguish between the two views.

---

[10] For some additional research on the property tax, see Zodrow (2008) and my papers with my former graduate student Athiphat Muthitacharoen (Muthitacharoen and Zodrow, 2010, 2012).

Finally, I also show that even if all of the stringent assumptions of the benefit view are satisfied, the large and differentiated intrajurisdictional capitalization effects that occur with a property tax-financed increase in local public services imply that the property tax is *not* a benefit tax for such increases; rather, it only becomes a benefit tax for future home purchasers — after the modeled intrajurisdictional capitalization effects occur.

5. Tax Competition

The phenomenon of tax competition has attracted a great deal of attention in recent years, both at the subnational level, where it often takes the form of state and local governments offering tax and other concessions to attract mobile firms to their jurisdictions, and at the national level, where corporate income tax rates have declined steadily, partially reflecting the efforts of countries competing to attract foreign direct investment. The final section of the book contains some of my work in this area.

5.1. *Interjurisdictional tax competition*

Drawing on some earlier work (Zodrow and Mieszkowski, 1983), Peter and I also collaborated on what has been my most influential paper, an article that appeared in the *Journal of Urban Economics* in 1986 (Chapter 17). This paper, entitled "Pigou, Tiebout, Property Taxation, and the Underprovision of Local Public Goods," builds on two classic propositions of public finance: the claim by Pigou (1947) that public services will be underprovided when financed by distortionary taxes, and the emphasis by Tiebout (1956) on the importance of interjurisdictional competition in determining the level of local public services.

Specifically, we construct a model of a national system of independent local governments in which the national capital stock is fixed but capital is perfectly mobile across jurisdictions, and each local government relies on the property tax to finance local public services. We begin with an initial equilibrium in which all local public services are financed with non-distortionary lump-sum taxes and then analyze the effects of property tax finance when the "permitted level" of lump-sum taxation is reduced. We assume that each local jurisdiction is small relative to the rest of the economy and model tax competition along Cournot–Nash lines, as each government sets its tax policies under the assumption that other governments hold their taxes constant. Within this context, we show that the forces of interjurisdictional tax competition — specifically, each government's concern that property taxation of mobile capital will drive such capital out of the taxing jurisdiction and into neighboring jurisdictions — result in an equilibrium in which each government underprovides local public services (although the national allocation of capital is not affected, since each jurisdiction acted in the same manner).

Our formulation, along with the complementary work of Wilson (1986), has often been described as the standard "workhorse model"[11] of a voluminous and still growing literature on tax competition among local, state, and national governments. Indeed, when I presented an address at the 2009 NTA annual conference honoring Peter on receiving the Holland Medal, I was pleased to note that our model had been extended in a multitude of directions. Specifically, quoting from that speech, I observed that,

> Among others, these extensions include "asymmetric tax competition" between large and small jurisdictions, the introduction of multiple goods with trade, the allowance of taxes on variable labor supply, the assumption of imperfectly mobile capital some of which may be owned by foreigners, the allowance of differences in tastes for public services, the inclusion of spillovers and scale economies in the provision of public goods, the addition of income uncertainty, and most importantly, consideration of the tendency toward overprovision of public services due to Leviathan tendencies on the part of local governments which can be tempered by interjurisdictional tax competition. And, although this article was written in the context of state and local governments in a federal system, more recently it has been applied to analyze tax competition among nations, especially within the European Union. I'm pretty sure Peter would agree that it has been extremely gratifying to see the many fascinating directions taken in the still-growing tax competition literature.

[11] In a recent review, Keen and Konrad (2012) describe our combined work as the "ZMW model" — despite my wife Dorey's exhortations, I have resisted the temptation to call the ZMW model "the ultimate tax competition machine"!

The following year, in a paper that builds on Zodrow (2003b), I survey the tax competition literature as well as the literature on the closely related topic of the extent of international capital mobility in a paper that appeared in a 2010 special issue of the *National Tax Journal* — excerpts of which appear as Chapter 18 in this book. Given space limitations, I will only list the topics discussed in this survey. For the survey of capital mobility, I examine the tax sensitivity of foreign direct investment, recent empirical evidence on the incidence of the corporate income tax on labor (implied by capital mobility), and the implications of saving and investment correlations for international capital mobility. For the tax competition survey, I discuss theoretical models of tax competition, the evolution of corporate tax rates in the presence of tax competition, empirical evidence of strategic interactions among governments in setting tax rates on capital reflective of tax competition, and tax competition in allowing tax avoidance.

5.2. *Tax competition in business public services*

In the tax competition paper described above, Peter and I focus on the case in which local governments provide public services financed with property taxes to local residents, where we show that, within the context of our model, interjurisdictional tax competition unambiguously leads to under-provision of such services. However, we also discuss the case in which local public services are provided to businesses, where we obtain more mixed results. I extend the analysis of tax competition for business public services in a paper with a former graduate student, Elisabeth Gugl, who is now an associate professor at the University of Victoria (Chapter 19).

In this paper, Elisabeth and I investigate the claim made by several prominent public finance experts that, in the absence of the assessment of explicit benefit taxes or user charges on businesses, broad-based taxes on local production, such as an origin-based VAT, are an attractive option. The rationale underlying this argument is that such production taxes are relatively efficient "benefit-related" taxes (Bird, 2000; Hines, 2003) and, in particular, that they are preferable on efficiency grounds to a tax on mobile capital such as that typically analyzed in the tax competition literature.

Accordingly, we construct a model of interjurisdictional tax competition similar to that described above, except we assume that local tax revenues, obtained from either a production tax or a capital tax, are used to finance the purchase of business public services, which then become an input into the production function of local firms. Our results provide some support for the idea that a production-based tax may be viewed as a "benefit-related" tax, although only under special circumstances does a production tax substitute perfectly for an explicit user charge. More generally, the characteristics of the firm's production function — specifically, its log modularity properties — play the key role in determining the relative efficiency properties of production-based taxes and capital taxes. The log modularity properties of the production function with respect to capital and business public services indicate how the elasticity of output with respect to increases in business public services varies at different levels of the amount of capital employed in production. Specifically, if the production function is log modular (log submodular, log supermodular) in capital and business public services, then the elasticity of output with respect to business public services is constant (decreases, increases) as the capital employed in production increases.

We show that in the special case of a production function that is log modular in capital and the public service (e.g., a Cobb–Douglas production function), a production tax is effectively a benefit tax and is thus entirely analogous to a user charge for public services that ensures an efficient level of public service provision. In contrast, in this case a capital tax always leads to underprovision of business public services and is thus an inefficient tax. By comparison, if the production function is log submodular in capital and public services (e.g., a CES production function with an elasticity of substitution greater than one), a production tax is inefficient and leads to underprovision of the public service, but it results in less underprovision and thus is less inefficient than a capital tax. Finally, although we show that the production tax leads to overprovision of public services in the case of a log supermodular production function (e.g., a CES production function with an elasticity of substitution less than one), the effect of a capital tax on public services in this case is theoretically ambiguous; this implies that a ranking of the relative efficiency properties of the two taxes is impossible without further restrictions on the production technology. In a companion paper (Gugl and Zodrow, 2015), however, we provide a wide variety of simulations using the CES production function which indicate that in those instances in which capital taxes are more efficient than the production tax, the efficiency gains from capital rather than production taxation are modest.

This chapter, like many in this book, reflects a collaborative effort. I have been fortunate throughout my career to have had the opportunity to work with many extremely gifted and unfailingly congenial colleagues, ranging from my early mentors Charlie McLure and Peter Mieszkowski (my own powerhouse "M&M Boys" — a reference that may be lost on all but diehard baseball fans from my generation) to my former student and current colleague at the Baker Institute for Public Policy at Rice, John Diamond (the formidable "Johnny D" on the golf links). My career has been immeasurably enriched by these fruitful collaborations, and this book is a testament to my debt of gratitude to these cherished colleagues and friends.

References

Aaron, Henry J., 1985. "Some Further Thoughts on Recapture of Excess Depreciation." *Tax Notes* (July 15), 315–321.

Aaron, Henry J., Leonard Burman, and William G. Gale, 2007. *Taxing Capital Income.* Urban Institute, Washington, DC.

Ahsan, Syed M., 1989. "Choice of Tax Base Under Uncertainty: Consumption or Income?" *Journal of Public Economics* 40(1), 99–134.

Ahsan, Syed M., 1990. "Risk-Taking, Savings, and Taxation: A Re-examination of Theory and Policy." *Canadian Journal of Economics* 23(2), 408–433.

Altshuler, Rosanne, Richard M. Bird, Malcolm Gillis, Arnold C. Harberger, Gary Hufbauer, Charles E. McLure, Jr., Jack Mintz, and George R. Zodrow, 2012. *Amici Curiae Brief Filed (August 8, 2012) in Support of Petitioners, PPL Corp and Subsidiaries v. Commissioner of Internal Revenue, Supreme Court of the United States.*

Bird, Richard M., 2000. "Subnational VATs: Experience and Prospects." *Proceedings of the Annual Conference on Taxation and Minutes of the Annual Meeting of the National Tax Associations*, pp. 223–228.

Bird, Richard M., and Oliver Oldman, 1990. *Readings on Taxation in Developing Countries*, fourth edition. The Johns Hopkins University Press, Baltimore, MD.

Blinder, Alan S., 2018. *Advise and Dissent: Why America Suffers When Economics and Politics Collide.* Basic Books, New York, NY.

Bradford, David F., 1978. "Factor Prices May Be Constant but Factor Returns Are Not." *Economics Letters* 1(3), 199–203.

Bradford, David F., and the U.S. Treasury Tax Policy Staff, 1984. *Blueprints for Basic Tax Reform*, second edition. Tax Analysts, Arlington, VA.

Diamond, John W., and George R. Zodrow, 2007. "Economic Effects of a Personal Capital Income Tax Add-On to a Consumption Tax." *Finanzarchiv* 63(3), 374–395.

Diamond, John W., and George R. Zodrow, 2008. *Fundamental Tax Reform: Issues, Choices and Implications*. MIT Press, Cambridge, MA.

Diamond, John W., and George R. Zodrow, 2013. "Promoting Growth, Maintaining Progressivity, and Dealing with the Fiscal Crisis: CGE Simulations of a Temporary VAT Used for Debt Reduction." *Public Finance Review* 41(6), 852–884.

Diamond, John W., and George R. Zodrow, 2014. "Dynamic Macroeconomic Estimates of the Effects of Chairman Camp's 2014 Tax Reform Discussion Draft." Baker Institute for Public Policy Working Paper, Rice University, Houston, TX.

Diamond, John W., and George R. Zodrow, 2015. "Modeling U.S. and Foreign Multinationals in a Dynamic OLG-CGE Model." Baker Institute for Public Policy Working Paper, Rice University, Houston, TX.

Diamond, John W., and George R. Zodrow, 2018. "The Effects of Carbon Tax Policies on the U.S. Economy and the Welfare of Households." Center on Global Energy Policy Report, Columbia University School of International and Public Affairs, New York, NY.

Diamond, John W., George R. Zodrow, Thomas S., Neubig, and Robert J. Carroll, 2014. "The Dynamic Economic Effects of a U.S. Corporate Income Tax Rate Reduction." In Diamond, John W., and George R. Zodrow (eds.), *Pathways to Fiscal Reform in the United States*. MIT Press, Cambridge, MA, pp. 343–406.

Echavarría, Juan José, and George R. Zodrow, 2005. "Foreign Direct Investment and the Business Tax in Colombia." In Bird, Richard M., James M. Poterba, and Joel Slemrod (eds.), *Fiscal Reform in Colombia: Problems and Prospects*. MIT Press, Cambridge, MA, pp. 153–190.

Feldstein, Martin S., 1976a. "Compensation in Tax Reform." *National Tax Journal* 29(2), 123–130.

Feldstein, Martin S., 1976b. "On the Theory of Tax Reform." *Journal of Public Economics* 6(1–2), 77–104.

Fischel, William A., 1975. "Fiscal and Environmental Considerations in the Location of Firms in Suburban Communities." In Mills, Edwin S., and

Wallace E. Oates (eds.), *Fiscal Zoning and Land Use Controls*. Lexington Books, Lexington, MA, pp. 119–173.

Fischel, William A., 2001. "Municipal Corporations, Homeowners, and the Benefit View of the Property Tax." In Oates, Wallace E. (ed.), *Property Taxation and Local Government Finance*. Lincoln Institute of Land Policy, Cambridge, MA, pp. 34–77.

Fox, William F., and Matthew Murray, 1997. "The Sales Tax and Electronic Commerce: So What's New?" *National Tax Journal* 50(3), 573–592.

Graetz, Michael J., 1979. "Implementing a Progressive Consumption Tax." *Harvard Law Review* 92(8), 1575–1661.

Gordon, Roger H., 1985. "Taxation of Corporate Capital Income: Tax Revenues versus Tax Distortions." *Quarterly Journal of Economics* 100(1), 1–27.

Goolsbee, Austan, 2000. "In a World Without Borders: The Impact of Taxes on Internet Commerce." *Quarterly Journal of Economics* 115(2), 561–576.

Gugl, Elisabeth, and George R. Zodrow, 2015. "Competition in Business Taxes and Public Services: Are Production-based Taxes Superior to Capital Taxes?" *National Tax Journal* 68(3S), 767–802.

Hall, Robert E., and Alvin Rabushka, 1995. *The Flat Tax,* second edition. Hoover Institution Press, Stanford, CA.

Hamilton, Bruce W., 1975. "Zoning and Property Taxation in a System of Local Governments." *Urban Studies* 12, 205–211.

Hamilton, Bruce W., 1976. "Capitalization of Intrajurisdictional Differences in Local Tax Prices." *American Economic Review* 66(5), 743–753.

Harberger, Arnold C., 1962. "The Incidence of the Corporate Income Tax." *Journal of Political Economy* 70(3), 215–240.

Hendrix, Michele, and George R. Zodrow, 2003. "Sales Taxation of Services: An Economic Analysis." *Florida State Law Review* 30 (Spring), 411–433.

Hettich, Walter, 1979. "A Theory of Partial Tax Reform." *Canadian Journal of Economics* 12(4), 692–712.

Hines, James R. Jr., 2003. "Michigan's Flirtation with the Single Business Tax." In Ballard, Charles L., Paul N. Courant, Douglas C. Drake, Ronald C. Fischer, and Elisabeth R. Gerber (eds.), *Michigan at the Millennium: A Benchmark and Analysis of its Fiscal and Economic Structure*. Michigan State University Press, East Lansing, MI, pp. 603–628.

Joint Committee on Taxation, 2005. "Macroeconomic Analysis of Various Proposals to Provide $500 Billion in Tax Relief." JCX-4-15. Joint Committee on Taxation, Washington, DC.

Joint Committee on Taxation, 2017. "Macroeconomic Analysis of the 'Tax Cuts and Jobs Act' as Ordered Reported by the Senate Committee on

Finance on November 16, 2017." JCX-61-17. Joint Committee on Taxation, Washington, DC.

Keen, Michael, and Kai A. Konrad, 2012. "The Theory of International Tax Competition and Tax Coordination." In Auerbach, Alan J., Raj Chetty, Martin Feldstein, and Emmanuel Saez (eds.), *Handbook of Public Economics*, Volume 5. Elsevier Publishing, Amsterdam, Netherlands, pp. 257–328.

McLure, Charles E., Jr., 1988. "The 1986 Act: Tax Reform's Finest Hour or Death Throes of the Income Tax?" *National Tax Journal* 41(93), 303–315.

McLure, Charles E., Jr., and George R. Zodrow, 1991. "Tax Reform in Colombia: Process and Results." In Khalilzadeh-Shirazi, Javad, and Anwar Shah (eds.), *Tax Policy in Developing Countries*. World Bank, Washington, DC, pp. 1–22.

McLure, Charles E., Jr., and George R. Zodrow, 1994. "The Study and Practice of Income Tax Policy." In Quigley, John M., and Eugene Smolensky (eds.), *Modern Public Finance*. Harvard University Press, Cambridge, MA, pp. 165–209.

McLure, Charles E., Jr., and George R. Zodrow, 1996a. "Creditability Concerns Doom Bolivian Tax." *Tax Notes International* (March 11), 825–829.

McLure, Charles E., Jr., and George R. Zodrow, 1996b. "A Hybrid Approach to the Direct Taxation of Consumption." In Boskin, Michael J. (ed.), *Frontiers of Tax Reform*. Hoover Institution Press, Stanford, CA, pp. 70–90.

McLure, Charles E., Jr., and George R. Zodrow, 1997. "Thirty Years of Tax Reform in Colombia." In Thirsk, Wayne (ed.), *Recent Experience with Tax Reform in Developing Countries*. World Bank, Washington, DC, pp. 57–125.

McLure, Charles E., Jr., and George R. Zodrow, 1998. "The Economic Case for Foreign Tax Credits for Cash Flow Taxes." *National Tax Journal* 51(1), 1–22.

McLure, Charles E., Jr., and George R. Zodrow, 2007. "Consumption-Based Direct Taxes: A Guided Tour of the Amusement Park." *Finanzarchiv: Public Finance Analysis* 63(2), 285–307.

McLure, Charles E., Jr., Jack Mutti, Victor Thuronyi, and George R. Zodrow, 1990. *The Taxation of Income from Business and Capital in Colombia*. Duke University Press, Chapel Hill, NC.

Mieszkowski, Peter, 1972. "The Property Tax. An Excise Tax or a Profits Tax?" *Journal of Public Economics* 1(1), 73–96.

Mieszkowski, Peter, and George R. Zodrow, 1989. "Taxation and the Tiebout Model: The Differential Effects of Head Taxes, Taxes on Land Rents and Property Taxes." *Journal of Economic Literature* 27(3), 1098–1146.

Mieszkowski, Peter, and George R. Zodrow, 1985. "The Incidence of a Partial State Corporate Income Tax." *National Tax Journal* 38(4), 489–496.

Muthitacharoen, Athiphat, and George R. Zodrow, 2010. "The Efficiency Costs of a Local Property Tax." In Bahl, Roy, Jorge Martinez-Vazquez, and Joan Youngman (eds.), *Challenging the Conventional Wisdom on the Property Tax*. Lincoln Institute of Land Policy, Cambridge MA, pp. 15–42.

Muthitacharoen, Athiphat, and George R. Zodrow, 2012. "Revisiting the Excise Tax Effects of the Property Tax." *Public Finance Review* 40(5), 555–583.

Nelson, Jaeger, and Kerk Phillips, 2019. "Macroeconomic Effects of Reducing OASI to Payable Benefits: A Comparison of Seven Overlapping-Generations Models." *National Tax Journal*, December, forthcoming.

Oates, Wallace E., 1994. "Federalism and Government Finance." In Quigley John S., and Eugene Smolensky (eds.), *Modern Public Finance*. Harvard University Press, Cambridge, MA, pp. 126–161.

Oates, Wallace E., and William A. Fischel, 2016. "Are Local Property Taxes Regressive, Progressive, or What?" *National Tax Journal* 69(2), 415–434.

Pigou, A. C., 1947. *A Study in Public Finance*. Macmillan, London.

President's Advisory Panel on Federal Tax Reform, 2005. *Simple, Fair, and Pro-Growth: Proposals to Fix America's Tax System*. U.S. Government Printing Office, Washington, DC.

Ross, Stephen and John Yinger, 2000. "Sorting and Voting: A Review of the Literature on Urban Public Finance." In Cheshire, Paul, and Edwin S. Mills (eds.), *Handbook of Regional and Urban Economics*, Volume 3. North Holland, Amsterdam, pp. 2001–2060.

Sarkar, Shounak, and George R. Zodrow, 1993. "Transitional Issues in Moving to a Direct Consumption Tax." *National Tax Journal* 46(3), 359–376.

Tiebout, Charles M., 1956. "A Pure Theory of Local Expenditures." *Journal of Political Economy* 64(5), 416–424.

U.S. Department of the Treasury, 1977. *Blueprints for Basic Tax Reform*. U.S. Government Printing Office, Washington, DC.

White, Michelle J., 1975. "Firm Location in a Zoned Metropolitan Area." In Mills, Edwin S., and Wallace E. Oates (eds.), *Fiscal Zoning and Land Use Controls*. Lexington Books, Lexington, MA, pp. 175–202.

Wildasin, David E., 1986. *Urban Public Finance*. Harwood, New York, NY.

Wilson, John D., 1986. A Theory of Interregional Tax Competition. *Journal of Urban Economics* 19(3), 296–315.

Zodrow, George R., 1980. "Optimal Tax Reform: The Case of Property Tax Equalization." *Proceedings of the Seventy-Third Annual Conference on Taxation*. National Tax Association, Columbus, OH, pp. 240–250.

Zodrow, George R., 1984. "The Incidence of Metropolitan Property Tax Base Sharing and Rate Equalization." *Journal of Urban Economics* 15(2), 210–229.

Zodrow, George R., 1985. "Partial Tax Reform: An Optimal Taxation Perspective." *Canadian Journal of Economics* 18(2), 335–346.

Zodrow, George R., 1986. "Implementing Tax Reform: The Intergenerational Carryover Problem." *National Tax Journal* 39(4), 419–433.

Zodrow, George R., 1990. "The Choice between Income and Consumption: Efficiency and Horizontal Equity Aspects." In Cnossen, Sijbren, and Richard M. Bird (eds.), *The Personal Income Tax: Phoenix from the Ashes?* North Holland, Amsterdam, pp. 85–115.

Zodrow, George R., 1997a. "On the Transition to Indirect or Direct Consumption-Based Taxation." In Krever, Richard (ed.), *Tax Conversations: Essays in Honour of John G. Head*. Kluwer Law International, London, pp. 27–59.

Zodrow, George R., 1997b. "Reflections on the Consumption Tax Option." In Head, John G., and Richard Krever (eds.), *Taxation Towards 2000*. Australian Tax Research Foundation, Sydney, pp. 46–79.

Zodrow, George R., 1999. *State Sales and Income Taxes*. Texas A&M Press, College Station, TX.

Zodrow, George R., 2001. "Reflections on the New View and the Benefit View of the Property Tax." In Oates, Wallace E. (ed.), *Property Taxation and Local Government Finance*. Lincoln Institute of Land Policy, Cambridge MA, pp. 79–111.

Zodrow, George R., 2002. "Transitional Issues in the Implementation of a Flat Tax or a Retail Sales Tax." In Zodrow, George R., and Peter Mieszkowski (eds.), *United States Tax Reform in the 21st Century*. Cambridge University Press, Cambridge, UK, pp. 245–283.

Zodrow, George R., 2002/2003. "Prospects for Consumption-Based Tax Reform in the United States." *Finanzarchiv* 59(2), 264–294.

Zodrow, George R., 2003a. "Alternative Forms of Direct Consumption Taxes: The Croatian Approach." In Ahlheim, Michael, Heinz-Dieter Wenzel, and Wolfgang Wiegard (eds.), *Tax Policy: Theoretical Foundations and Practical Applications*. Springer, Berlin, pp. 391–413.

Zodrow, George R., 2003b. "Tax Competition and Tax Coordination in the European Union." *International Tax and Public Finance* 10(6), 651–671.

Zodrow, George R., 2006. "Capital Mobility and Source-Based Taxation of Capital Income in Small Open Economies." *International Tax and Public Finance* 13(2/3), 269–294.

Zodrow, George R., 2008. "The Property Tax Incidence Debate and the Mix of State and Local Finance of Local Public Expenditures." *CES-ifo Economic Studies* 53(4), 1–27.

Zodrow, George R., 2010. "International Taxation and Company Tax Policy in Small Open Economies." In Claus, Iris, Norman Gemmell, Michelle Harding, and David White (eds.), *Tax Reform in Open Economies: International and Country Perspectives*. Edward Elgar Publishing, Northampton, MA, pp. 109–134.

Zodrow, George R., and Charles E. McLure, Jr., 1991. "Implementing Direct Consumption Taxes in Developing Countries." *Tax Law Review* 46(4), 405–487.

Zodrow, George R., and John W. Diamond, 2013. "Dynamic Overlapping Generations Computable General Equilibrium Models and the Analysis of Tax Policy." In Dixon, Peter B., and Dale W. Jorgenson (eds.), *Handbook of Computable General Equilibrium Modeling*, Volume 1. Elsevier Publishing, Amsterdam, Netherlands, pp. 743–813.

Zodrow, George R., and Peter Mieszkowski, 1983. "The Incidence of the Property Tax: The Benefit View versus the New View." In Zodrow, George R. (ed.), *Local Provision of Public Services: The Tiebout Model after Twenty-Five Years*. Academic Press, New York, pp. 109–129.

About the Author

George R. Zodrow is Cline Professor and Chair of the Department of Economics, and Faculty Scholar, Center for Public Finance, Baker Institute for Public Policy, at Rice University. He is also an International Research Fellow at the Centre on Business Taxation at Oxford University. Zodrow is the recipient of the 2009 Steven D. Gold Award, presented by the National Tax Association, the National Conference of State Legislatures, and the Association for Public Policy Analysis and Management, for his contributions to the theory and practice of state and local fiscal policy. His articles have appeared in numerous scholarly publications and books on taxation, and he has written and edited several books on tax issues. He recently served for ten years as editor of the *National Tax Journal* and has also been an editor of the "Policy Watch" section of *International Tax and Public Finance*. Zodrow was a visiting economist at the U.S. Treasury Office of Tax Analysis in 1984–85 during the preparation of Treasury I, the precursor to the Tax Reform Act of 1986, and has been involved in tax reform projects in numerous countries. He received his Ph.D. from Princeton University.

Part I

Optimal Tax Reform: Transitional Issues in Implementing Tax Reform

Chapter 1

Implementing Tax Reform*,†

George Zodrow

Rice University

The implementation of unanticipated changes in the tax structure results in essentially arbitrary redistributions of income. If the government is concerned about inducing such redistributions, the method of implementing tax reform is crucial; specifically, the redistributions can be reduced by altering the timing and extent of enactment of reform — postponing, phasing-in, or partially enacting the tax reform measure — at the cost of reducing the efficiency gains which would be obtained with immediate full enactment. The analysis indicates that, under fairly plausible conditions, immediate partial enactment is the optimal reform implementation policy; numerical simulations suggest that such a policy can significantly increase the social welfare gain obtained with postponed full enactment.

1. Introduction

The optimal taxation literature has generated a variety of prescriptions for optimal tax "design" — the design of tax systems which finance a

*This chapter is reproduced from *National Tax Journal*, **34**(4), 401–418, 1981.

†Drawn from thesis that won the 1980 NTA-TIA Doctoral Dissertation Award.

fixed level of government services at minimal social cost (for surveys, see Mirrlees (1976) and Sandmo (1976). However, as pointed out by Feldstein (1976a), these results are derived without consideration of the transitional problems of moving an economy from an initially suboptimal equilibrium to the tax design optimum when lump sum redistributions are infeasible. He stresses the need for a theory of optimal tax "reform" which would properly account for the fact that implementing efficiency-enhancing reforms induces redistributions of income which are essentially arbitrary and thus socially undesirable. Feldstein specifies a social welfare function which can be used to aggregate the net individual utility gains and losses caused by a reform in order to determine its social desirability. The method of implementing tax reform is crucial in the analysis, as the magnitudes of the income redistributions and efficiency gains which would be induced by an immediate movement to the tax design optimum can be altered by changing the time path of reform. Specifically, the redistributions can be reduced by altering the timing and extent of enactment of reform — postponing, phasing-in, or partially enacting the tax reform measure — at the cost of reducing the efficiency gains which would be obtained with immediate full enactment.

In this paper, I use the analytical framework developed by Feldstein to consider alternate methods of implementing tax reform. Within the context of a perfect information, instantaneous adjustment model, I show that under fairly plausible conditions the policy of immediate partial enactment (for example, the partial reduction of a distortionary tax differential, leaving the remaining differential in perpetuity) is the optimal implementation policy, dominating both phasing-in and postponing reform.

This result provides a counter-argument to Feldstein's (1976a, 1976b) suggestion that the optimal reform implementation policy may be postponed full enactment (current enactment of a movement to the tax design optimum with a future effective date), which reduces the individual utility gains and losses associated with immediate full enactment by a factor of proportionality that increases with the length of the postponement. The intuition behind the optimality of immediate partial enactment is that the first movements toward the tax design optimum result in relatively large marginal efficiency gains which dominate the effects of the associated redistributions on the social welfare function; these gains should be captured immediately rather than postponed. However, as one approaches full enactment, the marginal efficiency gains from reform become small, and, at some point, it is optimal from a social viewpoint simply to forego the incremental redistributions associated with further movements toward the tax design optimum, rather than just reducing them by postponed enactment.

Similar results obtain in two extensions of the basic model. First, I show that if the government is constrained to move eventually to the tax design optimum, immediate partial enactment is the optimal phasing-in policy. Second, I show that the basic result still obtains if social concern about the distribution of income is included in the analysis. Feldstein advocates an "impersonal justice" approach to the evaluation of tax reform proposals, where the government is indifferent to the actual utility levels of the individuals who experience the redistributions caused by the enactment of reform. Immediate partial enactment is still optimal when I modify his theoretical framework to study a "distributional justice" case so that, for example, the government is more averse to inducing an arbitrary loss of a given magnitude if it is experienced by a relatively poor individual.

In the following two sections, I describe the model utilized in the paper and define the optimal tax reform problem within the context of the model. In Section 4, I describe the conditions under which immediate partial enactment is the optimal reform implementation policy, using Feldstein's "impersonal justice" approach to the analysis of tax reform. The extensions to the case where the government is constrained to eventual full enactment of reform at a fixed future date, and to the "distributional justice" case are presented in Sections 5 and 6. The results of some numerical simulations are provided in Section 7 in order to suggest the magnitudes of the social welfare gains that can be obtained with the various reform implementation options, while Section 8 offers some conclusions. Details of the model used in the simulations, as well as a description of the incidence of tax reform in the model, are provided in the Appendix.

2. The Model

I consider the optimal implementation of tax reform within the context of the following model. There are N individuals in an economy who act to maximize an identical utility function which is linear in income. Equilibria in the economy are defined by a general equilibrium system of equations known to all agents. A fixed amount of tax revenue must be raised and the government is assumed to have only two taxes at its disposal. In this case, equilibria are defined by a single exogenous tax variable (T), as the other tax rate must adjust to balance the government budget. The government thus can calculate the pattern of individual utilities $U^i(T)$ for any value of T.

Two values of the exogenous government control variable provide reference points for the analysis — the tax design optimum and the tax rate in the initial equilibrium. For the majority of the paper, I shall follow Mirrlees (1976) and define the tax design optimum (T_d) as the value of the exogenous variable which maximizes the unweighted sum of the individual utility levels of the economy's residents; in this case, the tax design optimum corresponds to the allocative efficiency optimum for the economy. I consider an alternate definition of the tax design optimum in Section 6 when the distributional justice case is analyzed.

The initial equilibrium (T_o) is assumed to differ from the tax design optimum. I arbitrarily assume that $T_o < T_d$, so that the relevant "tax rate interval" is $T_o \leq T \leq T_d$; partial enactment of tax reform refers to an increase in the tax rate from T_o by an amount less than $(T_d - T_o)$, and full enactment of reform refers to an increase in the tax rate to T_d.

To further simplify the analysis, I assume that all individuals can be divided into two groups — one group composed of N_G identical unambiguous "gainers" from reform ($dU^G/dT = dU^i/dT > 0, i = 1,...,N_G$) and a second group of N_L identical unambiguous "losers" from reform ($dU^l/dT = dU^l/dT < 0, i = N_G + 1,...,N = N_G + N_L$). The net individual utility changes dU^G/dT and dU^L/dT each have two components. Both gainers and losers share in the marginal allocative efficiency gain from reform, which is positive at T_o and declines monotonically to zero at T_d,[1] while

[1]The classic example of this pattern for the efficiency effects of taxation is provided by Harberger (1974), who shows that the efficiency loss caused by a tax distortion is proportional to the square of the distortion.

each marginal movement toward T_d causes a pure redistribution from losers to gainers. Note that I assume that the marginal redistribution dominantes the marginal efficiency gain for the losers from reform ($dU^L/dT < 0$).

A crucial feature of the analysis is the calculation of the net individual utility changes which correspond to any time path of the exogenous tax variable T. I make two simplifying assumptions to facilitate this calculation. First, I assume that the economy moves instantaneously and costlessly from one equilibrium to the next at the actual time of a tax change. Second, I assume that the net utility changes associated with any future time path of the exogenous tax variable are perfectly capitalized as one-time windfall gains or losses when the reform policy is announced; note that this assumption implies that the reform is completely unanticipated.[2] Under these circumstances, the implementation of tax rates T_1, T_2,... at times t_1, t_2... will cause changes in the present value of individual utility (ΔPV^i) given by:

$$\begin{aligned}\Delta PV^i &= \int_{t_1}^{\infty}\left[U^i(T_1)-U^i(T_o)\right]\exp(-nt)\,dt \\ &\quad+\int_{t2}^{\infty}\left[U^i(T_2)-U^i(T_1)\right]\exp(-nt)\,dt+\cdots \\ &=\left[U^i(T_1)-U^i(T_o)\right]S_1/n \\ &\quad+\left[U^i(T_2)-U^i(T_1)\right]S_2/n+\cdots, \qquad (1)\end{aligned}$$

where n is the social discount rate and $S_k = \exp(-nt_k)$ are the "speed of enactment factors" ($0 \leq S_k \leq 1$) for the delayed implementation times $t_k(k = 1,2,\ldots)$.

To summarize briefly, tax reform is defined as a marginal movement toward the tax design optimum along the tax rate interval $T_o \leq T \leq T_d$. Adjustment from one equilibrium to the next in response to changes in the tax structure is instantaneous and costless. The reform policy is unanticipated prior to its announcement, but the net effects of any time path

---

[2]The assumption that tax changes are completely unanticipated is obviously a strong one. The equity argument against immediate full enactment of reform clearly loses strength if the risks of tax changes are correctly perceived and thus reflected in asset prices. The importance of this point varies with the specific reform proposal being considered, as it depends on the extent to which it is reasonable to assume that the reform has been anticipated. For a further discussion of this issue, see Feldstein (1976a).

of reform are perfectly capitalized (according to Eq. (1)) at the time of the policy announcement. These effects can be viewed as windfall gains to one group of N_G identical "gainers" from reform and windfall losses to a second group of N_L identical "losers" from reform.

3. The Optimal Tax Reform Problem

I assume that the government is concerned about two effects of a movement toward the tax design optimum in the model described above. The first is the allocative efficiency gain from reform; if efficiency gains were the only concern of the government, an immediate movement to the tax design optimum would be the optimal tax reform policy.

However, I assume that the government is concerned also about a second effect of reform, *the horizontal equity effect* of the essentially arbitrary utility gains and losses which accompany unexpected changes in an existing tax structure. The equity problem associated with an immediate movement to the tax design optimum is that the incidence of tax reform is essentially capricious in many cases. This is especially true for changes in capital and land taxation where, if asset prices accurately reflect future net returns, the owners of an asset at the time of the enactment of a tax advantage capture all of its benefits. As assets change hands, the correspondence between current owners and the individuals who received the tax advantage will become so small that the incidence of tax reform designed to eliminate the "tax break" can be characterized as capricious. Capricious incidence, particularly when the capitalized amounts involved are fairly large, is a strong equity argument against tax reform.[3]

Governmental concern about the arbitrary incidence of reform makes the timing and extent of enactment of reform critical, as postponed or partial enactment may be desirable to reduce the arbitrary redistributions associated with an immediate movement to the tax design optimum. The optimal tax reform problem is the selection of the time path of changes in the tax structure which strikes the best compromise between the maximum efficiency gains obtained with an immediate movement to the tax

[3] See Feldstein (1976a, 1976b), for a detailed discussion of the capricious nature of the incidence of tax reform.

design optimum and the zero level of redistributions implied by remaining at the initial equilibrium.

To formalize the problem, I follow Feldstein in analyzing tax reform proposals using the following modified version of the general additive social welfare function used in the optimal taxation literature[4]:

$$W = \frac{1}{(1-e)} \sum_i [(U_r + \Delta PV^i)^{1-e} - 1], \quad 0 \leq e \leq \infty \qquad (2)$$

where e is the constant elasticity of the marginal social valuation of individual utility and U_r is a common reference utility level.

In this approach, the e parameter is a measure of the degree of social concern about the arbitrary redistributions caused by tax reform. If $e = 0$, the utility changes experienced by the gainers and losers from reform are weighted equally from a social viewpoint; that is, only efficiency considerations are relevant to the government so that the optimal tax reform policy is immediate full enactment — an immediate movement to the tax design optimum. However, with a concave welfare function ($e > 0$), social equity concern about arbitrary redistributions is included in the welfare function, as arbitrary losses are weighted (negatively) more than proportionately, while windfall gains are weighted less than, proportionately. Since the concavity of the social welfare function increases as e increases, larger values of e imply greater social concern about the arbitrary nature of the redistributions which are caused by a change in the tax structure.

The U_r parameter is an arbitrary reference utility value used to scale the magnitudes of the present values of individual utility changes ΔPV^i caused by any time path of reform. I consider the case where U_r is the present value of a lifetime stream of the mean utility level in the initial equilibrium; this is approximated as $U_r = \bar{U}/n$ where $\bar{U}$ is the mean utility level in the initial equilibrium. Note in particular that the use of a common reference utility value implies that the government is unconcerned about the actual initial utility levels of the individuals who experience

[4] See Atkinson and Stiglitz (1980) for a discussion of the properties of this social welfare function.

windfall gains and losses as a result of the tax change. Instead, the social welfare function is simply a construct used to evaluate the magnitudes of individual utility changes implied by any particular tax reform proposal, independently of the utility levels of the individuals who actually experience the changes; all individuals are treated, in Feldstein's words, with "impersonal justice."[5]

Thus, the optimal tax reform problem is constructed so that it is equivalent to the optimal tax design problem when the government is concerned only with efficiency ($e = 0$). However, when there is social concern about arbitrary redistributions ($e > 0$), the optimal tax reform problem is the selection of the implementation times t_k (the speed of enactment factors S_k) and the corresponding tax rates T_k which generate the pattern of individual utility changes ΔPV^i which maximizes the optimal tax reform welfare function W.

4. The Optimality of Immediate Partial Enactment

Feldstein suggests postponed full enactment of reform (current announcement of a movement to the tax design optimum with a future effective date) as a reform implementation policy when $e > 0$. This approach limits the government to a single choice variable — the selection of the implementation time t^* (and the associated S^*) to move to the tax design optimum in order to maximize

$$Wp = \frac{1}{1-e}\sum_i \{[U_r + (U^i(T_d) - U^i(T_o))S^*/n]^{1-e} - 1\} \tag{3}$$

Thus, the only option available to the government is to reduce proportionately the gains and losses implied by a movement to $T_{d;}$ the factor of proportionality increases with the length of the postponement. In this section, I argue that postponed full enactment will never be the solution to the optimal tax reform problem posed in the previous section, and I describe

[5] See Feldstein (1976b) for a defense of the impersonal justice approach to the analysis of tax reform.

the conditions under which immediate partial enactment (an immediate movement to T*, $T_o < T^* < T_d$) is the optimal reform implementation policy.[6]

First, note that the construction of the problem insures that some enactment of reform will be desirable. Since U_r is the common reference point for both the gainers and the losers from reform, the marginal individual utility changes are weighted equally at T_o where there are no accumulated redistributions; since the marginal efficiency gain is positive at T_o, a marginal increase in T, regardless of when it is put into effect, will increase the measure of social welfare W.

Second, similar reasoning shows that neither postponed nor immediate full enactment of reform to the tax design optimum T_d is desirable. At T_d, the sum of the net marginal effects on individual utilities is zero (a pure redistribution) since the marginal efficiency effect is zero. However, the utility gains and losses accumulated as the tax rate is increased from T_o toward T_d insure that the net social valuation of the marginal redistributions at T_d will be negative, regardless of when the movement of T_d. might be enacted. Thus, the last incremental movement to T_d must be socially undesirable; instead, the optimal implementation strategy is one of partial enactment to the point where the efficiency gain is large enough at the margin to outweigh the net negative effect of the redistributions implied by a further incremental movement toward the tax design optimum.

It is considerably more difficult to make general analytical statements about the optimal implementation of partial enactment of reform. The crucial determinant of the optimal time path of reform is the pattern of the marginal individual utility changes (dU^G/dT and dU^L/dT) at each equilibrium along the tax rate interval ($T_o < T < T_d$); it is possible to construct situations where all three of the possible partial enactment implementation options (immediate, postponed and phased-in partial enactment) are optimal.

However, it is fairly simple to put a plausible restriction on the pattern of the marginal individual utility changes along the tax rate interval such

---

[6] For a formal proof of the results presented in this section, see Zodrow (1981).

that immediate partial enactment is the optimal implementation policy. The key variable is the "aggregate marginal utility tradeoff ratio,"

$$R(T) = -\frac{N^G dU^G/dT}{N^L dU^L/dT}, \tag{4}$$

which is the ratio of the aggregate marginal utility gain to the aggregate marginal utility loss at each value of T along the tax rate interval. A sufficient condition to insure the optimality of immediate partial enactment is that R(T) decline monotonically over the tax rate interval to $R(T_d) = 1$. It is quite plausible, although not unambiguously true, that this condition will be satisfied, as the aggregate marginal efficiency gain, $(N^G\ dU^G/dT + N^L\ dU^L/dT)$, declines monotonically to zero at $T = T_d$.[7]

To see the intuition behind the optimality of immediate partial enactment when R(T) declines monotonically over the tax rate interval, note that R(T) is independent of the time of enactment of the movement to T, and consider the desirability of phasing-in reform. The necessary condition for a multi-step phasing-in reform policy to be optimal is that at each value of the tax rate T_k:

$$R(T_k) = \left[\frac{U_r + \Delta PV^G}{U_r + \Delta PV^L}\right]^e; \tag{5}$$

that is, the aggregate marginal utility tradeoff ratio must be equal at each value of the tax rate along a multi-step tax reform path.[8] If this condition were not satisfied, say, for a two-step tax path, a marginal adjustment in the two tax rates would increase social welfare. Clearly, if R(T) declines

[7] The effects of an incremental movement toward T_d can be decomposed into a pure marginal redistribution between the gainers and losers $[\tau(T)]$ and the marginal efficiency gain $[\varepsilon(T)]$. Denoting $\theta^G(T)$ and $\theta^L(T)$ as the gainers' and losers' share of the marginal efficiency gain, $R(T) = -(\tau + \theta^G\varepsilon)/(-\tau + \theta^L\varepsilon)$. Treating θ^G and θ^L as constants, R(T) declines monotonically over the tax rate interval unless the marginal redistribution τ declines rapidly; my experience to date with general equilibrium simulations of the type described in Section 7 suggests that this is unlikely to occur, as τ tends to be approximately constant or to increase as T_d is approached.

[8] Equation (5) is obtained by setting the partial derivative of Eq. (2) with respect to each tax rate T_k equal to zero.

monotonically, the optimal partial enactment policy will be a one-step policy to a unique T*, $T_o < T^* < T_{d.}$

This result obtains because postponing reform does not alter R(T) for any T in the tax rate interval. Accordingly, if a marginal movement beyond T* was undesirable at the time of the movement to T*, it will still be undesirable if postponed. Moreover, since the individual tradeoff ratio is declining, all finite reductions beyond T* will be even less desirable. Thus, nothing can be gained by phasing-in reform beyond T*.

The final implication of a monotonically declining aggregate marginal utility tradeoff ratio is that the optimal one-step partial implementation policy will be enacted immediately. Postponement of a movement from T_o to T* is desirable only to reduce proportionately the magnitude of the associated redistributions. However, if R(T) is declining, it is preferable to reduce these redistributions simply by reducing the extent of reform and then enacting it immediately — this eliminates the less desirable utility changes (a relatively low tradeoff ratio) while enacting the more desirable utility changes (a relatively high tradeoff ratio) as soon as possible.

Thus, immediate partial enactment is the optimal tax reform implementation policy in the two-group case if the aggregate marginal utility tradeoff ratio declines monotonically between the initial equilibrium and the tax design optimum.[9] In particular, postponed full enactment is undesirable because it constrains the tax rate variable to be T_d, so that the only way to reduce the arbitrary redistributions associated with full enactment is to postpone the entire movement from T_o to T_d. It is preferable to relax the requirement of full enactment. This permits immediate enactment of reform where R(T) is high (the marginal efficiency gains from the reduction of a tax distortion are large when the distortion is large while the accumulated gains and losses are small) and eliminates the requirement that reform be pursued to the point where R(T) is equal to its minimum value of one (the marginal efficiency gain declines to zero at T_d while the accumulated gains and losses increase with each incremental movement toward T_d).

[9] In the multi-group case, immediate partial enactment is optimal if the sum of the marginal individual utility changes, weighted by the social marginal valuation of changes in individual utility, declines monotonically over the tax rate interval.

However, the implementation policy of immediate partial enactment is not necessarily optimal when R(T) does not decline monotonically between T_o and T_d. The following two examples illustrate this point.[10]

First suppose that the pattern of individual marginal utility changes along the tax rate interval is such that R(T) does not decline monotonically but increases monotonically to $\tilde{T}$, $T_o < \tilde{T} < T_d$, and then declines monotonically to T_d.[11] Suppose further that the optimal immediate partial enactment would be to T* ($T^o < T^* < \tilde{T}$). In this case delayed partial enactment to some T′ such that R(T′) > R(T*) may be desirable as it permits additional reform beyond T* to take advantage of the higher marginal tradeoff ratio, while reducing the magnitudes of the redistributions associated with the relatively low marginal tradeoff ratios between T_o and T*.

Second, suppose that R(T) declines monotonically to $\tilde{T}$, $T_o < \tilde{T} < T_d$, at which point R(T) increases discontinuously to $R(\tilde{T})$, and then declines monotonically to T_d.[12] Suppose further that the optimal immediate partial enactment would be to T* ($T_o < T^* < \tilde{T}$), where $R(\tilde{T}) > R(T^*)$. In this case, a two-step reform implementation policy of immediate reform to T_1 ($T_o < T_1 < T^*$), followed by delayed or phased-in reform to T_2 ($\tilde{T} < T_2 < T_d$) could be optimal. Such a phasing-in policy captures the high marginal tradeoff ratios between T_o and T_1 and between $\tilde{T}$ and T_2 while reducing the magnitudes of the redistributions associated with the relatively low marginal tradeoff ratios between T_1 and $\tilde{T}$ (recall that $R(T_1) = R(T_2)$ for the optimal T_1 and T_2).

Thus, the optimality of immediate partial enactment cannot be assumed. However, the above two examples were contrived to illustrate this point and seem to be atypical; a monotonically declining R(T) has been characteristic of all of the general equilibrium models with which I have experimented to date.

---

[10] See Zodrow (1981) for further details and numerical examples of these two cases.

[11] Such a pattern for R(T) obtains if the marginal efficiency gain declines linearly along the tax rate interval to zero at T_d, while the marginal redistribution decreases linearly from T_o to $\tilde{T}$ and is constant from $\tilde{T}$ to T_d.

[12] Such a pattern for R(T) obtains if the marginal efficiency gain declines linearly along the tax rate interval to zero at T_d, while the marginal redistribution is constant between T_o and $\tilde{T}$ and constant at a lower level between $\tilde{T}$ and T_d.

In the following two sections, I describe extensions of the analysis of tax reform presented above. First, I consider the implications of constraining the government to full enactment of a movement to the tax design optimum at a fixed future date; in this case, the relevant question is the optimal phasing-in of reform prior to the fixed full enactment date. Second, I describe how distributional concerns on the part of the government can be included in the analytical framework. In particular, I relax the assumption that only efficiency is considered in the definition of the tax design optimum and the assumption that the government is indifferent to the utility levels of the individuals who actually experience gains and losses as a result of tax reform. Thus, I consider optimal tax reform within a "distributional justice" context, in contrast to the "impersonal justice" approach advocated by Feldstein.

5. Optimal Phasing-in of Reform Prior to a Fixed Full Enactment Date

In the previous section, the government was assumed to be unconstrained in its choice of time path for the exogenous tax variable. Suppose instead that the government, for some reason, is constrained to full enactment of reform at a fixed future date. For example, an eventual movement to the tax design optimum may be judicially mandated or dictated by political considerations. Alternatively, note that the analysis assumes infinitely-lived governments or that future governments will support the tax reform policies of the current government. In practice, the current government may believe that future governments will be less likely to alter the tax structure if the economy is at the tax design optimum when power is transferred; accordingly, the current government may impose the constraint of eventual full enactment by the time they anticipate that the transfer of power will take place.[13]

In any case, under these circumstances, the case for immediate partial enactment when R(T) declines monotonically over the tax rate interval is only slightly altered. The requirement that full reform be enacted at a fixed

[13]Thus, as noted by Feldstein (1976b), an advantage of full enactment is that it eliminates one potential source of future horizontal inequities.

future date constrains the government to inducing a minimum level of redistributions so that the marginal individual utility changes are no longer weighted equally at T_0 as in the unconstrained case. As a result, it is possible that, even at T_0 where R(T) is at its maximum, this implied level of redistributions will be sufficiently large that the marginal tradeoff ratio will be too small to justify any phasing-in of reform prior to the fixed full enactment date.[14] However, if any phasing-in of reform is desirable, the remainder of the argument presented above is unchanged. That is, the optimal reform implementation policy will be one of some immediate partial enactment prior to the fixed full enactment date with no further phasing-in of reform. Note, however, that the extent of partial enactment will be less than in the unconstrained case due to the redistributions implied by the mandated eventual movement to T_d.

6. The Distributional Justice Case

The analysis thus far has dealt exclusively with the "impersonal justice" approach to the analysis of tax reform advocated by Feldstein. Introducing distributional concerns into the governmental optimization process alters the analytical framework described above in two important ways.

First, distributional concerns must be taken into account in the definition of the tax design optimum. The standard approach taken in the optimal taxation literature is to assume that the government selects its tax structure (T_d') to maximize the following weighted sum of individual utility levels:

$$W_D = \frac{1}{1-e'}\sum_i \{[U^i(T_d')]^{1-e'} - 1\}, \quad 0 \le e' < \infty \tag{6}$$

where e′ is the elasticity of the social marginal valuation of individual utility.[15] (The case where e′ = 0 and the individual utility functions are

[14] In terms of Eq. (5), $R(T_0)$ is less than $[(U_r + \Delta PV^G)/(U_r + \Delta PV^L)]^e$ evaluated at the values of ΔPV^G and APV^L implied by the fixed future movement to the tax design optimum with no phasing-in of reform; this implies the corner solution of no partial enactment prior to the fixed full enactment date.

[15] For example, see Atkinson and Stiglitz (1980).

linear in income corresponds to the impersonal justice case examined above, where the tax design optimum was defined solely with respect to efficiency considerations.) Thus, even if efficiency considerations alone dictate the elimination of any tax differential in the model described in Section 2, the tax design optimum in the distributional justice case could specify a tax differential which would have the effect of raising the utility levels of the relatively poor individuals in the economy.[16]

Second, distributional concerns must be included in the formulation of the optimal tax reform problem in order to reflect governmental concern about the utility levels of the individuals who actually experience gains and losses from a movement toward the tax design optimum. This is done by replacing the common reference utility level U_r in the impersonal justice formulation (Eq. (2)) with the actual individual utility levels in the initial equilibrium. That is, the government chooses its reform implementation policy to maximize

$$W' = \frac{1}{1-e}\sum_i [(U_r^i + \Delta PV^i)^{1-e} - 1], \quad e' \leq e < \infty \tag{7}$$

where U_r^i is the present value of each individual's lifetime utility if the initial equilibrium is unchanged, the ΔPV^i are again the capitalized present values of the individual utility changes associated with any time path of tax reform (as given by Eq. (1)), and e' is the value of e used in the definition of the tax design optimum. If $e = e'$, an immediate movement to the "distributional justice" case tax design optimum is the optimal tax reform implementation policy;[17] there is no social concern about the arbitrary redistributions of income caused by reform. This concern is introduced into the optimal tax reform problem when $e > e'$ (the concavity of the welfare function is increased). For individuals at the same initial utility level, a utility gain (loss) of a given magnitude is socially weighted less (more) than in the definition of the tax design optimum, as in the impersonal justice case (when $e > 0$). However, the point of reference for the

---

[16] I assume that the optimal tax design problem has a unique solution, although, as pointed out by Harris (1975), this is by no means certain.

[17] If $e = e'$, W' in Eq. (7) reduces to W_D in Eq. (6).

social evaluation of each utility change is based on the individual's actual initial utility level rather than the common reference level used in the impersonal justice case. For example, an arbitrary loss of a given magnitude will have a smaller negative impact on the social welfare function if it is suffered by a relatively rich individual. Thus, when $e > e'$, the government is always concerned about inducing arbitrary redistributions of income, but redistributions of a given magnitude have a larger impact on the governmental objective function if they are experienced by relatively poor individuals.

Once the analytical structure of the optimal tax reform problem has been modified to include distributional concerns as described above, the case for the optimality of immediate partial enactment is only slightly altered. Suppose that the tax rate interval is $T_o \leq T \leq T'_d$. In the distributional justice case, the marginal utility changes implied by a movement from the initial equilibrium T_o are not weighted equally as they were in the impersonal justice case (since each individual's reference utility value is U^i_r. rather than a common value U_r as in Equation (2)). Thus, for a high enough value of e, no reform may be optimal. However, if some movement from the initial equilibrium is desirable, and if the aggregate marginal utility ratio (which is defined precisely as in the impersonal justice case) is monotonically declining over the tax rate interval, the arguments supporting the optimality of the policy of immediate partial enactment are still valid; accordingly, the optimal implementation policy will be immediate partial enactment to T^*, $T_o < T^* < T'_d$.

Thus, the extension of the results to the impersonal justice case is straightforward. Note that both the impersonal justice and distributional justice approaches to the analysis of tax reform require interpersonal cardinal utility comparisons. The choice between the two approaches requires a social judgment as to the appropriate way to weight the reform-induced redistributions which occur to individuals at different utility levels. Feldstein argues that a "procedure of ignoring income differences is of course common to most legislative and judicial procedures," and thus that the government should be indifferent to the actual utility levels of the individuals who experience the redistributions induced by the enactment of reform.[18] Also, it is clear from the discussion in Section 3 that the

[18] See Feldstein (1976b, p. 100) for further elaboration.

enactment of tax reform is not, in general, an appropriate way to remedy distributional inequities, as the incidence of reform will be arbitrary even within income classes.

Nevertheless, it is by no means obvious that simply ignoring distributional considerations in the analysis is appropriate. Distributional questions have frequently been emphasized in the optimal taxation literature (for example, see Atkinson (1973)) and distributional concerns frequently pervade legislative debate on a variety of issues. Also, academic studies of policy questions frequently include a distributive component; for example, both Arrow and Kalt (1979) and Loury (1981) use an income-weighting process in assessing the effects of changes in energy policy in the area of petroleum price deregulation. Thus, I feel that distributional questions are likely to arise in the evaluation of most tax reforms, so that the distributional justice approach is a relevant extension of Feldstein's framework for the analysis of tax reform.

7. Numerical Simulation Results

In this section, I report the results of some simulations with a simple general equilibrium model which provide a rough indication of how the social welfare gains obtained from the enactment of tax reform vary with the method of implementation. I compare the social welfare gains obtained with immediate full enactment, postponed full enactment, and immediate partial enactment in the impersonal justice case, the impersonal justice case when the government is constrained to full enactment at an arbitrary future date, and the distributional justice case.

The model[19] has two jurisdictions, each with a fixed land supply. The supply of capital to the two jurisdictions is perfectly elastic and capital is perfectly mobile between the two jurisdictions. Profit-maximizing firms produce a single good (the numeraire) in both jurisdictions using capital and land; the production function is Cobb–Douglas. Government services are modeled as purchases of the consumption good and are provided as a pure public good to residents of both jurisdictions. These purchases are financed by property taxation of land and capital in both jurisdictions. The

[19]The equations of the model are listed in the appendix, along with the parameter values used in the simulations.

initial equilibrium is characterized by a property tax differential across the two jurisdictions; the tax reform question addressed is the reduction of this differential, holding the service level constant. The tax rate in the initially low-tax jurisdiction is the exogeneous government control variable (T), while the tax rate in the initially high-tax jurisdiction must adjust to satisfy the revenue constraint.[20]

7.1. *The impersonal justice case*

For the impersonal justice case, land ownership in the initially high-tax jurisdiction is divided equally among N_G identical individuals and land ownership in the initially low-tax jurisdiction is divided equally among N_L identical individuals; no individual owns land in both jurisdictions. All capital is owned by nonresidents of the two jurisdictions and the government is assumed to include only the $N(N = N_G + N_L)$ landowners in its welfare calculations. In the single good model, the individual utility level of the landowners is equal to the income from their land holdings. The "reference" income level in the social welfare calculations for the impersonal justice case is the present value of a lifetime income stream equal to the mean income level in the initial equilibrium; this is approximated as $\tilde{Y}/n$ where $\tilde{Y}$ is mean yearly income and n is the discount rate.

The tax design optimum (T_d) in the impersonal justice case corresponds to the allocative efficiency optimum of "tax equalization"; that is, the endogenous tax rate in the initially high-tax jurisdiction falls as the tax rate in the initially low-tax jurisdiction is raised, and the unweighted sum of the utilities of the N landowners is maximized when the two tax rates are equal.[21] As the tax rate in the initially low-tax jurisdiction is increased from its initial value of T_o along the tax rate interval of $T_o \leq T \leq T_d$, all N landowners share in the efficiency gains from reform in proportion to their income shares, while the redistributions which occur are from

[20] The model described above is a simplified version of a model used to analyze the optimal implementation of metropolitan property tax base sharing and rate equalization; see Zodrow (1980).

[21] See the Appendix for a proof.

Table 1.1.
Social Welfare Gains — Impersonal Justice Case[a]

e-Index of Social Concern about Redistributions	% Welfare Change with Immediate Full Enactment	% Welfare Change with Postponed Full Enactment	Optimal Postponement (years)	% Welfare Change with Immediate Partial Enactment	% Original Tax Differential Remaining	Welfare Gain Ratio Immediate Partial vs. Postponed Full
0	1.14	1.14	0	1.14	0	1.00
0.5	1.63	1.63	0	1.67	12.6	1.03
1.0	2.13	2.13	0	2.35	24.3	1.10
1.5	2.52	2.52	0	3.19	32.1	1.27
2.0	2.62	2.69	1.7	4.10	37.6	1.52
2.5	2.29	2.86	4.3	5.03	40.5	1.76
3.0	1.41	3.03	6.3	5.95	46.6	1.96
3.5	–0.08	3.18	8.1	6.81	49.9	2.14
4.0	–2.21	3.31	9.6	7.61	53.3	2.30

[a]For example, for e = 3, immediate full enactment of a movement to the tax design optimum results in a social welfare increase of 1.41 percent (all welfare changes are expressed as a percentage of the level of social welfare with no reform, leaving the initial tax differential in perpetuity), full enactment after a postponement of 6.3 years results in a 3.03 percent increase in welfare, and immediate partial enactment (reducing the original tax differential by 53.4 percent and leaving the remaining 46.6 percent In perpetuity) increases welfare by 5.95 percent. The welfare increase with immediate partial enactment is nearly twice that obtained with postponed full enactment (5.95/3.03 = 1.96).

landowners in the initially low-tax jurisdiction to landowners in the initially high-tax jurisdiction.[22]

The relative magnitudes of the welfare gains in the impersonal justice case obtained from immediate full enactment, postponed full enactment, and immediate partial enactment are given in Table 1.1 for a range of values of e. For the parameter values chosen, the aggregate marginal utility tradeoff ratio R(T) declines monotonically to one at $T = T_d$, so immediate partial enactment is the optimal implementation policy.

Several features of the results presented in Table 1.1 are of interest. First, as noted above, the largest welfare improvements for all values of $e > 0$ are obtained with the reform implementation policy of immediate

[22]This is also proved in the appendix.

partial enactment. Note that the welfare improvements obtained with immediate partial enactment relative to those obtained with postponed full enactment increase as the concavity of the welfare function increases. That is, as social concern about arbitrary redistributions caused by reform increases, it becomes relatively more important to relax the full enactment constraint and instead to permit some immediate incremental reform. For example, for e = 1(2, 3), immediate partial enactment results in a 10 percent (52 percent, 96 percent) larger welfare gain than postponed full enactment. Note also that the remaining tax differential increases as e increases; as social concern about redistributions increases, the extent of the optimal immediate partial enactment decreases.

Second, note that the optimal postponement becomes positive only for a sufficiently concave welfare function (the values of e ≥ 2). Thus, postponement is an improvement over immediate full enactment only in these cases, while immediate partial enactment is preferable to immediate full enactment for all values of e > 0. For example, for e = 1.5, the policy of postponed full enactment cannot increase the welfare gain obtained with immediate full enactment, while immediate partial enactment (an immediate elimination of 67.9 percent of the original tax differential) results in a welfare gain more than 26 percent larger than that obtained with immediate full enactment.

Finally, note that for sufficiently concave welfare functions (e = 3.5, e = 4.0), immediate full enactment actually results in a welfare loss. In these cases, tax reform is undesirable unless postponed considerably (8.1 and 9.6 years) or unless partial reform is implemented immediately; the latter policy clearly results in much larger welfare gains.

7.2. *Phasing-in reform prior to a fixed full enactment date*

Results for the impersonal justice case when the government is constrained to full enactment of reform at a fixed future date are presented in Table 1.2. The simulation is identical to the one described in the previous section, except that the government must implement a movement to the tax design optimum of full tax equalization by the end of a fixed time period; this time period is arbitrarily chosen to be five years.

Table 1.2.
Social Welfare Gains — Government Constrained to Full Enactment After Five Years

e-Index of Social Concern about Redistributions	% Welfare Change with Immediate Full Enactment[a]	% Welfare Change with Postponed Full Enactment	Optimal Postponement (years)	% Welfare Change with Immediate Partial Enactment	% Original Tax Differential Remaining	Welfare Gain Ratio Immediate Partial vs. Postponed Full
0	1.14	1.14	0	1.14	0	1.00
0.5	1.63	1.63	0	1.65	14.8	1.01
1.0	2.13	2.13	0	2.22	26.8	1.05
1.5	2.52	2.52	0	2.83	37.6	1.12
2.0	2.62	2.69	1.7	3.33	46.6	1.24
2.5	2.29	2.86	4.3	3.66	56.9	1.28
3.0	1.41	2.98	5.0	3.74	64.6	1.26
3.5	−0.08	2.88	5.0	3.56	68.9	1.24
4.0	−2.21	2.52	5.0	3.09	73.6	1.23

[a]Welfare changes are expressed as a percentage of the level of social welfare with no reform.

The basic pattern of the results is similar to that in the unconstrained impersonal justice case. In particular, the largest welfare gains are obtained with the policy of immediate partial phasing-in of reform prior to the fixed full enactment date, and the extent of partial reform decreases as the concavity of the social welfare function increases.

However, constraining the government to full enactment within five years changes the nature of the results in two important ways. First, the maximum welfare improvements are reduced relative to the unconstrained case presented above, as the government must eventually move to the tax design optimum even though, as explained in Section 4, such a movement is never desirable. Note that for each value of e the extent of partial enactment is also reduced; since the government must impose the redistributions implied by full enactment after five years, the losses (gains) induced by immediate phasing-in of reform are weighted more heavily (lightly) than in the unconstrained case so that less partial reform is enacted.

Second, recall that the welfare improvements obtained with immediate partial enactment relative to those obtained with postponed full enactment increased as e increased in the unconstrained impersonal justice case. The same result obtains in the constrained case only as long as the constraint is non-binding in the calculation of the optimal postponement — that is, as long as the optimal postponed full enactment delay is less than five years. In these cases, immediate phasing-in of reform followed by full enactment at the end of five years increases welfare in two ways. First, immediate phasing-in of reform increases welfare by permitting immediate enactment of reform where the marginal efficiency gains are relatively large. Second, delaying full enactment (by the difference between five years and the optimal postponement period) increases welfare by reducing the gains and losses implied by the eventual movement to the tax design optimum which causes relatively large accumulated redistributions and relatively small marginal efficiency gains. However, when the optimal postponement period is greater than or equal to the maximum allowable delay of five years, none of the potential gains from delaying full enactment can be realized. Thus, one of the advantages of immediate phasing-in of reform prior to the fixed full enactment date in comparison to postponing reform is eliminated. As a result, the ratio of the welfare gains (in the last column of Table 1.2) declines as e increases, once the unconstrained optimal postponement period exceeds five years. In fact, recall that social concern about the redistributions implied by the mandated movement to full equalization after five years means that the losses associated with immediate phasing-in of reform are weighted more heavily than the gains at T_0 (where they were equally weighted in the unconstrained case). For a high enough value of e, this concern will imply that any immediate phasing-in of reform is undesirable, as explained in Section 5. In this case, the government will not be able to increase the welfare gain obtained with postponed full enactment after the five year delay.

7.3. *The distributional justice case*

Results in the distributional justice case are presented in Table 1.3. In this case, the government is again assumed to be unconstrained in its choice of tax reform implementation policy. The simulation differs from the impersonal justice case in three ways.

Table 1.3.
Social Welfare Gains — Impersonal Justice Case (e′ = 0.5)

e-Index of Social Concern about Redistributions	% Welfare Change with Immediate Full Enactment[a]	% Welfare Change with Postponed Full Enactment	Optimal Postponement (years)	% Welfare Change with Immediate Partial Enactment	% Excess Tax Differential Remaining[b]	Welfare Gain Ratio Immediate Partial vs. Postponed Full
0.5	1.52	1.52	0	1.52	0	1.00
1.0	1.80	1.80	0	1.84	11.7	1.02
1.5	1.93	1.93	0	2.18	24.7	1.13
2.0	1.77	1.77	0	2.46	35.6	1.39
2.5	1.22	1.39	3.4	2.69	43.6	1.93
3.0	0.20	1.04	7.3	2.84	47.9	2.72
3.5	−1.35	0.73	11.3	2.90	52.5	3.97
4.0	−3.45	0.46	15.5	2.89	57.3	6.26

[a]Welfare changes are expressed as a percentage of the level of social welfare with no reform.
[b]The excess tax differential refers to the difference between the original tax differential and the optimal tax differential (the tax differential which maximizes Equation 6 when e′ = 0.5).

First, landowners in the initially high-tax jurisdiction are assumed to have an additional source of income such that they are relatively wealthier than the landowners in the initially low-tax jurisdiction.[23] Second, the tax design optimum is no longer the allocative efficiency optimum of tax equalization. Instead, as explained in Section 6, the tax design optimum is the value of the exogenous tax rate which maximizes W_D as given in Eq. (6) for e′ > 0. The results reported in Table 1.3 assume e′ = 0.5 which results in a tax rate interval of $T_o \leq T \leq T_d' < T_d$. That is, since the residents of the initially low-tax jurisdiction are relatively poor, the tax design optimum in the distributional justice case calls for a tax differential favoring the relatively poor jurisdiction rather than full equalization ($T_d' < T_d$). However, the initial equilibrium is assumed to be characterized by an even larger differential favoring the poor jurisdiction ($T_o < T_d'$), so that full

[23]For example, landowners in the initially high-tax jurisdiction could own some capital; since the return on capital is assumed fixed in the model, this would be equivalent to an exogenous source of income.

enactment of reform refers to a reduction of the initial differential to the "optimal" differential.

Third, in the impersonal justice case, the various reform implementation policies are evaluated according to the welfare criterion specified by Eq. (7). Since the welfare function is concave, a gain to an individual is still valued less than proportionately while a loss to the same individual is valued more than proportionately. However, the "reference" income level in the welfare calculation is the present value of a lifetime income stream equal to the individual's income level in the initial equilibrium (denoted as Y^G/n (Y^L/n) for the individuals in the initially high (low)-tax jurisdiction who are gainers (losers) from reform). Hence, in the distributional justice case, the gains from reform are weighted less than in the impersonal justice case since they accrue to relatively wealthy individuals.

Increasing social concern about the redistributions caused by reform is associated with values of e in Table 1.3 which are increasingly higher than $e' = 0.5$, and full enactment of reform refers to the elimination of 83 percent of the original tax differential. Given this interpretation, the pattern of the results in the distributional justice case is identical to the impersonal justice case. The largest welfare improvements are obtained with immediate partial enactment, the improvement obtained with immediate partial enactment relative to the gain obtained with postponed full enactment increases as social concern about redistribution increases, and the extent of immediate partial enactment decreases as e increases. Postponement is preferable to immediate full enactment only for a sufficiently concave welfare function, while immediate partial enactment is preferable to immediate full enactment for all values of $e > e' = 0.5$. Finally, immediate full enactment again can result in a welfare loss for a sufficiently concave welfare function; both postponed full enactment and immediate partial enactment yield welfare gains in these cases, although the latter policy is clearly preferable.

8. Conclusion

I have considered the optimal implementation of tax reform proposals within the context of an instantaneous adjustment, perfect information model where changes in the tax structure are unanticipated. The analysis shows that immediate partial enactment is the optimal method of implementing reform in a variety of situations involving different governmental objective functions and constraints; the numerical simulations suggest that immediate partial enactment yields substantially larger welfare gains than the alternate implementation policy of postponed full enactment. The basic intuition behind the optimality of immediate partial enactment is that the first movements toward the tax design optimum result in relatively large marginal efficiency gains which dominate the effects of the associated redistributions on the social welfare function; these gains should be captured immediately rather than postponed. However, as one approaches full enactment, the marginal efficiency gains from reform become small, and, at some point, it is optimal from a social viewpoint simply to forego the incremental redistributions associated with further movements toward the tax design optimum, rather than just reducing them by postponed enactment. This result obtains in (i) Feldstein's "impersonal justice" case, where the government is indifferent to the actual utility levels of the individuals who experience utility changes as a result of reform, (ii) the case where the government is constrained to eventual full enactment at a fixed future date (immediate partial enactment is the optimal phasing-in policy), and (iii) the "distributional justice" case where the government is concerned about the utility levels of the individuals who actually experience the redistributions. The numerical results suggest that sizable welfare gains, relative to those obtained with postponed full enactment, may be obtained with immediate partial enactment in all three cases.[24]

Administrative and political considerations strengthen the conclusion that immediate partial enactment is the optimal implementation policy. From an administrative viewpoint, immediate partial enactment would appear to be superior to a complicated phasing-in policy. Moreover, data presented by Bloom, Ladd, and Yinger (1980) support the assumption that the effects of actual tax changes are capitalized into property values

[24]"Note that the welfare improvements cited are clearly upper limits, as the assumption of instantaneous adjustment biases the optimal implementation result in the direction of immediate enactment by ignoring adjustment costs; I am currently investigating the optimal implementation of reform in models with adjustment costs.

but suggest that the effects of tax changes announced more than one year ahead of their enactment are not perfectly capitalized; this phenomenon would tend to make the calculation of the optimal postponement period rather tenuous.[25] Finally, immediate partial enactment may be a more realistic tax reform goal, as small changes seem to be more readily attainable within the political process than large ones.

Appendix

The seven equations of the general equilibrium model used in the simulations reported in Section 6 are as follows:

$$X_1 = K_1^a V_1^{1-a} \tag{A.1}$$

$$X_2 = K_2^a V_2^{1-a} \tag{A.2}$$

$$K_1/V_1 = [r(1 + P_1)/a]^{[1/(a-1)]} \tag{A.3}$$

$$K_2/V_2 = [r(1 + P_2)/a]^{[1/(a-1)]} \tag{A.4}$$

$$X_1 = (1 + P_1)(rK_1 + s_1V_1) \tag{A.5}$$

$$X_2 = (1 + P_2)(rK_2 + s_2V_2) \tag{A.6}$$

$$G = P_1\,(rK_1 + s_1V_1 + P_2\,(rK_2 + s_2V_2) \tag{A.7}$$

where X_j = production of the (numeraire) composite good in jurisdiction j
K_j = capital used in production of good X_j
V_j = fixed land supply in jurisdiction j
r = exogenously determined net return to capital
s_j = net return to land in jurisdiction j
P_j = ad valorem property tax rate in jurisdiction j
G = fixed total government purchases of the composite good
a = capital share parameter in the Cobb-Douglas production function.

Equations (A.1) and (A.2) are the production equations, while Eqs. (A.3) and (A.4) are the profit-maximizing factor demands. Equations (A.5) and (A.6)

[25] This point was first made by Helen Ladd; see Ladd (1980).

are implied by the assumptions of perfect competition and constant returns to scale production functions, and Eq. (A.7) is the government budget constraint.

The effects of a change in the tax structure in the model can be seen by totally differentiating the above system (see Ballentine and Eris (1975) or Vandendorpe and Friedlaender (1976) for details of general equilibrium differential incidence analysis) and solving for the elasticities of the factor price changes with respect to an increase in the relatively low tax rate P_2 (the "^" notation indicates logarithmic differentiation):

$$\hat{s}_1 = [y_{V2}(d_1+d_2)/(d_1 f_{V2}) + E](1 \hat{+} P_2) \quad \text{(A.8)}$$

$$\hat{s}_2 = [-y_{V1}(d_1+d_2)/(d_1 f_{V2}) + E](1 \hat{+} P_2), \quad \text{(A.9)}$$

where

$y_{Vi} = s_i V_i/(s_1 V_1 + s_2 V_2) = s_i V_i/Y \qquad i = 1, 2$

$f_{Vi} = s_i (1 + P_i)V_i/X_i \qquad i = 1, 2$

$d_i = (s_i V_i - P_i r K_i)/Y \qquad i = 1, 2$

$E = (P_1 - P_2)\,[(1 - f_{V1})/f_{V1}]\,y_{V1} y_{V2}/(d_1 f_{V2}).$

Thus, y_{Vi} is the income share of landowners in jurisdiction i in total landowner income, and f_{Vi} is the land share of gross production costs in jurisdiction i. Differentiating the government budget constraint yields:

$$-(d_1/f_{V1})(1 \hat{+} P_1) - (d_2/f_{V2})(1 \hat{+} P_2) = 0.$$

Thus $(-d_i/f_{Vi})$ is the elasticity of the government budget deficit with respect to a change in the tax rate in jurisdiction i, holding the other tax rate constant; I assume that each $d_i > 0$, that is, neither jurisdiction's tax rate is so high that a reduction in its tax rate increases its revenues. Finally, the aggregate marginal efficiency gain is equal to the increase in landowners' total income ($Y = s_1V_1 + s_2V_2$):

$$\hat{Y} = y_{V1}\hat{s}_1 + y_{V2}\hat{S}_2 = E(1 \hat{+} P_2).$$

Hence E can be termed "efficiency effect" of reform; since E is positive as long as $P_1 > P_2$, the allocative efficiency optimum is tax equalization.

The effects of an increase in P_2 on individual landowners (where landowners in jurisdiction 1 (2) are the gainers (losers) from reform) are given by:

$$dU^G = s_1(V_1/N_G)\hat{s}_1$$
$$dU^L = s_2(V_2/N_L)\hat{s}_2.$$

As noted in the text, the effects of reform can be split into two components; these correspond to the two terms in each bracket in Eqs. (A.8) and (A.9). The first term in each expression is the redistributive effect of reform, as an increase in P_2 causes a pure redistribution from landowners in jurisdiction 2 to landowners in jurisdiction 1:

$$N_G\ s_1\ (V_1/N_G)\ y_{V2}\ (d_1 + d_2)/d_1 f_{V2}$$
$$-N_L\ s_2\ (V_2/N_L)\ y_{V1}\ (d_1 + d_2)/d_1 f_{V2} = 0.$$

The second term in each expression shows that all landowners share in the efficiency gain in proportion to their shares in total land income:

$$[N_G\ s_1\ (V_1 N_G)/Y]E + [N_L\ s_2\ (V_2/N_L)/Y]E = E.$$[26]

The parameter values used in the simulations are $a = 0.8$, $V_1 = V_2 = 1$, $N_G = N_L = 100$, $r = 0.233$. The discount rate is assumed to be 9 percent and the initial property tax structure assumes a tax rate of 6 percent in the high-tax jurisdiction ($P_1 = 0.40$) and a tax rate of 3 percent in the low-tax jurisdiction ($P_2 = 0.25$).

In the impersonal justice case, the tax design optimum of property tax equalization occurs at $P_1 = P_2 = 0.294$, which implies a tax rate interval of $0.250 \le P_2 \le 0.294$. In the distributional justice case, the residents of the initially high-tax jurisdiction are assumed to have an exogenous source of income such that they would be fifty percent wealthier than the residents of the initially low tax jurisdiction in the equalized equilibrium; in this case, the tax design optimum is $P_d' = 0.282$ (the tax design optimum calls

[26] For the parameter values chosen, the efficiency gains never dominate the redistributive losses for landowners in the initially low-tax jurisdiction, who can be unambiguously classified as "losers" from reform ($dU/dT < 0$ for $T_o \le T \le T_d$).

for a tax differential of $P_1 - P_2 = 0.025$ which favors the relatively poor jurisdiction) and the tax rate interval is $0.250 \leq P_2 \leq 0.282$.

Acknowledgments

Research support from the National Science Foundation (Grant DAR-80011842) is gratefully acknowledged. This paper is based on my dissertation; I would like to thank David Bradford, Wallace Oates and Edwin Mills for their guidance and the NBER and the Sloan Foundation for financial support. I also benefited from the suggestions of Thomas McCaleb, Peter Mieszkowski, and especially Helen Ladd, whose comments on this paper as well on my dissertation (see Ladd (1980)) were extremely useful. Finally, I would like to thank Jackie Drane and Tom Herzfeld for research assistance.

References

Arrow, Kenneth J. and Joseph P. Kalt, *Petroleum Price Regulation: Should We Decontrol?* (Washington: American Enterprise Institute, 1979).

Atkinson, Anthony B., How Progressive Should Income Tax Be? in J. Michael Parkin, Editor, *Essays in Modem Economics* (London: Longmans, 1973).

Atkinson, Anthony B. and Joseph E. Stiglitz, *Lectures on Public Economics* (New York: McGraw-Hill, 1980).

Ballentine, J. Gregory and Ibrahim Eris, On the General Equilibrium Analysis of Tax Incidence, *Journal of Political Economy* 84 (February, 1975): 1–25.

Bloom, Howard S., Helen F. Ladd and John Yinger, Intrajurisdictional Property Tax Capitalization, Report for U.S. Department of Housing and Urban Development Grant H-2915RG (August, 1980).

Feldstein, Martin S., Compensation in Tax Reform, *National Tax Journal* 29 (June, 1976a): 123–130.

Feldstein, Martin S., On the Theory of Tax Reform, *Journal of Public Economics* 6 (July–August, 1976b): 77–104.

Harberger, Arnold C., Taxation, Resource Allocation and Welfare, in Arnold C. Harberger, *Taxation and Welfare* (Boston: Little, Brown and Company, 1976).

Harris, Richard G., A Note on Convex-Concave Demand Systems, Queen's University, Discussion Paper No. 197 (1975).

Ladd, Helen F., Discussion, *Proceedings of the Seventy-Third Annual Conference on Taxation,* National Tax Association-Tax Institute of America (November, 1980): 251–252.

Loury, Glenn C., An Analysis of the Efficiency and Inflationary Impact of the Decontrol of Natural Gas Prices, National Gas Supply Association (April, 1981).

Mirrless, James A., Optimal Tax Theory: A Synthesis, *Journal of Public Economics* 6 (November, 1976): 327–358.

Sandmo, Agnar, Optimal Taxation: An Introduction to the Literature, *Journal of Public Economics* 6 (July–August, 1976): 37–54.

Vandendorpe, Adolph L. and Ann F. Friedlaender, Differential Incidence in the Presence of Initial Distorting Taxes, *Journal of Public Economics* 6 (October, 1976): 205–229.

Zodrow, George R., Optimal Tax Reform: The Case of Property Tax Equalization, *Proceedings of the Seventy-Third Annual Conference on Taxation,* National Tax Association-Tax Institute of America (November, 1980): 240–250.

Zodrow, George R., On the Optimal Timing and Extent of Enactment of Tax Reform, working paper, Rice University (January, 1981).

Chapter 2

Optimal Tax Reform in the Presence of Adjustment Costs*

George R. Zodrow

U.S. Treasury Office of Tax Analysis, Washington, DC 20220, USA
Rice University, Houston, TX 77251, USA

The optimal implementation of an efficiency-enhancing capital taxation reform is examined when the government is concerned about arbitrary reform-induced redistributions and investment causes firms to incur adjustment costs. Theoretical results indicate that immediate partial enactment of reform is optimal with concave adjustment costs, while with convex adjustment costs, the optimal reform implementation policy is either (i) immediate partial enactment with sufficiently low adjustment costs, (ii) phased-in partial enactment with intermediate adjustment costs, or (iii) postponed partial enactment with sufficiently high adjustment costs. Numerical results suggest that, relative to the optimal one-step implementation policy, little is gained by phasing-in reform.

*This chapter is reproduced from *Journal of Public Economics*, **27**(2), 211–230, 1985.

1. Introduction

The important differences between optimal tax reform (the most effective method of reforming an existing tax structure) and optimal tax design (the selection of an optimal tax structure irrespective of initial conditions) have been the subject of several recent papers. Two main strands of this literature can be identified. The first, initiated by Guesnerie (1977), focuses on the conditions under which tax reform is Pareto-improving; although quite interesting, these conditions are sufficiently restrictive to rule out most tax reform proposals.

Accordingly, the second strand focuses on cases where reform has a net positive effect — according to some social welfare criterion — but causes individual losses as well as gains (and compensatory lump-sum transfers are infeasible).[1] Feldstein (1976a, 1976b) argues persuasively that such gains and losses should be a source of social concern as they are essentially government-induced arbitrary redistributions of income which violate commonly accepted notions of horizontal equity.[2] On this view the critical distinction between optimal tax design and optimal tax reform is clear. The optimal tax design theorist selects a tax structure to maximize a social welfare function; if the existing tax system differs from the optimal one, immediate reform is appropriate. In contrast, even if the optimal tax reform theorist agrees on the 'tax design optimum', postponing, phasing-in, or partially enacting a movement to the tax design optimum is preferred to immediate enactment — the associated reduction in the present value of social welfare gains[3] is acceptable in order to reduce the magnitudes of the reform-induced redistributions.

---

[1] Compensatory lump sum transfers are assumed to be politically infeasible. See Feldstein (1976a) for a discussion of compensation and tax reform.

[2] This argument rests on two assumptions which are maintained throughout my analysis. First, the tax change must be unanticipated so that the effects of the tax change are not reflected in asset prices (see Feldstein, 1976a for a discussion of this point). Second, asset prices must reflect the capitalized value of tax advantages and the existing tax structure must have been in effect long enough that many assets have changed hands since its enactment; in this case, the incidence of reform is capricious, as the correspondence between asset owners and those who benefited from the tax break is low (see Feldstein, 1976b).

[3] This discussion refers to the standard optimal tax design social welfare function, rather than the optimal tax reform objective function discussed below and in Feldstein (1976b).

Feldstein suggests that, from an optimal tax reform perspective, postponed full enactment — current enactment of a movement to the tax design optimum with a future effective date — may be the optimal reform implementation policy since it reduces the present value of all gains and losses proportionately. Arguing along similar lines, the U.S. Treasury (1977) and the Institute for Fiscal Studies (1978) both recommend a ten-year phasing-in period to reduce the redistributions associated with implementing their proposed reforms.

In an earlier paper (Zodrow, 1981), I argued that immediate partial enactment — for example, the partial reduction of a distortionary tax differential, leaving the remaining differential in perpetuity — is the optimal reform implementation policy, dominating both postponing and phasing-in reform. The intuition behind this result is that the first movements toward the tax design optimum result in relatively large marginal efficiency gains which dominate the negative effects of the associated redistributions; these gains should be captured immediately rather than postponed or phased-in. Then, as full enactment is approached, the marginal efficiency gains from further reform become small and, at some point, it is optimal to forgo them in order to avoid the associated incremental redistributions (rather than just reducing these redistributions with postponed or phased-in enactment).

However, this analysis assumes that the economy adjusts instantaneously and costlessly to tax changes. This is a troublesome assumption, since the enactment of many tax reform proposals would involve substantial resource reallocation. By neglecting the adjustment costs implicit in tax reform-induced resource reallocation, the analysis may be biased toward the immediate enactment option since postponing or phasing-in reform may reduce these adjustment costs.

Accordingly, the purpose of this paper is to consider the optimal implementation of reform within the context of a model which explicitly includes adjustment costs.[4] The analysis focuses on reforms which improve the efficiency of capital allocation in an economy where adjustment costs

[4] Most previous tax reform studies also ignore adjustment costs. An exception is the analysis of Fullerton (1983). His approach is quite different in emphasis from this study in that he simply assumes immediate enactment and infinite net adjustment costs (all reallocation

are incurred in effecting such a reallocation. Two types of adjustment costs have been analyzed in the literature. Most studies assume that adjustment costs are convex, while Rothschild (1971) argues that indivisibilities and economies of scale in the investment process imply concave adjustment costs; both concave and convex adjustment costs are analyzed in this paper.

Since the focus of the paper is the evaluation of efficiency-enhancing reforms which improve capital allocation, I utilize, without modification, Feldstein's (1976b) analytical framework. This approach assumes that the government is (i) concerned only with efficiency in selecting the tax design optimum, and (ii) indifferent to the actual utility levels of the individuals who experience the arbitrary reform-induced redistributions. I have shown elsewhere (Zodrow, 1981, 1985) how the analytical framework can be modified to allow for equity considerations in the selection of the tax design optimum as well as social concern about two experiences the redistributions;[5] these extensions are not considered here.

The paper is organized as follows. The optimal tax reform problem is reviewed in Section 2, and the model is presented in Section 3. Analytical results are provided in Section 4 while numerical simulation results are presented in Section 5. A concluding section comments on the generality of the model used in the analysis and summarizes the general inferences that can be drawn from the results presented in the paper.

2. Specification of the Optimal Tax Reform Problem

Since the distinction between optimal tax design and optimal tax reform is discussed by Feldstein (1976b) and Bittker (1980), only a brief treatment which stresses the analytical differences between the two approaches

---

occurs through replacement investment) and then considers the implications for the efficiency gains from tax reform.

[5] In these analyses, the tax design optimum is selected to maximize the standard optimal taxation social welfare function characterized by a diminishing social marginal valuation of individual utility (see Atkinson, 1973 or Atkinson and Stiglitz, 1980), while the optimal tax reform objective function is based on the assumption that the government is more averse to an arbitrary loss of a given magnitude if it is suffered by a relatively poor individual.

is presented here. Also, see Zodrow (1981) for a detailed formulation of the optimal tax reform problem.

Consider an economy with a fixed number (P) of individuals, indexed by i, each with a single-period utility function U^i defined over private good consumption.[6] The government has two tax instruments and must finance a fixed level of services. Since one of the tax instruments must adjust endogenously to balance the government budget, the other tax instrument, denoted as T, is the only government control variable.

The standard optimal tax design problem (see Atkinson and Stiglitz, 1980 for a thorough discussion) is to determine the tax design optimum T^* which maximizes a social welfare function which aggregates the individual utility levels. Tax reform is desirable if the existing tax structure, denoted as T^0, differs from T^*. Suppose that $T^0 < T^*$. The optimal tax reform problem is to determine the best way to increase T along the interval $T^0 \leqq T \leqq T^*$. Immediate movement to T^* may be inappropriate for two reasons, as postponed, phased-in or partial enactment of reform may be desirable (i) to reduce the magnitudes of the reform-induced redistributions of income, and/or (ii) to reduce the costs of adjustment incurred due to reform-induced factor reallocation.

The government's optimization problem is formulated as follows. Suppose the tax structure can be changed at F points in time t_j, where $t_1 = 0$ and $\Delta t = t_j - t_{j-1}$, $j = 2,..., F$, defines a 'period'. The tax structure is unchanged beyond time t_F.[7] At each time t_j, the government increases T by an amount $X_j \geqq 0$, where

$$\sum_{j=1}^{F} X_j \leqq (T^* - T^0). \tag{1}$$

The following definitions will be useful. Full enactment of reform occurs when Eq. (1) is an equality, while a strict inequality denotes partial enactment. Phased-in reform occurs when any two X_j are non-zero.

[6] Government services, which are held constant throughout the analysis, are not included in the individual utility function; alternatively, the individual utility function is separable in public and private goods.

[7] Thus, I assume an infinitely-lived government or that future governments honor the current government's commitments.

Immediate enactment implies only X_1 is non-zero, while postponed enactment occurs when only one X_1, $j = 2,\ldots,F$ is non-zero. Note that immediate, phased-in and postponed enactment may be partial or full. The time path of reform is described by the vector

$$X = (X_1, \ldots, X_F). \tag{2}$$

The government is assumed to be able to calculate the present values of the individual utility changes ($V^i(X)$) associated with any time path of reform; the $V^i(X)$ will hereafter be referred to as the capital gains and losses induced by reform. The optimal tax reform problem is the selection of X to maximize an objective function $W(X)$ which aggregates the $V^i(X)$. Specifically, following Feldstein, $W(X)$ is the following modified version of the standard optimal tax design social welfare function:

$$W(X) = \frac{1}{1-\varepsilon}\sum_{i=1}^{P}\{[B + V^i(X)]^{1-\varepsilon} - 1\}, \qquad 0 \leqq \varepsilon < \infty, \tag{3}$$

where the constants ε and B are parameters which reflect governmental attitudes about the effects of tax reform.[8]

In this formulation, ε is a constant elasticity parameter which serves as an index of the degree of social concern about the arbitrary redistributions caused by reform; it is the absolute value of the elasticity of the social marginal valuation of changes in the 'scaled' individual capital gain or loss expressions ($B + V^i$), where the B-scaling process is described below. Increasing values of this elasticity parameter (increasing concavity of the optimal tax reform social welfare function) imply greater social concern about the arbitrary nature of reform-induced redistributions, as individual capital losses (gains) are weighted more (less) than proportionately in the social aggregation process.[9]

---

[8] Note that the one is subtracted in Eq. (3) so that the welfare function is well defined when $\varepsilon = 1$; in this case, Eq. (3) becomes the sum of the natural logarithms of the ($B + V^i$) expressions. See Atkinson and Stiglitz (1980) for elaboration of this point, as well as a thorough discussion of the properties of the optimal tax design social welfare function analogous to Eq. (3).

[9] Thus, the ε parameter, which reflects social aversion to arbitrary redistributions in the optimal tax reform problem, is analogous to the elasticity of the marginal social valuation

If $\varepsilon = 0$, maximizing Eq. (3) is equivalent to maximizing the sum of the $V^i(X)$ — there is no social concern about inducing redistributions. Moreover, if the pattern of utilities in each period is a function only of the tax structure in that period — as is the case if there are no adjustment costs — then the optimal reform implementation policy is immediate full enactment.

The determination of the optimal reform implementation policy is more difficult if there are adjustment costs and/or there is social concern about redistributions ($\varepsilon > 0$). Adjustment costs make utility in each period a function of the entire tax path X and, when $\varepsilon > 0$, reform-induced capital gains and losses are weighted in the social aggregation process. In both cases, postponed, phased-in or partial enactment may be desirable.

Finally, the B parameter is an arbitrary reference base used to scale the magnitudes of the $V^i(X)$; for example, Feldstein suggests setting B equal to the mean utility level in the initial equilibrium. Relatively large values of B make any reform-induced capital gains and losses relatively small, so that the 'weighting' process described above is less important (when $\varepsilon > 0$), and postponed, phased-in or partial enactment of reform becomes less desirable. Note that B is the same for all individuals so that, as noted in the introduction, this approach evaluates reform-induced capital gains and losses independently of individual utility levels.

3. Modeling Capital Tax Changes in a Simple Economy

In this section, I construct a model of the investment effects of capital taxation reform; the model chosen is the simplest one which includes the three effects of reform emphasized above — efficiency gains, pure redistributions and adjustment costs — within a dynamic general equilibrium framework. The model is limited to two periods which is sufficient to explore the critical question of whether immediate, phased-in, or postponed enactment of full or partial reform is optimal; the two-period assumption is relaxed in the simulation results.

---

of individual utility, which reflects social aversion to inequality in the optimal tax design problem.

Consider a perfectly competitive, single-good economy with two jurisdictions, labeled J1 and J2. The good is produced with one variable factor, hereafter referred to as capital, and one fixed factor, hereafter referred to as land. The only taxes are specific taxes on capital in the two jurisdictions. In the initial tax-distorted equilibrium, the tax rate in J1 (T_{10}) is arbitrarily assumed to be greater than the tax rate in J2 (T_{20}) so that the initial capital stock in J1 (K_{10}) is smaller than the capital stock in J2 (K_{20}). The amount of land in each jurisdiction is fixed at one unit.

There are a fixed number of firms (M, N) in the two jurisdictions J1 and J2. Within a jurisdiction, each firm is identical, with a fixed supply of land ($1/M$, $1/N$) and an initial capital stock (K_{10}/M, K_{20}/N). All firms produce output with a constant returns to scale production function using capital and land; there is no depreciation. Each firm faces identical costs of adjustment which are a function of firm investment in period *t;* adjustment costs are symmetric for investment and disinvestment.

There is a fixed number (P) of consumers, with utility assumed to equal net income for each. There are two groups of consumers — one group of P_1 identical individuals, each of which owns $1/P_1$ units of land in J1, and a second group of P_2 identical individuals, each of which owns $1/P_2$ units of land in J2 ($P = P_1 + P_2$). No individual owns land in both jurisdictions, and each owns $(K_{10} + K_{20})/P$ of the initial capital stock.

Government services are modeled as public purchases of the production good. Capital tax revenues must finance a fixed level of public services (G) in each period.

Since I assume for simplicity that the 'future' can be modeled as two periods, the endogenous and exogenous variables change at only two points in time, $t_1 = 0$ and $t_2 = \Delta t$. The exogenous government tax variable is assumed to be the tax rate in the high tax jurisdiction J1; thus, the tax rates in J1 in the two periods are $T_{11} - T_{10} - X_1$ and $T_{12} = T_{10} - X_1 - X_{2,}$ where $X_1 \geqq 0$ and $X_2 \geqq 0$ are incremental tax reductions. I assume further that the initial tax rate in J1 is not so high that tax cuts increase revenues originating in J1. Thus, the tax rate in J2 in the two periods must rise endogenously to $T_{21} = T_{20} + Z_1$ and $T_{22} = T_{20} + Z_1 + Z_{2,}$ where $Z_1 \geqq 0$ and $Z_2 \geqq 0$ are incremental tax increases.

The endogenous responses of Z_1 and Z_2 are based on two assumptions. First, I assume that firms can purchase capital at a fixed rental rate R. Second, I adopt a somewhat unconventional government budget constraint. In each period, tax reductions in J1 must be offset by tax increases in J2 sufficient to finance the fixed level of government services G. At this point, the improved capital allocation within the two jurisdiction economy implies that the increase in demand for capital in J1 is larger in absolute value than the decrease in demand for capital in J2. I assume that the tax rate in J2 is further increased until these two changes in capital demand are equal in absolute value, with the excess tax revenues being given to landowners in J2 — that is, the government adjusts the endogenous tax rate to keep the economy's capital stock fixed.[10]

Thus, assuming a constant discount factor ρ, the optimization problem facing an infinitely-lived profit-maximizing representative firm $m(=1,\ldots,M)$ in J1 is to choose investment in the two periods, $I_1^m \geqq 0$ and $I_2^m \geqq 0$, and thus capital stocks $K_{11}^m = K_{10}/M + I_1^m$ and $K_{12}^m = K_{10}/M + I_1^m + I_2^m$ to maximize

$$\pi^m(I_1^m, I_2^m) = \delta[F(K_{11}^m) - (R+T_{11})K_{11}^m] - \delta C(\mathrm{I}_1^m) \\ + (\delta/\rho)[F(K_{12}^m) - (R+T_{12})K_{12}^m] - \delta^2 C(\mathrm{I}_2^m), \tag{4}$$

where $\delta = 1/(1+\rho)$, $F(\cdot)$ is the production function with the fixed land argument suppressed, $C(\cdot)$ is the cost of adjustment function, and the production good is the numeraire.

Similarly, a representative firm n in J2 chooses disinvestment in the two periods, $I_1^n \geqq 0$ and $I_2^n \geqq 0$, and thus capital stocks $K_{21}^n = K_{20}/N - I_1^n$ and $K_{22}^n = K_{20}/N - I_1^n - I_2^n$, to maximize

$$\pi^n(I_1^n, I_2^n) = \delta[F(K_{21}^n) - (R+T_{21})K_{21}^n] - \delta C(I_1^n) \\ + (\delta/\rho)[F(K_{22}^n) - (R+T_{22})K_{22}^n] - \delta^2 C(I_2^n). \tag{5}$$

[10] Note that this simplifying assumption violates, in a different context, the ban on lump-sum redistributions. However, the amounts involved are very small (see Zodrow, 1984 for numerical estimates in a similar model) and this approach (as shown below) clearly separates the redistributive and efficiency-enhancing effects of reform; a more conventional budget constraint is used in the simulations without changing the nature of the results.

The assumed governmental behavior implies:

$$I_1 = MI_1^m = NI_1^n, \tag{6}$$

$$I_2 = MI_2^m = NI_2^n. \tag{7}$$

Denote the total capital stocks in each jurisdiction as $K_{11} = K_{10} + I_1, K_{12} = K_{10} + I_1 + I_2, K_{21} = K_{20} - I_1$ and $K_{22} = K_{20} - I_1 - I_2$.

Firm behavior differs in the convex and concave adjustment cost cases, as shown in the following two subsections. The discussion below frequently draws on results presented in Rothschild (1971).

3.1. *Convex adjustment costs*

In this case, the properties of the adjustment cost function $C(\Omega)$, for a level of firm investment Ω, are assumed to be

$$C(0) = C'(0) = 0, \quad C'(\Omega) \gtreqqless 0 \quad \text{if} \quad \Omega \gtreqqless 0, \quad C''(\Omega) > 0, \tag{8}$$

where the primes denote differentiation. Since $C'(0) = 0$, any tax change will induce a change in the capital stock. Moreover, a straightforward extension of results presented by Rothschild shows that any tax change will induce an investment response in both periods; that is, convex adjustment costs imply interior solutions to the firm's optimization problem.

Since $F'(\cdot)$ is homogeneous of degree zero, the first order conditions for representative firm m can be written:

$$\delta[F'(K_{11}) - C'(I_1/M)] + (\delta/\rho)F'(K_{12}) = \delta(R + T_{11}) + (\delta/\rho)(R + T_{12}), \tag{9}$$

$$(\delta/\rho)F'(\mathrm{K}_{12}) - \delta^2\mathrm{C}'(I_2/M) = (\delta/\rho)(R + T_{12}); \tag{10}$$

the firm invests until the discounted value of the marginal product of the investment, net of adjustment costs, equals the discounted marginal cost. The analogous expressions for firm n, substituting from Eqs. (6) and (7), are

$$\delta[F'(K_{21}) - C'(I_1/N)] + (\delta/\rho)F'(K_{22}) = \delta(R + T_{21}) + (\delta/\rho)(R + T_{22}), \tag{11}$$

$$(\delta/\rho)F'(K_{22}) + \delta^2C'(I_2/\mathrm{N}) = (\delta/\rho)(R + T_{22}). \tag{12}$$

For any X_1, X_2, Eqs. (9)–(12) specify a system of four equations in I_1, I_2, Z_1 and Z_2; *I* assume the existence of a unique equilibrium.

To simplify notation, denote $f_{11} = -F''(K_{11})$, $f_{12} = -F''(K_{12})$, $f_{21} = -F''(K_{21})$, $f_{22} = -F''(K_{22})$, $c_{11} = C''(I_1/M)/M$, $c_{12} = C''(I_2/M)/M$, $c_{21} = C''(I_2/N)/N$, $c_{22} = C''(I_1/N)/N$. Totally differentiating Eqs. (9)–(12) and solving yields the investment responses to exogenous tax changes:

$$\partial I_1/\partial X_1 = (f_{12} + c_{12})/D, \tag{13}$$

$$\partial I_2/\partial X_1 = (f_{11} + c_{11} - f_{12})/D, \tag{14}$$

$$\partial I_1/\partial X_2 = \delta c_{12}/D, \tag{15}$$

$$\partial I_2/\partial X_2 = (f_{11} + c_{11})/D, \tag{16}$$

where $D = (f_{11} + c_{11})(f_{12} + \rho\delta c_{12}) + \delta f_{12} c_{12} > 0$.

3.2. *Concave adjustment costs*

The properties of the adjustment cost function are the same as Eq. (8), except $C''(\Omega) < 0$ and $C'_+(0) > 0$ and $C'_-(0) < 0$. Rothschild shows that, in this case, the total investment response (if any) to a single tax change occurs in the period of the tax change (since the marginal adjustment cost at zero investment is non-zero, small tax changes may induce no investment). Denote $\tilde{X}_1$ and $\tilde{X}_2$ as the minimum incremental reductions in the J1 tax rate required to induce some investment. The investment response to a change in only X_1 is obtained by differentiating Eq. (11) and evaluating at $X_2 = 0$ to yield:

$$\partial I_1 / \partial X_1 = (1+\rho)/[(1+\rho) f_{11} + c_{11}], \qquad X_1 \geqq \tilde{X}_1. \tag{17}$$

Similarly, differentiating Eq. (12) and evaluating at $X_1 = 0$ yields:

$$\partial I_2 / \partial X_2 = 1/(f_{12} + \rho\delta\, c_{12}), \qquad X_2 \geqq \tilde{X}_2. \tag{18}$$

Note that $f_{11} = f_{12}$ and the second order conditions insure that the denominators in Eqs. (17) and (18) are positive.

Corner solutions are also possible with phasing-in of reform. Of critical importance in the following section is the investment response to tax changes when $X_1 > \tilde{X}_1$ and $X_2 = \tilde{X}_2$. Differentiating Eqs. (9)–(12) and evaluating at $X_2 = \tilde{X}_2$ yields:

$$\partial I_1/\partial X_1 = (f_{11} + c_{12})/D', \tag{19}$$

$$\partial I_2/\partial X_1 = 0, \tag{20}$$

$$\partial I_1/\partial X_2 = \delta c_{12}/D', \tag{21}$$

$$\partial \mathrm{I}_2/\partial \mathrm{X}_2 = (f_{11} + c_{11})/D', \tag{22}$$

where $f_{11} = f_{12}$ at $\tilde{X}_2$ and $D' = (f_{11} + c_{11})(f_{12} + \rho\delta c_{12}) + \delta f_{12} c_{12}$. The second order conditions for firm optimization ensure that D', $(f_{11} + c_{11})$ and $(f_{11} + c_{12})$ are positive.

4. Optimal Tax Reform Results

Recall that all factors are locally owned, individual utility is equal to net income, and efficiency is the sole criterion for the optimal taxation problem. Under these circumstances the tax design optimum prescribes equalization of the capital tax rates — the government should lower T_1 (with T_2 rising endogenously as described above) until the two rates are equal.

Calculation of the V^i expressions is straightforward; since R is constant, the only asset price changes are due to changes in land rents in the two jurisdictions. Assuming that firm profits after taxes and adjustment costs are equally distributed among firm landowners, the V^i are

$$\begin{aligned} V^1 = (1/P_1)\{&\delta[F(K_{11}) - (R + T_{11})K_{11} - MC(I_1/M)] \\ &+ (\delta/\rho)[F(K_{12}) - (R + T_{12})K_{12}] - \delta^2 MC(I_2/M) - S_1\}, \end{aligned} \tag{23}$$

$$\begin{aligned} V^2 = (1/P_2)\{&\delta[F(K_{21}) - (R + T_{21})K_{21} - NC(I_1/N)] + (\delta/\rho)[F(K_{22}) \\ &-(R + T_{22})K_{22}] - \delta^2 NC(I_2/N) - S_2\} + (1/P_2)\{\delta[T_{11}K_{11} + T_{21}K_{21}] \\ &+ (\delta/\rho)[T_{12}K_{12}] + T_{22}K_{22} - (T_{10}K_{10} + T_{20}K_{20})/\rho\}, \end{aligned} \tag{24}$$

where S_1 and S_2 are land rents in the initial equilibrium and $V^1(V^2)$ refers to the capital gain (loss) which accrues to a representative landowner in J1 (J2). Note that the second term in braces in Eq. (24) represents the rebate of excess tax revenues to landowners in J2, which is assumed to be sufficiently small that $V^2 < 0$.

The marginal changes in V^1 and V^2 are obtained by differentiating Eqs. (23) and (24) and substituting from Eqs. (9)–(12) to yield:

$$\partial V^1/\partial X_1 = (1/P_1)R_1, \tag{25}$$

$$\partial V^2/\partial X_1 = -(1/P_2)R_1 + (1/P_2)E_1, \tag{26}$$

$$\partial V^1/\partial X_2 = -(1/P_1)R_2, \tag{27}$$

$$\partial V^2/\partial X_2 = -(1/P_2)R_2 + (1/P_2)E_2, \tag{28}$$

where (defining $\Delta T_1 = T_{11} - T_{21}$ and $\Delta T_2 = T_{12} - T_{22}$):

$$R_1 = \delta K_{11} + (\delta/\rho)K_{12},$$

$$R_2 = (\delta/\rho)K_{12},$$

$$E_1 = \delta\Delta T_1(\partial I_1/\partial X_1) + (\delta/\rho)\,\Delta T_2\,(\partial I_1/\partial X_1 + \partial I_2/\partial X_1),$$

$$E_2 = \delta\Delta T_1(\partial I_1/\partial X_2) + (\delta/\rho)\,\Delta T_2\,(\partial I_1/\partial X_2 + \partial I_2/\partial X_2).$$

The analytical separation of the effects of reform into redistributions and efficiency gains is clear in these expressions. The R_1 and R_2 terms represent pure redistributions from landowners in J2 to landowners in J1; these redistributions cancel in the aggregate. The E_1 and E_2 terms represent the net efficiency gains from reform which accrue solely to landowners in J2.

I consider the optimal tax reform problem for the concave and convex adjustment cost cases in turn. Throughout the analysis, I assume that the government optimization problem is well-behaved in the sense that a solution which satisfies the Kuhn-Tucker conditions is the unique optimum.[11]

---

[11] Although a unique optimum characterizes all simulation results reported in Section 5, existence and uniqueness are not guaranteed in these types of problems; see Atkinson and Stiglitz (1980).

4.1. *Concave adjustment costs*

The concave adjustment cost case is straightforward because an immediate one-step implementation policy is always optimal. I assume the government considers only reforms sufficiently large to induce capital reallocation; otherwise, there would be no efficiency gains and reform would be undesirable. Thus, if X_1 and X_2 are non-zero, $X_1 \geqq \tilde{X}_1$ and $X_2 \geqq \tilde{X}_2$. A one-step solution with $X_1^* > \tilde{X}_1$ is optimal if, evaluating at $\tilde{X}_2$.

$$\partial W/\partial X_1 = \alpha^1(\partial V^1/\partial X_1) + \alpha^2(\partial V^2/\partial X_1) = 0, \tag{29}$$

$$\partial W/\partial X_2 = \alpha^1(\partial V^1/\partial X_2) + \alpha^2(\partial V^2/\partial X_2) \leqq 0, \tag{30}$$

where $\alpha^1 = (B + V^1)^{-\varepsilon}$ and $\alpha^2 = (B + V^2)^{-\varepsilon}$ are the marginal social weights for the individual gains and losses induced by reform. Note that $\alpha^1 < \alpha^2$ once any reform occurs (when $\varepsilon > 0$), which corresponds to the weighting process described in Section 2. From Eqs. (29) and (30), immediate one-step enactment is optimal if

$$\alpha^2/\alpha^1 = \phi_1(X_1^*, \tilde{X}_2) \geqq \phi_2(X_1^*, \tilde{X}_2), \tag{31}$$

where $\phi_1 = -(P_1\partial V^1/\partial X_1)/(P_2\partial V^2/\partial X_1)$ and $\phi_2 = -(P_1\partial V^1/\partial X_2)/(P_2\partial V^2/\partial X_2)$; thus, $\phi_1(\phi_2)$ is the aggregate marginal tradeoff ratio of capital gains to capital losses in response to changes in $X_1(X_2)$.

Substituting from Eqs. (19)–(22) into Eqs. (25)–(28) — recall that at $X_2 = \tilde{X}_2$, $K_{11} = K_{12}$ and $f_{11} = f_{12}$ — indicates that Eq. (31) is satisfied if

$$\rho(\Delta T_1 - \Delta T_2)K_{11}f_{11} - (1+\rho)\Delta T_2 K_{11}c_{11} \geqq 0, \tag{32}$$

which always holds as an inequality so that a one-step policy is optimal.

The intuition behind this result is as follows. With no adjustment costs, the aggregate marginal tradeoff ratio is unchanged by postponement as both gains and losses are reduced proportionately so that Eq. (31) is satisfied as an equality; thus, if a marginal movement toward the tax design optimum is ever desirable, it is desirable immediately.[12] Concave

[12] See Zodrow (1981) for details of the argument for one-step enactment with no adjustment costs.

adjustment costs strengthen this argument for two reasons. First, the finite tax changes required before any investment is induced in period two ($\Delta T_1 - \Delta T_2 > 0$) imply redistributions without any efficiency gains and are thus undesirable — the first term in Eq. (32). Second, it is preferable that all investment occur in one period to take advantage of the concavity of the adjustment cost function ($c_{11} < 0$) — the second term in Eq. (32).

When $\varepsilon = 0$ ($\alpha^1 = \alpha^2 = 1$), immediate elimination of the tax differential is optimal since, substituting from Eq. (17) into Eq. (29),

$$\frac{\partial W}{\partial X_1} = \frac{(1+\rho)/\rho}{(1+\rho)f_{11} + c_{11}} \Delta T_1, \qquad X_1 \geqq \tilde{X}_1, \tag{33}$$

is positive until the capital tax differential is eliminated.[13]

When $\varepsilon > 0$, the expression analogous to Eq. (33) is

$$\frac{\partial W}{\partial X_1} = (\alpha^1 - \alpha^2)\left[\delta K_{11} + \left(\frac{\delta}{\rho}\right) K_{12}\right] + \alpha^2 \frac{(1+\rho)/\rho}{(1+\rho)f_{11} + c_{11}} \Delta T_1. \tag{34}$$

Since $(\alpha^1 - \alpha^2) < 0$, complete elimination of the tax differential cannot be optimal since $\partial W/\partial X_1 < 0$ when $\Delta T_1 = 0$; the marginal redistribution is negatively weighted and cannot be offset by the marginal net efficiency gain since it is zero.

Note, however, that no reform may be optimal. Since a finite tax change is required to stimulate some investment, the associated redistributions imply that $\alpha^1 < \alpha^2$. Thus if $\partial W / \partial X_1 / \leqq 0$ at $\tilde{X}_1$, the marginal efficiency gain at $\tilde{X}_1$ is too small to justify any reform. Barring this circumstance, the optimal implementation policy with concave adjustment costs and social concern about redistributions is immediate partial enactment to the point where Eq. (34) is zero.

4.2. *Convex adjustment costs*

In contrast to the concave case, with convex adjustment costs and a zero marginal adjustment cost at zero investment, some implementation of

[13] Note that, due to the nature of the adjustment process for the endogenous tax parameter, tax equalization will not occur at the zero adjustment cost tax design optimum.

reform is always optimal. Since no redistributions have been accumulated, the α- weights are equal, the marginal redistributions cancel, and a reduction in the initial tax differential results in a marginal efficiency gain.

When $\varepsilon = 0$, the optimal implementation policy is again immediate elimination of the tax differential. In this case,

$$\partial W/\partial X_1 = [\delta \Delta T_1(f_{12} + c_{12}) + (\delta/\rho)\Delta T_2(f_{11} + c_{11} + c_{12})]/D, \tag{35}$$

$$\partial W/\partial X_2 = [\delta^2 \Delta T_1 c_{12} + (\delta/\rho)\Delta T_2(f_{11} + c_{11} + c_{12})]/D; \tag{36}$$

both expressions are unambiguously positive until the differential is eliminated, and immediate enactment is optimal because $\partial W/\partial X_1 - \partial W/\partial X_2 \geqq 0$. Thus, if the government is concerned solely with efficiency, the tax differential should be eliminated immediately; individual firms will take convex adjustment costs into account when they optimally phase-in investment, so that phasing-in of reform by the government is unnecessary.

The case where $\varepsilon > 0$ is more complicated. It is straightforward to show that no full enactment policy can be optimal. Immediate full enactment is optimal only if, at $\Delta T_1 = \Delta T_2 = 0$,

$$\partial W/\partial X_1 = (\alpha^1 - \alpha^2)[\delta K_{11} + (\delta/\rho)K_{12}] = 0, \tag{37}$$

which is never satisfied since $(\alpha^1 - \alpha^2) < 0$. Postponed (phased-in) full enactment is optimal if, at $\Delta T_1 > 0$ and $\Delta T_2 = 0$, $\phi_1 \leqq \phi_2$ is satisfied as an inequality (equality). Substituting from Eqs. (13)–(16) into Eqs. (25)–(28) when $\Delta T_2 = 0$ indicates that $\phi_1 \leqq \phi_2$ only if

$$\Delta T_1[(K_{12} - K_{11})\rho\delta c_{12} + K_{12} f_{12}] \leqq 0; \tag{38}$$

which is never satisfied since $(K_{12} - K_{11}) > 0$. Thus, all the full enactment reform implementation options can be ruled out — full enactment is never desirable because the marginal net efficiency gain of the last incremental tax change is zero, but the associated marginal redistributions have a net negative effect on social welfare.

However, any of the three partial enactment options — immediate, phased-in, or postponed — may theoretically be the optimal reform implementation policy with convex adjustment costs. Immediate partial enactment is optimal if $\phi_1 \geqq \phi_2$ at $X_1 > 0$ and $X_2 = 0$, phased-in partial enactment is optimal if $\phi_1 = \phi_2$ at $X_1 > 0$ and $X_2 > 0$, and postponed partial enactment is optimal if $\phi_1 \leqq \phi_2$ at $X_1 = 0$ and $X_2 > 0$.

The intuitive interpretation of these conditions is as follows. Substituting from Eqs. (25)–(28) reveals that

$$\phi_1 \gtreqless \phi_2, \quad \text{as} \quad E_1/E_2 \gtreqless R_1/R_2. \tag{39}$$

Thus, immediate partial enactment is optimal if, at $X_1 > 0$ and $X_2 = 0$, postponement reduces the marginal net efficiency gains from reform proportionately more than the associated reduction in the marginal redistributions. Similarly, phased-in (postponed) partial enactment is optimal if, at $X_1 > 0$ and $X_2 > 0$ (at $X_1 = 0$ and $X_2 > 0$), postponing reform reduces the marginal net efficiency gains proportionately the same as (less than) the associated marginal redistributions.

From Eqs. (25)–(28), postponing reform reduces the marginal redistributions by a proportionality factor λ, where $0 < \lambda = (1 + \rho K_{11}/K_{12})^{-1} < 1$; thus,

$$R_1/R_2 = 1/\lambda > 1. \tag{40}$$

However, the effect of postponement on the marginal net efficiency gain is more complicated. Substituting from Eqs. (13)–(16) and Eqs. (25)–(28) yields:

$$\frac{E_1}{E_2} = \frac{\rho \Delta T_1(f_{12} + c_{12}) + \Delta T_2(f_{11} + c_{11} + c_{12})}{\rho \Delta T_1(\delta c_{12}) + \Delta T_2(f_{11} + c_{11} + \delta c_{12})} > 1, \tag{41}$$

which depends on the properties of the production and adjustment cost functions.

Rearranging Eqs. (40) and (41) indicates that $\phi_1 \gtreqless \phi_2$ as

$$\begin{aligned}[K_{12} f_{12} \Delta T_1 - K_{11} f_{11} \Delta T_2] + (K_{12} - K_{11})\delta c_{12} \\ \times(\rho \Delta T_1 + \Delta T_2) - K_1 c_{11} \Delta T_2 \gtreqless 0.\end{aligned} \tag{42}$$

Suppose that the production function is quadratic, so that $f_{11} = f_{12}$. In this case, since $\Delta T_1 > \Delta T_2$ and $K_{12} > K_{11}$, only the third term in Eq. (42) is negative. Thus, if the marginal adjustment cost does not increase too rapidly in the first period (c_{11} is sufficiently small), immediate partial enactment is optimal. Conversely, if the marginal adjustment cost increases sufficiently rapidly in the first period, phased-in or postponed partial enactment is optimal, as the social benefits of the associated reduction in the redistributions associated with reform are greater than the social costs of reducing the present value of the reform-induced net efficiency gains.

Condition Eq. (42) suggests that (i) for sufficiently low c_{11}, the optimum is the corner solution ($X_2 = 0$) of immediate partial enactment; (ii) there may be a range of intermediate values of c_{11}, where the optimum is the interior solution ($X_1 > 0$ and $X_2 > 0$) of phased-in partial enactment; and (iii) for sufficiently large c_{11}, the optimum is the corner solution ($X_1 = 0$) of delayed partial enactment.[14] However, this pattern is only suggested by Eq. (42) and the optimal reform implementation policy must be determined in each case by substituting in the relevant production and adjustment cost functions. Simulation results for such an experiment are reported in the following section.

5. Simulation Results

To provide a rough idea of the importance of phasing-in reform in the presence of convex adjustment costs, the results of some simulation experiments are reported in this section. Optimal tax paths are calculated and the social welfare improvements obtained from phasing-in reform, relative to those obtained with the alternative one-step implementation options of immediate partial enactment, postponed partial enactment and postponed full enactment, are examined.

---

[14] A similar result regarding the theoretical ambiguity of the optimal phasing-in policy is obtained when the government, for political or administrative reasons, is constrained to full enactment by the end of the second period. For example, if, contrary to the assumption in footnote 7, the current government is concerned that future governments will not maintain its policies, it may feel constrained to full enactment by the end of its tenure in order to reduce the possibility of future unexpected changes in the tax structure. In the present context, this is modeled by constraining the government's tax rates and the firm's capital stocks to equal their values at the tax design optimum by the end of the second period.

In the simulation model, three of the more restrictive assumptions utilized in the analytical model are relaxed.[15] First, to obtain more realistic investment time paths, the time horizon for firms is divided into five rather than only two periods. Thus, the firm objective functions are the five-period analogues of Eqs. (4) and (5).

Second, K is assumed fixed rather than held constant with the somewhat contrived procedure described above. The resulting small changes in R (see below) are assumed to have no effect on government and firm discounting which occurs at a constant annual rate (ρ) of 4 percent.

Third, with K fixed, I adopt a more conventional budget constraint as the government simply must finance G in each period. To simplify the computations, the government is limited to a single endogenous tax variable Z_1; the government thus chooses $T_{11} = T_1 - X_1$ in the first period and $T_{12} = T_1 - X_1 - X_2$ in periods two through five, with $T_{21} = T_2 + Z_1$ obtaining in each period. I thus assume the government can borrow and lend outside the system at constant ρ in balancing its five-period budget; such an assumption must be made if the tax structure is to remain unchanged after the second period since capital reallocation continues after that point.

Otherwise, the model is as described above. The functional forms and parameter values used in the simulations are as follows. The production function is Cobb-Douglas with a capital share parameter of 0.8, and the adjustment cost function is quadratic. Since the number of firms and individuals in each jurisdiction is arbitrary, I simply assume $M = N = P_1 = P_2 = 1$; these assumptions maximize the likelihood that phasing-in is required, since they result in the maximum concentration of adjustment costs and income redistributions. The equal-rate tax design optimum is assumed to have a capital tax rate of 0.150 relative to $R = 0.355$; the initial equilibrium is assumed to be characterized by a sizable tax differential, as $T_{10} = 0.200$ and $T_{20} = 0.126$.[16]

---

[15] Results which were qualitatively similar to those presented here were obtained in numerical simulation experiments with the simpler model described in Section 3.

[16] These assumptions imply $K = 20.0$, $G = 3.0$, and $K_{10} = 6.5$, $K_{20} = 13.5$ and $R = 0.350$ in the initial equilibrium.

Periods one through four are each five years long, so the fifth and final period begins at year twenty. Optimal tax paths and the associated welfare gains are shown as a function of adjustment costs and e in Table 2.1; note that the interval for the J1 tax rate is from the initial value of 0.200 to the tax design optimum of 0.150.[17]

The numerical simulation results are in accordance with the three theoretical predictions in Section 4. First, immediate full enactment is optimal when $\varepsilon = 0$, regardless of adjustment costs (C/E). Second, if $C/E = 0$, immediate full enactment is optimal when $\varepsilon = 0$, and immediate partial enactment is optimal when $\varepsilon > 0$. Thus, neither adjustment costs nor social concern about reform- induced redistributions independently warrant phasing-in of reform. Third, when both $\varepsilon > 0$ and $C/E > 0$, immediate partial enactment is optimal for zero or low values of C/E,[18] phased-in partial enactment is optimal for intermediate values of C/E, and postponed partial enactment is optimal for sufficiently large values of C/E.

Four results related to the pattern of welfare improvements are interesting and intuitively plausible. First, the welfare gains from optimal implementation of reform (when $\varepsilon > 0$ and $C/E > 0$), relative to postponed full enactment, increase with e (holding C/E constant), as increasing social concern about redistributions makes pursuing reform to the point of full enactment less desirable.[19] Second, although phasing-in is theoretically optimal whenever $\Delta W_3 > 0$, the gains from phased-in partial enactment are quite small relative to the optimal one-step implementation policy ($\Delta W_3 < 1$ percent always); this suggests little would be lost by following a strategy of immediate partial enactment with low adjustment costs and postponed partial enactment with large adjustment costs.[20] Third, when $\varepsilon = 0$ and immediate full enactment is optimal, ΔW_1 falls as C/E increases;

[17] Following Feldstein (1976b), the welfare function reference base B is set equal to mean income in the initial equilibrium.

[18] Immediate partial enactment is optimal for positive but sufficiently low levels of adjustment costs; the results in Table 2.1 suggest that, in terms of the discussion in Section 4, the interior solution for X_1 occurs at a fairly low level of adjustment costs.

[19] Note that the postponed full enactment is arbitrarily chosen to occur in period three, rather than at an optimally chosen point in time; postponed full enactment thus serves as an arbitrary benchmark.

[20] The critical value of C/E occurs when $\Delta W1$ is first less than $\Delta W2$.

Table 2.1.
Optimal Policies and Welfare Gains

ε	C/E	T_{11}*	ΔW_1	T_{12}*	ΔW_2	T_{11}**	T_{12}**	ΔW_3
0	0	0.150	10.3	0.150	0	0.150	0.150	0
0	0.05	0.150	6.5	0.150	0	0.150	0.150	0
0	0.10	0.150	4.2	0.150	0	0.150	0.150	0
0	0.15	0.150	3.0	0.150	0	0.150	0.150	0
0	0.20	0.150	2.3	0.150	0	0.150	0.150	0
0.25	0	0.158	8.9	0.153	0.6	0.158	0.158	0
0.25	0.02	0.158	6.1	0.153	0.6	0.159	0.158	0.01
0.25	0.04	0.158	4.3	0.153	0.6	0.164	0.157	0.07
0.25	0.06	0.159	2.8	0.153	0.7	0.168	0.157	0.21
0.25	0.08	0.159	1.6	0.153	0.9	0.173	0.157	0.43
0.25	0.10	0.159	0.8	0.154	1.2	0.183	0.156	0.43
0.25	0.15	0.161	–0.2	0.155	2.1	0.200	0.155	0
0.25	0.20	0.162	–0.1	0.157	3.4	0.200	0.157	0
0.5	0	0.163	14.4	0.159	8.1	0.163	0.163	0
0.5	0.02	0.164	12.2	0.159	8.1	0.167	0.163	0.05
0.5	0.04	0.164	10.5	0.159	8.4	0.171	0.163	0.23
0.5	0.06	0.165	9.4	0.159	9.0	0.180	0.162	0.66
0.5	0.08	0.165	8.9	0.160	10.0	0.190	0.161	0.21
0.5	0.10	0.166	9.0	0.160	11.3	0.200	0.160	0
0.5	0.15	0.167	11.6	0.162	15.8	0.200	0.162	0
0.5	0.20	0.169	17.1	0.164	22.2	0.200	0.164	0
0.75	0	0.168	28.6	0.164	23.9	0.168	0.168	0
0.75	0.02	0.168	26.7	0.164	23.9	0.172	0.167	0.08
0.75	0.04	0.168	25.6	0.164	24.7	0.178	0.167	0.44
0.75	0.06	0.169	25.6	0.164	26.2	0.188	0.166	0.42
0.75	0.08	0.170	26.6	0.165	28.5	0.200	0.165	0
0.75	0.10	0.170	28.7	0.165	31.6	0.200	0.165	0
0.75	0.15	0.172	38.1	0.167	42.2	0.200	0.167	0
0.75	0.20	0.174	53.6	0.169	57.4	0.200	0.169	0

(*Continued*)

Table 2.1.
(*Continued*)

ε	C/E	T_{11}*	ΔW_1	T_{12}*	ΔW_2	T_{11}**	T_{12}**	ΔW_3
1.0	0	0.171	49.7	0.167	46.7	0.171	0.171	0
1.0	0.02	0.171	48.4	0.167	46.8	0.177	0.170	0.12
1.0	0.04	0.172	48.4	0.167	48.2	0.183	0.170	0.66
1.0	0.06	0.172	50.0	0.168	50.9	0.196	0.168	0.08
1.0	0.08	0.173	53.3	0.168	55.0	0.200	0.168	0
1.0	0.10	0.174	58.3	0.169	60.4	0.200	0.169	0
1.0	0.15	0.176	77.5	0.171	79.3	0.200	0.171	0
1.0	0.20	0.178	107.1	0.173	106.4	0.200	0.173	0

Notation

ε = index of social concern about arbitrary redistributions.
C/E = ratio of present values of adjustment costs to efficiency gains with immediate full enactment.
T_{11}* = optimal tax rate with immediate partial enactment.
ΔW_1 = percentage welfare improvement with immediate partial enactment, relative to postponed full enactment.
T_{12}* = optimal tax rate with postponed partial enactment.
ΔW_2 = percentage welfare improvement with postponed partial enactment, relative to postponed full enactment.
T_{11}** = optimal first-period tax rate with phasing-in.
T_{12}** = optimal second-period tax rate with phasing-in.
ΔW_3 = percentage welfare improvement with phasing-in, relative to optimal one-step policy, i.e. relative to immediate (postponed) partial enactment if ΔW_1 is greater (less) than ΔW_2.

thus, abstracting from the extent of enactment, postponement is relatively less undesirable as it mitigates the effects of increasing adjustment costs. Fourth, for $\varepsilon > 0$, ΔW_2 increases as C/E increases; thus, abstracting from the timing of enactment, partial enactment is relatively more desirable as moving toward full enactment implies incurring increasing marginal adjustment costs to obtain relatively small marginal net efficiency gains.[21]

Finally, note three features of the optimal tax rate patterns. First, the optimal tax rates always increase as ε increases (holding C/E constant), as

[21] Indeed, for the larger values of ε, the fact that the values of ΔW_1 and ΔW_2 do not differ drastically suggests that the major welfare gain obtained from the optimal implementation of reform is from partial instead of full enactment, rather than from the timing of partial enactment.

greater social aversion to inducing redistributions implies less reform. Second, the optimal extent of immediate and postponed partial enactment declines as *C/E* increases, as increasing adjustment costs reduce the marginal net efficiency gains from enactment and make reform less desirable. Third, when phasing-in is optimal, the pattern, relative to immediate partial enactment, is to implement less reform in the first period ($T_{11}^{**} > T_{11}^{*}$) but to implement more reform eventually ($T_{12}^{**} < T_{11}^{*}$), as permitting phasing- in results in a reduction in reform-induced adjustment costs. Once the gains from phasing-in are exhausted, T_{12}^{**} rises as *C/E* increases, as in the case of postponed partial enactment.

6. Conclusion

I have examined the optimal implementation of tax reform in a model with adjustment costs when the government is concerned about arbitrary reform-induced redistributions. The model is most directly relevant for capital taxation reforms where reform-induced reallocation of the capital stock causes firms to incur adjustment costs; examples would include reform proposals to eliminate or reduce corporate income taxation, to equalize the taxation of capital income across industries, and to equalize the taxation of capital income across political jurisdictions with regional or metropolitan property tax base sharing plans.

However, the analysis applies generally to any reform where one factor of production is fixed while a second factor is mobile, subject to either concave or convex adjustment costs. Thus, with an appropriate definition of factors, the analysis could apply to the optimal implementation of non-capital taxation reforms which cause factor reallocation subject to adjustment costs; examples would include the elimination of federal income tax deductibility for state and local taxes (which would cause factor reallocation across states in response to changes in effective tax differentials) and the elimination of deductions for business meals and entertainment (which would cause factor reallocation out of the restaurant and entertainment industries). Also, it would be fairly straightforward to modify the model to consider reforms which improve efficiency by eliminating distortions in consumer prices but also induce adjustment costs; for example, the taxation of a wide variety of currently untaxed fringe benefits would eliminate price distortions which bias consumption toward goods which are provided as fringe benefits, but adjustment costs would be incurred as companies providing pensions, and life, health and property and casualty insurance companies changed their policies and procedures.

Several general inferences can be drawn from the results presented in this paper. The optimal tax reform problem is structured so that social concern about arbitrary reform-induced redistributions is sufficient to make full enactment of reform suboptimal regardless of how it is phased-in or delayed. The analysis suggests that neither adjustment costs nor concern about redistributions independently warrant delay or phasing-in of reform; immediate full enactment is optimal regardless of adjustment costs if there is no concern about redistributions, and immediate partial enactment is optimal if there is concern about redistributions without adjustment costs. Also, neither delay nor phasing-in is desirable if adjustment costs are concave as immediate partial (full) enactment is optimal if there is (no) concern about redistributions.

However, the interaction between adjustment costs and concern about redistributions is sufficient to make either phased-in or postponed partial enactment optimal if adjustment costs are convex and sufficiently large. Phasing-in is theoretically optimal under 'intermediate' levels of adjustment costs — those which are sufficiently large that some delay is desirable so that firms can postpone some capital reallocation, but sufficiently small that simply postponing reform results in too large a reduction in capital reallocation and the associated net efficiency gains. However, numerical simulation results suggest that the additional welfare gains obtained from phasing-in reform, relative to the gains obtained with the optimal one-step implementation policy of either immediate or postponed partial enactment, are quite small; indeed, they may easily be outweighed by the additional administrative costs associated with a multi-step phasing-in reform implementation policy.

Thus, the analysis suggests that for convex adjustment costs, little would be lost by following a reform implementation strategy of immediate partial enactment with small adjustment costs and postponed partial enactment with sufficiently large adjustment costs. Since the numerical results presented by Fullerton (1983) suggest that, even for large tax changes, most capital reallocation could be done with replacement investment, adjustment costs for net investment (analyzed in this paper) may be sufficiently small that immediate partial enactment is optimal or nearly so. Otherwise, the existence of significant convex adjustment costs implies that some delay of partial enactment is desirable, while the numerical results suggest that the argument for phasing-in partial enactment, rather than simply postponing it, may be rather weak.

Acknowledgments

Research support from the National Science Foundation (Grant SES80-11482) and from the Office of Tax Analysis is gratefully acknowledged. I have benefited from the research assistance of Mine Yucel, from the comments of James Alm, Peter Mieszkowski and the participants in the 1984 TRED Conference on The Political Economy of Tax Change, and from extended discussions with Katherine Rey. The views expressed are my own and do not reflect U.S. Treasury Policy.

References

Atkinson, Anthony B., 1973, How progressive should income tax be? in: Michael Parkin and A.R. Nobay, eds., *Essays in modern economics* (Longman, London).

Atkinson, Anthony B. and Joseph E. Stiglitz, 1980, *Lectures on public economics* (McGraw-Hill, New York).

Bittker, Boris I., 1980, Equity, efficiency, and income tax theory. Do misallocations drive out inequities?, in: Henry J. Aaron and Michael J. Boskin, eds., *The economics of taxation* (The Brookings Institution, Washington).

Feldstein, Martin S., 1976a, Compensation in tax reform, *National Tax Journal* 29, 123–130.

Feldstein, Martin S., 1976b, On the theory of tax reform, *Journal of Public Economics* 6, 77–104.

Fullerton, Don, 1983, Transition losses of partially mobile industry-specific capital, *Quarterly Journal of Economics* 98, 107–125.

Guesnerie, Roger, 1977, On the direction of tax reform, *Journal of Public Economics* 7, 179–202.

Institute for Fiscal Studies, 1978, *The structure and reform of direct taxation: Report of a committee chaired by Professor J.E. Meade* (Allen and Unwin, London).

Rothschild, Michael, 1971, On the cost of adjustment, *Quarterly Journal of Economics* 85, 605–622.

U.S. Treasury, 1977, *Blueprints for basic tax reform* (Government Printing Office, Washington).

Zodrow, George R., 1981, Implementing tax reform, *National Tax Journal* 34, 401–418.

Zodrow, George R., 1984, The incidence of metropolitan property tax base sharing and rate equalization, *Journal of Urban Economics* 15, 210–229.

Zodrow, George R., 1985, Partial tax reform. An optimal taxation perspective, *Canadian Journal of Economics* 18, 335–346.

Chapter 3

Grandfather Rules and the Theory of Optimal Tax Reform*

George R. Zodrow

Economics Department, Rice University, Houston, TX 77251-1892, USA

This paper analyzes grandfather rules (GR) within the context of the 'optimal tax reform' problem and a reform that eliminates differential capital taxation. Two general conclusions are suggested. First, GR can be a very effective reform implementation tool. Appropriately structured GR can convert potential 'losers' from reform into gainers so that the reform becomes Pareto-improving; alternatively, GR can often be used to distribute the gains from reform more equitably. Second, GR should nevertheless be used with caution. Market adjustments often imply that losses are sufficiently small that little grandfathering is needed; moreover, the effects of GR are very sensitive to the length of time they are in force, and their implementation may lead to efficiency losses.

---

*This chapter is reproduced from "Grandfather Rules and the Theory of Optimal Tax Reform," *Journal of Public Economics*, **49**(2), 163–190, 1992.

1. Introduction

The important distinction between optimal tax design and optimal tax reform (OTR) is well established. Optimal tax design involves the selection of an optimal tax structure, subject to constraints on revenue, tax instruments and the behavior of economic agents; initial conditions are irrelevant.[1] In contrast, the theory of OTR considers the problem of reforming an existing tax system, as it focuses on the best way to move from an initially suboptimal equilibrium toward the tax design optimum (Feldstein, 1976b and Zodrow 1985a). The tax reforms suggested by the two approaches are generally quite different. For example, Diamond and Mirrlees (1971) suggest that maintaining any level of factor taxation is generally undesirable in an optimal taxation framework in which social welfare is defined with respect to a long-run equilibrium. In contrast, Feldstein (1976b) and Zodrow (1981, 1985b) argue that delaying or even forgoing complete elimination of factor taxes may be desirable if the government is concerned with the losses such a reform may impose on the owners of partially (or completely) immobile capital in the initial equilibrium.

Three approaches have been used in attacking the OTR problem. The first assumes instantaneous adjustment and focuses on conditions under which tax reform is Pareto-improving (Guesnerie, 1977, Diewert, 1978, Dixit, 1979, Weymark, 1979). However, these conditions are sufficiently restrictive to preclude most reform proposals. Moreover, the assumption of instantaneous adjustment is suspect, especially if reform increases capital taxes in specific industries and thus would likely cause losses for owners of immobile capital in those industries.

The remaining two approaches can be characterized as the 'compensation' method and the 'reform implementation' approach. They share two essential assumptions. First, both assume that tax reform increases social welfare but is not Pareto-improving — that is, reform increases aggregate welfare but causes individual welfare losses as well as gains. Second, they

[1] Mirrlees (1976), Sandmo (1976), Atkinson and Stiglitz (1980), Auerbach (1985) and Stern (1987) provide surveys of this voluminous literature.

assume that the government is, as a matter of policy, averse to such reform-induced losses and gains.

As noted above, the first assumption seems uncontroversial. However, the second is more tenuous. Feldstein (1976b) argues that government aversion to reform-induced losses and gains is reasonable if they are caused by unanticipated tax changes, since such arbitrary and capricious redistributions due to government actions are undesirable from a social viewpoint. Although this argument has been questioned (Graetz, 1977), it is reasonably compelling under certain conditions (Goode, 1987). In addition, concern about reform-induced redistributions is generally in accord with political realities. Political processes may hinder or even rule out reforms that increase overall social welfare but also cause some individuals to experience losses; this is especially likely to be true if, as is often the case, the gains from reform are widely distributed while the losses are highly concentrated (perhaps among politically powerful special interests). Together, these two assumptions imply that the government should consider the negative effects of reform-induced redistributions when contemplating tax changes. Note that this line of reasoning is the analog in the case of taxation to the rationale commonly used to justify the payment of compensation to the losers from public expenditure projects (Cordes and Weisbrod, 1979, 1985).

The 'compensation' approach to solving the OTR problem is to use direct governmental compensation to eliminate or reduce reform-induced losses (Feldstein, 1976a). Compensation is clearly related to the Pareto-improving criterion, as lump-sum compensation could in principle convert any efficiency-enhancing reform into a Pareto-improving tax change. However, such schemes are commonly difficult to design and implement, may involve significant administrative costs and, as noted by Feldstein (1976b, p. 98), 'may always be politically impossible'. The 'windfall recapture tax' proposed by the U.S. Treasury (1985) provides a recent example of an application of the compensation principle, although in the form of 'negative' compensation for a reform-induced windfall gain (Aaron, 1985, Zodrow, 1988). The rejection of this proposal reinforces the notion that direct application of the compensation principle is politically impossible.

The 'reform implementation' approach assumes compensation is infeasible and examines how tax changes might be implemented so as to reduce reform-induced losses and gains. Previous research has focused on how the government can alter the timing and extent of enactment of reform to maximize the following 'OTR' social welfare function:

$$W = [1/(1-e)]\sum_{i=1}^{i=N}[(B+V_i)^{1-e} - 1], \quad 0 < e < \infty, \tag{1}$$

where V_i is the reform-induced gain or loss experienced by individual i, N is the number of individuals in the economy, e is an index of social aversion to arbitrary redistributions ($e = 0$ corresponds to no concern while increasing values of e indicate increasing aversion), and B is an arbitrary value (such as mean annual income) used to scale the magnitudes of the V_i. This function aggregates reform-induced gains and losses in such a way that losses are weighted more than gains; in particular, the weighting process is non-linear so that an individual loss of size $2X$ has a more negative effect on social welfare than do two individual losses each of size X.

The OTR social welfare function is thus designed to reflect social aversion to arbitrary redistributions, especially relatively large ones. It implies that an efficiency-enhancing reform that increases total income may nevertheless be undesirable because the welfare-weighted losses exceed the welfare-weighted gains. Alternatively, note that pure redistributions have an unambiguously negative effect on social welfare, so that a reform will be desirable only if the positive effect of reform-induced efficiency gains more than offsets the negative effect of the pure redistributions. Thus, the goal of this approach is to alter the timing and extent of reform so that reform-induced losses are reduced optimally — to maximize the welfare-weighted sum of gains and losses (1) — even though this implies that aggregate (unweighted) efficiency gains will also be reduced.[2]

Results in this area are quite varied, as solutions to these optimization problems depend to a great extent on the specific reform being considered

---

[2] For further discussion of this objective function, see Feldstein (1976b) and Zodrow (1985a). The particular form used in Eq. (1) follows Feldstein in assuming the government has an 'impersonal' notion of justice, as its aversion to reform-induced redistributions is independent of the income or utility levels of the individuals experiencing the redistributions. Distributional concerns can be introduced by weighting the gains and losses, as described in Zodrow (1985a).

and the model used to analyze its effects. Recommended solutions include postponed full enactment (Feldstein, 1976b), immediate partial enactment (Zodrow, 1981), and phased-in partial (or full) enactment (Zodrow, 1985b, 1986).

Although these analyses provide a wide variety of results about the optimal implementation of tax reform, limiting the set of available instruments to the timing and extent of enactment of reform is rather troublesome, as it ignores a commonly used alternative. Specifically, none of the studies cited above considers the use of grandfather rules (hereafter, GR) — special provisions that have the effect of granting existing assets future tax treatment in accordance with pre-reform law. This omission is a rather glaring one, as the use of GR is perhaps the most common legislative tool utilized in reducing the windfall gains and losses caused by reform. For example, during the recent tax reform experience in the United States, GR were at various times recommended for reforms proposed in a large number of areas, including the tax treatment of depreciable assets, assets eligible for the investment tax credit, expenditures that qualify for rapid amortization, multiperiod production contracts, installment sales, intangible drilling costs newly subject to the minimum tax, interest expenses incurred by depository institutions to carry tax-exempt bonds, net operating losses of depository institutions, interest income on life insurance policies and certain annuities, losses of property and casualty insurance companies, non-governmental purpose tax-exempt bonds, at-risk rules for real estate, certain retirement savings plans, and the taxation of foreign income. Given their widespread use, an analysis of GR within the context of the OTR problem seems highly desirable; such an analysis is the primary purpose of this study.[3]

Following the 'compensation' and 'reform implementation' approaches, the analysis of GR assumes that reform causes both individual gains and losses, and that the government is averse to such redistributions. Although GR will be treated as an alternative means of implementing reform, they could also be viewed as an indirect form of compensation. The analysis considers two alternative government objectives. The first assumes

[3] Graetz (1977, pp. 60–63) describes some of the problems involved in designing GR, and notes that such 'transitional mechanisms ... merit additional study'.

that — due to social concern about causing capital owners any reform-induced losses whatsoever or in order to obtain political support for reform — the government uses GR to make the reform a Pareto-improving one; that is, it uses GR to expand the set of Pareto-improving reforms. The second objective follows the 'reform implementation' approach as the government chooses its GR to maximize the OTR social welfare function Eq. (1) in which losses are weighted more heavily than gains.

The effects of GR are modeled in two ways. In the first case, 'ideal' GR result in lump-sum transfers that reverse reform-induced redistributions without causing efficiency losses. Such GR would clearly be an effective solution to the OTR problem. However, although such ideal GR are possible in theory, it may be difficult to design them in practice. Accordingly, the second case considers 'imperfect' GR that reduce efficiency gains in addition to offsetting reform-induced redistributions. Also, it should be noted that administrative costs are ignored in both cases — a potentially serious omission since GR may add significant administrative complexity.

Before proceeding further, it will be useful to describe in very general terms the model of tax reform analyzed in the paper. Since demands for GR are most common for changes in the tax treatment of capital assets, the reform considered is a change in the taxation of capital income. The reform causes capital owners to experience capital gains and losses, the calculation of which reflects reform-induced changes in the discounted present values of net income flows within the context of a model in which adjustment costs imply that capital reallocation is limited to replacement investment.[4] In addition, all changes are assumed to apply to both new and old capital; note, however, that capital taxation reforms also might apply only to new capital, in which case the reform-induced redistributions would differ from those analyzed below. Since the effects of the latter type

[4]The total capital stock is assumed to be fixed, and the capital gains and losses reflect changes in net returns to partially immobile capital during the transition to the new equilibrium. Note that this income-based approach differs from the analysis of Summers (1981), who calculates reform-induced wealth changes in the presence of capital adjustment costs using a 'q-theory' approach in which the capital stock varies and the after-tax return to capital is fixed.

of reform have received considerable attention recently (Auerbach and Kotlikoff, 1983), a brief discussion of these two types of reforms is in order.

The redistributions caused in the model by a reform that applies to both new and old capital are straightforward. For example, if tax rates on a particular sector are raised, the present value of the net income generated by assets in that sector falls, owners of the assets suffer capital losses, and GR are used to reduce such losses. In contrast, suppose that the effective tax rate on new investment in a particular sector is reduced (say, due to the introduction of accelerated depreciation) but the tax treatment of old capital in that sector is unchanged. In this case the equilibrium gross returns for a new marginal investment decline and, since both new and existing assets receive these new lower returns, existing assets will experience a capital loss. To offset this loss, GR would have to have effects similar to extending the more generous new tax treatment to existing assets.

The analysis in this paper considers the former type of reform for a number of reasons. Most importantly, it is tax increases that apply to both new and old capital that give rise to most demands for GR, and it is for such changes that the enactment of GR occurs most frequently. Indeed, the most common popular rationale for GR is that it is unfair to increase the taxation of existing formerly tax-preferred assets 'in the middle of the game'. In addition, many reforms typically apply to both new and old capital; in the recent U.S. experience, these include changes in (1) tax rates, (2) a wide variety of accounting rules, (3) limitations on deductions of interest expense, and (4) the treatment of losses. Moreover, even tax reductions that nominally apply only to new capital may effectively apply to both new and old capital if asset sales transform 'old' assets into 'new' ones and transactions costs and 'recapture' penalties are not prohibitively high. Thus, capital tax changes that apply to both new and old capital seem to be most relevant for an analysis of GR.

Nevertheless, GR could in principle also be applied for tax reforms that apply only to new capital. This idea suggests at least two directions for future research. First, the model used in this paper could be applied to the analysis of GR for such reforms. This would be fairly straightforward theoretically; as noted above, GR for a tax reduction on new capital in a sector would involve something like extending some of the new preferential treatment to existing capital. In practice, however, such an approach would involve several difficulties. Most importantly, the rationale underlying GR in the case of reforms that apply only to new capital is sufficiently subtle and counter-intuitive that it would be difficult to generate political support for such rules, so that their enactment seems unlikely. In addition, the general equilibrium calculations required to determine the appropriate GR are more complicated and uncertain and thus less likely to be generally accepted than in the case of reforms that apply to both new and old capital.

Second, an alternative means of addressing the OTR problem is to combine reforms so as to minimize reform-induced losses. For example, to the extent that such policies would be consistent with overall reform goals, a tax increase on both new and old capital in a particular sector (which causes windfall losses for assets in that sector) could be combined with a general tax increase on new capital (which causes windfall gains for existing capital) so as to minimize reform-induced capital losses. An analysis of such reform 'packages' is a promising avenue for future research.

The paper is organized as follows. Section 2 provides additional details on the government objective functions used in the paper and describes the model. Parameter values and results for optimal GR are presented in Section 3, and analogous results for suboptimal GR are discussed in Section 4. A concluding section summarizes the implications of the study.

2. A Model of Grandfather Rules and Optimal Tax Reform

2.1. *Governmental objectives*

Both governmental objectives described above require the determination of treatment the individual losses and gains, V_i, induced by any particular reform (including the effects of its GR). An equivalent variation measure is used to calculate these effects; specifically,

$$V_i = \int_0^\infty EV_i(t)\,\mathrm{e}^{-\mu t}\,\mathrm{d}t, \tag{2}$$

where $EV_i(t)$ is the equivalent variation associated with the reform at time t for individual i, and μ is the discount rate. The analysis assumes a relatively high value of $\mu = 0.25$ for several reasons.[5] For example, it is often asserted that elected officials are myopic in evaluating the future effects of current policy changes. Alternatively, individuals may also heavily discount reform-induced gains and losses, either as a matter of taste, or because they expect the current reform to be temporary, or due to uncertainty regarding the accuracy of predictions of future values of economic variables.

Given V_i, specification of the two alternative government objectives is straightforward. If the reform is to be Pareto-improving, the government sets its GR such that $V_i > 0$ for all i. Under the OTR social welfare function approach, the government should choose its GR to maximize Eq. (1). Note that in general an implication of this objective function is that a change in the way that reform is implemented that results in larger windfall losses for certain individuals may nevertheless be acceptable if it is accompanied by sufficiently large increases in the welfare of other individuals. However, as will be shown below, GR can convert the losers from reform into gainers in the current model. In this case, Eq. (1) implies that keeping GR in force beyond the point at which reform becomes Pareto-improving may be desirable — even if it causes efficiency losses — if it redistributes income to the relatively small gainers from reform from the relatively large gainers; that is, the government desires a more equitable distribution of the gains from reform.

2.2. *Description of the model*

Since GR have taken many forms, it is far from clear precisely how they should be modeled. However, most GR have three basic features in common. First, they generally attempt to identify income (or deductions) attributable to capital assets existing prior to the enactment of a reform,

[5]Thus, the discount factor applied to changes occurring more than a few years in the future is quite low; for example, at five years the discount factor is 0.286. The simulation results reported below are not overly sensitive to variations in the discount rate in the neighborhood of $\mu = 0.25$.

especially those assets that are relatively immobile. Second, they attempt to insulate the income/costs from the perceived negative effects of the reform; the most common approach is to design special provisions so that pre-reform tax will apply. Third, GR commonly apply for only a finite period of time; in addition, GR are often phased out over that time period.

In this paper I construct a simple dynamic general equilibrium model that captures these three features of GR in a stylized fashion. The model is a fairly standard two-sector, perfectly competitive, dynamic, general equilibrium model of a closed economy with a perfectly mobile factor (labor) and a factor (capital) that is immobile at any point in time but depreciates over time.

The public sector is characterized as follows. The level of government expenditures, G, is a fixed fraction, ϕ, of total income, Y_T, and is used to fund lump-sum per capita rebates. Revenues come solely from capital income taxes and the government budget must be balanced at each point in time. In the initial long-run equilibrium (prior to the enactment of reform at time $t = 0$), the capital income tax rate in sector one, T_1^0 is higher than the rate in sector two, T_2^0; that is, there is a tax preference for investment in sector two, with a corresponding disincentive for investment in sector one. The single tax rate which, if applied uniformly to all capital income in both sectors, would satisfy the budget constraint in a long-run 'equalized' equilibrium is denoted as T^*.

The reform analyzed is the elimination of this tax preference in a balanced- budget context; specifically, at time $t = 0$, T_2 is permanently raised to T^*, with an endogenous reduction in T_1 to balance the budget, until the two rates are equalized in the final long-run equilibrium.[6] Such a tax change is typical of recent 'revenue neutral' or balanced-budget reforms designed to improve resource allocation. For example, an explicit goal of the recent U.S. reform was the elimination of differential taxation of capital income in a revenue neutral context (McLure and Zodrow, 1987).

Such a tax change is also typical of reforms that generate demands for GR, as the elimination of differential tax treatment reduces the after-tax income of the owners of the relatively immobile capital in sector two — at least until a new long-run equilibrium is attained. Such individuals will

[6]To simplify notation, time indices are used only when needed to prevent ambiguity.

experience a reform-induced loss if the present value of the short-run losses outweighs the present value of the long run gains. It is the desire to eliminate or reduce these windfall losses that leads to demands for GR for the income attributable to capital invested in sector two at the time of the implementation of reform. The GR analyzed in this paper are designed to achieve this effect.

Details of the model are as follows. Two commodities (indexed by $j = 1,2$) are produced using capital and labor. For tractability and to identify clearly the effects of GR, the production technology is Cobb-Douglas with a labor share equal to α_j. The total supply of labor, L, is fixed, and labor is perfectly mobile earning wage w in both sectors. The total supply of capital, K, is also fixed. However, capital depreciates at a constant rate δ per period (in both sectors). Capital owners have an outside source of income that just covers depreciation on their capital, and reinvest an amount exactly sufficient to maintain their capital holdings at a constant level. Although somewhat arbitrary, these assumptions greatly simplify the analysis, as gross capital returns can be interpreted simultaneously as including an amount sufficient to cover depreciation and as representing the income available to pay taxes and to fund the consumption of capital owners.

Imperfect capital mobility is introduced by assuming that capital reallocation (from sector two to sector one in response to an increase in T_2) is limited to replacement investment, δK_2.[7] Note that, since capital is partially immobile, the returns to capital, r_1, r_2, will differ across the sectors until a long-run equilibrium is reached, $r_1 = r_2 = r$. The price of labor is the numeraire, $w = 1$.

All consumers maximize a standard utility function defined over consumption of the two commodities, which are purchased at prices p_j. The functional form is again Cobb-Douglas, with consumption shares β_1 and $\beta_2 = 1 - \beta_1$. Consumers are differentiated only according to factor ownership in the initial equilibrium, and there are three representative 'types' of consumers — owners of capital in sector one in the initial equilibrium

[7]That is, the adjustment costs associated with any further reallocation are assumed to be prohibitively high. Zodrow (1985b) considers adjustment costs in a similar model of tax reform.

(indexed by $i = 1$ and referred to as 'I1's'), owners of capital in sector two ($i = 2$, I2's), and owners of labor ($i = 3$,I3's). The total numbers of consumers of each type is N_i, with the total number of consumers equal to $N = N_1 + N_2 + N_3$.

Since the reform increases T_2, the GR to be analyzed apply to income attributable to capital in sector two in the initial equilibrium, K_2^0, and are introduced into the model as follows. First, since it seems reasonable that GR should account for depreciation, the amount of capital in sector two that qualifies for special treatment at any point in time is reduced to reflect depreciation. Second, consistent with the discussion above, GR specify that income attributable to grandfathered capital in sector two should be taxed at the pre-reform rate, T_2^0, rather than the rate existing in that time period, $T_2(t)$. Finally, the key choice variable for the government is the amount of time over which the GR apply, which is denoted as t^* years. Thus, at any point in time t, the amount of capital subject to GR is $K_2^G(t) = \mathrm{K}_2^0\, \mathrm{e}^{-\delta t}\theta(t)$, where $\theta(t) = 1$ over the time period the GR apply ($0 \leqq t < t^*$) and $\theta(t) = 0$ once the GR are no longer in force ($t \geqq t^*$). It will be convenient to define $\tilde{T}_2$ as the tax rate actually applied to capital in sector two that is potentially subject to GR, or $\tilde{T}_2(t) = T_2^0\theta(t) + \mathrm{T}_2(t)[1 - \theta(t)]$; thus $\tilde{T}_2 = T_2^0$ when GR are in force and $\tilde{T}_2 = T^*$ after they expire.

The capital reallocation induced by reform is assumed to follow a simple pattern, as firms originally in sector two allocate all replacement investment to sector one until the final equilibrium capital stock in sector two, K_2^* is reached; that is, K_2 is constrained to a suboptimally high level until time $t_c = \ln(K_2^0/K_2^*)/\delta$. Since replacement investment is not subject to GR, and GR are in effect for a finite (and, as will be shown below, a relatively short) period of time, this seems reasonable.[8] Thus, for $t < t_c$, the economy is in a 'constrained' equilibrium as $K_2(t) = K_2 e^{-\delta t}$ approaches K_2^*, and for $t \geqq t_c$, the economy is in the 'unconstrained' equilibrium ($K_2 = K_2^*$).

[8] Note, however, that in the presence of GR, $T_1 > T^*$ (even though $T_2 = T^*$), and if GR were in effect for a sufficiently long period it might become optimal for firms to delay the reallocation of capital to sector one. The analysis assumes that GR are never in effect long enough for this to occur; this assumption is not problematical in all of the simulations reported below.

Before proceeding further, note that the assumptions of the model are chosen to increase the likelihood that the optimal capital stock in sector two at any given time will be lower than the actual capital stock, so that the case for GR is as strong as possible. For example, prohibitively high adjustment costs preclude more rapid attainment of a long-run equilibrium through new investment, as does a fixed capital stock. Similarly, a closed economy implies that the time needed to adjust to a long-run equilibrium will be longer than if the economy were open; in particular, reductions in would be expected to increase capital imports in an open economy setting. Note, however, that the effect on optimal GR of 'opening' the economy is likely to be relatively small, since the main feature of the model that gives rise to the need for GR — the fact that capital cannot be reallocated quickly enough out of the sector in which taxes are rising — is not altered by moving from a closed to an open economy model. Also, since the empirical literature suggests elasticities of substitution in production between 0.5 and 1.0, a Cobb–Douglas production function implies that the reform-induced reallocation of capital will be relatively large. In addition, the time period over which GR apply is limited rather than being in force over the entire life of the asset. Finally, individual ownership of assets and thus reform-induced losses are concentrated.

The Cobb–Douglas assumptions imply that the evolution of the model over time is fairly straightforward.[9] In particular, for all t, total income, government expenditures, and labor in each sector are constant, so that commodity prices are a function only of capital stocks in each sector,

$$p_j(t) = \alpha_j^{-\alpha_j}(\beta_j Y_T)^{1-\alpha_j}\left[K_j(t)^{-(1-\alpha_j)}\right], \tag{3}$$

and net returns to capital in each sector, exclusive of any grandfather payments, are functions of only the tax rates and the capital stocks in each sector:

$$r_j(t) = (1-\alpha_j)\beta_j Y_T / \{[1+T_j(t)][K_j(t)]\}. \tag{4}$$

[9] In the interest of brevity, equations are presented only for the essential variables of the model; details of the fairly straightforward manipulations are presented in the working paper version of the paper, which is available from the author.

The use of GR naturally implies a higher equilibrium T_1, with budget balance implying $T_1 = T_1^0$ with GR (in which case reform narrows the tax differential to $T_1^0 - T^*$, and $T_1 = T^*$ in the absence of GR.

Consider first the unconstrained or long-run equilibrium in the absence of GR.[10] In such an equilibrium, r is the same across the two production sectors and equals

$$r_1(t) = r_2(t) = r = f_K Y_T / K; \tag{5}$$

$f_K = (1 - \alpha_1)\beta_1 + (1 - \alpha_2)\beta_2 - \phi$ is the constant capital share of total income. Commodity prices are

$$p_1(t) = \alpha_1^{-\alpha_1}(r\beta_1)^{1-\alpha_1}\{(1-\alpha_1)\beta_1 + (1-\alpha_2)\beta_2 T_2(t)/[1+T_2(t)] - \phi\}^{-(1-\alpha_1)} \tag{6}$$

and

$$p_2(t) = \alpha_1^{-\alpha_2}(r\beta_2)^{1-\alpha_2}\{(1-\alpha_2)\beta_2/[1+T_2(t)]\}^{-(1-\alpha_2)}. \tag{7}$$

Note that an increase in T_2 unambiguously increases p_2 and lowers p_1.

In the constrained equilibrium, the capital stock in sector two is simply $K_2(t) = K_2^0 e^{-\delta t}$. A fixed total capital stock of course implies that the capital stock in sector one is $K - K_2(t)$. However, the analysis is greatly simplified if this is approximated in exponential growth form as $K_1(t) = K_1^0 e^{-\gamma\delta t}$, where $\gamma = \ln(K_1^* / K_1^0)/(\delta t_c)$ is set so that the approximation is exact at $t = t_c$.[11] Substituting into (3) yields the time path of commodity prices:

$$p_1(t) = p_1^0 e^{-\gamma\delta(1-\alpha_1)t}, \tag{8}$$

$$p_2(t) = p_2^0 e^{\delta(1-\alpha_2)t}, \tag{9}$$

---

[10] As will be shown below, there is no need for GR in the unconstrained equilibrium as all individuals gain from reform. For future reference, these expressions consider long-run equilibria in which $T_1 > T_2$.

[11] Thus, the approximation is exact at the beginning and end of the period in which K_2 is constrained; in the simulations reported below, it is usually accurate within 1–2 percent, with a maximum error of 4 percent.

$$p_j^0 = [\alpha_j \beta_j / (\alpha_1 \beta_1 + \alpha_2 \beta_2)]^{1-\alpha_j} (L/K_j^0)^{1-\alpha_j} / \alpha_j, \qquad j = 1,2. \qquad (10)$$

Note that commodity prices are independent of changes in GR. Substituting into (4) yields net returns to capital in each sector (exclusive of payments under the GR) of

$$r_1(t) = \{(1-\alpha_1)\beta_1 + (1-\alpha_2)\beta_2 \tilde{T}_2(t)/[1+T_2(t)] - \phi\}(Y_T/K_1^0)e^{-\gamma\delta t} \qquad (11)$$

and

$$r_2(t) = \{(1-\alpha_2)\beta_2/[1+T_2(t)]\}(Y_T/K_2^0)e^{\delta t}. \qquad (12)$$

Consider next the gains and losses caused by implementing reform. Letting $Y_i(t)[Y_i^0]$ equal the income level of individual i (including a lump-sum rebate of $\phi Y_T/N$) under the reformed [initial] tax structure, the equivalent variation measure used to calculate these welfare changes is

$$EV_i(t) = C_i[p_1(t), p_2(t), Y_i(t)] - Y_i^0, \qquad (13)$$

where $C_i(t)$ is the indirect compensation function (Varian, 1984, p. 264) which in the Cobb–Douglas case is

$$C_i(t) = [p_1^0/p_1(t)]^{\beta_1}[p_2^0/p_2(t)]^{\beta_2} Y_i(t). \qquad (14)$$

The compensation functions when K_2 is constrained (denoted by c superscripts) are

$$\begin{aligned} C_1^c(t) &= a_1 e^{\varepsilon\delta t} + b_1 e^{(\varepsilon-\gamma)\delta t}, \\ a_1 &= \phi Y_T/N, \\ b_1 &= \{(1-\alpha_1)\beta_1 + (1-\alpha_2)\beta_2 \tilde{T}_2(t)/[1+T_2(t)] - \phi\}(Y_T/N_1), \end{aligned} \qquad (15)$$

$$\begin{aligned} C_2^c(t) &= a_2 e^{\varepsilon\delta t} - b_2 e^{(\varepsilon-\gamma)\delta t}, \\ a_2 &= a_1 + [(1-\alpha_1)\beta_1 + (1-\alpha_2)\beta_2 - \phi](Y_T/N_2), \\ b_2 &= b_1(N_1/N_2), \end{aligned} \qquad (16)$$

$$C_3^{\mathrm{C}}(t) = Y_3^0 \mathrm{e}^{\varepsilon\delta t}. \tag{17}$$

where $\varepsilon = \gamma\beta_1(1 - \alpha_1) - \beta_2(1 - \alpha_2)$. Alternatively, the compensation functions when K_2 is unconstrained (denoted by u superscripts) are

$$C_i^{\mathrm{u}}(t) = a_{\mathrm{u}} Y_i(t),$$
$$a_{\mathrm{u}} = \left\{\frac{(1-\alpha_1)\beta_1 + (1-\alpha_2)\beta_2 T_2(t)/[1+T_2(t)] - \phi}{(1-\alpha_1)\beta_1 + (1-\alpha_2)\beta_2 T_2^0/(1+T_2^0) - \phi}\right\}^{(1-\alpha_1)\beta_1} \times \left\{\frac{(1+T_2^0)}{[1+T_2(t)]}\right\}^{(1-\alpha_2)\beta_2}. \tag{18}$$

Substituting into Eq. (2) demonstrates that the individual gains and losses caused by reform are

$$V_i = \int_0^\infty EV_i(t)\mathrm{e}^{-\mu t}\,\mathrm{d}t = \int_0^{tc} C_i^{\mathrm{c}}(t)\mathrm{e}^{-\mu t}\,\mathrm{d}t + \int_{tc}^\infty C_i^u(t)\mathrm{e}^{-\mu t}\mathrm{d}t - Y_i^0/\mu. \tag{19}$$

2.3. *The effects of changes in the government control variables*

To see the effects of implementing reform, consider the changes in EV_i (and thus in V_i) with respect to changes in the government's control variables. Thus, in the unconstrained equilibrium,

$$\partial EV_i^u/\partial T_2 = C_i^u(t)[(1-\alpha_2)\beta_2/(1+T_2)^2](T_1 - T_2) > 0. \tag{20}$$

That is, a reduction in the tax differential improves the capital allocation and increases the welfare of all individuals. Accordingly, there is no need for GR in a long-run equilibrium. Note that since r is fixed, the efficiency gain is due to an improved price structure rather than an income increase.

Alternatively, in the constrained equilibrium, the effects of an increase in T_2 are

$$\partial EV_1^{\mathrm{c}}/\partial T_2 = (1/N_1)R_{\mathrm{T}}, \tag{21}$$

$$\partial EV_2^c/\partial T_2 = -(1/N_2)R_T,$$
$$R_T = (p_1^0/p_1)^{\beta_1}(p_2^0/p_2)^{\beta_2}[(1-\alpha_2)\beta_2/(1+T_2)^2]$$
$$\times Y_T N e^{-\gamma\delta t}[1-\theta(1+T_2^0)], \qquad (22)$$

$$\partial EV_3^c/\partial T_2 = 0. \qquad (23)$$

Thus, when capital is fixed, reform causes a pure redistribution among capital owners and has no effect on suppliers of labor (I3's). In the absence of GR ($\theta = 0$), raising T_2 causes a pure redistribution from I2's (owners of capital in sector two) to I1's (owners of capital in sector one). GR are designed to mitigate this redistribution; indeed, in the presence of GR ($\theta = 1$), reform causes the opposite redistribution, as increasing T_2 implies larger GR payments to I2's and a higher T_1.

The critical government control variable is the length of time over which GR are in effect (t^*). The effects of more GR (which, as noted above, occur only when the economy is in a constrained equilibrium) can be seen by examining the effects of an increase in θ on the EV_i, which are

$$\partial EV_1^c/\partial\theta = -(1/N_1)R_\theta, \qquad (24)$$

$$\partial EV_2^c/\partial\theta = (1/N_2)R_\theta,$$
$$R_\theta = (p_1^0/p_1)^{\beta_1}(p_2^0/p_2)^{\beta_2}[(1-\alpha_2)\beta_2/(1+T_2)]$$
$$\times Y_T e^{-\gamma\delta t}(T_2 - T_2^0)], \qquad (25)$$

$$\partial EV_3^c/\partial\theta = 0. \qquad (26)$$

Thus, GR have no effect on I3's, and result in a pure redistribution from I1's to I2's that acts to offset the losses experienced as a result of the increase in T_2.

2.4. *Optimal grandfather rules*

As discussed above, the analysis considers two governmental objectives. The first is to set the GR so that the reform becomes Pareto-improving. Substituting from Eqs. (15)–(18) into Eq. (19) and setting

$V_1 = 0$ yields the optimal period of time that GR should be in effect;[12] this implies

$$
\begin{aligned}
& t_1^* = (\ln\psi_1)/\psi_2, \\
& \psi_1 = \{a_2[1 - e^{(\varepsilon\delta - \mu)t_c}]/(\varepsilon\delta - \mu) - b_2^0/\psi_2 + b_0^* e^{[(\varepsilon-\gamma)\delta - \mu]t_c}/\psi_2 \\
& \quad - a_u Y_2 e^{-\mu t_c}/\mu + Y_2^0/\mu\}/[(b_2^* - b_2^0)/\psi_2], \\
& \psi_1 = (\varepsilon - \gamma)\delta - \mu.
\end{aligned} \tag{27}
$$

The alternative policy is to set the GR to maximize the OTR social welfare function Eq. (1). In this case, Eq. (1) depends only on the length of time GR are in effect (t_2). Differentiating Eq. (1) yields

$$
\partial W/\partial t_2 = \sum_{i=1}^{i=N} \omega_i \partial V_i/\partial t_2, \qquad \omega_i = (B + V_i)^{-e}, \tag{28}
$$

where ω_i indicates the relative social weight attached to a marginal change in the gain or loss experienced by individual *i.* Since introducing GR causes only pure redistributions from I1's to I2's, and has no effect on I3's, the first- order condition for the optimal t_2 is

$$
\omega_1 N_1 \partial V_1/\partial t_2 + \omega_2 N_2 \partial V_2/\partial t_2 = 0. \tag{29}
$$

However, since implementing GR causes only pure redistributions, Eq. (29) implies that $\omega_1 = \omega_2$ which in turn implies $V_1 = V_2$. Thus there is a unique optimal value t_2^* — independent of the value of e — at the point at which $V_1 = V_2$. As noted above, this implies that GR are used to increase the gain experienced by I2's (at the expense of reducing the gain for Il's) until the gains are equal.

The optimal t_2^* is thus determined by setting $V_1 = V_2$ and solving, which yields

$$
\begin{aligned}
& t_0^* = (\ln\psi_3)/\psi_2, \\
& \psi_3 = \{[(1-\alpha_1)\beta_1 + (1-\alpha_2)\beta_2 - \phi](Y_T/N_2)[1 - e^{(\varepsilon\delta - \mu)t_c}]/(\varepsilon\delta - \mu) \\
& \quad - b_1^0(N/N_2)/\psi_2 + b_1^*(N/N_2)e^{\psi_2 t_c}/\psi_2 \\
& \quad + a_u(Y_1 - Y_2)e^{-\mu t_c}/\mu - (Y_1^0 - Y_2^0)/\mu\}/[(b_1^* - b_1^0)(N/N_2)\psi_2].
\end{aligned} \tag{30}
$$

---

[12] Another interpretation of this policy is that the government maximizes V_1 subject to $V_2 \geqq 0$.

3. Results on Optimal Grandfather Rules

3.1. *Parameter values*

Parameter values are chosen to be 'plausible' and also to give rise to capital reallocations sufficiently large that they would likely spark demands for GR. Labor shares in production costs are $\alpha_1 = 0.7$ and $\alpha_2 = 0.3$, with a relatively large capital share in sector two suggesting a potentially significant need for GR. For individual tastes, a low $\beta_2 = 0.3$ results in a relatively large reallocation of capital from sector two when an initial tax differential of any given size is eliminated, so that the amount of time (t_c) that K_2 is constrained is fairly long and GR are again potentially attractive. The rate of capital depreciation, δ, is critical, as relatively low values of δ also imply a large t_c; the results consider a range of values from the very low rate of $\delta = 0.1$ (long-lived structures depreciate at roughly a 3 percent rate) to $\delta = 0.20$ (short-lived equipment).[13]

The initial tax rates are $T_1^0 = 0.5$ and $T_2^0 = 0$. Note that such a relatively large differential is not entirely unrealistic; for example, in the United States, investment in owner-occupied housing is subsidized while estimates of the total tax burden on corporate investment of 30 percent or more are common. The price of capital is set equal to one in the initial equilibrium. This implies $K = 100$, $L = 165.7$, and $Y_T = 285.7$. The tax rates chosen imply that $\phi = 0.07$, which in turn implies $G = 20$.

Since distributional issues are not addressed in the OTR social welfare function Eq. (1), individual incomes are of fairly little concern. Accordingly, the number of individuals of each type is simply set so that initial incomes are roughly equal. This implies $N_1 = 4$, $N_2 = 6$, $N_3 = 17$, and thus $N = 27$.

3.2. *Initial and final equilibria*

These parameters imply an initial equilibrium with $K_1^0 = 40$, $K_2^0 = 60$, $L_1 = 140$, $L_2 = 25.7$, $p_1^0 = 2.08$ and $p_2^0 = 1.84$. Tax rate equalization with a balanced budget constraint occurs at $T_1 = T_2 = T^* = 0.2$. In the long run,

[13] Note that the rationale for reform would disappear if $\delta = 0$ (land), since there would be no reallocation of capital and thus no efficiency gains when the tax differential was eliminated.

Table 3.1.
Simulation Results Without Grandfather Rules.

δ	V_1/Y_1^0	V_2/Y_2^0	t_c
0.01	0.412	−0.272	18.2
0.02	0.362	−0.235	9.12
0.03	0.318	−0.203	6.08
0.04	0.282	−0.177	4.56
0.05	0.253	−0.155	3.65
0.06	0.229	−0.138	3.04
0.07	0.209	−0.123	2.60
0.08	0.193	−0.111	2.28
0.09	0.179	−0.101	2.03
0.10	0.167	−0.092	1.82
0.15	0.126	−0.062	1.21
0.20	0.103	−0.045	0.91

this reform results in a significant reallocation of capital, as K_2 drops by 16.7 percent to $K_2^* = 50$, and K_1 increases by 25 percent to $K_1^* = 50$.[14] The reform reverses the order of relative consumer prices, as $p_1^* = 1.95$ and $p_2^* = 2.09$. In terms of efficiency gains, the aggregate equivalent variation for an immediate movement to the final tax-equalized equilibrium is 2.46 or 12.3 percent of government tax revenues. Note that since all three types of individuals have a higher utility level in the final equilibrium, the model focuses clearly on issues related to GR, as all welfare losses arise from the (temporary) immobility of capital in sector two rather than from any general equilibrium changes in factor returns or commodity prices.

Table 3.1 presents some illustrative examples of the effects on individual welfare changes of implementing the capital tax equalization reform in the absence of GR. These are significant for low values of the rate of economic depreciation δ, but fall rapidly as δ increases. For example, when $\delta = 0.1$, I1's experience a gain equal to 41.2 percent of annual income in the initial equilibrium, while I2's suffer a loss equal to 27.2 percent of annual

[14] Production in sector two (one) falls (increases) by nearly 12 (7) percent.

income. However, when $\delta = 0.03$, V_1 falls to 31.8 percent of annual income while V_2 is 20.3 percent of annual income, and when $\delta = 0.10$, V_1 is 16.7 percent of annual income while the loss experienced by I2's is 9.2 percent of annual income. These losses — even for fairly rapid rates of depreciation such as $\delta = 0.10$ — appear to be sufficiently large to spark demands for GR. The length of time K_2 is constrained, t_c, also falls quickly as δ increases. For example, when $\delta = 0.03$, $t_c = 6.1$ years. However, when $\delta = 0.10$, t_c falls to only 1.8 years, and when $\delta = 0.20$, $t_c = 0.91$.

3.3. *Results*

Results on optimal GR as a function of δ are presented in Table 3.2. These show t_1^*, the amount of time GR need to be in force to convert the reform to a Pareto-improving one, and t_2^*, the length of time GR must be in effect for the reform to maximize the OTR social welfare function Eq. (1). The amount of time the economy is in a constrained equilibrium, t_c, is also shown; as argued above, $t_1^* < t_2^* < t_c$. In addition, results are also presented for X_1 (X_2), defined as the ratio of the gain to II's when GR are in effect for t_1^* (t_2^*) years to the gain without such rules.

Table 3.2.
Optimal Grandfather Rules.

δ	t_1^*	t_2^*	t_3	t_c	X_1	X_2
0.01	6.46	6.76	6.97	18.2	0.034	0.014
0.02	3.67	3.97	4.18	9.12	0.078	0.031
0.03	2.49	2.79	3.00	6.08	0.124	0.050
0.04	1.85	2.15	2.36	4.56	0.169	0.068
0.05	1.45	1.75	1.96	3.65	0.213	0.085
0.06	1.17	1.47	1.68	3.04	0.256	0.102
0.07	0.97	1.27	1.48	2.60	0.297	0.119
0.08	0.82	1.12	1.33	2.28	0.337	0.135
0.09	0.70	1.00	1.21	2.03	0.375	0.150
0.10	0.61	0.90	1.11	1.82	0.413	0.165
0.15	0.31	0.61	0.82	1.22	0.581	0.232
0.20	0.17	0.46	0.67	0.91	0.724	0.289

Several features of these results are noteworthy. First, the values of t_1^* are fairly small — on the order of 20–40 percent of t_c. Moreover, t_1^* falls rapidly as δ increases; that is, the need for GR declines as the immobility of K_2 becomes less problematical. For example, when $\delta = 0.03$, GR need be in effect for only 2.5 years to convert the capital tax equilibrium reform into a Pareto-improving one. When $\delta = 0.07$ (0.10), t_1^* falls to only 1.0 (0.6) years.

Second, GR dramatically reduce the gains experienced by I1's, especially for low δ; for example, when $\delta = 0.03$, the introduction of GR that convert the reform into a Pareto-improving one reduces the gain experienced by I1's to slightly more than 10 percent of the gain in the absence of such rules ($X_1 = 0.12$); when $\delta = 0.1, X_1$ increases to 0.413. The intuition behind this result is that GR eliminate the redistributive component of the gain to I1's, leaving only the relatively small component attributable to increased efficiency; moreover, since the relative size of the efficiency component increases as δ increases (even though the absolute size of V_1 falls), X_1 increases also.

Third, the values of t_2^*, the length of time GR must be in force for the reform to maximize Eq. (1), are only very slightly greater than the optimal t_1^*. For example, when $\delta = 0.03$, $t_2^* = 2.8$ while $t_1^* = 2.5$; similarly, when $\delta = 0.10$, $t_2^* = 0.9$ while $t_1^* = 0.6$. The essential difference between the two reform implementation objectives is that under the Pareto-improving reform, none of the efficiency gain accrues to I2's, while if the government is choosing its GR to maximize Eq. (1), it keeps GR in effect until I2's share in the efficiency gain to the point at which $V_1 = V_2$. Since the marginal redistribution associated with GR is considerably larger than the marginal efficiency gain, GR must be kept in effect for only a slightly longer period of time (relative to the time required for a Pareto-improving reform) for this to occur. However note that the increase in time the GR are in effect significantly reduces the relative gain experienced by Il's, as much of their already small efficiency gain is redistributed to I2's. For example, when $\delta = 0.03$ and the time GR are in effect increases from t_1^* to t_2^*, V_1 falls from 12.4 to only 5.0 percent of the gain experienced in the absence of GR. As in the case of the Pareto-improving reform, the need for GR declines (t_2^* falls) as δ increases.

A fourth result is obtained by examining the values of t_3, which is defined as the amount of time GR must be in effect for the associated redistributions from I1's to I2's to be so great that I1's actually become losers from reform ($V_1 < 0$). The results indicate that GR need be in effect for only a slightly longer period of time than t_2^* (and thus t_1^*) for this rather perverse result to obtain. For example, when $\delta = 0.03$, $t_3 = 3.0$ while $t_2^* = 2.8$; similarly, when $\delta = 0.10$, $t_3 = 1.1$ while $t_2^* = 0.9$. Thus, the effects of GR are very sensitive to the amount of time such rules are in effect. Indeed, in all cases the difference between t_3 and t_1^* is very small at roughly 0.5 years.

The intuition behind this result is similar to that described above. Specifically, the difference between t_2^* and t_3 is small because the marginal redistribution associated with GR is considerably larger than the marginal efficiency gain, and the remaining efficiency gains received by I1's are fairly small when GR are kept in effect for t_2^* years. Accordingly, if GR are kept in effect for only a slightly longer period of time (relative to t_2^*), the associated redistribution from I1's to I2's will eliminate entirely the gain experienced by the former group. These results suggest that GR must be used with extreme caution, as it is easy to 'overshoot' the desired amount of reform and convert the reform to one in which the perceived gainers from reform (I1's) actually become losers.

4. Suboptimal Grandfather Rules

The previous results examined the need for and efficacy of GR when such rules were 'ideal' in that they caused only pure redistributions between the two types of capital owners. However, it seems likely GR often would not be so well-structured and instead would also cause efficiency losses. In the model detailed above this is most likely to occur if GR are left in effect too long, so that they reduce the speed of the reallocation of capital from sector one to sector two by delaying the elimination of the tax differential and thus result in smaller reform-induced efficiency gains.

Note that this does not occur because replacement investment remains in sector two in order to benefit from payments under the GR; such a result is precluded by the assumption that the amount of capital in sector two eligible for GR declines at the rate of depreciation.[15] Instead, the efficiency costs of extending GR beyond the optimal time arise as follows. Recall that as long as GR are in effect, $T_1 > T^*$ (even though $T_2 = T^*$) since the grandfather payments to owners of capital in sector two are financed with higher capital taxes on sector one. If this period is sufficiently long, then enough capital will be reallocated to sector one such that, given $T_1 > T^*$, the tax incentive for further reallocation will be eliminated before the final equalized equilibrium is reached.

One way this might occur is if GR are phased out slowly. As noted above, transition rules often include phased-out GR. In this section the model is revised to include a phase-out of GR that causes efficiency losses, and the implementation of such 'suboptimal' GR is studied.

4.1. *Revisions of the basic model*

The easiest way to introduce phased-out GR in the model is to assume that the amount of capital in sector two eligible for GR that actually receives such treatment is phased out at a constant rate ρ. In this case, $\theta(t) = \lambda e^{-\rho t}(0 \leqq \lambda \leqq 1)$, where λ reflects the extent to which GR are adopted, given that they are to be phased out at rate ρ. This approach implies that the amount of capital in sector two that is subject to GR is $K_2^G(t) = K_2^0 \lambda e^{-(\rho+\delta)t}$.

The phase-out rate ρ presumably would be fairly large, as GR typically are not maintained for long periods of time. Moreover, ρ is chosen so that the optimal reallocation of capital follows a simple path analogous to that described in Section 2. Specifically, the economy is assumed to be in a 'constrained' equilibrium in which $K_2(t) = K_2^0 e^{-\delta t}$ until time t' when a long-run equilibrium consistent with $\theta(t')$, $T_1(t')$ and $T_2(t') = T^*$ is reached. For all $t > t'$, the economy remains on an 'unconstrained' long-run equilibrium path as $T_1(t)$ falls toward T^* as the GR are phased out. The phase-out rates used in the simulations ($\rho = 0.25$ and $\rho = 0.50$) are consistent with this path of capital reallocation. Note that these rates

[15] Note, however, that another way to introduce suboptimal GR that would lead to efficiency losses would be to apply GR to all capital in sector two, as such provisions would slow the reallocation of capital to sector one in response to the enactment of reform.

are arbitrary, as the optimal GR policy involves no phasing out; phasing out of GR is introduced into the model solely to examine the effects of suboptimal GR that reduce reform-induced efficiency gains as well as redistributions.

The equations of the model for the case in which GR are phased out are quite similar to those detailed above. In the constrained equilibria, the expressions are the same except that $\theta(t)$ is defined as noted above. In the unconstrained equilibria, the critical variable in modifying Eqs. (10)–(14) is $\Omega(t)=[T_2(t)-T_2^0]K_2^G(t)/K$, which approaches zero with time. The net return to capital is the same in both jurisdictions, but is lower than the final equilibrium value due to the misallocation of capital attributable to the GR; specifically, with $r(t)$ as defined in Eq. (4),

$$r'(t) = r(t)/[1 + \Omega(t)]. \tag{31}$$

Similarly, the adjustment to the more efficient commodity price structure is slower, as

$$p_j'(t)=\alpha_j^{-\alpha j}(\beta_j Y_T)^{(1-\alpha_j)}[K_j'(t)]^{-(1-\alpha_j)}, \tag{32}$$

and $K_2'(t)>K_2(t)$; $K_1'(t)<K_1(t)$ as the suboptimal use of GR delays the reallocation of capital in response to the efficiency-enhancing capital tax equalization reform. Note that all variables converge to the analogous values in Eqs. (5)–(7) as time increases and Ω approaches zero.

The government's choice variable is thus λ, given the choice of ρ. In the constrained equilibria, the changes in the EV_i are analogous to those in Eqs. (15)–(17). In the unconstrained case,

$$\begin{aligned}\partial EV_3^u/\partial\lambda &= -E_\lambda' Y_3,\\ E_\lambda' &= (p_1^0/p_1)^{\beta_1}(p_2^0/p_2)^{\beta_2}[(1-\alpha_2)\beta_2/(1+T_2)]\\ &\quad [\Omega/(1+\Omega)](T_1-T_2)/\lambda,\end{aligned} \tag{33}$$

$$\begin{aligned}\partial EV_1^u/\partial\lambda &= -R_\lambda'/N_1 - E_\lambda' Y_1,\\ R_\lambda' &= (p_1^0/p_1)^{\beta_1}(p_0^0/p_2)^{\beta_2} rK_1^0[\Omega/(1+\Omega)]/\lambda,\end{aligned} \tag{34}$$

$$\partial EV_2^u/\partial\lambda = R_\lambda'/N_2 - E_\lambda' Y_2. \tag{35}$$

Thus, the implementation of GR has two effects. The first is an efficiency loss, E'_λ that is borne by all three types of individuals in proportion to income, as GR retard the elimination of the capital tax differential and thus perpetuate the associated commodity tax distortion; the magnitude of this effect increases with the size of the tax differential. The second effect is, as in the case of optimal GR, a pure redistribution, R'_λ, from I1's to I2's. The magnitude of this redistribution increases with the fraction of the capital stock subject to GR; that is, it increases as Ω increases.

The government again pursues one of two objectives. First, it may choose λ such that the reform becomes a Pareto-improving one; this value is denoted as λ_1^*. Second, it may choose λ to maximize the OTR social welfare function Eq. (1). This value, which is denoted as λ_2^*. satisfies

$$\omega_1 N_1 \partial V_1/\partial\lambda + \omega_2 N_2 \partial V_2/\partial\lambda + \omega_3 N_3 \partial V_3/\partial\lambda = 0. \tag{36}$$

That is, λ_2^* reflects the extent of enactment of GR such that the sum of the socially weighted (by w_i,) marginal changes in individual gains and losses is zero. Numerical solutions to Eq. (36) are shown below. However, the intuition behind the solutions is as follows. Recall that in the case of optimal GR, maximizing Eq. (1) implied setting GR such that $V_1 = V_2$. Following the same strategy in this case would not be optimal; at the value of λ (say, λ_E) at which $V_1 = V_2$, the redistributive effects on social welfare of a marginal increase in λ would cancel exactly, but all of the efficiency component would have a negative effect. Thus, the enactment of GR must stop at a value smaller than λ_E. However, to the extent that the efficiency gains from reform are fairly small relative to the redistributions, λ_2^* will approach λ_E. This is especially true for large values of e, in which case the government is concerned primarily with the adverse effects of reform-induced redistributions rather than the positive effects of efficiency gains. This pattern of results is in fact reported below.

4.2. *Results*

Results for the Pareto-improving extent of enactment of phased-out GR (λ_1^*) as a function of δ are shown in the second column of Table 3.3. In contrast to the previous results, it is not necessarily the case that GR can

Table 3.3.
Suboptimal Grandfather Rules ($\rho = 0.25$); Optimal λ_2^* as a Function of e and δ.

δ	λ_1^*	λ_E	λ_3	e: 0	0.05	0.1	0.3	0.5	0.7	0.9	1.0	1.5	2.0	3.0	5.0
0.01	—	—	—	0	1	1	1	1	1	1	1	1	1	1	1
0.02	—	—	—	0	1	1	1	1	1	1	1	1	1	1	1
0.03	0.87	0.98	—	0	0.91	0.94	0.96	0.96	0.97	0.97	0.97	0.97	0.97	0.97	0.97
0.04	0.71	0.83	0.91	0	0.70	0.75	0.80	0.81	0.81	0.82	0.82	0.82	0.82	0.82	0.82
0.05	0.59	0.73	0.82	0	0.54	0.62	0.68	0.70	0.70	0.71	0.71	0.72	0.72	0.72	0.72
0.06	0.51	0.66	0.76	0	0.42	0.59	0.61	0.62	0.62	0.63	0.63	0.64	0.64	0.64	0.65
0.07	0.44	0.60	0.71	0	0.35	0.43	0.52	0.55	0.56	0.57	0.57	0.58	0.59	0.59	0.59
0.08	0.38	0.55	0.67	0	0.29	0.36	0.46	0.49	0.51	0.52	0.52	0.53	0.53	0.54	0.54
0.09	0.33	0.51	0.64	0	0.24	0.33	0.41	0.44	0.46	0.47	0.47	0.48	0.49	0.50	0.50
0.10	0.29	0.48	0.61	0	0.20	0.28	0.38	0.41	0.43	0.44	0.44	0.45	0.46	0.46	0.46
0.15	0.13	0.36	0.53	0	0.10	0.16	0.25	0.29	0.30	0.31	0.32	0.33	0.34	0.34	0.35
0.20	0.02	0.29	0.48	0	0.06	0.10	0.18	0.21	0.23	0.24	0.24	0.26	0.26	0.27	0.28

convert the reform into a Pareto-improving one; in particular, for $\delta \leqq 0.02, V_2 \leqq 0$ even if $\lambda = 1$. This result obtains because GR are phased out at the rate $\rho = 0.25$, and thus may be insufficient to eliminate all losses to I2's (even if phased out over an infinite time period) especially if λ is sufficiently low that the losses suffered by I2's in the absence of GR are relatively large. Since GR reduce efficiency gains (some of which accrue to I2's) it is also more difficult to eliminate the loss to I2's with GR in this case. Note that λ_1^* declines fairly rapidly with increases in δ; indeed, the reform is almost Pareto-improving even in the absence of GR for $\delta = 0.2$. As above, these results simply reflect the fact that more rapid depreciation implies less need for GR.

The third column of Table 3.3 provides values of λ_E, which is the extent of enactment of GR such that $V_1 = V_2$. Recall that λ_E provides an upper limit for λ_2^*. This relationship is in fact observed as λ_2^* (the last 12 columns of Table 3.3) approaches as λ_E increases, and the two are almost identical when $e = 5$ for all values of δ. Also included in Table 3.3 are values of λ_3, defined as the extent of enactment of GR such that II's are actually converted to losers from reform. As in the case of optimal GR, it is possible that 'too much' grandfathering will give this rather perverse result. For the parameter values shown, this can occur for all values of $\delta \geqq 0.04$. Note that λ_3 also declines as δ increases, and thus the need for GR declines. As expected, $\lambda_1^* < \lambda_E < \lambda_3$.

The remainder of Table 3.3 presents values of λ_2^* as a function of δ and e. Note first that if $e = 0, \lambda_2^* = 0$ and no GR are enacted. In this case the government is concerned only with efficiency gains and GR are undesirable because they reduce such gains. The remaining results assume $e > 0$, so that the government is averse to reform-induced redistributions. Note that $\lambda_1^* > \lambda_2^*$ in a small number of cases — those in which $0.04 \leqq \delta \leqq 0.15$ when $e = 0.05$ (and sometimes when $e = 0.1$). Thus, for sufficiently low values of e, the optimal extent of GR [that maximizes Eq. (1)] can be less than that required to convert the reform into a Pareto-improving one. In these cases the government is not very averse to reform-induced redistributions, and is willing to limit the extent of GR to avoid efficiency losses, even though such a policy implies I2's will be losers from reform.

An interesting result is that the extent of enactment of GR can be relatively small — even though such rules are phased out at a fairly rapid rate — especially for large values of δ. For example, for $\delta = 0.05, \lambda_2^*$ varies from 0.54 to 0.72, while for $\delta = 0.1$, λ_2^* varies from 0.20 to 0.46. This result suggests that — as in the case of optimal GR — the need for GR is limited, especially if rapid depreciation rates suggest rapid market adjustments and GR impose efficiency costs.

In addition, the results indicate that the need for GR decreases significantly as δ increases. As discussed above, a relatively large δ implies faster capital reallocation and thus smaller reform-induced redistributions, so that the enactment of GR that postpone efficiency gains becomes less desirable. Moreover, as δ increases, λ_2^* falls increasingly below λ_E for the smaller values of e, reflecting the greater magnitude of the efficiency costs of GR and thus less willingness on the part of the government to move toward a solution where V_1 approximates V_2 (unless e is very large).

Note also that λ_2^* increases as e increases. A relatively large e implies that the government is more willing to accept efficiency losses in order to mitigate the effects of reform on I2's. As described above, there are two interpretations of the OTR social welfare function Eq. (1) in this case. In the relatively few cases in which $\lambda_2^* < \lambda_1^*$, the standard interpretation is appropriate — the government chooses its reform implementation methods to trade off reduced efficiency gains against reduced redistributions from I1's to I2's. However, in the vast majority of the cases (that are characterized by $\lambda_2^* > \lambda_1^*$), the best interpretation of Eq. (1) is that the government weighs gains to individuals who are the small (large) gainers from reform more (less) heavily, and that the government is willing to forgo some efficiency gains to redistribute the gains from reform more uniformly. Larger values of e reflect an increased willingness to make this particular trade off.

In addition, the results for λ_2^* are considerably more sensitive to δ than to the choice of e (which varies over the sizable range 0–5). Thus, once it is established that the government has some aversion to reform-induced redistributions, one can arrive at an estimate of λ_2^* even if the precise value of e is unclear, as long as one knows the value of δ with reasonable accuracy. Such a result would appear to be quite useful, given the inherent difficulties in calculating the value of e.

Finally, Table 3.4 presents results for λ_2^* when GR are phased out at the faster rate of $\rho = 0.50$. The pattern of the results is the same as above. However, in all cases the optimal extent of enactment of GR is considerably greater than when $\rho = 0.25$, as more rapid phasing out of GR implies

Table 3.4.

Suboptimal Grandfather Rules ($\rho = 0.50$); Optimal λ_2^* as a Function of e and δ.

δ	λ_2^*	λF	λ3	e 0	0.05	0.1	0.3	0.5	0.7	0.9	1.0	1.5	2.0	3.0	5.0
0.01	—	—	—	0	1	1	1	1	1	1	1	1	1	1	1
0.02	—	—	—	0	1	1	1	1	1	1	1	1	1	1	1
0.03	—	—	—	0	1	1	1	1	1	1	1	1	1	1	1
0.04	—	—	—	0	1	1	1	1	1	1	1	1	1	1	1
0.05	0.86	—	—	0	0.98	1	1	1	1	1	1	1	1	1	1
0.06	0.72	0.93	—	0	0.78	0.85	0.90	0.91	0.92	0.92	0.92	0.92	0.92	0.92	0.93
0.07	0.61	0.84	0.99	0	0.66	0.74	0.79	0.80	0.81	0.82	0.82	0.82	0.83	0.83	0.83
0.08	0.53	0.77	0.93	0	0.56	0.60	0.70	0.72	0.73	0.74	0.74	0.75	0.75	0.75	0.76
0.09	0.45	0.71	0.88	0	0.46	0.56	0.62	0.65	0.66	0.67	0.68	0.68	0.69	0.69	0.70
0.10	0.39	0.66	0.84	0	0.37	0.47	0.58	0.60	0.62	0.62	0.63	0.63	0.64	0.64	0.65
0.15	0.17	0.49	0.71	0	0.18	0.26	0.37	0.41	0.43	0.44	0.44	0.46	0.47	0.47	0.47
0.20	0.02	0.39	0.65	0	0.10	0.16	0.26	0.30	0.32	0.33	0.34	0.35	0.36	0.37	0.37

fewer efficiency losses so that GR are more desirable; that is, as the speed of the inherently suboptimal phase-out increases, the enactment of GR approaches the optimal policy analyzed in Section 3. The differences in the extent of enactment can be considerable. For example, for $e = 1$ and $\delta = 0.05$ (0.10), λ_2^*, increases from 0.71 (0.44) when $\rho = 0.25$ to 1.0 (0.63) when $\rho = 0.5$.

4.3. *A note on grandfathering vs. phasing-in reform*

In this paper, GR are the only instrument available to the government; in particular, the reform is characterized by $T_2 = T^*$ for all $t > 0$. As noted in the Introduction, this approach is markedly different from that used in previous analyses, which have ignored GR and instead focused on phasing-in, delaying or partially enacting reform — that is, choosing $T_2(t)$ to maximize Eq. (1). A natural extension of the approach used in this paper is to combine the two instruments and examine how optimal GR are affected if $T_2(t)$ is also a government control variable. Although a complete examination of this issue is beyond the scope of this paper, the following analysis is suggestive.

Consider first the case in which GR are designed optimally (Section 3) to maximize Eq. (1). In this case, supplementing GR with a phasing-in of reform $T_2(t) < T^*$ for some time $t < t_2^*$ — is undesirable. In the presence of GR ($\theta = 1$), Eq. (21) and Eq. (22) show that a reduction in T_2 causes a redistribution from I2's to I1's; such a redistribution is clearly undesirable as it increases rather than mitigates the redistributions caused by the enactment of reform.

The case in which GR are designed suboptimally (Section 4) is more difficult to analyze. For example, suppose that the government is still constrained to full tax equalization or enactment of $T_2(t) = T^*$ by time $t = \tau$, but may phase in reform by enacting $T_2(t) = T_2'$ for $0 \leqq t \leqq \tau$, $0 \leqq T_2' < T^*$; that is, the government chooses λ and T_2' to maximize (Eq. 1). Since GR are phased out, $\theta(t) < 1$ for $t > 0$. Thus, R_T in Eq. (21) and Eq. (22) will be positive if $\theta < 1/(1+T_2^0)$. In this case the redistributions from I1's to I2's caused by phasing-in reform (in the constrained equilibrium) are desirable as they partially reverse the redistributions caused by increasing T_2 while reducing T_1. Thus phasing-in reform is likely to be a useful supplement to

GR. Intuitively, phased-out GR are problematic because they cause efficiency losses. If phasing-in of reform occurs while the economy is in a constrained equilibrium, reform-induced redistributions are reduced at no efficiency cost. This is desirable because it reduces the need for GR and the associated efficiency losses.[16] This brief analysis suggests that if GR are implemented suboptimally, it may be useful to supplement them with phasing-in of reform; further examination of this issue is left to future research.

5. Conclusion

Despite the frequent use of GR, the effects of such rules have received little attention. This paper analyzed the effect of GR within the context of the 'optimal tax reform' problem. Since the model is quite specialized, care must be exercised in drawing inferences from the results. Indeed, an obvious direction for future research is the analysis of specific GR for specific reforms in more general models. Nevertheless, several conclusions are suggested for those situations in which the use of GR can be approximated by the stylized approach described above.

The most important conclusion is that carefully constructed GR are a highly effective reform implementation tool. Indeed, in the model analyzed, appropriately structured GR can generally convert potential 'losers' from reform into gainers. An interesting implication is that, rather than describing reforms as desirable if direct compensation from gainers to losers were theoretically possible (Hicks, 1939, Kaldor, 1939), the use of GR is an indirect means of introducing such compensation; as a result, reforms can be Pareto-improving even without any direct compensation. GR thus can be effective in minimizing political opposition to efficiency-enhancing tax reforms.

Appropriately structured GR also provide an effective reform implementation tool if the government objective is the standard OTR social welfare function. In this case the interpretation of the OTR problem in the presence of GR generally differs from the traditional one of balancing

[16] Note, however, that phasing in reform can also cause efficiency losses if it occurs when the economy is in an unconstrained equilibrium.

reduced efficiency gains against reduced redistributions. Rather, the problem is to implement the reform such that the gains from reform are distributed equitably; in this context, GR are desirable because they redistribute gains from the 'big' gainers from reform to the 'small' gainers, although this redistribution may occur at the cost of delaying some aggregate efficiency gains. That is, the OTR social welfare function implies that the government wishes to distribute the gains from reform more uniformly, and is willing to forgo some efficiency gains to do so.

However, the analysis also suggests at least three reasons why caution should be exercised in implementing GR (especially if they involve large administrative costs). The first issue is the length of time GR should be in effect. The model indicates that, although owners of immobile capital initially in tax-preferred activities do experience short-run losses, several factors mitigate these losses. Specifically, the outflow of capital from the formerly tax-advantaged sector increases short-run returns to the capital that remains. In addition, since some of the capital initially in the tax-preferred sector is reallocated to the formerly tax-disadvantaged sector, owners of such capital benefit from the newly lower taxes and relatively high returns in the latter sector. Moreover, at some point a long-run equilibrium will be attained, and reform-induced efficiency gains are shared by all individuals. The analysis suggests that these factors are sufficiently important that reform-induced losses, while large enough to concern a government averse to such redistributions, are not so large that GR need be in effect for extended periods of time. For example, in the model analyzed in this paper — which is characterized by many assumptions designed to make GR desirable — reform-induced losses ranged from 10 to 20 percent of annual income (for depreciation rates between 3 and 10 percent), and the length of time that GR needed to be in effect varied from slightly over half a year to nearly three years.

A second reason for caution is that the effects of GR are very sensitive to the length of time they are in force. In particular, the results suggest that it is easy to 'overshoot' the optimal extent of enactment of GR and convert the apparent gainers from reform into losers. For example, in the simulations reported, keeping GR in effect for only half a year 'too long' was sufficient to convert a Pareto-improving reform to one in which the apparent gainers from reform were converted to losers. Such sensitivity suggests that erring on the side of too little enactment of GR may be wise.

Finally, a third reason for caution is that the use of GR may cause efficiency losses. For example, in the case studied above, phased-out GR reduce revenues in one sector and thus require higher and more distortionary tax rates in the other sector. Such effects also suggest that restraint in the use of GR is appropriate.

Acknowledgements

Research support from the National Science Foundation (Grant SES-8606730) is gratefully acknowledged. The paper has been greatly improved in response to the comments of an anonymous referee. I have also benefited from the comments of Peter Mieszkowski, from the research assistance of T. Ligeralde and O. Hendrick, and from extended discussions with Laura Noel.

References

Aaron, H.J., 1985, Some further thought on recapture of excess depreciation, Tax Notes (July 15), 315–321.

Atkinson, A.B. and J.E. Stiglitz, 1980, *Lectures on public economics*. McGraw-Hill: New York.

Auerbach, A.J., 1985, The theory of excess burden and optimal taxation, in: AJ. Auerbach and M. Feldstain, eds., *Handbook of public economics*, Vol. I (North-Holland, Amsterdam).

Auerbach, A.J. and L.J. Kotlikoff, 1983, Investment versus saving incentives: The size of the bang for the buck and the potential for self-financing business tax cuts, in: L.H. Meyer, ed., *The economic consequences of government deficits* Kluwer-Nijhoff: Boston.

Cordes, J.J. and B.A. Weisbrod, 1979, Governmental behavior in response to compensation requirements, *Journal of Public Economics* 11, 47–58.

Cordes, J.J. and B.A. Weisbrod, 1985, When government programs create inequities: A guide to compensation policies, *Journal of Policy Analysis and Management* 4, 178–195.

Diamond, P.A. and J.A. Mirrlees, 1971, Optimal taxation and public production, *American Economic Review* 61, 8–27 and 261–278.

Diewert, W.C., 1978, Optimal tax perturbations. *Journal of Public Economics* 10, 139–177.

Dixit, A.K., 1979, Price changes and optimum taxation in a many-person economy, *Journal of Public Economics* 11, 143–157.

Feldstein, M.S., 1976a, Compensation in tax reform, *National Tax Journal* 29, 123–130.

Feldstein, M.S., 1976b, On the theory of tax reform, *Journal of Public Economics* 6, 77–104.

Goode, R., 1987, Disappointed expectations and tax reform, *National Tax Journal* 40, 159–169.

Graetz, M.J., 1977, Legal transitions: The case of retroactivity in income tax reform, *University of Pennsylvania Law Review* 126, 47–87.

Guesnerie, R., 1977, On the direction of tax reform, *Journal of Public Economics* 6, 77–104.

Hicks, J.R., 1939, The foundations of welfare economics, *Economic Journal* 49, 696–712.

Kaldor, N., 1939, Welfare propositions of economics and interpersonal comparisons of utility. *Economic Journal* 49, 549–552.

McLure, C.E., Jr. and G.R. Zodrow, 1987, Treasury 1 and the tax reform act of 1986: The economics and politics of tax reform, *Journal of Economic Perspectives* 1, 37–58.

Mirrlees, J., 1976, Optimal tax theory: A synthesis, *Journal of Public Economics* 6, 327–358.

Sandmo, A., 1976, Optimal taxation: An introduction to the literature, *Journal of Public Economics* 6, 327–358.

Stern, N.H., 1987, The theory of optimal commodity and income taxation: An introduction, in: D. Newbery and N.H. Stern, eds., *The theory of taxation for developing countries*. Oxford University Press for the World Bank: New York.

Summers, L.H., 1981, Taxation and corporate investment: A *q*-theory approach, *Brookings Papers on Economic Activity* 2, 67–127.

U.S. Treasury, 1985, *The president's proposals to the congress for fairness, growth and simplicity*. Government Printing Office: Washington, DC.

Varian, H.R., 1984, *Microeconomic analysis*. Norton: New York.

Weymark, J.A., 1979, A reconciliation of recent results in optimal taxation theory, *Journal of Public Economics* 12, 171–189.

Zodrow, G.R., 1981, Implementing tax reform, *National Tax Journal* 401–418.

Zodrow, G.R., 1985a, Partial tax reform: An optimal taxation perspective, *Canadian Journal of Economics* 18, 335–346.

Zodrow, G.R., 1985b, Optimal tax reform in the presence of adjustment costs, *Journal of Public Economics* 27, 211–230.
Zodrow, G.R., 1986, Implementing tax reform: The intergenerational carryover problem, *National Tax Journal* 34, 419–433.
Zodrow, G.R., 1988, The windfall recapture tax: Issues of theory and design, *Public Finance Quarterly* 16, 387–424.

Chapter 4

Consumption Tax Reform: Changes in Business Equity and Housing Prices*

John W. Diamond[1]

Baker Institute for Public Policy and Economics Department
Rice University, Houston, TX 77005, USA

George R. Zodrow

Economics Department and Baker Institute for Public Policy
Rice University, Houston, TX 77005, USA

---

*This chapter is reproduced from *Fundamental Tax Reform: Issues, Choices and Implications*, edited by John W. Diamond and George R. Zodow, MIT Press, 2008, pp. 227–251. Please note that the appendix to the paper is not included (although citations to the appendix remain).

[1]We have benefited from the comments of Len Burman and Alan Viard and the participants of a conference on 'Is It Time for Fundamental Tax Reform? The Known, the Unknown and the Unknowable,' sponsored by the Tax and Expenditure Policy Program of the James A. Baker III Institute for Public Policy, Rice University, Houston Texas. The views expressed in this paper are those of the authors and do not necessarily reflect those of the Baker Institute for Public Policy.

1. Introduction

Fundamental tax reform, often defined as replacing the income tax with some form of consumption-based taxation, has been discussed in both academic and policy circles in the United States for some time. The 2005 report of the President's Advisory Panel on Federal Income Tax Reform discussed a consumption-based tax — the Progressive Consumption Tax (PCT) option, modeled after the X-Tax created by the late David Bradford (1986, 2005) — at length but ultimately decided against recommending this alternative.[2] Proponents of consumption-based reforms argue that they would generate a variety of benefits, and there is a voluminous literature examining the relative advantages and disadvantages of income and consumption taxes in terms of efficiency (especially with respect to reducing tax biases against saving and investment and promoting economic growth), horizontal and vertical equity (including views of vertical equity that take a lifetime rather than an annual perspective), and simplicity in administration and compliance.[3]

These familiar issues will not be revisited in this paper. Rather, the focus of this study is on an analysis of two transitional issues that often arise in discussions of the feasibility of consumption tax reforms: (1) the potential reform-induced decline in the price of owner-occupied housing attributable to the enactment of a consumption tax that eliminates the preferential tax treatment of housing under the current income tax, and (2) the tendency of such a reform to impose a one-time windfall loss on the owners of existing business equity capital. These issues have played an important and controversial role in the tax reform debate. Some observers have argued that the prospect of large reform-induced windfall losses would create a huge impediment to the enactment of reform; in marked contrast, others have stressed that such losses create the potential for larger long run efficiency gains from reform while simultaneously mitigating the distributional problems associated with the lower marginal tax rates at the top of the income distribution and the generous treatment of

[2] See Zodrow and McLure (2006) and the other analyses cited therein for discussions of the panel's report.

[3] For example, see the paper in this volume by Auerbach and the papers in Boskin (1996), Aaron and Gale (1996), Zodrow and Mieszkowski (2002b), and Aaron, Burman and Steuerle (forthcoming).

capital income that characterize a consumption tax. The Flat Tax is the primary reform considered in this paper because it (as well as its variants such as the X-Tax) is among the most often-discussed consumption tax proposals, its enactment is believed to raise the most troublesome transitional issues among the various consumption-based tax reform options, and it is the main reform analyzed in existing studies of the effects of fundamental reform on the housing values (Gravelle, 1996; Capozza, Green and Hendershott, 1996).

An analysis of the transitional effects of implementing a Flat Tax provides an excellent example of the central theme of this volume — attempting to discern what is known, unknown and unknowable about the desirability of enacting fundamental tax reform in the U.S. Some might argue that the magnitudes of such transitional effects are inherently unknowable — that there is simply too much uncertainty regarding the appropriate modeling of economic behavior and the existing empirical estimates of key parameters that describe individual behaviors that are necessary to construct reasonable estimates of these effects, at least in the foreseeable future.[4] Although we recognize these difficulties, our own perspective is that it is preferable to view continuing efforts to model economic behavior as gradually moving us along a spectrum from the unknown to the known, even if the latter can never realistically be fully attained. In particular, as economic models capture more elements of reality and empirical estimates of behavioral parameters are further refined, the range of what is unknown about the effects of fundamental tax reform, including its transitional effects, will be narrowed. The evolution over time of such analyses is a critical element in the policy making process. It is clear that if policy makers wait for definitive answers about what is known about the effects of fundamental tax reform, the status quo will simply be enshrined forever. However, enough is known about the problems of the existing income tax system that maintaining the status quo is not an attractive option. Accordingly, movements along the spectrum from the unknown toward the known will clarify, and perhaps strengthen, the case for

[4] See Kotlikoff (1998), Gravelle (2006) and Diamond and Zodrow (2006) for recent discussions of the validity of using dynamic overlapping generations computable general equilibrium models of the type constructed in this paper to analyze the effects of tax reforms, including discussions of the various assumptions made in such models (as noted by Burman in this volume).

fundamental reform, and help to define which approach to reform is the most appropriate. Beyond that, it remains to be seen whether at some point it will be perceived by most observers that enough is known about the effects of fundamental tax reform to make it a reasonable and advisable course of action.

Part of this process is reflected in a wide variety of studies that have examined the effects of consumption tax reforms, some of which have considered transitional effects, and define what is currently known and unknown about these effects. For example, Auerbach (1996) and Altig, Auerbach, Kotlikoff, Smetters and Walliser (2001) (hereafter, AAKSW) use computable general equilibrium simulation models to compare the effects of revenue neutral moves from an income tax to several potential consumption-based tax systems, including estimates of the transitional effects of such a reform on asset prices. These models are significantly extended versions of the Auerbach-Kotlikoff (1987) model, and include 12 income groups within each of 55 age cohorts, a Social Security and Medicare system, an endogenous bequest motive, and various existing tax preferences under the income tax. However, these models are characterized by a single production sector and thus cannot be used to estimate reform-induced effects on housing values or other disaggregated asset price effects. In contrast, the model constructed by Fullerton and Rogers (1993) has many sectors including housing; however, the Fullerton-Rogers model is not well suited to the analysis of transitional issues because it calculates equilibria only once every five years after the enactment of reform and, by assuming myopic expectations, tends to systematically overstate transitional problems. Several other studies, including Capozza, Green, and Hendershott (1996), hereafter CGH, Bruce and Holtz-Eakin (1999), hereafter BHE, and Gravelle (1996), analyze the effects of consumption taxes on house values, but do so only in the context of partial equilibrium models.

The model constructed in this paper is designed to expand what is known about the transitional effects of consumption tax reform, by examining the effects of the enactment of a Flat Tax on the prices of both housing and other capital assets in the context of a fully specified general equilibrium model. The analytical framework is a perfect foresight dynamic overlapping generations model with no uncertainty and three production sectors — a composite consumption good, owner-occupied housing and rental housing. Asset price effects — for both types of housing and for business equity — are calculated explicitly. Equilibria are calculated for every year after the enactment of a reform (which is assumed to be permanent), so that the transition path of the economy can be observed in annual increments. However, unlike the AAKSW and FR models, the model utilized in this paper has not yet been extended to include multiple income groups within each generation.[5]

Our simulation results on the changes in business equity and housing prices associated with the enactment of a consumption-based flat tax reform can be summarized as follows. The reform results in a long increase in GDP of nearly 5 percent, long-run increases in investment that range from about 2 percent in owner-occupied housing to 15–17 percent in the other two production sectors, and a long run increase in welfare of nearly 3 percent. However, these gains come at the expense of one-time windfall losses experienced by the (primarily elderly) owners of business equity. These losses are greater than those predicted in some other recent studies, but not nearly as large as those predicted by partial equilibrium models that ignore a wide variety of factors that tend to mitigate asset price declines in our general equilibrium model. These results suggest special transition rules should be used with caution, especially since they significantly reduce the long run gains obtained from reform. Nevertheless, a reasonably strong case for transitional relief can be made for business assets with large amounts of remaining basis, especially in the rental housing sector. Our analysis also suggests that the negative effects on house values of reducing tax preferences for owner-occupied housing under a flat tax would be relatively small once all general equilibrium effects are taken into account. Finally, it is interesting to note that the effects of adjustment costs — at least if they are symmetric across production sectors — tend to cancel, as higher adjustment costs mitigate the fall in the value of business equity but exacerbate declines in the values of owner-occupied housing, in both cases

[5] In addition, the model does not allow for different types of capital or endogenous growth, and thus cannot analyze the efficiency costs of differential taxation of different types of capital under the income tax, or any efficiency gains that might arise if reform-induced increases in investment increased the technological growth rate. Also, because the model assumes perfect certainty, the wage insurance properties of alternative tax systems cannot be analyzed. Finally, the current version of the model assumes a closed economy, and thus abstracts from international flows of capital and goods and services in response to the enactment of reform.

by slowing down the reallocation of capital from owner-occupied housing to the other production sectors. Thus, explicitly accounting for such differential asset price effects is essential to accurately estimating the welfare effects of fundamental tax reform.

The paper is organized as follows. The following section considers the nature of the windfall tax on the owners of existing business equity capital that tends to occur under a consumption tax, while the third section discusses the potential effects of a consumption-based tax reform on the price of owner-occupied housing. Section 4 outlines the model used in the study; details of the model and the calibration of the initial equilibrium are provided in an appendix. The fifth section discusses the simulation results, and the final section concludes and suggests directions for future research.

2. Effects on the Prices of Business Assets

Much of the concern about the transition from the current income tax to a consumption tax has focused on the potential one-time windfall loss imposed on the owners of existing capital assets (other than owner-occupied housing). For example, under the Flat Tax, allowing expensing is equivalent in present value to exempting from taxation the normal rate of return on all new investments. However, in the absence of transition rules under the Flat Tax, firms would not be allowed to deduct the remaining basis of existing assets, although the returns earned by such assets (and the proceeds of asset sales) would be included in the tax base. As a result, the rate of return on existing assets would fall relative to the return on new investments, and arbitrage across new and existing assets would imply that the value of existing assets would fall; Gravelle (1996) constructs a simple model in which the decline is proportional to the rate of tax. Moreover, as long as the general price level remained unchanged under the Flat Tax, lenders would be insulated from this loss since the nominal value of outstanding bonds would be fixed; thus the entire reform-induced one-time windfall loss would be borne by business equity holders.[6] (Note that, as

[6] Since the Flat Tax is similar in structure to the current income tax in that taxes on wages are collected at the individual level so that wage contracts are expressed on a pre-tax basis, most observers have argued that the implementation of this reform would not have much

will be discussed later, owners of owner-occupied housing would not be subject to this particular one-time tax; under both the existing income tax and the Flat Tax, owner-occupiers are neither taxed on the imputed rents from owner-occupied housing nor allowed expensing or depreciation deductions for housing purchases, and completely or largely escape the tax on capital gains from home sales).

However, as described by Zodrow (2002), this analysis ignores a wide variety of other factors associated with the implementation of a Flat Tax that would also affect existing business capital owners, most of which would act to reduce the one-time windfall tax on existing assets or offset its negative welfare effects. A partial list of these factors — all of which are considered in our model — includes: (1) the costs of adjusting the capital stock, which would allow the owners of capital to earn above-normal returns on both existing assets and new investments during the period of transition to the new post-reform equilibrium[7]; (2) a short-run (and perhaps a long-run) increase in the after-tax rate of interest, which would allow the owners of capital to earn a higher after-tax rate of return on existing assets and new investments; (3) the reduction under a lower-rate flat tax of the expected tax on assets that were allowed accelerated depreciation allowances, including 'bonus depreciation' and expensing of investments in research and development or advertising, under the current income tax[8]; and (4) the efficiency gains obtained from eliminating distortions of saving and investment decisions and reducing distortions of the labor-leisure choices, as well as from improvements in the allocation of capital across business sectors.[9]

---

of an impact on the price level. Under these circumstances, Gravelle (1996) argues that asset prices would fall by a factor equal to $t/(1-b)$, where t is the tax rate under the Flat Tax and b is the debt/asset ratio.

[7]We follow the conventional approach and assume that the costs of adjusting the capital stock are quadratic; for discussion of alternative approaches, see Hassett and Newmark (this volume).

[8]This point is stressed by Lyon and Merrill (1999).

[9]The model tends to overstates transitional losses for two additional reasons. First, to the extent the 'new view' of dividend taxation is accurate, the enactment of a consumption tax reform would benefit existing assets by removing individual level taxation of dividends that is capitalized into current asset prices; see Auerbach (1996). Because the model is based on

Several studies have attempted to predict the net effect of some of these factors on asset values. For example, AAKSW find that the implementation of the Flat Tax reduces average asset values in the year of the reform by 3.6 percent when adjustment costs are considered, and by 10 percent in the absence of adjustment costs. Auerbach (1996) finds that implementing a Flat Tax would cause average asset values to decline initially by 5.7 percent without adjustment costs but to increase by 3 percent in the presence of adjustment costs. These findings suggest that the magnitude of the reform-induced windfall losses imposed on business equity assets are much smaller, and may even be fully offset, once the factors noted above are considered.

Note that these findings do not consider potentially important differences in reform-induced asset price changes across different types of assets. This is especially true for the case of owner-occupied housing, where the reform-induced asset price changes are fundamentally different than those for other assets. In addition, capital reallocation across sectors coupled with adjustment costs play an important role in determining the asset price effects that arise when existing and new investments earn above normal rates of return during the transition to the post-reform equilibrium.

3. Effects on the Price of Owner-Occupied Housing

A second contentious issue associated with implementing a consumption-based tax reform is its potentially negative effect on the price of

---

the 'traditional' view of dividend taxation, it does not capture this effect. One potential extension of the model is to allow some 'traditional view' firms and some 'new view' firms, consistent with the evidence presented in Auerbach and Hassett (2003). Second, as stressed by Hubbard (2002), the primary difference between income and consumption taxes is that only the latter exempts normal returns to capital; by comparison, above-normal returns and the returns to risk-taking are treated similarly under income and consumption taxes, so that little change in the tax treatment of these components of the return to capital would result from reform. Since the model is characterized by perfect competition and certainty, it does not consider these factors. In particular, as discussed by Auerbach (this volume), treating all of the return to capital as normal returns in the simulations of the effects of tax reform may significantly overstate the gains that could be achieved with a consumption tax reform.

owner-occupied housing. As noted previously, such a price decline is not a special case of the one-time reform-induced levy on business equity capital. Rather, this price decline is due to a reform-induced increase in the user cost of housing, as perceived by the owner-occupier, which arises primarily because (1) normal returns to business equity investments are effectively untaxed under the Flat Tax, making such investments relatively more attractive and raising the opportunity cost of equity-financed investment in owner-occupied housing, and (2) deductions for mortgage interest and property taxes are eliminated.[10] The increase in the user cost of owner-occupied housing that would occur under the Flat Tax would tend to reduce the demand for owner-occupied housing, which in turn would tend to result in a decline in the price of owner-occupied housing in the short run. In the long run, the quantity of housing and the cost of housing would return to an equilibrium reflecting production costs, including the cost of land, and the absence of taxation.

Several analysts have commented on the impact of consumption tax reforms on housing prices, and the range of predicted effects is large. An analysis conducted by Data Resources Incorporated (Brinner *et al.*, 1995) predicts that the present value of the loss of mortgage interest and property tax deductions alone would cause the aggregate value of owner-occupied housing to decline by 15 percent. CGH (1996) predict that implementing a Flat Tax would reduce owner-occupied housing prices by an average of 20 percent, assuming that interest rates fall by one percentage point. By comparison, Gravelle (1996) and BHE (1999) argue that both the short-run and the long-run effects of a Flat Tax on housing prices would be fairly small. Similarly, Hall (1997) argues that implementation of the Flat Tax would result in a rather modest decline in the aggregate price of housing, assuming a two percentage point decline in the interest rate.

The case for large consumption tax reform-induced declines in housing prices is illustrated by CGH (1996). They estimate the reform-induced change in the price of owner-occupied housing using an asset market equilibrium model that incorporates a perfectly inelastic supply of

[10]The user cost of owner-occupied housing is defined as the sum of the opportunity cost of the homeowner's equity, the after-tax cost of mortgage interest, depreciation and maintenance expenditures, and (arguably) property tax payments.

residential land. Given this assumption, a change in the tax treatment of owner-occupied housing must be fully capitalized into the price of owner-occupied housing. Their model predicts that implementing the Flat Tax at a rate of 17 percent, holding constant the before-tax rate of interest, would reduce owner-occupied housing prices by an average of 29 percent. However, since they believe some reduction in interest rates is likely, they report that the average house price would decline by 20 (9) percent if the before-tax interest rate declines by 1 (2) percentage point(s).[11,12]

Other studies cast doubt on such large price declines, and shift the focus to the dynamic factors that would mitigate the effects of a consumption tax reform on the price of housing. For example, BHE (1999) employ a dynamic simulation model of the owner-occupied housing market that is capable of analyzing the partial equilibrium transition path of enacting a Flat Tax on the price of owner-occupied housing.[13] In their model, housing supply is modeled using a Cobb–Douglas production function that depends on inputs of structures and land, thus capturing the fact, stressed by CGH (1999), that the supply response of land is more inelastic than the supply response of structures. They assume an elasticity of supply for land equal to 0.2 and an elasticity of supply for structures equal to 0.8.[14]

[11] They also note that housing price effects would vary widely across geographical areas, and that the largest price declines in percentage terms would occur for expensive urban homes that are typically owned by individuals with high marginal tax rates.

[12] Holtz-Eakin (1996) notes in his comments on the CGH paper that calculations with more recent data suggest much smaller price declines, e.g., only 15 percent rather than 29 percent under a Flat Tax reform with no decline in interest rates.

[13] BHE implicitly make the assumption that the Federal Reserve would accommodate the Flat Tax, which would imply that the price level — including the price of new and thus (in equilibrium) existing owner-occupied housing — would increase proportionally by the rate of the tax (this is an unusual assumption (Diamond and Zodrow, 1998) which we do not adopt in our analysis). Note, however, that this one-time increase in the price of housing does not reflect a change in the real value of owner-occupied housing; rather, as described above, it reflects the fact that owner-occupied housing is not subject to the potential capital levy associated with the implementation of a consumption tax. Any decline in the real price of owner-occupied housing in the BHE (1999) model reflects the changes in consumer demand stressed by CGH (1996).

[14] CGH (1998) argue that the large supply elasticities used in this study are responsible for the small impacts of reform on housing prices. They suggest that the structures elasticity might be on the order of 0.02 and the land elasticity could be even lower.

Their results indicate that the short-run impact of enacting a 17 percent Flat Tax, assuming the before-tax rate of interest is constant, would be a 10 percent increase in the nominal price of owner-occupied housing. This implies that the real price of owner-occupied housing would decline by roughly 6 percent. In the long run, a smaller stock of capital would be employed in the production of owner-occupied housing and nominal housing prices would increase by 17 percent, leaving real housing prices unchanged. Most of the adjustment in this model occurs within 10 years of the reform.[15]

Gravelle (1996) also finds that switching to a Flat Tax would likely have a small effect on the price of owner-occupied housing in the short run and a very small effect in the long run. She argues that several factors would mitigate the decline in the price of owner-occupied housing in the short run. These factors include reductions in new construction, the propensity for owners to temporarily remove existing houses from the market in response to temporary price declines, the conversion of owner-occupied houses to rental houses, and short-run technology and capacity constraints that limit profitable investment in other sectors.

Starting with a set of worst-case assumptions — the supply of housing is perfectly inelastic, housing demand is unit elastic, and the before-tax interest rate is constant — Gravelle finds that owner-occupied housing prices would fall by 22 percent. Modifying the assumptions to reflect the fact that the short-run supply of housing is not perfectly inelastic and that interest rates are likely to decline if a Flat Tax were implemented moderates the decline in the price of housing. If the elasticity of supply for owner-occupied housing is increased from zero to 0.5, the decline in housing prices is reduced from 22 to 13 percent. If the supply of housing is unit elastic and the interest rate falls by one-percentage point, then the decline in the price of owner-occupied housing is reduced from 22 to 5 percent. Gravelle argues that in the long run the impact of a consumption tax reform on the price of owner-occupied housing is likely to be very small since the supply of housing is more elastic in the long run.

---

[15] Somewhat surprisingly, this model yields a nominal short-run increase in the price of owner-occupied housing that is quite similar to the single-factor version of their model that ignores land. However, in the two-factor model the adjustment period is roughly twice as long as in the model that ignores land.

The housing component of the model used in this paper captures most of the important factors discussed by Brinner *et al.* (1995), CGH (1996), BHE (1999) and Gravelle (1996). The model explicitly accounts for changes in the level of new investment and the reallocation of the existing capital stock across the business and both owner-occupied and rental housing sectors, and examines the effects of the costs of adjusting the capital stock. In addition, changes in consumer demands across rental and owner-occupied housing, including those changes attributable to the elimination of deductibility of home mortgage interest and property taxes, as well as changes in demands for the composite good, are considered. It should be noted, however, that a weakness of the approach used in the model is that land is not modeled explicitly. Instead, the difficulties of converting land used initially for owner-occupied housing to other uses are captured indirectly by including the costs of adjusting the housing capital stock in the analysis. These costs are assumed to be symmetric — that is, to follow the same quadratic pattern for both declines and increases in investment, relative to the steady state level — and reflect the costs of reducing the level of new investment, reducing the level of replacement investment, converting owner-occupied housing to rental housing, and finally, if necessary, converting owner-occupied housing to production of the composite good.

4. Model Structure and Calibration

The distinguishing feature of the analytical approach used in this paper is the treatment of owner-occupied and rental housing markets in the context of a dynamic overlapping-generations life-cycle computable general equilibrium model that explicitly calculates reform-induced changes in all asset values during the transition to a consumption tax reform. As noted previously, the model has three production sectors — owner-occupied housing, rental housing, and a composite good sector that includes all non-housing goods and services. The time path of investment demands in all three sectors is modeled explicitly, taking into account capital stock adjustment costs. On the consumption side, the current tax advantage of owner-occupied housing relative to other assets is taken into account in modeling the demands for the three goods. Thus, the model allows for a fairly detailed description of the both the transitional and the long run effects of implementing a consumption-based tax reform on the prices of housing and business assets, including both a composite good and rental housing. At the same time, however, the treatment of housing is less detailed than in some of the partial equilibrium studies noted above, since land is not considered and the model does not allow for multiple income groups within each generation. This section outlines the basic structure of the model, which combines various features from similar and well-known models constructed by Auerbach and Kotlikoff (1987), Goulder and Summers (1989), Goulder (1989), Keuschnigg (1990), Fullerton and Rogers (1993) and Hayashi (1982). More detailed descriptions of the model and the calibration of the initial equilibrium are provided in the appendix, and the complete details are provided in Diamond and Zodrow (2005).

4.1. *The composite good production sector*

Firms in the composite good production sector produce output using a CES (constant elasticity of substitution) production function with capital and labor as inputs. Firms are assumed to choose the time path of investment to maximize the present value of firm profits or, equivalently, maximize firm value, net of all taxes and subject to quadratic costs of adjusting the capital stock. Total taxes in the composite good production sector include the corporate income tax or the business component of the flat tax and state and local property taxes. Each firm is assumed to maintain a fixed debt/asset ratio and pay out a constant fraction of earnings after taxes and depreciation in each period.

The model assumes individual level arbitrage, which implies that the after-tax return to bonds must equal the after-tax return received by the shareholders of the firm. The value of the firm in the composite good sector equals the present value of all future net distributions to the owners of the firm.

4.2. *The owner-occupied and rental housing production sectors*

Housing is produced in the owner-occupied and rental housing production sectors where, following Goulder and Summers (1989) and Goulder

(1989), rental housing is produced by non-corporate landlords and owner-occupied housing is produced by the owners. The technology used in the production of rental housing and owner-occupied housing is assumed to be identical — capital and labor combined in the same CES production function. Landlords and owner-occupiers are also are assumed to choose time paths of investment to maximize the equivalent of firm value, net of total taxes.

In the case of the rental housing sector, the firm is modeled as a non-corporate firm, which implies that landlords are simply taxed at the individual level. In the owner-occupied housing sector, the tax burden takes into account the facts that imputed rents are untaxed and maintenance expenditures are not deductible, while mortgage interest and property taxes are deductible. The optimal investment path is calculated as above.

4.3. *Individual behavior*

On the individual side, the model has a dynamic overlapping generations framework with fifty-five generations alive at each point in time. There is a representative individual for each generation, who has an economic life span (which begins upon entry into the work force) of fifty-five years, with the first forty-five of those years spent working, and the last ten years spent in retirement. Individual tastes are identical so that differences in behavior across generations are due solely to differences in lifetime budget constraints. An individual accumulates assets from the time of 'economic birth' that are used to finance both consumption over the life cycle, especially during the retirement period, and the making of bequests. The model follows Fullerton and Rogers (1993) in including a relatively primitive 'target model' of bequests, with the real values of bequests assumed to be fixed and thus unaffected by changes in economic conditions, including changes in income.

The consumer is assumed to choose the time paths of consumption and leisure to maximize rest-of-life utility, which is a discounted sum of annual utilities, subject to a lifetime budget constraint that requires the present value of lifetime wealth including inheritances to equal the present value of lifetime consumption including bequests. Annual utility is assumed to be a CES function of consumption of an aggregate consumption good and leisure The aggregate consumption good is modeled as a CES function of the composite good and aggregate housing services (including a minimum purchase requirement for both goods), with aggregate housing services in turn modeled as CES function of owner-occupied and rental housing services. In addition, the model includes a simple social security system, government purchases of the composite good, transfer payments, a hump-backed wage profile over the life cycle, a progressive tax on wage income, and constant average marginal tax rates applied to interest income, dividends, and capital gains.

5. Simulation Results

The reform simulated is the replacement of the federal income tax system (but not the payroll tax) with a revenue neutral Hall and Rabushka (1995) flat tax that applies a constant rate to a comprehensive measure of household labor incomes, with an exemption amount that is initially set at $20,000 per household,[16] and business real cash flow, which allows expensing of all non-financial business purchases and ignores financial flows and thus does not allow deductions for interest expense. The reform is assumed to be unanticipated and enacted immediately. Since adjustment costs are critical for analyzing transitional effects but there is uncertainty about the magnitude of these effects, simulation results are presented for the cases of no adjustment costs, intermediate adjustment costs, and high adjustment costs.[17] The assumption of a comprehensive flat tax base, which follows the admittedly highly optimistic Hall and Rabushka (1995) approach of assuming taxation of all fringe benefits, elimination of all deductions, and elimination of the Earned Income Tax Credit, implies that the required flat tax rate is relatively low — it ranges from 21.0–22.3 percent

[16]The exemption amount grows at the steady state growth rate of the economy.

[17]The simulation results are typically be presented as ranges for the range of adjustment costs noted above; unless otherwise noted, the first number corresponds to the value with high adjustment costs, and the second number corresponding to the value with no adjustment costs.

in the year of reform, depending on the level of adjustment costs, and gradually declines to a steady state value of 20.1 percent.[18] The following discussion begins with a summary of the macroeconomic effects of the enactment of such a flat tax on prices, output, investment and the allocation of capital, and then examines the changes in business equity prices and housing prices that are the focus of the analysis, as well as the associated intergenerational redistributions.

5.1. *Macroeconomic effects on prices, output, investment and capital allocation*

Tables 4.1–4.3 show that the general time paths of the wage rate and interest rate are similar for all three levels of adjustment costs. In the year of enactment of the flat tax, the before-tax wage rate declines initially by 0.5–0.6 percent, as labor supply increases immediately by 1.8–2.0 percent, depending on the level of adjustment costs, while the capital stock is initially fixed. The increase in labor supply is a result of both an increase in the after-tax wage rate and an increase in the after-tax interest rate that causes individuals to substitute future consumption and leisure for current consumption and leisure.[19] Note that part of the increase in the wage rate and the resulting increase in labor supply is attributable to the reform-induced reallocation of capital from owner-occupied housing into the much more labor-intensive production of the composite good (discussed below), which stimulates the demand for labor. The wage rate then rises over time as increased saving leads to a higher capital-labor ratio. In the long run steady state, the before-tax wage rate is 4.2 percent higher and the capital-labor ratio is 8.8 percent higher than in the initial steady state.

[18]The associated payroll tax rate necessary to fund the pre-reform level of social security benefits is 9.5 percent in the year of reform and 9.2 percent in the long run equilibrium.
[19]Note that the net-of-tax wage actually decreases for generations that are near the age of retirement at the time of reform. They have low wages, due to the 'humped-back' nature of their wage profile, and thus face higher marginal tax rates under the flat tax than under the progressive income tax rate structure in the initial equilibrium. This effect is far outweighed by the increase in the net-of-tax wage for all younger generations. In addition, labor supply increases due to an income effect as the increase in the after-tax interest rate reduces the present value of future labor earnings.

The before-tax interest rate is 1.3 percentage points lower in the long run steady state, with more than half of the decline occurring within 10 years after reform. The after-tax interest rate initially increases by 0.9–1.6 percentage points, depending on the level of adjustment costs, and then declines steadily to a value 0.2 percentage points higher than in the initial steady state.

Gross domestic product (GDP) increases by 1.0–1.3 percent in the year of reform and by 4.9 percent in the long run. Even for the highest level of adjustment costs, most of the increase in GDP (4.2 percent) occurs within 20 years of the enactment of reform, as labor supply and aggregate investment increase and as capital is reallocated among the three production sectors. In the composite good sector, output is 1.4–1.5 percent larger in the year of reform and 5.2 percent larger in the long run steady state. In the rental housing sector, output decreases by 0.0–1.4 percent in the year of reform, and increases by 1.2 percent in the long run steady state. In the owner-occupied housing sector, the change in output ranges from an increase of 0.1 percent to a decline of 1.5 percent in the year of reform, and is 3.6 percent larger in the long run steady state.

Investment in the composite good sector increases by 11.4–44.6 percent in the year of reform, and then gradually falls to a level that is 16.9 percent higher than in the initial steady state. Investment in the rental housing sector increases by 18.9–52.8 percent in the year of reform and by 15.0 percent in the long-run steady state. Investment in owner-occupied housing decreases by 8.4–100.5 percent in the year of reform, and increases by 2.3 percent in the long run steady state.[20] Investment in owner occupied housing returns to its level in the initial steady state within three to eleven

[20] Recall that this dramatic reduction in investment reflects not only the elimination of new and replacement investment in owner-occupied housing in the year of reform but also the conversion of some owner-occupied housing to rental housing. The analysis assumes that such conversions would qualify for consumption tax treatment. Although such treatment is consistent with consumption tax treatment, it creates the potential for huge tax deferrals. Accordingly, some proposals, including the progressive consumption tax option discussed by the recent presidential tax reform panel, limit expensing to assets purchased from other businesses. This would create a tax bias against conversions of owner-occupied housing, implying larger adjustment costs in the housing sector. However, only a very small level of

years after reform. These changes in investment imply a short-run increase in the savings rate of roughly 6.2–12.3 percent and a long-run increase in the savings rate of 8.4 percent.

The increase in investment in the composite good and rental housing sectors and the initial decline in investment in owner-occupied housing occur for two reasons. First, eliminating the tax on the normal rate of return to investment as well as the gradual decline in interest rates reduces the cost of capital and thus increases the optimal level of investment in the composite good and rental housing sectors relative to the initial steady state. Second, the reduction of the relative tax advantage of owner-occupied housing at the individual level due to the elimination of deductions for home mortgage interest and property taxes reduces demand for such housing and thus encourages a reallocation of capital from the owner-occupied housing sector to the composite good and rental housing sectors, and thus also increases investment in these sectors.

One of the economic benefits of fundamental tax reform is a more efficient allocation of capital across the housing and composite good sectors, but this naturally comes only with a reduction in investment in owner-occupied housing during a transition period following reform. The capital stocks in the composite good and rental housing sectors increase in every year after reform in relation to the initial steady state, and are 16.9 and 15.0 percent larger, respectively, in the long run steady state. By comparison, in the owner-occupied housing sector, the stock of capital declines in relation to the initial steady state, as capital is reallocated from the owner-occupied housing to the rental housing and composite good sectors. Five years after the reform is enacted, the capital stock in the owner-occupied housing sector is 1.0–6.1 percent smaller than in the initial steady state, although it is 2.3 percent larger in the long run steady state. In the long run steady state, the share of the capital stock in the owner-occupied housing sector falls from 40.4 to 37.3 percent, while the share of composite good capital increases from 48.3 to 51.0 percent, and the share of rental housing capital increases modestly from 11.3 to 11.7 percent.

---

adjustment costs is required in the model to limit disinvestment in the owner-occupied housing sector to declines in new and replacement investment.

5.2. *The effects of reform on business equity prices and housing values*

As noted previously, the transition to a consumption tax raises some interesting issues. Some observers have argued that, in the absence of special transition rules, the windfall losses experienced by the owners of corporate equity and owner-occupied housing would be sufficiently large to make the enactment of a consumption tax reform politically infeasible. Others have countered that such windfall losses would be desirable, because they would act to offset the reduction in progressivity associated with the flat tax, attributable to reducing the marginal tax rates on the wealthy and eliminating the taxation of the normal returns to capital. Yet others have concluded that these transitional problems are overstated, and that the enactment of a consumption tax reform would have little effect — or might even increase — the values of business assets and owner-occupied housing In this section, we examine the effect of a flat tax reform on asset values within the context of our model.

Table 4.1 shows the effects of implementing reform if adjustment costs are set approximately to zero and there are no transition rules. In this case, the average value of equity in the composite good production sector (average *Q*) decreases by 16.5 percent in the year of reform, while the average value of equity in the rental housing sector (where remaining basis is relatively large) decreases by 29.9 percent. The effects of reform on the value of equity in the owner-occupied sector are much more modest, where home equity values initially fall by 2.9 percent which, with a debt-asset ratio of 0.35, is equivalent to a 1.9 percent decline in the total value of owner-occupied housing; equity values return to their initial levels by the fourth year after the reform.[21]

These windfall losses in the composite good and rental housing sectors are moderated when adjustment costs are added to the analysis, since the reallocation of capital to these sectors is slowed, allowing existing

[21] In the long run, the value of average Q in the owner-occupied sector returns to its initial steady state value since there are no business level taxes in this sector. By comparison, the value of average Q in the other two sectors, which is adjusted for business tax factors, declines in the long run as a result of the more generous treatment of investment in these sectors under the Flat Tax.

Table 4.1.
Base Case Simulation — No Adjustment Costs

Years after Enactment	0	1	2	4	6	10	20	50	100
Interest rate									
After-tax	0.3	1.4	1.6	1.3	1.0	0.6	0.3	0.2	0.2
Before-tax	−1.2	−0.1	0.2	−0.2	−0.5	−0.9	−1.2	−1.3	−1.3
Prices									
RH service	−1.4	−2.7	−4.1	−6.0	−7.2	−9.1	−11.2	−11.7	−11.7
OH service	−1.4	4.3	7.7	9.2	7.9	5.1	2.1	1.4	1.3
Wage rate	−0.5	0.8	1.7	2.6	3.0	3.5	4.1	4.2	4.2
Labor supply	1.8	1.9	2.0	2.1	2.1	2.0	1.8	1.8	1.8
Tax rates									
Flat tax	22.3	22.3	21.8	21.1	20.8	20.5	20.2	20.1	20.1
Payroll	7.1	7.0	6.9	6.8	6.8	6.8	6.8	6.7	6.7
Investment									
NH	44.6	35.4	27.6	19.8	17.9	17.7	17.1	17.0	16.9
RH	52.8	52.9	44.1	31.8	27.2	23.9	17.5	15.3	15.0
OH	−100.5	−55.0	−19.6	11.3	15.7	11.7	5.0	2.5	2.3
Capital stock									
NH	0.0	4.7	8.0	11.4	12.9	14.6	16.5	16.9	16.9
RH	0.0	2.0	4.0	6.7	8.5	11.0	14.1	14.9	15.0
OH	0.0	−3.9	−5.8	−6.1	−4.6	−1.9	1.4	2.2	2.3
Tobin's *Q*									
NH	−16.5	−19.9	−20.8	−20.4	−19.8	−19.2	−18.8	−18.7	−18.7
RH	−29.9	−31.4	−31.4	−30.4	−29.8	−29.4	−29.0	−28.9	−28.9
OH	−2.9	−2.4	−1.3	0.2	0.5	0.4	0.1	0.0	0.0
Firm value									
NH	−16.5	−16.1	−14.5	−11.3	−9.4	−7.4	−5.4	−4.9	−4.9
RH	−29.9	−30.0	−28.7	−25.8	−23.9	−21.6	−19.0	−18.4	−18.3
OH	−2.9	−6.2	−7.0	−5.9	−4.1	−1.5	1.5	2.2	2.3
Output									
GDP	1.0	2.2	3.1	4.0	4.3	4.5	4.8	4.9	4.9
NH	1.4	2.6	3.4	4.3	4.6	4.8	5.1	5.2	5.2
RH	−1.4	−0.8	−0.4	0.2	0.4	0.7	1.0	1.2	1.2
OH	−1.5	0.3	1.5	2.7	3.0	3.1	3.5	3.6	3.7

assets to earn above-normal returns during the transition. In the case of moderate adjustment costs, shown in Table 4.2, the average value of equity in the composite good production sector falls by 10.4 percent in the year of reform, while the average value of equity in the rental housing sector falls by 26.3 percent. By comparison, adjustment costs — which are assumed to be symmetric across all sectors — slow down the reallocation of capital out of the owner-occupied housing sector, increasing windfall losses in that sector. This effect is magnified by higher interest rates during the transition. With moderate adjustment costs, the average value of equity in the owner-occupied housing sector initially falls by 4.2 percent, which is equivalent to a 2.7 percent decline in the total value of owner-occupied housing, and it now takes five years for the average value of equity in the owner-occupied housing sector returns to its initial value.

In the high adjustment costs case, shown in Table 4.3, the above-normal returns earned during the transition imply that the average value of equity of firms in the composite good production sector only decreases by 0.1 percent in the year of reform, while the decline in the average value of equity in the rental firm sector is reduced to 19.9 percent. In this case, the average value of housing equity falls by 5.1 percent in the year of reform, which is equivalent to a 3.3 percent decline in the total value of owner-occupied housing.

Thus, our results suggest that implementing a Flat Tax would decrease the total value of owner-occupied housing by 1.9 to 3.3 percent in the year of reform, depending on the level of adjustment costs. In the year of reform, the before-tax interest rate falls by about 1.2 percentage points in our simulations. By comparison, allowing for a two-percentage point decline in the before-tax rate of interest, CGH predict an average decline in the value of owner-occupied housing of 9 percent, three to four times the magnitude of our estimates.[22] Assuming no change in the before-tax rate of interest, BHE estimate that nominal house values would increase by 10 percent in the year of reform, which translates to a 5.9 percent decline in real house values given that the price level increases by 17 percent, still somewhat larger than those predicted by our model. Thus, our

[22] With no change in the before-tax interest rate, CGH estimate a 29 percent decline in the value of owner-occupied housing.

Table 4.2.
Base Case Simulation — Moderate Adjustment Costs

Years after Enactment	0	1	2	4	6	10	20	50	100
Interest rate									
After-tax	0.2	1.0	1.3	1.2	1.0	0.7	0.3	0.2	0.2
Before-tax	−1.3	−0.5	−0.2	−0.3	−0.5	−0.8	−1.2	−1.3	−1.3
Prices									
RH service	−0.9	−1.8	−2.6	−4.2	−5.6	−7.8	−10.5	−11.6	−11.7
OH service	−0.9	1.2	3.0	5.1	5.8	5.4	2.9	1.5	1.3
Wage rate	−0.6	0.2	0.8	1.7	2.3	3.1	3.9	4.1	4.2
Labor supply	2.0	2.0	2.0	2.0	2.0	1.9	1.8	1.8	1.8
Tax rates									
Flat tax	21.4	21.7	21.6	21.3	21.0	20.6	20.2	20.1	20.1
Payroll	7.1	7.0	7.0	6.9	6.9	6.8	6.8	6.7	6.7
Investment									
NH	23.5	22.8	21.7	19.9	18.8	17.7	16.9	17.0	16.9
RH	32.1	33.6	33.1	30.5	27.9	24.2	18.0	15.4	15.0
OH	−33.6	−26.3	−18.2	−5.9	1.1	6.4	5.1	2.6	2.3
Capital stock									
NH	0.0	2.5	4.6	8.0	10.3	13.2	15.9	16.8	16.9
RH	0.0	1.2	2.5	4.7	6.6	9.5	13.2	14.8	15.0
OH	0.0	−1.3	−2.2	−3.2	−3.2	−2.2	0.6	2.1	2.3
Tobin's *Q*									
NH	−10.4	−13.8	−15.5	−17.0	−17.7	−18.2	−18.6	−18.6	−18.7
RH	−26.3	−27.9	−28.4	−28.4	−28.4	−28.4	−28.7	−28.9	−28.9
OH	−4.2	−4.0	−3.0	−1.0	0.2	1.0	0.6	0.1	0.0
Firm value									
NH	−10.4	−11.7	−11.6	−10.4	−9.2	−7.5	−5.7	−5.0	−4.9
RH	−26.3	−27.0	−26.6	−25.1	−23.6	−21.6	−19.3	−18.4	−18.3
OH	−4.2	−5.3	−5.2	−4.2	−3.1	−1.2	1.2	2.2	2.3
Output									
GDP	1.2	1.8	2.3	3.1	3.7	4.2	4.7	4.9	4.9
NH	1.5	2.1	2.6	3.4	3.9	4.5	5.0	5.2	5.2
RH	−0.9	−0.6	−0.3	0.2	0.5	0.7	1.1	1.2	1.2
OH	−0.9	−0.1	0.7	1.8	2.5	3.0	3.5	3.6	3.7

Table 4.3.

Base Case Simulation — High Adjustment Costs

Years after Enactment	0	1	2	4	6	10	20	50	100
Interest rate									
After-tax	0.3	0.8	0.9	0.9	0.8	0.7	0.4	0.3	0.2
Before-tax	−1.2	−0.7	−0.6	−0.6	−0.6	0.8	−1.1	−1.2	−1.3
Prices									
RH service	0.0	−0.6	−1.1	−2.1	−3.1	−4.8	−7.8	−10.9	−11.7
OH service	0.1	0.8	1.4	2.4	3.1	3.9	3.9	2.2	1.4
Wage rate	−1.6	−0.2	0.1	0.7	1.2	2.0	3.1	4.0	4.2
Labor supply	1.9	1.9	1.9	1.9	1.9	1.9	1.8	1.8	1.8
Tax rates									
Flat tax	21.0	21.3	21.3	21.2	21.0	20.8	20.4	20.2	20.1
Payroll	7.1	7.0	7.0	7.0	6.9	6.9	6.8	6.8	6.7
Investment									
NH	11.4	11.8	12.2	12.8	13.4	14.3	15.4	16.7	16.9
RH	18.9	19.1	19.2	19.2	19.0	18.7	17.1	15.5	15.0
OH	−8.4	−7.7	−6.7	−4.6	−3.0	−0.4	1.9	2.6	2.3
Capital stock									
NH	0.0	1.2	2.3	4.3	6.1	8.9	13.0	16.3	16.9
RH	0.0	0.7	1.4	2.8	4.0	6.1	10.0	13.9	14.9
OH	0.0	−0.3	−0.6	−1.0	−1.3	−1.4	−0.6	1.5	2.3
Tobin's *Q*									
NH	−0.1	−2.8	−4.6	−7.0	−8.9	−11.6	−15.6	−18.2	−18.6
RH	−19.9	−21.2	−21.9	−22.5	−23.1	−24.0	−26.1	−28.3	−28.9
OH	−5.1	−5.1	−4.5	−2.9	−1.6	0.2	1.5	0.7	0.0
Firm value									
NH	−0.1	−1.6	−2.4	−3.0	−3.3	−3.8	−4.6	−4.9	−4.9
RH	−19.9	−20.6	−20.7	−20.4	−20.0	−19.3	−18.7	−18.3	−18.3
OH	−5.1	−5.4	−5.0	−3.9	−2.8	−1.1	0.9	2.2	2.3
Output									
GDP	1.3	1.6	1.8	2.3	2.7	3.3	4.2	4.8	4.9
NH	1.5	1.7	2.0	2.5	2.9	3.5	4.4	5.1	5.2
RH	0.0	0.1	0.3	0.6	0.7	0.9	1.2	1.3	1.2
OH	0.1	0.5	0.8	1.4	1.9	2.5	3.4	3.7	3.7

estimates suggest that reform-induced declines in the prices of owner occupied housing would be modest, consistent with the conjectures of Hall (1997) and Gravelle (1996).[23] In addition, we find that the period of transition would be roughly half as long as suggested by BHE. With moderate (high) adjustment costs, the decrease in the average value of owner-occupied housing dissipates within 7 (12) years of the reform, which is similar to the results with low and high supply elasticities presented by Bruce and Holtz-Eakin (1999). On the other hand, the declines in the values of rental housing are relatively large under all scenarios. This suggests that, even though most discussion of transitional issues in the housing market has focused on owner-occupied housing, the transitional problems and thus the case for transition relief is strongest in the rental housing sector.

5.3. *Welfare analysis*

Figure 4.1 presents the intergenerational welfare effects of implementing the Flat Tax in the model, calculated as equivalent variations and expressed as percentage changes of remaining lifetime utility, using a measure of lifetime resources including the value of leisure across all generations; these changes take into account all reform-induced welfare gains and losses considered in the model. The general pattern of welfare changes is similar under the varying levels of adjustment costs; however, the magnitudes and signs of the net welfare change vary considerably with the assumed level of adjustment costs for a particular generation. For example, the generation of age 54 in the year of enactment experiences a net welfare loss of 1.8 percent under the assumption of high adjustment costs and a net welfare loss of 11.3 percent with no adjustment costs. This reflects the fact that as the level of adjustment costs increases the one-time windfall tax on existing capital owners is potentially fully offset by above normal

[23] Note, however, that these are average figures and thus do not capture the variation in housing price changes that would occur in different regions of the country; in particular, one would expect larger housing price declines in areas that have experienced recent rapid growth in housing prices and have homes that are owned predominantly by individuals in relatively high tax brackets.

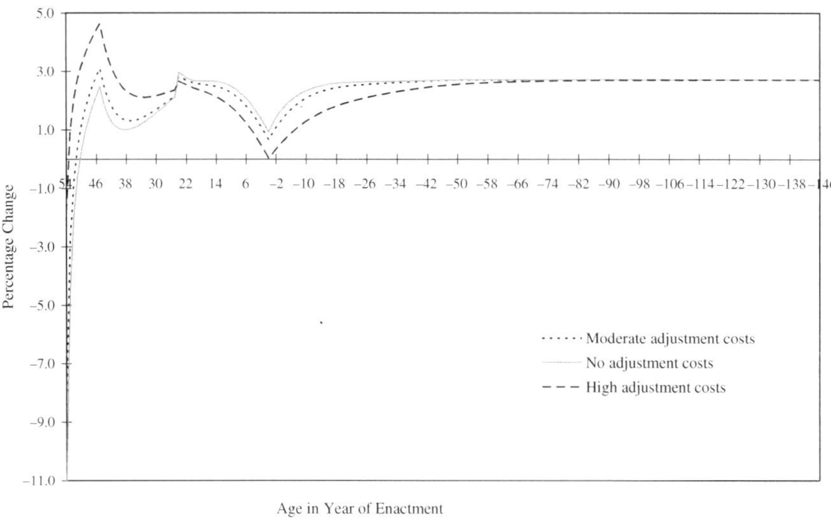

Figure 4.1.
Equivalent Variation for a Flat Tax Reform

returns on new and existing investments. Note that for those who are retired at the time of reform (between the economic ages of 45 and 54), as the age in the year of enactment decreases the net welfare gain increases; this occurs because the retired generations with longer life spans after reform receive inframarginal returns and a higher after-tax interest rate on their remaining financial wealth over a longer period of time.

The net welfare gains decline steadily for generations that are approximately within 7 to 12 years of retirement, depending on the levels of adjustment costs. This pattern of welfare gains is due primarily to two factors. First, replacing the federal income tax system with the Flat Tax raises the marginal tax rate of labor income for generations that are near retirement, since the wage profile has a 'humped-back' shape and the income tax rates are structured in a progressive manner in the initial income tax steady state.[24] Second, the initial decrease in the wage rate tends to have a larger impact on older and middle-aged generations since

[24] For generations within 7 years of retirement, implementing the Flat Tax actually raises the marginal tax rate on labor income due to the humped-back wage profile and the progressive income tax rates in the initial income tax steady state.

they have fewer years to benefit from the higher wage rates several years after reform, and during these years they are faced with the higher marginal tax rates on wage income near retirement. For this reason, the welfare gains of younger individuals in the age range from 25 to 35 are larger the longer they have to benefit from higher wages and reductions in their marginal tax rates in their prime working years.

As discussed above, since the model assumes a 'target' bequest, older generations are not allowed to pass on part of any windfall gains or losses to their heirs. Thus, the generation of economic age 25 in the year of enactment experiences a discontinuous increase in net welfare since it is the first generation to receive an inheritance after reform and thus will benefit from the above normal returns on business equity during the transition period. Generations older than age 25 would have received their inheritance before the reform and thus would suffer a welfare loss since their inherited asset would be subject to the one time tax at the time of reform. The steady decline in the welfare gain for individuals younger than age 25 reflects the fact that these individuals would hold their inherited assets a shorter period of time over the transition period and thus would experience smaller welfare gains relative to older generations age 25 and younger. Net welfare continues to decline until the efficiency effects of reform begin to dominate other welfare effects. The discontinuity at age zero reflects the fact that generations born after reform can plan optimally over their entire life without any unexpected changes in the tax system. In the long run steady state, the increase in net welfare is equal to 2.7 percent of remaining lifetime utility.

The relatively large net welfare gains (and smaller net welfare losses) in this study as compared to some of the other studies cited above are partially attributable to the increased efficiency gains that result from explicitly modeling the elimination of tax distortions of investment across the composite good, rental housing, and owner-occupied housing sectors. Furthermore, with higher levels of adjustment costs, the rate at which investment is reallocated across the three sectors tends to occur less rapidly. This leads to higher inframarginal returns and thus larger increases (smaller decreases) in the total real value of equity in the composite good and rental housing sectors. This study suggests that in this case these gains tend to almost completely offset the one-time tax on existing assets; at the same time, however, it must be noted that the relevance of these results are called into question by recent results which suggest that adjustment costs are significantly smaller than once believed (Hall, 2004).

6. Conclusion

This paper examines the transitional effects of implementing a specific type of consumption tax reform — a Hall–Rabushka Flat Tax — on the values of business equity and housing prices. The analysis is conducted within the context of a dynamic overlapping generations computable general equilibrium model that includes a corporate sector that produces a composite good as well as non-corporate rental and owner-occupied housing production sectors and allows for the costs of adjusting all capital stocks in response to the enactment of the reform.

Our results suggest that such a reform would potentially cause a one-time windfall loss to be experienced by the (primarily elderly) owners of existing business equity. However, the loss is smaller than predicted by partial equilibrium models, and is mitigated once the acceleration of deductions under the current tax system, general equilibrium effects on interest rates, reform-induced efficiency gains, and investment adjustment costs are considered. This suggests that special transition rules should be used with some caution, especially since they significantly reduce the long-run gains that can be attained from reform — a line of argument that is strengthened by the fact that several factors (noted above) that would mitigate transitional losses are not considered in our model but weakened by recent empirical evidence that suggests that adjustment costs are relatively small.

Nevertheless the asset price declines at the time of reform are greater in our model than in some other studies such as Auerbach (1996) and AAKSW, presumably because of differences in estimates of remaining basis. It is clear that the estimate of remaining basis under the current tax system is the crucial piece of information in estimating the asset price declines associated with consumption tax reform. The amount of the undepreciated basis of depreciable assets under the current tax system is an issue that is knowable, although it is subject to some uncertainty because of a lack of data, and should be a focus of future research. Our welfare losses are far greater than those reported by Auerbach (1996) and AAKSW. This, however, is entirely attributed to the fact that our model assumes target bequests, so that elderly individuals experiencing an asset price decline must maintain a constant bequest and therefore experience very large declines in consumption.[25]

In general, the case for transition relief is strongest for business assets with large amounts of remaining basis which, in our model, is primarily the rental housing sector. At the same time, our analysis suggests that the negative effects of reducing the tax preference for owner-occupied housing that exists under the current income tax system would be relatively small once all general equilibrium effects are taken into account. Thus, our analysis suggests that reform-induced transitional problems in the housing market are significantly more severe for rental housing than for owner-occupied housing. It is also noteworthy that the effects of adjustment costs — at least if they are symmetric across production sectors — tend to cancel to some extent, as higher adjustment costs mitigate the fall in value of business equity but exacerbate declines in the values of owner-occupied housing, in both cases by slowing down the reallocation of capital from owner-occupied housing into rental housing and the corporate production sector. Thus, explicitly accounting for these differential asset prices effects is essential to estimating accurately the potential welfare gains and losses associated with the enactment of consumption-based tax reforms.

Our analysis has been conducted within the framework of a single representative individual in each generation. An additional critical issue is the distribution of these welfare changes across lifetime income groups taking into account differences in investment patterns across income groups, especially since lower and middle income groups hold disproportionately large shares of their investment portfolios in owner-occupied housing relative to the upper income groups and the relative importance of tax-deferred assets varies across income groups. Another critical issue is the differential treatment during the transition of different types of capital as well as different business sectors. These topics are the focus of ongoing research.

In closing, we hope that this paper has contributed to moving the understanding of the effects of fundamental tax reform modestly along

[25] We are currently modifying the model to include a more realistic bequest motive.

the spectrum from the unknown to the known. It must be admitted that such analyses include simplifying assumptions about factors that are essentially unknowable. In particular, our analysis, like most others, assumes that any fundamental tax reform that is implemented would last forever. Past history, including the events following the enactment of the Tax Reform Act of 1986, clearly imply that such an assumption is highly optimistic. The potential for an unraveling of the effects of fundamental tax reform might be reduced by the introduction of supermajority requirements for adding preferences or raising tax rates or the reintroduction of 'pay-as-you-go' budget rules (Bradford, 2005; Auerbach and Hassett, 2005a); moreover, such provisions may be politically more palatable as part of a fundamental reform of the tax structure than under, for example, a more incremental reform of the existing income tax system. Nevertheless, the evolution of the tax system in future years is inherently unknowable, and the prospect of future tax 'deforms' suggests that the potential gains from enacting fundamental tax reform may be overstated in analyses such as the one in this study.

More generally, the validity of analyses using overlapping generations computational general equilibrium analyses such as ours ranges somewhere between the unknown and the known. Such models have certainly gained wide acceptance in the economics profession and among policymakers, and some support for their use is provided by recent empirical analyses which suggest that sufficiently rich life-cycle models explain consumption and saving behavior reasonably well (Scholz, Seshadri and Khitatrakun, 2006). At the same time, the behavioral assumptions underlying life-cycle models are strong, and often called into question by the relatively new behavioral economics literature discussed by McCaffery (this volume).

In addition, considerable uncertainty surrounds a wide variety of issues raised by such models, and there are many outstanding questions about (1) the parameter estimates used in simulations of these models, especially since some recent econometric estimates of several key parameters vary considerably from the conventional wisdom, (2) the saving behavior of the wealthy, especially the very wealthy, who determine much of what happens to aggregate saving in the economy, and (3) the determinants of bequest behavior. Although many may debate whether the answers to these questions are unknown or known, they are in principle knowable — and their resolution will be the focus of much research as the debate on fundamental tax reform in the U.S. and elsewhere continues.

Acknowlegdments

We have benefited from the comments of Len Burman and Alan Viard and the conference participants. The views expressed in this chapter are those of the authors and do not necessarily reflect those of the Baker Institute for Public Policy.

References

Aaron, Henry J. and William G. Gale, 1996. *Economic Effects of Fundamental Tax Reform* (Washington DC: Brookings Institution).

Altig, David, Alan J. Auerbach, Laurence J. Kotlikoff, Kent A. Smetters and Jan Walliser, 2001. "Simulating Fundamental Tax Reform in the United States," *American Economic Review* 91: 574–595.

Auerbach, Alan J., 1996. "Tax Reform, Capital Allocation, Efficiency, and Growth," in Henry J. Aaron and William G. Gale (eds.), *Economic Effects of Fundamental Tax Reform* (Washington DC: Brookings Institution).

Auerbach, Alan J. and Kevin A. Hassett, 2003. "On the Marginal Source of Investment Funds," *Journal of Public Economics* 87: 205–232.

Auerbach, Alan J. and Kevin A. Hassett, 2005. "Conclusion," in Alan J. Auerbach and Kevin A. Hassett (eds.), *Toward Fundamental Tax Reform* (Washington DC: AEI Press), pp. 149–158.

Auerbach, Alan J. and Laurence J. Kotlikoff, 1987. *Dynamic Fiscal Policy* (Cambridge MA: Harvard University Press).

Boskin, Michael J., 1996. *Frontiers of Tax Reform* (Palo Alto, CA: Hoover Institution Press).

Bradford, David F., 1996. "Consumption Tax Alternatives: Implementation and Transition Issues," in Michael J. Boskin (ed.), *Frontiers of Tax Reform* (Palo Alto, CA: Hoover Institution Press).

Bradford, David F., 2005. "A Tax System for the Twenty-First Century," in Alan J. Auerbach and Kevin A. Hassett (eds.), *Toward Fundamental Tax Reform* (Washington DC: AEI Press), pp. 81–94.

Bruce, Donald and Douglas Holtz-Eakin, 1999. "Fundamental Tax Reform and Residential Housing," *Journal of Housing Economics* 8: 249–271.

Brinner, Roger, Mark Lansky and David Wyss, 1995. "Market Impacts of Flat Tax Legislation," *DRI/McGraw-Hill U.S. Review* (June).

Capozza, Dennis R., Richard K. Green, and Patric H. Hendershott, 1996. "Taxes, Mortgage Borrowing and Residential Land Prices," in Aaron, Henry J. and William G. Gale (eds.), *Economic Effects of Fundamental Tax Reform* (Washington DC: Brookings Institution).

Cappozza, Dennis R., Richard K. Green, and Patric H. Hendershott, 1998. "Tax Reform and House Prices: Large or Small Effects," National Tax Association Proceedings 1998.

Chirinko, Robert S., 2002. "Corporate Taxation, Capital Formation, and the Substitution Elasticity between Labor and Capital," *National Tax Journal* 55 (June) 339:55.

Cummins, Jason, Kevin Hassett, and R. Glenn Hubbard, 1994. "A Reconsideration of Investment Behavior Using Tax Reforms as Natural Experiments," *Brookings Papers on Economic Activity*, Issue 2: 1–74.

Davis, Steven J. and Magnus Henrekson, 2004. "Tax Effects on Work Activity, Industry Mix and Shadow Economy Size: Evidence from Rich Country Comparisons," *National Bureau of Economic Research Working Paper No. 10509.*

Diamond, John and George R. Zodrow, 1998. "Housing and Intergenerational Redistributions Under a Consumption Tax Reform," *National Tax Association Proceedings* 1998.

Diamond, John and George R. Zodrow, 2005. "Description of the Tax Policy Advisers General Equilibrium Model," Manuscript, Rice University.

Diamond, John and George R. Zodrow, 2006. "Reflections on the Use of Life-Cycle Computable General Equilibrium Models in Analyzing the Effects of Tax Reform," *NTA Network*, National Tax Association, April 2006, pp. 3–4.

Engen, Eric and William Gale, 1996. "The Effects of Fundamental Tax Reform on Saving," in Aaron, Henry J. and William G. Gale, *Economic Effects of Fundamental Tax Reform* (Washington DC: Brookings Institution).

Fullerton, Don and Diane Lim Rogers, 1993. *Who Bears the Lifetime Tax Burden?* (Washington, DC: Brookings Institute).

Gale, William G., Scott Houser and John K. Scholz, 1996. "Distributional Effects of Fundamental Tax Reform," in Aaron, Henry J. and William G. Gale, *Economic Effects of Fundamental Tax Reform* (Washington DC: Brookings Institution).

Gentry, William and R. Glenn Hubbard, 1997. "Distributional Implications of Introducing a Broad-Based Consumption Tax," in James M. Poterba (ed.), *Tax Policy and the Economy* (Cambridge MA: National Bureau of Economic Research).

Goulder, Lawrence H., 1989. "Tax Policy, Housing Prices, and Housing Investment," *National Bureau of Economic Research Working Paper 2814.*

Goulder, Lawrence H., and Lawrence H. Summers, 1989. "Tax Policy, Asset Prices, and Growth," *Journal of Public Economics* 38: 265–296.

Gravelle, Jane G., 1996. "The Flat Tax and Other Proposals: Effects on Housing," *Congressional Research Service Report for Congress Number 96-379E.*

Gravelle, Jane G., 1994. *The Economic Effects of Taxing Capital Income* (Cambridge MA: MIT Press).

Gravelle, Jane G., 2006. "Feasible but Hard-to-Believe Models: Computable General Equilibrium Intertemporal Models," *NTA Network*, National Tax Association, January 2006, pp. 3–4.

Hall, Robert E. and Alvin Rabushka, 1985. *The Flat Tax.* (Stanford: Hoover Institution Press). Second edition, 1995.

Hall, Robert E., 1997. "The Effects of Tax Reform on Prices and Asset Values," in James M. Poterba (ed.), *Tax Policy and the Economy* (Cambridge MA: National Bureau of Economic Research).

Hall, Robert E., 2004. "Measuring Factor Adjustment Costs," *Quarterly Journal of Economics* 119: 889–927.

Hendershott, Patric H. and Sheng Cheng Hu, 1981. "Inflation and Extraordinary Returns on Owner-Occupied Housing: Some Implications for Capital Allocation and Productivity Growth," *Journal of Macroeconomics* 3: 177–203.

Hayashi, Fumio, 1982. "Tobin's Marginal q and Average q: A Neoclassical Interpretation," *Econometrica* 50: 213–224.

Holtz-Eakin, Douglas, 1996. "Comment," in Aaron, Henry J. and William G. Gale, *Economic Effects of Fundamental Tax Reform* (Washington DC: Brookings Institution).

Hubbard, R. Glenn, 2002. "Capital Income Taxation in Tax Reform: Implications for Analysis of Distribution and Efficiency," in George R. Zodrow and Peter Mieszkowski (eds.), *United States Tax Reform in the 21st Century* (Cambridge UK: Cambridge University Press).

Jorgenson, Dale W. and Kun-Young Yun, 2001. *Investment*, Vol. 3, (Cambridge, MA: The MIT Press).

Kotlikoff, Laurence J., 1998. "The A-K Model: Its Past, Present and Future," *National Bureau of Economic Research Working Paper 6684.*

Kotlikoff, Laurence J., 2005. "Simulating the Dynamic Micro and Macroeconomic Effects of the FairTax," *National Bureau of Economic Research Working Paper W11858.*

Kueschnigg, Christian, 1990. "Corporate Taxation and Growth: Dynamic General Equilibrium Simulation Study," *Simulation Models in Tax and Transfer Policy* (edited by Johann Brunner and Hans-Georg Petersen, Campus Verlag), 245–278.

Lyon, Andrew B. and Peter R. Merrill, 2001. "Asset Price Effects of Fundamental Tax Reform," in Kevin A. Hassett and R. Glenn Hubbard (eds.), *Transition Costs of Fundamental Tax Reform*, Washington, DC: The AEI Press.

Muthitacharoen, Athiphat and George R. Zodrow, forthcoming. "State and Local Taxation of Business Property: A Small Open Economy Perspective," *Proceedings of the Ninety-Eighth Annual Conference on Taxation*, National Tax Association.

Poterba, James M., 1992. "Taxation and Housing: Old Questions, New Answers," *American Economic Review* 82: 237–242.

Prescott, Edward C., 2005. "The Elasticity of Labor Supply and the Consequences for Tax Policy," in Alan J. Auerbach and Kevin A. Hassett (eds.), *Toward Fundamental Tax Reform* (Washington DC: AEI Press), pp. 123–134.

Rosen, Harvey S., 1985. "Housing Subsidies: Effects on Housing Decisions, Efficiency, and Equity," in Alan J. Auerbach and Martin Feldstein, *Handbook of Public Economics*, Vol. 1, (North-Holland: Elsevier Science Publishers B.V.).

Ring, Raymond R., Jr., 1999. "Consumer's and Producer's Share of the General Sales Tax," *National Tax Journal* 52: 79–90.

Shapiro, Matthew D., 1986. "The Dynamic Demand for Capital and Labor," *Quarterly Journal of Economics* 101:513–542.

U.S. Bureau of Economic Analysis, 2004. "National Income and Product Accounts," *Survey of Current Business*, Vol. 84: 11 (November).

Zodrow, George R., 2002. "Transitional Issues in the Implementation of a Flat Tax or a National Retail Sales Tax," in George Zodrow and Peter Mieszkowski (eds.), *United States Tax Reform in the 21st Century* (Cambridge UK: Cambridge University Press).

Zodrow, George R. and Michael F. Williams, 1998. "Intergenerational Transitional Issues in the Implementation of a National Retail Sales Tax," Manuscript, Rice University.

Zodrow, George R. and Peter Mieszkowski, "Taxation and the Tiebout Model: The Differential Effects of Head Taxes, Taxes on Land Rents and Property Taxes," *Journal of Economic Literature*, Vol. 27: 3 (September 1989), pp. 1098–1146.

Zodrow, George R. and Peter Mieszkowski (eds.), 2002. *United States Tax Reform in the 21st Century* (Cambridge UK: Cambridge University Press).

Zodrow, George R. and Peter Mieszkowski, 2002a. "The Fundamental Question of Fundamental Tax Reform," in George Zodrow and Peter Mieszkowski (eds.), *United States Tax Reform in the 21st Century* (Cambridge UK: Cambridge University Press).

Part II
Consumption Taxation

Chapter 5

Should Capital Income Be Subject to Consumption-Based Taxation?*

George R. Zodrow

Economics Department and Baker Institute for Public Policy
Rice University, Houston, TX 77005, USA

In 2005, the report of the President's Advisory Panel on Federal Tax Reform proposed two alternative approaches to tax reform. If implemented, both plans would move the tax system farther away from the full taxation of capital income that is the hallmark of a true income tax. However, the panel did not recommend enacting a true consumption tax — instead, both proposals are hybrid income-consumption taxes. The report thus highlights the uncertainty regarding the appropriate tax treatment of capital income, the focus of this book. This chapter examines the central issue the panel faced — whether to implement full-scale consumption-based taxation of capital income.

*This chapter is reproduced from *Taxing Capital Income*, edited by H. J. Aaron, L. Burman and C. E. Steuerle, Urban Institute Press, 2007, pp. 49–81.

1. Introduction

Not surprisingly, separating the topic of this part, "should we tax capital income," — from the other topics in this book ("do we" and "can we" tax capital income) is difficult. After all, a key argument proponents of consumption-based taxation make is that accurately measuring and taxing capital income is difficult, especially in the face of increasing international capital mobility and tax-sheltering activity, and that, in practice, much capital income escapes taxation under the income tax. This chapter, however, ignores these issues and assumes that accurately taxing capital income at a reasonable cost is possible. It considers several preliminary issues and then turns to an analysis of the desirability of consumption-based taxation of capital income.

1.1. *Is a "pure" consumption tax more likely than a "pure" income tax?*

Experience has shown taxing all income as accrued is difficult. Practical requirements for a tax based on realizations — loosely speaking, actual sales — rather than on accrued values, plus the difficulties in measuring economic depreciation and adjusting for inflation, make accurate income measurement exceedingly difficult.[1] By comparison, similar conceptual issues do not beset a consumption-based tax.[2] Of course, "real world" consumption taxes would be more complex than their idealized versions, especially if the United States' trading partners continued to rely on income taxes. Moreover, many of the implementation problems that plague the income tax also arise under a consumption tax.[3] Nevertheless, consumption is inherently easier to measure than income.

---

[1] For example, see Kleinbard (2007) and Roin (2007) for discussions of the difficulties of taxing capital income; Shakow (1986) and Auerbach and Bradford (2004) discuss how a comprehensive income tax might be implemented.

[2] See Bradford (1986) for a classic exposition of this argument. More recently, McCaffery (2005, 809) argues that a "great deal and possibly all of the mind-numbing complexity of America's largest and least popular tax follows from the decision to have a progressive personal income tax." Shaviro (2004, 92) stresses that "a consumption tax could offer enormous simplification advantages."

[3] Schler and Bankman (2007) address these issues in the context of a version of the X tax. In addition, Weisbach (2000), McLure and Zodrow (1996), and Feld (1995) discuss problems that would arise in implementing the flat tax, while Bradford (1996b) discusses

Beyond measurement issues, both the corporate and individual income taxes are riddled with special deductions, exemptions, and other forms of preferential tax treatment, most of which would be eliminated under current consumption-tax reform proposals (and could also be eliminated under an income tax reform). Could any consumption tax reform that survived the political process maintain "purity?" Several factors suggest some room for cautious optimism. Under the corporate tax, a uniform marginal effective tax rate of zero on all forms of investment could serve as a natural floor to preferential tax treatment, at least if there were greater political resistance to outright subsidies than to mere reductions in tax liabilities, especially given current budget exigencies.[4] Of course, recent reforms — including (temporary) accelerated depreciation, extensions of small business expensing, and reductions in tax rates on capital gains and dividends — were not accompanied by limits on the deductibility of interest expenses, as is required to avoid negative effective tax rates. Nevertheless, in the 1980s, public outcries at the tax sheltering and tax loss trading associated with negative effective tax rates at the business level provide some support for the notion of a "zero rate floor" as they prompted passage of the Tax Reform Act of 1986 and the elimination of the safe-harbor leasing provisions of the Economic Recovery Tax Act of 1981.

There is less cause for optimism on the individual side. Pressure to maintain popular deductions would be intense under any fundamental tax reform, although the lure of lower tax rates and the prospect of significant simplification would hopefully offset some of this pressure. Some limits on current deductions might be palatable, especially if the limits target higher-income taxpayers who benefit most from rate reductions. For

problems raised by the taxation of financial institutions under prepaid consumption tax plans. Ginsburg (1995) analyzes issues raised by the USA tax proposal (which combined a business level value-added tax with an individual level cash flow tax), and Murray (1997) addresses problems in implementing a national retail sales tax. Slemrod (2005) discusses the desirability of, and problems raised by, removing popular tax preferences, and Hubbard (2005a) discusses the administrative problems of integrating the corporate and individual income tax systems.

[4] Note that if favorable treatment of some narrow classes of investment were deemed desirable (e.g., in research and development in order to capture significant positive externalities), carefully targeted expenditure programs could be utilized rather than general tax preferences.

example, the "upside-down subsidy" nature of the current deduction for home mortgage interest implies benefits highly concentrated among the wealthy (Carasso, Steuerle, and Bell 2005). Proposals to convert the deduction to a credit subject it to a cap and eliminate it for second homes — as the president's tax reform panel recommends — might be feasible as a means of reducing top rates.

Introducing super-majority requirements for raising rates or adding preferences and reenacting "pay-as-you-go" budget rules would also help limit tax preferences. Legislators might be more likely to enact these budget rules under a large-scale reform of the tax structure than under a more modest income tax reform (Auerbach and Hasset 2005; Bradford 2005). Finally, in addition to eliminating current deductions, legislators could introduce new (perhaps capped) deductions for investments in human capital that are not only politically popular, but have the advantage of being consistent with the principles of consumption-based taxation (Judd 2001). To sum up, there are several reasons why a new consumption tax, enacted in the context of fundamental tax reform, might attain a greater degree of "purity" than would be possible under an incremental reform of the current income tax. Of course, whether such arguments prove compelling in the end, and whether such reforms would be sustainable, is highly speculative.[5]

Would a consumption tax be less susceptible to the tax sheltering activity that has plagued the income tax?[6] Some tax experts argue that many tax sheltering schemes, most of which involve manipulations of provisions related to the taxation of capital income, would not be possible under a consumption tax (Bankman 2004). But the validity of this argument in the "real world" would depend a great deal on the specific

[5] International experience with the VAT may also be instructive in this regard. Although VATs are never completely uniform, preferences take the form of applying zero rates to certain commodities (typically on distributional grounds) or exempting certain activities (typically on distributional or administrative grounds), rather than business subsidies that give rise to negative marginal effective tax rates.

[6] This is clearly related to the more general issue of whether a consumption tax would be simpler than an income tax, discussed by Slemrod (1996) and Gale and Holtzblatt (2002).

details of the plan enacted.[7] For example, some argue that the flat tax and the X tax are more easily evaded than other consumption tax options, primarily because they are "open" tax systems that allow business deductions even when there are no offsetting inclusions (e.g., purchases from individuals, tax-exempt institutions, or foreigners).[8] Similarly, Schler and Bankman (2007) identify sheltering opportunities under the flat tax and the X tax.

Thus, the relative importance of sheltering opportunities under the income tax and the various consumption tax options is unclear, partly because there is so little international experience with direct consumption taxes.[9] It is important to note, however, that the economic models of income and consumption taxation described in this chapter assume effective enforcement and thus do not take into account differences in susceptibility to tax sheltering.

1.2. *Consumption-based and income-based taxation of capital income*

The essential difference between consumption and income-based taxes is in how they treat capital income. Although consumption taxes are often described as exempting the capital income included in the base of an income tax, the differences in tax treatment under the two approaches

[7] For example, McLure and Zodrow (1996) argue for a modified version of the X tax that would tax both real and financial transactions at the business level partly on the grounds that it would be less susceptible to evasion and avoidance, especially on international transactions.

[8] By comparison, under the credit-method VAT utilized in Europe and elsewhere, firms get credits on their purchases only to the extent that they have invoices showing that their suppliers have paid the tax (McLure 1987).

[9] A related question is why this international experience is so limited (beyond the extensive international experience with indirect consumption taxation in the form of the VAT), with the primary examples being the ACE (allowance for corporate equity) taxes implemented in Croatia, Brazil, Italy, and Austria (Genser, forthcoming). One factor played a critical role in halting several consumption tax reforms: the reasonable concern that the U.S. Internal Revenue Service would not deem a consumption-based business cash flow tax (e.g., under a flat tax, an X tax, or an expenditure tax) to be creditable against the domestic tax liability of U.S. multinationals (McLure and Zodrow 1998).

are subtler than this simple characterization suggests. The purchases of investment goods, for instance, are not included in a consumption tax, either due to immediate deductions (expensing), exemptions, or credits. Such treatment is more generous than the treatment provided under an income tax, which allows only deductions for economic depreciation. More specifically, allowing expensing is sufficiently generous to exempt only the normal return to investment.[10] However, as the recent literature has stressed, capital income consists of four conceptually separate components.[11] The risk-free return that compensates individuals for deferring consumption, often described as the "return to waiting," is tax exempt under a consumption tax but is fully taxed under a comprehensive accrual income tax. In contrast, the tax treatments of the other three components of capital income — above-normal returns and the returns to risk taking, which include the expected risk premium and returns that reflect good or bad luck — are similar under income and consumption taxes. Thus, the difference between the tax treatment of capital income under income and consumption taxes is limited to taxation of the risk-free return, which is fully taxed under income taxes and exempt under consumption taxes.

The implications of this point are quite interesting and have not been fully investigated. Risk-free real returns to capital have historically been quite low, especially in periods of high inflation, with average rates ranging from roughly 0.5 to 3 percent (Avi-Yonah 2004). This suggests that the literature may have overstated differences between income and consumption taxes.[12] In particular, most computer simulation models assume perfect competition, ignore uncertainty, and thus may overstate how much capital income is taxed under the income tax, as well as the efficiency gains obtained by moving to a consumption tax. On the other hand, since these models usually ignore inflation, they also understate

[10] See Zodrow and McLure (1991) for a demonstration of this point.

[11] See Weisbach (2004) and Hubbard (2005b) for comprehensive recent discussions, including demonstrations of all the basic points asserted in the text; see also Bradford (1986), Bankman and Griffith (1992), and Hubbard (2002).

[12] Weisbach and Bankman (2005) and McCaffery (2005) stress this point. Note, however, that this argument in no way implies that the taxation of normal returns to capital is a trivial issue; see Aaron's comments in the concluding section.

how much normal returns to capital are taxed under an unindexed income tax. Sorting out these effects is a useful avenue for future research.

1.3. *International issues*

Increasing globalization also plays a critical role in the debate on the appropriate taxation of capital income (see Roin 2007). Many administrative problems would arise if the United States implemented a consumption-based direct tax system while its trading partners continued to tax income. In particular, avoidance schemes based on the differential treatment of capital income would be problematic under certain forms of consumption taxation, and the transfer pricing problems that plague the income tax would also arise in certain cases (Avi-Yonah 2004; Bradford 2003; McLure and Zodrow 1996; Weisbach 2000). Yet adoption of a consumption tax would also allow substantial simplification of international tax rules (Ballard 2002; Weisbach 2000).

From a theoretical perspective, globalization reinforces the case for consumption-based tax treatment of capital income. In particular, the optimal tax rate on capital income is zero for countries that are small open economies and thus face a fixed after-tax return to internationally mobile capital (Gordon 1986; Razin and Sadka 1991).[13] A fixed international rate of return implies that taxes cause capital outflows that lower the productivity of immobile factors in the taxing country — especially land and relatively immobile labor — and thus lower wages and land rents by the full amount of the tax plus its efficiency cost (excess burden). The clear implication is that, solely from the viewpoint of the residents of the taxing country, it is preferable simply to tax local residents directly.[14] This strong result has been qualified in various ways in the literature (see Zodrow 2006). Nevertheless, on balance, international capital

[13]This applies only for production-based taxes on capital income. By comparison, taxes on the capital income of all of a nation's residents, regardless of where it is earned, is in principle desirable but in practice exceedingly difficult to implement.

[14]This result is closely related to the international tax competition literature; see Zodrow (2003) for a recent discussion.

mobility strengthens the case for consumption-based tax reform (see Ballard 2002).

2. An Overview of the Literature

The debate on the relative merits of income and consumption taxation has generated a voluminous literature.[15] This section focuses on three important sets of results in the literature on optimal capital income taxation, as well as various qualifications to those results, and then considers some additional issues.

2.1. *Results from infinite horizon models analyzing efficiency issues*

The most striking result in this literature involves optimal capital and wage income taxation in models with individuals assumed to have infinite lifetimes. Such models can be loosely justified as representing a parent whose welfare depends on her children's welfare, on her grandchildren's welfare, etc. Within this context, several researchers have shown that, in the long run, the optimal capital income tax rate is zero (Chamley 1986; Judd 1985).[16] The intuition behind this result is straightforward. By reducing the after-tax interest rate, a capital income tax raises the price of future consumption. Although this distortion may be modest over the short term, it grows exponentially with time, so that even a small capital income tax rate will eventually be highly distortionary. Since the individuals in these models have perfect foresight over an infinite lifetime, such a tax highly distorts their consumption patterns, with significant declines in saving and capital accumulation.

Indeed, one infinite horizon model that includes both representative workers and capitalists shows that the negative effects of a capital income tax on labor productivity and wages are so great that the optimal capital

[15] For recent surveys, see Zodrow and McLure (1991), Gravelle (1994), Gordon (2000), Judd (2001), McCaffery (2005) and Weisbach and Bankman (2005).

[16] For recent extensions, see Lucas (1990); Chari, Christiano, and Kehoe (1994); and Judd (1997, 1999).

income tax rate is zero even if the government is concerned only about the welfare of workers (Judd 1985). A second message of the infinite horizon models is that, even though capital income taxation should be avoided entirely in the long run, existing capital should be taxed to the maximum extent feasible, since such taxation represents a "lump sum" or nondistortionary source of revenue.[17]

The large saving responses that characterize infinite horizon models imply that consumption tax reforms would yield large growth effects (Engen, Gravelle, and Smetters 1997).[18] Yet the policy implications of these results are open to debate. In particular, some researchers argue that returns to human capital investments should also be exempt from tax (Jones, Manuelli, and Rossi 1993; Milesi-Ferretti and Roubini 1998). To the extent the costs of obtaining human capital are foregone earnings, this is not an issue since such costs are effectively "deductible." However, if the direct costs of making an investment in human capital (e.g., tuition, books, and fees) are not deductible, the logic underlying the zero capital income tax result also implies that the associated wage income should not be taxed. That is, tax exemption of the income to physical capital under a consumption tax should be accompanied by deductibility of the direct costs of investing in human capital, at least to the extent such investments do not reflect consumption expenditures (Judd 2001).

More importantly, many observers hesitate to draw policy implications from models that assume infinitely lived individuals. Beyond questions on the validity of using this representation of altruism across generations, such models cannot address the critical issues related to the

[17] Although the practical relevance of this result is generally limited, it is interesting to note that implementing a consumption tax may, depending on transition rules, achieve this result; this point is investigated further in the discussion of transition issues below. Note also that such a policy suffers from a "time inconsistency problem" in that although it may, in principle, be desirable to impose a huge tax on existing capital as part of an agreement to exempt future returns to capital, investors will understandably be suspicious that future governments will renege on the agreement and tax future accumulations of capital, in which case, the predicted positive effects on saving and capital accumulation will not fully materialize.

[18] Indeed, Lucas (1990, 314) argues that consumption tax reform would trigger "the largest genuinely free lunch I have seen in 25 years in this business."

intergenerational redistribution and transitional problems consumption tax reforms raise. Accordingly, most policy analyses of consumption tax reforms have focused on life-cycle models with an overlapping generations structure.[19]

2.2. *Results from life-cycle models analyzing efficiency issues*

The basic structure described above also characterizes the simplest version of the traditional life-cycle model, except that the representative individual has a two-period life cycle: supplying labor (demanding leisure), purchasing goods, and saving during the earnings period, and drawing down savings during the retirement period. A tax on wage income in this context is equivalent to a uniform consumption tax in the two periods, while a tax on capital income effectively acts as a tax on future consumption. The optimal capital income tax problem is thus analogous to the issue of whether uniform or differential taxation of consumption commodities is desirable. As is well known, uniform commodity taxation is efficient only under certain circumstances. Specifically, the optimal capital income tax rate is zero (implying uniform taxation of consumption in both periods, as would occur under a consumption or wage tax) only if first and second period consumption are equally complementary with leisure.[20]

[19] Note, however, that the insight that capital income taxes are highly distortionary for individuals with long time horizons is still relevant, if to a lesser degree, in lifecycle models. Indeed, because lifecycle models often assume away intergenerational altruism entirely, they may be understating the gains from consumption tax reform.

[20] For example, see Feldstein (1978), Bradford (1980), King (1980) and, in an explicitly dynamic context, Atkinson and Sandmo (1980). Goods that are complements tend to be consumed together. More formally, leisure and a consumption good are complements if an increase in the price of the consumption good reduces the demand for leisure (and thus increases labor supply).

The intuition underlying this result reflects a balancing of two considerations. Uniform taxation of consumption tends to be efficient, as it avoids tax distortions of intertemporal consumption allocation decisions. However, the inability to tax leisure directly implies that taxation of consumption goods will inefficiently reduce labor supply, so that differential taxation of consumption goods will be desirable if it can be used to offset the tax-induced increase in leisure demand and the associated reduction in labor supply. If consumption in each of the two periods is equally complementary to leisure and thus

The conditions for the optimality of uniform commodity taxation require that decisions on choices among consumption commodities must be separable, or independent of the decision on how much labor to supply (leisure to demand). Also, individual tastes must be homothetic with respect to the consumption goods, which implies that increases in wealth are distributed proportionately across consumption in all periods (Auerbach 1979). There is, of course, no guarantee that individual tastes will satisfy these two conditions, although such an assumption is plausible at least to a first approximation.[21] In sum, the simple two-period model arguably suggests a presumption that an optimal tax system exempts capital income from taxes.

The applicability of the simple two-period model, however, is limited. A more complete analysis requires that a more detailed model of individual life-cycle optimization be combined with production and incorporated into an overlapping-generations, general equilibrium structure of the economy. These concerns are addressed in an overlapping generations model, constructed in 1981 by Lawrence H. Summers, comprised of life-cycle savers who have a 50 year adult life (the last 10 of which are spent in retirement), supply labor inelastically, and experience exponential wage growth (Summers 1981). The Summers model emphasizes that increasing the tax rate on capital income reduces the after-tax discount rate individuals use in estimating their human wealth — the present value of all future labor earnings — when making consumption and savings decisions. The resulting increase in human wealth prompts greater consumption early in life and thus, less saving. Simulations suggest that this human wealth effect is highly significant, implying that consumption tax reform would result in large steady state welfare gains. For example, in one central case, the enactment of a cash flow consumption tax results in a steady state welfare gain equal to 11.2 percent of lifetime income.[22] A wage tax reform

affects labor supply in the same way, any rationale for differential taxation disappears, and uniform commodity taxation (a capital income tax rate of zero) is optimal.

[21] For example, Atkinson and Stiglitz (1980, 437) conclude that separability is "an assumption that has been made in nearly all studies of demand and labor supply functions."

[22] One reason for the large welfare gains obtained with a consumption tax reform is that the size of the existing capital stock under the income tax is suboptimal in the Summers model; such an assumption seems plausible and is consistent with the often-expressed

in the Summers model would also increase steady state welfare but to a significantly smaller extent (7 percent of lifetime income), since existing capital is not subject to tax.[23]

The Summers model sparked a great deal of interest and additional research, most prominently the overlapping-generations, general equilibrium model constructed in 1987 by Auerbach and Kotlikoff.[24] This model allows labor-leisure choices in each period, assumes a "humpbacked" wage profile over the life cycle taken from the labor economics literature, and uses more conservative parameter values than those Summers utilizes.

As a result of these and other differences from the Summers model, the welfare gains obtained from a consumption tax reform in the Auerbach–Kotlikoff model are more moderate. For example, in a base case analysis, a cash flow consumption tax increases steady state welfare by 2.3 percent of the present value of "lifetime resources," which includes the value of leisure and is therefore a broader measure of welfare than that used by Summers.[25] A more recent version of the model estimates that implementing a retail sales tax or a value-added tax would increase long-run steady state welfare by 1.9 percent of lifetime resources; this corresponds to an efficiency gain for all future generations, holding constant the utility levels of all individuals alive at the time of enactment, equal to

---

concern that the United States saves and invests too little. Note, however, that many non-tax government policies also affect the level of saving and the size of the capital stock, making it difficult to ascertain whether the capital stock is too large or too small.

[23]This highlights the point, noted above, that a significant fraction of the efficiency gains obtained from a consumption tax reform is attributable to a one-time "hit" on old capital, reminiscent of the tax on existing capital that characterizes the infinite horizon models. In addition, Summers assumes that the government's budget must be balanced each year. As a result, any policy that defers taxes, such as a cash flow consumption tax or an income tax, will stimulate additional savings as individuals must save to finance the payment of future taxes; this additional savings would not occur under a wage tax reform, which reduces savings effects and thus the long run welfare gains associated with its enactment.

[24]The model is described in Auerbach and Kotlikoff (1987). See Auerbach (1996) for a recent analysis of fundamental tax reform using the Auerbach and Kotlikoff model and Kotlikoff (1998) for a discussion of its evolution.

[25]By comparison, for the same reasons as in the case of the Summers model, the enactment of a wage tax (again without a complementary business tax) reduces welfare by 0.9 percent of the present value of lifetime resources.

6.4 percent of lifetime resources. By comparison, the Hall–Rabushka flat tax, due to its standard deduction and personal exemptions, results in smaller welfare and efficiency gains, as steady state welfare increases by 1.6 percent and the efficiency gain is more than halved to 2.8 percent. Reform-induced efficiency gains thus vary significantly across consumption tax reforms; in addition, these analyses show that adding progressivity and transition rules significantly reduces efficiency gains.[26]

2.3. *Results from models analyzing efficiency and equity issues*

Equity concerns are also central to the debate on the desirability of taxing capital income. The literature has addressed issues of both horizontal equity (equal treatment of equals) and vertical equity (progressivity).

2.3.1. *Equal treatment of equals*

Before equity issues can be addressed, the period over which ability to pay tax is to be measured must be determined. If this period is a single year, then potential rather than actual annual consumption is a plausible measure of ability to pay, and a comprehensive measure of income that includes all accrued capital income, often referred to as Haig–Simons income, is typically viewed as the appropriate tax base. In this case, horizontal equity implies that individuals with the same comprehensive income in a given year should pay the same tax.

However, consumption tax proponents have questioned the rationale underlying the Haig–Simons ideal. In particular, the basic life-cycle model implies that individual welfare is a function of consumption over the lifetime rather than annual income (Bradford 1980). In this case, the

---

[26] Indeed, Auerbach also estimates that the efficiency gains associated with implementing the USA tax (Weidenbaum 1996), which provides for transition rules and multiple individual tax rates that range up to 40 percent as well as a variety of other features, are only 0.1 percent of lifetime resources.

A separate issue is whether the optimal capital income tax is zero in such overlapping generations models. Erosa and Gervais (2002) and Garriga (2003) show that this is not necessarily the case because individual utility functions are not necessarily characterized by separability in leisure and consumption. However, their "optimal" capital income tax rates are relatively small.

appropriate measure of ability to pay is an individual's "endowment" — the present value of lifetime wage earnings — and capital income merely represents compensation for deferred consumption.[27] On this view, a tax on consumption and a tax on wages satisfy horizontal equity, as the lifetime tax burdens under each approach equal the product of the tax rate and the present value of the endowment, independent of individual consumption and saving decisions. By comparison, an income tax taxes the return to saving, penalizing savers. Many researchers argue that a consumption tax is therefore the preferable option on horizontal equity grounds.

A more contentious issue is whether this argument should be extended to multiple generations, implying that economic resources should not be taxed until consumed.[28] Some tax experts argue the "dynastic" view — that bequests should be tax exempt as they represent a transfer of potential consumption to heirs. According to this view, under a prepaid tax like the flat tax or the X tax, inheritances should not be included in the tax base of the recipient (since the tax has already been paid); similarly, under a postpaid expenditure tax, "withdrawals" used to fund bequests should not be taxed, and inheritances should be taxed only when consumed. The sales tax or value-added tax approaches are inherently consistent with the dynastic view of equity, as tax is not assessed until consumption actually occurs.

By comparison, the "lifetime endowment" view of equity underlying the life-cycle model described above argues that people should be taxed on all resources available during their lives, including inheritances, whether used for consumption or bequests. Therefore, the correct base for measuring ability to pay tax is lifetime income, including inheritances (Aaron and Galper 1985). Under a prepaid tax like the flat tax or the X-tax, both the recipient and the donor will pay tax on intergenerational transfers. Under a postpaid expenditure tax, "withdrawals" used to fund bequests should be taxed and should also be in the recipient's tax base. Proponents of the

---

[27] As explained below, when the basic lifecycle model is extended to include bequests and inheritances, the value of the individual endowment should include inheritances, and bequests should (arguably) be treated as consumption.

[28] See Zodrow and McLure (1991) for further discussion.

dynastic equity view argue that such treatment creates a tax bias against saving and transfers in the form of bequests relative to other forms. In contrast, proponents of the lifetime endowment equity view argue that such treatment is essential to ensure all individuals with the same lifetime resources are treated equally (and to limit transfers of huge fortunes across generations). The choice between the two approaches obviously involves personal value judgments. However, it is important to note that the choice between the dynastic and lifetime endowment views of equity has similar implications for the designs of both income and consumption taxes, and is relevant primarily to the extent that capital income taxation is perceived to supplement poorly administered estate taxes (or to substitute for non-existent estate taxes).[29]

2.3.2. *Progressivity*

Progressivity is also a contentious issue in the income versus consumption tax debate. Although a complete exploration of the optimal progressivity of the tax system is beyond the scope of this chapter, the following discussion examines whether capital income taxation is necessary to achieve an appropriate level of progressivity.

In a seminal paper published in 1976, Atkinson and Stiglitz construct a model of optimal commodity and wage taxation. The Atkinson and Stiglitz model focuses on whether differential commodity taxation is desirable to achieve a society's equity goals if wages are taxed optimally and individuals differ only in their skill and wage levels. Within this

[29] Cremer, Pestieau, and Rochet (2003) show that capital income taxation may be desirable in a version of the Atkinson and Stiglitz (1976) model, modified to include bequests that are by assumption tax exempt, if the equity gains from indirectly taxing inherited wealth offset the efficiency costs of reducing saving and investment. Note also that capital income taxation can be justified as a proxy for a wealth tax that is assessed on the grounds that wealth confers utility beyond its consumption value in the form of prestige, security, and power, including political power (Carroll 2000). However, consistent with the dynastic view of equity, Shaviro (2004) argues that such benefits reflect only the value of future consumption, which would be taxed fully under a consumption tax (although there would be no reduction in wealth accumulation under a consumption tax, in contrast to the case under an effective capital income tax).

context, differential commodity taxation is unnecessary if the conditions for uniform commodity taxation (described above) are satisfied. The intuition behind this striking result is that an appropriately progressive wage tax can achieve all distributional goals since individuals differ only in their skill levels and at any given skill level all individuals have the same earnings and consumption pattern.

A number of recent papers provide qualifications to the Atkinson and Stiglitz result. For example, if demands for leisure and consumption goods vary within a given skill class, differential commodity taxes may further the redistribution that occurs under the progressive wage tax. In a dynamic context, the implication is that, with more saving and higher levels of welfare, taxes on saving are desirable (Saez 2002). The practical relevance of this result, however, is open to question. With low national savings rates being a perennial concern, the desirability and political feasibility of a policy designed explicitly to penalize savers seems highly questionable (Bankman and Weisbach 2005; Naito 1999; Saez 2004; Stiglitz 1982).

Consumption-based taxation would thus appear preferable to income taxation in terms of providing equal treatment of equals, and progressivity goals in principle could be achieved with a suitably progressive consumption-based tax, such as the X tax or a progressive expenditure tax.[30] Indeed, a tax system that at least roughly replicates the progressivity of the current tax system across income classes seems a prerequisite for reform in most (although by no means all) circles, and such a constraint was imposed on the deliberations of the president's tax reform panel.[31] Such a result also cannot be obtained with a flat tax or a national retail sales tax (or VAT) plus rebate plan, as numerous studies have demonstrated that these plans

[30] Note that in addition to the vertical equity rationale, progressive taxation effectively provides social insurance against income fluctuations (Varian 1980).

[31] Note, however, that even a "distributionally neutral" consumption tax reform will cause redistributions within income classes. Moreover, since low-income individuals pay little or no income tax and middle-income individuals already largely receive consumption tax treatment since most of their saving is in housing or retirement plans (see Toder and Rueben 2007), these redistributions will be concentrated in the upper-income classes, especially at the very top. One could argue that as long as reform is roughly distributionally neutral in the bottom four quintiles, redistributions among the top quintile may be of relatively little social concern.

involve a shift in tax burden from the very wealthy to a broadly defined middle class (Feenberg, Poterba, and Mitrusi 1997; Mieszkowski and Palumbo 2002).[32] Such a redistribution of tax burdens is undesirable, especially in light of the dramatic increase in income inequality over the past 30 years. Indeed, this concern is sufficiently important that Robert Hall, one of the creators of the original flat tax plan, now argues that a "tax design to fit the times might have two or even three different tax rates at the personal level" (Hall 2005, 75).

A natural question is whether the current distribution of the tax burden could in practice be replicated under a progressive consumption-based tax. Recent increases in income inequality are due primarily to an explosion in compensation of the wealthy, while capital income has become increasingly less concentrated over time (Piketty and Saez 2003). As long as a consumption tax system subjects executives' compensation to the same level of tax as current law — for example, by including executive pay in the form of stock options in the individual-level tax — maintaining progressivity under a consumption tax should be feasible.[33] Still, replicating current tax burdens would require a progressive consumption tax rate with potentially high maximum tax rates. For example, one static revenue estimate of the effects of implementing an X tax with no transition relief while maintaining current tax preferences concludes that a revenue- and distributionally neutral reform would require a corporate tax rate and a top individual rate of 44 percent (see Toder and Rueben 2007). Such static estimates, however, are subject to the criticisms that they miss the primary advantages of a consumption tax reform, including its efficiency-enhancing behavioral responses, and overstate the regressivity of consumption taxes by focusing on annual rather than lifetime incidence measures.

---

[32] As Fullerton and Rogers (1993) discuss, lifetime incidence analyses are preferable to studies based on annual income because they limit mismeasurement due to income fluctuations attributable to cyclical and lifecycle factors. For a dissenting view, see Barthold (1993).

[33] Note that one potential advantage of the postpaid expenditure tax approach is that it may be relatively less susceptible to evasion in the form of converting labor income to exempt capital income (Weisbach 2000), although many such strategies are limited under the prepaid flat tax and X taxes by setting the top individual tax rate equal to the flat business tax rate.

These issues are addressed in a 2001 analysis that extends the Auerbach and Kotlikoff (1987) model to include 12 lifetime income groups (10 deciles, with the top (bottom) decile split into the top (bottom) 2 percent and the remaining 8 percent) (Altig *et al.* 2001). Simulations with this model indicate that using an X tax with a top marginal rate of 30 percent results in a long-run increase in output of 6.4 percent, coupled with long-run welfare increases for each of the 12 lifetime income classes of between 1 and 2 percent of full lifetime resources (including leisure). However, the transitional losses for the elderly that accompany these gains at the time of reform range between 1 and 2 percent of remaining lifetime utility; moreover, other simulations suggest that adding transition relief would significantly reduce, and perhaps even reverse, these long-run, steady-state welfare gains.

In addition, estimates of the regressivity of implementing a consumption tax are reduced by taking into account that high-income households often receive capital income as returns to risk-taking and economic rents, which are taxed similarly under income and consumption taxes. One estimate suggests this factor reduces the decline in the tax share paid by the top 5 percent of the net worth distribution by more than a third, relative to an analysis that assumes a consumption tax exempts all capital income (Gentry and Hubbard 1997).

Several researchers have investigated how much capital income is actually taxed under the current income tax (see Slemrod 2007). One study found that an X tax implemented in 1983 would have raised no additional personal and corporate income tax revenues, and that the tax burden on lower-income investors who tend to hold taxable bonds was greater than on higher-income investors who tend to borrow heavily to invest in assets that generate more lightly taxed capital gains (Gordon and Slemrod 1988).[34] A subsequent analysis of the 1995 tax system showed a

[34] Indeed, McCaffery (2005) argues that wealthy individuals can largely avoid taxation over their lifetimes by following a strategy of investing in, and then holding until death, assets that generate capital gains while financing current consumption with debt. See Gravelle's comments to Part 1 of the book, "Taxing Capital Income", for a critique of this approach that concludes that it understates how much capital income is taxed under the current income tax.

similar distributive pattern for capital income taxes in the lower- and middle-income classes, but also showed that very high income taxpayers bore a significant portion of the capital income tax burden that year (Gordon, Kalambokidis, and Slemrod 2004). Indeed, in 2004, replacing the income tax with an X tax regime would have cost only $63.8 billion (less than 7 percent of combined personal and corporate annual income tax revenues) (Gordon *et al.* forthcoming).[35]

Finally, most dynamic models of consumption tax reform allow for only a single production good and do not capture the economic efficiency gains that arise from taxing investment more uniformly under a consumption tax, especially investment in owner-occupied housing, relative to other forms of investment.[36]

Although any conclusion from these analyses is tentative, they suggest that a progressive consumption tax reform could be designed without causing huge redistributions of income across income classes, at least if the growth effects such models predict in fact materialize and transition relief is limited. The reform would also have to be well-designed to improve

[35]These authors also find that expanding prepaid savings accounts, as was proposed in 2004 and is currently being discussed, could result in a situation where the taxation of capital income loses revenue. This dramatically illustrates the point that piecemeal reforms that cobble together various elements of a consumption tax reform but do not include all of its features, including especially the elimination of interest deductibility, can be highly undesirable. In particular, the "five easy pieces" approach (Christian and Robbins 2002) — which would reduce rates (and eliminate the estate tax), allow expensing, and exempt capital income from taxation at the individual level without providing for consumption-based tax treatment of interest expense — loses revenue and creates arbitrage opportunities without gaining the advantages of consumption-based taxation in providing uniform tax treatment of all saving and investment decisions and a simplified tax system.

[36]Note that such gains would not be obtained under an income tax reform — although more uniform treatment of business investment could be achieved (if economic depreciation were measured accurately and the appropriate adjustments for inflation were made), a move to more comprehensive taxation of business income would exacerbate the already large tax bias favoring owner-occupied housing over other forms of investment. The net result would likely be a relatively small efficiency gain or an efficiency loss. Note also that additional efficiency gains could be obtained with reforms that would reduce the consumption distortions of the existing income tax, especially those attributable to tax preferences for fringe benefits; these potential efficiency gains, however, could be achieved with either income or consumption tax reforms, and would face the same political obstacles in either case.

economic efficiency. Yet, since considerable uncertainty remains about the accuracy of these models' predictions, implementing a slightly more progressive system than such models predict may be advisable to avoid unanticipated income redistributions (Auerbach and Hassett 2005).

2.4. *Additional issues*

The literature on income and consumption taxation has considered a host of additional issues relevant to the debate.

2.4.1. *The size of behavioral responses*

One issue is whether the behavioral responses that the simulation models predict, especially labor supply and saving responses, are unreasonably large. Empirical estimates of labor supply responses to changes in taxation are typically low (Ballard 2002; Bernheim 2002; Engen, Gravelle, and Smetters 1997; Gravelle 2002). Some simulated effects of consumption tax reforms are significantly larger than the current econometric literature implies. For example, one infinite-horizon study estimates that enacting a pure flat rate national retail sales tax with no exemptions or rebates would, in the short run, increase investment nearly 80 percent and labor supply 30 percent, and, in the long run, boost investment roughly 16.5 percent and labor supply 15 percent (Jorgenson and Wilcoxen 2002). Large, although typically more moderate, responses also characterize some life-cycle models, especially in the short run.[37]

Two factors, however, mitigate the validity of this criticism. First, as noted above, much recent literature has adopted more conservative assumptions in both model structure — for example, life-cycle rather than infinite-horizon models, perfect foresight rather than myopic expectations, and more careful modeling of the consumption tax-type features of the current income tax — and in parameter choices, resulting in more

[37] See Gravelle (2002) for an extended discussion of this and other issues raised by the use of computable general equilibrium model to analyze the effects of consumption tax reforms.

moderate behavioral responses, especially in the long run.[38] Second, the current econometric literature may not adequately capture the behavioral responses that would occur under fundamental tax reform. Econometric estimates of the response of saving to changes in the after-tax rate of return may inadequately capture the human wealth effect (Summers 1988). Recent research that examines differences in labor supply in the United States and Europe suggests that long-run labor supply responses to tax changes are considerably greater than those found in the microbased empirical literature, which typically studies data over a much shorter time period (Prescott 2005).

2.4.2. *Alternative models of saving*

Most analyses discussed in this chapter are based on the individual life-cycle model. Since this approach represents the "workhorse" model of individual behavior in neoclassical economics, this emphasis is not surprising. However, several researchers have suggested such models may present an incomplete picture of individual saving behavior.[39]

One argument is that saving reflects a precautionary motive, as individuals attempt to protect themselves against fluctuations in earnings and an uncertain lifetime (Engen and Gale 1996). When precautionary saving is added to a standard life-cycle model, the savings responses induced by a consumption tax reform fall dramatically, since precautionary saving is relatively unresponsive to changes in after-tax rates of return. As a result, the efficiency gains from switching to a consumption tax are significantly smaller than in alternative analyses that do not consider precautionary

[38] The assumption of myopic expectations tends to overstate the short-run responses to the enactment of the consumption tax reform because individuals and firms do not take into account in their behavioral responses the decline in the interest rate over time that occurs with capital accumulation. More careful modeling of the many consumption tax-type features of the current hybrid income tax implies that enacting a consumption tax would change the current system less than if it were a true income tax (Engen and Gale 1996).

[39] Indeed, Altig *et al.* (2001) note that in their simulations, they use a relatively low value of the intertemporal elasticity of substitution, a key parameter in determining saving responsiveness, to compensate for the lack of non-lifecycle saving motives in their model.

saving. The efficiency case for consumption tax reform is correspondingly weakened.

In addition, some individual saving may be undertaken to meet a goal that is fixed in dollar terms.[40] In this case, a consumption tax reform may reduce saving, as a higher after-tax rate of return helps achieve the savings target. One estimate attributes approximately a third of aggregate wealth to such precautionary saving motives, which again implies that life-cycle models overstate the savings responses that would occur with a consumption tax reform (Carroll and Samwick 1998). However, a more recent study places this figure at a much lower 10 percent (Hurst *et al.* 2005).

Another issue is that individuals may not be as free to borrow at any point in their life-cycle, especially early in life, as most analyses assume. Reform-induced efficiency gains might be muted if a large number of credit-constrained individuals, who consume all their after-tax earnings, are negatively affected by higher wage or consumption taxes under a consumption tax reform. However, a progressive consumption tax could address such liquidity problems by reducing tax rates on lower-income, credit-constrained individuals, an approach preferable to a progressive income tax that distorts individuals' saving decisions. Further, problems with liquidity constraints can be addressed more directly with transfer programs such as the earned income tax credit and presumably have been alleviated in recent years by easier access to credit card debt and tax-favored home equity loans (Hubbard and Judd 1986).

Uncertainties about future income levels could also make some capital income taxation desirable for credit-constrained individuals if it reduces the saving of individuals who save too much due to concern about future income declines (Aiyagari 1994; Chamley 2001). However, the desirability and political feasibility of a tax policy designed explicitly to penalize savers in the current low-saving environment is open to serious question.

Another potentially serious concern is that individual saving behavior is far more erratic than economic simulation models predict. Specifically, the relatively new field of behavioral economics has suggested new models that have implications for modeling individual saving behavior (Bernheim 1997, 2002). To cite one example, individual decisions may reflect a

[40] Samwick (1998) examines such "target saving."

balancing of the desire for immediate gratification against the desire to engage in more prudent behavior by saving for the future. In this case, tax preferences for savings under the income tax imply government encouragement of saving that may successfully sway behavior away from immediate consumption, which such features as restrictions and penalties on withdrawals from tax-preferred savings plans and systematic payroll deductions for savings may reinforce. If such features are eliminated under a consumption tax reform, saving might decline. In particular, since employer-provided pensions would lose their relative tax advantage under a consumption tax reform, employers might reduce the extent of pension coverage (Bernheim 1997). As a result, savings might fall because some people would no longer be constrained to save more than they desired or be penalized for withdrawals from savings to finance current consumption. However, such effects might be partially, or even fully, offset if a consumption tax reform were perceived as government encouragement of all forms of saving.

2.4.3. *Transitional issues*

Transitional issues present a formidable obstacle to enacting consumption tax reform. Most analyses have focused on two issues.[41] First, in the absence of transition rules, a consumption tax might result in a one-time fall in equity prices. Under a value-added tax or national retail sales tax, inflation in the form of a one-time, tax-induced increase in consumer prices would reduce the purchasing power of existing real assets. Under the direct consumption tax options, such as the flat tax, X tax, or expenditure tax, the relative value of existing capital would decline because remaining depreciation deductions would be denied while competing investments in new capital would be expensed; an equilibrium with equal after-tax returns on both new and old assets could occur only if the prices of old assets fell.[42] Second, a consumption tax might also push down the

[41] For example, see Sarkar and Zodrow (1993), Bradford (1996a), Pearlman (1996), Shaviro (2000), and Zodrow (1997, 2002).

[42] Note that existing assets could be put on an equal footing with new assets only if the remaining basis were expensed at the time of enacting a consumption tax reform.

price of existing owner-occupied housing, which would lose its current tax advantages. Some observers have suggested that the asset prices could plunge 20 to 30 percent (Cappoza, Green, and Hendershott 1996; Gravelle 1995).

However, these analyses neglect certain offsetting factors (Bruce and Holtz-Eakin 1999; Lyon and Merrill 2001; Zodrow 2002). Equity price declines, for instance, would be mitigated by the costs of adjusting the capital stock in response to reform, which imply that existing capital would earn above-normal returns during the transition to a new equilibrium. Simulation results suggest that adjustment costs alone play a significant role in reducing and, in some cases, eliminating reform-induced declines in equity values (Altig *et al.* 2001; Auerbach 1996).

Numerous factors, such as declines in interest rates and reductions in the supply of owner-occupied housing, would mitigate any tendency for house prices to fall (Diamond and Zodrow 1999; Gravelle 1996). One simulation suggests that the declines in the price of owner-occupied housing could be on the order of 3 to 5 percent, far smaller than those suggested above, and would dissipate relatively quickly over time (Diamond and Zodrow 2005).

Thus, transition problems may not be a "show stopper" for fundamental tax reform; indeed, transition relief should be minimized since transition rules significantly reduce the efficiency gains obtained from such a reform (Zodrow 2002). The relatively harsh transition rules that accompanied the enactment of the Tax Reform Act of 1986 suggest that transition relief could be limited under a consumption tax reform. However, political realities suggest that some transition rules are inevitable and will eliminate the need to create complex rules that limit attempts to avoid a one-time, reform-induced transition "hit" on existing capital (Pearlman 1996; Shaviro 2000; Weisbach 2003). If so, the costs of such transition rules should be kept to a minimum by using targeted grandfather rules (Zodrow 1992). For example, transition relief could be limited to allowing continued depreciation allowances only on long-lived assets, especially since recent equipment purchases have benefited from bonus depreciation. In addition, transition rules could be coupled with compensating provisions. For example, under the flat tax or X tax, phased-out deductions for home mortgage interest could be accompanied by similarly phased-out taxation of the associated interest income, and expensing of new investment might be limited to a fraction of the purchase price for firms with significant continuing deductions for depreciation on existing investment (Hall and Rabushka 1995).

3. Conclusion

The debate on whether capital income should be subject to consumption-based taxation has raged for many years. It is likely to intensify as the United States examines various options for fundamental tax reform, including those the president's tax reform panel proposed in 2005. What lessons can be drawn from the voluminous literature on this subject?

The theoretical literature generally supports consumption-based taxation of capital income. Infinite horizon models provide the most clearcut result — a long-run optimal capital income tax rate of zero — due to ever-increasing distortions of future consumption and saving decisions. A similar result can be obtained in the context of life-cycle models, although it is more tenuous as it depends on unproven but plausible assumptions on individual tastes. In terms of tax fairness, consumption-based taxation provides for more equal treatment of equals, and a central theoretical result indicates that under the same assumptions on individual tastes, progressivity goals can be achieved with progressive direct taxes on consumption. Further, the low level of revenues capital income taxation collects under the current income tax suggests that approximating the current distribution of the tax burden is less difficult than might appear under a consumption tax. These results on the taxation of labor income are especially important to the current debate, as recent increases in income inequality are largely attributable to an explosion in executive compensation. Consumption taxes are also inherently simpler than taxes based on income, although some of this advantage would be muted as "pure" proposals for reform are modified to accommodate a variety of real-world complications and political pressures. Indeed, one critical factor in advancing the debate is the ongoing development of more fully specified reform proposals, with the work of David Bradford on his celebrated X tax — which formed the basis of one of the two reform proposals made in 2005 by the president's panel on tax reform — setting the standard for such endeavors.

The results of large-scale computer simulation models have played an important role in buttressing the case for consumption tax reform. Many of these models indicate that such a reform would generate impressive improvements in economic performance and gains in economic welfare, especially in the long run. Yet, these gains are significantly muted, and in a few cases, even reversed, once reform is accompanied by transition rules to protect old capital and as the progressivity of the tax system increases. This suggests that transition relief should be kept to a minimum in implementing a consumption tax reform. In addition, keeping rates relatively low by eliminating tax preferences at the business level and severely limiting them at the individual level, especially at the high end of the income distribution where the gains from reform are concentrated, is critical to attaining efficiency gains and achieving rough distributional neutrality. It is equally important to note that current models do not capture all of the potential efficiency gains from fundamental tax reform and so may understate the potential for such gains. Items often not considered (depending on the model) include the gains attributable to an improved allocation of capital across sectors, especially across housing and nonhousing production and across the corporate and noncorporate sectors, the benefits of increased inflows of foreign capital, the gains from eliminating financing distortions, the potential gains from a well-designed and simpler tax system that would require less resources for compliance and administration and be less susceptible to avoidance and evasion, and any positive additional benefits (e.g., on the growth rate of technological innovation) from tax-induced increases in investment (Stokely and Rebelo 1995).

This chapter suggests two directions for future research to clarify the main issues in the ongoing debate on fundamental tax reform.[43] The first is continued evolution of computer simulation models to capture more fully reform-induced efficiency gains and distributional effects on both current and future generations, and as many of the "real world" complications of reform as possible. The second is continued development of the structural details of consumption tax reform proposals to understand more clearly their economic effects and how effectively they would cope with various real-world complications, and to help in choosing among the prototypes for

[43] See also Zodrow and Mieszkowski (2002).

reform. Finally, it is important to note that piecemeal changes in the general direction of consumption tax reform run the risk of losing revenues and creating arbitrage opportunities while falling short of attaining all the potential gains that a well-designed reform package might achieve — gains that must be achieved for a consumption tax to be a desirable approach to reform.

Acknowledgments

I would like to thank Alan Auerbach, Len Burman, John Diamond and Joel Slemrod for helpful comments, Kevin Grahmann for outstanding research assistance at the beginning stages of this project, and Athiphat Muthitacharoen for his invaluable help in bringing this chapter to completion.

References

Aaron, Henry J., and Harvey Galper. 1985. *Assessing Tax Reform.* Washington, DC: Brookings Institution Press.

Aiyagari, S. Rao. 1994. "Uninsured Idiosyncratic Risk and Aggregate Saving." *Quarterly Journal of Economics* 109:659–684.

Altig, David, Alan J. Auerbach, Laurence J. Kotlikoff, Kent A. Smetters, and Jan Walliser. 2001. "Simulating Fundamental Tax Reform in the United States." *American Economic Review* 91:574–595.

Andrews, William D. 1974. "A Consumption-Type or Cash Flow Personal Income Tax." *Harvard Law Review* 87:1113–1188.

Atkinson, Anthony B., and Agnar Sandmo. 1980. "Welfare Implications of the Taxation of Savings." *Economic Journal* 90:529–549.

Atkinson, Anthony B., and Joseph E. Stiglitz. 1976. "The Design of Tax Structure: Direct versus Indirect Taxation." *Journal of Public Economics* 6:55–75.

———. 1980. *Lectures on Public Economics.* New York: McGraw-Hill.

Auerbach, Alan J. 1979. "A Brief Note on a Nonexistent Theorem about the Optimality of Uniform Taxation." *Economic Letters* 3:49–52.

———. 1996. "Tax Reform, Capital Allocation, Efficiency, and Growth." In *Economic Effects of Fundamental Tax Reform,* edited by Henry J. Aaron and William G. Gale (29–73). Washington, DC: Brookings Institution Press.

Auerbach, Alan J., and David F. Bradford. 2004. "Generalized Cash-Flow Taxation." *Journal of Public Economics* 88:957–980.

Auerbach, Alan J., and Kevin A. Hassett. 2005a. "Conclusion." In *Toward Fundamental Tax Reform,* edited by Alan J. Auerbach and Kevin A. Hassett (149–158). Washington, DC: AEI Press.

———. 2005b. *Toward Fundamental Tax Reform.* Washington, DC: AEI Press.

Auerbach, Alan J., and James R. Hines. 2002. "Taxation and Economic Efficiency." In *Handbook of Public Economics,* vol. 4, edited by Alan J. Auerbach and Martin Feldstein (1347–1421). Amsterdam: Elsevier.

Auerbach, Alan J., and Laurence J. Kotlikoff. 1987. *Dynamic Fiscal Policy.* Cambridge, UK: Cambridge University Press.

Avi-Yonah, Reuven S. 2004. "Risk, Rents, and Regressivity: Why the United States Needs Both an Income Tax and a VAT." *Tax Notes International* 37(December 20): 177–195.

Balcer, Yves, Irwin Garfinkel, Kathy J. Krynski, and Efraim Sadka. 1983. "Income Redistribution and the Structure of Indirect Taxation." In *Social Policy Evaluation: An Economic Perspective,* edited by Elhanan Helpman, Assaf Razin, and Efraim Sadka (279–297). New York: Academic Press.

Ballard, Charles L. 1990. "On the Specification of Simulation Models for Evaluating Income and Consumption Taxes." In *Heidelberg Congress on Taxing Consumption,* edited by Manfred Rose (147–188). Berlin: Springer-Verlag.

———. 2002. "International Aspects of Fundamental Tax Reform." In *United States Tax Reform in the 21st Century,* edited by George R. Zodrow and Peter Mieszkowski (109–139). Cambridge, UK: Cambridge University Press.

Bankman, Joseph. 2004. "The Tax Shelter Problem." *National Tax Journal* 57:925–936.

Bankman, Joseph, and Thomas Griffith. 1992. "Is the Debate between an Income Tax and a Consumption Tax a Debate about Risk? Does It Matter?" *Tax Law Review* 47:377–406.

Barthold, Thomas A. 1993. "How Should We Measure Distribution?" *National Tax Journal* 46:291–299.

Bernheim, B. Douglas. 1997. "Taxation and Saving: A Behavioral Perspective." In *Proceedings of the Eighty-Ninth Annual Conference on Taxation.* Washington, DC: National Tax Association.

———. 2002. "Taxation and Saving." In *Handbook of Public Economics,* vol. 3, edited by Alan J. Auerbach and Martin Feldstein (1176–1207). Amsterdam: Elsevier.

Blumenthal, Marsha, and Joel Slemrod. 1995. "The Compliance Cost of Taxing Foreign-Source Income: Its Magnitude, Determinants, and Policy Implications." *International Tax and Public Finance* 2:37–54.

Bond, Stephen R., Michael P. Devereux, and Malcolm J. Gammie. 1996. "Tax Reform to Promote Investment." *Oxford Review of Economic Policy* 12:109–117.

Boskin, Michael J., ed. 1996. *Frontiers of Tax Reform.* Stanford: Hoover Institution Press.

Bradford, David F. 1980. "The Case for a Personal Consumption Tax." In *What Should Be Taxed: Income or Expenditure?* edited by Joseph Pechman (77–113). Washington, DC: Brookings Institution Press.

———. 1986. *Untangling the Income Tax.* Cambridge, MA: Harvard University Press.

———. 1987. "On the Incidence of Consumption Taxes." In *The Consumption Tax: A Better Alternative,* edited by Charles E. Walker and Mark A. Bloomfield (243–261). Cambridge, MA: Ballinger.

———. 1996a. "Consumption Taxes: Some Fundamental Transition Issues." In *Frontiers of Tax Reform,* edited by Michael J. Boskin (123–150). Stanford: Hoover Institution Press.

———. 1996b. "Treatment of Financial Services under Income and Consumption Taxes." In *Economic Effects of Fundamental Tax Reform,* edited by Henry J. Aaron and William G. Gale (437–460). Washington, DC: Brookings Institution Press.

———. 2003. "Addressing the Transfer-Pricing Problem in an Origin-Basis X Tax." *International Tax and Public Finance* 10:591–610.

———. 2005. "A Tax System for the Twenty-First Century." In *Toward Fundamental Tax Reform,* edited by Alan J. Auerbach and Kevin A. Hassett (81–94). Washington, DC: AEI Press.

Bruce, Donald, and Douglas Holtz-Eakin. 1999. "Fundamental Tax Reform and Residential Housing." *Journal of Housing Economics* 8:249–271.

Burton, David, and Dan Mastromarco. 1997. "Emancipating America from the Income Tax: How a National Sales Tax Would Work." Policy Analysis No. 272. Washington, DC: Cato Institute.

Capozza, Dennis R., Richard K. Green, and Patric H. Hendershott. 1996. "Taxes, Mortgage Borrowing, and Residential Land Prices." In *Economic Effects of Fundamental Tax Reform,* edited by Henry J. Aaron and William G. Gale (171–198). Washington, DC: Brookings Institution Press.

Carasso, Adam, C. Eugene Steuerle, and Elizabeth Bell. 2005. "Making Tax Incentives for Homeownership More Equitable and Efficient." Discussion Paper No. 21. Washington, DC: Urban–Brookings Tax Policy Center.

Carroll, Christopher D. 2000. "Why Do the Rich Save So Much?" In *Does Atlas Shrug: The Economic Consequences of Taxing the Rich,* edited by Joel Slemrod (465–484). Cambridge, MA: Harvard University Press.

Carroll, Christopher D., and Andrew A. Samwick. 1998. "How Important Is Precautionary Saving?" *Review of Economics and Statistics* 80:410–419.

Chamley, Christophe. 1986. "Optimal Taxation of Capital Income in General Equilibrium with Infinite Lives." *Econometrica* 54:607–622.

———. 2001. "Capital Income Taxation, Wealth Distribution, and Borrowing Constraints." *Journal of Public Economics* 79:55–69.

Chari, V. V., Lawrence J. Christiano, and Patrick J. Kehoe. 1994. "Optimal Fiscal Policy in a Business Cycle Model." *Journal of Political Economy* 102:617–652.

Christian, Ernest, and Gary Robbins. 2002. "Stealth Approach to Tax Reform." *Washington Times,* November 1.

Cnossen, Sijbren. 2000. "Taxing Capital Income in the Nordic Countries: A Model for the European Union?" In *Taxing Capital in the European Union,* edited by Sijbren Cnossen (180–213). Oxford: Oxford University Press.

Coakley, Jerry, Farida Kulasi, and Ron Smith. 1998. "The Feldstein-Horioka Puzzle and Capital Mobility: A Review." *International Journal of Finance and Economics* 3:169–188.

Cremer, Helmuth, Pierre Pestieau, and Jean-Charles Rochet. 2003. "Capital Income Taxation when Inherited Wealth Is Not Observable." *Journal of Public Economics* 87:2475–2490.

Diamond, John, Craig Johnson, and George R. Zodrow. 1997. "Bequests, Saving, and Taxation." In *Proceedings of the Eighty-Ninth Annual Conference on Taxation.* Washington, DC: National Tax Association.

Diamond, John W., and George R. Zodrow. 2005. "Consumption Tax Reform and Corporate Equity and Housing Prices." Unpublished manuscript, Rice University.

Engen, Eric M., and William G. Gale. 1996. "The Effects of Fundamental Tax Reform on Saving." In *Economic Effects of Fundamental Tax Reform,* edited by Henry J. Aaron and William G. Gale (83–112). Washington, DC: Brookings Institution Press.

Engen, Eric M., Jane Gravelle, and Kent Smetters. 1997. "Dynamic Tax Models: Why They Do the Things They Do." *National Tax Journal* 50:657–682.

Erosa, Andres, and Martin Gervais. 2002. "Optimal Taxation in Life-Cycle Economies." *Journal of Economic Theory* 105:338–369.

Evans, Owen J. 1983. "Tax Policy, the Interest Elasticity of Saving, and Capital Accumulation: Numerical Analysis of Theoretical Models." *American Economic Review* 73:398–410.

Feenberg, Daniel R., Andrew W. Mitrusi, and James M. Poterba. 1997. "Distributional Effects of Adopting a National Retail Sales Tax." In *Tax*

Policy and the Economy, vol. 11, edited by James M. Poterba (49–89). Cambridge, MA: MIT Press.

Feld, Alan L. 1995. "Living with the Flat Tax." *National Tax Journal* 48(4): 603–617.

Feldstein, Martin. 1978. "The Welfare Cost of Capital Income Taxation." *Journal of Political Economy* 86:29–51.

Feldstein, Martin, and Phillipe Bacchetta. 1991. "National Saving and International Investment." In *National Saving and Economic Performance*, edited by B. Douglas Bernheim and John B. Shoven (201–220). Chicago: University of Chicago Press.

Feldstein, Martin, and Charles Horioka. 1980. "Domestic Savings and International Capital Flows." *Economic Journal* 90:314–329.

Fullerton, Don, and Diane Lim Rogers. 1993. *Who Bears the Lifetime Tax Burden?* Washington, DC: Brookings Institution Press.

———. 1996. "Lifetime Effects of Fundamental Tax Reform." In *Economic Effects of Fundamental Tax Reform,* edited by Henry J. Aaron and William G. Gale (321–347). Washington, DC: Brookings Institution Press.

Gale, William G. 2005. "Tax Reform Options in the Real World." In *Toward Fundamental Tax Reform,* edited by Alan J. Auerbach and Kevin A. Hassett (34–47). Washington, DC: AEI Press.

Gale, William G., and Janet Holtzblatt. 2002. "The Role of Administrative Issues in Tax Reform: Simplicity, Compliance, and Administration." In *United States Tax Reform in the 21st Century,* edited by George R. Zodrow and Peter Mieszkowski (179–214). Cambridge, UK: Cambridge University Press.

Gale, William G., and Joel Slemrod. 2001. *Rethinking Estate and Gift Taxation.* Washington, DC: Brookings Institution Press.

Garriga, Carlos. 2003. "Optimal Fiscal Policy in Overlapping Generations Models." Unpublished manuscript, Florida State University.

Genser, Bernd, forthcoming. "The Dual Income Tax: Implementation and Experience in European Countries," *Finanzarchiv.*

Gentry, William M., and R. Glenn Hubbard. 1997. "Distributional Implications of Introducing a Broad-Based Consumption Tax." In *Tax Policy and the Economy,* vol. 11, edited by James M. Poterba (1–47). Cambridge, MA: MIT Press.

Gillis, Malcolm, Peter Mieszkowski, and George R. Zodrow. 1996. "Indirect Consumption Taxes: Common Issues and Differences among the Alternative Approaches." *Tax Law Review* 51(Summer): 725–774.

Ginsburg, Martin D. 1995. "Life under a Personal Consumption Tax: Some Thoughts on Working, Saving, and Consuming in Nunn-Domenici's Tax World." *National Tax Journal* 68:585–602.

Gordon, Roger H. 1986. "Taxation of Investment and Savings in the World Economy." *American Economic Review* 76:1086–1102.

———. 1992. "Can Capital Income Taxes Survive in Open Economies?" *Journal of Finance* 47:1159–1180.

———. 2000. "Taxation of Capital Income vs. Labour Income: An Overview." In *Taxing Capital in the European Union,* edited by Sijbren Cnossen (15–45). Oxford: Oxford University Press.

Gordon, Roger H., and James R. Hines Jr. 2002. "International Taxation." In *Handbook of Public Economics,* vol. 4, edited by Alan J. Auerbach and Martin Feldstein (1935–96). Amsterdam: Elsevier.

Gordon, Roger H., and Joel Slemrod. 1988. "Do We Collect Any Revenue from Taxing Capital Income?" In *Tax Policy and the Economy*, vol. 2, edited by Lawrence H. Summers (89–130). Cambridge: National Bureau of Economic Research.

Gordon, Roger H., Laura Kalambokidis, and Joel Slemrod. 2004. "Do We Now Collect Any Revenue from Taxing Capital Income?" *Journal of Public Economics* 88:981–1009.

Gordon, Roger H., Laura Kalambokidis, Jeffrey Rohaly, and Joel Slemrod. Forthcoming. "Toward a Consumption Tax and Beyond." *American Economic Review, Papers and Proceedings* 94:161–165.

Goulder, Lawrence H., John B. Shoven, and John Whalley. 1983. "Domestic Tax Policy and the Foreign Sector: The Importance of Alternative Foreign Sector Formulations to Results from a General Equilibrium Tax Analysis Model." In *Behavioral Simulation Methods in Tax Policy Analysis,* edited by Martin Feldstein (333–368). Chicago: University of Chicago Press.

Graetz, Michael J. 2005. "A Fair and Balanced Tax System for the Twenty-First Century." In *Toward Fundamental Tax Reform,* edited by Alan J. Auerbach and Kevin A. Hassett (48–69). Washington, DC: AEI Press.

Gravelle, Jane G. 1994. *The Economic Effects of Taxing Capital Income.* Cambridge, MA: MIT Press.

———. 1995. "The Flat Tax and Other Proposals: Who Will Bear the Tax Burden?" Congressional Research Service Report for Congress, No. 95-1141E. Washington, DC: U.S. Library of Congress.

———. 1996. "The Flat Tax and Other Proposals: Effects on Housing." Congressional Research Service Report for Congress, No. 96-379E. Washington, DC: U.S. Library of Congress.

———. 2002. "Behavioral Responses to a Consumption Tax." In *United States Tax Reform in the 21st Century,* edited by George R. Zodrow and Peter Mieszkowski (25–54). Cambridge, UK: Cambridge University Press.

Grubert, Harry, and John Mutti. 1985. "The Taxation of Capital Income in an Open Economy: The Importance of Resident-Nonresident Tax Treatment." *Journal of Public Economics* 27:291–309.

Hall, Robert E. 2005. "Guidelines for Tax Reform: The Simple, Progressive Value-Added Consumption Tax." In *Toward Fundamental Tax Reform,* edited by Alan J. Auerbach and Kevin A. Hassett (70–80). Washington, DC: AEI Press.

Hall, Robert E., and Alvin Rabushka. 1983. *Low Tax, Simple Tax, Flat Tax.* New York: McGraw-Hill.

———. 1995. *The Flat Tax.* Stanford: Hoover Institution Press.

Harberger, Arnold C. 1995. "The ABCs of Corporate Tax Incidence: Insights into the Open-Economy Case." In *Tax Policy and Economic Growth,* edited by American Council for Capital Formation (51–73). Washington, DC: ACCF Center for Policy Research.

Hubbard, R. Glenn. 2002. "Capital Income Taxation in Tax Reform: Implications for Analysis of Distribution and Efficiency." In *United States Tax Reform in the 21st Century,* edited by George R. Zodrow and Peter Mieszkowski (89–108). Cambridge, UK: Cambridge University Press.

———. 2005a. "Economic Effects of the 2003 Partial Integration Proposal in the United States." *International Tax and Public Finance* 12:97–108.

———. 2005b. "Would a Consumption Tax Favor the Rich?" In *Toward Fundamental Tax Reform,* edited by Alan J. Auerbach and Kevin A. Hassett (81–94). Washington, DC: AEI Press.

Hubbard, R. Glenn, and Kenneth L. Judd. 1986. "Liquidity Constraints, Fiscal Policy, and Consumption." *Brookings Papers on Economic Activity* 2001(1): 1–50.

Hurst, Erik, Annamaria Lusardi, Arthur Kennickell, and Francisco Torralba. 2005. "Precautionary Savings and the Importance of Business Owners." NBER Working Paper No. 11731. Cambridge, MA: National Bureau of Economic Research.

Institute for Fiscal Studies (Meade Commission). 1978. *The Structure and Reform of Direct Taxation.* London: George Allen & Unwin.

Jones, Larry E., Rodolfo E. Manuelli, and Peter E. Rossi. 1993. "Optimal Taxation in Models of Endogenous Growth." *Journal of Political Economy* 101:485–517.

Jorgenson, Dale W., and Peter J. Wilcoxen. 2002. "The Economic Impact of Fundamental Tax Reform." In *United States Tax Reform in the 21st Century,* edited by George R. Zodrow and Peter Mieszkowski (55–88). Cambridge, UK: Cambridge University Press.

Judd, Kenneth L. 1985. "Redistributive Income in a Simple Perfect Foresight Model." *Journal of Public Economics* 28:59–83.

———. 1997. "The Optimal Tax Rate for Capital Income is Negative." NBER Working Paper No. 6004. Cambridge, MA: National Bureau of Economic Research.

———. 1999. "Optimal Taxation and Spending in General Competitive Growth Models." *Journal of Public Economics* 71:1–26.

———. 2001. "The Impact of Tax Reform in Modern Dynamic Economies." In *Transition Costs of Fundamental Tax Reform,* edited by Kevin A. Hassett and R. Glenn Hubbard (5–53). Washington, DC: AEI Press.

Kaplow, Louis. 2004. "On the Undesirability of Commodity Taxation Even When Income Taxation Is Not Optimal." Discussion Paper No. 470. Cambridge, MA: John M. Olin Center for Law and Economics.

King, Mervyn A. 1980. "Savings and Taxation." In *Public Policy and the Tax System,* edited by G. A. Hughes and G. M. Heal (1–35). London: Allen and Unwin.

Kleinbard, Edward D. 2007. "Designing an Income Tax on Capital." Chapter 4 in *Taxing Capital Income*, edited by Henry J. Aaron, Leonard E. Burman and C. Eugene Steverle (165–210). Urban Institute Press, Washington DC.

Kotlikoff, Laurence J. 1996. "Saving and Consumption Taxation: The Federal Retail Sales Tax Example." In *Frontiers of Tax Reform,* edited by Michael J. Boskin (160–80). Stanford: Hoover Institution Press.

———. 1998. "The A-K Model — Its Past, Present, and Future." NBER Working Paper No. 6684. Cambridge, MA: National Bureau of Economic Research.

Lawrence, Emily C. 1991. "Poverty and the Rate of Time Preference: Evidence from Panel Data." *Journal of Political Economy* 99(1): 54–77.

Lucas, Robert E. Jr. 1990. "Supply-Side Economics: An Analytical Review." *Oxford Economic Papers* 42:293–316.

Lyon, Andrew B., and Peter R. Merrill. 2001. "Asset Price Effects of Fundamental Tax Reform." In *Transition Costs of Fundamental Tax Reform,* edited by Kevin A. Hassett and R. Glenn Hubbard (58–91). Washington, DC: AEI Press.

McCaffery, Edward J. 2005. "A New Understanding of Tax." *Michigan Law Review* 103:807–938.

McLure, Charles E. Jr. 1987. *The Value-Added Tax: Key to Deficit Reduction?* Washington, DC: AEI Press.

McLure, Charles E. Jr., and George R. Zodrow. 1996. "A Hybrid Approach to the Direct Taxation of Consumption." In *Frontiers of Tax Reform,* edited by Michael J. Boskin (70–90). Stanford: Hoover Institution Press.

McLure, Charles E. Jr., Jack Mutti, Victor Thuronyi, and George R. Zodrow. 1990. *The Taxation of Income from Business and Capital in Colombia: Fiscal Reform in the Developing World.* Durham, NC: Duke University Press.

Mieszkowski, Peter, and Michael G. Palumbo. 2002. "Distributive Analysis of Fundamental Tax Reform." In *United States Tax Reform in the 21st Century,* edited by George R. Zodrow and Peter Mieszkowski (140–178). Cambridge, UK: Cambridge University Press.

Milesi-Ferretti, Gian M., and Nouriel Roubini. 1998. "On the Taxation of Human and Physical Capital in Models of Endogenous Growth." *Journal of Public Economics* 70:237–254.

Murray, Matthew N. 1997. "Would Tax Evasion and Tax Avoidance Undermine a National Retail Sales Tax?" *National Tax Journal* 50:167–182.

Naito, Hisahiro. 1999. "Re-Examination of Uniform Commodity Taxes under a Nonlinear Income Tax System and Its Implication for Production Efficiency." *Journal of Public Economics* 71:165–188.

Nielsen, Soren Bo, and Peter Birch Sorensen. 1994. "On the Optimality of the Nordic System of Dual Income Taxation." *Journal of Public Economics* 63:311–329.

Pearlman, Ronald A. 1996. "Transition Issues in Moving to a Consumption Tax: A Tax Lawyer's Perspective." In *Economic Effects of Fundamental Tax Reform,* edited by Henry J. Aaron and William G. Gale (393–427). Washington, DC: Brookings Institution Press.

Piketty, Thomas, and Emmanuel Saez. 2003. "Income Inequality in the United States, 1913–1998." *Quarterly Journal of Economics* 118:1–39.

Prescott, Edward C. 2005. "The Elasticity of Labor Supply and the Consequences for Tax Policy." In *Toward Fundamental Tax Reform,* edited by Alan J. Auerbach and Kevin A. Hassett (123–134). Washington, DC: AEI Press.

Razin, Assaf, and Efraim Sadka. 1991. "International Tax Competition and Gains from Tax Harmonization." *Economics Letters* 37:69–76.

Roin, Julie A. 2007. "Can Income from Capital Be Taxed? An International Perspective." Chapter 5 in *Taxing Captial Income*, edited by Henry J. Aaron, Leonard E. Burman and C. Eugene Steverle (211–240). Urban Institute Press, Washington DC.

Roubini, Nouriel, and Gian Milesi-Ferretti. 1998. "On the Taxation of Human and Physical Capital in Models of Endogenous Growth." *Journal of Public Economics* 70:237–254.

Saez, Emmanuel. 2002. "The Desirability of Commodity Taxation under Nonlinear Income Taxation and Heterogeneous Tastes." *Journal of Public Economics* 83:217–230.

Saez, Emmanuel. 2004. "Direct or Indirect Tax Instruments for Redistribution: Short-Run versus Long-Run." *Journal of Public Economics* 88:503–18.

Samwick, Andrew A. 1998. "Tax Reform and Target Saving." *National Tax Journal* 51:621–635.

Sarkar, Shounak, and George R. Zodrow. 1993. "Transitional Issues in Moving to a Direct Consumption Tax." *National Tax Journal* 46:359–376.

Schler, Michael L. and Joseph Bankman. 2007. "Tax Planning Under the Flat Tax." Chapter 6 in *Taxing Capital Income*, edited by Henry J. Aaron, Leonard E. Burman and C. Eugene Steverle (245–284). Urban Institute Press, Washington DC.

Seidman, Laurence S. 1983. "Taxes in a Life Cycle Growth Model with Bequests and Inheritances." *American Economic Review* 73:437–441.

Shakow, David J. 1986. "Taxation without Realization: A Proposal for Accrual Taxation." *University of Pennsylvania Law Review* 134:1111–1205.

Shaviro, Daniel. 2000. *When Rules Change: An Economic and Political Analysis of Transition Relief and Retroactivity.* Chicago: University of Chicago Press.

———. 2004. "Replacing the Income Tax with a Progressive Consumption Tax." *Tax Notes* 102 (April 5): 91–162.

Slemrod, Joel. 1996. "Which Is the Simplest Tax System of Them All?" In *Economic Effects of Fundamental Tax Reform,* edited by Henry J. Aaron and William G. Gale (355–384). Washington, DC: Brookings Institution Press.

———. 2005. "My Beautiful Tax Reform." In *Toward Fundamental Tax Reform,* edited by Alan J. Auerbach and Kevin A. Hassett (135–148). Washington, DC: AEI Press.

———. 2007. "Does the United States Tax Capital Income." Chapter 1 in *Taxing Capital Income*, edited by Henry J. Aaron, Leonard E. Burman and C. Eugene Steverle (3–30). Urban Institute Press, Washington DC.

Sorensen, Peter Birch. 1994. "From a Global Income Tax to the Dual Income Tax: Recent Reforms in the Nordic Countries." *International Tax and Public Finance* 1:57–79.

Starrett, David A. 1988. "Effects of Taxes on Saving." In *Uneasy Compromise: Problems of a Hybrid Income-Consumption Tax,* edited by Henry J. Aaron,

Harvey Galper, and Joseph Pechman (237–68). Washington, DC: Brookings Institution.

Steuerle, Eugene C. 2004. *Contemporary U.S. Tax Policy.* Washington, DC: Urban Institute Press.

Stiglitz, Joseph E. 1982. "Self-Selection and Pareto Efficient Taxation." *Journal of Public Economics* 17:213–240.

Stokey, Nancy L., and Sergio Rebelo. 1995. "Growth Effects of Flat-Rate Taxes." *Journal of Political Economy* 103:519–550.

Summers, Lawrence H. 1981. "Capital Taxation and Accumulation in a Life Cycle Growth Model." *American Economic Review* 74:533–544.

———. 1988. "Comment." In *Uneasy Compromise: Problems of a Hybrid Income-Consumption Tax,* edited by Henry J. Aaron, Harvey Galper, and Joseph A. Pechman (259–265). Washington, DC: The Brookings Institution.

Toder, Eric and Kim Rueben. 2007. "Should we Eliminate Taxation of Capital Income." Chapter 3 in *Taxing Capital Income*, edited by Henry J. Aaron, Leonard E. Burman and C. Eugene Steverle (89–142). Urban Institute Press, Washington DC.

U.S. Department of the Treasury. 1977. *Blueprints for Basic Tax Reform.* Washington, DC: U.S. Government Printing Office.

———. 1992. *Integration of the Individual and Corporate Tax Systems: Taxing Business Income Once.* Washington, DC: U.S. Government Printing Office.

Varian, Hal. 1980. "Redistributive Taxation as Social Insurance." *Journal of Public Economics* 14:49–68.

Weidenbaum, Murray. 1996. "The Nunn-Domenici USA Tax: Analysis and Comparisons." In *Frontiers of Tax Reform,* edited by Michael J. Boskin (54–69). Stanford: Hoover Institution Press.

Weisbach, David A. 2000. "Ironing Out the Flat Tax." *Stanford Law Review* 52:599–664.

———. 2003. "Fundamental Tax Reform: Does the X-tax Mark the Spot?" *SMU Law Review* 56:201–238.

———. 2004. "The Non-Taxation of Risk." *New York University Tax Review* 58:1–57.

Weisbach, David A., and Joseph Bankman. 2005. "The Superiority of a Consumption Tax over an Income Tax." Unpublished manuscript, University of Chicago Law School and Stanford Law School.

Zodrow, George R. 1992. "Grandfather Rules and the Theory of Optimal Tax Reform." *Journal of Public Economics* 49:163–190.

———. 1997. "On the Transition to Indirect or Direct Consumption-Based Taxation." In *Tax Conversations: A Guide to the Key Issues in the Tax Reform Debate,* edited by Richard Krever (27–59). London: Kluwer Law International.

———. 2002. "Transitional Issues in the Implementation of a Flat Tax or a National Retail Sales Tax." In *United States Tax Reform in the 21st Century,* edited by George R. Zodrow and Peter Mieszkowski (245–283). Cambridge, UK: Cambridge University Press.

———. 2003. "Tax Competition and Tax Coordination in the European Union." *International Tax and Public Finance* 10:651–671.

———. 2006. "Capital Mobility and Source-Based Taxation of Capital Income in Small Open Economies." *International Tax and Public Finance* 13: 269–294.

Zodrow, George R., and Charles E. McLure Jr. 1991. "Implementing Direct Consumption Taxes in Developing Countries." *Tax Law Review* 46(Summer):407–487.

Zodrow, George R., and Peter Mieszkowski. 2002a. "The Fundamental Question in Fundamental Tax Reform." In *United States Tax Reform in the 21st Century,* edited by George R. Zodrow and Peter Mieszkowski (1–24). Cambridge, UK: Cambridge University Press.

Chapter 6

A Hybrid Consumption-Based Direct Tax Proposed for Bolivia*

Charles E. McLure, Jr.[†] and George R. Zodrow[‡]

[†]*Hoover Institution, Stanford, CA 94305-6010, USA*
[‡]*Rice University, Houston, TX 77005, USA*

In 1994 the authors designed a consumption-based direct tax for the government of Bolivia. The proposal combined yield exemption treatment (exemption of interest income and no deduction for interest expense) of individuals with consumed income tax treatment (taxation or deduction of the net proceeds of borrowing and lending, as well as interest income and expense) of business. This article explains why taxation based on cash flow has administrative and economic advantages over a conventional income tax and why the hybrid system proposed is preferable to either pure form of consumption-based tax.

Keywords: consumption tax; cash-flow tax

*This chapter is reproduced from *International Tax and Public Financer,* **3**(1), 97–112, 1996.

1. Introduction

During 1994 the government of Bolivia was under pressure from the International Monetary Fund to introduce a corporate income tax to increase its tax revenues. (In 1986, Bolivia had repealed its previous income tax, which did not yield significant revenue due to evasion, and replaced it with a tax on the net assets of businesses; this tax has suffered from similar problems.) Rather than simply proposing adoption of a conventional income tax, President Gonzalo Sanchez de Lozada expressed interest in a cash-flow tax on business, which he saw as more conducive to saving and investment. We assisted the government in designing such a tax, coupled with a complementary tax on the labor income of individuals. (Professor Peter Byrne of the Harvard International Tax Program prepared a draft law based on that design, as well as assisting us with legal issues during the design stage.) Together these can be seen as constituting a system of direct taxation of consumption.

This effort ultimately came to naught. Because of concern that the United States Internal Revenue Service would not allow foreign tax credits for the proposed business cash-flow tax, the government of Bolivia eventually proposed (and the Congress adopted) a conventional income tax (IT). Even so, the experience was beneficial, as it provided insights into the relative advantages of various forms of direct consumption-based taxation. This paper reports on the lessons gained from that experience, which is relevant for advanced countries, as well as less developed ones.[1] Since much of what follows summarizes previous literature, it is intentionally brief; while nonspecialists may find it incomplete, it contains ample references.

In prior work for the government of Colombia, we considered two alternative ways of imposing a direct consumption-based tax; both allow immediate deductions (expensing) for all nonfinancial expenditures, but they differ in their treatment of debt and interest; these differences are described in detail below (see McLure, Mutti, Thuronyi, and Zodrow, 1990; McLure and Zodrow, 1990; Zodrow and McLure, 1991). All previous proposals for direct consumption taxes, including ours, have been based on the (perhaps implicit) assumption that debt and interest should

[1] Indeed, we have proposed a variant of the hybrid consumption tax developed in Bolivia for enactment in the United States. See McLure and Zodrow (forthcoming).

be treated symmetrically under the business and individual parts of such a system if the parts were to mesh in the sense of achieving desirable economic results and avoiding complexity and opportunities for evasion or avoidance. However, in the course of reexamining these two options while designing a tax reform plan for Bolivia, we were struck by the fact that most of the critical relative advantages of one approach are concentrated in the business component of the tax, while the relative advantages of the other approach were most important for the individual level tax. This led us to propose that the Bolivian government consider a "hybrid consumption tax" that combines the best features of the two approaches. We believe that the hybrid is superior to either pure form of direct consumption tax because it avoids problems peculiar to one or the other of the two approaches, without introducing insurmountable new problems.

Section 2 briefly contrasts the two pure forms of consumption-based tax, the hybrid consumption-based tax proposed to the government of Bolivia, and a conventional income tax. Section 3 summarizes the benefits of a consumption-based direct tax, especially in the virtually unique situation of present-day Bolivia. Section 4 indicates how the hybrid version overcomes problems that plague the pure forms of direct consumption-based tax and describes how we would deal with problems encountered under our hybrid approach. In what follows we use the term *yield exemption tax* (YET) to describe one of the pure forms of consumption-based tax and the term *consumed income tax* (CIT) to describe the other; we call the tax we proposed in Bolivia the *hybrid consumption tax* (HCT).

2. Competing Alternatives

Consumption-based direct taxation, in its various forms, is perhaps most easily understood by contrasting it with a conventional income tax. This also allows clarification of the differences among the various forms of consumption-based taxes.

2.1. *Real transactions*

Under the conventional income tax, business taxpayers maintain depreciation accounts for depreciable assets and use inventory accounts to calculate the cost of goods sold. By comparison, under a consumption-based direct tax, an immediate deduction (expensing) is allowed for the full amount of all legitimate business-related purchases.

2.2. *Debt and interest*

Whereas all consumption-based taxes treat "real" activities in the same way, each differs from the income tax in unique ways in its treatment of financial transactions.[2] Under an income tax, interest expense is deductible and interest income is taxable; by comparison, principal transactions in debt have no tax consequences.

In contrast, the CIT approach to the direct taxation of consumption provides cash-flow treatment of borrowing and lending (CFTBL). Interest income and expense are treated as under the income tax.[3] But, unlike with the income tax, taxpayers must include the proceeds of borrowing in the base of the CIT and can deduct repayments of debt principal. Analogously, taxpayers engaged in lending, including financial institutions, are allowed to deduct the principal of amounts loaned, and repayments of principal received are included in the tax base.

By comparison, the yield exemption tax is much simpler, as it ignores both principal and interest.[4] Indeed in our work in Colombia we called it the *simplified alternative tax* to emphasize its simplicity.

---

[2] An exception to this general statement is the *S-based tax* on distributions from businesses to individuals examined by the Meade Commission (see Institute for Fiscal Studies, 1978). We do not discuss that approach, which has been given little consideration in either the academic literature or policy circles.

[3] Examples of CIT proposals include the cash-flow alternative described in U.S. Treasury Department (1977), the R + *F*-based tax (on *real plus financial transactions)* proposed by the Meade Commission (Institute for Fiscal Studies, 1978), and the proposal in Aaron and Galper (1985).

[4] Examples of YET proposals include the yield exemption alternative described in U.S. Treasury Department (1977), the R-based tax (on "real" transactions) proposed by the Meade Commission (Institute Jar Fiscal Studies, 1978), the *flat taxes* proposed by Hall and Rabushka (1995) and by U.S. House Majority Leader Armey, the *X-tax* proposed by Bradford (1986), and the *simplified alternative tax* proposed for Colombia in McLure, Mutti, Thuronyi, and Zodrow (1990).

Table 6.1.
Treatment of Depreciable Assets, Inventories, Debt, and Interest Under an Income Tax and Three Consumption Tax Schemes

		Alternative Forms of Consumption-Based Direct Tix		
	Income Tax (IT)	Tax on Consumed Income (CIT)	Yield Exemption Tax (YET)	Hybrid Consumption Tax (HCT)
Depreciable assets	Depreciation allowances	Expensing	Expensing	Expensing
Additions to inventory	Inventory accounting	Expensing	Expensing	Expensing
Receipt of principal (by borrowers or lenders)	Exempt	Taxable	Exempt	Business: taxable Individual: exempt
Disbursement of principal (by lenders or borrowers)	Exempt	Deductible	Nondeductible	Business: deductible Individual: nondeductible
Interest income	Taxable	Taxable	Exempt	Business: taxable Individuals: exempt
Interest expense	Deductible	Deductible	Nondeductible	Business: deductible Individuals: nondeductible

The above descriptions of the treatment of debt and interest do not distinguish between businesses and individuals; they apply equally to financial transactions of both. The critical feature of the hybrid consumption tax we developed in our work in Bolivia is that it makes such a distinction. Specifically, it applies the CFTBL characteristic of the CIT to the debt and interest of businesses, but YET treatment to the debt and interest of individuals.[5] Table 6.1 describes the characteristics of the four basic tax systems.

[5]The Unlimited Savings Allowance (USA) Tax System (1995) proposed by U.S. Senators Nunn and Dominici can be seen as a form of hybrid that crosses the two pure forms of

3. Advantages of Consumption-Based Taxation

Economists commonly emphasize the economic benefits of consumption-based taxation.[6] By comparison, we have emphasized that consumption-based taxation is inherently simpler than income taxation (see McLure, 1988; McLure and Zodrow, 1990).[7]

3.1. *Economic advantages*

A standard theorem in the public finance literature is that the marginal effective tax rate (METR) on income from capital under a consumption-based tax is zero.[8] In contrast, the marginal effective tax rate on income from equity-financed investment under an income tax (ignoring the effects of inflation and assuming that depreciation allowances are based on economic depreciation) reflects the combined effect of business taxation at the statutory rate and individual level taxation of dividends and capital gains; by comparison, because interest payments are deductible to the firm, the METR on debt-financed investment reflects only taxation at the statutory individual tax rate applied to interest income.[9] Unless significant tax preferences cause taxable income to be well below economic income, the marginal effective tax rate on the returns to saving and investment is considerably greater under the income tax than the zero rate implied by a direct consumption tax. Thus, an income tax creates a tax bias

---

consumption taxation in the opposite way, applying YET treatment to businesses and CIT treatment to individuals. Since this approach postdates our work in Bolivia and the preparation of this paper, it is not discussed here. It appears, however, that many of the problems we were trying to avoid with the HCT plague the USA Tax.

[6] For recent discussions of these argumerts, see Zodrow and McLure (1991), Zodrow (forthcoming), and Jorgenson (forthcoming).

[7] The simplicity advantages of direct consumption taxes have also been emphasized by Bradford (1986). For contrasting views, see Mintz and Seade (1991), Tait (1992), and Shome and Schutte (1993).

[8] The METR is the percentage by which tax reduces the rate of return on an investment; it can exceed 100 percent, or it can be negative — which implies that "taxation" actually produces a subsidy. See King and Fullerton (1984) for a description of the METR methodology.

[9] See Zodrow and McLure (1991) for numerical examples illustrating these points.

against saving, while a consumption-based tax is neutral between current and future consumption.[10]

Another complicating factor arises because the tax base is smaller under a consumption-based tax than under the income tax, which implies that rates must be higher to raise a given amount of revenue. This, in turn, implies that the disincentive for work effort, relative to current consumption, is somewhat greater under the consumption-based tax than under the IT. But a consumption tax distorts the tradeoff between current labor and future consumption less than an income tax. The net effect on economic welfare is theoretically ambiguous and depends on the values of parameters about which there is little evidence.[11] Nevertheless, many economic models suggest that welfare would be higher under the more nearly neutral consumption-based tax (see Jorgenson, forthcoming).

Because the METR under consumption-based taxation is zero, it is sometimes thought that such a tax cannot add much to the progressivity of the tax system. This is not necessarily true. First, a direct consumption-based tax can be made progressive through the use of an appropriately graduated rate structure at the individual level. Second, in many countries income tax preferences, combined with a wide variety of tax-sheltering devices, create METRs that are negative; these commonly benefit the wealthy disproportionately. By comparison, under a properly designed consumption-based tax, all taxpayers are subject to a marginal effective tax rate of zero on capital income and inframarginal returns (economic profits) are subject to tax.

3.2. *Simplicity*

Consumption-based taxation is inherently simpler than the income tax for three reasons. First, *inflation* distorts the measurement of income under

[10] This result is often interpreted as implying that saving, investment, and economic growth would be greater under a consumption-based tax than under an income tax; however, the magnitudes (and even the signs) of these effects are not clear on either theoretical or empirical grounds. Bar an early exposition of this point, see Feldstein (1978). For a discussion of more recent theoretical and empirical results, see Zodrow (forthcoming) and the references cited therein.

[11] See King (1980) and Bradford (1980a, 1980b) or, for a simplified exposition, McLure (1980).

the income tax. By comparison, measurement of the tax base of a consumption-based tax is immune to inflation (except that occurring during the year of acquisition of an asset or a liability, a problem we ignore in what follows). Consider the case of real assets: tax is levied on purely inflationary capital gains; the cost of depreciable assets cannot be recovered tax-free in a system that bases depreciation allowances on historical costs, with no adjustment for inflation; and deductions for the cost of goods sold from inventories are less than the real cost of the goods, except (approximately) in the case of last-in, first-out inventory accounting.[12] Because of the use of expensing under the consumption-based tax, inflation has no opportunity to erode the value of depreciation and additions to inventory. Because capital gains are exempt (under the YET) or have no basis (under the CIT), there can be no taxation of purely inflationary capital gains.

Real interest income and expense are overstated in a system that taxes nominal interest income and allows a deduction for nominal interest expense. The YET avoids this problem by exempting interest income and allowing no deduction for interest expense. The CIT treats interest income and expense as under the income tax, but includes the value of debt transactions in the tax base. The resulting overstatement of interest income or expense is offset by the erosion of the real principal amount of debt.[13]

The avoidance of complex *timing issues* is the second major simplicity advantage of consumption-based taxation. Under an income tax, it is necessary to know when to recognize income for tax purposes and when to allow deductions. These questions must be answered in such a way that taxable income reflects economic income accurately, if equity and economic neutrality are to be achieved. Unfortunately, a multitude of timing

---

[12] LIFO is sometimes advocated as a substitute for indexed FIFO (first-in, first-out) inventory accounting. In fact, LIFO eliminates the effects of shifts in relative prices, as well as those of inflation. For a more complete discussion of the need for inflation adjustment under an income tax and of several ways to achieve it, see McLure, Mutti, Thuronyi, and Zodrow (1990, Ch. 7).

[13] For a comparison of the "old" view of the need for integration to reduce the double taxation of income from equity-financed investment (assumed in the text) and the "new" view, which argues that double taxation is not important for investment financed with retained earnings, see Zodrow (1991).

issues are either inherently very difficult to answer (such as economic depreciation and the time pattern of income earned in a construction project extending over several years), administratively difficult (original issue discount and capitalization of costs, including those of inventories), or both. Consumption-based taxes, being based on annual cash flow, avoid timing issues.

Finally, *double taxation of dividends* occurs under an income tax, in the absence of explicit measures designed to "integrate" the individual and business level taxes. Whereas double taxation is unfair and distorts the financial choices of firms, integration is complex, even if limited to dividends (see McLure, 1979; U.S. Department of the Treasury, 1992). This problem is avoided under a consumption-based tax; the YET exempts dividends at the individual level, and the same result is effectively achieved under the CIT, which only taxes income that is consumed.

3.3. *Relating the HCT to the VAT*

These simplifications are formidable advantages of any consumption-based tax, relative to the IT; the next section compares the complexity/simplicity of the various types of consumption-based taxes in detail. Before leaving the present general discussion of the simplicity advantages of direct consumption-based taxation, it is useful to consider another issue, the possibility of relating the base of a consumption-based direct tax to that of the value added tax (VAT).

Although consumption-based "direct" taxes are similar in appearance to the conventional income tax, they are actually more closely related to the "indirect" value added tax in both concept and structure.[14] As under the VAT, both receipts and expenditures are reported on a cash-flow basis; that is, there are no deductions for depreciation and no inventory accounting.

[14] Although the terms in quotation marks are quite slippery and hard to define, the following characterizations seem reasonable. An indirect tax is based on transactions and is borne by individuals indirectly in the form of higher prices for consumer goods or lower factor returns. A direct tax is assessed directly on individuals and thus can be personalized to reflect differences in individual circumstances through the use of deductions, exemptions, and progressive marginal tax rates as desired.

Thus it would be possible to employ many of the same (or similar) accounting concepts (such as taxable receipts and creditable/deductible expenditures) and similar declarations under both taxes.[15] Leaving aside for the moment the treatment of international trade, the primary differences under the YET version of consumption-based taxation are (1) the deduction of labor costs and (2) the deduction of land purchases and the inclusion of the proceeds of land sales. In the case of the CIT and the HCT there would be two additional adjustments: (3) the inclusion of interest income, repayments of amounts loaned, and the proceeds of borrowing, and (4) the deduction of interest expense, amounts loaned, and repayments of amounts borrowed. While the YET is clearly the easiest to relate to the VAT, our HCT utilizes the CIT approach at the business level because the YET suffers from the problems to be described in the next section.

International trade deserves special attention. Under the VAT, as commonly applied, imports are taxed and exports are zero rated. (That is, no tax is collected on exports, but credit is allowed for VAT paid by exporters on their purchases.) This application of *border-tax adjustments* (taxation of imports and rebate of tax on exports) produces a *destination-principle* tax, in which goods enter international trade tax-free and taxation is based on consumption, instead of production. The alternative is to employ the *origin principle;* under it, value added before the import stage is exempt and exports are taxed. Thus taxation is based on production.

For several reasons we have assumed that a cash-flow tax would be an origin-based tax. First, the General Agreement on Tariffs and Trade allows border tax adjustments only for indirect taxes. While it is unclear exactly what this means, it is unlikely that a cash-flow tax would be judged to be an indirect tax.[16] Second, and perhaps as important, we think it unlikely that Bolivia would want to relinquish revenues from application of the cash flow tax to exports in exchange for revenues from cash flow taxation of imports.

[15] Under the commonly applied *credit method,* VAT is levied on all sales and businesses are allowed a credit for all purchases. Under the *subtraction method* VAT, tax is levied on the difference between business purchases and sales.

[16] For an attempt to read the tea leaves of history to determine what the framers of GATT meant by this terminology, see Floyd (1973) and Hufbauer (1995).

Table 6.2.
Calculation of Consumption-based Tax, from VAT Base

Taxable Receipts	Deductible Expenditures
Receipts subject to VAT, including zero-rated goods such as exports	Expenditures generating VAT credits, including imported inputs
+ Any exempt sales	+ Deductible labor costs
+ Proceeds of land sales	+ Land purchases
= Receipts taxable under YET	= Deductible expenditures under YET
+ Amounts borrowed	+ Repayments of amounts borrowed
+ Repayments of amounts loaned	+ Amounts loaned
+ Interest income	+ Interest expense
= Receipts taxable under CIT and HCT	= Deductible expenditures under CIT and HCT

If it were going to do that, it might better simply raise the VAT rate. Thus, we have assumed that in calculating liability for the consumption-based tax, exports would be added to receipts subject to VAT, imports would be exempt, and imported business inputs would be deductible.

The base of the three consumption-based taxes can be calculated by adjusting the base of the VAT, as shown in Table 6.2. This makes it possible to combine reporting of both taxes on one form. Thus compliance with one of these taxes (and audit of one) would greatly facilitate compliance with (and audit of) the other.

3.4. *The unique case of Bolivia*

Of all the countries of the world, Bolivia in 1994–1995 offered perhaps the best opportunity to enact a consumption-based tax. As in virtually all developing countries, the simplicity and economic advantages of the consumption-based tax — especially the fact that it does not penalize saving and investment, as does an income tax — are extremely important. Bolivia lacks the administrative capacity to implement an income tax effectively, and it needs the saving and investment that an income tax would discourage. But the Bolivia of 1994–1995 was unique in four important respects.

First, initial interest in a cash-flow tax came directly from the president, a successful ex-businessman who is convinced of the merits of the tax and enjoys considerable popular support; it did not arise from the bowels of the Finance Ministry or from a report submitted by foreign advisers. Thus the chances of enactment were probably considerably better than usual.

Second, because Bolivia had no corporate income tax, there was no concern that enactment of the consumption-based direct tax would reduce the progressivity of the tax system, as is often the case; indeed, by taxing economic rents, it probably would have increased progressivity.

Third, the base of the existing VAT in Bolivia is extremely comprehensive. As a result, the similarities between the base of the VAT and base of the proposed HCT are as great or greater than they would be in virtually any country in the Third World. Thus the argument made above — that administration of and compliance with the two taxes can largely be accomplished simultaneously — was particularly compelling in the case of Bolivia.[17] Moreover, this feature implies that it would have been possible to implement the HCT much more quickly than a new IT.[18]

Finally, because there was no income tax, the transition problems that plague most proposals to substitute a consumption-based tax for the income tax would be much less serious than usual.

Against all these advantages must be placed a problem that plagues all attempts to enact a consumption-based direct tax — the risk that the U.S. government would not allow foreign tax credits for such a tax. Of course,

---

[17] One reviewer of an earlier draft of this paper has asked how Bolivia has been able to administer a comprehensive VAT, given that it has been unable to administer its other taxes well. Two responses seem appropriate. First, we do not claim that Bolivia has administered its VAT well — only that it could administer the combination of the VAT and HCT better than the combination of the VAT and IT. Second, it is generally not as difficult to administer a comprehensive VAT as to administer one shot through with exemptions.

[18] One reviewer has asked why Bolivia should enact a consumption-based direct tax, instead of simply raising the rate of its VAT, and has identified two possible reasons — "to engineer a more progressive tax system and, by means of the foreign tax credit, to capture some of the tax revenues being sent abroad by multinationals." Because the individual income tax that would have accompanied the HCT accommodates exemptions and graduated rates, it is more progressive than the VAT. Also, it is irresponsible to "leave money on the table," by not including in the tax system a component that would be eligible for the foreign tax credit (FTC). McLure and Zodrow (1996) explain why consumption-based direct taxes should be eligible for the FTC.

this risk, which proved to be dispositive in the decision not to propose the HCT, is not unique to Bolivia.

4. Advantages of the Hybrid Consumption Tax

For the reasons presented below, we believe that the HCT is superior to either the "pure" CIT or the "pure" YET from the standpoint of ease of administration and compliance.[19] Such considerations are particularly important in developing countries in which the skills needed for effective administration and successful compliance are scarce; accordingly, we believe that the HCT is especially appropriate for implementation as the system of direct taxation in developing countries. Nevertheless, the hybrid approach does create some problems related to the interlace between the business and individual level taxes. These are also explored below.

4.1. *The business-level tax*

Our proposal calls for the use of CFTBL characteristic of the CIT at the business level. Opponents of the CIT inevitably note the complexity and unfamiliarity of CFTBL. However, this complexity, as well as the costs of adapting to CFTBL, would be much less of a problem for businesses than for individuals; many firms maintain comprehensive (and commonly computerized) records detailing all aspects of their borrowing and lending transactions. (Actually, all that is needed is comparative balance sheets showing year-to-year changes in net indebtedness.) At the same time, applying CFTBL at the business level avoids the following important problems that would arise if loans were ignored at the business level, as under the YET.

4.1.1. *Exemption of financial intermediation*

Applying YET treatment to businesses would imply that the interest-rate spread earned by financial institutions would be entirely exempt from tax.[20] Such treatment would probably be perceived to be unfair and thus

---

[19]This section draws heavily on a more detailed presentation of the advantages of the HCT presented in McLure and Zodrow (forthcoming).

[20]The same problem occurs under a VAT (see Hoffman, Poddar, and Whalley, 1987).

would be highly unpopular. Although a separate tax could be assessed on financial institutions under a YET, this would add complexity and possibly distort the allocation of resources across financial and nonfinancial activities. In marked contrast, the interest-rate spread earned by financial institutions is taxed automatically under CFTBL.

4.1.2. *Treatment of firms with negative cash flow*

Mary firms would experience negative cash flow (NCF) under a consumption-based business tax, since such a tax allows expensing (rather than deductions for economic depreciation). In principle, NCFs pose no problems, as long as they can be refunded or carried forward with nominal interest to reduce future tax liability or carried back to previous years. However, in practice, governments around the world have been very reluctant to allow either refunds or carryforward with interest. Unfortunately, the denial of refunds and carryforward with interest on NCFs creates serious problems for a consumption-based business tax; in particular, it increases the effective tax rate (moving the tax system in the direction of income taxation) and creates artificial incentives for mergers, takeovers, buyouts, and attempts to transfer NCFs among firms.

Even if carryforward of NCFs with interest were allowed, the choice of the appropriate interest rate would be controversial, and it seems likely that the rate used would be less than the opportunity cost of funds for most if not all firms. Thus, the problems noted above would still exist, although they would be less important.

An important advantage of CFTBL is that the inclusion of loan proceeds in the tax base for debt-financed investment would significantly reduce the likelihood that firms would be in an NCF position. Thus, all the problems noted above would be much less likely to occur than under the YET approach, which ignores loan transactions.

4.1.3. *Revenue consequences*

A related problem with the absence of CFTBL under the YET is that government revenues would be lower during the first few years following its enactment than would be the case under the HCT. Although these revenue shortfalls would be recouped in future years, the implied temporary increase in the budget deficit might cause significant financial, economic, and political problems during the first few critical years following a consumption tax reform.

4.1.4. *Tax avoidance opportunities*

An equally serious problem with the YET approach is that it creates a variety of potentially serious opportunities tax avoidance. The relevant techniques, outlined below, would take advantage of the asymmetry implied by the facts that (1) under the YET, interest income is exempt while other receipts are taxable and interest expense is nondeductible while other expenses are deductible, and (2) other entities not subject to the YET are typically indifferent between interest income and other receipts and between interest expense and other expenses. These entities include foreign firms, tax-exempt institutions (to the extent that their noninterest income would not be subject to a tax on unrelated business income) and, in some cases, individuals subject to the individual component of the YET. By comparison, these problems do not arise under CFTBL, which implies symmetric treatment of all these items of income and expense.

These avoidance techniques fell into two general categories and can be illustrated using the following examples, in which Firm A is subject to the YET, while Entity B is not. In the first case, Firm A sells its output to Entity B and arranges for a reduced price in exchange for either (1) an above-market interest rate on a loan that it extends to B (such as an installment sale or other type of seller financing), or (2) a below-market interest rate on a loan from B to A. Firm A clearly benefits from lower taxable receipts, while Entity B is indifferent to this manipulation.[21]

[21] If B were a foreign firm subject to income taxation, the lower deductions for inputs purchased from A would be offset by either (1) higher interest deductions on the loan from A, or (2) lower interest income on the loan to A. If B is a tax-exempt institution, none of the differences in prices has any tax consequences. Note also the first scheme applies for consumer sales to individuals, who would be indifferent to lower sales prices coupled with higher interest rates (say, on installment sales) that were equivalent in present value terms.

In the second general category of avoidance schemes, Firm A arranges to pay higher prices on its purchases from Entity B in exchange for either (1) a lower interest rate on a loan from B to A, or (2) a higher interest rate on a loan from A to B. In this case, Firm A benefits because its deductions for inputs are higher, while the differences in interest payments have no effect on tax liability; at the same time, Entity B is again indifferent to the price manipulation.[22]

Such avoidance techniques would be difficult to police. In principle, it would be possible to combat such abuses through the use of measures such as interest-rate ceilings and floors or requirements that loans between parties that are engaged in trade with each other be treated on a cash-flow basis. But such methods involve significant complexities. By comparison, none of these issues arise under CFTBL, which applies uniform treatment to interest income and other receipts and to interest expense and other deductions.

The need to distinguish between payment of deductible interest and payment of nondeductible dividends is a major disadvantage of applying CFTBL to businesses. This problem does not arise under the YET approach, since neither interest nor dividends is deductible. Nevertheless, on balance, the CIT approach to the taxation of business seems to be significantly superior to the YET approach on administrative grounds.

4.2. *The individual level tax*

By comparison, CFTBL would be difficult to apply at the individual level, and the additional complexity would be costly in the sense that it would in many cases be borne by individuals who are relatively less capable than most firms in dealing with tax complexity. Accordingly, we believe that the YET is preferable to the CIT as an individual level tax. Our arguments are described below; these arguments are particularly compelling in the context of a developing country with limited administrative and compliance capabilities.

---

[22] Note that opportunities to engage in such manipulation of prices would imply that a YET would create a tax incentive for firms to engage in tied sale/loan transactions, including leases.

4.2.1. *Simplicity*

Most important, the tax treatment of individuals under the YET is far simpler than under the CIT. The YET avoids the considerable administrative problems of tracking interest income, capital gains, and the return of initial investments. It also avoids the problems associated with including the proceeds of loans in the tax base under the CIT, which would be an unpopular and dramatic departure from current practice. Considerable amounts of additional record keeping (by many individuals who would normally keep minimal records on such transactions) would be required if repayment of debt were to be deductible, as prescribed under the CIT. Finally, complex withholding on consumption loans and "negative withholding" on principal and interest repayments on such loans would in principle be required under the CIT. (A standard problem in applying graduated tax rates to a global concept of income is caused by the fact that the payor of interest, unlike the payor of wages, does not know the tax rate at which to withhold tax on interest. Under the CIT this problem would be aggravated by the need to withhold tax — or refund it — on principal transactions.)

4.2.2. *Tax abuses*

CFTBL under the CIT, coupled with progressive marginal tax rates, would create opportunities for abuse in the form of loans at below-market interest rates to lower-bracket children, retired parents, or relatives. Similarly, cash-flow treatment would create opportunities for tax base shifting to low-bracket family members, as transactions would be structured so that deductions accrued to family members in high tax brackets and returns to those in low brackets.

4.2.3. *Problems with limited YET treatment of loans*

Some proponents of the CIT have argued that these problems could be largely avoided by allowing individuals to ignore some minimum level of loans (such as US$20,000 in the United States) for tax purposes. Although such an approach would in principle simplify compliance for many taxpayers, the limit would introduce new record-keeping requirements and confusion and would be difficult to enforce. In addition, taxpayers might attempt (either intentionally or unwittingly) to take deductions for the repayment of principal and interest on loans that did not qualify for CFTBL. Moreover, allowing cash flow and yield exemption treatment of loans simultaneously would create tax avoidance opportunities. For example, individuals subject to CFTBL could defer tax liability by extending very short-term, end-of-year loans to individuals subject to YET treatment; indeed, tax liability could be deferred indefinitely by repeating the transaction every year.

4.2.4. *International manipulations*

International complications would also exist under the individual cash-flow approach. The most troublesome would arise if individuals could borrow abroad without including the proceeds of the foreign loan in their tax base (either legally or illegally with little chance of detection). In this case (as above), such individuals could defer tax liability indefinitely by borrowing abroad and investing the funds domestically. Moreover, individuals who could borrow abroad outside their cash-flow accounts would find it easy to reduce their tax burden by "self-averaging" — taking deductions for domestic investments financed with foreign debt incurred when their marginal tax rates are relatively high and making withdrawals from their cash-flow accounts to repay the foreign debt when their marginal tax rates are relatively low. "Self-averaging," which is a standard feature of the cash-flow approach, is often viewed as highly desirable (for example, see U.S. Department of the Treasury, 1977). But allowing greater access to this tax-saving device only to those able to borrow abroad would probably (and with justification) be viewed as unfair and undesirable. Yet it would be extremely difficult to restrict. In addition, if returns to foreign investments, including loans made abroad, were ignored (or underreported) under the CIT system, a significant avoidance opportunity would arise to the extent that deductions for saving could be allocated to the domestic cash-flow account, with the returns allocated abroad. Finally, to preclude individuals from taking deductions for saving and then avoiding tax by emigrating, transfers abroad from cash flow accounts would have to be taxable; such treatment would also increase the complexity of the cash flow approach.

4.2.5. *Other issues*

Several observers have argued that the cash-flow approach at the individual level is preferable because it results in larger steady state welfare gains (for example, see Summers, 1981; Auerbach and Kotlikoff, 1987).[23] However, we believe that this result is predicated on several questionable assumptions. First, it assumes that existing savings accumulated from after-tax income would be taxed under the CIT when withdrawn, rather than being withdrawn on a tax-free basis; this seems highly unlikely from a political perspective. Second, it assumes that existing accrued gains would be untaxed if the YET were adopted; this also seems fairly unlikely from a political standpoint. Third, such analyses assume that the government would not offset lower private saving under the YET with higher public saving (deficit reduction); although this assumption is certainly more plausible, deficit reduction could in principle be required. Other transitional problems would be significant, but broadly similar, under the two approaches (see Sarkar and Zodrow, 1993).

Income averaging also occurs more easily under the cash-flow approach than under the YET. However, given recent reductions in rate differentials, the differences between the two approaches would not appear to be significant on this score.[24]

Finally, since the CIT assesses tax on the basis of the actual outcomes of risky investments, is often perceived to be fairer than the YET, which exempts all returns. However, this difference is more apparent than real in many important cases; indeed, if the government is not able to spread risk

[23] The discussion of this point is relevant primarily where an individual income tax is being replaced by a CIT.

[24] It has commonly been assumed that pensions would be treated on a cash-flow basis, even under the yield exemption approach; in that case, the differences would be even smaller. However, the attention recently devoted to front-loaded IRAs — essentially YET treatment of one form of saving for retirement — suggests that this assumption may not be valid.

any better than the private sector, the two approaches are equivalent, even in the presence of uncertain returns to investment (see Zodrow, 1995).

4.3. *The business/individual tax interface*

Although we believe that the proposed Hybrid Consumption Tax is preferable to either of the two "pure" forms of direct taxation of consumption, the differential treatment of debt and interest across firms and individuals described above creates several possibilities for tax avoidance. These opportunities also exist for transactions between firms subject to CFTBL and other entities that are outside the tax system and thus not subject to such treatment. Special rules are required to eliminate or greatly reduce the potential for tax avoidance.[25]

4.3.1. *Loans made to CFTBL firms by entities outside the system*

Loans extended to firms subject to CFTBL by entities not subject to such treatment — such as foreigners, tax-exempt institutions and individuals subject to the YET — pose several problems. The most difficult issue arises when the "outside" entities also have an equity interest in the firm, since the firm will face a strong tax incentive to convert nondeductible dividends into deductible interest payments, and the outside entity will generally be indifferent to this substitution. This difficult problem would presumably be attacked with regulations designed to prevent the recharacterization of equity as debt, as well as provisions such as "thin capitalization" rules. The income tax laws of many countries contain such provisions. This problem is avoided under the YET, which allows a deduction for neither dividends paid nor interest expense.

Firms subject to CFTBL would also face a tax incentive to overstate the interest rate on loans from outside entities, provided that some means of compensating the firm in a way that would not be detected by the tax authorities could be found. The primary problem would involve the substitution of overstated interest on loans from individual owners for lower taxable wages or salary. Accordingly, the proposed treatment under the

[25] For a more complete discussion of these issues, see McLure and Zodrow (forthcoming).

HCT is that contributions of debt to a firm by its individual owners would be treated as equity contributions; that is, the proceeds of the contribution and subsequent repayments of both principal and interest would have no tax consequences. Indeed, if deemed necessary to avoid the complexity of identifying individual owners, all loans by individuals to firms subject to CFTBL could be treated as equity contributions.[26]

4.3.2. *Loans extended by CFTBL firms to entities outside the system*

Loans extended by firms subject to CFTBL to outside entities also pose some problems. Fortunately, the most important category of such loans for nonfinancial firms — seller financing, including installment sales — poses no problems under the HCT, as the conceptually correct treatment could be achieved simply by including all receipts from seller-financed sales in the firm's cash flow tax base. Similarly, leasing would pose no problems, since all lease payments would simply be included in the base of the tax.

However, other types of loans raise two troublesome problems. First — and analogous to the case described above — firms subject to CFTBL would face a strong tax incentive to make loans at below-market interest rates to entities outside the tax system, as long as the entity could compensate the firm in some way that would not be detected by the tax authorities; in the most extreme example of this strategy, the outside entity could default on the loan. The primary problem area — aside from fraudulent transactions — would be loans to employees at below-market interest rates coupled with lower wages.

The second problem is that firms subject to CFTBL could defer their tax liability by making very short-term, end-of-year loans to outside entities. Moreover, this process could continue indefinitely with a series of such short-term, end-of-year loans.[27]

[26] Similarly, financial institutions would have to be precluded from paying above-market rates on deposits held by related parties, including employees. Note that if avoidance in this area proved problematical, this admittedly harsh treatment could be applied to all loans to firms subject to CFTBL by related — or even unrelated — tax-exempt institutions and/or foreign entities.

[27] Note that loans between firms subject to CFTBL at the same tax rate are not problematical, apart from the fact that they could be used to shift losses among firms, which is

None of the potential ways of dealing with either or both of these two problems is particularly attractive. We recommend the fairly draconian approach of applying income tax treatment to all loans (other than for seller financing) extended by nonfinancial firms to entities not subject to CFTBL — no deduction for loans extended, no inclusion of loan principal repayments, and full inclusion of interest income. This would eliminate both problems, but at the costs of adding some administrative complexity in terms of tracking two different types of loans and creating a strong tax bias against such loans, including loans to foreigners and loans to individuals that do not involve seller finance. (An exception might be allowed for the purchase of foreign debt.) For most firms, this bias would not be unimportant since they typically would not extend loans other than those associated with seller financing.

Note also that the issue of the indefinite deferral of tax liability through the use of shortterm loans also arises for bank deposits by firms subject to CFTBL. Since it seems likely that one would want to limit the extent to which firms subject to CFTBL could shift their tax liability to financial institutions, income tax treatment could also be applied to short-term deposits (such as 180 days or less).

Finally, note that the same problems arise for loans by financial institutions to entities outside the HCT. In this case, it is clear that income tax treatment could not be extended to such loans, since they are an essential component of the business activity of the financial institution. The problem of below-market interest rates could be treated by the prohibition of preferential rates on loans to related parties, including employees. In addition, it might well prove necessary to prorate the deductions allowed for loans outside of the system across the current year and the following year, depending on the month (or even the week) in which the loan was issued. Such complexity might well be required to limit tax avoidance by financial institutions and would be much less problematic than if the proposed treatment were applied to all firms subject to CFTBL.

---

arguably desirable since it would mitigate any problems associated with carrying forward losses with nominal interest.

5. Concluding Remarks

Influential policy makers in the United States have recently expressed serious interest in shifting reliance to (or toward) consumption-based taxation. These include Bill Archer, chair of the House Ways and Means Committee; Dick Armey, House Majority Leader; and Senators Sam Nunn and Pete Dominici.[28] Most attention has focused on a consumption-based direct tax that employ the yield exemption method. Whether or not the United States makes such a shift, other countries are likely to consider such an alternative, if only because of its increased visibility. We believe that the hybrid consumption tax we proposed for Bolivia would be a superior choice for any country considering this option.

Acknowledgments

The authors would like to thank Chairat Aemkulwat for research assistance.

References

Aaron, Henry J., and Harvey Galper. (1985). *Assessing Tax Reform*. Washington DC: Brookings Institution.

Auerbach, Alan J., and Laurence J. Kotlikoff. (1987). *Dynamic Fiscal Policy*. Cambridge, MA: Harvard University Press.

Boskin, Michael J. (Forthcoming). *Frontiers of Tax Reform*. Palo Alto, CA: Hoover Institution Press, Washington, DC, May 11.

Bradford, David F. (1980a). "The Case for a Personal Consumption Tax." In Joseph A. Peckhan (ed.), *What Should Be Taxed: Income or Expenditure?* (pp. 75–125). Washington, DC: Brookings Institution.

Bradford, David F. (1980b). "The Economics of Tax Policy Towards Savings." In George M. von Furstenburg (ed.), *The Government and Capital Formation*. Cambridge, MA: Ballinger.

---

[28] See the papers and speeches in Boskin (forthcoming). Senator Bob Packwood, chair of the Senate Finance Committee, was on record as supporting such an approach until expelled from the Senate.

Bradford, David F. (1986). *Unentangling the Income Tax.* Cambridge, MA: Harvard University Press.

Feldstein, Martin. (1978). "The Rate of Return, Taxation, and Personal Savings." *Economic Journal* 88 (September), 29–35.

Floyd, Robert H. (1973). "GATT Provisions on Border Tax Adjustments." *Journal of World Trade Law* 7(5) (September/October), 489–499.

Hall, Robert E., and Alvin Rabushka. (1995). *The Flat Tax* (2nd ed.). Stanford, CA: Hoover Institution Press.

Hoffman, Lorey Arthur, S.N. Poddar, and John Whalley. (1987). "Taxation of Banking Services Under a Consumption Type, Destination Basis VAT." *National Tax Journal* 40(4) (December), 547–554.

Hufbauer, Gary Clyde. (1995). *Fundamental Tax Reform and Border Tax Adjustments.* Washington, DC: Institute for International Economics.

Institute for Fiscal Studies. (1978). *The Structure and Reform of Direct Taxation.* London: Allen and Unwin.

Jorgenson, Dale W. (Forthcoming). "The Economic Impact of Fundamental Tax Reform." In Michael Boskin (ed.), *Frontiers of Tax Reform.* Palo Alto, CA: Hoover Institution Press.

King, Mervyn A. (1980). "Savings and Taxation." In G.A. Hughes and G.M. Heal (eds.), *Public Policy and Taxation* (pp. 1–35). London: Allen and Unwin.

King, Mervyn, and Don Fullerton. (1984). *The Taxation of Income from Capital: A Comparative Study of the U.S., U.K., Sweden, and West Germany.* Chicago: University of Chicago Press.

McLure, Charles E., Jr. (1979). *Must Corporate Income Be Taxed Twice?* Washington DC: Brookings Institution.

McLure, Charles E., Jr. (1980). "Taxes Saving, and Welfare: Theory and Evidence." *National "Tax Journal* 34(3) (September), 311–320.

McLure, Charles E., Jr. (1987). *The Value Added Tax: Key to Deficit Reduction?* Washington, DC: American Enterprise Institute.

McLure, Charles E., Jr. (1988). "The 1986 Act: Tax Reform's Finest Hour or Death Throes of the Income Tax?" *National Tax Journal* 41(3) (September), 303–315.

McLure, Charles, E., Jr. (1993). "Economic, Administrative, and Political Factors in Choosing a General Consumption Tax." *National Tax Journal* 46(3) (September), 345–358.

McLure, Charles E., Jr., Jack Mutti, Victor Thuronyi, and George Zodrow. (1990). *The Taxation of Income from Business and Capital in Colombia.* Durham, NC: Duke University Press.

McLure, Charles E., Jr., and George R. Zodrow. (1990). "Administrative Advantages of the Individual Tax Prepayment Approach to the Direct

Taxation of Consumption." *Heidelberg Congress on Taxing Consumption* (pp. 335–382). New York: Springer-Verlag.

McLure, Jr., Charles E., Jr., and George R. Zodrow. (1996). "The Economic Case for Foreign Tax Credits for Cash Flow Taxes." Xeroxed.

McLure, Charles E., Jr., and George R. Zodrow. (Forthcoming). "A Hybrid Approach to the Direct Taxation of Consumption." In Michael Bo skin (ed.) *Frontiers of Tax Reform.* Palo Alto, CA: Hoover Institution Press.

Mintz, Jack M., and Jesus Seade. (1991). "Cash Flow or Income? The Choice of a Base for Company Taxation." *World Bank Research Observer* 6 (July), 177–190.

Sarkar, Shounak, and George R. Zodrow. (1993). "Transitional Issues in Moving to a Direct Consumption Tax." *National Tax Journal* 46(3) (September), 359–376.

Shome, Parthasarathi, and Christian Schutte. (1993). "Cash-Flow Tax." International Monetary Fund Working Paper WP/93/2 (January).

Summers, Lawrence H. (1981). "Capital Taxation and Accumulation in a Life Cycle Growth Model." *American Economic Review* 71 (September), 533–544.

Tait, Alan A. (1992). "A Not-So-Simple Alternative to the Income Tax for Socialist Economies in Transition: A Comment on McLure." *World Bank Research Observer* 7 (July), 239–248.

U.S. Department of the Treasury. (1977). *Blueprints for Basic Tax Reform.* Washington, DC: U.S. Government Printing Office. Also available as D.F. Bradford and the U.S. Treasury Tax Policy Staff, *Blueprints for Basic Tax Reform* Arlington, VA: Tax Analysts, 1984.

U.S. Department of the Treasury. (1984). *Tax Reform for fairness, Simplicity, and Economic Growth.* Washington, DC: U.S. Government Printing Office.

U.S. Department of the Treasury. (1992). *Integration of the Individual and Corporate Tax Systems.* Washington, DC: U.S. Government Priming Office.

"Unlimited Savings Allowance (USA) Tax System." (1995). *Tax Notes* 66(11) (March 10), 1,485–1,575.

Zodrow, George, R. (1991). "On the 'Traditional' and 'New' Views of Dividend Taxation." *National Tax Journal* 44 (December), 497–509.

Zodrow, George, R. (Forthcoming). "Reflections on the Consumption Tax Option." In John G. Head (ed.), *Taxation Towards 2000.* Sydney: Australian Tax Foundation.

Zodrow, George R. (1995). "Taxation, Uncertainty, and the Choice of a Consumption Tax Base." *Journal of Public Economics* 58, 257–265.

Zodrow, George R., and Charles E. McLure, Jr. (1991). "Implementing Direct Consumption Taxes in Developing Countries." *Tax Law Review* 46(4) (Summer), 405–487.

Chapter 7

US Supreme Court Unanimously Chooses Substance over Form in Foreign Tax Credit Case: Implications of the PPL Decision for the Creditability of Cash-flow Taxes*

Charles E. McLure, Jr.

Senior Fellow Emeritus, Hoover Institution
Stanford University, Stanford, CA, USA

Jack Mintz

Palmer Chair, School of Public Policy
University of Calgary, Alberta, Canada

George R. Zodrow (Corresponding Author)

Cline Professor, Economics Department, and Rice Scholar,
Baker Institute for Public Policy
Rice University, Houston, TX, USA;
International Research Fellow, Centre for Business Taxation
Oxford University, Oxford, England
zodrow@rice.edu

*This chapter is reproduced from *International Tax and Public Finance*, **22**(5), 887–907, 2015.

In a recent unanimous decision in the PPL case, the US Supreme Court ruled that a one-time retroactive British "Windfall Tax" levied on 32 public utilities that were privatized between 1984 and 1996 was eligible for the US foreign tax credit (FTC). The Court rejected the contention of the US Internal Revenue Service that eligibility for the FTC should be governed by the legislative form of the tax rather than its economic substance. This decision could have far-reaching implications for the creditability of taxes that are not ordinarily thought to be income taxes, including various cash-flow business taxes that are key elements of several proposals recommending replacement of the income tax with a consumption-based tax. This article examines these issues, arguing that one and arguably both of the most common forms of cash-flow consumption-based taxes should be creditable; it also discusses questions that remain about the interpretation of key regulatory requirements that govern creditability.

Keywords: US Supreme Court PPL decision; windfall profits tax; foreign tax credit; cash flow tax; rent tax

1. Introduction

On May 20, 2013, in the PPL case,[1] the US Supreme Court ruled, in a unanimous decision, that a one-time retroactive British tax levied on 32 public utilities that were privatized between 1984 and 1996 — known as the Windfall Tax — was eligible for the US foreign tax credit (FTC). The Court rejected the contention of the US Internal Revenue Service that eligibility for the FTC should be governed by the legislative form of the tax rather than its economic substance. Questions remain, however, about the interpretation of key regulatory requirements that govern creditability.

The PPL decision could have far-reaching implications for the creditability of taxes that are not ordinarily thought to be income taxes, including various cash-flow business taxes that are key elements of several proposals recommending replacement of the income tax with a consumption-based tax. Indeed, in an amicus brief in support of the respondent (Alstott *et al.*

[1] *PPL Corp. et al, v. Commissioner of Internal Revenue*, 569 US _____ (2013).

(2013, p. 3)), a group of eight distinguished law school professors and one economist warned that a decision for the taxpayer could "extend the foreign tax credit well beyond its statutory scope of income and excess profits taxes to a whole host of taxes on value and perhaps even to consumption taxes, none of which have ever been creditable."

This article examines these issues, drawing in part on arguments made in Altshuler *et al.* (2012), an amicus brief filed in support of the petitioners in the PPL case in which all three of the authors of this paper participated. Section 2 provides background information; it summarizes the US statute and regulations governing creditability, the provisions of the UK's Windfall Tax, the arguments of the taxpayer and the government in the PPL case, and why the US Supreme Court agreed to consider the creditability of such a seemingly unimportant tax. Section 3 summarizes the most relevant arguments presented by Alstott *et al.*, the Supreme Court's opinion written by Justice Thomas, the concurring opinion written by Justice Sotomayor, and some questions left unanswered by the *PPL* decision, including the interpretation of the regulatory provisions mentioned above. Section 4 summarizes the experience of the present authors when they considered recommending that various foreign countries enact cash-flow taxes and considers the implications of *PPL* for the creditability of cash-flow taxes. Section 5 considers some sector-specific cash flow taxes and other taxes broadly similar to cash flow taxes that have been deemed creditable by the US and also examines the warning that taxes on value could be deemed creditable. Section 6 concludes.

2. Background

2.1 *The US statute and regulations*

The United States allows credit against US tax liability for certain taxes paid to foreign governments, including taxes paid by foreign subsidiaries of US companies. The US Internal Revenue Code (IRC), Section 901, states that income, war profits, and excess profits taxes are creditable. The regulations that interpret the statute (IRC Section 1.901), which lump these three types of taxes together as "income taxes," state that whether a tax is creditable depends on its "predominant character," which must be "that of an income tax in the US sense." Generally, a tax "either is or is not an income tax, in its entirety, for all persons subject to the tax."

The "predominant character" criterion is met if the tax "is likely to reach net gain in the normal circumstances in which it applies." To fulfill the latter requirement, (1) gain must be realized (the realization requirement), (2) gross receipts cannot exceed actual values (the gross receipts requirement), and (3) recovery of all significant expenses must generally be allowed (the net income requirement). These requirements are intended to prevent FTCs being claimed for taxes that are not levied on net income (e.g., taxes on gross income) and for taxes whose base exceeds income in the US sense (for example, by taxing gain that has not been realized, overstating gross receipts, or understating deductions). An exception to the generally applicable net income rule would seem to be crucial for the creditability of some forms of cash-flow taxes: the net income rule is deemed to be satisfied even if recovery is not allowed for all expenses, as long as other allowances compensate for their absence.

2.2 *The UK Windfall Tax*

As part of the Thatcher government's efforts to reduce direct government participation in the British economy, the UK privatized 32 public utilities between 1984 and 1996. During an "initial period" following privatization, commonly about four years, the privatized companies were not subject to rate regulation. During this period the companies were not allowed to raise rates, but also were not required to reduce them. By becoming more efficient, the companies increased profits substantially, giving rise to complaints that the values at which the companies were privatized were too low. When it came into power in 1997, the Labour government imposed the Windfall Tax, to deliver on a campaign promise to claw back the excess profits earned during the initial period following privatization.

Formally, the tax was levied on the difference between two values: a calculated figure defined as the "value in profit-making terms" and the lower "flotation value" or privatization value. The Windfall Tax can be described by the following formula:

$$Tax = 0.23\left[(365 \times 9 \times P/D) - FV\right] = 0.23\left\{9\left[\frac{P}{(D/365)}\right] - FV\right\}, \quad (1)$$

where

D is the number of days in the taxpayer's initial period,
P is the total amount of profits earned during that period, and
FV is flotation value.

The term 9[P/(D/365)] defines value in profit-making terms. It reflects an estimate of the value of the firm, calculated as the product of an implicit price-earnings ratio (9) and the average annual earnings of the firm [P/(D/365)] during the initial period. The tax was thus 23% of the difference between the value in profit-making terms and the flotation value. The assumed price-earnings ratio used (9) was the minimum value realized by the 32 privatized companies.

2.3 *The taxpayer's position*

Of the 32 privatized companies, 27 had initial periods of four years, and three more had initial periods that differed only slightly from four years. Only one, Railtrack, had a significantly shorter initial period, 316 days. (One company had no tax liability.) The taxpayer PPL, the American part-owner of one of the privatized companies, argued that an initial period of four years was the normal circumstances in which the tax applied. Based on this reasoning it argued that, with insignificant rounding, Eq. (1) could be rewritten as:

$$Tax = 0.23[9/4 \times P - FV] \quad (2)$$

or as:

$$Tax = 0.5175\ [P - 0.444 \times FV]. \quad (2a)$$

This equation refers to tax paid during the entire four-year initial period. To convert it to an annual tax on excess profits in each of the four years, it can be rewritten as follows:

$$Tax_i = 0.5175\ [P_i - 0.111 \times FV], \tag{2b}$$

where Tax_i is the annual tax and P_i represents profits in each of the four years, considered individually. This expression implies that the tax was 51.75% of the excess of profits over 11.1% of flotation value. PPL thus contended that the Windfall Tax was in fact a tax on excess profits, emphasizing that Eq. (2b) is precisely the form excess profits taxes commonly take.[2]

2.4 *The government's position*

Although the government stipulated to the accuracy of the taxpayer's mathematical manipulations of Eq. (1), it objected that the rewritten formulas were neither "the statutory equivalent of the equation set forth in the [Windfall Tax] Act" nor "an appropriate application of the equation in the Act" and argued that the stipulations are "irrelevant and immaterial." It argued that the form of the tax, and not its economic substance, should determine credibility, going so far as to argue before the Tax Court that "[t]he words of the UK statute are the 'substance' of this tax." (emphasis in original) In other words, the Windfall Tax was levied

[2] As stressed by Goldin (2010), assuming that D is fixed in moving from Eqs. (1) to (2) such that $D/365 = 4$ implies that the tax specified in Eqs. (2a) and (2b) is based on average profit per day rather than actual profit. This creates some anomalies for companies whose initial period is not four years, as the tax due will not change even if actual profits change as long as profits per day are unchanged. Goldin provides some numerical examples illustrating this point; for example, he shows that total profits can increase (for a firm with an initial period greater than four years) but tax can fall if profits per day decline. Because all but one of the 32 privatized firms that paid tax under the Windfall Tax had initial periods that either equaled or closely approximated four years, the tax calculated using Eqs. (2a) of (2b) are a very close approximation to the tax that would be due under a windfall profits tax imposed on actual profits, analogous to that specified in Eq. (2b). For such firms, it is reasonable to argue that the Windfall Tax had the "predominant character" of an income tax. However, as will be discussed below, this is not the case for Railtrack, which had an initial period of only 316 days, but was treated as an "outlier" that could be ignored for the purpose of determining creditability.

on the difference in two values, not excess profits, and therefore was not creditable.[3] Crucially, the government did not question PPL's position that an initial period of four years was the normal circumstances in which the tax was imposed, agreeing that "outliers" — taxpayers with unusual circumstances — could be ignored. In other words, it conceded that Eq. (1) could be rewritten as Eq. (2).

2.5 *The circuit court split*

In two cases involving identical issues, the Tax Court found for the taxpayers. When the government appealed the Tax Court decisions, one circuit court of appeals found for the government (in *PPL)* and one for the taxpayer (in *Entergy*) — both in unanimous decisions. PPL appealed the former decision to the Supreme Court and the government appealed the latter. The Supreme Court agreed to hear the cases to resolve this circuit court split and thereby prevent the untenable situation in which creditability would depend on which circuit court's ruling applied to a particular taxpayer. The Supreme Court's decision in favor of PPL meant that the government lost its appeal in the Entergy case.

3. The Supreme Court Decision

Before turning to the Supreme Court's decision, it will be useful to summarize the position taken in the amicus brief prepared by Alstott *et al.* (2013).

3.1 *The Alstott et al. amicus brief*

Adding emphasis that does not appear in the regulations, Alstott *et al.* stated in their amicus brief, "Treasury regulations under § 901 are clear: With exceptions not relevant here, 'a tax either is or is not an income tax in its entirety for *all* persons subject to the tax.'" (Brief of Alstott *et al.* in

[3]The government also argued that the realization, gross receipts, and net income standards for determining creditability were not met. These arguments, which the Court rejected, are not considered further. In the form presented in *PPL*, they have no relevance for the questions considered in the remainder of this article.

support of respondent, at 17.) In other words, to be creditable, a tax must be an income tax, as defined by the regulations, for all taxpayers. (It is unclear how the professors who prepared the brief would square this unequivocal view with the regulation's clear reference to only "the normal circumstances in which it [the tax] applies.") This view implies that "outliers" cannot be ignored in determining whether a tax is creditable. For Railtrack, with its initial period of only 316 days, the effective tax rate on "excess profits" would be 239.1 percent, rather than 51.75 percent, as in Eqs. (2a) and (2b). The brief concluded that, because income tax rates do not exceed 100 percent, the Windfall Tax was not an income tax and thus was not creditable.

3.2 *The Court's opinion*

The Court had no difficulty rejecting the government's position that form, not substance, should determine the creditability of a tax. Its opinion states:

> The Commissioner argues that any algebraic rearrangement is improper, asserting that US courts must take the foreign tax rate as written and accept whatever tax base the foreign tax purports to adopt. As a result, the Commissioner claims that the analysis begins and ends with the Labour government's choice to characterize its tax base as the difference between "profit-making value" and flotation value. Such a rigid construction is unwarranted. It cannot be squared with the black-letter principle that "tax law deals in economic realities, not legal abstractions." Given the artificiality of the U. K.'s method of calculating purported "value," we follow substance over form and recognize that the Windfall Tax is nothing more than a tax on actual profits above a threshold.[4] (internal citations omitted)

In reaching its decision, the Court rejected the emphasis on "all" added by Alstott *et al.* in quoting the regulations. It stated (p. 5), "... a foreign tax

[4] *PPL Corp. et al, v. Commissioner of Internal Revenue*, *supra* n. 1, at 10–11. The Court noted (*id.*, at 8) that "the Labour government's conception of 'profit-making value' as a backward-looking analysis of historic profits is not a recognized valuation method; instead, it is a fictitious value calculated using an imputed price-to-earnings ratio."

that operates as an income, war profits, or excess profits tax *in most instances* is creditable, even if it may affect a handful of taxpayers differently. Creditability is an all or nothing proposition." (emphasis added) Although the Court mentioned (p. 204, note 6) the Alstott *et al.* argument that the two outliers changed the predominant character of the Windfall Tax, the Court did not take it into account, noting that the government had not preserved this argument in its briefing before either the appeals court or the Supreme Court.

3.3 *Justice Sotomayor's concurring opinion*

Justice Sotomayor found the Alstott *et al.* argument "persuasive," but did not base her analysis on it because the government had agreed that outliers should be disregarded in determining the "predominant character" of a tax. She observed (p. 2), in remarks that seem relevant for the analysis in the remainder of this article, "The challenge in applying predominant character analysis will sometimes lie in determining whether and how such outlier taxpayers affect the characterization of a given tax."

3.4 *Unanswered questions*

The Supreme Court answered unequivocally the most important question raised by *PPL*: whether the IRS can base the creditability of a tax on its form. But it left important questions unanswered, because the government did not raise them. In particular, how does one determine the "predominant character" of a tax? Do the words "normal circumstances in which it applies" mean what they seem to mean, or can outliers make a tax non-creditable, as argued by Alstott *et al.*? What distinguishes normal from abnormal circumstances?

Another question that did not arise in *PPL* is important for present purposes. The regulations state:

> A foreign tax law that does not permit recovery of one or more significant costs or expenses, but that provides allowances that effectively compensate for nonrecovery of such significant costs or expenses, is considered to permit recovery of such costs or expenses.

The regulations do not explain how to determine whether allowances "effectively compensate for nonrecovery" of significant costs or expenses. (The UK Petroleum Revenue Tax discussed below provides an example of such compensation.) But if the timing of allowed and disallowed deductions differs, the only method of evaluation that is consistent with the principle cited by the Court that "tax law deals in economic realities ..." is to examine the present values of such deductions. That is the approach taken in the next section.

4. The Creditability of Cash-flow Taxes

Whether cash-flow taxes would be eligible for the FTC offered by the United States has long been subject to uncertainty. McLure and Zodrow have encountered this issue in several countries, including Bolivia, Colombia, Jamaica, Kazakhstan, and Russia.[5] Most significantly for present purposes, in 1994, presaging the government's position in *PPL*, a representative of the US Internal Revenue Service (IRS) told McLure and Zodrow — and the president of Bolivia at the time, Gonzalo Sánchez de Lozada — that a cash-flow tax the president was seriously considering would not be creditable because, at the IRS, "we look at form, not substance".[6] The concern that the proposed cash-flow tax would not be creditable in the US was sufficiently great that it doomed the proposal — even though many US firms, including potential investors in Bolivia, already had more FTCs than they could use (they were in an excess "FTC position"), so that additional credits would have been of relatively little value.

Even though many US firms still have excess credits, in many cases creditability remains a critical issue — primarily for capital-importing countries in which the predominant source of foreign direct investment is, at least potentially, US multinationals that are not in an excess foreign tax credit position.[7] The PPL decision may open the way for such countries

[5]McLure (2013) provides an overview of this experience; for a more detailed review, see McLure and Zodrow (2007).

[6]This episode is discussed in McLure and Zodrow (1996, 1998).

[7]A separate issue is whether a cash-flow tax would also be deemed non-creditable by other capital-exporting countries with FTC systems, compounding the problems associated with

to introduce some forms of cash-flow taxation as a general corporate tax, as they may be much less uncertain about whether the tax will be creditable and less fearful that it will not be.[8] (The PPL decision reinforces the impression gained from the fact that the IRS has not yet ruled that a cash-flow-based minimum tax enacted in Mexico in 2008 is not creditable.) Given the manifest economic and simplification benefits of such taxes,[9] this could produce an important gain in world welfare. Moreover, given the paucity of "real world" cash-flow taxes, other than sector-specific resource rent taxes based on cash flows enacted in the resource sectors of various countries, other countries considering adopting similar taxes — including the United States, which is the source of many such reform proposals — could learn from the experience of early adopters. This section considers whether, under the statute and the regulations interpreting them and in light of the Court's ruling in *PPL* emphasizing substance over form in deciding issues of creditability, various types of cash-flow taxes should be creditable in the United States.

4.1 *Background on the economic substance of various business taxes*

4.1.1 *Overview*

Before discussing the creditability of cash-flow taxes, it may be useful to provide a brief overview of the basic properties of both income-based and consumption-based business taxes.[10] The key similarities and differences between the two approaches lie in their treatment of the normal and

non-creditability in the US. This issue is rapidly becoming moot, however, as many capital-exporting countries, most prominently Japan and the United Kingdom, have in recent years moved to "territorial" tax systems under which active foreign-source income is largely exempt from domestic tax and foreign taxes are no longer credited against home tax liabilities.

[8] Arguably the US government should not oppose creditability for cash-flow taxes, since the amount of potentially creditable tax paid under a cash-flow tax will generally be significantly less than under an income tax levied at the same rate.

[9] These advantages are discussed in detail by Zodrow and McLure (1991), who focus on the benefits of consumption-based taxation in a developing country context.

[10] See Zodrow (2007) and Auerbach (2008) for further discussion of the differences between income-based and consumption-based taxes.

above-normal returns to both equity-financed and debt-financed investment.[11] The two forms of consumption-based taxation are similar in that they both tax all above-normal returns or economic rents and exempt from tax the normal return to debt-financed investment; they are thus also often described as rent-based taxes. (Both types of returns may or may not be taxed under the personal income tax; we focus only on business-level taxation in this discussion.) The essential difference between the two forms of taxation lies in their treatment of the normal return to equity-financed investment, which is taxed under an income tax but is effectively exempt under a consumption-based business tax. Since the latter is thus a tax on economic rents, it can be viewed as an "excess profits" tax that taxes all above-normal returns and exempts all normal returns — identical in substance if not in form to the more conventional excess profits taxes described above. These propositions can be illustrated with an analysis that calculates the costs of capital and the marginal effective tax rates (METRs) under the various taxes.[12]

An METR analysis is useful for this purpose because it calculates the effective tax rate applied to a "marginal" investment that just covers the opportunity costs of its investors — that is, the normal return to investment — and thus determines the equilibrium level of investment in the economy.[13] The calculation takes into account not only the statutory tax rate but also the details of the system of business taxation, including

[11]The normal return refers to the average economy-wide risk-free rate of return to investment. We abstract from uncertainty in this paper. Note, however, that both income-based and consumption-based business taxes tax the returns to risk taking and that, depending on the provisions dealing with losses, taxpayers and governments share in the losses to risky investments. The primary difference under the two approaches is that the government also effectively shares in the cost of an investment (i.e., it acts as a silent partner in the investment with an ownership share equal to the tax rate) under rent-based business taxes that allow expensing and full offset of losses, for example, by carrying forward losses at a factor equal to one plus the time value of money (the riskless bond rate); by comparison, such cost sharing does not occur under an income tax. When the government fully shares in both gains and losses incurred, the consumption-based tax provides an implicit deduction for the cost of risk (Mintz 1995).

[12]In the calculations below, we adopt the simplest METR approach that illustrates the essential differences between income-based and rent-based taxes; for more thorough discussions, see Devereux and Griffith (2003) and Klemm (2008).

[13]Note, however, that the location decisions of firms that earn above normal rents are also affected by the statutory tax rate, since that is the rate that is generally applied to above

deductions for investment in capital assets and inventory, investment tax credits, and the treatment of various forms of finance, etc. An METR of zero implies that the deductions allowed under the tax system are sufficiently large that the normal return to investment is exempt from tax while above-normal returns are subject to tax at the statutory rate (since they are not offset by any deductions). By comparison, an METR equal to the statutory rate implies that both above-normal and normal returns are fully taxed at the statutory rate.

Since the details of METR analysis are well known (Boadway, Bruce, and Mintz, 1984; King and Fullerton, 1984), we only outline the approach for depreciable capital assets here. Consider an investment that costs q, lasts forever but depreciates exponentially at rate δ, and has a marginal revenue product c. We also assume there is no inflation so that nominal and real returns on assets are the same. The firm finances a fraction b of the investment using debt at an interest rate i (the return to bond holders) and finances the remainder $(1 - b)$ with equity at a cost of ρ (the return paid as dividends or capital gains to shareholders). The firm faces a corporate income tax with a statutory tax rate τ; the tax system allows deductions for economic depreciation but has no additional investment incentives. (With no inflation, tax and economic depreciation are identical for depreciation at rate δ.) The treatment of debt and equity finance under the corporate tax system is specified by two parameters: $\varphi_D = 1$ ($\varphi_D = 0$) if interest expense is (not) deductible, and $\varphi_E = 1$ ($\varphi_E = 0$) if the opportunity cost of equity capital is (not) deductible. The discount rate for the firm, which reflects a weighted average of its costs of debt and equity finance taking into account whether such costs are deductible, is thus

$$r = b(1-\varphi_B\tau)i + (1-b)(1-\varphi_E\tau)\rho. \tag{3}$$

4.1.2 *The income tax*

Consider first a traditional or "classical" income tax that allows deductions for economic depreciation and for interest expense ($\varphi_D = 1$) but not for the

normal profits (Devereux and Griffith, 1998, 2003). Given the location decision, the METR is then the key factor in determining the level of investment.

cost of equity ($\varphi_E = 0$), which implies a discount rate of $r = b(1 - \tau)i + (1 - b)\rho$. For a marginal investment made at time $t = 0$, the cost of the investment must equal the present value of after-tax returns over the (infinite) lifetime of the investment, or

$$q = (1-\tau)\int_0^{\infty} ce^{-\delta t}e^{-rt}dt + \tau\int_0^{\infty} \delta qe^{-\delta t}e^{-rt}dt, \quad (4)$$

that is, the cost of the asset must equal the present value of after-tax gross receipts net of the value of depreciation deductions. Solving for the cost of capital $c/q - \delta$ (the before-tax return to the investment net of depreciation) yields

$$\frac{c}{q} - \delta = \frac{r}{1-\tau} = \frac{b(1-\tau)i + (1-b)\rho}{1-\tau}. \quad (5)$$

In the absence of taxes ($\tau = 0$), this expression reduces to $c/q - \delta = bi + (1 - b)\rho$, which simply states that the marginal return on a dollar of investment must just cover its opportunity costs. With the income tax, consider first the case of all debt finance ($b = 1$). In this case, $c/q - \delta = i$, which implies that the cost of capital is unchanged for a fully debt-financed investment under the income tax, since all of the returns on the marginal investment are paid out as deductible interest expense. This in turn implies that the METR, defined as the difference between the before-tax return net of depreciation ($c/q - \delta = i$) and the amount paid to investors (i), divided by the former, is zero: an income-based corporate tax does not impose a burden on the marginal debt-financed investment. By comparison, for a fully equity-financed investment ($b = 0$), Eq. (5) becomes $c/q - \delta = \rho/(1 - \tau)$. The cost of capital is thus increased by a factor of $1/(1 - \tau)$, and the METR for a fully equity-financed investment under the income is

$$\text{METR}_E^{IT} = \frac{\rho/(1-\tau) - \rho}{\rho/(1-\tau)} = \tau, \quad (6)$$

that is, the METR equals the statutory corporate income tax rate. Thus, as noted above, a traditional income tax subjects to full taxation all above-normal returns and the normal return to equity-financed investment, while exempting the normal return to debt-financed investment.

4.1.3 *The allowance for corporate equity (ACE) tax*

The allowance for corporate equity (ACE) tax was developed simultaneously by the Institute for Fiscal Studies (1991) and by a German group headed by Manfred Rose (Rose, 1994, 1999; Rose and Wiswesser, 1998), which first implemented the tax in Croatia as an "interest-adjusted profits tax." It was later adopted in whole or part in several countries, including Belgium, Brazil, and Italy (Genser and Reutter, 2007). The ACE tax is basically a traditional income tax, complete with deductions for depreciation[14] and interest expense, supplemented by an additional deduction for the opportunity cost of corporate equity capital; the latter is equal to the product of what is sometimes termed the "protective" rate of interest — which corresponds to the normal return to capital above — and the value of a firm's equity capital. The ACE thus treats equity and debt finance on equal terms by allowing a deduction for the opportunity cost of each form of finance.

The ACE is easily incorporated into our cost of capital/METR analysis, since it implies that the return to equity investors on the marginal investment is fully deductible ($\varphi_E = 1$), while interest expense continues to be deductible ($\varphi_D = 1$). Everything else remains the same as under the income tax; in particular, equity returns in excess of those earned on a marginal investment are taxed. In this case, the firm's discount rate becomes $r = (1 - \tau)[bi + (1 - b)\rho]$. An analogous analysis implies that the ACE has no effect on the cost of capital ($c/q - \delta = i$ for debt finance and $c/q - \delta = \rho$ for equity finance), and the METRs on both debt-financed and equity-financed investments are zero. Despite its superficial resemblance to an income tax, the ACE is thus a rent-based business tax: it taxes all above-normal returns at the statutory rate and exempts the normal return on both debt-financed and equity-financed investment, and can thus be viewed as a tax on economic rents or an excess profits tax.

---

[14] One difference between the two taxes is that under the income tax depreciation deductions are typically based on historical values regardless of when they are used, while under the ACE tax losses are carried forward with interest so that any unused deductions are effectively adjusted for the time value of money.

4.1.4 *The R-base cash-flow tax*

We now turn to the cash-flow taxes that are the focus of our analysis. Cash-flow taxes are distinguished by the allowance of immediate expensing for all purchases of capital assets, rather than deductions for depreciation and inventory accounting (loosely speaking, the tax base is cash flowing in and out of the business). The simplest form of cash-flow taxation is, using the terminology of the Meade Report (Institute for Fiscal Studies 1978), an R-base cash-flow tax, under which the tax base includes only the cash flow of "real" transactions and ignores borrowing and lending (and thus does not allow deductions for interest expense). The best known tax reform proposals that include R-Base cash-flow business taxes are the flat tax advocated by Hall and Rabushka (1995) and its graduated-rate relative, the X-Tax favored by Bradford (1986, 2005). Since neither interest expense nor the opportunity cost of equity capital are deductible, the firm's discount rate is the same as in the no-tax case, $r = [bi + (1 - b)\rho]$. Thus, with expensing under an R-Base cash-flow tax, Eq. (4) becomes

$$q = (1-\tau)\int_0^{\infty} ce^{-\delta t}e^{-rt}\,dt + \tau q, \tag{7}$$

and the cost of capital is

$$\frac{c}{q} - \delta = r, \tag{8}$$

indicating that, as in the case of the ACE tax, the R-Base cash-flow tax does not affect the cost of capital, resulting in METRs of zero for both debt-financed and equity-financed investment. The intuition underlying these results is that (1) for debt finance, the benefit of allowing expensing rather than deductions for depreciation offsets the cost of not allowing interest deductions, and results in the same METR of zero that occurs under both the income tax and the ACE, and (2) for equity finance, the same logic applies with respect to a comparison with the ACE (expensing compensates for the lack of a deduction for the opportunity cost of equity) and, in comparison to the income tax, the relative benefit of expensing is sufficiently large to reduce the METR to zero under the R-Base cash-flow tax as compared to an METR equal to the statutory rate under the income tax.

4.1.5 *The R+F-base cash-flow tax*

The Meade Report also discusses the option of a cash-flow tax on both real and financial transactions, which it terms the "R+F-Base" cash-flow tax; well known proposals that incorporate an R+F-Base business tax are the "consumed income tax" discussed by the US Treasury (1977) and the "lifetime income tax" proposed by Aaron and Galper (1985).[15] This tax is identical to the R-Base cash-flow tax, except that (1) the proceeds of borrowing and repayments of interest and principal associated with previous loans issued are included in the tax base, and (2) interest expense and repayments of loan principal are deductible, as are amounts lent. These exceptions, however, have no effect on the tax base in present value terms, so that the cost of capital (r) and the METRs on both debt-financed and equity-financed investment (zero) are the same as in the case of the R-Base cash-flow tax.

To see this, consider the case of borrowing to finance an investment. Suppose that the fraction of the value of an asset financed with debt is constant at b over the life of the asset, which requires that the loan be repaid at the rate of depreciation, δ. In this case, the net effect on the cash-flow tax base of the specified treatment of loans — in present value terms, assuming that the firm discounts all cash flows related to the loan at the interest rate i[16] — is

$$bq - \int_0^\infty \delta\, bqe^{-\delta t} e^{-it}\, dt - \int_0^\infty ibqe^{-\delta t} e^{-it}\, dt, \tag{9}$$

where the first term reflects the initial inclusion of the proceeds of the loan in the cash-flow tax base, and the second (third) term reflects the present value of the deductions for the repayment of principal (interest expense) over the life of the investment. Since this expression reduces to zero

$$bq - \frac{\delta\, bq}{\delta + i} - \frac{ibq}{\delta + i} = 0, \tag{10}$$

---

[15] A third cash-flow tax discussed by the Meade Report (Institute for Fiscal Studies 1991), the "S-Base" cash-flow tax which is assessed on only on net distributions to shareholders, is equivalent to the R+F-Base Tax.

[16] Since the deductibility of interest acts to offset in part the inclusion of the proceeds of the loan in the tax base, the appropriate discount rate for debt finance is the before-tax interest rate and, assuming that the firm equalizes the costs of debt and equity finance, $i = \rho$, so $r = i$.

the treatment of loans under the R+F-base tax has no impact on cash flow in present value terms, so that the R-Base and R+F-Base are equivalent in terms of having no effect on the equilibrium cost of capital (r), which in turn implies that the METRs on debt-financed or equity-financed investment are zero under both regimes — as they are under the ACE tax.

These results on the fundamental properties of a business income tax and the three forms of consumption-based business taxes are summarized in Table 7.1.

Table 7.1.
Properties of Income-Based and Consumption-Based Taxes

Transactions and Types of Returns	Type of Business-Level Tax			
	Income Tax	ACE Tax	R-Base Tax	R+F-Base Tax
Treatments of transactions				
Depreciable assets	Depreciation, typically based on historical values	Depreciation, with adjustment for time value of money	Expensed	Expensed
Inventory	Inventory accounting	Inventory accounting, with adjustment for time value of money	Expensed	Expensed
Borrowing/receipt of debt repayment	Ignored	Ignored	Ignored	Taxable
Lending/debt repayment	Ignored	Ignored	Ignored	Deductible
Interest received	Taxable	Taxable	Exempt	Taxable
Interest paid	Deductible	Deductible	Non-deductible	Deductible
Imputed return to equity	None	Deductible	None	None
Marginal effective tax rates (METRs)				
Normal returns: equity	Statutory rate	Zero	Zero	Zero
Normal returns: debt	Zero	Zero	Zero	Zero
Supranormal returns (economic rents): equity	Statutory rate	Statutory rate	Statutory rate	Statutory rate
Supranormal returns (economic rents): debt	Zero	Zero	Zero	Zero

4.2 *Implications of the analysis for the creditability of the various taxes*

4.2.1 *The ACE tax*

Creditability has never been an issue for the various ACE taxes enacted in several countries, including Croatia, Italy, Brazil, Belgium (Genser and Reutter, 2007). Because the ACE tax includes both deductions for depreciation and interest expense, it has always been deemed to have the predominant character of an income tax, clearly satisfying the realization, gross receipts, and net income criteria. Although one could easily argue that the additional deduction for the opportunity cost of equity under the ACE results in a measure of net income that is too small, the statute is written and has been interpreted as requiring only that deductions be sufficiently large to avoid imposing a tax on gross income. For example, the UK corporate income tax in the mid-1980s allowed expensing, but the creditability of the UK tax was never at issue. This and the granting of creditability to various ACE taxes implies that the IRS has already — on numerous occasions — deemed creditable a consumption-based tax that imposes tax only on above-normal returns and exempts normal returns.[17]

4.2.2 *Resource rent taxes*

Numerous countries, including Australia, Canada, Norway, and the UK, utilize cash flow-based taxes, often referred to as "resource rent taxes," to assess tax on the "net profit" or "economic rents" earned by resource companies, that is, returns in excess of a threshold rate of return, where investments are measured on a cash flow basis.[18] These taxes have been deemed creditable in several cases but not always. In *Inland Steel Co. v. United States*,[19] the Ontario Mining Tax on mining profits, defined gross of interest expense, depletion and royalties, was found to be not creditable since

[17] As noted above, the IRS has also not deemed the cash flow minimum tax utilized in Mexico to be non-creditable.

[18] Chen and Mintz (2013) discuss aspects of royalty systems in Australia, Canada, Norway and United Kingdom that resemble features of cash flow taxation.

[19] *Inland Steel Co. v. United States*, 677 F.2d 72 (Ct. Cl. 1982).

the tax did not reach "net gain". However, in *Texasgulf Inc. v. Comm'r*,[20] the same Ontario Mining Tax was found to be creditable since its allowances for processing costs were in excess of other disallowed expenses. The Tax Court also ruled in *Phillips Petroleum Co. v. Commissioner* in 1993 that the Norwegian supplementary cash-flow tax on offshore petroleum was creditable. Similarly, the UK Petroleum Revenue Tax (PRT), which is a cash flow based tax that allows deductions for capital costs and also allows an "uplift allowance" equal to 35 percent of most capital expenditures that was deemed to compensate for the PRT's lack of interest deductions, was deemed creditable in *Exxon Corporation vs. Commissioner.*[21] More generally, in a recent survey of resource rent taxes, Land (2010, p. 257) concludes that "Creditability issues no longer appear to be a factor that would inhibit the use of a [sic] conventionally designed resource rent taxes in host countries, although it is a matter to be examined with regard to different home tax jurisdictions and any double taxation agreement in place or under negotiation ..." Although these resource taxes are sector-specific rather than generally applicable cash flow taxes, they provide additional examples of cash-flow based rent-taxes that the IRS has deemed creditable.

4.2.3 *Creditability of the R-base cash-flow tax*

In our view, an R-Base cash-flow tax should clearly be a creditable tax. Three related — and individually compelling — arguments support this position.

First, even though the R-Base cash-flow tax does not satisfy the net income standard because it disallows a deduction for interest expense, the analysis above demonstrates clearly that allowing expensing rather than deductions for economic depreciation more than compensates for the lack of recovery of interest expense. (The METRs are zero for debt-financed investment for both income and R-Base taxes, and the METR of zero for equity-financed investment under the R-Base tax is lower than the METR under the income tax, which equals the statutory rate.)

---

[20] *Texasgulf Inc. v. Comm'r*, 172 F.3d 209 (2nd Cir. 1999).

[21] For further details on the creditability of the UK PRT and other broadly similar taxes, see Gesualdi (2013).

Thus, the fact that, for purposes of satisfying the net income requirement, the regulations allow the absence of the deductibility for an expense (interest expense) to be offset by another compensating deduction (the excess of expensing over deductions for depreciation), implies the R-Base cash-flow tax should be creditable.

Second, under the normal circumstance in which an R-Base cash-flow tax is applied it is economically equivalent to the ACE tax. Since the IRS has deemed numerous version of the ACE tax to be creditable, the emphasis of the Supreme Court in the *PPL* decision on economic substance over legislative form implies that the tax should be creditable: even though the R-Base tax may differ in form from the ACE tax, the economic equivalence of the two taxes implies that if one is creditable, both should be creditable. (The same logic arguably applies for the numerous sector-specific resource rent taxes that have also been deemed to be creditable.)

Third, the analysis above demonstrates that the R-Base cash-flow tax, like the ACE tax, is a consumption-based tax that taxes above-normal returns while exempting normal returns for both debt-financed and equity-financed investments. It is thus effectively a tax on above-normal returns, that is, on excess profits, and as such should be a creditable tax under the clear meaning of IRC Section 902. Such an interpretation would clearly be consistent with the logic of the *PPL* decision.[22]

---

[22] Grubert (2005) argues that the importance of the creditability of cash flow taxes is often overstated because creditability is not likely to affect decisions regarding investments earning above normal returns or economic rents. His argument has two components. First, for investments earning completely immobile location-specific rents (e.g., due to access to local markets or the use of local resources), the standard theory of the taxation of monopoly profits implies that investment decisions will not be affected as long as the combined tax rate is less than 100 percent. Second, for investments earning highly mobile firm-specific rents (e.g., due to intellectual property or other unique intangible assets), Grubert argues that all of the rents should be paid to the parent firm as deductible royalties, so that no tax will be collected by the source country and again investment decisions will not be distorted. These arguments are open to debate, since few rents are completely immobile and all rents are not likely to be paid out as royalties — certainly not to the relatively high-tax United States. Further, as shown by Leechor and Mintz (1993), a cash flow tax in a capital importing country is not neutral if the capital exporting country uses a deferral approach to tax corporate income. Specifically, the investment and financing decisions of

4.2.4 *Creditability of the R+F-Base cash-flow tax*

The arguments for creditability are less transparent in the case of the R+F-Base cash-flow tax and, in comparison to the R-Base tax, the R+F-Base is considerably less likely to be deemed creditable by the IRS. Nevertheless, in our view, this consumption-based tax should also be a creditable tax.

Note first that the second and third arguments in the previous section apply with full force to the R+F-Base cash-flow tax. Since the tax is economically equivalent to the R-Base tax and thus to the creditable ACE tax, the Court's emphasis on substance over form implies that the R+F-Base tax should also be creditable. And, since the R+F-Base tax is thus also a tax on economic rents or above-normal returns, it should be creditable as an excess profits tax.

The critical problem for the creditability of the R+F-Base tax is that the inclusion of both the proceeds of net loans (loans net of financial asset purchases) and repayments of loan principal (net of financial asset sales) in the cash-flow tax base implies that it does not satisfy the realization requirement for creditability since these cash-flow items are not treated as realization events under a conventional income tax. However, we would argue that this should not necessarily be dispositive in determining the creditability of the tax. Although the form of the tax is clearly problematical given existing regulations, the analysis above demonstrates that its substance is not. In particular, the inclusion of loan proceeds in the tax base is fully offset in present value terms by subsequent deductions for repayments of principal and interest, and the inclusion of repayments of principal (and interest) in the tax base is fully offset in present value terms by an earlier deduction for lending. Thus, at least in present

---

the subsidiary will affect the tax imposed by the capital exporting country on repatriated dividends; it will thus distort decisions regarding the allocation of capital across the capital exporting and capital importing countries, thereby undermining the validity of the Grubert argument. More importantly, all three of our arguments presented above, which are constructed within the context of the determination of creditability under current law, are not affected by the Grubert analysis, which is conducted in the context of a redesign of the international tax system that emphasizes minimizing behavioral distortions, including those regarding the international allocation of investment.

value terms (although not in annual terms), these inclusions do not violate the realization requirement over the life of a loan. Indeed, as shown above, if all of the features of the tax are taken into account, the tax base is smaller than the typical tax on net income, despite these inclusions that are not normally treated as realization events under the income tax. Moreover, again emphasizing substance over form, one could apply an analog to the "compensating deduction" regulation noted above in the case of the absence of interest deductions under the R-Base tax. That is, although relative to a conventional income tax the tax base under the R+F-Base is too large due to the inclusion of the proceeds of borrowing, that is compensated for by subsequent additional deductions for the repayment of principal (not allowed under an income tax) and interest. Similarly, the inclusion of repayments of principal is offset by earlier deductions for lending (also not allowed under an income tax). Accordingly — although admittedly inconsistent with the current form of the regulations — the inclusion of these two items in principle should not be dispositive in determining the creditability of the tax. Although these positions may strain the Court's emphasis on substance over form in the *PPL* case, the arguments are compelling from the perspective of the economic substance of the tax.

It could also perhaps be argued that, if a sufficiently small amount of investment is debt-financed, the inclusion of the proceeds of borrowing and the repayment of debt under the R+F-Base cash-flow tax would not cause the realization requirement to be violated, making the predominant character of the R+F-Base tax that of an income tax. This is what McLure and Zodrow found in Bolivia in 1994, where relatively low levels of debt implied that, for the nation's largest taxpayers, the base of an R+F-Base cash-flow tax would have been only three to six percent larger than that of an income tax.[23] It would, however, be difficult to know what are the "normal circumstances" in which a tax applies and to identify outliers, especially since reliance on debt — and thus presumably creditability — could change over time. Worse, an R+F-Base tax structured in a given way might seem to satisfy the realization test in one country, but not in another, because of differences in reliance on debt. This seems to be an

[23] McLure and Zodrow (1998, pp. 10–11).

untenable state of affairs. It seems better to base creditability on principles that apply universally, such as the fact that expensing compensates for the lack of an interest deduction under R-based cash-flow tax — and on the analogous present-value analysis of the R+F Base tax presented above, than on empirical relations that are not the same for all taxpayers or in all countries and will change over time.

5. A Brief Commentary on Two Points Raised by Alstott *et al.*

Alstott *et al.* (2013, p. 3) assert that acceptance of the arguments made by PPL would in effect "extend the foreign tax credit well beyond its statutory scope of income and excess profits taxes to a whole host of taxes on value and perhaps even to consumption taxes, none of which have ever been creditable." We examine this contention in this section.

5.1 *The lack of international experience with generally applicable cash-flow taxes*

In our view, the Alstott *et al.* assertion that direct consumption-based taxes have never been creditable, seems disingenuous for two reasons. First, as discussed above, the ACE taxes enacted by numerous countries, while not based on cash flow, are consumption-based taxes that tax above-normal returns at the statutory rate and exempt normal returns; all of these taxes have been deemed creditable by the IRS. Also, as noted above, cash flow based taxes on resource rents in many countries, including Australia, Canada, Norway, and the UK, have been deemed creditable.

Second, opportunities for determining the creditability of generally applicable cash-flow consumption-based business taxes have been virtually non-existent, as no country that relies heavily on investment from the United States and has been well-advised has ever introduced such a cash-flow consumption-based business tax, given the uncertainty that the tax might not be creditable (and, as we now know, the likelihood that the IRS would deny creditability). It is, of course, possible — or even likely in light of the PPL decision — that a taxpayer with expert counsel making the kind of arguments based on economic substance presented above could prevail, at least for certain types of cash-flow taxes. But the price that both countries and taxpayers would be forced to "pay to play" — the risk of double taxation because of ineligibility for the FTC — has always been deemed to be too high. For example, in one important oil-producing country, a major oil company headquartered in the United States told one of the authors (McLure) to "back off" from proposing a cash-flow tax, because they did not wish to take the risk of paying billions of dollars in tax that might not be creditable. Indeed, forging ahead to introduce a cash-flow tax that might not be creditable could have a chilling effect on investment from the United States, so it is not surprising that prior to the *PPL* decision virtually all countries had been unwilling to do so.

5.2 *Creditability of taxes on value*

Although we obviously agree that an implication of the *PPL* decision is that consumption-based cash-flow taxes may — and should — become creditable, the Alstott *et al.* brief also suggests that, since any tax on value can be approximated as a tax on income, the decision may have adverse revenue consequences by facilitating the conversion of non-creditable value-based taxes into creditable income or excess profits taxes. Although this is a possibility, the converse is true as well — one could approximate an income tax or an excess profits tax as a value-based tax and make it non-creditable. Given this inherent ambiguity,[24] the key factor in determining whether any tax should be creditable would, at least in the first instance, seem to have to be simply whether it is in actuality based on income, excess profits, or value. The fact that the Windfall Tax was based on profits rather than value thus clearly suggests that the Court was correct it determining that it should be creditable.

[24] Indeed, Viard (2013) argues that the ambiguity that inevitably arises by arbitrarily allowing creditability for income taxes but not for asset taxes is a fatal flaw of the foreign tax credit system, which he argues should be replaced by an exemption system or a preferential rate for foreign source income — an issue that we do not address here, but which is discussed comprehensively by Grubert and Altshuler (2013).

Moreover, even if interpreted as an approximation to a tax on value, the Windfall Tax clearly did not accurately measure the value differential it claimed to capture — the difference in value attributable to lax regulation over the initial four-year period following privatization. Instead, because it applied a fixed price-equity ratio to average earnings over the period of lax regulation, the Windfall Tax formula approximated the change in value that would have occurred had the lax regulations counterfactually remained in place forever.[25] It is thus exceedingly difficult to argue that the base of the Windfall Tax even approximately captured the undervaluation due to lax regulation. By comparison, as shown above, it is straightforward to demonstrate that, with the appropriate rate adjustment, the Windfall Tax formula can be interpreted as a reasonable approximation to an excess profits tax. Thus the Court's decision to treat the Windfall Tax as a creditable excess profits tax is eminently reasonable. By comparison, the fact that even if interpreted as a valuation formula the Windfall Tax did not accurately measure the value differential it claimed to capture makes it unclear what implications, if any, the *PPL* decision might have for the possibility of the conversion of non-creditable taxes on value to creditable income or excess profits taxes.

6. Concluding Remarks

The Supreme Court's resounding rejection of the doctrine of form over substance in its *PPL* decision is consistent with a long legal tradition supporting the importance of the economic substance of business transactions over their form. The decision is thus inconsistent with claims that creditability should be denied for cash-flow business taxes simply because their form is not identical to that of a conventional income tax, and indeed suggests that at least some forms of cash-flow taxation may be creditable. Indeed, in this paper we argue that the PPL decision suggests that the two most common forms of cash-flow business taxation — the

[25] In the appendix, we construct a simple example in which the Windfall Tax formula results in a tax base that is too large, relative to an accurate measure of the difference in value attributable to lax regulation over the initial four-year period following privatization, by a factor of roughly three.

R-Base version, which ignores loans and thus does not allow deductions for interest expense, and the R+F-base version, which includes the proceeds of loans in the tax base and allows deductions for repayment of both interest and principal — should be creditable against the domestic tax liability of US multinationals. Adoption of this position would in turn imply that the US IRS could no longer effectively act as a unilateral GATT for taxes; that is, the IRS could no longer make it unattractive, or at least extremely risky, for foreign governments who rely on investment from US multinationals to adopt business cash flow taxes simply because they do not fit the mold of conventional income taxes.

Appendix

The argument underlying the Windfall Tax is that profits P^H during an initial four-year period of lax regulation were too high relative to the normal profits P^N that would have been obtained in those years, and in fact were obtained in subsequent years, under more appropriate regulation. Thus, assuming constant profits of both types and a constant interest rate r, the value of the firm with lax regulation in the first four years can be approximated by

$$V^{rH} = \left[\frac{P^H}{(1+r)} + \frac{P^H}{(1+r)^2} + \frac{P^H}{(1+r)^3} + \frac{P^H}{(1+r)^4}\right] + \left[\frac{P^N}{(1+r)^5} + \cdots\right],$$

while the value of the firm, had the appropriate regulations been in place initially, can be approximated by the so-called "flotation value" of the value firm

$$FV = \left[\frac{P^N}{(1+r)} + \frac{P^N}{(1+r)^2} + \frac{P^N}{(1+r)^3} + \frac{P^N}{(1+r)^4}\right] + \left[\frac{P^N}{(1+r)^5} + \cdots\right] = \frac{P^N}{r}.$$

Thus, if the base of the Windfall Tax were designed to capture the undervaluation due to lax regulation, the base would be the difference between these two expressions. Given the assumption that $r = 11.1\%$, or the inverse of the assumed price-earnings ratio of 9, this difference can be approximated as

$$V^H - FV = \left[3P^H + 6P^N\right] - 9P^N = 3(P^H - P^N); \quad r = 0.111, \ 1/r = 9.$$

Instead, by multiplying average earnings during the lax regulation period by the price-earnings ratio, the Windfall Tax formula essentially and counterfactually assumes that lax regulations are maintained indefinitely and the firm is able to earn P^H forever. In terms of this example, the base of the Windfall Tax is approximately

$$B^{WT} = 9P^H - FV = 9(P^H - P^N) = 3(V^H - FV),$$

that is, the base of the Windfall Tax is roughly three times the appropriate level. It is thus exceedingly difficult to argue that the base of the Windfall Tax even approximately captures the undervaluation due to lax regulation.

By comparison, neglecting discounting over the first four years of lax regulation, a reasonable base for an excess profits tax over the four years of lax regulation in this case would be

$$EP = 4(E^H - E^N) = 4[E^H - r(E^N / r)] = 4[E^H - r(FV)].$$

The formula for the Windfall Tax is consistent with this formulation, once the statutory tax rate of 23% is multiplied by the factor (9/4) to yield an effective excess profits tax rate of 51.75%, or

$$Tax = 0.23[(9E^H - FV] = [(0.23)(9/4)]\{(4/9)[(9E^H - (FV)]\}$$

$$= [(0.23)(9/4)]\{4[(E^H - r(FV)]\}$$

$$= 0.5175\{4[(E^H - r(FV)]\}, \quad r = 1/9,$$

that is, the product of the effective excess profits tax rate and the excess profits tax base. Thus, apart from the lack of discounting over the first four years, the Windfall Tax formula corresponds to the correct excess profits tax formula, providing strong evidence that it should be creditable as an excess profits tax. (Taking into account discounting, the multiplicative factor on the expression for *EP* above should be 4 instead of 3, and the Windfall Tax would be too high, relative to the correct excess profits tax, by one-third (4/3 – 1), far smaller than the error in the case of the undervaluation interpretation.)

References

Aaron, H.J. and Galper, H. (1985). *Assessing tax reform.* Washington, DC: Brookings Institution Press.

Alstott, A., Chirlestein, M., Desai, M., Graetz, M., Halperin, D., Kane, M., Lokken, L., Peroni, R., and Warren, A. (2013). Amici curiae brief filed (January 18, 2013) in support of respondent, PPL Corp and Subsidiaries v. Commissioner of Internal Revenue, Supreme Court of the United States.

Altshuler, R., Bird, R.M., Gillis, M., Harberger, A.C., Hufbauer, G.C., McLure, C.E. Jr., Mintz, J., and Zodrow, G.R., (2012). Amici curiae brief filed (August 8, 2012) in support of petitioners, PPL Corp and Subsidiaries v. Commissioner of Internal Revenue, Supreme Court of the United States.

Auerbach, A.J. (2008). Tax reform in the twenty-first century. In J.W. Diamond and G.R. Zodrow (Eds.), *Fundamental tax reform: Issues, choices and implications* (pp. 27–59). Cambridge MA: MIT Press.

Boadway, R.W., Bruce, N., and Mintz, J. M. (1984). Taxation, inflation, and the marginal tax rate on capital for the Canadian mining industry. *Canadian Journal of Economics* 17, 62–79.

Bradford, D.F. (1986). *Untangling the income tax.* Cambridge, MA: Harvard University Press.

Bradford, D.F. (2005). A tax system for the twenty-first century. In A.J. Auerbach and K.A. Hassett (Eds.), *Towards fundamental tax reform.* Washington: American Enterprise Institution.

Devereux, M.P. and Griffith, R. (1998).Taxes and the location of production: Evidence from a panel of U.S. multinationals. *Journal of Public Economics* 68(3), 335–367.

Devereux, M.P. and Griffith, R. (2003). Evaluating tax policy for location decisions. *International Tax and Public Finance* 10(2), 107–126.

Genser, B. and Reutter, A. (2007). Moving toward dual income taxation in Europe. *Finanzarchiv* 63(3), 436–456.

Gesualdi, C. (2013). After *PPL*: How to bring congressional intent back to the foreign tax credit applicability decision. *Tax Notes International,* 71, 355–365.

Goldin, J. (2012). Reconsidering substance over form in PPL. *Tax Notes* 137 (December 12), 1229–2232.

Grubert, H. (2005). Tax credits, source rules, trade, and electronic commerce: Behavioral margins and the design of international tax systems. *Tax Law Review* 58(2), 149–190.

Grubert, H., and Altshuler R. (2013). Fixing the system: An analysis of alternative proposals for the reform of international tax. *National Tax Journal* 66 (3), 671–712.

Hall, R.E. and Rabushka, A. (1995). *The flat tax*. Stanford, CA. Hoover Institution Press.

Institute for Fiscal Studies (1991). *Equity for companies: A corporation tax for the 1990s*. London: Institute for Fiscal Studies.

Klemm, A. (2007). Effective average tax rates for permanent investment. IMF Working paper WP/08/56. Washington DC: International Monetary Fund.

King, M., and Fullerton, D. (1984). *The taxation of income from capital*. Chicago: University of Chicago Press.

Land, B.C. (2010). Resource rent taxation: Theory and experience. In P. Daniel, M. Keen, and C. McPherson (Eds.), *The taxation of petroleum and minerals: Principles, problems and practice*. New York: Routledge.

Leechor, C., and Mintz J. (1993). "On the taxation of multinational investment when the capital exporting country uses the deferral method." *Journal of Public Economics*, 51,1, 75–96.

McLure, C.E. Jr. (2013). Reflections on the PPL decision and its implications for the creditability of cash-flow taxes. *Tax Notes*, 71, 141–43.

McLure, C.E. Jr. and Zodrow, G.R. (1996). A hybrid consumption-based tax proposed for Bolivia. *International Tax and Public Finance*, 3, 97–112.

McLure, C.E. Jr. and Zodrow, G. R. (1998). The economic case for foreign tax credits for cash flow taxes. *National Tax Journal* 51(1), 1–22.

McLure, C.E. Jr. and Zodrow, G. R. (2007). Consumption-based direct taxes: A guided tour of the amusement park. *Finanzarchiv*, 63, 285–307.

Mintz, J. (1995). "The corporation tax: A survey," *Fiscal Studies*, 16(4), 23–68.

Mintz, J. and Chen, D. (2012). Capturing economic rents through royalties and taxes. *SPP Research Papers,* 5(30), The School of Public Policy, University of Calgary,

Rose, M. (1994). Tax reform in Eastern Europe: Economic concept and administrative feasibility. In O. Gans (Ed.), *Policy reform and structural adjustment: The cases of Malaysia, Hungary, China, Peru and Sri Lanka* (pp. 41–62). Heidelberg: Heidelberg Studies in Applied Economics and Rural Institutions.

Rose, M. (1999). "Recommendations on taxing income for countries in transition to market economies." In M. Rose (Ed.), *Tax reform for countries in transition to market economies* (pp. 23–62). Stuttgart: Lucius and Lucius.

Rose, M. & Wiswesser, R. (1998). Tax reform in transition economies: Experiences from participating in the Croatian tax reform process of the 1990s. In P.B. Sorensen (Ed.), *Public finance in a changing world*. Macmillan Press, Houndmills.

US Treasury (1977). *Blueprints for basic tax reform*. Washington: USGPO.

Viard, A. D. (2103). PPL: Exposing the flaws in the foreign tax credit. *Tax Notes* (April 29), 553–566.

Zodrow, G.R. (2007). Should capital income be subject to consumption-based taxation? In H J. Aaron, L. Burman, and C. E. Steuerle (Eds.), *Taxing capital income*. Washington: Urban Institute Press.

Zodrow, G.R. and McLure, C.E. Jr. (1991). Implementing direct consumption taxes in developing countries. *Tax Law Review*, 46, 405–427.

Chapter 8

Taxation, Uncertainty and the Choice of a Consumption Tax Base*

George R. Zodrow

Economics Department, Rice University, Houston, TX 77251-1892, USA

Several observers have concluded that the equivalence between the cash flow and wage tax approaches to direct consumption taxation breaks down in the presence of uncertainty, as individuals with extraordinarily large gains are treated too generously under the latter approach. In particular, Ahsan (*Journal of Public Economics*, 1989, 40, 99–134; *Canadian Journal of Economics*, 1990, 23, 408–433) contends that equivalence obtains only if returns in excess of a safe rate of return are included in the wage tax base. This paper constructs an alternative and arguably more plausible model under which full equivalence between the two approaches obtains even in the presence of uncertainty. It also derives Ahsan's result in a more general context, and demonstrates that the divergence between the two analyses is

*This chapter is reproduced from *Journal of Public Economics*, **58**(2), 257–265, 1995.

attributable to different assumptions regarding the cost to the government of an uncertain revenue stream.

Keywords: Consumption tax equivalence results; Taxation and saving; Tax with uncertainty

1. Introduction

The question of whether income or consumption is the preferable base for direct taxation has sparked extended debate.[1] The issue is complicated by the existence of two alternative methods of implementing a consumption tax. The 'expenditure tax' approach allows individuals a deduction for saving, with full taxation of withdrawals of both the amounts saved and all earnings; since the tax base is net cash flow, this method is also called the 'individual cash flow' (ICF) approach. Under certain circumstances, including constant tax rates and certain returns, the ICF approach effectively exempts capital income from tax, as the benefit of tax deferral at the time of saving exactly offsets in present value future taxation of all withdrawals. This suggests that a 'wage tax' approach, which simply exempts capital income, provides an alternative means of implementing a consumption- based tax; indeed, under these same circumstances, the two approaches are equivalent in the sense that they result in tax burdens that are equal in present value (although the timing of tax payments is different) and identical individual consumption paths and utility levels.[2] This second approach is also termed the 'individual tax prepayment' (ITP) approach to a consumption tax since, relative to the ICF tax, tax liability is 'prepaid' — no deduction is allowed for saving so subsequent taxation of withdrawals is unnecessary.

Several observers, however, have argued that this equivalence breaks down in a critical fashion in the presence of uncertainty, as extraordinarily large returns to 'lucky' investors will be entirely untaxed under the ITP approach, but such returns are included in the base of the ICF tax.[3] For example, the U.S. Treasury (1977, pp. 128–129) argues that under the ITP

[1] For example, see the papers in Pechman (1980) and Rose (1990).

[2] For a discussion of these points and some illustrative examples, see Zodrow and McLure (1991).

[3] Similarly, 'unlucky' investors will be able to deduct losses only under the ICF approach.

approach, "The major disadvantage … is that … lucky investors might become very rich and owe no additional tax liability on future consumption of their wealth … ." Similarly, Graetz (1979) argues that fairness requires that taxpaying capacity be evaluated only on the basis of actual outcomes (that is, using an ex post measure such as the ICF approach), rather than on the basis of opportunities (that is, using an ex ante measure such as the ITP tax).

Other analysts, including Aaron and Galper (1985), Bradford (1986), and Zodrow and McLure (1991), conclude that this distinction is overstated. They argue that individuals subject to an ICF tax will anticipate future taxes on withdrawals and will increase the amount saved in the risky asset, relative to the ITP tax; each of these authors constructs simple numerical examples for which individual consumption outcomes are identical under the two approaches.[4]

However, in two provocative papers Ahsan (1989, 1990) has constructed a model that he argues provides a formal proof of the Treasury/Graetz position. Specifically, he concludes that the ITP approach is equivalent to the ICF tax only if extraordinary capital gains — those in excess of a safe or riskless rate of return — are included in the tax base under the ITP approach; he calls this the 'modified wage tax' (MWT) approach.[5] This result is of course entirely consistent with the rationale underlying the Treasury/Graetz argument, as it requires 'lucky' investors to pay an extra tax on extraordinary gains under the modified version of the ITP tax.

This result is troublesome for advocates of the ITP approach, since its simplicity advantages relative to the ICF tax — due largely to the absence of capital income in the base — would evaporate under the MWT.[6] Indeed, the need to identify and tax only the 'extraordinary' component of investment returns under the MWT would likely render it more complicated than the ICF tax. Since some observers argue that the latter approach is too

[4] Note that Bradford *et al.* (1984, pp. 115–116) accept this line of reasoning in the revised edition of *Blueprints* (U.S. Department of Treasury, 1977).

[5] Alternatively, an ITP tax is equivalent to an ICF tax only if the latter exempts extraordinary gains from taxation.

[6] McLure and Zodrow (1990) discuss the relative simplicity advantages of the ITP approach.

complicated to be practical, this suggests that considerations of tax simplicity may preclude a direct consumption tax.

However, in this paper I argue that such a conclusion is premature, and is arguably a misleading guide to tax policy. I construct an alternative (more general) model under which full equivalence between the ICF and ITP taxes obtains even in the presence of uncertainty. The key assumption of this model is that an uncertain revenue stream is costly to the government, so that it discounts future revenues at the expected rate of return in the economy rather than at the riskless rate; I also show, within the context of the same model, that Ahsan's result obtains only when the government is assumed to be able to absorb such risk costlessly.

2. Equivalence Results

2.1. *Equivalence of the ICF and ITP taxes with uncertainty*

The model used in this paper is a generalized version of the Ahsan model. Individuals are expected utility maximizers, and utility is a strictly concave function of consumption in two periods, C_1 and C_2.[7] There are two assets — a safe asset with a certain return r, and a risky asset with an uncertain return x.[8] The fraction of total saving invested in the risky asset is α. Labor supply is exogenous, with first-period income Y and no second-period income. Consumption is taxed at rate t_C under the ICF approach, and wages are taxed at rate t_W under the ITP approach; the ICF tax has full loss offset. Individuals thus choose α and C_1 to maximize

$$E(U\{C_1, [(1 - t_W)Y/(1 + t_C) - C_1][1 + r + \alpha(x - r)]\}), \tag{1}$$

where the individual budget constraint implies the second argument is C_2, and $t_C = 0$ under the ITP approach while $t_W = 0$ under the ICF approach. The first-order conditions for α and C_1 are

$$E\{U_2 \cdot [(1 - t_W)Y/(1 + t_C) - C_1](x - r)\} = 0, \tag{2}$$

---

[7] Ahsan considers the special case in which the utility function can be expressed in the form $g(C_1) + E[h(C_2)]$. Government services are assumed to be additively separable in the utility function in both formulations.

[8] As will be shown (footnote 10), the extension to the case of many risky assets is straightforward.

$$E\{U_1 - U_2 \cdot [1 + r + \alpha (x - r)]\} = 0. \qquad (3)$$

In the absence of uncertainty, constant government revenues (in present values) require[9]

$$(1 - t_W) = 1/(1 + t_C) \Rightarrow t_W = t_C/(1 + t_C). \qquad (4)$$

Suppose Eq. (4) also holds with uncertainty. If so, Eqs. (2) and (3) are identical under the ICF and ITP regimes, implying identical optimal values of α and C_1. Moreover, since saving under the ITP tax is $S_W = (1 - t_W)Y - C_1$ and saving under the ICF tax is $S_C = Y - (1 + t_C)C_t$, it is clear that

$$S_C = (1 + t_C)S_W \qquad (5)$$

when Eq. (4) is satisfied; that is, as suggested above, saving increases under the ICF tax — by a factor of $(1 + t_C)$ relative to the ITP tax — in anticipation of the larger future taxes that must be paid under the former tax regime. In addition, since α is identical in both cases, the amounts invested in the risky and safe assets also increase equiproportionately under the ICF tax.[10]

The critical issue is thus the validity of Eq. (4) in the presence of uncertainty. Under the ITP method, the present value of revenues (which are collected entirely in the first period), is simply $R_W = t_W Y$. Under the ICF tax, the expected present value of revenues is $R_C = t_C\,[C_1 + E(C_2)/(1 + \rho)]$, where ρ is the government's discount rate. Substituting for C_2 (as in Eq. (1)) and simplifying yields

$$R_C = [t_C/(1 + t_C)]\theta Y + t_C C_1(1 - \theta), \qquad (6)$$

where $\theta = E[1 + r + \alpha (x - r)]/(1 + \rho)$. Thus, Eq. (4) obtains under the equal expected revenue constraint $R_W = R_C$ if the government discount rate equals the expected return to saving, or $\rho = r + E[\alpha(x - r)]$.

---

[9] For example, see Atkinson and Stiglitz (1980, pp. 69–70).

[10] Note that this result can easily be extended to the case of many risky assets. For $k = 1, \ldots, K$ risky assets, there are K conditions analogous to (2) — one for each α_k, the share of saving in an asset with a risky return x_k. The equivalence result still obtains, however, as the $K + 1$ first-order conditions are identical under the ICF and ITP taxes.

This rather plausible condition can be interpreted in several ways. One interpretation is that the deduction for saving under the ICF tax effectively makes the government a silent partner in risky investments, sharing in both gains and losses.[11] Accordingly, the government should in this case account for the uncertainty of future revenues by discounting them at the expected rate of return in the economy (rather than the riskless rate);[12] such an approach is consistent with several recent analyses, including Mayshar (1977), Mintz (1981), Bulow and Summers (1984), Gordon (1985) and Hamilton (1987), who argue that the government cannot absorb risk costlessly.[13] For example, Gordon (1985, pp. 5–6) concludes that "risk in government tax revenues is as costly to bear as privately traded risks" since governments bear the risks of "random tax rates on other income, random government expenditures, or random government deficits". An alternative interpretation is that the revenues which are obtained earlier under the ITP approach than under the ICF tax can be invested by the government to yield a return equal to the expected private rate of return in the economy. Such a view is also a plausible one, and is generally consistent with some recent results on relative returns to public and private investment.[14]

Thus, when the government accounts for the costs of uncertain future revenues by discounting them at the expected rate of return, full equivalence between the ITP and ICF approaches is established. That is, consumption in both periods and the expected present value of government revenues are identical under both consumption tax regimes.[15]

---

[11] This point is well known in the consumption tax literature; for example, see Zodrow and McLure (1991).

[12] Similarly, Summers (1987) argues that firms should use a relatively high discount rate for uncertain cash flows.

[13] These studies effectively assume that individuals face perfect capital markets and are sufficiently diversified that aggregate uncertainty is not reduced when risk is transferred from private individuals to the government; see Hamilton (1987).

[14] See Aschauer (1989) and the papers in Munnell (1990) for discussions of this controversial issue.

[15] However, note that the private valuations of taxes paid in the two cases depend on the individual discount rate.

2.2. *Equivalence of the ICF approach and the MWT*

In contrast, Ahsan concludes that equivalence obtains between the ICF tax and the MWT. His analysis follows earlier analyses of taxation and risk-taking, including Domar and Musgrave (1944), Mossin (1968), Stiglitz (1969) and Arrow and Lind (1970), in assuming the government can absorb risk costlessly.[16] In this case, the appropriate government discount rate is the riskless rate of return ($\rho = r$), and the above analysis indicates that if (4) were satisfied, expected revenue would be lower under the ITP tax than under the ICF alternative (since future revenues under the latter tax are discounted at a lower rate). Accordingly, Ahsan argues that the wage tax base must be expanded to include extraordinary gains ($x - r$) to obtain equivalence with the ICF; his result can be generalized within the context of the model utilized in this paper as follows.

Consider the model detailed above for the case in which α_R is the absolute amount of saving invested in the risky asset. In this case, individuals choose α_R and C, to maximize

$$E(U\{C_1, [(1 - t_W)Y/(1 + t_C) - C_1(1 + r) + [(1 - t_W)/(1 + t_C)\alpha_R(x - r)]\}), \tag{1'}$$

where the second argument is again C_2, taking into account the individual budget constraint under the taxation of extraordinary returns ($x - r$) at rate t_W under the MWT. In this case, the first-order conditions for α_R and C_1 are

$$E\{U_2 \cdot [(1 - t_W)/(1 + t_C)](x - r)\} = 0, \tag{2'}$$

$$E\{U_1 - U_2 \cdot (1 + r)\} = 0. \tag{3'}$$

If Eq. (4) is satisfied, then Eqs. (2′) and (3′) imply that the optimal α_R and C_1 are identical under the ICF and MWT taxes. In addition, since saving under the ICF approach is $S_C = Y - (1 + t_C)C_1$, and saving under the MWT approach is $S_M = (1 - t_W)Y - C_1$, $S_C = (1 + t_C)S_M$ when Eq. (4) is

---

[16] This assumption is at the opposite extreme from that made by the studies noted in the previous subsection — individuals are not perfectly diversified and government risk-spreading reduces aggregate uncertainty costlessly.

satisfied. Thus, relative to the MWT, saving goes up proportionately (by a factor of $(1 + t_C)$) under the ICF approach; however, since α_R is constant, all of the increase in saving goes into the safe asset.

To determine the validity of Eq. (4), note that expected revenues under the MWT — under the assumption that the government discounts future revenues at the riskless return r — are

$$R_M = t_W\{Y + E[\alpha_R(x - r)]/(1 + r)\}. \tag{7}$$

Substituting for C_2 into $R_C = t_C[C_1 + \mathrm{E}(C_2)/(1 + r)]$ and simplifying shows that Eq. (4) implies $R_M = R_C$.

Thus, when the government discounts future revenues at the riskless rate of return, the ICF approach is equivalent to the MWT. It is interesting to note that the MWT is constructed so that the behavioral response that is critical to establishing the equivalence between the ICF and ITP approaches in the previous subsection — an increase in investment in the risky asset under the ICF tax in anticipation of future larger tax payments — does not occur; all of the increase in saving that occurs when switching from the MWT to the ICF tax goes into the safe asset.

3. Conclusion

In summary, this paper identifies conditions under which the well-known equivalence between the ICF and the ITP approaches to the direct taxation of consumption in the presence of certain returns to investment also obtains in the presence of uncertainty; the key assumption is that the government cannot absorb risk costlessly and accounts for the costs of uncertain revenue streams by discounting future revenues at the expected rate of return. By comparison, if the government can absorb risk costlessly it should discount future uncertain revenues at the riskless rate of return. This implies that the expected present value of revenue is lower under the ITP tax than under the ICF approach, and the government must alter the structure of the ITP tax to obtain an equivalent amount of revenue. Ahsan (1989, 1990) shows that one way this might be done is by including extraordinary capital gains in a 'modified wage tax'. However, 'equivalence' might also be established in alternative ways; in particular, rates under the ITP tax could simply be raised to reflect the absence of costless government risk-sharing, relative to the ICF tax; such an approach would have the clear administrative advantage of avoiding attempts to characterize returns as 'normal' and 'extraordinary'. In any case, the nature of the equivalence results presented above clearly depends on the extent to which the government can absorb risk costlessly; although this issue clearly is still controversial, there seems to be increasing support in the literature for the view that bearing such risk imposes costs on the government.

The results of the paper also highlight an important feature of cash flow taxes. Such taxes are often asserted to generate positive revenues by taxing economic rents or above-normal returns to risky investment.[17] However, this is true only in the limited sense that such revenues reflect economic rents or above-normal returns on the government's share of the investment (which arises due to deductions for expensing rather than for economic depreciation under a cash flow tax). Indeed, the above analysis demonstrates that government revenues are zero in present value terms for above-normal returns to risky investment if the government discounts uncertain future revenues at the expected rate of return. Thus, a cash flow tax does not affect private rates of return and thus does not reduce the rate at which private investors earn economic rents or above-normal returns; only the private share of the investment is reduced.[18]

Finally, two additional qualifications to the equivalence between the ICF and ITP taxes should be noted. First, equivalence does not obtain under a progressive tax system, since tax rates will differ across periods under the ICF tax. Second, although the assumption that rates of return are independent of the level of private investment is often plausible, it may be inappropriate in the case of unique investment opportunities (e.g. entrepreneurial innovation).[19] Investigation of the importance of these points is left to future research.

---

[17] For a recent example, see Musgrave (1992, p. 180).

[18] For further discussion of this point, see Zodrow and McLure (1991).

[19] Note, however, that such issues are avoided under an ITP tax to the extent that many investment activities, including those of entrepreneurs, are subject to a business level cash flow tax that complements ITP treatment at the individual level. See Hall and Rabushka (1985), Bradford (1986) and McLure *et al.* (1990).

Acknowledgments

I have benefited greatly from the comments of two anonymous referees and from discussions with Charles McLure and Peter Mieszkowki. Any remaining errors are my own.

References

Aaron, H.J. and H. Galper, 1985, *Assessing tax reform* (Brookings Institution, Washington, DC).

Ahsan, S.M., 1989, Choice of tax base under uncertainty: Consumption or income, *Journal of Public Economics* 40, 99–134.

Ahsan, S.M., 1990, Risk-taking, savings, and taxation: A re-examination of theory and policy, *Canadian Journal of Economics* 23, 408–433.

Arrow, K. and R. Lind, 1970, Uncertainty and the evaluation of public investment decisions, *American Economic Review* 60, 364–378.

Aschauer, D.A., 1989, Is public expenditure productive?, *Journal of Monetary Economics* 23, 177–200.

Atkinson, A.B. and J.E. Stiglitz, 1980, *Lectures on public economics* (McGraw-Hill, New York).

Bradford, D.F., 1986, *Untangling the income tax* (Harvard University Press, Cambridge, MA).

Bulow, J.I. and L.H. Summers, 1984, The taxation of risky assets, *Journal of Political Economy* 92, 20–39.

Domar, E.D. and R.A. Musgrave, 1944, Proportional income taxation and risk taking, *Quarterly Journal of Economics* 58, 382–422.

Gordon, R.H., 1985, Taxation of corporate capital income: Tax revenues versus tax distortions, *Quarterly Journal of Economics* 100, 1–27.

Graetz, M.J., 1979, Implementing a progressive consumption tax, *Harvard Law Review* 92, 1575–1661.

Hall, R.E. and A. Rabushka, 1985, *The flat tax* (Hoover Institution Press, Stanford).

Hamilton, J.H., 1987, Taxation, savings, and portfolio choice in a continuous time model, *Public Finance* 42, 264–282.

Mayshar, J., 1977, Should the government subsidize risky projects?, *American Economic Review* 67, 20–28.

McLure, C.E., Jr. and G.R. Zodrow, 1990, Administrative advantages of the individual tax prepayment approach to the direct taxation of consumption, in:

M. Rose, ed., *Heidelberg Congress on taxing consumption* (Springer-Verlag, Berlin).

McLure, C.E., Jr., J. Mutti, V. Thuronyi and G.R. Zodrow, 1990, *The taxation of income from business and capital in Colombia* (Duke Univ. Press, Chapel Hill).

Mintz, J.M., 1981, Some additional results on investment, risk taking, and full loss offset corporate taxation with interest deductibility, *Quarterly Journal of Economics* 96, 631–642.

Mossin, J., 1968, Taxation and risk taking: An expected utility approach, *Economica* 35, 74–82.

Munnell, A.H., 1990, ed., *Is there a shortfall in public capital investment?* (Federal Reserve Bank of Boston, Boston).

Musgrave, P.B., 1992, Substituting consumption-based direct taxation for income taxes as the international norm: A comment, *National Tax Journal* 45, 179–184.

Pechman, J.A., 1980, What should be taxed: Income or expenditure? (Brookings Institution, Washington, DC).

Rose, M., 1990, ed., *Heidelberg Congress on taxing consumption* (Springer-Verlag, Berlin).

Stiglitz, J.E., 1969, Effects of wealth, income, and capital gains taxation on risk taking, *Quarterly Journal of Economics* 83, 263–83.

Summers, L.H., 1987, Investment incentives and the discounting of depreciation allowances, in: M. Feldstein, ed., *The effects of taxation on capital accumulation* (Univ. of Chicago Press, Chicago).

U.S. Department of Treasury, 1977, *Blueprints for basic tax reform* (Government Printing Office, Washington, DC). Revised second edition issued as D.F. Bradford and the U.S. Treasury Tax Policy Staff, 1984 (Tax Analysts, Arlington, VA).

Zodrow, G.R. and C.E. McLure, Jr., 1991, Implementing direct consumption taxes in developing countries, *Tax Law Review* 46, 405–487.

Chapter 9

Optimal Commodity Taxation of Traditional and Electronic Commerce*

George R. Zodrow

Economics Department and Baker Institute for Public Policy
Rice University, Houston, TX 77005, USA

This paper examines theoretical arguments supporting preferential sales tax treatment of electronic commerce, using a version of the standard optimal commodity tax model that includes distributional concerns, tax-exempt goods, a subset of individuals with highly elastic demand for Internet goods (which are close but imperfect substitutes for similar goods sold by traditional retailers), and relatively high administrative costs of taxing electronic commerce. The analysis concludes that tax exemption of electronic commerce is unlikely to be even close to optimal, with the optimal tax differentials calculated suggesting that the traditional prescription of uniform taxation of traditional and electronic commerce should not be over ridden by optimal taxation concerns.

*This chapter is reproduced from *National Tax Journal*, **59**(1), 7–31, 2006.

1. Introduction

A great deal of attention has recently been focused on state sales taxation of electronic commerce, with numerous papers (including the December 2001 special issue of the *National Tax Journal*) and at least three high level groups (the National Tax Association Communications and Electronic Commerce Tax Project, the U.S. Advisory Commission on Electronic Commerce, and the Streamlined Sales Tax Project) exploring various aspects of this issue. Views on the appropriate sales tax treatment of electronic commerce range across a broad spectrum. For example, the "majority proposal" of the Advisory Commission on Electronic Commerce (2000) would, if adopted, virtually eliminate sales taxation of remote electronic commerce (sales over the Internet from vendors outside of the taxing jurisdiction) and reduce the taxation of local electronic commerce. In particular, one recommendation that could lead to significant revenue losses would allow out-of-state online retailers to own conventional "bricks and mortar" affiliates in a state without triggering a requirement to collect use tax (a tax on sales from remote vendors that complements the sales tax), even if the in-state affiliate accepts refunds and performs warranty work on products purchased from the online retailer.

In marked contrast, McLure (2000) argues that the sales tax issues raised by the advent of electronic commerce merely highlight the long-standing problems of the state sales and use tax system, and that now is a propitious time for fundamental reform. He proposes an "ideal retail sales tax" system consistent with the basic principles of sales taxation long advocated by public finance economists[1] — uniform taxation of a comprehensive consumption tax base on a destination basis, that is, with the revenues accruing to the state in which consumption occurs. Under McLure's approach, all states would agree on a common base that would include all consumption items, including services consumed by individuals, with each state then free to set its own rate. All businesses would be issued a uniform exemption certificate, and their purchases of all business inputs (defined as only those deductible under the federal income tax) would be tax exempt. Under this approach, all electronic commerce between businesses would be tax exempt, while all electronic commerce between businesses

[1] See Fox and Luna (2003) for a recent example.

and consumers — and indeed all remote sales to consumers, including those made via mail order, telemarketing and television shopping networks — would be fully taxed. Other proposals fall between these two ends of the spectrum, including the model legislation proposed by the Streamlined Sales Tax Project (2001), as well as proposed treatments suggested by Fox and Murray (1997) and Mikesell (2000).

A central issue in all of these discussions is whether preferential sales tax treatment is desirable for electronic commerce. Zodrow (2000) argues that most of the arguments made supporting such preferential treatment, including the often-cited network externality argument (examined in Zodrow, 2002[2]), do not survive close scrutiny — or are at least highly suspect — and are thus unlikely to justify over-riding the traditional presumption for uniform sales taxation of all consumption expenditures. However, two of these arguments are potentially valid.

The first is that the administrative and compliance costs associated with applying the sales tax to electronic commerce — at least from remote vendors — are especially large, so that exemption from the requirement to collect use tax is appropriate.[3,4] Under the current sales tax system, this

[2] Zodrow (2002) argues that although in principle the existence of beneficial network externalities in the network of computers that form and provide access to the Internet may provide a rationale for preferential tax treatment of electronic commerce designed to encourage the expansion of the network to its efficient size, this argument is weak under the current circumstances, especially given the recent rapid growth of the Internet. Moreover, even if such a tax preference were deemed desirable, sales tax exemptions of remote (or even all) e-commerce are a very poorly targeted, expensive and thus undesirable means of accounting for network externalities. In particular, tax exemption (or subsidization) of Internet access fees would be a much more targeted response to the issues raised by the existence of significant network externalities; note that the argument for such treatment is relatively stronger for fees for access to broadband, as the network of broadband users is still relatively small. The fact that such treatment already characterizes most US states — and because new taxes on Internet access are prohibited under the Internet Tax Freedom Act — further weakens the case for any additional preferential treatment of electronic commerce.

[3] Vendors deemed to have a physical presence (nexus) within a taxing jurisdiction are required to collect tax on remote sales. However, since many Internet vendors have nexus in very few states, much of electronic commerce currently escapes sales tax.

[4] Note that these differentially high administrative costs would typically arise for tax collection by all remote vendors and are presumably less important for Internet sellers who have nexus in a taxing jurisdiction. Thus, although the text will follow common usage and

argument has proved to be a compelling one. In particular, the US Supreme Court has issued multiple rulings, most recently in its 1992 decision in *Quill Corp. v. North Dakota*, stating that requiring vendors without nexus in the taxing jurisdiction to collect use tax on remote sales is sufficiently complicated that it represents an unconstitutional restriction of interstate commerce. This complexity arises primarily because sales taxes are imposed by some 8,000 different entities, including state and local governments and various special taxing jurisdictions, with large variations in tax rates, bases, and administrative rules (including procedures for filing, exempting sales, registration, sourcing sales and audit). In addition, the existence of digital goods, as well as the anonymity that sometimes characterizes Internet transactions (customers and vendors whose locations are uncertain or transactions conducted using anonymous "electronic cash" accounts) complicates enforcement even if it is legally required.

Note, however, that the practical importance of these problems is not obvious. For example, most transactions involve credit card purchases from well-established vendors, and widespread use of traceable electronic transactions may in fact facilitate tax collection (Bird, 2003). In addition, firms can purchase — or state governments can provide (free or at nominal cost) — computer software that will calculate tax liability for remote sales, and firms with little in the way of remote sales would be exempt under the de minimis rules provided by most proposals to tax remote sales. Moreover, the US states are currently involved in an ambitious effort — the Streamlined Sales Tax Project (SSTP) — designed to simplify and unify the state sales tax system while allowing states flexibility in setting rates, presumably in the hope that a sufficiently uniform system will prompt Congress or the Supreme Court to require the collection of use tax by remote vendors (McLure, 2002). Nevertheless, it is certainly possible that imposing sales taxation on electronic commerce is — and will continue to be for the foreseeable future — somewhat more costly than taxing sales from "bricks and mortar" establishments located within a taxing jurisdiction, and that this potentially provides a rationale for preferential tax treatment.

---

discuss differential treatment in terms of traditional and electronic commerce, it should be remembered that the key distinction is between local and remote vendors.

Second, preferential treatment of electronic commerce may be desirable due to optimal commodity tax considerations. It is possible to construct scenarios under which uniform taxation of all consumption commodities is optimal, even purely from an efficiency perspective.[5] The key factor is the interaction between the demands for the various taxable commodities and the demand for untaxed leisure. If consumer tastes are such that leisure and consumption commodities are separable, then uniform taxation is desirable to avoid distortions in consumer choices across the various consumption commodities — the standard case for uniform treatment. This tendency toward uniformity is reinforced by several practical considerations. Differential tax rates are difficult to administer, as they inevitably raise extremely troublesome classification issues and create incentives for tax avoidance and evasion. Moreover, "real world" commodity tax differentials are more likely to reflect political factors than optimal tax considerations, and thus reduce rather than enhance economic efficiency. As emphasized by Slemrod (1990), adherence to the principle of uniform taxation thus provides a critical "anchor" against the entreaties of special interests for preferential (and typically highly inefficient) tax treatment.[6]

Nevertheless, as is well known from this literature, a uniform commodity tax structure is generally not optimal, so that preferential treatment of electronic commerce is certainly a theoretical possibility (Auerbach and Hines, 2002). However, a consensus has not yet emerged on whether the standard optimal taxation arguments for differential taxation imply that preferential treatment of electronic commerce is desirable. For example, in a comprehensive review of the optimal taxation literature and its application to the taxation of electronic commerce, Bruce, Fox and Murray (2003) stress that differential commodity taxes arise primarily due to differences in relative substitutability with

[5] In general, the addition of an income tax, not considered in this analysis, would also make it less likely that differential commodity taxation would be desirable (Saez, 2002, 2004; Kaplow, 2004).

[6] For further discussions of the practical difficulties of implementing commodity tax differentials and the administrative case for uniform taxation, see Harberger (1990) and Slemrod (1990).

untaxed leisure (Corlett and Hague, 1953), and that this substitutability will assuredly be quite similar for commodities that differ only in whether they are purchased online or in a traditional retail outlet. (Note that this efficiency argument for differential taxation arises not only for leisure but for any goods that are untaxed, including those that are exempt for distributional or social reasons.) Bruce, Fox and Murray also note that purchases over the Internet may be more elastic than similar purchases at a traditional retail outlet, so that preferential treatment may in theory be desirable, since another familiar optimal tax rule — which implies that optimal commodity tax rates should be set to cause equiproportionate reductions in compensated demands to minimize efficiency costs — tends to prescribe relatively low tax rates for goods with high own-price demand elasticities. For example, Goolsbee and Zittrain (1999, p. 418) suggest that "if the price elasticities of Internet customers and retail customers are very different it may actually be efficient to allow those with high elasticities to have lower rates ... the least distortive tax would be the one with high rates on those people who would not change their behavior." Their argument draws on earlier work by Sandmo (1981), who considers optimal linear income taxation in a model with two groups of individuals, one of which may engage in work in an informal labor market where the tax on labor income can be collected only at a differentially high administrative cost. Sandmo shows that, apart from equity concerns, a relatively low (expected) tax rate on labor income in the tax-evading informal sector may be desirable on efficiency grounds if the own-price supply elasticity of labor to that sector is sufficiently large.[7] By analogy, Goolsbee and Zittrain (1999) argue that relatively low tax rates on electronic commerce may be desirable, again apart from equity concerns, since empirical evidence suggests that those individuals who avoid tax by purchasing goods over the Internet tend to be highly price responsive (Goolsbee, 2000). The argument is that high taxes on electronic commerce will tend to significantly distort the behavior of individuals who are Internet shoppers

[7] Specifically, the own price elasticity of supply of labor to the informal sector must exceed the absolute value of the cross-price elasticity of labor supply to the regular market with respect to the net wage in the informal market.

and thus will have a high efficiency cost, relative to taxation of sales from traditional retailers, where the elasticity of demand is presumably lower.

The results discussed thus far focus on efficiency issues. However, equity concerns, based on the notion that the social marginal utility of income declines with income, have also been incorporated into the optimal commodity taxation literature (Diamond, 1975). The central message of this literature is that, in addition to the efficiency considerations discussed above, commodity tax rates should be differentially high on goods consumed disproportionately by those with relatively high incomes.[8] Goolsbee and Zittrain (1999) demonstrate that individuals who shop on the Internet tend to be high income and relatively well educated, as Internet shoppers on average have approximately $22,000 more in annual income and nearly two more years of education. However, they also note that this differential is declining over time. Thus, as argued by Fox and Murray (2003), equity concerns are likely to imply that differentially high tax rates on electronic commerce will be appropriate, with this distinction declining over time.

It must be stressed, however, that all of these arguments are fairly conjectural since, as observed by Bruce, Fox and Murray (2003, p. 27), "Despite the large number of articles in the optimal tax literature that have addressed the issue of neutral commodity taxation, none have addressed the idea of non-neutral taxation of two units of the same good which are obtained for final consumption via different modes of purchase." The purpose of this paper is to attempt to fill this void in the literature, and shed some additional light on the question of whether the theory of optimal commodity taxation, taking into account equity concerns, the relatively high own-price elasticities of individuals who are Internet shoppers,

---

[8] Note that this line of reasoning is diametrically opposed to the "digital divide" argument which contends that preferential tax treatment of electronic commerce is desirable because it should facilitate use of the Internet by lower-income individuals. McLure and Hellerstein (2004) argue convincingly that this argument is not compelling, as preferential tax treatment for electronic commerce is an extremely poorly targeted and thus very expensive means of promoting use of the Internet by low-income individuals or achieving any distributional goals. Accordingly, the digital divide argument is not considered in the model utilized in this paper.

and potentially differentially high costs of administering taxation of electronic commerce, implies that preferential treatment of electronic commerce is desirable.

The analysis adapts the standard optimal commodity taxation model (as described in detail in Auerbach and Hines (2002) in their review of the optimal taxation literature), to consider multiple goods that are close substitutes in their physical attributes, but are less than perfect substitutes because they differ in terms of their mode of purchase and other attributes such as ease of shopping, purchase and return, ability to "touch and feel" the good, and delivery costs, times and uncertainties, etc. In addition, the standard model is modified (1) to include distributional concerns, following Diamond (1975), (2) to include goods that are exempt from tax for social, political or administrative reasons, (3) to consider an economy in which only a subgroup of individuals purchases goods over the Internet, with the demand for such goods exhibiting a relatively high own-price elasticity, following the argument of Goolsbee and Zittrain (1999) and the model of Sandmo (1981) where only a subgroup of the population works in the informal labor market, and (4) to include differentially high costs of administering and complying with sales taxation of goods purchased over the Internet, following Kaplow (1990) who includes administrative costs in the optimal commodity tax problem, extending the analysis of Sandmo (1981) to the case of sales taxation.

It should be noted that the standard optimal taxation analysis adopted in this paper assumes that the commodity tax rates applied to both traditional and electronic commerce are perfectly flexible. In practice, the critical issue is much more likely to be whether electronic commerce (involving remote vendors) should be entirely tax exempt or should be taxed at the same rate as traditional commerce, rather than whether electronic commerce should receive a preferential rate.[9] Nevertheless, optimal taxation analysis can be quite informative to the policy debate. In particular, if the optimal tax rates for electronic commerce tend to cluster either around the standard rate applied to traditional commerce or around zero,

[9] In particular, legal issues involving the Commerce Clause as well as provisions requiring uniform taxation in many state constitutions are likely to preclude preferential rates in many cases.

then the analysis would provide strong support for full taxation or tax exemption, respectively.

The paper is organized as follows. The following section describes the theoretical optimal commodity taxation model, outlined above, that is applied to analyze the question of the desirability of preferential sales tax treatment of electronic commerce, and derives the expression that determines the optimal taxation of traditional and electronic commerce in the context of that model. Section 3 provides some illustrative calculations of the key result of the optimal commodity taxation model analysis, attempting to shed some light on the relative magnitudes of the various effects, as well as the central issue of whether, on balance, preferential taxation or tax exemption of electronic commerce seems likely to be desirable. A concluding section summarizes the results.

2. The Model and the Solution of the Optimal Tax Problem

2.1. *The model*

The model is a modified version of the standard single-period optimal commodity taxation model with fixed producer prices described in Auerbach and Hines (2002).[10] Individuals are assumed to maximize a standard utility function defined over several consumption goods and leisure. There is no source of exogenous income and only commodity taxes are allowed. There are two types of individuals in the economy, A and B, and the number of each type of individual, N^A and N^B, is fixed. Individuals of type A never purchase goods over the Internet, while individuals of type B are frequent users of the Internet and often make purchases on line.

[10] Since Auerbach and Hines provide a detailed treatment of the basic optimal commodity taxation problem, the derivations of the results are only outlined here; derivations of the results in this paper are also provided in Zodrow (2005). The model of consumer behavior utilized is also generally similar to that used by Alm and Melnick (2003) in their empirical analysis of the sensitivity of the demand for Internet goods to preferential tax treatment, except that it treats traditional goods and Internet goods as close rather than perfect substitutes and allows for leisure and a separate good that is exempt from sales tax for distributional or social reasons.

These rather stark assumptions both simplify the model and allow for clear analogies to the similar model of Sandmo (1981). However, they admittedly are fairly stringent, especially since one would expect that the number of individuals making online purchases (as well as the set of goods sold over the Internet as defined below) would increase over time.

In addition to leisure, which is the numeraire with a fixed price w, there are four types of consumer goods in the economy. Goods x_E are exempt from commodity taxation, either for distributional reasons (they are consumed disproportionately by the poor), social reasons (e.g., health care, education), administrative reasons (e.g., some services), political reasons (e.g., services from owner-occupied housing), or some combination of the above. Goods x_N are never sold on the Internet, either for technical or historical reasons, and are not closely substitutable for goods sold over the Internet. The remaining two categories of goods were the focus of the discussion above — goods that are sold both by traditional or "bricks and mortar" retailers and over the Internet. The model, following the argument made by proponents of preferential treatment of electronic commerce, makes the admittedly controversial assumption that these goods can be treated as separate commodities. Specifically, goods x_I are assumed to be sold only on the Internet, while goods x_S are sold only by traditional retailers. These two goods are assumed to be close but not perfect substitutes, differing only in mode of purchase and other attributes such as the nature and ease of shopping, purchase and return, the ability to "touch and feel" the good, and delivery costs, times and uncertainties, etc.[11] Because of their similarities, these two goods (x_S and x_I) are assumed to have very similar cross-price elasticities with the other two types of goods and with leisure.

---

[11] As noted by Bruce, Fox and Murray (2003), this assumption can be cast in the framework of Lancaster (1966), who argues that it is the attributes of a good, rather than the good itself, that determine consumer welfare. Whether the differences between otherwise identical goods purchased over the Internet and from traditional retailers are sufficiently important to merit treatment as different goods is open to debate — and, if not, then any potential case for preferential taxation of electronic commerce on optimal tax grounds vanishes. Nevertheless, the "different goods" argument has some plausibility and will, at least for purposes of argument, be made in this paper. Indeed, the general strategy utilized in the paper will be to attempt to avoid any potential bias against preferential tax treatment of electronic commerce by adopting assumptions that tend to favor such treatment.

Consumer prices for these four consumption goods are denoted as p_i, $i = E, N, S, I$. Producer prices are assumed to be fixed, and denoted as q_i, $i = E, N, S, I$. There are two commodity tax (i.e., retail sales tax) rates in the model — t is applied to the taxable goods sold by traditional retailers (x_N and x_S) and τ is applied to the goods sold over the Internet (x_I). Goods x_E and leisure are untaxed. Under a uniform tax on (taxable) commodities, $\tau = t$, while preferential tax treatment of electronic commerce implies that $\tau < t$.

The N^A individuals of type A thus have an indirect utility function $V^A(w, q_E, q_N + t, q_S + t)$ while the N^B individuals of type B have utility $V^B(w, q_E, q_N + t, q_S + t, q_I + \tau)$. The government must raise a fixed amount of revenue, R, net of administrative costs, using only the two sales tax instruments t and τ.

Raising revenues from sales taxation also results in administrative and compliance costs. The nature of these costs, in particular the differences in the functional relationships between these costs and the tax revenues raised from traditional and electronic vendors, is unclear, although one would expect that tax compliance costs would exhibit declining marginal costs for both traditional and electronic vendors. The common perception, discussed above, is that such costs would be higher for e-commerce due to the need to comply with use taxes and regulations in many different jurisdictions and because a disproportionately large fraction of e-commerce sales are attributable to relatively small vendors, and this may very well be the case. On the other hand, with the appropriate sales and use tax compliance software, these differences may be small especially for larger vendors — and irrelevant for the many smaller vendors which would be excluded by de minimis rules. Indeed, for firms, even relatively small ones, engaged purely in electronic commerce who already have accurate records on mailing and billing addresses on all their customers for all sales, the additional costs of collecting use taxes may be less than the costs of sales tax compliance for a traditional retailer.[12] In any case, the analysis in this paper will

[12] A separate issue is the one-time set-up costs that would be incurred by currently tax exempt remote electronic vendors, which are ignored in the analysis in this paper (which, as noted above, does not explicitly consider the issue of whether electronic commerce should be taxed at all but rather the question of whether it should receive a significantly

assume that the marginal costs of compliance are either the same or greater for electronic vendors than for traditional vendors. Specifically, total administrative costs (C_t) of taxing goods sold by traditional retailers are assumed to be a function of the total revenue raised, with marginal costs (c_t) positive and constant or declining with revenues, or

$$C_t = C_t(R_t) = C_t[t(N^A x_N^A + N^B x_N^B + N^A x_S^A + N^B x_S^B)];\ c_t = \frac{dC_t}{dR_t} > 0,\ c_{tt} \leq 0.$$

Similarly, suppose that administrative costs for taxing Internet sales (C_τ) are a (different) function of total revenue raised, also with positive and constant or declining marginal costs, or

$$C_\tau = C_\tau(R_\tau) = C_\tau(\tau N^B x_I^B); \quad c_\tau = \frac{dC_\tau}{dR_\tau} > 0, \quad c_{\tau\tau} \leq 0,$$

and that marginal costs may be higher than for goods purchased from traditional retailers ($c_\tau \geq c_t$).

2.2. *The optimal tax result*

Following the standard optimal commodity taxation approach with heterogeneous consumers (Diamond, 1975), the government is assumed to maximize a weighted sum of individual utilities, where distributional

preferential rate). These fixed set-up costs should presumably be amortized over many future years (and arguably compared to similarly amortized fixed costs already incurred by traditional retailers in complying with existing sales taxes), but in any case typically would not appear in the optimal tax conditions derived below, which are functions of marginal costs. In any case, the omission of these fixed costs is not particularly problematic, since they typically would range from one to three years of annual software costs, so that their amortized value would not be large relative to annual costs. Moreover, set-up costs are largest for relatively small firms without existing enterprise software, many of which would be exempt from the requirement to collect use tax due to de minimis rules. For larger firms, especially those with enterprise software from an established vendor (e.g., Oracle or SAP), set-up costs would be at the lower end of this range. (These rough approximations were generously provided by Mr. Charles Collins of Taxware.) Note also that these figures suggest that tax compliance costs for firms engaging in electronic commerce — like tax compliance costs in general — result in a modest barrier to entry for the industry.

weights γ^A and γ^B reflect the marginal social valuation of utility changes for the two individuals. Thus, the Lagrangian for the government is

$$L = N^A\gamma^A V^A(w, q_E, q_N + t, q_S + t) + N^B\gamma^B V^B(w, q_E, q_N + t, q_S + t, q_I + \tau)$$
$$+\lambda\left\{\begin{array}{l} t(N^A x_N^A + N^B x_N^B + N^A x_S^A + N^B x_S^B) + \tau N^B x_I^B \\ -\{R + C_t[t(N^A x_N^A + N^B x_N^B + N^A x_S^A + N^B x_S^B)] + C_\tau \tau[N^B x_I^B] \end{array}\right\} \quad (1)$$

The government chooses its two tax rates t and τ under the assumption of fixed producer prices (with units chosen so that prices equal one) to maximize Eq. (1). Substituting from Roy's identity, the Slutsky equation and the definitions of total consumption levels of the three taxable goods — $x_N = N^A x_N^A + N^B x_N^B$; $x_S = N^A x_S^A + N^B x_S^B$; $x_I = N^B x_I^B$ — into the resulting first order conditions (and using the symmetry of the Slutsky matrix and the Slutsky adding up conditions for each type of individual) yields

$$\left\{\begin{array}{ll} -N^A[x_N^A(\varepsilon_{Nw}^A + \varepsilon_{NE}^A) & \\ \quad + x_S^A(\varepsilon_{Sw}^A + \varepsilon_{SE}^A)] & \\ -N^B[x_N^B(\varepsilon_{Nw}^B + \varepsilon_{NE}^B + \varepsilon_{NI}^B) & N^B(x_N^B\varepsilon_{NI}^B + x_S^B\varepsilon_{SI}^B) \\ \quad + x_S^B(\varepsilon_{Sw}^B + \varepsilon_{SE}^B + \varepsilon_{SI}^B)] & \\ -N^B x_I^B(\varepsilon_{Iw}^B + \varepsilon_{IE}^B + \varepsilon_{II}^B) & N^B x_I^B \varepsilon_{II}^B \end{array}\right\}\left\{\begin{array}{l} (1-c_t)t/(1+t) \\ (1-c_\tau)\tau/(1+\tau) \end{array}\right\}$$

$$= (-1)\left\{\begin{array}{c} \dfrac{\lambda(1-c_t)-\beta_N}{\lambda}x_N + \dfrac{\lambda(1-c_t)-\beta_S}{\lambda}x_S \\ \dfrac{\lambda(1-c_\tau)-\beta_I}{\lambda}x_I \end{array}\right\} \quad (2)$$

where ε_{ij}^h is the compensated cross price elasticity for individual h of good i with respect to the price of good j with the price of leisure w, and

$$\beta_N = \frac{N^A x_N^A}{x_N}\beta^A + \frac{N^B x_N^B}{x_N}\beta^B; \quad \beta_S = \frac{N^A x_S^A}{x_S}\beta^A + \frac{N^B x_S^B}{x_S}\beta^B;$$

$$\beta_I = \frac{N^B x_I^B}{x_I}\beta^B = \beta^B$$

are the social marginal utilities of revenues from taxing the three taxable goods, where α^h is the marginal utility of income for individual h, and

$$\beta^A = \gamma^A \alpha^A + \lambda(1-c_t)t\left(\frac{\partial x_N^A}{\partial M^A} + \frac{\partial x_S^A}{\partial M^A}\right);$$

$$\beta^B = \gamma^B \alpha^B + \lambda(1-c_t)t\left(\frac{\partial x_N^B}{\partial M^B} + \frac{\partial x_S^B}{\partial M^B}\right) + \lambda(1-c_\tau)\tau\frac{\partial x_I^B}{\partial M^B}$$

are the net social marginal valuations of income to individuals A and B, including the additional net tax revenues, taking into account administrative costs, generated from purchases of taxed goods financed with the additional income.

The matrix of the coefficient determinant (D) is positive because the Slutsky matrix is negative semi-definite, and in general each of the terms in the right hand side expressions is positive (Auerbach and Hines, 2002).[13] Solving for the two tax rate terms, defining the individual consumption shares of the two goods sold by traditional retailers as $f_j^h = N^h x_j^h / (x_N + x_S)$, $j = N, S$, $h = A, B$, and the weighted cross price elasticity of the consumption of the taxed goods with respect to the prices of leisure and the untaxed good as

$$\varepsilon^* = f_N^A(\varepsilon_{Nw}^A + \varepsilon_{NE}^A) + f_S^A(\varepsilon_{Sw}^A + \varepsilon_{SE}^A) + f_N^B(\varepsilon_{Nw}^B + \varepsilon_{NE}^B) + f_S^B(\varepsilon_{Sw}^B + \varepsilon_{SE}^B),$$

yields the optimal taxation expression that determines the conditions under which preferential treatment of Internet commerce may be desirable:

$$\frac{\tau}{1+\tau} = \frac{(1-c_t)}{(1-c_\tau)}\frac{t}{1+t} - \frac{x_I(x_N + x_S)}{D(1-c_\tau)}\left\{\begin{array}{l}\left[\begin{array}{l}\dfrac{\lambda(1-c_t)-\beta_N}{\lambda}\dfrac{x_N}{x_N + x_S} \\ + \dfrac{\lambda(1-c_t)-\beta_S}{\lambda}\dfrac{x_S}{x_N + x_S}\end{array}\right](\varepsilon_{Iw}^B + \varepsilon_{IE}^B) \\ -\left[\dfrac{\lambda(1-c_\tau)-\beta_I}{\lambda}\right]\varepsilon^*\end{array}\right\}. \quad (3)$$

[13]These conditions are satisfied for all the numerical results reported in Section 4.

2.3. *Interpreting the result*

The following discussion provides an interpretation of the key optimal commodity tax rate expression Eq. (3), considering first the case of no distributional concerns and uniform administrative costs, and then examining the effects of relaxing each of these two assumptions.

2.3.1. *A Benchmark Case*

Consider first the case in which administrative costs are the same for sales taxation of traditional retailers and Internet sales and the net social marginal valuations of income for the two individuals are identical ($\beta^A = \beta^B = \beta$). Then $c_t = c_\tau = c$; $\beta_N = \beta_S = \beta_I = \beta$. In this case, Eq. (3) becomes

$$\frac{\tau}{1+\tau} = \frac{t}{1+t} - \frac{x_I(x_N + x_S)}{D(1-c)}\left[\frac{(1-c)-\beta}{\lambda}\right][(\varepsilon_{Iw}^B + \varepsilon_{IE}^B) - \varepsilon^*].$$

This result is the two-person analog to the familiar Corlett-Hague result when both leisure and one of the consumption goods (x_E) are untaxed. That is, neglecting distributional concerns and differences in administrative costs, if the Internet good is more substitutable for leisure or the untaxed good, with the cross-price elasticities between the taxed goods and leisure and the untaxed good weighted as shown in the definition of ε^* (that is, $(\varepsilon_{Iw}^B + \varepsilon_{IE}^B) - \varepsilon^* > 0$), then the Internet good should be taxed less (complements with the untaxed good and leisure should be taxed more).[14]

Although it is stated differently, this condition captures the essence of the argument stressed by Goolsbee and Zittrain (1999) that preferential taxation of electronic commerce may be desirable if the own-price elasticity of demand for Internet goods is relatively high for individuals who make purchases over the Internet. Note first that the result from Sandmo (1981) on which Goolsbee and Zittrain base their conclusion is a rather weak one. Sandmo considers optimal linear income taxation in

[14] Note that this reasoning suggests that a potential argument for differentially higher taxation of electronic commerce (not considered in the model utilized in this paper) is that the convenience of shopping over the Internet allows leisure time to be used more productively, so that goods purchased over the Internet are more likely to be complementary to leisure.

a model with two groups of individuals, only one of which may engage in work in an informal labor market where the tax on labor income is relatively easily avoided and thus can be collected only at a differentially high administrative cost. The model allows differential taxation of labor in the formal and informal markets, once differences in audit probabilities are taken into account. Sandmo shows that the (expected) tax rate on labor in the informal market should be lower than the tax rate in the formal market if the elasticity of labor supply to the informal market with respect to the tax rate in that market is sufficiently large (in absolute value). However, the magnitude of this elasticity must be compared to the cross-price elasticity of labor supply to the formal market with respect to the tax rate in the informal market. That is, preferential tax treatment of wage income earned in the informal sector is desirable only if a tax increase in the informal sector causes a reduction in labor supply to that sector that exceeds in magnitude the associated increase in labor supply to the formal sector. In other words, if taxation of the informal sector merely reallocates labor from the informal to the formal market, then uniform taxation is desirable, regardless of the magnitude of the own-price elasticity of labor supply to the informal sector; preferential taxation of the informal sector is desirable only if it results in a net increase in labor supply.[15]

The condition presented above implies a similar result. Consider first the cross-price elasticities involving leisure demand/labor supply effects. Preferential taxation of the Internet goods is desirable if it will have a relatively negative effect on the demand for leisure (Internet goods are substitutes for leisure) and thus a relatively large positive effect on labor supply, which will more than offset the negative effect on labor supply of taxing goods supplied by traditional retailers — that is, only if the net labor supply effect is positive (just as in the Sandmo (1981) analysis of preferential taxation of labor in the informal sector). If instead, the Internet good and

[15] Sandmo also derives a second result, which indicates that under certain conditions the tax rate on labor in the formal sector should be lowered if the elasticity of labor supply to the tax-evading informal market is sufficiently large. In this case, the potential for evasion increases the overall efficiency cost of labor income taxation so that greater reliance on lump sum taxation is desirable in the model. The option of lump sum taxation, however, is assumed to be unavailable in the model utilized in this paper.

goods sold by traditional retailers are equally substitutable for leisure, then uniform taxation is desirable, regardless of the magnitude of the own-price elasticity of demand for the Internet good. For the case analyzed in this paper, this result is augmented by the need to consider cross-price effects with the tax-exempt good, where again preferential taxation of the Internet goods is desirable only if it will have a relatively large negative effect on demand for the untaxed good.

This condition can also be related more clearly to the argument made by Goolsbee and Zittrain in an even more specialized case of the model. Suppose that among the three taxed goods (x_N, x_S, and x_I), all cross-price effects are zero except for the cross-price elasticities between the Internet good x_I and x_S (which are large by assumption), and all income effects are zero. In this case, $\varepsilon^* = (-\varepsilon_{NN}) + (-\varepsilon_{SS}) - f_S^B \varepsilon_{SI}^B$. Substituting, the optimal tax rate expression Eq. (3) becomes

$$\begin{aligned}
\frac{\tau}{1+\tau} - \frac{t}{1+t} &= \frac{x_I(x_N + x_S)}{D(1-c)}\left[(1-c) - \frac{\beta}{\lambda}\right] \\
&\quad \times \left\{ [(-\varepsilon_{NN}) + (-\varepsilon_{SS}) - f_S^B \varepsilon_{SI}^B] - [(-\varepsilon_{II}^B) - \varepsilon_{IS}^B] \right\} \\
&= \frac{x_I(x_N + x_S)}{D(1-c)}\left[(1-c) - \frac{\beta}{\lambda}\right][(-\varepsilon_{NN}) + (-\varepsilon_{SS}) - f_S^B \varepsilon_{SI}^B][(-\varepsilon_{II}^B) - \varepsilon_{IS}^B] \\
&\quad \times \left[\frac{1}{(-\varepsilon_{II}^B) - \varepsilon_{IS}^B} - \frac{1}{(-\varepsilon_{NN}) + (-\varepsilon_{SS}) - f_S^B \varepsilon_{SI}^B}\right].
\end{aligned}$$

In the absence of any cross price effects, this is simply the Ramsey inverse elasticity rule — the tax rate on the good with the relatively high own-price elasticity should have the lower tax rate, as the tax rates, expressed as a percentage of price, are proportional to the inverses of the compensated demand elasticities. This is the point stressed by Goolsbee and Zittrain. That is, if the own-price elasticity of the Internet good is large, relative to the own price elasticities of the other taxable goods, optimal tax considerations will tend to imply relatively low tax rates on electronic commerce. However, this result must be tempered by efficiency concerns about distorting consumption between goods sold over the Internet and their substitutes — the standard efficiency concern that if the Internet good is a close substitute for other taxed goods, preferential treatment of the Internet good will cause a large distortion of demand and thus large efficiency losses. This concern is captured by the fact that the own-price effects are tempered by the cross-price effects as indicated above. In addition, as long as the size of the market for Internet goods is relatively small, then $\varepsilon_{SI}^{B} = \varepsilon_{IS}^{B} p_I x_I / (p_S x_S) << \varepsilon_{IS}^{B}$. Thus, it is reasonable to assume that $\varepsilon_{IS}^{B} >> f_S^B \varepsilon_{SI}^{B}$, and efficiency concerns about distorting consumer decisions regarding purchases from Internet firms rather than traditional retailers work in the direction of increasing the taxation of Internet goods (rather than simply equalizing the two tax rates), thus tempering or reversing any tendency for a tax advantage for Internet goods due to a relative high own price elasticity.[16]

To sum up, in the benchmark case that neglects distributional concerns and differences in administrative costs, preferential treatment of electronic commerce is desirable only if the Internet good is more substitutable for leisure or the untaxed good, relative to the two other taxed goods in the model. This result simultaneously captures the concept that differential taxation is desirable only if it provides an indirect means of taxing goods that are untaxed, as well as the concept that preferential taxation of e-commerce may be desirable if the own-price elasticity of demand for Internet goods is relatively large, but that this concern must be weighed against efficiency concerns about distorting consumer decisions regarding purchases from Internet firms rather than traditional retailers.

Distributional Concerns

Consider next the role played by distributional concerns. Thus, suppose that the distributional weights (the β's, which include the effects of different individual propensities to consume taxed goods) are different, but the administrative costs of taxing traditional and electronic commerce are still equal. Then the optimal tax rate expression becomes

$$\frac{\tau}{1+\tau} = \frac{t}{1+t} - \frac{x_I(x_N + x_S)}{D(1-c)}[(\varepsilon_{Iw}^{B} + \varepsilon_{IE}^{B}) - \varepsilon^*]$$

$$+ \frac{x_I(x_N + x_S)}{D(1-c)}\left[\left(\frac{\beta_N}{\lambda}\frac{x_N}{x_N + x_S} + \frac{\beta_S}{\lambda}\frac{x_S}{x_N + x_S}\right)(\varepsilon_{Iw}^{B} + \varepsilon_{IE}^{B}) - \frac{\beta_I}{\lambda}\varepsilon^*\right].$$

[16] Note that this argument implies that it is likely that $(-\varepsilon_{NN}) + (-\varepsilon_{SS}) - f_S^B \varepsilon_{SI}^B > 0$.

The third term on the right hand side captures the effects of adding distributional concerns. Suppose, consistent with the empirical data described previously, that the Internet good is consumed primarily be relatively wealthy individuals. In that case, β_I will be relatively low in comparison to β_N and β_S.[17] As a result, the third term is more likely to be positive, which will tend to increase the tax rate applied to the Internet good (τ). That is, distributional concerns temper the traditional Corlett-Hague argument expressed in the second term on the right side of the equation. Thus, even if Internet goods are substitutes with leisure and/or the untaxed goods and would thus tend to be taxed preferentially, distributional concerns will temper this result and may imply that goods sold over the Internet should be taxed more heavily than goods sold by traditional retailers if the difference in the distributional weights applied to the two individuals is sufficiently large.

Administrative Cost Differentials

Suppose next that distributional concerns are ignored ($\beta^A = \beta^B = \beta$, so that $\beta_N = \beta_S = \beta_I = \beta$), but the administrative costs of taxing Internet goods are greater than those associated with taxing goods sold by traditional retailers ($c_\tau > c_t$).[18] Then the optimal tax rate expression becomes

$$\frac{\tau}{1+\tau} = \frac{(1-c_t)}{(1-c_\tau)}\frac{t}{1+t}$$

$$-\frac{x_I(x_N + x_S)}{D(1-c_\tau)}\left\{\left[(1-c_t) - \frac{\beta}{\lambda}\right](\varepsilon^B_{Iw} + \varepsilon^B_{IE}) - \left[(1-c_\tau) - \frac{\beta}{\lambda}\right]\varepsilon^*\right\}.$$

The first term on the right side of this equation reflects the effects of administrative cost differentials, neglecting the cross price elasticity effects of the taxed goods with the untaxed good and leisure. In this case, if the administrative costs of taxing Internet goods are relatively high ($c_\tau > c_t$),

---

[17] Note that this characterization assumes that the income effect terms in the definitions of the β's do not dominate the distributional terms.

[18] This discussion is similar to the analysis of optimal commodity taxation in the presence of administrative costs in Kaplow (1990).

such goods should be taxed at a higher rate. That is, neglecting cross-price effects, uniform taxation would be desirable except for the administrative cost differential, which argues for higher taxes on Internet goods to discourage their consumption and thus lower average administrative costs. Thus, arguments which suggest that preferential taxation of electronic commerce is necessarily desirable because the administrative costs of such taxation are relatively high do not take into account that the lower prices associated with lower taxation of electronic commerce will stimulate demand for goods for which tax collection costs are relatively high.

The second term on the right side indicates that the conventional argument that high administrative costs imply that preferential tax treatment is optimal may nevertheless still be valid. This term shows that differential administrative costs change the weighting of the cross-price effects of the taxed goods with the untaxed good and leisure, which tend to reduce (increase) τ if the Internet good is more (less) substitutable with the untaxed good and leisure. When the administrative costs of taxing Internet goods are relatively high ($c_\tau > c_t$), then the weight attached to the term involving the cross-price elasticities of the Internet good with the untaxed good and leisure (the first term in brackets) is relatively large, implying that preferential taxation of Internet goods is more likely to be desirable (as long as $\varepsilon_{Iw}^{B} + \varepsilon_{IE}^{B} > 0$). More generally, these results indicate that if the administrative and compliance costs of taxing the Internet good are relatively large, the cross-price effects of this good with leisure and other untaxed goods are even more important in choosing an optimal tax structure.[19]

Thus, to sum up, adding differential administrative costs to the model has two potentially offsetting effects. On the one hand, preferential taxation

[19] Of course, these results depend on the specific form of administrative costs used in the model. For example, if the issue were framed as extending uniform taxation to more goods sold over the Internet and the administrative costs associated with doing so increased more than proportionately, then the extent of base expansion, generally desirable on efficiency grounds, would be limited by increasing marginal administrative costs (Yitzhaki, 1979). On the other hand, the analysis also does not consider the fact that administrative costs tend to increase with the existence of rate differentials, as goods must be allocated to different tax classes. If this factor were considered, there would be an additional tendency toward uniform rates.

of traditional commerce is desirable to discourage consumption of Internet goods that are characterized by differentially high administrative costs. On the other hand, preferential treatment of electronic commerce is more likely to be optimal in the presence of relatively high administrative costs if Internet goods are more substitutable with leisure and the untaxed good.

3. Some Illustrative Examples

The above discussion indicates that, as is inevitably the case for optimal tax problems, the final results are theoretically ambiguous and depend on the values of various key parameters. In particular, expression Eq. (3) indicates that the case for or against preferential tax treatment of electronic commerce is especially ambiguous with respect to efficiency and administrative cost considerations, while distributional concerns suggest that preferential taxation is not desirable. The following section attempts to shed some additional light on this issue, by performing some calculations of this optimal tax condition for various parameter values. This section presents some sample calculations for the tax rates t and τ, using the optimal tax condition Eq. (3) and a balanced budget requirement under which the combined revenues from any configuration of taxation of traditional and electronic commerce equals the revenues, net of administrative costs, in the initial equilibrium. The measure of preferential treatment for Internet goods is defined as the tax differential favoring electronic commerce, as a percentage of the tax rate applied to traditional commerce, or $\phi = (t - \tau)/t$. Expressed in percentage terms, if $\phi = 100$ the optimal tax structure implies tax exemption for electronic commerce, uniform treatment is reflected as $\phi = 0$, and $\phi < 0$ ($\phi > 100$) implies that electronic commerce should be taxed more heavily than traditional commerce (subsidized).

The calculations are based on parameter values taken from the empirical literature when available and plausible parameter values when empirical data are not available. The analysis uses a partial equilibrium approach that ignores general equilibrium reactions between changes in the tax rates and various parameter values (such as income shares, income and price elasticities, marginal utilities of income, the marginal efficiency cost of taxation and, for purposes of the government budget constraint, the sizes of the sales tax bases), all of which are assumed to be unaffected by the simulated tax rate changes. It should thus be viewed as only suggestive of the optimal tax differentials that might arise in a more complete general equilibrium analysis, which could also be utilized to calculate the changes in excess burden associated with various tax structures. Given the considerable uncertainty surrounding the parameter values used, the calculations are performed for a range of parameter values.

3.1. *Parameter values*

The parameter values used in the calculations were obtained as follows. In its study *A Nation Online: How Americans are Expanding Their Use of the Internet*, the U.S. Department of Commerce (2002) reports that in September 2001, 53.9 percent of the population (of age 3 and over) was using the Internet. Among Internet users, 39 percent of individuals are making online purchases. Thus approximately 21% of the population are Internet shoppers (.21 = .39 × .539), and 79% are not. Accordingly, the calculations assume $N^A/N = 0.79$ and $N^B/N = 0.21$. Assuming that these ratios can be applied directly to households (they are calculated for individuals) and using the 2001 figure for a population of 109.3 million households (U.S. Bureau of the Census, 2004–05), this implies $N^A = 86.3$ million and $N^B = 23.0$ million.[20]

Goolsbee and Zittrain (1999) provide information, based on 1997 data collected by Forrester Research, grouped by individuals who use and do not use the Internet. In particular, they report that the average income of individuals who do not use the Internet was $35,600, while the average income of Internet users was $57,200. Converting these figures to

[20]These figures are of course already dated. Note, however, that the optimal taxation results derived above depend primarily on the various own-price and cross-price elasticities and other parameters, rather than the absolute amount of goods sold over the Internet (which is any case calculated below using more recent 2003 data). Note in particular that in the optimal tax expression (3) the value of the denominator D is proportional to total internet purchases which thus fall out of the expression, so that total Internet sales enter into (3) only indirectly as reductions in purchases of substitutable goods; the effect of total purchases of Internet goods on the optimal tax differential should thus be relatively small, since they are relatively small in comparison to purchases of substitutable goods (and in comparison to the sum of purchases of all non-substitutable and substitutable goods).

2001 dollars yields values of \$39,300 and \$63,100. The ratio of the latter to the former is 1.6. Since data presented in U.S. Department of Commerce (2002) indicate that use of the Internet by lower income households has increased more rapidly in the intervening years (and since the consumption/income ratio declines with income), the assumed ratio of consumption expenditures of group *B* to group *A* is adjusted downward slightly to 1.5.[21]

With total personal consumption expenditures, exclusive of sales taxes paid, of \$7,045 billion in 2001 (U.S Department of Commerce, 2002), these assumptions imply that the total consumption levels of groups *A* and *B* are \$5,037 billion and \$2,008 billion. This consumption must be allocated among the four different goods in the model. Given the degree of aggregation in these data, any such allocation will of course be quite arbitrary; the definitions are chosen so that the amount of personal expenditures that could potential be made over the Internet is fairly broad. Using the consumption expenditures classifications used in the National Income and Product Accounts, exempt goods (X_E) are defined as food, housing, transportation and medical care, goods that are not substitutable for goods purchased over the Internet (X_N) as defined as motor vehicles[22] and parts, energy goods and services, recreation, other services[23] and other household operation items, and goods that are substitutable for goods purchased over

[21] Note that these figures are used as the consumption of individuals of type A and type B. This assumes that consumption is proportional to income for the two groups, and that the income levels of Internet shoppers are the same as those of Internet users. Goolsbee and Zittrain (1999) show that the variation in Internet usage across income groups is far greater than the variation in purchasing over the Internet, given Internet usage (although their results indicate that high income Internet users are somewhat more likely to be Internet shoppers).

[22] Although there is a small trade in motor vehicles over the Internet, such purchases are typically fully subject to either sales tax or a similar motor vehicle tax when the vehicle is registered. Thus, since most motor vehicle are not purchased over the Internet and all motor vehicles are subject to sales or motor vehicle taxes, motor vehicles are included in the group of goods that are not substitutable for goods purchased over the Internet and fully taxed at rate the standard sales tax rate *t*.

[23] Since most states are increasing the extent to which they tax consumer services (Hendrix and Zodrow, 2003), consumer services other than housing, transportation and medical care as treated as taxed goods, although this categorization is obviously fairly arbitrary.

the Internet or are actually purchased over the Internet (X_S and X_I) are defined as furniture and other household equipment, clothing and shoes, and all other durable and non-durable goods. The latter category must be divided between X_S and X_I. Although Internet sales, especially of consumer goods, are still relatively small (Cline and Neubig, 1999), they are growing rapidly. Since the projections of Bruce and Fox (2000) suggest potentially taxable sales of consumer goods over the Internet in 2003 of about $130 billion (slightly under 10 percent of all consumer expenditures in categories X_S and X_I), this figure is used in allocating goods between the two groups.[24] Bruce and Fox (2000) indicate that the average US state sales tax rate (t) is 6.38 percent, and that about 21 percent of potentially taxable consumer sales over the Internet are taxed, either because the selling firm has nexus in the consumer's state of residence or because the state collects use tax, implying an effective tax rate on such sales (τ) of 1.33 percent. The implied level of sales tax revenue, given the division of goods specified above, is $223.3 billion, yielding total gross consumer expenditures of $7,269 billion.[25]

Expenditures on consumer goods are allocated between the two groups A and B using data from Jorgenson (1997), which provides expenditure shares and income elasticities by income level for the classification of goods in the National Income and Product Accounts; these data are interpolated to fit the four-good classification system and the aggregate consumption levels, including sales taxes, for the two expenditure groups as described above.[26] The results of this interpolation are presented in Table 9.1. The resulting expenditure shares are fairly similar, with the

---

[24] Although this estimate, which is adjusted to reflect the larger values in unpublished data cited by Bruce and Fox (2000), is on the high end of existing estimates, especially when compared with Cline and Neubig (1999), it is used in the spirit of increasing the likelihood that preferential tax treatment of electronic commerce will be desirable in the optimal tax framework.

[25] This figure is not directly comparable to actual revenues, since the tax bases in this analysis are so approximate and sales taxation of business purchases is ignored; nevertheless, this figure is very close to the actual level of general sales tax revenues in 2001 (U.S. Bureau of the Census, 2004–05).

[26] Although these data are quite dated (1972), they provide the only information on expenditures shares and income elasticities by income and by commodity group that I was able to find.

Table 9.1.
Expenditure Shares and Income Elasticities

Consumption Good	Expenditure Share, Group A	Expenditure Share, Group B	Income Elasticity Group A	Income Elasticity Group B
X_E	0.495	0.421	0.673	0.554
X_N	0.334	0.326	0.995	0.912
X_S	0.171	0.189	1.955	1.857
X_I	0	0.064	0	1.857

Table 9.2.
Consumption Expenditures by Group

Consumption Good	Total Expenditures ($ billion)	Share of Total Consumption	Expenditures of Group A ($ billion)	Expenditures of Group B ($ billion)
X_E	3,442	0.474	2,569	873
X_N	2,412	0.332	1,735	677
X_S	1,283	0.176	890	392
X_I	132	0.018	0	132
Total	7,269	1.000	5,194	2,074

lower-income individuals in Group *A* spending a somewhat larger fraction of their income on exempt goods and the higher-income individuals in Group *B* spending a somewhat larger share of income on goods that can be purchased over the Internet and their substitutes. The income elasticities range from 0.5–2.0, with the lower-income individuals in Group *A* having a higher-income elasticity for exempt goods and both groups having relatively high income elasticities for goods substitutable with goods that can be purchased over the Internet.

The figures on expenditure shares by type of individual can then be used to calculate the distribution of the total consumption of the two groups across the four goods. The results of this calculation are presented in Table 9.2. Note that by assumption only individuals in Group *B* have expenditures on consumption of good X_I.

The remaining parameters needed for the calculation of the optimality condition (3) are the various own-price and cross-price elasticities.

Only limited evidence is available on these, so in many cases calculations are performed for a range of plausible values. As noted above, the results presented in Goolsbee (2000) suggest a very high own-price elasticity of Internet goods — in the context of the model utilized in this paper, the estimated reduction in Internet purchases due to the taxation of electronic commerce implies an average own-price demand elasticity roughly on the order of $\varepsilon_{II}^{B} = -4.0$. By comparison, Alm and Melnik (2003), using a more recent and comprehensive data set, present results that suggest a much lower own-price demand elasticity for Internet goods, on the order of one-fourth that estimated by Goolsbee (2000). However, since the implications of a high own-price demand elasticity for Internet goods are the focus of this paper — and in the spirit of making assumptions which tend to make the strongest case for preferential treatment of electronic commerce — the analysis will assume the higher value in the simulations presented below.

Another key parameter is the cross-price elasticity of the various goods with leisure and the tax-exempt good. Fullerton and Rogers (1993) use an elasticity of substitution between consumption and leisure of 0.50 in their lifetime tax incidence general equilibrium model which, with the CES utility function they employ and a time endowment equally split between consumption and non-market activity, implies a compensated cross-price elasticity of demand with leisure of 0.25.[27] Accordingly, 0.25 is used as the benchmark value for the compensated cross-price elasticities of the various goods with leisure. Since the tax-exempt good consists primarily of basic necessities, the analysis assumes that the compensated demand for this good is inelastic with respect to own price and is not affected by the prices of the other goods; that is, all compensated cross-price elasticities involving the tax-exempt good and the other goods are assumed to be zero. Finally, in the absence of a compelling argument otherwise and because this cross-price elasticity is of less importance in the optimal taxation analysis than those of the Internet good and its substitutes, the compensated cross-price elasticity of the goods that are

[27] By comparison, Altig *et al.* (2001) assume an elasticity of substitution between consumption and leisure of 0.8 with approximately 40 percent of the time endowment devoted to labor supply; using these alternative values has only a minor impact on the results.

assumed to be not substitutable with the goods sold over the Internet with respect to the price of the Internet good is also assumed to be zero.

For administration and compliance costs, Slemrod and Bakija (1996) report from a sample of eight states that administrative costs under the state sales tax were between 0.4–1.0 percent of revenues and compliance costs were between 2–3.8 percent in seven of those states. Accordingly, the analysis assumes that marginal costs are constant with $c_t = 0.035$, which is near the midpoint of this range, and that c_T is some multiple of c_t.

Consider next the social welfare optimization problem. The analysis assumes that the individual utility functions, which are characterized by heterogeneous preferences, are cardinalized so that the marginal utility of income for both types of individuals is one and that these marginal utilities of income do not vary with the tax rates; this implies that differences in individual preferences do not by themselves (in the absence of any social concerns about the distribution of income) give rise to tax differentials.[28] The analysis initially assumes no social weighting ($\gamma^A = \gamma^B = 1$), but also considers various weighting schemes that place a lower weight γ^B on the relatively higher income individuals. For the calculation of λ, the marginal social cost of raising revenue, the marginal excess burden of the system of sales taxes is assumed to be constant at 10 percent and administrative and compliance costs are as described above. This figure is roughly consistent with general equilibrium results on the efficiency costs of a national value-added tax presented by Ballard, Scholz and Shoven (1987), adjusted upward to reflect variation in sales tax rates across the states and the fact that much of the sales tax in the U.S. functions as a distortionary cascading tax on business inputs.[29] Finally, the various β values (2–3) are calculated using these values and the expenditure shares and income elasticities presented in Table 9.1.

---

[28] See Boadway, Marchand, Pestieau and del Mar Racionero (2002) for a discussion of such cardinalization for social welfare optimization with individuals with heterogeneous preferences.

[29] Recall that Ring (1999) estimates that 60 percent of the state sales tax base consists of consumer purchases. The resulting cascading of tax burden implies that the US state sales the tax system is considerably more inefficient than the truly consumption-based VAT studied by Ballard, Scholz and Shoven (1987).

3.2. *Results*

The first set of results establishes a benchmark case, in which distributional concerns are ignored, administrative and compliance costs for taxing Internet goods are assumed to equal those for traditional commerce, and the compensated cross-price elasticities for goods X_N, X_S (for both types of individuals) and X_I (for individuals of type *B*) with respect to leisure are set equal to 0.25. In this benchmark case, which is designed to maximize the optimality of equal taxation, the optimal tax rate on Internet goods is 6.08 percent, slightly less than the tax rate on traditional goods of 6.20 percent. This slight differential reflects the fact that even though $\gamma^A = \gamma^B = 1$, $\beta^B/\lambda = 0.952$ is slightly larger than $\beta^A/\lambda = 0.947$ because individuals of type *B* are slightly more likely to spend additional income on taxed goods. As a result, slightly preferential tax treatment of Internet goods is desirable because it provides more income to individuals of type *B*, who in turn spend it disproportionately on taxed goods. The resulting "optimal" tax differential of 0.12 percentage points (or a value of $\phi = 1.8$ percent) due to this factor is, however, negligible.

Consider next variations in the degree of substitutability of Internet goods for leisure $\left(\varepsilon_{IW}^{B}\right)$.[30] Larger (smaller) values of this elasticity should lead to lower (higher) tax rates on Internet goods, as they are less (more) complementary with leisure, and this pattern is observed in Table 9.3. However, variations in the cross-price elasticity over a considerable range $\left(-0.50 < \varepsilon_{IW}^{B} < 1.0\right)$ lead to only moderate variation in the tax rates, as the

Table 9.3.
Variations in Substitutability of X_I for Leisure

ε_{IW}^{B}	−0.50	−0.25	0.00	0.25	0.50	0.75	1.00
t	6.17%	6.18%	6.19%	6.20%	6.21%	6.22%	6.23%
τ	6.83%	6.58%	6.34%	6.08%	5.85%	5.60%	5.35%
$t-\tau$	−0.65%	−0.40%	−0.14%	0.12%	0.37%	0.62%	0.88%
ϕ	−10.5%	−6.4%	−2.3%	1.8%	5.9%	10.0%	14.1%

[30] All variations in the relative substitutability of the Internet good for leisure (or for the untaxed good) are assumed to be accompanied by identical variations for the closely substitutable good X_S.

optimal tax differentials vary from –0.65 to 0.88 percentage points, with the e-commerce tax preference measure (ϕ) clustering in the neighborhood of zero (–10.5% < ϕ < 14.1%), indicating that the optimal tax preference for Internet goods is at most about 14 percent for the range of parameter values analyzed, and should in fact be negative for the values of $\varepsilon^B_{Iw} < 0.25$, reflecting a surtax as large as nearly 11 percent.

The optimality condition Eq. (3) also indicates that the cross-price elasticity of the Internet good with untaxed goods is also an important parameter in determining the extent of taxation of electronic commerce. Although the base case assumption that this elasticity is zero seems plausible, a higher (lower) values of ε^B_{IE}, for any given value of ε^B_{Iw}, would tend to imply lower (higher) taxation of the Internet good, as it would be less (more) complementary with the untaxed good. This is demonstrated in Table 9.4, which gives the optimal tax differentials for the same range of ε^B_{Iw}, that is, $-0.50 < \varepsilon^B_{IE} < 1.00$, when $\varepsilon^B_{IE} = 0.25$ rather that the benchmark value of $\varepsilon^B_{IE} = 0$. As expected, this increases the likelihood that preferential taxation of electronic commerce is desirable, although the effects are fairly modest. Specifically, the optimal tax differentials now vary from –0.40 to 1.13 percentage points, with the e-commerce tax preference measure (ϕ) shifting up about 4 percentage points, as it varies from (–6.4% < ϕ < 18.2%). Thus, in this case, the maximum optimal tax preference for Internet goods increases from around 14 percent to roughly 18 percent for the range of parameter values analyzed, and is negative only for the negative values of ε^B_{Iw}, with a maximum surtax of 6.4 percent.

The effect of adding distributional concerns to the analysis is less ambiguous and somewhat more significant. Suppose that social concern about the (current) fact that Internet users are relatively high income

Table 9.4.

Variations in Substitutability of X_I for Leisure ($\varepsilon^B_{IE} = 0.25$)

ε^B_{IW}	–0.50	–0.25	0.00	0.25	0.50	0.75	1.00
t	6.18%	6.19%	6.20%	6.21%	6.22%	6.23%	6.24%
τ	6.58%	6.34%	6.09%	5.85%	5.60%	5.35%	5.10%
$t-\tau$	–0.40%	–0.14%	0.11%	0.37%	0.62%	0.88%	1.13%
ϕ	–6.4%	–2.3%	1.8%	5.9%	10.0%	14.1%	18.2%

Table 9.5.
Variations in Social Weight on Higher Income Individuals ($\gamma^A = 1.0$, $\varepsilon^B_{IW} = 0.25$, $\varepsilon^B_{IE} = 0$)

γ^B	1.00	0.95	0.90	0.80	0.70	0.60	0.50
t	6.20%	6.18%	6.16%	6.14%	6.13%	6.12%	6.11%
τ	6.09%	6.75%	7.19%	7.75%	8.08%	8.31%	8.47%
$t-\tau$	0.11%	–0.57%	–1.03%	–1.61%	–1.96%	–2.19%	–2.36%
ϕ	1.8%	–9.3%	–16.8%	–26.2%	–31.9%	–35.8%	–38.5%

individuals is expressed by utilizing weights in the social welfare function such that $\gamma^B < \gamma^A = 1$. Although the appropriate weights, if any, are inherently subjective, a value of γ^B outside the range of $0.5 \leq \gamma^B \leq 1$ seems implausible, especially since the consumption levels of the two groups are not radically different (recall that the consumption level of group B is 1.5 times the consumption of group A).[31] Table 9.5 provides results for this variation in γ^B for the benchmark case in which $\varepsilon^B_{IW} = 0.25$ (and $\varepsilon^B_{IE} = 0$). These results demonstrate that such weighting significantly affects the optimal tax differential, implying a surtax on the Internet good — since it is consumed disproportionately by the relatively high income group — that goes as high as 2.4 percentage points. Similarly, the e-commerce tax preference measure ϕ is negative for all values of $\gamma^B < 1$, implying surtaxes that range up to 38.5 percent.

Differential administrative and compliance costs also play an important role in determining the optimal tax rate on Internet goods. For example, consider the benchmark case ($\varepsilon^B_{IW} = 0.25, \varepsilon^B_{IE} = 0, \gamma^A = \gamma^B = 1.0$), and suppose that the marginal administrative and compliance costs of taxing Internet goods are somewhere between equal to and twice the costs for other goods of 3.5 percent of revenues ($c_t = 0.035$). Table 9.6 presents the results for this case.

These results suggest that differentially high administrative and compliance costs for taxing Internet goods put moderate downward pressure

[31]The maximum differential in the distributional weights shown in Table 9.5 corresponds roughly to a social welfare function with an elasticity of the marginal social valuation of individual utility of one, as a fifty percent increase in an individual's consumption gives rise to a fifty percent reduction in the individual's social weight.

Table 9.6.
Variations in Administrative and Compliance Costs for X_I
($c_t = 0.035$, $\varepsilon^B_{IW} = 0.25$, $\varepsilon^B_{IE} = 0$, $\gamma^A = \gamma^B = 1.0$)

c_τ	0.035	0.040	0.045	0.050	0.055	0.060	0.070
t	6.20%	6.21%	6.21%	6.22%	6.22%	6.23%	6.24%
τ	6.09%	6.00%	5.90%	5.80%	5.70%	5.60%	5.39%
$t-\tau$	0.11%	0.21%	0.31%	0.41%	0.52%	0.62%	0.84%
ϕ	1.8%	3.4%	5.0%	6.7%	8.3%	10.0%	13.5%

on τ. In particular, although there is a tendency for higher administrative and compliance costs to lead to higher tax rates on Internet goods in order to discourage consumption of goods with high tax administration costs, this effect is outweighed by the interaction between the higher administrative and compliance costs and the cross-price elasticity effects in Eq. (3), as described above. The net result is that the optimal sales tax differential favoring Internet goods increases monotonically, ranging from 0.11–0.84 percentage points, with the Internet good preference parameter ranging from $1.8\% \leq \phi \leq 13.5\%$. Nevertheless, given the significant increase in costs at the high end of this spectrum (a doubling from 3.5 to 7.0 percent of total revenues), the fact that the optimal tax preference for Internet goods is a maximum of less than 14 percent suggests that higher administrative and compliance costs by themselves do not justify a significant preference for electronic commerce.

A wide variety of interactions among the various parameters can also be examined. Consider first the interactions between variations in administrative and compliance costs and differences in the cross-price elasticities of the Internet good with leisure and untaxed goods. These are explored in Table 9.7, which examines the effects of higher administrative and compliance costs for the case in which the Internet good relatively substitutable with leisure and the untaxed good ($\varepsilon^B_{IW} = 0.75$, $\varepsilon^B_{IE} = 0.25$), and in Table 9.8 which illustrates the case in which the Internet good is relatively complementary for these goods ($\varepsilon^B_{IW} = -0.25$, $\varepsilon^B_{IE} = -0.25$). These results indicate that the differences in cross-price elasticities have the expected effect on the optimal tax rates on Internet goods. When Internet goods are relatively substitutable with leisure and the untaxed good, preferential

Table 9.7.
Variations in Administrative and Compliance Costs for X_I
($c_t = 0.035$, $\varepsilon^B_{IW} = 0.75$, $\varepsilon^B_{IE} = 0.25$, $\gamma^A = \gamma^B = 1.0$)

c_τ	0.035	0.040	0.045	0.050	0.055	0.060	0.070
t	6.23%	6.24%	6.24%	6.25%	6.25%	6.26%	6.27%
τ	5.35%	5.22%	5.08%	4.94%	4.80%	4.66%	4.36%
$t-\tau$	0.88%	1.02%	1.16%	1.31%	1.46%	1.60%	1.91%
ϕ	14.1%	16.3%	18.6%	20.9%	23.3%	25.6%	30.4%

Table 9.8.
Variations in Administrative and Compliance Costs for X_I
($c_t = 0.035$, $\varepsilon^B_{IW} = -0.25$, $\varepsilon^B_{IE} = -0.25$, $\gamma^A = \gamma^B = 1.0$)

c_τ	0.035	0.040	0.045	0.050	0.055	0.060	0.070
t	6.17%	6.18%	6.18%	6.18%	6.19%	6.19%	6.20%
τ	6.83%	6.77%	6.72%	6.66%	6.61%	6.55%	6.43%
$t-\tau$	−0.65%	−0.59%	−0.54%	−0.48%	−0.42%	−0.36%	−0.23%
ϕ	−10.5%	−9.6%	−8.7%	−7.7%	−6.8%	−5.8%	−3.7%

taxation of Internet goods is always desirable, with differentials that range from 0.88–1.91 percentage points (Table 9.7). Even in this case, however, the maximum value of the Internet good tax preference parameter ϕ for the range of parameters considered is still at most roughly 30 percent. In contrast, when Internet goods are relatively complementary with both leisure and the untaxed good, the effects of increases in administrative costs are never strong enough to offset the tendency to tax leisure complements at differentially higher rates, with surtaxes on Internet goods ranging from 10.5 to 3.7 percent (Table 9.8).

Finally, the interaction between distributional concerns and differential administrative costs is examined in Tables 9.9 and 9.10. Consider first the benchmark case ($\varepsilon^B_{IW} = 0.25$, $\varepsilon^B_{IE} = 0$) but suppose that administrative and compliance costs for taxing Internet goods are twice those for other goods ($c_t = 0.035$, $c_\tau = 0.070$), and the range of distributional weights is the same as in Table 9.5. The results for this case are given in Table 9.9, and suggest that distributional concerns rapidly outweigh

Table 9.9.
Variations in Social Weight on Higher Income Individuals
($\gamma^A = 1.0, c_t = 0.035, c_\tau = 0.070, \varepsilon^B_{IW} = 0.25, \varepsilon^B_{IE} = 0$)

γ^B	1.00	0.95	0.90	0.80	0.70	0.60	0.50
t	6.24%	6.20%	6.18%	6.16%	6.14%	6.13%	6.12%
τ	5.39%	6.28%	6.87%	7.60%	8.05%	8.34%	8.55%
$t-\tau$	0.84%	–0.07%	–0.68%	–1.45%	–1.91%	–2.21%	–2.43%
ϕ	13.5%	–1.2%	–11.1%	–23.5%	–31.0%	–36.1%	–39.7%

Table 9.10.
Variations in Social Weight on Higher Income Individuals
($\gamma^A = 1.0, c_t = 0.035, c_\tau = 0.070, \varepsilon^B_{IW} = 0.75, \varepsilon^B_{IE} = 0.25$)

γ^B	1.00	0.95	0.90	0.80	0.70	0.60	0.50
t	6.27%	6.23%	6.20%	6.17%	6.15%	6.14%	6.13%
τ	4.36%	5.49%	6.25%	7.20%	7.78%	8.17%	8.45%
$t-\tau$	1.91%	0.74%	–0.04%	–1.03%	–1.63%	–2.03%	–2.32%
ϕ	30.4%	11.9%	–0.7%	–16.8%	–26.6%	–33.1%	–37.9%

the effects of differential administrative costs, as the optimal tax rate on Internet goods roughly equals the rate on other goods for $\gamma^B = 0.95$ ($\phi = -1.2\%$) and the optimal tax preference parameter for the Internet good indicates a surtax of nearly 40 percent when $\gamma^B = 0.5$.

This strong result is only tempered somewhat if Internet goods are relatively substitutable for leisure and untaxed goods. To take the case among those analyzed thus far most favorable to a tax preference for electronic commerce, suppose that $\varepsilon^B_{IW} = 0.75, \varepsilon^B_{IE} = 0.25$ and administrative costs for taxing Internet goods are still double those of other goods ($c_t = 0.035$, $c_\tau = 0.070$). In this case, even though the tax preference parameter is roughly thirty percent in the absence of distributional concerns, such concerns are sufficiently important to result in a roughly uniform taxation for $\gamma^B = 0.9$ ($\phi = -0.04\%$), and the tax preference parameter indicates a surtax on Internet goods of nearly 38 percent when $\gamma^B = 0.5$.

4. Conclusion

The goal of this research was to identify the factors that determine whether preferential taxation of electronic commerce is desirable from an optimal taxation perspective and provide some calculations that illustrate the implications of plausible values for these factors. The model constructed built on existing results from the literatures on optimal commodity taxation including both efficiency and equity concerns, taxation and administrative costs, and the taxation of electronic commerce. The analysis stressed a balancing of the tendency toward uniform taxation due to efficiency concerns about distorting consumer decisions across consumption commodities as well as the essential physical similarity of goods sold over the Internet and by traditional retailers against the tendency for differential taxation attributable to differences between the goods, including differences in various demand elasticities, distributional preferences and administrative and compliance costs. The analysis identified the parameters that are critical in characterizing these offsetting tendencies, and provided some illustrative calculations as a means of determining their net effects and thus ascertaining whether it appears that uniform or preferential taxation of electronic commerce is desirable.

The results indicate that, as is generally the case in optimal taxation problems, the optimal tax treatment of traditional and electronic commerce varies considerably depending on key parameter values (highlighting the need for more empirical data on these parameters), implying preferential tax treatment of electronic commerce in some cases and higher taxes in others. Nevertheless, even though the assumptions of the model were generally chosen to maximize the likelihood that preferential treatment of electronic commerce would be desirable, the results suggest that, in the practical terms of the current debate, uniform tax treatment of traditional and electronic commerce is much more likely to be desirable than tax exemption (or, alternatively, a significant tax preference for e-commerce). In none of the cases analyzed did the optimal tax rate approach zero, with the largest "optimal" tax preference for electronic commerce on the order of 30 percent, and many much less than that. A key factor leading to prescriptions for moderate preferential treatment of sales over the Internet was relatively high administrative and compliance costs, lending some credence to the argument that uniform taxation is much more likely to be desirable if advances in computer software or simplification efforts such as those proposed and to some extent implemented under the Streamlined Sales Tax Project (or even more radical proposals for simplification such as that advanced by McLure (2000)) are successful in reducing the costs of administering and complying with taxation of sales over the Internet. On the other hand, differentially higher taxation of Internet goods was also optimal in a variety of cases, with the always controversial addition of distributional concerns playing a large role in prescribing relatively high tax rates on Internet goods, and in some cases resulting in surtaxes in the neighborhood of 35–40 percent. Indeed, the simplest characterization of the results presented in this paper is that the optimal tax rates on electronic commerce tend to cluster around the rate applied to traditional commerce. Thus, on balance, it seems clear that tax exemption of Internet goods is very unlikely to be even close to optimal, and the optimal differentials calculated in this paper suggest that it is unlikely that the traditional prescription of uniform taxation should be overridden by optimal taxation concerns, especially once the administrative and political difficulties of implementing differential taxation are taken into account.

Acknowledgments

Research support from the American Tax Policy Institute is gratefully acknowledged. An earlier version of this paper was presented at a conference sponsored by ATPI in Washington, DC on July 8, 2004 at which I received many helpful comments, especially from my discussants Joseph Cordes and Tom Neubig. I have also benefited from the comments of Charles McLure and two anonymous referees, and from the research assistance of Joyce Tung, Joe Vavra and Michele Hendrix. Finally I would like to extend special thanks to Charles Collins of Taxware for his help with information on the costs of applying state sales and use taxes to electronic commerce.

References

Advisory Commission on Electronic Commerce. *Report to Congress*. <http://www.ecommercecommission.org/acec_report.pdf>, 2000.

Alm, James and Mikhail I. Melnick. Sales Taxes and the Decision to Purchase Online. Manuscript, Georgia State University, 2003.

Altig, David, Alan J. Auerbach, Laurence J. Kotlikoff, Kent A. Smetters and Jan Walliser. Simulating Fundamental Tax Reform in the United States. *American Economic Review* 91(2001): 574–595.

Auerbach, Alan J. and James R. Hines. Taxation and Economic Efficiency. In *Handbook of Public Economics, Volume 3*, edited by Alan J. Auerbach and Martin Feldstein. New York: Elsevier, 2002.

Ballard, Charles L., John Karl Scholz and John B. Shoven. The Value-Added Tax: A General Equilibrium Look at Its Efficiency and Incidence. In *The Effects of Taxation on Capital Accumulation*, edited by Martin Feldstein. Chicago: University of Chicago Press, 1987.

Bird, Richard. Taxing Electronic Commerce: The End of the Beginning? *International Tax Program Paper 0502.* Toronto: University of Toronto International Tax Program, 2003.

Boadway, Robin, Maurice Marchand, Pierre Pestieau and Maria del Mar Racionero. Optimal Redistribution with Heterogeneous Preferences for Leisure. *Journal of Public Economic Theory* 4 (2002): 475–498.

Bruce, Donald and William F. Fox. E-Commerce in the Context of Declining State Sales Tax Bases. *National Tax Journal* 53 (2000): 1373–1388.

Bruce, Donald, William F. Fox and Matthew Murray. To Tax or Not To Tax? The Case of Electronic Commerce. *Contemporary Economic Policy* 21 (2003): 25–40.

Cline, Robert J. and Thomas S. Neubig. The Sky is Not Falling: Why State and Local Revenues Were Not Significantly Affected in 1998. *State Tax Notes* 43 (1999).

Corlett, W. and D. Hague. Complementarity and the Excess Burden of Taxation. *Review of Economic Studies* 21 (1953): 21–30.

Diamond, Peter A. A Many-Person Ramsey Tax Rule. *Journal of Public Economics* 4 (1975): 335–342.

Fox, William F. and Matthew Murray. The Sales Tax and Electronic Commerce: So What's New? *National Tax Journal* 50 (1997): 573–592.

Fox, William F. and LeAnn Luna. Taxing E-Commerce: Neutral Taxation if Best for the Industry and the Economy Manuscript, University of Tennessee at Knoxville, 2003.

Fullerton, Don and Diane Lim Rogers. *Who Bears the Lifetime Tax Burden?* Washington DC: The Brookings Institution, 1993.

Goolsbee, Austan. In a World Without Borders: The Impact of Taxes on Internet Commerce. *Quarterly Journal of Economics* 115 (2000): 561–576.

Goolsbee Austan and Jonathan Zittrain. Evaluating the Costs and Benefits of Taxing Internet Commerce. *National Tax Journal* 52 (1999): 413–428.

Harberger, Arnold. The Uniform Tax Controversy. In *Public Finance, Trade and Development*, edited by Vito Tanzi. Detroit, MI: Wayne State University Press, 1990.

Hendrix, Michele and George R. Zodrow. Sales Taxation of Services: An Economic Analysis. *Florida State Law Review* 30 (2003): 411–433.

Jorgenson, Dale J. *Welfare, Volume 1: Aggregate Consumer Behavior.* Cambridge, MA: MIT Press, 1997.

Kaplow, Louis. Optimal Taxation with Costly Enforcement and Evasion. *Journal of Public Economics* 43 (1990): 221–236.

Kaplow, Louis. On the Undesirability of Commodity Taxation Even When Income Taxation is Not Optimal. *John M. Olin Center for Law and Economics,* Discussion Paper No. 470, 2004.

Lancaster, Kelvin J. A New Approach to Consumer Theory. *Journal of Political Economy* 74 (1966): 132–157.

McLure, Charles E., Jr. Rethinking State and Local Reliance on the Retail Sales Tax: Should We Fix the State Sales Tax or Discard It? *Brigham Young University Law Review.* 2000, pp. 77–137.

McLure, Charles E., Jr. Taxing Electronic Commerce: Legal, Economic, Administrative, and Political Issues. *Urban Lawyer* 34 (2002): 487–520.

McLure, Charles E., Jr. and Walter Hellerstein. Congressional Intervention in State Taxation: A Normative Analysis of Three Proposals. *State Tax Notes* 31 (March 1, 2004): 721–735.

Mikesell, John L. Remote Vendors and American Sales and Use Taxation: The Balance Between Fixing the Problem and Fixing the Tax. *National Tax Journal* 53 (2000): 1273–1286.

National Tax Association. *Communications and Electronic Commerce Tax Project: Final Report.* <http://www.ntanet.org/ecommerce/final.pdf>, 1999.

Ring, Raymond. Consumers' Share and Producers' Share of the General Sales Tax. *National Tax Journal* 52 (1999): 79–90.

Saez, Emmanuel. The Desirability of Commodity Taxation under Non-Linear Income Taxation and Heterogeneous Tastes. *Journal of Public Economics* 83 (2002): 217–230.

Saez, Emmanuel. Direct or Indirect Tax Instruments for Redistribution: Short-run versus Long-run. *Journal of Public Economics* 88 (2004): 503–518.

Sandmo, Agnar. Income Tax Evasion, Labour Supply, and the Efficiency-Equity Tradeoff. *Journal of Public Economics* 16 (1981): 265–288.

Slemrod, Joel. Optimal Taxation and Optimal Tax Systems. *Journal of Economic Perspectives* 4 (1990): 157–178.

Slemrod, Joel and Jon Bakija. *Taxing Ourselves: A Citizen's Guide to the Great Debate over Tax Reform.* Cambridge, MA: MIT Press, 1996.

Streamlined Sales Tax Project. *Streamlined Sales Tax System for the 21st Century.* <http://www.geocities.com/streamlined2000/>, 2001.

U.S. Bureau of the Census. *Statistical Abstract of the United States: 2004–2005.* Washington, DC: U.S. Bureau of the Census, 2004–2005.

U.S. Department of Commerce. *A Nation Online: How Americans are Expanding Their Use of the Internet.* Washington, DC: U.S. Department of Commerce, 2002.

Yitzhaki, Shlomo. A Note on Optimal Taxation and Administrative Costs. *American Economic Review* 69 (1979): 475–480.

Zodrow, George R. *State Sales and Income Taxes.* College Station: Texas A&M Press, 1999.

Zodrow, George R. Evaluating the Case for a Temporary Moratorium on the Taxation of Electronic Commerce. *State Tax Notes* 19 (December 4, 2000): 1515–1521.

Zodrow, George R. Network Externalities and Indirect Tax Preferences for Electronic Commerce. *International Tax and Public Finance* 10 (2002): 79–97.

Zodrow, George R. Optimal Commodity Taxation of Traditional and Electronic Commerce (Working Paper). Rice University, 2005.

Part III

Income Tax Reform

Chapter 10

Treasury I and the Tax Reform Act of 1986: The Economics and Politics of Tax Reform*

Charles E. McLure, Jr.† and George R. Zodrow‡

†*Senior Fellow at the Hoover Institution, Stanford University, Stanford, CA, USA*

‡*Associate Professor of Economics, Rice University, Houston, TX, USA*

During President Reagan's State of the Union Address in January 1984, he requested that Treasury Secretary Donald Regan prepare "a plan for action to simplify the entire tax code so that all taxpayers, big and small, are treated more fairly." In response, the Department of the Treasury spent ten months preparing a report to the President that has come to be called Treasury I (U.S. Department of the Treasury, 1984). This three-volume study explained the need for tax reform and the general directions such reform should take, provided a comprehensive set of proposals for reform of the income tax, and analyzed the feasibility and desirability of an American value-added tax. Following almost two years of public debate, the Tax Reform Act of 1986 (hereafter the 1986 Act) became law on

*This chapter is reproduced from *Journal of Economic Perspectives*, **1**(1), 37–58, 1987.

October 22, 1986. Though widely hailed as the most far-reaching reform of the nation's tax system since the 1940s, if not since the introduction of the income tax in 1913, the 1986 Act falls far short of the promise of Treasury I.

It is useful to devote attention to Treasury I, even though much of it failed to survive the legislative process. First, because Treasury I represented an attempt to formulate a workable tax system that closely approximates the economist's view of an ideal income tax, it is likely to condition future deliberations on tax reform both in the United States and in other countries. Second, the conceptually coherent proposals of Treasury I provide a standard against which to measure the hodge-podge of proposals that became law in the 1986 Act. Finally, a discussion of the decisions underlying Treasury I should prove informative to economists and political scientists interested in the process and substance of tax reform.

Before proceeding, a brief description of the process by which Treasury I was formulated may be of interest. The White House had no involvement in preparing Treasury I. Instead, the staff economists and lawyers in the Office of Tax Policy, under the direction of the Deputy Assistant Secretary for Tax Analysis (Charles McLure, a public finance economist), prepared proposals for consideration by the Assistant Secretary for Tax Policy (Ronald Pearlman, a tax attorney). Proposals approved by Pearlman were forwarded to Treasury Secretary Donald Regan and discussed in highly confidential meetings attended by Regan, his Deputy Secretary, the Undersecretary for Monetary Affairs (Beryl Sprinkel), the Commissioner of Internal Revenue (Roscoe Egger), the assistant secretaries for Economic Policy (Manuel Johnson), Legislative Affairs, Business and Consumer Affairs, and Press Relations, as well as Pearlman and McLure. Of the nine individuals advising the Secretary at these meetings, only three were tax experts; two (Sprinkel and Johnson) were economists without particular expertise in tax matters, but the other four were neither tax experts nor economists. However, in most cases Secretary Regan did accept the advice of his two chief tax policy advisers.

1. Critical Decisions on Tax Reform

Literally hundreds of decisions were made during the formulation of Treasury I, and many of these affected the final contours of tax reform.

The seven most critical decisions were: (1) to reform the basic structure of the income tax rather than relying on "add-on" or "back-stop" indirect measures; (2) to use income rather than consumption as the tax base; (3) to have a revenue neutral reform; (4) to have a distributionally neutral reform; (5) to strive for investment neutrality and thus eliminate opportunities for tax shelters; (6) to shift some of the burden of taxation from individuals to corporations; and (7) to implement reform quickly.

1.1. *Reforming the basic structure of the income tax*

The reform strategy chosen in Treasury I was a frontal attack on nearly all current law deviations of taxable income from real economic income. Efforts were made to match the timing of recognition of income and the deduction of related expenses, and to eliminate industry-specific tax preferences. Comprehensive inflation adjustment would have been applied to capital gains, interest income and expense, depreciation allowances, and the cost of goods sold from inventories. On the individual side, most tax credits and most exclusions, exemptions, and deductions not necessary for the accurate measurement of real economic income would have been eliminated or sharply curtailed, while personal exemptions and the zero-bracket amount would have been raised.

Achieving the overriding objective of taxing all real economic income consistently would reduce horizontal inequities (substantial differences in tax payments by families with equal real economic incomes), allow lower tax rates, reduce interference of the tax system in private market decision-making, reduce the importance of tax planning, simplify tax compliance, and improve both the actual and the perceived fairness of the tax system.[1]

Two alternative approaches were rejected in Treasury I. The first would have left the existing income tax more or less intact and concentrated on devising an alternative minimum tax that tracked economic

[1] For further elaboration on this objective and its reflection in the proposals of Treasury I, see U.S. Treasury Department (1984) and McLure (1986b). The political importance of the objective of "perceived" fairness is particularly apparent in the minimum tax provision of the 1986 Act which assesses tax on corporations on the basis of their reported book income.

income much more closely. Once the minimum tax was in place, its rates could be raised gradually, and those of the existing tax lowered, until the minimum tax superceded the existing system. But such an approach would require millions of taxpayers to calculate tax liability under two tax codes during a lengthy transition period. It was deemed to be politically unacceptable and too complex.

The second alternative was to set tougher limitations on deductions for artificial losses. Many tax preferences would be left intact under this approach, but taxpayers would be prohibited from using artificial accounting losses (resulting, for instance, from accelerated depreciation allowances coupled with interest deductions) to offset (or shelter) income from other sources. This approach was rejected both because it is more complicated than direct structural reform and because the arbitrary line-drawing it requires — distinguishing, for instance, "tax shelter" losses from "real economic" losses — is unfair and distortionary.

The 1986 Act is commonly portrayed as being similar in spirit to Treasury I, but actually the two differ in spirit and substance. Instead of fundamental reform, the 1986 Act is better characterized as using the revenues from elimination of most tax shelters, the investment tax credit, sales tax deductibility, and other politically vulnerable provisions to reduce tax rates dramatically. Reflecting political compromise that was almost totally absent in the development of Treasury I, the 1986 Act allows many sources and uses of income to remain tax-preferred. To eliminate or sharply curtail tax shelters, the 1986 Act combines the minimum tax and the limitation on artificial loss approaches, with all the complexity those approaches imply. For example, in attempting to limit artificial losses, the 1986 Act creates a new distinction between passive and active investment income and new restrictions on which types of interest expense are deductible. Distinctions like these lead to complexity, expensive compliance and enforcement procedures, and a multitude of traps for the unwary; furthermore, they generate an endless cycle of administratively cumbersome regulations, taxpayer schemes to recharacterize income and expenses, and use of mergers or "bundling" arrangements through financial intermediaries to circumvent the limitations. Finally, such distinctions distort economic decision-making; for example, some taxpayers will simply avoid many transactions that would subject them to these complex rules, including some of those that would otherwise make economic sense.

As a result, the 1986 Act provides little simplification, except for those removed entirely from the tax rolls or those who will no longer itemize deductions. For many taxpayers with upper-middle or high incomes or with substantial wealth, the effect of the tax system on economic decision-making will become more complicated, rather than less.

1.2. *Choosing income as the tax base*

The most fundamental decision made in formulating Treasury I — and for many, the most disappointing — was to propose a comprehensive tax on real economic income, rather than a tax on personal consumption or consumed income. The simplicity, equity, and efficiency advantages of consumption taxes have been detailed in the literature, and various consumption-based taxes have attracted broad support in both the academic and business communities (for an excellent recent exposition, see Bradford, 1986). However, the income tax has the obvious advantage of familiarity.[2] A great deal of experience has been acquired over the years with all practical aspects of income taxation, while no industrialized country has ever implemented a personal tax on consumption.[3]

But the choice of the income tax model reflected much more than familiarity; implementation of a consumption tax is more problematic than it may seem. For example, some consumption tax advocates would exempt from tax gifts and bequests transferred between individuals until

---

[2]Most of the following discussion is relevant primarily for a cash-flow tax on consumed income modeled after that outlined in *Blueprints for Basic Tax Reform* (U.S. Department of the Treasury, 1977), the approach that received most consideration by the Treasury Department. Some are equally applicable to a tax patterned after the so-called "Plan X" described in Bradford (1986), a multi-rate version of the flat tax reform proposal described in Hall and Rabushka (1983, 1985). The flat rate tax plan advocated by Hall and Rabushka would seriously violate distributional neutrality.

[3]For further discussion of the choice of an income-based tax and the role time constraints and staffing problems played in that choice, see McLure (1985, 1986b). Other determinants of that choice are discussed in U.S. Department of the Treasury (1984), Vol. 1, Chapter 3.

such transfers are consumed by the recipient. Others argue that a consumption tax would be acceptable only if gifts and bequests were included in the tax base of the donor or decedent (that is, treated as consumption of the transferor), and then taxed again when consumed by the recipient. Under such an approach the tax base would be the individual's lifetime endowment (see Aaron and Galper, 1985). Given the amounts of wealth held by high income families that passes from generation to generation, the treatment of gifts and bequests assumes major importance.

In this context, it is important to note that gift and estate taxes have been drastically reduced recently and that there is apparently an unwillingness to curb gift and estate tax loopholes that are now so generous that one expert has categorized gift and estate taxes as "voluntary" (see Cooper, 1979). Moreover, during the formulation of Treasury I, it was impossible to gain agreement for even extremely limited taxation of capital gains on assets transferred at death. Accordingly, if consumption had been chosen as the tax base, gifts and bequests would probably have been excluded on political grounds. At least some of those responsible for the formulation of Treasury I, agreeing with the "individual lifetime endowment" school of consumption tax advocates, thought such an outcome would be highly inequitable.

International considerations raised additional problems with moving to a consumption tax. First, bogus international transactions might be used to evade or defer indefinitely a tax on consumed income. For example, funds might be "invested" in a sham foreign subsidiary of a privately owned domestic corporation and then channeled back into the United States covertly to reappear as deductible saving. Stopping this form of abuse might require pervasive exchange controls. Second, all foreign tax treaties (since they are based on the income tax model) would have to be renegotiated, and provisions for unilateral relief of double taxation of foreign source income via the foreign tax credit would need to be revised. Such treaty negotiations could take years to complete, during which time the tax treatment of income from international investment would likely be under a cloud of uncertainty and controversy.

Also, a consumption tax might be difficult to sell to the American public. Shifting to a tax which imposes relatively greater burdens than current law during the high-debt years of relative youth and during retirement, when consumption is financed by drawing on previously accumulated assets, might be perceived as fundamentally unfair. This perception may reflect an implicit recognition that capital markets are not perfect, as assumed in most theoretical demonstrations of the superiority of consumption-based taxation.

Finally, numerous difficult transitional issues arise in moving to a consumption tax. In particular, many taxpayers nearing retirement would consider it unfair that earnings on which they had already paid tax would now be subject to a second consumption-based tax when spent.[4] It would not be simple to devise a scheme which would exempt consumption of a minimal amount of wealth accumulated from after-tax income, without exempting all consumption of existing assets.[5]

Of course, Treasury I was not a conceptually pure income tax. In particular, the tax-preferred status of pension plans was retained and opportunities to save in tax-advantaged individual retirement accounts (IRAs) were substantially increased. These provisions defer taxes on some savings, as would a tax on consumed income, without moving to a pure consumption tax. This break with income tax principles was not without cost, since these preferences distort portfolio choices and create opportunities for blatant tax arbitrage — for example, borrowing with tax-deductible interest (subject to the limitations proposed in Treasury I) to invest in a tax-advantaged IRA. Moreover, critics of IRAs argue that they provide

[4] Some consumption tax schemes have relatively low tax rates or can be shown (under certain assumptions) to increase the welfare of all future generations because they effectively impose a one-time wealth tax on current capital owners. This effect is questionable on equity grounds and, if widely recognized, would likely prompt a firestorm of political opposition.

[5] For example, the transition rules proposed by Aaron and Galper (1985) are fairly complex, as they involve a one-time establishment of basis of all assets, to be indexed by a factor related to market interest rates. These rules effectively grant consumption tax treatment immediately to existing assets, since they provide for immediate expensing (in present value terms) of all remaining basis. As a result, the Aaron-Galper transition proposal could be viewed as overly generous to owners of existing wealth; moreover, this problem would be magnified if their recommendation to deny all interest deductions on existing loans were not followed — a prospect which seems rather likely from a political perspective. For further discussion, see Zodrow (1986).

ineffective saving incentives; since much of the saving in such accounts would have occurred anyway, the subsidy is largely inframarginal.[6]

1.3. *Revenue neutrality*

During his debates with Walter Mondale, President Reagan left no doubt that he would not tolerate a tax increase masquerading as tax reform. On the other hand, most Treasury Department economists agreed that tax reform should not reduce revenues, given the size of the federal budget deficit. Thus, tax reform would have to be revenue neutral. Unfortunately, it is no simple matter to predict revenues or define revenue neutrality; moreover, revenue neutrality need not imply zero impact on the budget deficit. There are at least three major problems.

"Static" Revenue Estimation. Treasury Department economists have been severely criticized for employing "static revenue estimates," instead of estimates that reflect behavioral responses of individuals, firms, and all levels of government.[7] Supply-side economists argue that revenues are understated since more rapid growth induced by lower tax rates is not considered; others believe that revenues are overstated because new tax avoidance techniques cannot be predicted. The fact is that available

---

[6]These arguments have been used to justify the limitations on IRAs for higher income taxpayers contained in the 1986 Act. Inconsistent with these limitations, however, is the new law's decision to allow contributions of up to $7,000 (down from $30,000 under current law) to so-called 401(k) deferral plans, which Treasury I would have eliminated. The continued availability of 401(k) plans will put considerable pressure on all firms to set up such plans, distort firm compensation choices, add complexity, waste legal and accounting resources, and extend the benefits of consumption tax treatment of saving to only a relatively small (and commonly wealthy) subset of the population. Such a result is incompatible with true tax reform; the treatment of saving in deferral accounts should be simple and equally available to all taxpayers.

[7]In many cases this criticism is simply incorrect; some microeconomic adjustments are considered even though macroeconomic forecasts are not changed (see Nester, 1986). It should also be noted that virtually all of the revenue estimates presented in Treasury I and quoted here generally overstate the revenue consequences of individual provisions, because they are based on existing rates before the effect of lowering rates is calculated. If the proposed rates were adopted, the revenue gain or loss from not adopting the provision in question would ordinarily be substantially less.

economic models cannot accurately estimate all of the reactions to a reform package as comprehensive as Treasury I.

Static estimates are almost certainly wrong, but they are less subject to manipulation than are "dynamic" estimates. While the economists in the Office of Tax Analysis have traditionally been quite free from effective pressure to "shade" revenue estimates up or down for political purposes, they might be less successful in resisting such pressure in a world of widespread dynamic revenue estimation, which would inevitably entail making controversial assumptions concerning the dynamic responses of the economy to tax reform.

Appropriate Time Horizon. A reform package was defined to be revenue neutral if it produced substantially the same revenues as current law over the five-year budget period following enactment.[8] Clearly, this criterion could result in greater or smaller tax receipts than under current law in the long run. For example, the proposal by U.S. Representative Jack Kemp (R-New York) and Senator Robert Kasten (R-Wisconsin) to allow multi-year depreciation deductions equal in present value to "expensing" (immediate write-off of investment) would have been revenue neutral in the short run but would have involved large long run revenue losses due to much greater deductions for depreciation just beyond the five-year budget horizon. In the 1986 Act, a significant fraction of the increase in corporate taxes represents accounting changes that move tax revenues forward in time; this fact suggests that the increase in corporate tax revenues may be significantly less in the long run than suggested by the five-year estimates and that the tax reform adopted would not satisfy a longer run definition of revenue neutrality.

Indirect Budgetary Impacts. Treasury Department revenue estimates generally ignore indirect effects that tax reform would have on the budget deficit. These could either decrease or increase the deficit while not

[8]Though Treasury I did provide a few estimates of revenue effects of tax reform when "fully phased in" (and all estimates of distributional effects were made on this basis), it is fair to say that little attention was paid to the long run revenue implications of tax reform. In the debate on Treasury I opponents of reform (and the press) focused on the 37 percent increase in corporate taxes during the five-year budget period, rather than on the much smaller 24 percent increase when all proposals were fully phased in.

violating the specified standard of revenue neutrality.[9] For example, if Treasury I led to lower interest rates (as was widely predicted), it would reduce the deficit due to lower interest payments on the national debt. On the other hand, reducing some "tax expenditures" might lead to increased federal spending for the same purposes.

1.4. *Distributional neutrality*

Although not mandated by President Reagan, distributional neutrality was adopted as a reasonable "first-cut" objective of tax reform to divorce the technical issues of redefining the income tax base from the controversial political issue of the proper distribution of tax burdens across income classes (U.S. Department of the Treasury, 1984, p. I:15). However, when the tax burden shifts from individuals to corporations, as in Treasury I and all subsequent reform proposals, defining distributional neutrality becomes quite complicated for at least two reasons.

First, in order to answer questions about distribution, the increase in the corporate income tax must be attributed to individuals; but, as is well known, the incidence of the corporate income tax is very controversial. To make the question even more complex, much American capital is owned by pension funds and financial institutions on behalf of low and middle income individuals, by others in the nonprofit sector, and by foreigners. Those responsible for the Treasury Department proposals felt that they could not include in their analysis of proposals for tax reform either a long discourse on the incidence of the corporate income tax or distributional analyses based on alternative estimates of incidence. Nevertheless, it is important to note that, to the extent that the burden of corporate income taxes is more (less) progressive than the burden of individual income taxes,

---

[9]To the extent that the Treasury I reforms would increase the base for Social Security contributions (for example, by including certain fringe benefits in taxable income), Social Security tax revenues would be increased, unless compensating changes were made in tax rates applied to the Social Security base or in the base itself. No account was taken of these increases in revenues because, strictly speaking, modification of the Social Security base would require separate legislation; it would not result automatically from reform of the income tax base. No recommendations were made to assure such conformity because Social Security reform had recently been the subject of a major bipartisan agreement.

all proposed tax reforms would be more (less) progressive than suggested by the calculation using only individual income taxes.

Second, Treasury I and all subsequent reform packages defined distributional neutrality in the reform of the individual income tax as equal percentage reductions in tax liabilities at all income levels. A reasonable alternative is an equal percentage increase in after-tax incomes at all income levels (see Musgrave and Tun Thin, 1948). The implications of these two definitions differ substantially, as the definition of distributional neutrality adopted by the Treasury Department results in far greater tax reductions for high-income taxpayers than does adoption of the second alternative. In retrospect, it appears that the definition of distribution neutrality was chosen without full appreciation of the political importance of that decision.

1.5. *Investment neutrality and the elimination of tax shelters*

An evenhanded policy of neutrality toward economic decisions is likely to be a significant improvement over politically determined tax subsidies, even if some socially beneficial activities are denied preferential tax treatment. Thus preferential treatment of an investment activity was recommended in Treasury I only when dictated by compelling economic, administrative, or political arguments. The decision to design a neutral tax system had profound implications. Measures to assure economic neutrality toward investment decisions included indexed economic depreciation allowances, taxation of indexed capital gains at ordinary income tax rates, and inflation adjustment for interest income and expense.[10] Tax reform that would produce investment neutrality would also severely curtail, if not eliminate, opportunities for tax shelters. Given the popular perception of abuses associated with tax shelters, as well as the distortions of investment decisions they cause, greater neutrality was viewed as imperative. The magnitude of the horizontal inequities created by tax shelters is revealed by some simple statistics. About 11 percent of returns with total positive income (TPI, defined as the sum of positive income flows before

[10]These proposals would have reversed many of the changes made just five years earlier in the 1981 Economic Recovery Tax Act.

subtraction of negative income items such as partnership losses) in excess of $250,000 (or even in excess of $1 million) paid income taxes of less than 5 percent of TPI. By comparison, 47 percent of those with incomes in excess of $250,000 paid at least 20 percent of TPI in tax, and even returns with TPI of $30,000 to $75,000 paid an average of 13 percent of TPI in tax (U.S. Department of the Treasury, 1985, pp. 717–718). Clearly, the tax code offers some high income individuals a chance to avoid tax liability. Treasury I would have rectified this situation by taxing all real economic income uniformly and consistently. Whereas 27 percent of those with incomes between $100,000 and $200,000 and 49 percent of those with incomes in excess of $200,000 would have experienced decreases in taxes of at least 2 percent of economic income, about 15 percent of households in these income classes would have experienced tax increases of this magnitude (Department of Treasury, 1984, p. I:54).

Several prominent arguments for preferential treatment of investment deserve comment. Some argue that preferential tax treatment of equipment purchases is appropriate because most technological improvement is embodied in equipment and such technology creates external benefits. Even if these propositions were agreed to be valid, the appropriate tax treatment would be an incentive limited to investments especially likely to show such external benefits. The existing research and development tax credit was retained with modifications in both Treasury I and the 1986 Act partly on these grounds.

Others note that the combination of the investment tax credit and the accelerated cost recovery system of current law is a surrogate for expensing, which they assert is the appropriate way to treat depreciable assets for tax purposes. The problem with this view is that expensing generally makes sense only in a full-fledged consumption tax system; if grafted onto an income tax system in which interest expense is deductible, expensing results in low or negative marginal effective tax rates, misallocation of resources, inequity, and complexity. Once the tax on consumed income was rejected, it made no sense to consider expensing, and even accelerated depreciation was inconsistent with the principle of taxing real economic income.

Some observers view the acceleration of depreciation allowances as an ad hoc surrogate for explicit indexation of depreciation allowances. But a given pattern of accelerated depreciation makes sense only for a particular rate of inflation; at any other inflation rate depreciation allowances are either too generous or not generous enough. Treasury I reflected the judgement that the risks and costs of instability in the rate of inflation justify the introduction of an explicit system of indexation for depreciation allowances. Accordingly, Treasury I proposed to eliminate the investment tax credit, base depreciation allowances for tax purposes on the best available estimates of economic depreciation, and index those depreciation allowances for inflation.

The decision to tax all real economic income generated by depreciable assets did not extend to owner-occupied housing. The decision to maintain preferential treatment of housing provides an interesting example of how a seemingly simple political decision can have far-reaching economic implications. On February 18, 1981, President Ronald Reagan said: "The taxing power of government must be used to provide revenues for legitimate government purposes. It must not be used to regulate the economy or bring about social change."[11] Yet on May 10, 1984, in response to pressure from the National Association of Realtors, President Reagan promised not to eliminate the deduction for home mortgage interest. This promise guaranteed that the so-called "playing field" would not be level. While lower tax rates make all deductions less important, the distortion in favor of owner-occupied housing actually would have been accentuated by the subsequent decision that interest indexing could not be applied to interest on home mortgages.[12]

The sanctity of the home mortgage interest deduction posed a difficult question for tax reform. Given that the mortgage interest deduction could not be curtailed and that income from owner-occupied housing

[11] President Ronald Reagan, to a joint session of Congress on the program for economic recovery, February 18, 1981.

[12] Treasury I proposed that part of nominal interest expense would be nondeductible, but an exception was made for home mortgage interest, which would have remained fully deductible. The failure to index interest on home mortgages would have created substantial incentives for tax arbitrage, in the form of borrowing via unindexed mortgage debt for investment in indexed debt. For further discussion of the impact of the sanctity of the home mortgage deduction on the possibility of achieving the goals of tax reform, including a level playing field, see McLure (1986a).

could not be taxed, did it make sense to subject all other real economic income from capital to full taxation? The importance of such second-best considerations is indicated by calculations suggesting that the President's Proposals (1985), a watered-down version of Treasury I that did not go nearly as far in taxing real economic income, may have generated greater welfare gains than Treasury I (see, for example, the estimate in Fullerton, 1987). It was decided that these considerations did not overwhelm the case for a "nearly pure" comprehensive income tax. But critics who question the desirability of fully taxing non-housing capital while subsidizing capital investment in owner-occupied housing raise a valid and troublesome point.

Unfortunately, the 1986 Act may have accentuated the already overly favorable tax treatment of owner-occupied housing. Home mortgage debt will become relatively more attractive since interest on such debt (within certain limits) remains fully deductible, while consumer interest becomes non-deductible and deductions for interest incurred to finance most investments not yielding current income will be curtailed. Of course, these restrictions on consumer interest deductions will encourage individuals to finance consumption purchases with home equity loans and favor individuals who can substitute "business" borrowing for "consumption" borrowing.[13]

Moreover, the 1986 Act accentuates the favorable treatment of owner-occupied housing because of changes in capital gains taxation. While capital gains on virtually all assets will be taxed as ordinary income, those on owner-occupied housing will continue to qualify for extended rollover as long as the proceeds from a sale of one home are reinvested in another, and gains on sales of such homes by taxpayers over 55 years of age will

[13] Initially, it appeared that residents of states that prohibit home equity loans would be disadvantaged by this treatment. However, a last minute provision inserted in the 1986 Act by Texas Senator Lloyd Bentsen creates yet another type of fully deductible debt to be known as a "non-enforceable second mortgage." For tax purposes this new type of loan is similar to a home equity loan in that the 1986 Act allows home owners to borrow an amount equal to the purchase price of their home plus the cost of improvements less outstanding mortgages; however, it is a home mortgage loan in name only — and in its characteristic of full deductibility — since it cannot be secured by the residence. Such measures illustrate the arbitrary and complex treatment of interest under the 1986 Act.

continue to be largely tax-exempt. If inflation should again enter the double-digit range, the strong incentives that existed during the 1970s for excessive investment in owner-occupied housing will emerge again.

1.6. *Shifting the tax burden from individuals to corporations*

One of the hallmarks of Treasury I and its successors, including the 1986 Act, is a substantial shift of tax liabilities from individuals to corporations. The shift in Treasury I reflected several considerations.

A decision had already been made on neutrality grounds to eliminate or sharply curtail most tax preferences, including those of benefit primarily to the corporate sector, whether they benefited mainly single industries (defense contractors, insurance companies, banks and other financial institutions, the oil and gas industry, timber companies, etc.) or the entire corporate sector (the investment tax credit and the Accelerated Cost Recovery System). Eliminating these tax breaks without a shift from individual to corporate taxes could have produced a tax system with a lower corporate rate (28 rather than 33 percent), and higher individual rates (16, 28, and 37 percent rather than 15, 25, and 35 percent). This outcome was thought to be unacceptable for three reasons.

First, the gap between the corporate rate and the top individual rate had to be kept small to limit incentives for using the corporate form to avoid tax. A nine percentage point difference between corporate and individual rates was thought to be unacceptable. Second, a political judgement was made that a net tax reduction for individuals was necessary to create many more individual "winners" than "losers." Otherwise, since the losses would be more concentrated than the gains, the outcry from losers might have swamped any positive reactions from winners and tax reform would have been politically impossible. This strategy almost backfired when the increase in corporate taxes generated a firestorm of opposition.

Finally, aesthetics played at least a minor role in the choice of tax rates, and therefore in the shift of tax liabilities from individuals to corporations. Recalling the effectiveness of "10-5-3" as a rallying call during the 1981 quest for accelerated depreciation, it was felt that rates of 15, 25, and 35 percent had more aesthetic and political appeal than 16, 28, 37 — which one wag likened to signals called by a quarterback in a football game.

1.7. *Reform should be implemented quickly*

The existing tax system creates vested interests that stand to lose enormous amounts if the system is changed suddenly. More generally, any tax reform is likely to result in marked changes in the value of various assets. For instance, the repeal of the investment tax credit can be expected to benefit owners of old equipment, but to harm producers and purchasers of new equipment. Similarly, lowering tax rates confers windfall gains on owners of both physical and human capital, but for owners of capital specific to industries that lose tax preferences these may be offset by windfall losses.

If adequate provisions are not made for a fair and orderly transition to the post-reform tax system, political opposition to reform is likely to be formidable, and perhaps overwhelming. Transition provisions focus on ameliorating the reductions in wealth that accompany an unexpected change in the tax structure through measures such as grandfathering, phasing-in, and delaying the enactment of reform.[14] Such provisions should balance the benefits of reducing such losses against the costs of delaying the gains in efficiency, equity and simplicity which result from implementing reform (see Feldstein, 1976; Zodrow, 1981, 1985).

The Treasury I proposals attempted a fair and orderly transition, but generally erred in the direction of implementing reform too rapidly. There were two primary reasons for proposing a quick transition, in addition to the desire to capture the gains from reform quickly and the fear that post-ponements would provide time for opponents of reform to repeal various provisions. First, in some cases where special tax preferences were highly visible and had frequently been discussed as potential targets for reform, markets had presumably already adjusted to the possibility that these pro-visions would be repealed so that transitional relief was unnecessary. Second, a "tough" initial stance was deemed appropriate to provide a strong bargaining position for the negotiating which would surely follow the introduction of Treasury I.

In retrospect, the transition proposed in Treasury I may have been too rapid from a political point of view, since it resulted in unnecessary

---

[14] Concern is hardly ever shown for tax-induced increases in wealth; the windfall recapture tax recommended in the President's Tax Proposals (1985) was a notable exception.

controversy by focusing attention on the speed of implementation rather than the need for reform. For example, the proposed introduction of interest indexing was delayed for only two years. The rationale was that the interest rate reduction induced by enactment of Treasury I would result in the refinancing of most large existing loans and that investors in existing debt-financed business assets would receive an offsetting benefit from the taxation of the asset's income at a lower rate. The business community found this rationale to be inadequate and protested fiercely; in response, a modified ten-year phase-in transition rule was quickly announced.

However, the 1986 Act, in many respects, provides for an even more rapid transition than proposed in Treasury I. For example, the investment tax credit is repealed retroactively to January 1, 1986 (Treasury I called for only prospective repeal) and the deduction for state and local sales taxes is repealed immediately (rather than phased in over two years as was repeal of all state and local tax deductibility under Treasury I). Moreover, the four-year phase-in period for the new limits on the deduction of passive investment losses strikes some as being inappropriately short.

2. Major Proposals of Treasury I and How They Fared

This section discusses important individual provisions of Treasury I and how they were changed and amended in producing the Tax Reform Act of 1986. The discussion is separated into those topics dealing primarily with the measurement of business and capital income and those provisions affecting individuals.

2.1. *Business and capital income provisions*

The Treasury I proposals for the taxation of income from business and capital were an integrated and largely consistent attempt, based on the principles outlined above, to make the tax base resemble real economic income. Since the tax breaks that are the building blocks of tax shelters (acceleration of deductions and postponement of recognition of income, partial exclusion of long-term capital gains, and full deduction of nominal interest expense) would have been sharply curtailed, a minimum tax would have been unnecessary. Unfortunately, the 1986 Act did not follow this integrated and consistent approach.

Depreciable Assets. For the reasons described earlier, the Treasury I proposals focused on taxing real economic income. In contrast, the 1986 Act provides for accelerated depreciation allowances not indexed for inflation. Such treatment will result in distortions due to differential taxation of assets and industries, problems that will worsen if inflation increases or varies dramatically.[15]

The 1986 Act also lengthens depreciation lives and requires straight line depreciation for real estate. Moreover, the Act will eliminate capital gains treatment and limit interest deductions for real estate (although not as severely as for other passive income), reducing these offsets to relatively slow depreciation allowances. The net result will be to change commercial real estate (including rental housing) from a tax-advantaged to a tax-disadvantaged asset. This will imply a long period of economic transition for the real estate industry, which is already suffering from overbuilding (probably produced in part by anticipation that favorable treatment under the 1981 bill would be temporary).

Other Issues of Time Value. Depreciation is only the most widely discussed case of the general problem of accounting for expenditures incurred in one year that give rise to income over several subsequent years. Examples include the costs of developing oil and gas wells, mines, timber, vineyards, and so on. The common tax policy question is the appropriate time pattern for allowing such expenditures to be deducted. Current tax law allows immediate expensing of many of these expenditures. Treasury I proposed to bring tax accounting more nearly into line with economic reality — and with generally accepted accounting principles, which require that many such costs be capitalized and amortized over the life of the resulting asset.

The 1986 Act took a similar approach in that it requires that many expenses of this type be capitalized, including costs of production for additions to inventories. But the most notorious of all, intangible drilling costs in the oil and gas industry, will continue to be expensed if incurred

[15] For further elaboration of this argument and estimates of marginal effective tax rates for several inflation rates, see U.S. Department of the Treasury (1984, Vol. 2, Chapter 8).

by independent drillers. (Integrated producers must amortize 30 percent of intangible drilling costs over a five-year period, compared to 20 percent over three years under current law.) This tax subsidy is generally agreed to be a poor response to the "national security" problem of assuring an adequate energy supply; its continuation reflects a compromise with members of Congress from the "oil patch."

The other side of the coin is the question of when to recognize income that is earned through a process that lasts several years. The most apparent example of such "multi-period production" involves the income reporting of defense contractors, but the same problem arises for any construction activity extending over several years and for sales made on an installment basis. Under the completed contract method of accounting, taxpayers can defer tax on income from such contracts until they are completed. Although Treasury I did not eliminate the completed contract method, the 1986 Act will significantly curtail its benefits by requiring that taxpayers use the percentage completion method, under which income is recognized as the project proceeds, to calculate at least 40 percent of income from such contracts. These "timing" issues account for at least half of the $120 billion five-year net increase in revenues from corporations.

Capital Gains. Under pre-1987 law, 60 percent of long-term capital gains (gains on assets held for more than six months) are excluded from tax. Efforts to take advantage of this exclusion by recharacterizing ordinary income as long-term capital gain — and the corresponding attempts of the Internal Revenue Service to thwart such efforts — account for a substantial portion of the complexity of the U.S. tax system.

The two primary justifications commonly given for the exclusion are that it is an ad hoc adjustment for inflation and that it provides an incentive for entrepreneurship and risk taking. Treasury I dealt explicitly with the first problem by indexing the basis of capital assets, to eliminate the taxation of fictitious inflationary capital gains. The increase in complexity due to indexing would have been offset by the benefits of an improved measure of economic income and the elimination of incentives to recharacterize ordinary income as capital gains.

The effect of capital gains taxation on risk taking is a more complex issue. The arguments of Domar and Musgrave (1944) and the subsequent literature have made it clear that a proportional income tax with full loss offsets is likely to encourage risk taking. Since loss offsets are far from complete and the tax system is progressive, the net effect is not clear, either under the old law or the new. Although it was recognized that raising the capital gains rate might have an adverse effect on risk taking, those responsible for Treasury I decided that the known benefits of simplification and lower tax rates justified taking that risk.

However, Treasury I did not attempt to tax capital gains on an accrual basis rather than when recognized, as is required under a pure income tax. Taxation only upon realization creates inequities and encourages taxpayers to hold existing assets, rather than realize gains and reinvest proceeds in assets paying higher yields; these tendencies are aggravated by the failure to tax gains on assets transferred at death. (No tax is collected on such gains and the basis of the asset is "stepped up" to the value at death.) During the formulation of Treasury I several ways of dealing with those problems, including constructive (deemed) realization at death, were considered and rejected.[16]

In light of the outcry prompted by the Treasury I proposal to index capital gains against inflation and tax them at a maximum rate of 35 percent, the agreement under the 1986 Act to tax gains at a 33 percent maximum rate without indexing for inflation is quite amazing. From an economic standpoint, the failure to index against inflation can be justified only as an ad hoc method of offsetting the advantage of deferral of tax payments until a capital gain is realized. But this approach means that the effective tax rate paid on real capital gains will continue to depend on the rate of inflation. Full taxation of nominal gains, combined with the more stringent provisions for treatment of losses, implies that there will be major inequities and distortions in the pattern of investment, and that risk taking will be reduced. It would not be surprising — particularly if inflation accelerates — to see reintroduction of a capital gains exclusion.

[16] Accrual taxation of only securities listed on major exchanges — using "mark-to-market" techniques — would create an undesirable bias against investment in such securities, relative to investment in assets where accrual-based taxation is not administratively feasible. It should be noted that existing mark-to-market rules (in futures markets) are designed primarily to limit abuses rather than to meet the requirements for a consistent measure of annual economic income.

In addition, the failure to adopt constructive realization of capital gains at death renders questionable the taxation of gains on gifts of appreciated property given to charity under both Treasury I and the alternative minimum tax in the 1986 Act. It is justifiable on income measurement grounds not to allow a deduction if the associated income is never realized, and such a rule reduces the benefits of overvaluing donated property to evade taxes. But since gains are taxed when donated to charity during an individual's lifetime, but not when passed on to heirs at death, there will be incentives to delay or avoid charitable contributions.

Interest Income and Expense. The ad hoc adjustments for inflation provided by accelerated depreciation allowances and the partial exclusion of long term capital gains are quite imperfect, but at least they exist. In contrast, the inflationary component of nominal interest income receives no such adjustment; similarly, the entire amount of nominal interest expense is allowed as a deduction, with no adjustment for inflation. The result is substantial inequity and misallocation of resources. Tax shelters become especially attractive in times of high inflation, since borrowers can deduct the full amount of nominal interest expense and then benefit from accelerated deductions for depreciation (and similar expenses of multi-year production) and the partial exclusion of capital gains.

Treasury I proposed that both interest income and expense should be adjusted for inflation. This combination would sharply reduce the inequities, distortions, and opportunities for tax shelters that exist in current law. Moreover, since capital gains were to be indexed, indexation of interest was critical to remove the opportunity for arbitrage.

However, Treasury I did not follow the conceptually correct approach of excluding from income or disallowing deduction of an amount of interest equal to the product of the inflation rate and the outstanding principal of debt. This procedure was viewed as inordinately cumbersome from an administrative standpoint, since in principle it would involve applying an inflation adjustment factor to the principal (calculated on the annualized basis) of every credit arrangement in the economy; compliance would have been difficult except on loans involving financial institutions or other sophisticated borrowers or lenders. In practice it would likely have resulted in "indexed" and "unindexed" classes of loans which would have been somewhat arbitrary, difficult to monitor, and subject to abuse.

Instead, Treasury I proposed to disallow a fraction of all interest expense (and exclude the same fraction of interest income) equal to the rate of inflation divided by the sum of that rate plus 6 percent. This partial exclusion approach is only a rough approximation to accurate indexing of interest, and was chosen for simplicity.[17] The formula's use of 6 percent — a rate that is high relative to historical real interest rates — was chosen to err on the side of a smaller than appropriate disallowance of interest deductions (although this decision also implied a relatively small interest income exclusion).

The proposal for interest indexing was strongly opposed by those in the real estate and tax shelter industries. Moreover, the short transition period stirred opposition from firms with large outstanding indebtedness, especially public utilities. A surprising but frequently cited objection to interest indexing and all the other Treasury I inflation indexing proposals was that indexing creates uncertainty in the nominal amount of deductions available. The final blow to interest indexing was its cost. Because Treasury Department economists estimated that the inflation adjustment of interest income and expense would cost roughly $43 billion over the five-year period 1986–90, interest indexing was quite vulnerable.[18] It did not survive the initial process of political compromise leading to the President's Proposals (1985) and was not reinstated in the 1986 Act.

---

[17]The Treasury I proposal would clearly be inappropriate for financial institutions, which would benefit from partial exclusion of the spread in interest rates on funds borrowed and then loaned, even though the effects of inflation cancel in such a transaction. (The gain from the reduction in the real value of the principal amount borrowed is exactly offset by the loss from the reduction in the real value of the principal amount loaned.) This point was made abundantly clear by the fact that financial institutions did not oppose Treasury I despite various other proposals eliminating tax treatment benefitting them. Nevertheless, the imperfect partial exclusion approach, especially if modified so that only the equity investments of financial institutions (amounts loaned or invested net of amounts deposited in the institution) were indexed, would have been an improvement over current law which implicitly assumes that no inflation exists.

[18]U.S. Department of the Treasury (1984, p. I:247). In actuality, this revenue loss would occur entirely in fiscal years 1988–90, because implementation of interest indexing was not to occur until 1988. During both 1989 and 1990 revenue loss was estimated to be roughly $18 billion to $19 billion per year. This revenue loss may have been more than offset by savings on the cost of servicing the national debt.

Dividend Relief. Income from equity investment in the corporate sector is taxed twice, once when earned by the corporation, and again when distributed to shareholders. This "double taxation of dividends" creates a well-known set of inequities and distortions in resource allocation and the financial decisions of corporations (see McLure, 1979). To ameliorate these effects, Treasury I proposed a 50 percent corporate deduction for dividends paid.[19]

Dividend relief is enormously expensive; the proposal would reduce annual revenues by $31 billion in fiscal 1990, and still not be fully phased in. Moreover, much of this revenue loss would represent windfall gains to present owners of corporate shares; it would be an extremely inefficient way of achieving the benefits of increased equity finance or improved resource allocation associated with *de novo* enactment of an integrated corporate-personal income tax.

Those responsible for Treasury I seriously considered the possibility of allowing dividend relief only for newly issued shares, but rejected the idea, in part because of feared complexity and the potential for abuse through using nonprofit conduits to convert old shares that would not benefit from the deduction to new ones that would benefit.[20] Little attention was devoted to the possibility of fully integrating the corporate and personal income taxes, a conceptually correct approach that is generally agreed to be administratively infeasible for large publicly held corporations (see McLure, 1979, Chapter 5).

On a related topic, the authors of Treasury I recognized that many large limited partnerships resemble corporations, even to the point that shares are traded on major stock exchanges. Accordingly, it was proposed that such entities be subject to the corporation income tax, rather than

[19] A 100 percent deduction was avoided partly to reduce the revenue loss and partly to keep the rules simpler — since preference income would be presumed to be paid out last under rules governing the order of payout of dividends, these rules would come into play infrequently under a 50 percent deduction, but would affect many corporations under a 100 percent deduction. For further discussion of the difficulties caused by tax preferences, see McLure (1979, Chapter 4).

[20] A high tax on non-dividend distributions would forestall simply reorganizing to convert old shares to new. However, large nonprofit institutions could buy a controlling interest in a corporation, pay out all retained profits as untaxed dividends, and then reorganize.

being allowed the "conduit" treatment accorded partnerships under current law. Under "conduit" treatment, partnership income and losses are attributed directly to the partners, thereby avoiding the corporate tax on income while getting immediate deductions for losses. Such an approach would have severely restricted the use of the partnership form in tax shelter schemes.

The 1986 Act alters dramatically the incentives involved in choosing between corporate and non-corporate forms of business organization. Most obviously, tax shelter partnerships will be discouraged. But for other purposes, non-corporate forms of business organization may come to dominate corporate forms. The 1986 Act provides no relief from double taxation of dividends. Under current law most income retained by corporations is taxed at a 46 percent rate, whereas that earned by a partnership is taxed to individuals at rates as high as 50 percent. Under the new law these rates are changed to 34 percent and 28 or 33 percent, respectively. This shift in relative rates may lead to disincorporation in some cases, but this response will be limited by another 1986 reform (the repeal of the General Utilities doctrine) which provides for corporate taxation of gains on assets distributed to shareholders in liquidation. However, new business ventures may use such forms as master limited partnerships to take advantage of conduit treatment and lower individual rates. The long run economic consequences of this change in organizational form are not obvious.

Tax Exempt Bonds. One of the few major deviations of Treasury I from the principles of uniform taxation of real economic income was in the area of state and local bond interest. Repeal of the exemption of interest on state and local bonds issued for "governmental" or "public" purposes was not recommended, despite the strong economic case for doing so; the rational was that the exemption appeared "to be an accepted part of the fiscal landscape" (U.S. Department of the Treasury, 1984, p. I:135). But Treasury I recommended that the exclusion be repealed for "non-governmental" or "private purpose" bonds, defined as those where more than one percent of the proceeds were used directly or indirectly by any person other than a state or local government. The 1986 Act follows this general approach, but is more liberal in its threshold test of private purpose; moreover, a long list of exemptions are provided, for example, for tax-exempt organizations, rental housing, mass commuting facilities, airports, local utilities, water plants, and sewage and water treatment facilities.

The Treasury I decision to eliminate the exclusion for "private purpose" bonds was probably a mistake. Subsidized debt issued to support many activities which generate little or no external benefit (such as industrial development bonds and home mortgage subsidy bonds) would justifiably have been eliminated. However, some "private purpose" bonds are related to services characterized by substantial "publicness" that render them similar to services financed with general obligation bonds.[21] Though one might quarrel with a few of the choices of activities that will continue to benefit from the exclusion under the 1986 Act, it appears that in most cases the Congressional decision to continue the exclusion for private purpose bonds is not unreasonable — given the reluctance to eliminate the exclusion for general obligation bonds.

2.2. *Provisions affecting individuals*

Treasury I would have made substantial changes in the tax treatment of individuals by repealing or eliminating many exclusions, exemptions, deductions, and credits. The following discussion focuses on three base-broadening issues: fringe benefits, especially employer-provided health insurance, state and local taxes, and charitable contributions. It concludes with comments on the "hump-backed" rate structure of the 1986 Act.

Fringe Benefits. Many types of compensation are currently untaxed, with the largest category being employer-provided health insurance and group life insurance. As a result, there are substantial horizontal inequities between those who are paid in taxable and tax-exempt forms, and

[21] A convincing case can be made for the continuation of a federal subsidy only for activities generating substantial national benefit spillovers. But if the subsidy is to be continued for general obligation bonds, it seems sensible to judge the availability of the subsidy for "private purpose" bonds by the same standard as that used for general obligation bonds.

consumer choices are distorted in favor of goods and services that can be provided as untaxed fringe benefits.[22] Also, the exclusion of employer-provided fringes has regressive distributional consequences, since the value of the exclusion increases with the marginal tax bracket of the taxpayer. Treasury I proposed to eliminate the preferential treatment of many fringe benefits and curtail others. The net increase in annual revenues from these proposals would have been $24 billion in 1990.

The most important proposal was to tax health benefits in excess of $175 per month for a family ($70 for an individual). This approach was a compromise between the objective of taxing all income uniformly and consistently and the objection that doing so in the case of health insurance would lead to less reliance on employer-provided health benefits and to greater pressure for government-funded health insurance.

One of the most glaring deficiencies of the 1986 Act is that it makes no attempt to tax fringe benefits more fully. Particularly unfortunate is the refusal to curtail the tax advantages of so-called "cafeteria plans" which allow employees a choice between taxable cash and a wide variety of non-taxable fringe benefits. This decision is likely to lead to rapidly increasing erosion of the income tax (and Social Security tax) base as more and more forms of compensation are accorded tax exemption.

State and Local Taxes. The itemized deduction for state and local taxes reduces the effective price individuals who itemize pay for services provided by state and local governments; as a result, it acts a federal subsidy for the activities of those governments. If such services do not provide significant national spillovers, the subsidy provided through the itemized deduction for these taxes is likely to induce excessive allocation of resources to the state and local public sectors. Even if such national benefit spillovers exist, the itemized deduction is a peculiar means of compensating for them; the subsidy depends on the marginal tax rate of individuals, is nonexistent in the case of taxpayers who do not itemize deductions, and does not differentiate between activities deemed to have

[22] Recent arguments that such horizontal inequities are unimportant because taxpayers are free to choose among jobs with or without generous fringe benefit packages (see Feldstein, 1976) are of questionable relevance since they rest on the assumption that all individuals have the same tastes, abilities, and access to fringe benefits.

significant national externalities and purely "local" public goods (or even private ones provided by state and local governments).

Treasury I proposed that the deduction be eliminated on the grounds that most state and local expenditures do not have strong national benefit spillovers and those that do should be subsidized with direct Federal outlays. No distinction was made between types of taxes, because to do so would interject the federal government into the fiscal decisions of state and local governments and have capricious effects across states. The predicted increase in annual revenue by 1990 was $39 billion.

The 1986 Act repeals the deduction for state and local sales taxes, while leaving fully intact those for income and property taxes. This is a mistake, for the reasons given above. It would have been preferable to eliminate a given fraction of the itemized deduction (or provide a partial tax credit) for all state and local taxes.

Charitable Contributions. The itemized deduction for charitable contributions is commonly justified as a reflection of the external benefits associated with the activities of nonprofit organizations receiving the donations; it allows an element of personal control over altruistic activities absent in governmental programs with similar objectives. Treasury I proposed continuation of the deduction, in one of the few cases in which use of the tax system to encourage a particular economic activity was recommended. A conceptually more attractive approach would be to convert the deduction into a tax credit; this was rejected because of the desire to eliminate all credits (except that for foreign taxes) in order to remove at least this part of the camel's nose of tax subsidies from the tent of tax reform.

However, Treasury I would have limited the deduction in three ways, reflecting a compromise between the objectives of fairness and lower rates and the encouragement of nonprofit organizations. The deduction would not have been available to non-itemizers, itemizers would have been allowed to deduct only contributions in excess of two percent of adjusted gross income, and deductions for appreciated property would have been limited to the inflation-adjusted basis (usually the cost) of the asset. Only the repeal of the deduction for non-itemizers (and taxation of gifts of appreciated property under the individual alternative minimum tax) survived in the 1986 Act. Aside from the problems with taxing gifts of appreciated property mentioned above, such treatment does not seem to be an inappropriate resolution of a difficult tax policy problem with no obvious solution.

The Individual Rate Structure. The marginal tax rate structure of the 1986 Act — rates of 15, 28, 33 and 28 percent, with the 33 percent rate due to phasing out of the benefits of the 15 percent rate and personal exemptions for high income taxpayers — is extremely peculiar.[23] It began as a cosmetic ploy designed to make the package salable as a "two-rate" structure with a so-called "maximum" rate of 28 percent. This illusory maximum marginal rate seems to have been particularly important (and particularly deceiving) in the debate regarding raising the maximum tax rate on capital gains from its existing level of 20 percent; many apparently believed that the decision to tax capital gains as ordinary income — and perhaps tax reform itself — would unravel if this rate rose much above 28 percent. The equity implications of a lower marginal tax rate at the very highest income levels are troubling, especially since individuals in the income class of $100,000 and above receive larger percentage individual income tax cuts than taxpayers in the upper middle income classes.[24]

3. Concluding Remarks

The Tax Reform Act of 1986 has been characterized as a political miracle; in this view, it is amazing that Congress decided to pay attention to the general interest in tax neutrality and equity, rather than (for the most part) to the representatives of special interests. But it is also amazing that a better reform package could not be passed. Congress clearly wanted to eliminate the specter of wealthy individuals and profitable corporations

---

[23] Though the theory of optimal taxation suggests that a regressive rate structure may be appropriate at the top of the income distribution, it seems doubtful that this line of reasoning provided any part of the rationale for the decision. Even if such results had been considered, it is not clear that a regressive marginal rate structure would be implied for the U.S. income tax.

[24] Particularly anomalous is the fact that the regressive pattern of marginal rates produces an incentive for upper-middle income taxpayers to bunch into "28 percent years" capital gains and other income over which they can exercise discretion in timing, rather than allowing such income to be spread more evenly and taxed at the 33 percent rate.

paying little or no tax, yet it was unwilling to eliminate some forms of preferential treatment (such as depreciation allowances more rapid than economic depreciation) or to provide explicit indexing for interest income and expense. As a result, it was forced to adopt "backstop" provisions such as the beefed-up alternative minimum tax and the limitations on deductions for so-called passive losses and various types of interest expense — features that will add considerable complexity to the tax law. If, as some have said, the 1986 Act was an opportunity that occurs only once in each generation, it is hard to know whether to rejoice that the glass of tax reform is half full or bemoan the fact that it remains half empty.

For an economist it is troublesome to see how little influence economic arguments exerted once Treasury I went to the White House and considerations of politics and cosmetics became dominant.[25] On the other hand, it is gratifying that economists were influential within the Treasury Department, especially in making the case for consistent application of income tax principles that set the terms for the ensuing debate.

The Treasury I decision to follow the income tax pattern is the decision that will be debated the longest. It may be that it is simply too difficult to implement a reasonably consistent tax on annual real economic income. Certainly, more research needs to be devoted to the hard issues involved in the choice between income and consumption as bases for personal taxation, including transition issues, the consequences of alternative ways of treating gifts and bequests, and international issues.[26] But if

---

[25] Unfortunately, economic arguments sometimes affected the tax reform process in a negative way. A few weeks after the release of the Treasury I proposals, several macroeconomic forecasting firms issued forecasts warning of the undesirable economic effects of tax reform. However, macroeconomic models generally cannot adequately capture the economic benefits of tax reform, especially because such models do not distinguish between investments of differing marginal productivity or consumption of differing marginal benefits to consumers. Although also subject to limitations, general equilibrium models of the types constructed by Shoven, Whalley, Fullerton, Henderson and others that capture the benefits of improvements in resource allocation are much better suited to the task of evaluating tax reform (see Shoven and Whalley, 1984, and the references cited there). Nevertheless, because macroeconomic forecasting models are more familiar and more quickly available, they were far more influential in the early debates following the release of Treasury I.

[26] For a survey of these issues which compares alternative approaches to progressive consumption taxation, see Zodrow (1986).

Treasury I showed conclusively just how complex a relatively pure income tax can be, the Tax Reform Act of 1986 makes strikingly clear that a tax that is less pure is sure to be even more complicated.

References

Aaron, Henry J., and Harvey Galper, *Assessing Tax Reform.* Washington, D.C.: The Brookings Institution, 1985.

Bradford, David F., "The Case for a Personal Consumption Tax." In Pechman, Joseph A., ed., *What Should be Taxed: Income or Expenditure?* Washington: The Brookings Institution, 1980, pp. 75–113.

Bradford, David F., *Untangling the Income Tax.* Cambridge, MA: Harvard University Press, 1986.

Cooper, George, *A Voluntary Tax? New Perspectives on Sophisticated Estate Tax Avoidance.* Washington, D.C.: The Brookings Institution, 1979.

Domar, Evsey D., and Richard A. Musgrave, "Proportional Income Taxation and Risk-Taking," *Quarterly Journal of Economics, 58,* 388–422.

Feldstein, Martin S., "On Theory of Tax Reform," *Journal of Public Economics,* July 1976, *6,* 77–104.

Fullerton, Don, "The Indexation of Interest, Depreciation, Capital Gains, and Tax Reform in the United States," *Journal of Public Economics,* February, 1987, *32,* 25–51.

Hall, Robert E., and Alvin Rabushka, *Low Tax, Simple Tax, Flat Tax.* New York: McGraw-Hill, 1983.

Hall, Robert E., and Alvin Rabushka, *The Flat Tax.* Stanford, CA: Hoover Institution Press, 1985.

King, M. A., "Savings and Taxation." In Hughes, G. A., and G. M. Heal, eds., *Public Policy and the Tax System.* London: George Allen & Unwin, 1980.

McLure, Charles E., Jr., *Must Corporate Income Be Taxed Twice?* Washington: The Brookings Institution, 1979.

McLure, Charles E., Jr., "Reflections on Recent Proposals to Rationalize the U.S. Income Tax." Forthcoming in *Proceedings of the* 41*st Congress of the International Institution of Public Finance.* Madrid, August 26–30, 1985.

McLure, Charles E., Jr., "The Tax Treatment of Owner-occupied Housing: The Achilles' Heel of Tax Reform?" In Follain, James R., ed., *Tax Reform and Real Estate.* Washington: Urban Institute Press, 1986a, pp. 219–32.

McLure, Charles E., Jr., "Where Tax Reform Went Astray." Forthcoming in *Villanova Law Review, 31,* No. 6, 1986b.

Musgrave R. A., and Maung Tun Thin, "Income Tax Progression," 1929–48, *Journal of Political Economy*, December 1948, *56,* 498–514.

Nester, Howard, "Revenue Estimates — Macrostatic, Microdynamic." In *Proceedings of the Seventy-Ninth Annual Conference on Taxation of the National Tax Association-Tax Institute of America*, Hartford, November 9–12, 1986.

Pechman, Joseph A., ed., *What Should be Taxed: Income or Expenditure?* Washington: The Brookings Institution, 1980.

Shoven, John B., and John Whalley, "Applied General Equilibrium Models of Taxation and International Trade," *Journal of Economic Literature*, September 1984, *XXII,* 1007–51.

The President's Tax Proposals to the Congress for Fairness, Growth and Simplicity, Washington, D.C.: U.S. G. P. O., May 1985.

U.S. Congress, Committee on Ways and Means, *Proposals Relating to Tax Shelters and Other Tax-Motivated Transactions.* Washington, D.C.: U.S. G. P. O., February 17, 1984.

U.S. Department of the Treasury, *Blueprints for Basic Tax Reform.* Washington, D.C.: U.S. G. P. O., January 17, 1977. Also available as Bradford, David F., and the U.S. Treasury Department Staff, *Blueprints for Basic Tax Reform.* Arlington, VA: Tax Analysts, 1984.

U.S. Department of the Treasury, *Tax Reform for Fairness, Simplicity and Economic Growth.* Washington, D.C.: U.S. G. P. O., 1984.

U.S. Department of the Treasury, "Taxes Paid by High-Income Taxpayers and the Growth of Partnerships." Reprinted in *Tax Notes*, August 12, 1985, *28,* 717– 720.

Zodrow, George R., "Implementing Tax Reform," *National Tax Journal,* December 1981, *34,* 401–418.

Zodrow, George R., "Optimal Tax Reform in the Presence of Adjustment Costs," *Journal of Public Economics*, July 1985, *27,* 211–230.

Zodrow, George R., "Alternative Approaches to Progressive Expenditure Taxation." In *Proceedings of the Seventy-Ninth Annual Conference on Taxation of the National Tax Association-Tax Institute of America*, Hartford, November 9–12, 1986.

Chapter 11

The Windfall Recapture Tax: Issues of Theory and Design*

George R. Zodrow

Economics Department and Baker Institute for Public Policy
Rice University, Houston, TX 77005, USA

The May 1985 tax reform package issued by the Reagan administration included a proposal to assess a "windfall recapture tax" on owners of existing depreciable assets; this unique proposal was one of the most controversial elements of the recommended reforms. As the first attempt to apply the principle of compensation in tax reform, the windfall recapture tax presents a host of provocative theoretical questions regarding its efficiency and equity properties, and also raises many interesting questions regarding the practical design of such a tax. This article analyzes those questions and presents theoretical and numerical analyses of alternative design approaches.

Included among the recommendations of the Reagan administration in its May 1985 tax reform package was a novel proposal designed to "Deny Rate

*This chapter is reproduced from *Public Finance Quarterly*, **16**(4), 387–424, 1988.

Reduction Benefit Attributable to Excess Depreciation."[1] The proposal would have affected certain corporate and individual taxpayers who deferred income at relatively high prereform tax rates by taking accelerated depreciation allowances in excess of "economic" depreciation; it was designed to eliminate the windfall gain that would otherwise accrue to such taxpayers when this previously deferred income was included in the tax base (when economic depreciation exceeded depreciation allowances for tax purposes in the later years of the investment) at the significantly lower postreform rates recommended in the proposal. As detailed below, this was to be achieved by assessing a tax roughly equal to the product of the magnitude of the postreform rate reduction experienced by the taxpayer and the amount of "excess depreciation" taken in years prior to the enactment of reform. The proposal, which became known as the "windfall recapture tax," was not included in the Tax Reform Act of 1986. Nevertheless, it received serious consideration during the first few months following the release of the May 1985 Treasury reform package; indeed, despite predictions of immediate dismissal, the merits of the windfall recapture tax were debated at length, and serious consideration was given to expanding the measure to other windfalls generated by the implementation of reform.

The proposal for a windfall recapture tax proved to be a highly controversial one. In particular, many observers characterized the measure as simply a blatant attempt to inflate revenues to satisfy the constraint of revenue neutrality over the five-year budget period following the enactment of reform. Unfortunately, the focus on the revenue aspect of the proposal obscured to a large extent the more interesting economic question explored in this article — the desirability of using such a special and selective tax levy as a transitional tool in implementing tax reform. Although the windfall recapture tax did not survive the legislative process that led to the Tax Reform Act of 1986, the proposal is of considerable current interest for at least three reasons. First, as a unique tax reform proposal the windfall recapture tax raises a host of provocative theoretical questions regarding transitional equity in the implementation of tax reform; the efficiency and distributional properties of the proposal are also

---

[1] See U.S. Treasury (1985: 192–196). The proposal is described in detail in the following section.

of theoretical interest. Second, the structure for the windfall recapture tax proposed by the Treasury, as well as alternative structures recommended by other observers, raise interesting questions about the practical design of such a tax. Finally, the notion of attempting to recapture the benefits associated with unexpected reform-induced tax rate reductions is likely to reappear in subsequent tax reform debates, both in the United States and in other nations. Accordingly, the theoretical and practical issues raised by the proposed windfall recapture tax are still of considerable policy interest. These issues are the focus of this article.

The article is organized as follows. In the first section the general principles underlying the use of recapture taxes as a transitional tool in tax reform are described briefly, and the specific application of these principles in the Treasury windfall recapture tax is examined. The second section considers several theoretical issues raised by the proposed tax, while the third section discusses a variety of design issues raised by the Treasury proposal and alternative designs. Some simulation results for various designs of the windfall recapture tax are presented in the fourth section, and the final section offers some conclusions.

1. The Theory of Tax Reform and the Windfall Recapture Tax

1.1. *Transitional relief and the compensation principle*

The implementation of tax reform inevitably causes a wide variety of redistributions of income or wealth when the economy adjusts from the prereform to the postreform equilibrium. During the recent tax reform debate, the Treasury accepted the theoretical proposition articulated by Hochman (1974) and Feldstein (1976b) that such essentially arbitrary and capricious reform-induced redistributions are undesirable from a social viewpoint and should be limited through appropriate transition rules.[2] In

[2] Note that this viewpoint is not accepted universally in the literature. Graetz (1977) argues that tax changes are little different from most changes in public policy that cause redistributions and that the latter are generally uncompensated; thus individuals should rationally expect changes in tax laws and should not be insulated from the risks of the political

particular, an explicit goal of the November 1984 Treasury proposal (hereafter, Treasury I), as well as the May 1985 administration package (hereafter, Treasury II), was a "fair and orderly transition" to the new tax system. Implementation of the wide-sweeping tax changes proposed was perceived to involve the standard "optimal tax reform tradeoff" — that is, immediate implementation was desirable both on grounds of simplicity and to obtain reform-induced gains in efficiency and equity as soon as possible, but was viewed as undesirable because it maximized the arbitrary redistributions associated with reform.[3]

Such reform-induced redistributions can be reduced in a variety of ways. Grandfathering is perhaps the most frequently used transitional device; it was generally advocated, although subject to qualifications, by the Treasury in its well-known *Blueprints for Basic Tax Reform* (see D. F. Bradford and the U.S. Treasury Tax Policy Staff, 1984). Postponement has been advocated by Feldstein (1976b), who notes that such delay generally reduces reform-induced gains and losses proportionately. Elsewhere (Zodrow, 1981,1985a, 1986), I have analyzed the efficacy of phasing in or partially enacting reform to obtain an optimal balance

process any more than they are from the risks of the market. The Treasury I proposals arguably may be interpreted to accept this viewpoint in a few instances. For example, one justification for the fairly harsh transition rules proposed for the elimination of oil and gas preferences (immediate elimination), for the expansion of the interest limitation rules (a two-year phase-in), and for the taxation of certain large limited partnerships as corporations (full taxation in five years) could be that taxpayers should have reasonably expected some reforms in these particularly tax-advantaged or highly politicized areas. Note that to the extent such expectations exist, market returns should be higher to reflect the probability of tax changes, so that transitional relief is relatively less necessary. Nevertheless, both Treasury reports generally suggest acceptance of the argument that arbitrary reform-induced redistributions are undesirable and should be limited. Also, it is interesting to note that many of the transitional provisions of the Tax Reform Act of 1986 (e.g., retroactive repeal of the investment tax credit, immediate elimination of the deduction for state and local sales taxes, and only a four-year phase-in for the new limits on "passive" investment losses) seem to be relatively harsh; see McLure and Zodrow (1987) for further discussion.

[3] See Zodrow (1985b) for a discussion of the optimal tax reform tradeoff, the conditions under which reform-induced redistributions can appropriately be viewed as arbitrary, and a description of a method used to formalize the tradeoff. See also U.S. Treasury (1984, vol. 1: 229–232).

between reform-induced redistributions and efficiency gains; these analyses indicate that the optimal method of implementing reform generally depends on the nature of the reform-induced redistributions and whether adjustment costs are convex and sufficiently large. In most cases, concern about arbitrary reform-induced redistributions was reflected in the use of these standard transitional tools, as various provisions in both Treasury proposals recommended grandfathering or delayed or phased-in enactment.[4]

However, the windfall recapture tax proposed by the Treasury represents a rather different approach to achieving transitional equity in tax reform. The standard transitional approaches described above are designed to reduce the redistributions associated with reform either by exempting existing assets or by delaying the timing or reducing the extent of enactment of reform. However, in principle reform could be enacted immediately with no redistributions if individuals who suffered windfall losses were identified and compensated with revenues raised from taxation of individuals who enjoyed reform-induced windfall gains.[5] Feldstein (1976a) supports the notion of compensation where feasible, although he focuses on compensation of losers. However, the logic of compensation applies equally well to the taxation of windfall gains — even though in practice windfall losses receive much more attention and are the focus of virtually all special transitional provisions. This point is recognized explicitly in the "optimal tax reform" literature, where the objective function used to evaluate alternative methods of implementing reform weights losses more than proportionately and gains less than proportionately on the grounds that both types of redistributions are arbitrary and thus undesirable from a social viewpoint.[6] Thus in terms of the theory of tax reform the windfall recapture tax can be viewed as an application of the compensation principle to an unanticipated reform-induced windfall gain.

[4] See U.S. Treasury (1984, vol. 1: 233–243) and U.S. Treasury (1985: 437–451).

[5] Provided that reform improves social welfare, the magnitude of the gains will exceed the magnitude of the losses (either in dollar terms or as measured by a social welfare function) so that, neglecting administrative costs, such compensation is theoretically possible.

[6] See Feldstein (1976b) and Zodrow (1985b).

1.2. *Identifying the windfall*

The windfall gain subject to the proposed recapture tax arises because depreciation allowances for tax purposes, especially under the Accelerated Cost Recovery System (ACRS), are generally more accelerated than economic depreciation. The essence of the investment incentive provided with accelerated deductions is that "excess depreciation" — the difference between the accelerated depreciation allowances and those under economic depreciation — is granted in the early years of an investment, thus reducing taxable income in those years. Excess depreciation allowances are taken until the asset reaches its "crossover point," or the point in the later years of an investment when economic depreciation first exceeds tax depreciation (since the latter was accelerated to the early years of the investment). For ACRS assets, the crossover point generally occurs only after all ACRS deductions are exhausted.

The tax benefit of accelerated depreciation is thus frequently viewed as an interest-free loan; the loan accumulates during the "excess depreciation" years prior to the crossover point, when income is shielded from tax, and is repaid during the "deficient depreciation" years after the crossover point, when income for tax purposes is larger than it would be if economic depreciation deductions were being allowed. The benefit is thus the timing advantage of tax deferral.[7] In each period the value to the taxpayer of this interest-free "tax deferral loan" is equal to the product of the interest rate and the amount of the loan (defined as the product of the tax rate and the cumulative amount in that period of excess depreciation less any deficient depreciation). Tax rates are generally assumed to be constant over the entire life of the investment.

[7] Calculation of the benefits of accelerated depreciation also depends on the tax treatment of assets at disposition (which varies greatly across assets), especially the extent to which the excess of the selling price over basis is taxed as ordinary income rather than capital gain, and expected holding periods given these tax rules; for an example of such calculations for real estate, see Gordon, Hines, and Summers (1986). The discussion here generally assumes that assets are held for their economic lives or that there would be no advantage to early disposition; however, see the discussion of real estate in the following section under Modifications of the Treasury Proposal.

The windfall addressed by the recapture tax is the gain that would be conferred by rate reductions that occur after the investment is made. Excess depreciation deductions taken prior to the effective date of the rate reduction reduced income that was subject to tax at relatively high prereform rates. However, to the extent that the associated period of deficient depreciation would occur during the new low-tax regime, the loan would be "repaid" by taxing the previously deferred income at lower postreform rates. As a result, the investor in depreciable assets would receive a reduction in tax unexpected at the time the investment was made. In terms of the tax deferral loan analogy for a large corporation, a taxpayer taking out a loan at a 46% tax rate prior to the effective date of reform that was repaid after such date at the postreform tax rate of 33% would effectively be repaying the interest-free loan at 72 cents (0.33/0.46) on the dollar. Such an investor in depreciable assets would thus benefit not only from the tax deferral expected at the time the investment was made, but also from the postreform tax rate reduction that presumably was not expected at the time of investment.

Under the compensation principle, the windfall gain described above would seem to be a reasonable candidate for "negative" compensation or a recapture tax, as the rate reduction confers a significant windfall gain to the owners of existing depreciable assets. Although assumptions regarding the expectations of investors are necessarily speculative, a dramatic rate reduction from 46% to 33% seems unlikely to have been anticipated at the time of investment.

1.3. *The Treasury design*

The Treasury proposal to eliminate the windfall gain due to the combination of accelerated depreciation allowances and rate reduction was designed as follows. The benchmark for economic depreciation was taken to be the straight-line depreciation allowances used for calculating "earnings and profits" (E&P). Excess depreciation on an investment was defined as the difference between tax depreciation and E&P depreciation between January 1, 1980, and July 1, 1986, the proposed effective date of the rate reduction. For large corporations, the reduction in tax rates proposed under Treasury II was from 46% to 33%, a reduction of 13 percentage points. For the balance of the article, the case of such a large corporation will be the focus of discussion. However, the Treasury proposal also would affect certain wealthy individuals, who would experience a 15% tax rate reduction from 50% to 35%. (Small corporations and individuals not in top brackets generally would be excluded from the effects of the proposal by the generous exemption and exclusion described below.)

As described above, the basic intent of the proposal was to prevent the "tax deferral loan" associated with this amount of excess depreciation from benefiting from the 13% rate reduction from 46% to 33% when it was "repaid." This was achieved by including in income 40% of excess depreciation as defined above over the years 1986 to 1988 (12% in 1986, 12% in 1987 and 16% in 1988); the 40% inclusion, coupled with the new corporate rate of 33%, implied that excess depreciation was subject to a 13% recapture tax ($0.40 \times 0.33 = 0.132$). An income inclusion, rather than an additional tax, was used so that losses could offset the income inclusion. A generous exemption was allowed so that the tax would apply only to the largest corporations and wealthiest individuals, as only firms or individuals with $400,000 of total depreciation over the period were included; in addition, the first $300,000 of excess depreciation was excluded.

The windfall recapture tax was thus an application of the principle of compensation to certain taxpayers who would experience a windfall gain due to the dramatic reduction in individual and corporate tax rates proposed in Treasury II. Accordingly, although the windfall recapture tax was certainly a unique tax reform proposal, the idea of recapturing windfall gains was consistent with the principle of compensation advocated in the theoretical literature on tax reform. Moreover, as noted by Cordes and Weisbrod (1985), compensation for the effects of government actions outside the tax area has been fairly prevalent. Thus although the windfall recapture tax could be termed "unprecedented" and "revolutionary" as a specific tax reform proposal, it was not without theoretical justification or without precedent in government actions. In any case, regardless of the apparent novelty of the proposal, the two most critical questions are whether the rationale for the tax satisfied the theoretical requirements of a fair application of the compensation principle and whether the design of the tax was appropriate in terms of calculating accurately the windfall to be recaptured.

These two questions are the focus of this article.

2. Theoretical Issues

The primary theoretical issues raised by the windfall recapture tax are (1) the relevance of the compensation argument in the case of the particular windfall addressed by the tax, (2) the desirability of selective application of the compensation principle to a single windfall gain, and (3) the efficiency and distributional aspects of the proposal.[8]

2.1. *Relevance of the compensation argument*

The primary theoretical argument against the application of the compensation principle in this case is that investors expected only that the time pattern of depreciation deductions determined at the time of the investment would be honored, and that any changes in income tax rates would not trigger either recapture or compensation rules — income received in any year would always be taxed at the rates in effect in that year.[9] According

[8]The following issue is also of interest. Bell and Ooesterhuis (1985) observe that the appropriate measure for economic depreciation (used to measure the amount of "excess depreciation") is the Real Cost Recovery System (RCRS) proposed in Treasury I. (See U.S. Treasury, 1984, vol. 2: 152–172.) They note that the present value of the difference between ACRS and RCRS deductions is negative for equipment at sufficiently high rates of inflation, indicating no benefit to the taxpayer. They argue that if this difference in present values is negative even after the rate reduction, no windfall recapture tax is appropriate, and that in all other cases the size of the tax should be constrained to be no larger than the size of the benefit to the taxpayer, given the rate reduction. The above discussion of the compensation principle suggests that this argument is invalid. Given the tax structure existing at the time of investment, the implicit contract between the investor and government specified a series of depreciation deductions that were expected to be taken at the existing tax rate. The unexpected rate reduction would result in a windfall to the taxpayer, relative to the terms expected at the time of investment. The fact that the present value of that tax benefit attributable to ACRS may be negative is irrelevant; the taxpayer voluntarily agreed to a deferral "contract" with the government on those terms — presumably in exchange for the tax benefits of the investment tax credit — and the purpose of the recapture tax is to ensure that the terms of that deferral contract are honored. Thus it is theoretically possible that the tax benefit could initially be negative and only less negative (rather than positive) after the rate reduction. The theoretically correct recapture tax would ensure that the taxpayer experienced the full "negative tax benefit" expected at the time of investment.

[9]See Viard (1985).

to this view, the application of a recapture tax represents an unfair and retroactive levy on the owners of existing depreciable assets rather than a justifiable application of the compensation principle. This position is not completely without merit, as past tax rate changes have not resulted in applications of the compensation principle and, as noted above, assumptions about investors' expectations regarding future tax changes are always speculative.[10]

Nevertheless, it is difficult to conceive how a rational system of transitional rules could be based on the assumption that taxpayers would receive transitional relief if certain features of the tax law were changed but would be denied such relief for changes in other provisions. Instead, any practical and consistent approach would have to be based on the assumption that taxpayers expected continuation of existing law. Moreover, all of the theoretical work on implementing tax reform assumes that the rationale for special transitional rules is to protect implicit "contractual" agreements made between the investor and the government based upon "reliance" on current law, rather than on only certain provisions of current law.[11] Accordingly, the Treasury position that transitional rules should be based on the expectation of investor reliance of all aspects of current law, including the rate structure, seems reasonable — especially in the context of a fundamental reform that would result in an unprecedented reduction in corporate and individual tax rates and would require a large number of transitional rules.

2.2. *Selective application of the compensation principle*

A second criticism of the windfall recapture tax is considerably more telling. The Treasury proposal applies the compensation principle to a single windfall gain, although the proposed reform package would result in a

[10] In addition to the fact that general practice provides no support to the principle of recapture due to rate changes, Viard (1985) suggests that taxation of income deposited in IRAs at rates in force upon withdrawal supports the proposition of taxing income at whatever rate is in effect when it is earned. This position seems tenuous, since income averaging is an explicit goal of IRAs, while it is unlikely that Congress expected investors to benefit from rate reduction in 1986 when ACRS was enacted in 1981.

[11] See especially Feldstein (1976b) and Graetz (1977).

multitude of windfall gains and losses. Indeed, the implementation of the Treasury package would cause changes in the values of literally all the assets in the economy, as well as in the welfare of all individuals; such changes occur because after-tax returns to all activities would be altered, both as a result of changes in tax treatment as well as reform-induced general equilibrium changes in before-tax rates of return. To cite just a few examples, one would expect significant changes in individual wealth as a result of (1) the generally less favorable treatment of capital intensive industries, primarily attributable to the elimination of the investment tax credit, (2) the markedly less favorable treatment of rental real estate, attributable to changes in depreciation schedules, at-risk rules, and other provisions, (3) various changes in tax treatment specific to the energy industries, financial institutions, and industries characterized by multiperiod production processes, and (4) repeal of the deductibility of state and local taxes.[12]

In principle, all such wealth changes could theoretically be subject to compensation. In practice, calculation of all windfall gains and losses is theoretically infeasible as well as impossible from a practical standpoint because of the huge administrative costs involved. Thus the determination of which gains and losses will be subject to compensation is inevitably rather arbitrary.[13]

The Treasury effectively limited its application of the compensation principle to the case of income deferral (as described above), rather than considering the much broader category of situations in which an anticipated income stream benefits from an unexpected rate reduction or is changed by reform-induced general equilibrium price changes. Limiting compensation to cases of income deferral is arguably a reasonable approach for at least three reasons. First, cases of income deferral include many of the situations in which reform-induced changes in wealth are significant and capricious. Second, such a rule limits consideration to a class of cases where reform-induced changes in wealth are attributable to past rather

---

[12] For details of the relevant provisions, see U.S. Treasury (1985).

[13] A thorough discussion of which gains and losses should and should not be subject to compensation is beyond the scope of this article; for extended discussions of this critical issue, see Feldstein (1976a, 1976b), Graetz (1977), and Goode (1987).

than future actions; wealth changes in such cases are relatively easily to identify and thus have a more reasonable claim for compensation. For example, cases of income deferral are readily identified, while identifying cases in which taxpayers experience losses due to prospective tax changes (e.g., elimination of the investment tax credit) is a more tenuous process. Third, reform-induced gains or losses in cases of income deferral are more readily measured. That is, the gain or loss in a case characterized by previous deferral of a specific amount of tax liability is easier to measure than the gain or loss in a case in which future returns must be predicted.

Nevertheless, even within the limited domain of cases characterized by income deferral many other candidates for recapture were not proposed by the Treasury. For example, the compensation principle could be applied to income deferrals in the cases of expensing of intangible drilling costs and R&D expenditures, advertising and job-training expenditures that have effects lasting more than a year, loss carryforwards, installment sales, contracts using the "completed contract" method, bad debt reserves, and savings in retirement plans. The length of this list is not necessarily an argument against the windfall recapture tax. Instead, it suggests that the principle is applicable in areas other than depreciable assets and that, if the imposition of windfall recapture taxes in these areas is administratively feasible, the revenue potential of such taxes may be larger than is commonly believed.[14]

Thus although the particular windfall gain addressed by the proposed recapture rule is a highly significant one in revenue terms and is fairly easy to measure (provided there is a widely accepted standard of economic depreciation), the proposal is clearly subject to the telling criticism that it represents an unfair selective tax on a single reform-induced windfall gain. This criticism is tempered somewhat by the fact that windfall gains from investments made before 1980, as well as the income from existing investments, would benefit from rate reduction and because a host of other transition rules generally designed to ameliorate windfall

---

[14] However, the application of the compensation principle through recapture taxes in such areas may well be quite difficult from an administrative standpoint. This is especially true since calculation of the amount of windfall generally requires a measure of true economic cost (e.g., "true economic depreciation" of R&D and advertising expenditures).

losses without providing for direct compensation were proposed. Nevertheless, the election by Treasury to apply the compensation principle to only one gain and no losses is clearly open to criticism. In particular, it is quite conceivable that some taxpayers would have windfall losses caused by other reform measures (including the relevant transition rules) that would dwarf any gains due to the combination of accelerated depreciation allowances and rate reduction; such taxpayers would likely find recapture of their windfall gains coupled with no compensation for their windfall losses highly inequitable.

2.3. *Efficiency and distributional aspects of the proposal*

A major advantage of the windfall recapture tax is that it represents a rather close approximation to a lump sum tax — one that depends on previous investment decisions and thus does not affect future decisions — but does not have some of the characteristics that generally make such taxes undesirable. As is well known, the primary advantage of a lump sum tax is that it imposes no efficiency loss, since changes in behavior cannot reduce tax liability. This feature of the windfall recapture tax is particularly attractive in light of possible alternative sources of revenue — higher corporate rates or less generous depreciation allowances — that would affect future investment decisions.

Lump sum taxes are generally viewed as grossly unfair, either because they are arbitrary or because they are regressive. However, to the extent one accepts the logic of the compensation principle and the appropriateness of its application in the windfall recapture tax, the tax is an equitable form of lump sum tax since it eliminates an unfair windfall gain that would otherwise occur. Moreover, as noted by Viard (1985), the tax will be borne by corporate shareholders, many of whom are upper-income individuals, and by high-bracket investors in depreciable assets. Thus the tax is likely to be progressive rather than regressive, as is generally the case with lump sum taxes.

Of course, it is possible to conceive of ways that the windfall recapture tax might alter future investment decisions and thus not satisfy the requirements for a true lump sum tax.[15] Some taxpayers might relocate

[15] See Viard (1985) for further discussion.

abroad to avoid the tax, although generally this course of action seems farfetched. Investors might anticipate future recapture taxes and thus reduce investment — although they might equally well anticipate future rate increases coupled with "windfall loss compensation" based on the rationale underlying the windfall recapture tax, and thus increase investment due to reduced uncertainty regarding the tax treatment of their investments. To the extent the proposal is viewed simply as an arbitrary capital levy, investment may be reduced.[16] Finally, if investment is determined by cash flow rather than cost of capital considerations, investment could be reduced by the imposition of the tax; however, to the extent the tax simply replicated the present value of cash flow expected at the time of investment due to depreciation allowances while increasing cash flow due to lower taxation of the income from investment, any negative investment effects should be minimal. These points serve primarily to illustrate the familiar fact that a tax that is a perfect lump sum tax is impossible to design. Nevertheless, the windfall recapture tax would seem to be as close to a real-world approximation of a feasible lump sum tax as is realistically possible.

3. Design Issues

Even if one accepts the theoretical rationale for the windfall recapture tax, the Treasury proposal raises several critical design issues. These can be divided into two groups. The first consists of relatively straightforward design changes that were suggested as modifications of the basic Treasury framework for the windfall recapture tax; these changes would clearly improve the design of the recapture tax as they are both justifiable on theoretical grounds and practical in that they could be implemented easily and fairly. The second issue is a much more fundamental design change suggested by Aaron (1985). These two types of changes are considered in turn in the following subsections.

[16] Viard (1985) notes that investment in 1986 might have been reduced to avoid the recapture tax. He also tends to discount expectation effects on investment, arguing that future recapture taxes are doubtful since further tax cuts are unlikely in view of the deficit situation and future depreciation allowances would be less accelerated than under ACRS giving rise to a smaller windfall to recapture.

3.1. *Modifications of the Treasury proposal*

Discounting future windfall gains. As stressed by Stretch and Sunley (1985a), the Treasury proposal did not properly account for the time value of money, as it required repayment of excess depreciation in the first three years following enactment without discounting for the fact that most such repayments were scheduled to be made in years beyond this three-year horizon. As a result, it generally overstated the present value of liability due.[17] It is clear that discounting is appropriate from an economic perspective; indeed, this was recognized explicitly by Treasury.[18] The stated justification that ignoring discounting would be simpler from an administrative standpoint is not compelling, as the cost of any additional complexity would seem to be clearly offset by improved accuracy in the calculation of the tax. The appropriate discounting method is demonstrated below.

The choice of the measure of economic depreciation. The choice of E&P (earnings and profits) depreciation as the measure of economic depreciation was justified on simplicity grounds, since most firms already have to calculate E&P depreciation and thus would not have to recalculate a new measure of depreciation. However, the E&P standard of economic depreciation is a very slow measure and thus results in too much excess depreciation. The obvious solution is to use the Real Cost Recovery System (RCRS) proposed in Treasury I as the measure of real economic depreciation. Again, any costs attributable to increased complexity would seem to be more than offset by the benefits of accurate measurement. The effects of using RCRS in the calculation of the windfall recapture tax are explored below.

Although economic theory clearly indicates that the measure of economic depreciation should be indexed for inflation, persistent congressional reluctance to include indexing provisions in the measurement of capital income suggests that both indexed and nonindexed options should be considered.[19] This is done in the analysis below, where the unindexed option used as the measure of economic depreciation is unindexed RCRS.

---

[17] In a few cases the fact that the payment was spread over three years without requiring the payment of interest in the second and third years more than offset the lack of discounting, and the Treasury approach understated the present value of tax liability.

[18] See U.S. Treasury (1985: 196).

[19] Stretch and Sunley (1985b) argue that the choices for a benchmark for economic depreciation should be restricted to "depreciation systems that were commonly accepted at the

The treatment of real estate. The fact that the Treasury proposal applied to real estate is problematical, because in many cases the proposed windfall recapture tax was too harsh on a taxpayer who invested in a real estate asset on the expectation that the asset would be held for a period significantly shorter than its economic life (as determined by the life used in the measure of economic depreciation). Prior to 1986, all long-term gains on nonresidential real estate investment that were depreciated straight line using ACRS lives were taxed at capital gains rates.[20] Hendershott and Ling (1984) demonstrate that under most circumstances the optimal trading strategy for such property is to sell at the crossover point (when the depreciation deductions are exhausted). Those investors who elected straight line depreciation — rather than taking ACRS depreciation deductions on the expectation of taxation at ordinary income rates on all gains up to the difference between the original purchase price and tax basis at the time of sale — probably planned to follow some variant of such a strategy. That is, they expected to take excess depreciation deductions at their top-bracket individual rate of 50%, sell the property at or before the crossover point, and "repay" the tax deferral loan at the capital gains rate of 20%. Under these circumstances, the windfall would only be the 2.5% reduction in the maximum capital gains tax rate proposed in Treasury II, rather than the 13% assumed in the construction of the windfall recapture tax proposal.[21,22]

---

time the contract arose." However, the measurement of "excess depreciation" theoretically must be the difference between depreciation taken (the amount of receipts actually shielded from tax at the prereform rates) and the most accurate measure available of economic depreciation (the amount of receipts appropriately shielded from tax under an income tax system). The question of whether the accurate measure of economic depreciation was available to the taxpayer for tax depreciation purposes is irrelevant.

[20] Use of the term "recapture" is avoided in this discussion of taxation of certain gains on depreciable property at ordinary income tax rates in order to prevent any confusion with the windfall "recapture" tax.

[21] A similar point applies to investors who took ACRS deductions on residential real estate prior to 1986, who expected that only those gains corresponding to the difference between the original purchase price and the excess of ACRS depreciation deductions over straight line depreciation would be subject to taxation at ordinary income (rather than capital gains) tax rates.

[22] Note however that if even E&P straight line depreciation overstates economic depreciation for real estate (as is sometimes asserted), the amount of excess depreciation calculated

Although one can argue that such generous capital gains provisions under pre-1986 law were inappropriate, the rationale underlying the compensation principle requires that expectations based on the provisions of existing law be honored. Accordingly, the windfall recapture tax should be applied to real estate investments only if amended by exceptions that would take into account expected holding periods on such assets in light of the capital gains provisions of pre-1986 law.[23,24]

3.2. *The Aaron critique*

A more fundamental criticism was raised by Aaron (1985), who believes that the basic windfall recapture tax design proposed by Treasury was inappropriate. Aaron notes that the Treasury proposal considered only tax deferral loans "taken out" prior to the effective date of reform. He argues that the calculation of the windfall recapture tax should preserve the exact character of all of the tax deferral loans expected by the investor at the time of investment, including those taken out after the effective date of reform; he proposes an alternative calculation method that satisfies this criterion. This alternative approach is discussed in detail in this subsection, and numerical estimates of the amounts of tax raised using the Aaron method, relative to the amounts raised by the original Treasury proposal both with and without discounting, are provided in the following section.

---

by the Treasury method would be too low, which in turn would result in an understatement of the amount of the windfall.

[23] See McLure (1985).

[24] There is a limited amount of empirical evidence that supports the commonly held notion that investors tend to "churn" real estate assets — that is, sell them one or more times rather than holding them for their entire economic lives — as predicted by the theoretical analysis of Hendershott and Ling (1984). Gravelle (1985) estimates that the average holding period for multifamily residential real estate is roughly 20 years, considerably less than the 63-year truncated life used in the Treasury RCRS approximation to economic depreciation. Gordon, Hines, and Summers (1986) show that a significant portion of nonresidential real estate assets placed in service since the enactment of ACRS were depreciated straight line rather using ACRS deductions; they point out that such an election generally makes sense only if taxpayers expect to sell the assets at some point in the future and wish to avoid the taxation of gains at ordinary income tax rates on the future sale.

The discussion is facilitated by using the example of a \$1,000 asset with a 3-year ACRS life. A constant 4% real after-tax return and a constant 4% inflation rate are assumed. To focus attention on the effects of using the two alternative methods rather than the effects of using E&P depreciation in calculating the windfall recapture tax, economic depreciation is assumed to be measured according to the best available standard (RCRS) in the comparisons of the Treasury and Aaron approaches; the extension to the case where economic depreciation is calculated using the slower E&P measure is straightforward. The cases where the RCRS measure of economic depreciation is unindexed and indexed are considered in turn.

The unindexed case. The unindexed case is fairly straightforward, and clearly illustrates the concepts involved. Let A_i denote the ACRS deductions allowed in year i = 1,...,b, where b is the final year in which ACRS deductions are taken; thus b = 3 for the 3-year asset. For ACRS assets in the unindexed case, all years in which ACRS deductions are taken are years of excess depreciation. Thus years i = 1,...,b are years of excess depreciation, and the subsequent years of "deficient depreciation" can be indexed by j = 1,...,r, where (b + r) is the total number of years of RCRS deductions. Under RCRS, the 3-year ACRS asset would be depreciated over five years; let B_i denote the deductions allowed in years i = 1, 2, 3 and R_j(j = 1,2) be the deductions allowed in the two years after the ACRS deductions are exhausted (years four and five of the investment).

The appropriate values are thus $A_1 = 250.00$, $A_2 = 380.00$, $A_3 = 370.00$, $B_1 = 160.00$, $B_2 = 268.80$, $B_3 = 182.78$, $R_1 = 124.29$, and $R_2 = 264.13$. The associated amounts of excess depreciation $E_i = A_i - Bi$ are $E_1 = 90.00$, $E_2 = 111.20$, and $E_3 = 187.22$. The crossover point occurs after year three, and the amounts of "deficient depreciation" are simply R_j. By construction, the sum of the E_i equals the sum of the R_j. In terms of the tax deferral loan analogy, the principal amount of the loan is E_1 in year one, $E_1 + E_2$ in year two, $E_1 + E_2 + E_3$ in year three, $E_1 + E_2 + E_3 - R_1$ in year four, and $E_1 + E_2 + E_3 - R_1 - R_2 = 0$ in year five when the loan is completely repaid.

For purposes of modeling the effects of the recapture tax and comparing the Treasury and Aaron approaches, the tax benefit of accelerated depreciation is most easily interpreted as a sequence of loans granted in each of the b years prior to the crossover point. Thus for the three-year ACRS asset this modeling approach implies three loans. These loans are then repaid in the years after the crossover point. The amounts and timing of the repayment of each loan is specified by $a_{ij}R_j$, where the a_{ij} are "loan repayment coefficients," where the i refers to the year the loan was "taken out," and the j refers to the year the loan is to be "repaid." Thus $a_{ij}R_j$ represents the fraction of the "deficient depreciation" R_j that is allocated to the repayment of the loan taken out in year i. By construction, $\Sigma_i\, a_{ij} = 1$; that is, all R_j are allocated to the repayment of one of the b loans. Although the selection of the a_{ij} is somewhat arbitrary in the sense that any pattern of repayment could be specified, the analysis in this article adopts the intuitively appealing approach of assuming that the loans are repaid according to a "FIFO" or "first-in, first-out" criterion.[25] This approach follows Treasury as well as Stretch and Sunley (1985a) and, as discussed below, also has the advantage of limiting the number of years that must be included in the calculation of the tax under the Treasury approach.

Thus in the case of the three-year asset the excess depreciation taken in year one ($E_1 = 90.00$) is fully repaid in year four ($j = 1$), so $a_{11} = 90.00/124.29 = 0.724$ and $a_{12} = 0$. The excess depreciation taken in the second year of the investment ($E_2 = 111.20$) is partially repaid in year four ($a_{21} = 34.29/124.29 = 0.276$), with the remainder repaid in year five ($a_{22} = (111.20–34.29)/264.13 = 0.291$). Similarly, the excess depreciation taken in year three ($E_3 = 187.22$) is fully repaid in year five ($a_{31} = 0$ and $a_{32} = 187.22/264.13 = 0.709$).

[25] Note that alternative loan repayment allocation methods would yield different results. For example, prorating some portion of each loan repayment to each of the loans taken out prior to the crossover point would extend the number of years of repayment of loans taken out prior to the effective date of reform; this would have the effect of reducing the amount of the recapture tax calculated under the Treasury approach, since the repayments would be discounted more. A LIFO or "last-in, first-out" allocation method would result in an even larger reduction of the amount of the recapture tax, since loans taken out prior to the crossover point would be the last scheduled for repayment and thus would be discounted the most. Although there is no strong theoretical case for the FIFO approach, it has some intuitive appeal and also has the advantage of minimizing the number of years that must be included in the calculation of the recapture tax under the Treasury approach (see footnote 28 below for further discussion).

Under this approach, the present value LU_i of each of the i = 1,...,b unindexed tax deferral loans, calculated in year one, with constant tax rate t and a discount rate d equal to the real after tax rate of return, is given by

$$LU_i = t\left[(A_i - B_i)(1+d)^{-(i-1)} - \sum_j a_{ij} R_j (1+d)^{-(j+b-1)}\right], \quad i = 1,\ldots,b. \qquad (1)$$

For t = 0.46, d = 0.0816 (recall the assumptions of a constant 4% real after-tax rate of return and a constant 4% rate of inflation), and a $1,000 investment, this yields LU_1 = 0.46 (18.88) =8.69, LU_2 = 0.46 (19.54) = 8.99, and LU_3 = 0.46 (23.20) = 10.67. Thus the total tax value of the accelerated depreciation allowances in the unindexed case (VU) is

$$VU = \sum_i LU_i = 28.34. \qquad (2)$$

This method of calculating the value of accelerated depreciation allowances to the taxpayer is equivalent to two alternative approaches. First, the value can be calculated as the tax rate times the difference in the present values of the two streams of depreciation allowances, or

$$\begin{aligned} VU &= t\left\{\sum_i A_i (1+d)^{-(i-1)} - \left[\sum_i B_1 (1+d)^{-(i-1)} + \sum_j R_j (1+d) -^{(i+(b-1)}\right]\right\} \\ &= (0.46)\,(917.61 - 855.99) = 28.34. \end{aligned} \qquad (3)$$

Second, the value equals the interest rate times the present value of the amount of the outstanding "deferral loan" over the life of the investment, or

$$\begin{aligned} VU &= (d)(t)\ [E_1(1 + d)^{-1} + (E_1 + E_2)(1 + d)^{-2} \\ &\quad + (E_1 + E_2 + E_3)(1 + d)^{-3} + (E_1 + E_2 + E_3 - R_1)(1 + d)^{-4}] \\ &= (0.0816)\ (0.46)\ (755.17) = 28.34. \end{aligned} \qquad (4)$$

The indexed case. The tax deferral loan analogy can still be used when the measure of economic depreciation is indexed for inflation, although the approach must be modified to reflect the fact that the nominal amount "repaid" will exceed the nominal amount "borrowed."[26] Under (indexed)

---

[26] Stretch and Sunley (1985b) argue that the adoption of indexing in the measure of economic depreciation moves the analysis "away from the concept of accelerated depreciation

RCRS as proposed in Treasury I, the deductions allowed from income become $B_i(1 + \pi)^{1-1}$ for i = 1,..., b and R_j $(1 + \pi)^{j+b-1}$ for j = 1,..., r, where $\pi = 0.04$ is the assumed constant inflation rate. Thus allowing for inflation indexing in the measure of economic depreciation has two effects on the calculation of the "tax deferral loans" associated with accelerated depreciation. First, the amounts of the b loans are reduced (except for the first year) since the measured amount of excess depreciation is reduced. Second, the amounts of required loan repayments are larger in nominal terms and, with indexing, the total nominal amount to be repaid exceeds the total nominal amount of excess depreciation taken. Both of these effects act to reduce the value of the tax deferral loans associated with accelerated depreciation.

To construct the analogous tax deferral loan terms for the indexed case, assume that the "matching" of loans and repayments is the same as in the unindexed case, but both loans and repayments are subject to indexing as specified under RCRS. Thus all of the loan repayments in years after the crossover point, including the inflation adjustments, are allocated to loans taken out during years i = 1,..., b; the allocation is identical to the FIFO-type allocation described in the unindexed case, except the inflation adjustments are included. Thus the expression for each of the b indexed loans is

$$LI_j = t\{[A_i - B_i(1+\pi)^{i-1}](1+d)^{-(i-1)} - \sum_j a_{ij}R_j[(1+\pi)/(1+d)]^{(i+b-1)}\}, \quad i = 1,\ldots,b. \tag{5}$$

For a constant 4% inflation rate, this yields $LI_1 = 0.46\ (10.00) = 4.60$, $LI_2 = 0.46\ (-3.36) = -1.54$, and $LI_3 = 0.46\ (-12.75) = -5.86$, and the total tax value of the accelerated depreciation allowances in the indexed case (VI) is

$$VI = \sum_i LI_i = -2.80. \tag{6}$$

With indexing and a constant tax rate the value of the deferral loans is reduced; indeed, the value is negative in this case. As noted above, this

as an interest-free loan, inasmuch as the indexed depreciation allowances will exceed the original cost of the investment." As shown below, this is not necessarily the case; accelerated depreciation allowances can still be modeled as deferral loans, where the amounts loaned and repaid are interpreted as balances indexed for inflation.

result is not that unusual since, at inflation rates in the 4% to 5% range, RCRS is more generous than ACRS. Note that a negative present value at a constant tax rate does not imply that no windfall results from the tax rate reduction; the allowances under ACRS are still accelerated relative to RCRS in terms of their timing (even though they are worth less in present value terms), so that the windfall due to rate reduction still occurs.

Calculating the windfall recapture tax. The alternative approaches to calculating the amount of the windfall recapture tax recommended by Treasury and Aaron are fundamentally different. The Treasury approach, once properly adjusted to account for discounting as done above, requires that any loan taken out at a 46% rate be repaid at a 46% rate rather than at a 33% rate; that is, the amount of the tax deferral loan due to excess depreciation deductions taken when the tax rate was 46% should effectively be repaid (during the time of deficient depreciation deductions using the FIFO allocation technique described above) as if the tax rate were still 46%.

If the effective date of the rate reduction occurs at or after the crossover point of an asset, all the loans have been taken out and some of the repayment may have already occurred. (The Treasury and Aaron approaches yield identical results in these cases.) If the year of the rate reduction is denoted as j*, the amount of windfall recapture tax under the Treasury approach in the unindexed case (Wtu) — with discounting and in present values of the year in which the investment was made — is

$$W_{TU} = \sum_i \left\{ (0.13) \left[\sum_{j \geq j^*} a_{ij} R_j (1+d)^{-(j+b-1)} \right] \right\}. \tag{7}$$

Following the example used above, suppose the asset with a three-year ACRS life was purchased in 1983 and the effective date of the rate reduction was 1987. In this case, j* = 2, all three loans have been "taken out" and only one year of "loan repayment" remains. Thus in 1983 present values,

$$\begin{aligned} W_{TU} &= (0.13) \sum_i a_{i2} R_2 (1+d)^{-4} \\ &= 0.13\,(0.291 + 0.709)(264.13)(1.0816)^{-4} = 25.09, \end{aligned} \tag{7'}$$

or 34.34 in 1987 present values. Similarly, the recapture tax in the indexed case (W_{TI}) is

$$W_{TI} = \sum_{i} \left\{ (0.13) \left[\sum_{j \geq j^*} a_{ij} R_j [(1+\pi)/(1+d)]^{(j+(b-1)} \right] \right\}. \tag{8}$$

For the example of the three-year asset purchased in 1983 (j* = 2), this yields

$$\begin{aligned} W_{TI} &= (0.13) \sum_{i} a_{i2} R_2 [(1+\pi)/(1+d)]^4 \\ &= 0.13\,(0.291 + 0.709)\,(264.13)\,(1.04/1.0816)^4 = 29.35, \end{aligned} \tag{8'}$$

or 40.17 in 1987 present values.

Note that the amount of tax under the original Treasury plan is βW_{TU}, where $\beta = 0.3 + 0.3/(1+d) + 0.4/(1+d)^2$ is a factor reflecting the reduction in tax due to the three-year spread of tax liability under the original Treasury plan. For d = 0.0816, $\beta = 0.919$.

If the effective date of reform occurs prior to the crossover point, the Treasury approach would require repayment at a 46% rate only for the loans taken out prior to the effective date. If the effective date were in year i*, the amount of the windfall tax in the unindexed case (W_{Tu}), measured in present values of the year in the investment was made, is

$$W_{TI} = \sum_{i<i^*} \left\{ (0.13) \left[\sum_{j} a_{ij} R_j (1+d)^{-(j+b-1)} \right] \right\}. \tag{9}$$

For example, suppose the three-year asset was purchased in 1985 and the effective date of the rate reduction was 1987. In this case, i* = 3 and only two (of potentially three) deferral loans have been taken out at the pre-reform tax rate. Thus in 1985 present values,

$$\begin{aligned} W_{TU} &= \sum_{i=1,2} = \left\{ (0.13) \left[\sum_{j=1,2} a_{ij} R_j (1+d)^{-(j+2)} \right] \right\} \\ &= 0.13[(0.724 + 0.276)(124.29)(1.0816)^{-3} \\ &\quad + (0.291)(264.13)(1.0816)^{-4}] = 20.07, \end{aligned} \tag{9'}$$

or 23.49 in 1987 present values. Similarly, the windfall recapture tax in the indexed case (W_{TI}) is

$$W_{TI} = \sum_{i<i^*} \left\{ (0.13) \left[\sum_{j} a_{ij} R_j [(1+\pi)/(1+d)]^{(j+b-1)} \right] \right\}. \tag{10}$$

For the example of the three-year asset purchased in 1985 ($i^* = 3$), this yields

$$W_{TI} = \sum_{i=1,2} \left\{ (0.13) \left[\sum_{j=1,2} a_{ij} R_j [(1+\pi)/(1+d)]^{(j+2)} \right] \right\}$$

$$= 0.13[(0.724 + 0.276)(124.29)(1.04/1.0816)^3$$

$$+ (0.291)(264.13)(1.04/1.0816)^4] = 22.92, \qquad [10']$$

or 26.80 in 1987 present values.

This approach ensures that the loans taken out at a 46% rate prior to the effective date of reform are effectively repaid at a 46% rate, once the windfall recapture tax is assessed. However, note that this approach changes the terms of the loans scheduled to be taken out in the year i^* and subsequent years (until $i = b$); that is, such loans will now be taken out at a 33% rate, rather than the 46% rate the investor expected at the time of the investment.

As noted above, this aspect of the Treasury plan is the feature Aaron finds objectionable. He argues that the calculation of the windfall recapture tax should preserve the exact character of the tax deferral loans expected by the investor at the time of the investment; that is, the total value to the taxpayer of the accelerated depreciation allowances should be unchanged. Following the previous discussion of the determination of VU and VI, this would be equivalent to (1) holding constant the product of the initial tax rate and the difference between the present values of the accelerated depreciation allowances and the RCRS measure of economic depreciation, and to (2) holding constant the product of the interest rate and the present value sum of the amounts of the outstanding deferral loan in each period (defined as the product of the initial tax rate and the cumulative amounts of excess depreciation less any deficient depreciation in that period).

When the effective date of reform occurs at or after the crossover point, this exact preservation of the character of the tax deferral loans expected by the investor at the time of the investment is achieved. However, when the effective date occurs prior to the crossover point, Aaron argues that the windfall recapture tax should ensure that the loans taken out after the effective date are effectively taken out at a 46% rate. Thus Aaron's windfall recapture tax in the unindexed case (W_{AU}) — again, measured in present values of the year in which the investment was made — is

$$W_{AU} = -(0.13/0.46)\sum_{i \geq i^*} LU_i + W_{TU}. \tag{11}$$

For the example of the three-year asset purchased in 1985, $i^* = 3$ and the third deferral loan is taken out after the enactment of the rate reduction. Thus Aaron's windfall recapture tax (in 1985 present values) would be

$$\begin{aligned} W_{AU} &= -(0.13/0.46)\ LU_3 + W_{TU} \qquad (11') \\ &= -(0.283)\ (10.67) + 20.07 = 17.06, \end{aligned}$$

or 19.95 in 1987 present values. Similarly, in the indexed case Aaron's windfall recapture tax (W_{AI}) is

$$W_{AI} = -(0.13/0.46)\sum_{i \geq i^*} LI_i + W_{TI}. \tag{12}$$

For the example of the three-year asset purchased in 1985 ($i^* = 3$), this yields

$$\begin{aligned} W_{AI} &= -(0.13/0.46)\ LI_3 + W_{TI} \\ &= -(0.283)\ (-5.86) + 22.92 = 24.58, \qquad (12') \end{aligned}$$

or 28.74 in 1987 present values.

Note that the first terms in (11) and (12) ensure that the tax deferral loans taken out after the effective date are still taken out at a 46% rate; thus the conditions described above for an exact preservation of the character of the tax deferral loans expected by the investor at the time of the investment are satisfied. Aaron notes that this may result in a positive sum being due to the taxpayer as a result of the windfall recapture "tax."

A comparison of the two approaches. The rationale for Aaron's position is as follows. He argues that the purpose of the windfall recapture tax is to correct only for the windfalls that occur due to the mismeasurement of income implicit in accelerated depreciation allowances coupled with an unexpected rate reduction. Windfalls due to any other aspects of reform are not to be considered, but windfall losses (the reduction in the value of a tax deferral loan yet to be taken) should also be considered.

The Aaron position has considerable intuitive appeal, especially within the context of the "reliance on all aspects of current law" argument described above. Nevertheless, the position taken by Treasury has some advantages. Consider first the unindexed case, which, as argued above, is the likely political outcome. In this case, the value of the loan is positive, and the Aaron approach would result in a payment to the taxpayer for the loans taken out after the effective date of the rate reduction. However, the taxpayer is already receiving a windfall gain from the fact that the income from the investment is unexpectedly subject to tax at the lower 33% rate. In addition, Treasury II would raise effective tax rates for equipment. In the new equilibrium, gross income to equipment investments — new and existing — would be likely to increase in order to maintain after-tax rates of return. As a result, owners of existing equipment would receive a second windfall gain. (Note that this reasoning is analogous to the argument made by Auerbach and Kotlikoff [1983] who stress the windfall losses due to the effective tax rate reductions under ERTA in 1981.) In light of these two windfalls to investors in equipment, the imposition of a windfall recapture subsidy could well be viewed as undesirable from a policy standpoint. Nevertheless, since this argument relies on an evaluation of other windfalls caused by reform, the Treasury approach is clearly more susceptible than is the Aaron approach to the selective compensation critique described in the preceding section.

For structures, effective tax rates would decline modestly under Treasury II; thus, again applying the Auerbach-Kotlikoff reasoning, the resulting reduction in income would, in isolation, result in a windfall loss. However, other changes, such as the extension of "at risk" rules to real estate, the elimination of the Investment Tax Credit on the portions of structures that qualify for the credit, and the expanded interest limitation rule on limited partnership interest, might reverse this effect; that is, a larger income stream would be required to achieve the same rate of return on new investment. In any case, the net effect of these changes and the reduced tax rate on income is likely to be a windfall gain, so that the argument is still applicable, if with less force.

In the indexed case, the present values of some of the individual loans LL (as well as the total value of the tax deferral loans) can be negative, especially for short-lived assets. Under these circumstances, the Aaron approach could actually result in an additional tax on investors; that is, a loan with a negative present value would effectively be taken out at a 46% rather than a 33% rate as under the Treasury approach. As noted above, this additional tax can be justified — both on the grounds of keeping the terms of the loans invariant and as an offset to the windfall gains described above. Nevertheless, the tax on loans made after the effective date of reform could easily be viewed as overstepping the need to recapture windfall gains, especially when so many other windfall gains induced by reform are untaxed and many other windfall losses are uncompensated.

However, the most important advantage of the Treasury approach follows from the fact that the windfall recapture tax would almost certainly have to be assessed in the year or the first few years following the enactment of reform. Such timing would be necessary both to offset the revenues lost from delayed or phased-in implementation of various other provisions within the relevant budget period (e.g., five years for both Treasury packages), and to eliminate transitional provisions of the reform package in a reasonable amount of time.[27] Note that both the Treasury and Aaron approaches would require projections of tax rates and inflation rates (in the indexed case) in order to calculate the magnitude of the windfall recapture tax. However, the latter approach would require projections for a considerably longer period, since all tax deferral loans (not just the ones taken out before the effective date of reform) would have to be included

[27] Some observers argued that the existence of the windfall recapture tax indicated that the package of recommendations in Treasury I was not revenue neutral in the long run. A discussion of the revenue properties of the reform package is clearly beyond the scope of this article. However, it should be noted that the short run revenue gain attributable to the windfall recapture tax was at least partially offset by short run revenue losses attributable to many of the other transitional provisions of the package, including various provisions calling for phased-in or delayed implementation. Thus the windfall recapture tax did not necessarily imply a long run revenue shortfall.

in the calculation.[28] This feature increases the likelihood that the tax would be calculated incorrectly, especially for long-lived assets purchased just before the enactment of reform. It would be prudent from a policy as well as an administrative standpoint to avoid projection far into the future by simply avoiding assessing the tax on loans made after the effective date of reform; if tax rates were higher or inflation rates lower than projected, the Aaron approach would be much more likely to result in justified future claims for refunds of overassessed windfall recapture taxes.

Thus, although both the Treasury and Aaron approaches to calculating the magnitude of the windfall recapture tax have their advantages and disadvantages, the problems associated with basing a windfall recapture tax on inflation and tax rate projections far into the future arguably make the Treasury calculation method the preferable approach. In any case, an interesting question is the effect of the choice between the two methods on the revenue raised by the tax; this question is considered in the following section.

4. A Numerical Comparison of the Various Approaches

A numerical analysis of the magnitudes of the windfall recapture taxes under the various approaches discussed in this article is presented in Table 11.1. The numerical calculations consider a $1,000 investment made in the year indicated under the assumptions that the inflation rate is 4% and the real rate of return in 4%, so that the discount rate is 8.016%. The effective date of reform is assumed to be January 1, 1987, with "excess depreciation" defined over the period between January 1, 1981, and December 31, 1986. The data presented are the values of the recapture taxes (in 1987 present values) for the original Treasury proposal with E&P depreciation used as the base for economic depreciation and no discounting (W_T), the Treasury approach with discounting (W_{T^*}), the Treasury

[28] Note that an advantage of the FIFO allocation method is that the loans taken out before the effective date of reform are repaid as quickly as possible, so that fewer tax rate and inflation projections are required than with alternatives such as the LIFO or prorated allocation methods.

Table 11.1.
Comparison of Windfall Recapture Taxes

Year	W_T	W_{T*}	W_{TU}	W_{AU}	W_{TI}	W_{AI}
Asset: ACRS 3-Year (RCRS Class 1, E&P 5-Year)						
1981	0	0	0	0	0	0
1983	49.07	38.02	34.34	34.34	40.17	40.17
1985	46.14	38.48	23.49	19.95	26.80	28.74
Asset: ACRS 5-Year (RCRS Class 2, E&P 12-Year)						
1981	103.64	57.29	27.34	27.34	35.63	35.63
1983	81.50	49.70	19.79	16.59	24.90	27.56
1985	34.25	23.36	3.98	−2.83	4.85	10.08
Asset: ACRS 5-Year (RCRS Class 3, E&P 12-Year)						
1981	103.64	57.29	35.45	35.45	49.74	49.74
1983	81.50	49.70	30.22	23.64	39.52	39.78
1985	34.25	23.36	11.61	−1.63	14.32	15.24
Asset: ACRS 5-Year (RCRS Class 4, E&P 12-Year)						
1981	103.64	57.29	49.71	49.71	71.43	71.43
1983	81.50	49.70	40.63	33.31	55.57	55.34
1985	34.25	23.36	18.64	−0.66	23.63	20.54
Asset: ACRS 5-Year (RCRS Class 5, E&P 12-Year)						
1981	103.64	57.29	46.12	46.12	75.67	75.67
1983	81.50	49.70	41.95	26.51	62.28	54.53
1985	34.25	23.36	22.29	−12.88	29.24	12.79
Asset: ACRS 10-Year (RCRS Class 6, E&P 25-Year)						
1981	80.36	28.25	22.20	−0.43	41.77	33.10
1983	49.07	19.13	15.96	−15.18	27.76	15.44
1985	22.37	9.91	8.70	−29.28	13.89	−1.96
Asset: ACRS IS-Year (RCRS Class 7, E&P 35-Year)						
1981	57.95	13.71	10.80	−20.21	25.56	11.22
1983	35.98	9.41	7.94	−28.14	17.39	0.00
1985*	14.33	3.12	2.73	−34.85	6.28	−10.07

*Data assume an 18-year ACRS asset with a 35-year E&P life.

Note: 1987 present values, for a $1,000 investment made in year indicated, with $\pi = 0.04$, d = 0.0816, and an effective date of reform of 1/1/87. W_T = tax under original Treasury plan (E&P base and no discounting); W_{T*} = tax under Treasury approach with E&P base; W_{TU} = tax under Treasury approach with unindexed RCRS base; W_{AU} = tax under Aaron approach with unindexed-RCRS base: W_{TI} = tax under Treasury approach with indexed-RCRS base; W_{AI} = tax under Aaron approach with indexed-RCRS base.

and Aaron approaches with unindexed-RCRS as the base and discounting (W_{TU}, W_{AU}), and the Treasury and Aaron approaches with indexed-RCRS as the base and discounting (W_{TI}, W_{AI}).

In all cases, $W_{T*} < W_T$, since discounting uniformly reduces the size of the windfall recapture tax. (Theoretically this is not necessarily the case, because the reduction of tax due to the three-year spread of tax liability under the original Treasury proposal might outweigh the increase in tax due to the lack of discounting.) The magnitude of over-taxation without discounting increases with the life of the asset, as the loan repayments are scheduled to occur at times farther into the future so that discounting is relatively more important. As stressed by Stretch and Sunley (1985a), the magnitudes of overtaxation can be very large — for very long-lived assets, the undiscounted approach overstates tax liability by roughly a factor of four.[29] The absolute magnitude of the overstatement is larger the earlier the asset was placed in service, since such assets accumulated more excess depreciation.

In all cases, $W_{TU} < W_{T*}$, since using unindexed-RCRS rather than the slower E&P depreciation allowances as the measure of economic depreciation reduces the amount of the appropriate recapture tax. The magnitudes of the further tax reductions due to switching from E&P to unindexed-RCRS — with discounting in both cases — are significant in many cases, especially for shorter-lived assets where E&P allowances are particularly slow relative to unindexed RCRS. Again, the absolute magnitude of the tax increase — in this case, due to the use of E&P rather than unindexed-RCRS — is larger the earlier the asset was placed in service, since such assets accumulated more excess depreciation.

Consider next the differences between the Treasury and Aaron approaches. In the unindexed case, the present values of all tax deferral loans LU_i are positive. Thus for all cases where the effective date of reform occurs prior to the crossover point, the Aaron approach results in a smaller windfall recapture tax; in many cases a rebate (a negative tax) is appropriate.

[29]The numerical results presented here differ from those of Stretch and Sunley (1985a) because the effective date of reform is assumed to be six months later, the discount rate is 8.016% rather than 8.7% (they state they use a 9.2% rate, but actually use an 8.7% rate), and the figures are stated in 1987 rather than 1986 dollars.

The benefit to the taxpayer under the Aaron approach increases with the life of the investment and is greater the more recently the investment was placed in service, as more posteffective date loans with a positive present value are included in the calculation of the tax.

However, a characterization of the results in the theoretically correct indexed case is more difficult. For shorter-lived assets, the analysis suggests that the differences in the dollar values of the windfall recapture taxes calculated by the two approaches is not tremendously large and, for very short-lived assets (RCRS classes 1–3), the Aaron approach results in a larger windfall recapture tax. For longer-lived assets, the Aaron approach results in a smaller tax, although the absolute magnitudes of the tax reductions are still relatively small.

The intuition behind these results is as follows. As shown in Table 11.2, for shorter-lived assets the value of LI_i is positive for the loans that are scheduled to be taken out relatively early and negative for the loans scheduled to be taken out relatively late.[30] For assets with several years of ACRS deductions remaining at the effective date of reform, these two effects tend to cancel in the extra term that is included in the calculation of the tax under the Aaron approach (see the preceding section). Consequently, the net difference between the Treasury and Aaron approaches is relatively small for most short-lived assets. (If ACRS deductions are exhausted before 1987, the approaches yield identical results). For the very short-lived RCRS class 1–3 assets, the Aaron approach results in a larger windfall recapture tax, as primarily post-effective-date loans with a negative present value are included in the calculation.

In contrast, for longer-lived assets, the tax deferral loans generally all have positive present values. Thus longer-lived assets tend to have a lower tax under the Aaron approach as more post-effective-date loans with a positive present value are included in the calculation.

For longer-lived assets, the Aaron approach results in a larger reduction in the amount of windfall recapture tax (in percentage terms) for assets placed in service more recently, as more loans with a positive present value are included in the calculation. However, for shorter-lived assets the increase in tax under the Aaron approach is relatively larger for assets

[30] Note also that the sum of the loans is negative for RCRS class 1 and 2 assets; the implications of this result were discussed in the Theoretical Issues section.

Table 11.2.
Values of the Tax Deferral Loans

Asset: ACRS 3-Year (RCRS Class 1)

$\Sigma_i LI_i = (9.99 - 3.36 - 12.75) = -6.12$

Asset: ACRS 5-Year (RCRS Class 2)

$\Sigma_i LI_i = (5.34 - 6.91 - 9.01 - 10.45 - 14.93) = -35.96$

Asset: ACRS 5-Year (RCRS Class 3)

$\Sigma_i LI_i = (10.68 + 1.04 - 2.54 - 2.02 - 1.50) = 5.86$

Asset: ACRS 5-Year (RCRS Class 4)

$\Sigma_i LI_i = (16.73 + 12.86 + 10.41 + 8.64 + 1.26) = 49.91$

Asset: ACRS 5-Year (RCRS Class 5)

$\Sigma_i LI_i = (21.46 + 25.83 + 27.57 + 37.00 + 43.59) = 155.45$

Asset: ACRS 10-Year (RCRS Class 6)

$$\Sigma_i LI_i = (18.47 + 27.76 + 21.03 + 13.93 + 13.61 + 14.02 + 11.51 + 11.86 + 10.07 + 8.19) = 150.45$$

Asset: ACRS 15-Year (RCRS Class 7)

$$\Sigma_i LI_i = (15.90 + 29.65 + 24.86 + 19.84 + 14.75 + 14.06 + 9.44 + 8.92 + 8.56 + 8.32 + 8.21 + 7.79 + 6.79 + 5.86 + 5.00) = 187.95$$

Note: For a \$1,000 investment with RCRS base, $\pi = 0.04$, and $d = 0.0814$. Numbers in parentheses are the tax deferral loans issued in each year of excess depreciation, which correspond to ACRS years.

placed in service more recently, as more post-effective date loans with a negative present value are included in the calculation.

5. Conclusion

The Treasury and Aaron approaches to calculating the windfall recapture tax both represent reasonable ways of recapturing the windfall gain that accrues to taxpayers as a result of the combination of accelerated depreciation allowances and an unexpected rate reduction. The choice between the two rests on a determination of whether the tax (or subsidy) should be assessed on "tax deferral loans" taken out after the effective date of reform.

In either case, however, the windfall recapture tax represents an interesting development in the theory of transitional equity and tax reform. The equity rationale for the tax is reasonable — although such schemes will always be subject to the criticism that they are selective and thus unfair — and the incidence of the tax is likely to be quite progressive. On efficiency grounds, the windfall recapture tax has the distinct benefits of being an operational form of lump sum tax (apart from the caveats mentioned in the text), so that it does not distort the behavior of economic agents and thus does not have an excess burden.

The efficiency characteristics of the tax are particularly interesting if one views the windfall recapture tax as a quid pro quo for the accelerated depreciation schedules proposed in Treasury II (relative to the RCRS proposed in Treasury I).[31] Such an exchange should be viewed favorably by the many proponents of lower business taxes who criticized Treasury I for conferring a windfall benefit to old capital through rate reductions while harming new capital formation through a higher cost of capital. Such individuals should prefer the approach calling for the windfall recapture tax coupled with accelerated depreciation and lower rates, since it lowers the cost of capital for new investment while indirectly attacking the problem of a windfall gain attributable to lower tax rates on the income from old capital.

In any case, as noted by Aaron, a tax that imposes little or no efficiency cost and has a claim to being equitable should be not be quickly dismissed; it could be an important tool in the implementation of any fundamental tax reform that involves a large reduction in rates. Although the windfall recapture tax ultimately was dropped from the recent tax reform debate, the concerns that led to its proposal are likely to arise again in future discussions of tax reform. Accordingly, the windfall recapture tax is a proposal that deserves serious consideration.

Acknowledgments

[31] Such a view seems plausible since, in the House version of tax reform, elimination of the windfall recapture tax was accompanied by less accelerated depreciation allowances and higher corporate tax rates. See U.S. House of Representatives (1985).

Research support from the U.S. Treasury Office of Tax Analysis and from the National Science Foundation (Grant SES-8606730) is gratefully acknowledged. I have benefited from the comments of two anonymous referees, from discussions with Joseph Cordes, Michael Graetz, Walter Hettich, Harold Hochman, Peter Mieszkowski, and Thomas Neubig, and from the research assistance of Tony Ligeralde. The views expressed are my own and do not reflect U.S. Treasury policy.

References

Aaron, H. J. (1985) "Some further thoughts on recapture of excess depreciation." Tax Notes (July 15): 315–321.

Auerbach, A. and L. Kotlikoff (1983) "Investment vs. saving incentives: the size of the bang for the buck and the potential for self-financing business tax cuts," in L. H. Meyer (ed.), The Economic Consequences of Government Deficits. Boston: Kluwer-Nijoff.

Bell, J. C. and P. W. Ooesterhuis (1985) "The ACRS recapture tax: short-lived assets and phantom windfalls." Tax Notes (September 16): 1389–1492.

Bradford, D. F. and the U.S. Treasury Tax Policy Staff (1984) Blueprints for Basic Tax Reform. Washington, DC: Tax Analysts.

Cordes, J. J. and B. A. Weisbrod (1985) "When government programs create inequities: a guide to compensation policies." J. of Policy Analysis and Management 4: 178–195.

Feldstein, M. S. (1976a) "Compensation in tax reform." National Tax J. 29:123–130.

Feldstein, M. S. (1976b) "On the theory of tax reform." J. of Public Economics 98: 107–125.

Goode, R. (1987) "Disappointed expectations and tax reform." National Tax J. 40: 159–169.

Gordon, R. H., J. R. Hines, Jr., and L. H. Summers (1986) "Notes on the tax treatment of structures." Working paper 1896. National Bureau of Economic Research, Cambridge, MA.

Graetz, M. J. (1977) "Legal transitions: the case of retroactivity in income tax revision." University of Pennsylvania Law Rev. 126: 47–87.

Gravelle, J. G. (1985) "U.S. tax policy and rental housing: an economic analysis." Congressional Research Service Report 85-208E. Washington, DC: Government Printing Office.

Hendershott, P. H. and D. C. Ling (1984) "Trading and the tax shelter value of depreciable real estate." Working paper 1267. National Bureau of Economic Research, Cambridge, MA.

Hochman, H. M. (1974) "Rule change and transitional equity," in H. M. Hochman and G. E. Peterson (eds.) Redistribution Through Public Choice. New York: Columbia Univ. Press.

McLure, C. E., Jr. (1985) "Rationale underlying the treasury proposals," in Economic Consequences of Tax Simplification. Boston: Federal Reserve Bank of Boston.

McLure, C. E., Jr., and G. R. Zodrow (1987) "Treasury I and the Tax Reform Act of 1986: the economics and politics of tax reform." J. of Econ. Perspectives 1: 37–58.

Stretch, C. C. and E. M. Sunley (1985a) "Recapture of excess depreciation: what are the issues?" Tax Notes (June 24): 1501–1505.

Stretch, C. C. and E. M. Sunley (1985b) "Stretch and Sunley's recapture response." Tax Notes (July 15): 321.

U.S. House of Representatives (1985) Tax Reform Act of 1985. Washington, DC: Government Printing Office.

U.S. Treasury (1984) Tax Reform for Fairness Simplicity and Growth. Washington, DC: Government Printing Office.

U.S. Treasury (1985) The President's Tax Proposals to the Congress for Fairness, Growth and Simplicity. Washington, DC: Government Printing Office.

Viard, A. D. (1985) "The implementation and rationale of windfall recapture." Tax Notes (September 16): 1384–1388.

Zodrow, G. R. (1981) "Implementing tax reform." National Tax J. 34: 401–418.

Zodrow, G. R. (1985a) "Adjustment costs and the theory of optimal tax reform." J. of Public Economics 27: 211–230.

Zodrow, G. R. (1985b) "Partial tax reform: an optimal taxation perspective." Canadian J. of Economics 18: 335–346.

Zodrow, G. R. (1986) "Implementing tax reform: the intergenerational carryover problem." National Tax J. 39: 419–433.

Chapter 12

Balancing Act: Weighing the Factors Affecting the Taxation of Capital Income in a Small Open Economy*

Margaret K. McKeehan

Ph.D. Student, Department of Economics MS-22, Rice University, P.O. Box 1892, Houston, TX 77251, mkm1@rice.edu, (865) 607-0660

George R. Zodrow

Cline Professor, Department of Economics and Rice Scholar, Baker Institute for Public Policy, Rice University, International Research Fellow, Centre for Business Taxation Oxford University Department of Economics MS-22, Rice University, P.O. Box 1892, Houston, TX 77251, zodrow@rice.edu

Alternative economic theories yield dramatically different prescriptions for optimal capital taxation in small open economies. On the one hand, foreign firms, including those with investments that yield firm-specific

*This chapter is reproduced from *International Tax and Public Finance*, **24**(1), 1–35, 2017.

above-normal returns, have a large number of alternative investment opportunities; this suggests that the supply of foreign direct investment is highly elastic, which implies that small open economies should avoid imposing any source-based taxes on capital income. On the other hand, governments invariably want to tax any above-normal returns earned by location-specific capital, especially if the returns accrue to foreigners, and to take full advantage of the potential revenue increase from any "treasury transfer" effect that arises due to residence-based tax systems with foreign tax credits, such as that utilized by the United States. These factors suggest that investment is highly inelastic with respect to capital taxation, so that source-based capital income taxation is desirable; indeed, in one special case, the capital income tax rate for a small open economy should equal the relatively high US tax rate. Moreover, this difficult trade-off is in practice complicated by numerous additional factors: deferral of unrepatriated profits and cross-crediting of foreign tax credits for US multinationals, foreign direct investment from firms from countries that, unlike the United States, operate territorial systems, and the existence of opportunities for both international capital income shifting and labor income shifting. In this paper, we analyze optimal capital income taxation in a small open economy model that attempts to balance these conflicting factors.

Keywords: Optimal Taxation; Open Economy; Income Shifting; Corporate Taxation

1. Introduction

Under the appropriate assumptions, optimal tax theory provides a striking result on the use of source-based taxes on capital income such as the typical corporate income tax: in a small open economy that cannot affect the after-tax return to internationally mobile capital or the prices of tradable goods, the optimal capital income tax rate is zero (Gordon, 1986; Razin and Sadka, 1991; Zodrow and Mieszkowski, 1983).[1] This result does not rely on — although it is reinforced by — concerns about the negative effects of capital income taxation on domestic saving or the distortions of many types of investment decisions under the typical corporate

[1] For further discussion, see Zodrow (2010a, b).

income tax (Nicodème, 2008), or the tendency toward under-provision of public services financed with capital income taxes in the presence of international tax competition (Zodrow and Mieszkowski, 1986; Wilson, 1986). Instead, the argument follows from the assumption that the small open economy faces a perfectly elastic supply of highly mobile international capital. In this case, the imposition of a source-based tax on capital income will simply cause internationally mobile capital to migrate to other countries until its after-tax return in the taxing country increases to the internationally determined rate of return. This emigration of capital lowers the productivity of the fixed factors in the taxing country — land, labor (or at least relatively immobile labor), and any immobile capital — so that local factors of production ultimately bear the entire burden of the capital income tax, including both the revenue raised and the efficiency costs of the tax due to capital emigration (as well as the other distortionary costs noted above). Indeed, Harberger (1995, 2008) argues that immobile labor and land may bear more than one hundred percent of a corporate income tax in a small open economy, once general equilibrium effects across business sectors are considered.

This argument is reinforced by two additional considerations in the modern global economy. The first is a straightforward extension of the basic argument, applied to investments by multinational corporations (MNCs) that generate significant firm-specific economic rents; such rents are attributable to factors unique to the firm such as specialized and patented technological knowledge, superior managerial skills or production techniques, or valuable product brands, trademarks, reputations, and other intangible assets (Dunning, 1981). Moreover, there is some empirical evidence that the relative importance of such rents is increasing over time, as Auerbach (2006) shows that the dispersion of relative profitability for US corporations has increased significantly in recent years, suggesting an increase in the importance of investments that generate above-normal returns made by a relatively small number of highly profitable firms. Because such firm-specific capital is likely to be especially mobile and also may have the potential for significant increases in the productivity of local factors (e.g., it is most likely to be associated with high levels of technology transfer, access to skilled labor including highly effective management, and the generation of other external benefits including the creation of a competitive environment that fosters invention and innovation), concerns about tax-induced emigration of mobile capital may be especially pronounced for such investments, reinforcing the standard zero-tax argument (Gordon and Hines, 2002).

The second issue has been the focus of many recent policy discussions, most recently in the Base Erosion and Profit Shifting project of the Organisation for Economic Co-operation and Development (OECD) (2013). Specifically, the application of a relatively high corporate tax rate to the income of MNCs encourages them to engage in profit shifting, that is, to use various financial manipulations, including transfer pricing, the relocation of the ownership of intangibles, and the use of loan reallocations that facilitate interest stripping, to shift revenues to relatively low tax countries and deductions to relatively high-tax countries. There is considerable empirical evidence of income shifting (Clausing, 2011, 2016; Dowd, 2016), in particular that a relatively high statutory corporate tax rate encourages income shifting, since it is the statutory tax rate that determines the value to the firm of shifted revenues and deductions. Thus a desire to avoid creating incentives for income shifting also puts downward pressure on capital income tax rates.[2]

Despite these arguments, as well as empirical evidence of the importance of international tax competition (Devereux and Loretz, 2013), corporate income tax rates in small open economies have not in practice converged to zero (although they have declined on average over time). A wide variety of arguments have been offered in support of corporate taxation, all of which qualify the argument that a small open economy should exempt capital income from tax. Although it is difficult to judge the relative importance of each of these qualifications, the pervasiveness of corporate income taxation around the world suggests that together these arguments have been taken seriously by policymakers.

Perhaps the most important argument in support of a relatively high level of source-based capital income taxation is that it allows the government to obtain significant revenues from the taxation of location-specific economic rents. Such rents, which may accrue to both domestically-owned

---

[2] Furthermore, a low statutory rate may make a country attractive for investment by MNCs simply because it creates the potential for additional income shifting (Slemrod 1997).

firms and firms that are partially or fully owned by foreigners, can reflect resource rents as well as economic rents that arise because of factors such as local economies of agglomeration, productive government infrastructure, easier access to consumer markets (including those for financial services), lower transport costs, and inexpensive but relatively productive local factors of production including skilled labor — in addition to the ability to avoid trade barriers such as tariffs and quotas.

The taxation of location-specific economic rents provides an efficient and thus highly desirable source of revenue. Moreover, if these rents accrue to foreigners, such taxes are especially attractive from the perspective of the taxing country, as the burden of the tax on rents is borne by foreigners, while marginal domestic investment decisions are not distorted (Mintz, 1995). Indeed, empirical evidence suggests that a higher share of foreign ownership in a country tends to result in a higher average corporate income tax rate (Huizinga and Nicodème, 2006).

A second argument is related to the prevalence of income shifting noted above. Specifically, although a high domestic corporate tax rate tends to encourage more income shifting, the existence of income shifting to some extent mitigates the negative effect of a high statutory tax rate on foreign direct investment by MNCs, since firms know they will be able to avoid some of the costs of a high tax rate in a host country by shifting income to lower tax countries. Indeed, to the extent that such tax avoidance opportunities are available primarily to MNCs and such firms are more mobile than domestic companies, a relatively high statutory rate may be desirable as part of a strategy that attracts FDI at minimal revenue cost by imposing a high tax burden on relatively immobile domestic capital but a low effective tax burden, taking into account tax avoidance activities, on relatively mobile international capital (Hong and Smart, 2010; Gugl and Zodrow, 2006). An aggressive version of this strategy would include lax enforcement of the many rules currently used to limit tax avoidance by MNCs or even explicit regulations that facilitate such tax avoidance — the new variation of international tax competition stressed by Altshuler and Grubert (2006), which they note is exemplified by the long-time existence of the "check-the-box" rules in the United States.

A third argument for a relatively high corporate tax rate in a small open economy was once believed to be compelling, but has been declining in importance over time. Specifically, the "treasury transfer" argument suggests that a host country that imports capital primarily from countries that use residence-based corporate income tax systems and grant foreign tax credits (FTCs) should raise its tax rate approximately to the rate utilized by those countries, since such a rate increase will essentially transfer revenues from the treasury of the home countries to the treasury of the host country without having any deleterious effects on FDI (since the combined host and home countries tax burden borne by the MNC is always determined solely by the statutory tax rate of the home country).

The prospect of such a "free" source of tax revenue is naturally appealing and has been stressed in many tax policy discussions. However, there are at least three reasons the treasury transfer effect is often argued to be of limited relevance in the modern economy. First, because both Japan and the United Kingdom have recently switched to "territorial" tax systems under which foreign-source income is largely tax exempt, the United States is now the only major industrialized country that utilizes a residence-based tax system with an FTC. Thus, the treasury transfer argument is potentially relevant only for countries that import significant amounts of capital from the United States.[3] Second, because of various limitations placed on the use of foreign tax credits, many US multinationals are in an "excess foreign tax credit" position — that is, they already have more credits than they can use currently, so that additional credits are of limited value and a lower host country tax rate should attract additional FDI. Third, the importance of the treasury transfer effect is limited by the fact that host country taxes are assessed currently but foreign tax credits in the home country are not granted until the funds are repatriated to the parent firm. Indeed, under certain circumstances, a home country repatriation tax has no effect on investment financed with the retained earnings of the subsidiary (Hartman, 1985; Sinn, 1987) — although the relevance in practice of this proposition has been the subject of debate; in particular, Grubert and Altshuler (2013, Appendix A) argue that the

[3] Although the relative importance of FDI from the United States has of course declined in recent years, it is still significant in many countries. For example, the Economic Commission for Latin America and the Caribbean (2012) reports that the U.S. accounts for roughly a quarter of foreign direct investment in Latin America and the Caribbean.

Hartman-Sinn model is based on very restrictive assumptions and its predictions are inconsistent with the empirical data on repatriations.

It is also interesting to note, however, that the importance of the treasury transfer effect may be increasing — currently and perhaps to a significantly greater extent in the near future — for host countries with relatively low tax rates. Specifically, many capital-exporting countries have become increasingly concerned about revenue losses due to income shifting by multinationals, especially to very low rate tax haven countries, and are enacting, or considering the enactment of, what are broadly referred to as "anti-base-erosion" provisions (OECD, 2013). Although such provisions may take many forms, one common approach is to impose current home country taxes on income that is earned in relatively low-rate jurisdictions. For example, the new territorial tax system in Japan includes Controlled Foreign Company (CFC) provisions under which Japanese companies are required to report as domestic income taxable profits earned in any country with an effective tax rate of 20 percent or less (Deloitte, 2014).

Similar provisions have been proposed in the context of reform of the system of international taxation in the United States. For example, the discussion draft put forward by Representative Dave Camp includes an anti-base-erosion provision under which foreign-source income from intangibles derived from sales to foreign markets would be taxed in the United States in the year earned at a 15 percent rate, subject to credits for foreign taxes paid, while foreign-source income from intangibles derived from sales to the US market would be taxed in the year earned at a 25 percent rate — all relative to a proposed general corporate statutory tax rate of 25 percent.[4] The discussion draft released by Senator Max Baucus would tax all passive and highly mobile foreign-source income, as well as foreign-source income earned from selling goods and services back to the U.S., in the year earned at the statutory corporate tax rate, subject to credits for foreign taxes paid. Foreign-source income from products and services sold abroad would similarly be taxed currently, although at reduced

[4]Details of the Camp discussion draft are available at http://waysandmeans.house.gov/UploadedFiles/Statutory_Text_Tax_Reform_Act_of_2014_Discussion_Draft__022614.pdf.

rates.[5] Both of these proposals could significantly increase the relevance of the treasury transfer effect, although within the context of a lower US corporate tax rate.

Numerous other arguments support some source-based capital income taxation, often in the form of a corporate income tax. From a domestic perspective, a corporate income tax is often deemed to be desirable as a "backstop" to the personal income tax; that is, depending on relative personal and corporate tax rates, a corporate income tax may be desirable to prevent individuals from incorporating and deferring personal income tax on labor income by retaining the earnings in corporate form while financing any desired consumption with loans from their companies. In addition, the small open economy assumptions may be too extreme for some countries; Gravelle and Smetters (2006) stress that the economic effects of corporate income taxes differ significantly if capital is imperfectly mobile or if traded and domestically-produced goods are imperfect substitutes. Finally, a corporate income tax may be politically indispensable in many countries.

Relatively few papers have examined the interactions of these competing effects on capital income taxation from the perspective of an open economy. Four papers are particularly relevant to our analysis.

Gordon and Mackie-Mason (1995) consider the interaction of domestic income shifting and international income shifting. In their model, an optimal tax system balances the cost from individuals disguising labor income as capital income when the capital income tax rate is lowered against the benefit of an increase in the tax base due to reduced international income shifting.[6]

Huizinga and Nielsen (1997) examine optimal rules for separate taxes on all capital income and on above-normal profits in a small open economy model where foreigners own some of the domestic capital

---

[5] Details of the Baucus discussion draft are available at http://www.finance.senate.gov/imo/media/doc/Chairman's Staff International Discussion Draft Summary.pdf.

[6] See also Gordon and Slemrod (2000), who estimate the extent of income shifting between the personal and corporate income tax bases following the enactment of the Tax Reform Act of 1986, and Slemrod and Wilson (2009) who investigate the effects of such shifting in the presence of low-rate tax havens.

stock. They show that, as long as above-normal profits are taxed at rates less than one hundred percent, some source-based taxation of capital income is desirable to extract rents from foreign owners of domestic capital.

Becker and Fuest (2011) examine how differences in capital mobility and profitability affect the desirability of base broadening, rate reducing (BBRR) corporate reforms relative to introducing investment incentives. Specifically, they show that under certain circumstances a BBRR reform that involves a corporate rate reduction financed by less generous deductions for depreciation is preferable to increasing investment incentives if relatively more mobile firms are also more profitable than their relatively immobile competitors. The intuition is that a lower statutory rate is desirable to attract/retain the more mobile firms which are highly responsive to the statutory rate since that is the rate applied to its above-normal profits, even at the cost of reducing investment incentives (accelerated depreciation), which are relatively more important in determining the tax burden of the comparatively immobile less profitable firms.

Finally, Haufler and Schjelderup (2000) construct a model that includes foreign direct investment and the possibility of income shifting. Like Becker and Fuest (2011), they show that under certain circumstances a BBRR reform that involves a corporate rate reduction financed by less generous deductions for depreciation is desirable, as the gains from reducing income shifting are unambiguously larger than the costs of reducing investment incentives.

In a similar vein, we construct a simple theoretical model that illustrates how the government of a small open economy might balance some of the trade-offs involved in taxing capital income described above, and then simulate a more complicated version of the model to see how much optimal capital income tax rates might vary from zero under scenarios that take into account the interactions between the various factors analyzed.[7] We maintain the standard small open economy assumptions of

[7]To simplify the analysis, we model a single "capital income tax rate" (τ), which serves as a proxy for a combination of the various relevant tax rates. For example, the relevant capital income tax rate would be the statutory rate for equity-financed domestic

perfect mobility (of certain forms of) capital and perfect substitutability of domestic and foreign tradable goods in our model. In addition, we assume the economy is small enough that changes in domestic tax policy do not affect the determination of tax rates in other countries; that is, foreign countries do not respond strategically to the increase in the domestic tax rate, as foreign tax rates are treated as exogenous. In our base analytical model, we focus on the trade-offs involved in balancing (1) the costs of taxing highly mobile capital, including firm-specific capital earning above-normal returns, and (2) the costs of encouraging income shifting to lower-tax jurisdictions, against (3) the gains from taxing location-specific capital, some of which is foreign-owned, (4) the mitigating effects on tax-induced reductions of FDI of the presence income shifting possibilities, and (5) the potential for a treasury transfer effect. Our base model does not include explicit costs of income shifting or the potential for disguising labor income as capital income. However, we include these features in our computational model, which also includes ordinary capital in both production sectors, endogenous labor supply, a proportional labor income tax, and the possibility of direct taxation of location-specific capital.

The base analytical model confirms several general results, showing that some capital income taxation may be efficient in the presence of residual taxation or foreign ownership of location-specific capital. The computational model confirms and extends these observations, showing that foreign ownership and residual taxation can both generate large increases in the optimal capital income tax rate. However, these results are subject to various qualifications. If separate taxation of location-specific

---

investment under a system that measured real economic income accurately (e.g., with tax depreciation equal to inflation-adjusted economic depreciation and no other investment allowances). In practice, tax systems are far more complicated, with lower effective tax rates due to interest deductions for debt-financed investment and accelerated depreciation deductions, investment tax credits, etc. In addition, different tax rates are relevant at different margins — the statutory rate is most relevant for income shifting, some combination of the statutory rate and the effective tax rate is most relevant for investment of firm-specific capital, and the effective tax rate is most relevant for investment of ordinary capital. Note, however, that we do model explicitly the reduction in the effective capital income tax rate due to income shifting.

capital is feasible, foreign ownership does not notably increase the optimal general capital income tax rate. While residual taxation is shown to be an important consideration, changes in the foreign tax rate have minimal effects on the optimal domestic rate unless the two rates are very close to each other. The computational model also highlights the varying importance of income shifting activity. If individuals are able to easily disguise labor income as capital income, increasing capital income taxation becomes more desirable. However, greater international income shifting opportunities have only modest effects on the optimal capital income tax rate due to offsetting effects. While increases in income shifting imply the size of the tax base is more sensitive to capital income taxation, income shifting opportunities also lower the tax sensitivity of real investment (since firms know they will be able to lower their effective tax burden through income shifting) and increase the proportion of relatively immobile factors in the tax base.

We describe the structure of our base analytical model in the following section, and the characteristics of the solution for the optimal capital income tax rate in Section 3. The details of the expanded computational model are presented in Section 4, which also provides the results of simulating that model for the optimal capital income tax rate for a wide variety of parameter values. Conclusions and directions for future research are discussed in the final section.

2. The Base Model

Our base analytical model is designed to capture four of the primary factors that influence the optimal capital income tax rate in a small open economy: (1) immobile capital that earns location-specific rents, some of which may be owned by foreigners; (2) perfectly mobile foreign-owned capital that earns firm-specific rents; (3) the possibility of capital income shifting; and (4) the possibility of residual home country taxation of foreign-source income by countries that operate a residence-based system of taxation, such as the United States, or countries like Japan that have base erosion provisions that apply domestic tax on an accrual basis to income earned in host countries with sufficiently low tax rates, subject to foreign tax credits.

To capture these effects we construct a simple two-sector model. Sector one is a "domestic" sector that produces a non-traded good (X_1) using labor (L_1) and location-specific capital (*LSK*) that is fixed, immobile, and earns economic rents (ρ_L) that may be partially or completely foreign-owned. Sector two is a "multinational" sector that produces a traded good (X_2) using labor (L_2) and firm-specific capital (*FSK*) that is perfectly mobile, foreign-owned, and earns economic rents at an internationally determined rate of return (ρ_F). The price of the traded good (p_2) is also determined internationally, and it is possible that the small open economy may be either a net importer or a net exporter. The domestic good is produced using a constant returns to scale technology, $X_1 = F_1(L_1; LSK)$. The earnings of capital in the domestic sector are subject to capital income taxation at a statutory tax rate τ, so the profit-maximizing labor demand in sector one is the solution to $\max_{L_1}\{p_1X_1 - wL_1\}$, where p_1 is the market price of good one and w is the market wage. In equilibrium, the before-tax economic rents earned by *LSK* are $(1 + \tau)\rho_L LSK = p_1X_1 - wL_1$. Note that in order to simplify the model, we treat the corporate tax simply as applying to all capital income, and thus do not consider many complicating and distortionary features of actual corporate income taxes, including deductions for economic depreciation, accelerated depreciation deductions, investment tax credits and other investment preferences, the treatment of inflation, as well as differential treatment of equity and debt finance, especially deductions for interest expense.

Production in the multinational or traded goods sector is a function of the amounts of labor (L_2) and *FSK* utilized, $X_2 = F_2(L_2, FSK)$.[8] The

[8] Following the approach used in the CORTAX computable general equilibrium model constructed by Bettendorf *et al.* (2009) and de Mooij and Devereux (2011), we model the factor generating firm-specific rents as an explicit production input characterized by "fixed management capacity." That is, we assume a fixed amount of firm-specific capital (which includes a combination of factors such as unique managerial skills, production processes, and intangible capital) that must be allocated among different locations around the world. A similar approach is used by Becker and Fuest (2011), who consider "ownership skill" that creates above-normal returns, assuming first that the amount of this skill is fixed and must be allocated across countries, and then extending the analysis to the case in which ownership skill is unlimited. Devereux, Fuest, and Lockwood (2014) consider both cases as well as intermediate possibilities.

earnings of the firm-specific capital in the multinational sector are in principle also subject to the statutory capital income tax rate. However, a fraction (ϕ_S) of capital income in this multinational sector is shifted to a tax haven country with a relatively low tax rate τ_H; the fraction shifted is a function of the tax differential $\tau - \tau_H$. Only the unshifted share of capital income $(1 - \phi_S)$ is subject to the domestic tax. In addition, a fraction ϕ_F of the unshifted income is also subject to a current residual tax imposed by the foreign (home) country at tax rate τ_F. We assume that none of the capital income shifted to the tax haven is subject to a residual tax.

Consequently, the effective capital income tax rate in the multinational sector, taking into account income shifting to tax havens and residual home country current taxation, is $T_K = (1 - \phi_S)[\tau + \phi_F \max(\tau_F - \tau, 0)] + \phi_S\tau_H$. Given any level of *FSK*, the multinational firms in sector two choose labor to maximize profit. The amount of firm-specific capital invested is the amount consistent with after-tax earnings equal to the internationally-determined rate of return ρ_F, taking into account the demand for labor as a function of *FSK*. That is, the amount of firm-specific capital invested in the country is such that $\rho_F = (p_2X_2 - wL_2)/[(1 + T_K)FSK]$, where both X_2 and L_2 are functions of the firm-specific capital invested.

In the base model, we assume a single representative resident with inelastic labor supply. Consequently, the individual allocates income across consumption goods to maximize utility, producing the indirect utility function

$$v(p_1, I) = \max_{C_1, C_2}\{U(C_1, C_2) \mid I \geq p_1C_1 + p_2C_2\}, \tag{1}$$

where C_i is the consumption of good i, p_i is the market price of good i, and I is the individual's after-tax income. We hold government services (G) constant throughout the analysis and assume they are separable from consumption in the individual's welfare function. Income is composed of labor income and capital income, less any lump-sum taxes levied by the government, so that net income is

$$I = wL + \theta\rho_L LSK - t, \tag{2}$$

where t is the lump-sum tax, L is the fixed level of total labor supply, and θ is the share of location-specific capital that is owned domestically.

Government services are modeled as purchases of the tradable good, and government revenues are raised from capital income taxation of the returns to LSK and FSK and the lump-sum tax (which is a proxy for labor income taxation in the base model, given the assumption of an inelastic supply of labor). The government budget constraint is thus

$$p_2 G \leq \tau \rho_L LSK + (1-\phi_S)\tau \rho_F FSK + t. \tag{3}$$

Finally, since total labor supply (L) is fixed, equilibrium in the labor market requires $L_1 + L_2 = L$, and equilibrium in the domestic good market requires $C_1 = X_1$. Combining these two conditions with the first-order conditions for the consumer and producer optimization problems fully specifies the equilibrium in the model.

3. Properties of the Optimal Capital Income Tax Rate

3.1. *Characterizing the optimal capital income tax rate*

The government chooses its tax rates to maximize the utility of the representative resident while ensuring that revenues are sufficient to finance a fixed level of the separable public good (G), which is modeled as purchases of the output of the multinational sector. The government thus solves

$$\max_{\tau, t}\left\{v(p_1, I) + \lambda[p_2 G - \tau \rho_L LSK - \tau(1-\phi_S)\rho_F FSK - t]\right\},$$

where $v(p_1, I)$ is the individual indirect utility function, the government budget constraint is $p_2 G = \tau[\rho_L LSK + (1-\phi_S)\rho_F FSK] + t = R + t$, and R is capital income tax revenue. Since the lump-sum tax is always available to the government, the capital income tax will be used only if it can successfully extract resources from foreign investors, that is, if some of the tax burden can successfully be "exported" abroad. Note that the capital tax is applied to all unshifted capital income earned in the country. Substituting from the government budget constraint, the government's problem becomes

$$\max_{\tau} \nu(p_1, I);$$
$$I = (wL + \theta \rho_L LSK) - \{p_2 G - \tau[\rho_L LSK + (1-\phi_S)\rho_F FSK]\}. \quad (4)$$

Thus, since income is defined to include the head tax, any revenue shortfalls that arise due to outmigration of *FSK* or any declines in the return to *LSK* associated with increases in the capital income tax rate must be offset with head tax increases.

The first-order condition for the optimal capital income tax rate is

$$\frac{\partial v(p_1,I)}{\partial \tau} = \frac{\partial v}{\partial p_1}\frac{\partial p_1}{\partial \tau} + \frac{\partial v}{\partial I}\frac{\partial I}{\partial \tau} = -C_1\alpha\frac{\partial p_1}{\partial \tau} + \alpha\frac{\partial I}{\partial \tau}$$
$$= \alpha\left[\frac{1}{I}\frac{\partial I}{\partial \tau} - \left(\frac{p_1 C_1}{I}\right)\frac{1}{p_1}\frac{\partial p_1}{\partial \tau}\right] = 0$$

$$\frac{1}{\alpha}\frac{\partial v(p_1,\mathrm{I})}{\partial \tau} = \pi_I - \psi_{C_1}^{I}\pi_{p1} = 0, \quad (5)$$

using Roy's Identity, and defining π_I and π_{pI} as the tax semi-elasticities of the subscripted variables, $\psi_{C_1}^{I}$ as the expenditure share of good one, and α as the marginal utility of income. This condition reflects the standard result that the optimal capital income tax rate should be set to maximize the dollar value of individual utility at the margin, which requires that the change in real income, or the sum of the "sources" and "uses" effects on utility, equals zero. This expression can be interpreted in terms of several key tax semi-elasticities.

3.1.1. *Tax semi-elasticity of Income*

The tax semi-elasticity of income is

$$\pi_I = \psi_L^I \pi_w + \left[\psi_{LSK}^I + \left(\frac{R}{I}\right)\psi_{LSK}^R\right]\pi_{\rho L} + \left(\frac{R}{I}\right)\psi_{FSK}^R\left(\pi_{FSK} + \pi_{1-\phi S}\right) + \left(\frac{R}{I}\right)\frac{1}{\tau}, \quad (6)$$

where the various ψ's are factor shares in income or total capital income tax revenue (R). The tax semi-elasticity of income is thus determined by the changes in the returns to the two fixed factors in response to an increase in the capital income tax and the change in the head tax, which equals the change in capital tax revenues, taking into account the effects of the tax on *FSK* and ρ_L.

3.1.2. *Tax semi-elasticity of the wage*

To obtain the tax semi-elasticity of the wage, recall that in the multinational sector the effective tax rate on *FSK* is $T_K = (1 - \phi_S)[\tau + \phi_F \max(\tau_F - \tau, 0)] + \phi_S\tau_H$. We assume that $\tau_F > \tau$ for this derivation, so that

$$T_K = (1-\phi_S)(1-\phi_F)\tau + (1-\phi_S)\phi_F\tau_F + \phi_S\tau_H,$$

which implies that

$$\frac{\partial T_K}{\partial \tau} = (1-\phi_S)(1-\phi_F) + (1-\phi_S)[(1-\phi_F)\tau + \phi_F\tau_F - \tau_H]\pi_{1-\phi_S} \tag{7}$$

is a constant determined by the extent of income shifting and residual taxation. With constant returns to scale in labor and *FSK* in the multinational sector, differentiating the unit cost function with respect to τ for fixed ρ_F yields $\chi_{L2}\pi_w + \chi_{FSK2}\pi_{\rho_{FG}} = 0$, where the χ terms are gross factor shares in production costs and $\pi_{\rho_{FG}} = (\partial T_K/\partial\tau)/(1 + T_K)$ is the tax semi-elasticity of the gross rate of return to *FSK*. Thus, with a fixed commodity price and a fixed return to *FSK* in the multinational sector, any increase in the capital income tax burden is fully reflected in a reduction in wages — consistent with the traditional small open economy reasoning described above.

3.1.3. *Tax semi-elasticity of the price of good one*

Similarly, with constant returns to scale in labor and *LSK* in the domestic sector,

$$\pi_{p1} = \chi_{L1}\pi_w + \chi_{LSK1}\pi_{\rho LG} = \chi_{L1}\pi_w + \chi_{LSK1}\left(\pi_{\rho L} + \frac{1}{1+\tau}\right). \tag{8}$$

Thus, the tax semi-elasticity of the price of the domestic good is determined by a weighted average of the tax semi-elasticities of the gross prices of the two inputs, labor and location-specific capital.

3.1.4. *Tax semi-elasticity of the return to location-specific capital*

Differentiating the consumer's first-order condition for the domestic good yields $\pi_{C_1} = \left(\varepsilon_{11} - \eta_1 \psi^I_{C_1}\right)\pi_{p_1} + \eta_1 \pi_I$, where ε_{11} is the compensated elasticity of demand for good one and η_1 is the income elasticity of demand for good one. Substituting from Eq. (8) yields the price and income effects on the tax semi-elasticity of consumer demand C_1

$$\pi_{C_1} = \left(\varepsilon_{11} - \eta_1 \psi^I_{C_1}\right)\{\chi_{L1}\pi_w + \chi_{LSK1}[\pi_{\rho L} + 1/(1+\tau)]\} + \eta_1 \pi_I. \tag{9}$$

On the production side, differentiating the production function with fixed location-specific capital and solving for the tax semi-elasticity of labor demand yields

$$\pi_{X_1} = -\chi_{L1}\sigma_1\left(\pi_w - \pi_{\rho LG}\right), \tag{10}$$

where σ_1 is the Allen-Uzawa elasticity of substitution in production.[9] Since the consumption and production tax semi-elasticities of the domestic good are equal, equating Eqs. (9) and (10) and solving for the tax semi-elasticity of the net return to *LSK* yields

$$\pi_{\rho L} = \frac{\left(\varepsilon_{11} - \eta_1 \psi^I_{C_1} + \sigma_1\right)\chi_{L1}\pi_w + \eta_1 \pi_I}{\chi_{L1}\sigma_1 - \chi_{LSK1}\left(\varepsilon_{11} - \eta_1 \psi^I_{C_1}\right)} - \frac{1}{1+\tau}. \tag{11}$$

Note that in the case of Cobb–Douglas utility and production functions, this expression reduces to $\pi_{\rho L} = \pi_I - 1/(1+\tau)$, which indicates that — apart from the effects of changes in income — the gross return to *LSK* is fixed so that the owners of *LSK* bear the burden of the capital income tax in

[9]The Allen-Uzawa elasticity of substitution can be written as $[\partial \ln (x_i)/\partial \ln (P_j)]/S_j$, where x_i is the quantity of factor *i* used in production, p_j is the price of factor *j*, and S_j is the production cost share of factor *j*.

that sector. Otherwise, the first term in Eq. (11) reflects the net general equilibrium effects on the return to *LSK* of changes in relative prices on consumer demands and factor demands.

Substituting Eq. (11) into Eq. (8) implies that the tax semi-elasticity of the price of the domestic good is

$$\pi_{p_1} = \chi_{L1}\pi_w + \chi_{LSK1}\left[\frac{(\varepsilon_{11} - \eta_1\psi_{C_1}^I + \sigma_1)\chi_{L1}\pi_w + \eta_1\pi_I}{\chi_{L1}\sigma_1 - \chi_{LSK1}(\varepsilon_{11} - \eta_1\psi_{C_1}^I)}\right]. \qquad (12)$$

Note that an income increase thus results in an increase in the relative price of the domestic good (since the price of the multinational good is fixed).

3.1.5. *Tax semi-elasticity of firm-specific capital*

To solve for π_{FSK}, calculate the tax semi-elasticity of the multinational sector good using the labor market equilibrium equation and the tax semi-elasticity of per-unit labor demand, and substitute into the expression for the tax semi-elasticity of demand for *FSK* to yield

$$\pi_{FSK} = \frac{\lambda_1}{\lambda_2}\sigma_1\left(\pi_w - \pi_{\rho L} - \frac{1}{1+\tau}\right) + \sigma_2\left[\pi_w - \frac{1}{1+T_K}\left(\frac{\partial T_K}{\partial \tau}\right)\right], \qquad (13)$$

where $\lambda_1 = L_1/L$, $\lambda_2 = L_2/L$, and σ_1, σ_2 are the elasticities of substitution in production in the domestic and multinational sectors, respectively. In the Cobb–Douglas case, this reduces to

$$\pi_{FSK} = \left(1 + \frac{\lambda_1}{\lambda_2}\right)\pi_w - \left(\frac{\lambda_1}{\lambda_2}\right)\pi_I - \frac{1}{1+T_K}\left(\frac{\partial T_K}{\partial \tau}\right). \qquad (14)$$

The first term indicates that an increase in the wage reduces the relative price of *FSK* (since the price of the multinational good is fixed) and thus increases demand for *FSK*. The second term reflects the fact, noted above, that an increase in income results in an increase in the relative price of the domestic good and thus the demands for the factors producing that good, while decreasing relative factor demands for the factors producing the multinational sector good, thus putting downward pressure on the demand for *FSK*. The more general case reflects the additional net general equilibrium effects on the demand for *FSK* of changes in relative prices on consumer demands and factor demands.

3.1.6. *Solving for the optimal tax rate in the Cobb–Douglas case*

To make these expressions more tractable in solving for the optimal τ, suppose that the production functions are Cobb–Douglas with constant labor shares χ_{L1}, χ_{L2}, and the utility function is also Cobb–Douglas with constant expenditure shares $\psi^I_{C_1}, \psi^I_{C_2}$. In this case, the various tax semi-elasticities reduce to

$$\frac{\partial T_K}{\partial \tau} = (1-\phi_S)(1-\phi_F) + (1-\phi_S)[(1-\phi_F)\tau + \phi_F \tau_F - \tau_H]\pi_{1-\phi_S}$$

$$\pi_w = \frac{\chi_{FSK2}}{\chi_{L2}(1+T_K)}\left(\frac{\partial T_K}{\partial \tau}\right)$$

$$\pi_{\rho L} = \pi_I - \frac{1}{1+\tau}$$

$$\pi_{P_1} = \chi_{L1}\pi_w + (1-\chi_{L1})\pi_I$$

$$\pi_{FSK} = \left(1+\frac{\lambda_1}{\lambda_2}\right)\pi_w - \left(\frac{\lambda_1}{\lambda_2}\right)\pi_I - \frac{1}{1+T_K}\left(\frac{\partial T_K}{\partial \tau}\right)$$

$$\pi_I = \psi^I_L \pi_w + \psi^I_{LSK}\pi_{\rho L} + \left(\frac{R}{I}\right)\left[\psi^R_{LSK}\pi_{\rho L} + \psi^R_{FSK}(\pi_{FSK} + \pi_{1-\phi_S}) + \frac{1}{\tau}\right].$$

Substituting for $\pi_{\rho L}$ and π_{FSK} and solving for the tax semi-elasticity of income yields

$$D\tau\pi_I = \frac{R}{I} + \left[\psi^I_L + \left(\frac{R}{I}\right)\psi^R_{FSK}\left(\frac{\lambda_1}{\lambda_2} + \frac{1}{\chi_{FSK2}}\right)\right]\tau\pi_w$$
$$- \left[\psi^I_{LSK} + \left(\frac{R}{I}\right)\psi^R_{LSK}\right]\left(\frac{\tau}{1+\tau}\right) + \left(\frac{R}{I}\right)\psi^R_{FSK}\tau\pi_{1-\phi_S}, \qquad (15)$$

where $D = 1 - \psi^I_{LSK} - \left(\frac{R}{I}\right)\psi^R_{LSK} + \left(\frac{R}{I}\right)\left(\frac{\lambda_1}{\lambda_2}\right)\psi^R_{FSK}$. Substituting $\pi_{p1} = \chi_{L1}\pi_w + (1-\chi_{L1})\pi_I$ into the government's first-order condition for τ Eq. (5) and multiplying by $D\tau$ yields

$$D\tau\pi_I - D\left(\frac{\psi^I_{C_1}\chi_{L1}}{1-\psi^I_{C_1}\chi_{LSK1}}\right)\tau\pi_w = 0. \tag{16}$$

Substituting from the Cobb–Douglas tax semi-elasticity expressions above yields

$$\frac{R}{I} - \Omega_R\left(\frac{R}{I}\right) = \psi^I_{LSK}\left(\frac{\tau}{1+\tau}\right) + \Omega T_K\left(\frac{T}{1+T_K}\right)\left(\frac{\partial T_K}{\partial \tau}\right), \tag{17}$$

where

$$\Omega_R = \psi^R_{LSK}\left(\frac{\tau}{1+\tau}\right) + \psi^R_{FSK}\left[\frac{\lambda_1}{\lambda_2}\left(\frac{\chi_{FSK2}}{\chi_{L2}}\right) + \frac{1}{\chi_{L2}} - \tau\pi_{1-\phi_S}\right]$$

$$\Omega T_K = \left[\psi^I_L - \frac{D\psi^I_{C_1}\chi_{L1}}{1-\psi^I_{C_1}\chi_{LSK1}}\right]\left(\frac{\chi_{FSK2}}{\chi_{L2}}\right)$$

$$T_K = (1-\phi_F)(1-\phi_S)\tau + [(1-\phi_S)\phi_F\tau_F + \phi_S\tau_H].$$

Thus, at the capital income tax rate optimum, the static increase in revenue due to an increase in the tax rate (the first term in Eq. (17), *R/I*) is exactly offset by the net effect on real income, including endogenous adjustments in the head tax (Ω_R *R/I*), and the increase in taxation of capital in the domestic sector (the second-to-last term in Eq. (17)) and in the multinational sector (the last term in Eq. (17)).

3.2. *Properties of the optimal capital income tax rate*

In this section, we show that our optimality condition is consistent with the basic results discussed in the introduction on (1) zero capital income taxation, and (2) capital income taxation at the residual tax rate. First, divide the optimality condition Eq. (17) by τ and apply $R = \tau[\rho_L LSK + (1-\phi_S)\rho_F FSK]$ so that the optimality condition is well defined at $\tau = 0$,

$$\frac{\rho_L LSK + (1-\phi_S)\rho_F FSK}{I} - \left[\psi^I_{LSK} + \left(\frac{R}{I}\right)\psi^R_{LSK}\right]\left(\frac{1}{1+\tau}\right) + \left(\frac{R}{I}\right)\psi^{R\ \pi}_{FSK\,1-\phi_S}$$
$$-\left[\frac{D\psi^I_{C_1}\chi_{L1}}{1-\psi^I_{C_1}\chi_{LSK1}} - \psi^I_L - \left(\frac{R}{I}\right)\psi^R_{FSK}\left(\frac{\lambda_1}{\lambda_2} + \frac{1}{\chi_{FSK2}}\right)\right]\pi_w = 0. \tag{18}$$

When there is a zero capital income tax rate, $\psi_{LSK}^{R}=\psi_{FSK}^{R}=T_K=0$ and (18) simplifies to

$$\frac{\rho_L LSK+(1-\phi_S)\rho_F FSK}{I}-\psi_{LSK}^{I}=\left[\frac{\left(1-\psi_{LSK}^{I}\right)\psi_{C_1}^{I}\chi_{L1}}{1-\psi_{C_1}^{I}\chi_{LSK1}}-\psi_{L}^{I}\right]\pi_{w}. \quad (19)$$

Assuming that the tax rate in the tax haven is non-zero, $\tau_H > 0$, firms will not shift income to the tax haven if the change from $\tau = 0$ is small enough, $\pi_{1-\phi_S}=0|_{\tau=0}$. Additionally, at $\tau = 0$, no income shifting occurs ($\phi_S = 0$), reducing the wage expression to

$$\pi_{w}=-\frac{\chi_{FSK2}}{\chi_{L2}}(1-\phi_F). \quad (20)$$

Recognizing that $\psi_{C_1}^{I}\chi_{LSK1}=\psi_{LSK}^{I}/\theta, \psi_{C_1}^{I}\chi_{L1}=\psi_{L}^{I}\lambda_1$, and χ_{FSK2}/χ_{L2} = $\rho_F FSK/wL_2$ at $\tau = 0$, we can multiply this entire expression by $IL_2/\rho_F FSK$ to get

$$\frac{\psi_{LSK}^{I}I}{\rho_F FSK}\left(\frac{1-\theta}{\theta}\right)L_2+L_2=\left[L-\left(\frac{1-\psi_{LSK}^{I}}{1-\psi_{LSK}^{I}/\theta}\right)L_1\right](1-\phi_F), \quad (21)$$

which is the condition under which a zero capital tax rate is optimal. If all location-specific capital is owned domestically ($\theta = 1$), the optimality condition becomes

$$L_2 = (L - L_1)(1 - \phi_F)$$

and a zero capital income tax is optimal only if there is no foreign residual tax.

To consider the case where a portion of location-specific capital is not owned domestically, $\theta < 1$, rewrite the optimality condition to the form

$$\frac{\psi_{LSK}^{I}I}{\rho_F FSK}\left(\frac{1-\theta}{\theta}\right)L_2=\left[L-\left(\frac{1-\psi_{LSK}^{I}}{1-\psi_{LSK}^{I}/\theta}\right)L_1\right](1-\phi_F)-L_2. \quad (22)$$

As long as $\theta<1, 1-\psi_{LSK}^{I}>1-\psi_{LSK}^{I}/\theta$ so that $L-\left(\frac{I-\theta\rho_L LSK}{I-\rho_L LSK}\right)L_1<L_2$. Since $(1 - \phi_F) \leq 1$, this suggests the right-hand side of Eq. (22) is strictly negative, while $\theta < 1$ implies the left-hand side of Eq. (22) is strictly positive. Consequently, optimality condition Eq. (22) never holds if $\theta < 1$. This suggests that as long as any location-specific capital is foreign-owned, the optimal capital tax rate is non-zero, as a portion of location-specific capital represents immobile, foreign-owned, above-normal returns (assuming a non-zero tax rate in the tax haven). However, if all location-specific capital is owned domestically, the optimal capital tax rate is zero if there is no residual tax, under the baseline assumption $\tau_H > 0$.

We can also characterize the optimal capital income tax rate under full residual taxation. If all capital income earned in sector two is subject to residual taxation ($\phi_F = 1$) and the domestic tax rate is lower than the residual tax rate ($\tau < \tau_F$), the optimality condition Eq. (17) reduces to

$$\frac{1+\tau}{\theta+\tau} = \frac{\rho_L LSK}{\rho_L LSK + (1-\phi_S)\rho_F FSK}. \tag{23}$$

By definition, $0 \le \theta \le 1$ and the expression in Eq. (23) cannot hold as long as some income is unshifted, $\phi_S < 1$. Consequently, if there is full residual taxation, $\tau < \tau_F$ is not optimal as long as any capital income in sector two is unshifted when $\tau = \tau_F$.

4. Extended Model, Parameter Values, and Simulation Results

4.1. *Extended model*

In this section, we simulate an extended version of the model to obtain an idea of the magnitudes of the effects of the various factors on the optimal capital income tax rate. Specifically, we expand the individual's optimization problem to include endogenous labor supply, converting the head tax to a proportional tax on labor, and allow for the possibility of endogenous labor income shifting to the capital income tax base. Further, we add another factor in both production sectors — "ordinary" capital (K) that earns a normal rate of return (r); we assume that this factor is also perfectly mobile so that r is fixed. This implies that domestic production also includes internationally mobile capital, so that both production sectors are affected by the capital tax rate. Both sectors thus now employ three factors in production, which we model using CES production functions. Finally, we consider the effects on the optimal capital income tax rate of adding an explicit tax on location-specific capital as an additional tax instrument available to the government.

In the computational model, we use a utility function that enables calibration of the income elasticity of labor:

$$v(p_1, I) = \max_{C_1, C_2, L} \left\{ \alpha_{C1} \left(\frac{C_1^{1-1/\gamma_1}}{1-1/\gamma_1} \right) + \alpha_{C2} \left(\frac{C_2^{1-1/\gamma_2}}{1-1/\gamma_2} \right) + \alpha_L \left(\frac{(H-L)^{1-1/\gamma_L}}{1-1/\gamma_L} \right) \right\}$$

$$s.t. \quad I = wL + \theta \rho_L LSK + rK_d > p_1 C_1 + p_2 C_2; \;\; H \geq L. \tag{24}$$

All variables correspond to those used in the analytical model above, with the additional terms K_d and H indicating domestic ownership of capital and the labor endowment, respectively, with leisure defined as H–L. The wage rate in the individual problem remains net of tax and, as will be discussed below, includes any wages that are shifted to the business income tax base and thus subject to the capital income tax.

Both CES production functions now account for ordinary capital (K_1 and K_2), or

$$X_1 = \left[\alpha_1 K_1^{(\xi_1 - 1)/\xi_1} + \alpha_2 L_1^{(\xi_1 - 1)/\xi_1} + (1 - \alpha_1 - \alpha_2) LSK^{(\xi_1 - 1)/\xi_1} \right]^{\frac{\xi_1}{\xi_1 - 1}} \tag{25}$$

$$X_2 = \left[\beta_1 K_2^{(\xi_2 - 1)/\xi_2} + \beta_2 L_2^{(\xi_2 - 1)/\xi_2} + (1 - \beta_1 - \beta_2) FSK^{(\xi_2 - 1)/\xi_2} \right]^{\frac{\xi_2}{\xi_2 - 1}}, \tag{26}$$

where ξ_1 and ξ_2 are the elasticities of substitution in production for sectors one and two.

Turning next to extensions of the modeling of income shifting, Grubert and Altshuler (2013) argue that the costs associated with international income shifting are roughly quadratic.[10] Accordingly, we assume that multinationals engage in income shifting to maximize the increment

[10] Most of this discussion is included in their online Appendix A, http://econweb.rutgers.edu/altshule/Fixing-appendices.pdf.

in after-tax profits attributable to such shifting, subject to quadratic adjustment costs. Thus, the proportion of capital income shifted to a tax haven (ϕ_S) satisfies

$$\phi_S \in \max_{0 \le \phi_S \le 1} \left\{ \left[\left(\tau + \phi_F \max\left\{ \tau_F - \tau, 0 \right\} - \tau_H \right) \phi_S - \eta \phi_S^{\;2} \right] \left(rK_2 + \rho_F FSK \right) \right\}, \quad (27)$$

and the total per-unit cost of both types of capital to the multinational sector with income shifting is $1 + (1 - \phi_S)[\tau + \phi_F \max(\tau_F - \tau, 0)] + \phi_S \tau_H + \eta \phi_S^2$.

In the domestic economy, some individuals are assumed to be able to shift labor income to the business tax base when the capital income tax rate is lower than the labor income tax rate. Such shifting maximizes the associated increment in after-tax wage income, again subject to quadratic adjustment costs. Only a limited portion (ω_I) of labor income, corresponding roughly to the share of labor income earned from self-employment or in small closely-held corporations, can potentially be shifted. Consequently, the proportion of labor income shifted to the capital income tax base (ϕ_I) satisfies

$$\phi_I = \omega_I a \middle| a \in \max_{0 \le a \le 1} \left\{ a \left(\tau_L - \tau \right) wL - \mu a^2 wL \right\}. \quad (28)$$

With ϕ_E indicating the share of wage income exempt from labor taxation, the gross wage rate, including shifting costs, is $w_G = \phi_E w + (1 - \phi_E) w[(1 - \phi_I)(1 + \tau_L) + \phi_I (1 + \tau) \mu \phi_I^2]$. Government revenue comes from three tax instruments: a capital income tax, a labor income tax, and (in some cases) a direct tax on location-specific capital. A fixed share (ϕ_{LSK}) of *LSK* is subject to the direct tax, and any of these taxes paid are deductible from the capital income tax base, so the total tax revenue raised from location-specific capital income is $R_{LSK} = \phi_{LSK} [\tau_{LSK} + \tau(1 - \tau_{LSK})] \rho_L LSK + (1 - \phi_{LSK}) \tau \rho_L LSK$. Accounting for income shifting behavior, total revenue raised from the taxation of labor income is $R_L = \tau_L (1 - \phi_I) wL + \tau \phi_I wL$ and total revenue raised from ordinary and firm-specific capital income is $R = \tau\{r[K_1 + (1 - \phi_S)K_2] + (1 - \phi_S)\rho_F FSK\}$. In our simulations, we treat the location-specific capital tax rate as exogenous, effectively assuming there is a maximum feasible level of *LSK* taxation. The welfare-maximizing government chooses the capital income tax rate and the labor income tax rate according to

$$\max_{\tau_L, \tau} \left\{ v\left(p_1, I \right) \middle| p_2 G = R_L + R_{LSK} + R \right\}. \quad (29)$$

4.2. *Parameter values*

In this section, we describe the parameter values used in our model. In the simulations, we consider a wide range of values for numerous key parameters.

4.2.1. *Production function parameters*

The appropriate value for the elasticity of substitution in production is a contentious issue. Many simulation studies (e.g., Altig *et al.*, 2001; Fehr *et al.*, 2013) assume Cobb–Douglas production functions, and a relatively large degree of substitutability seems appropriate for our model given that two of our inputs are different types of capital. Accordingly, in our benchmark case, we assume a Cobb–Douglas production function, that is, a unitary elasticity of substitution in production. However, Chirinko (2002) argues that a much lower elasticity of substitution between capital and labor is appropriate; his preferred estimate is 0.4. Accordingly, we calibrate our simulation model for a wide range of substitution elasticities, varying from the Cobb–Douglas case ($\xi_1 = \xi_2 = 1$) to an elasticity of substitution in production as low as $\xi_1 = \xi_2 = 0.25$ (Table 12.1).

In a recent paper that documents the decline in the labor share of income since the 1980s, Karabarbounis and Neiman (2014) estimate a global corporate labor share of around 60 percent, and an overall labor share of around 52.5 percent. We assume that the labor share in sector one (the domestic sector) corresponds to the global share ($\alpha_2 = 0.525$) and the labor share in sector two (the multinational corporate sector) corresponds to the global corporate share ($\beta_2 = 0.60$).

Cronin *et al.* (2013) estimate that roughly 63 percent of corporate income is due to above-normal returns. Given a corporate labor income share of 60 percent, we choose the shares of ordinary capital and firm-specific capital to be consistent with the Cronin et al. estimate. That is, we choose our parameters so that the ratio of the total earnings attributable to above-normal returns to *FSK*, defined as the excess of actual returns to *FSK* over the returns to ordinary capital, to the total earnings from the normal returns to ordinary capital is 1.7 (= 0.63/(1 – 0.63)). This in turn implies that the ordinary capital and *FSK* shares in the MNC production function are $\beta_1 = 0.148$ and $1 - \beta_1 - \beta_2 = 0.252$. Similarly, assuming a labor share of 52.5 percent in the domestic sector implies $\alpha_1 = 0.176$ and $1 - \alpha_1 - \alpha_2 = 0.299$.

To calibrate the relative rate of return to *FSK*, we consider the literature studying the rate of return to investment in research and development. In a study of UK firms, Greenhalgh and Rogers (2006) find that the ratio of the shadow value of intangible to tangible assets is 3.5, but that this ratio varies considerably by sector, from 2.34 for software firms to 7.97 for production intensive firms. Following their baseline result, we set $r = 0.1$ and $\rho_F = 0.35$.

It is less clear how the rate of return to *LSK* should compare to the return to ordinary capital. Hou and Robinson (2006) find that in the United States firms in more concentrated markets earn lower stock market returns, while Gallagher, Ignatieva, and McCulloch (2015) find that in Australia firms in more concentrated markets are able to earn excess returns. Gallagher, Ignatieva, and McCulloch hypothesize that a more rigorous regulatory environment in United States explains this difference. Given this ambiguity, we choose a rate of return to *LSK* that is only 25 percent higher than the rate earned by ordinary capital, $\rho_L = 0.125$.

4.2.2. *Utility function parameters*

In 2012, foreign-controlled enterprises produced 37 percent of total GDP in the EU countries.[11] Accordingly, the MNC produces 37 percent of GDP in our base case. To achieve this, we set the consumption share parameters for the representative resident at $\alpha_{C1} = 6.15$ and $\alpha_{C2} = 4.08$. The various γ parameters determine the responsiveness of consumption and labor supply to changes in prices (including the wage) and income. We calibrate our demand price elasticity for the multinational good to −1.1 ($\gamma_2 = 1.22$), consistent with Senhadji's (1998) estimate that the average long-run price elasticity of import demand is slightly higher than one. Seale and Regmi (2006) estimate price elasticities across good types for a wide selection of countries; we select an intermediate value for the uncompensated price elasticity of the domestic good of −0.8 ($\gamma_1 = 0.615$).

---

[11] Authors' calculations based on data from Eurostat, http://ec.europa.eu/eurostat/data/database, "GDP and main components" and "Foreign control of enterprises by economic activity and a selection of controlling countries."

Turning to the labor supply parameters, in a Congressional Budget Office survey of recent research on labor supply elasticities, McClelland and Mok (2012) conclude that the substitution elasticity of labor supply for the total population in the U.S. is between 0.1 and 0.3, and that the income elasticity is between –0.1 and zero. Accordingly, we set the parameters of our utility function so that the labor supply substitution elasticity is 0.2, and the income elasticity is –0.05; this implies $\gamma_L = 0.413$ and $\alpha_L = 7.3$. Note that these parameter values yield an uncompensated labor supply elasticity of 0.15, a value that is consistent with the consensus estimates in McClelland and Mok (2012) and comparable to the value of 0.18 used by Jacobs (2009).

4.2.3. *Government spending and tax rates*

We fix government services, which are assumed to be separable from the individual utility function, at roughly 16 percent of national income. This is consistent with the average level (16.2 percent) reported by The World Bank's World Development Indicators for high-FDI countries between 2000 and 2013.[12]

As discussed above, our "capital income tax rate" is a proxy for several concepts of capital income taxation, including statutory and various effective tax rates. We calibrate our model at a capital tax rate of $\tau/(1 + \tau) = 0.18$, which reflects the average effective business-level capital income tax rate estimated by PricewaterhouseCoopers (2011) for high-FDI countries.[13] Under our base case assumption that the elasticity of substitution in production is $\xi_1 = \xi_2 = 1.0$, this implies a labor tax rate of $\tau_L/(1 + \tau_L) = 0.22$. This labor tax rate, which is endogenously determined to balance the government budget constraint, assumes that 35 percent of labor income is

[12] We identify high-FDI countries as those whose average (2000–2013) foreign direct investment (FDI) net inflows as a share of GDP are in the top 50% reported internationally. This corresponds to countries whose FDI net inflows average above 3.7% of GDP between 2000 and 2013. These data were obtained from http://databank.worldbank.org/data/reports.aspx?source=world-development-indicators.

[13] The unweighted average of effective tax rates for high-FDI countries (as defined in footnote 11) in this study is 17.5%, rising to 19.2% if the samples is restricted to countries with at least 10 observations.

exempted from the tax base ($\phi_E = 0.35$), reflecting provisions such as standard deductions, personal exemptions, and a variety of other deductions and exclusions. For example, in 2013, about 69 percent of the income reported on US tax returns was taxable, a figure that overstates the share of taxable income since filers with very low income levels are not required to file US tax returns.[14]

Globally, taxes on domestic natural resources vary considerably. In a recent survey, the International Monetary Fund (2012) reports high average effective tax rates on extractive industries. For the petroleum industry, these rates are generally between 65 and 85 percent of net present value. For mining industries, rates are somewhat lower, ranging from 45 to 65 percent. Accordingly, in our benchmark case, the direct tax on location-specific capital is set at 60 percent ($\tau_{LSK} = 0.6$). We initially assume that none of the location-specific capital is subject to this tax, $\phi_{LSK} = 0$, since *LSK* does not necessarily represent extraction activity, but consider the full range of possible values in our simulations ($0 \leq \phi_{LSK} \leq 1$).

As discussed in the introduction, in most circumstances the fraction of firm-specific capital that is subject to residual taxation in the home country (ϕ_F) is likely be relatively small. However, it may be significant for (1) countries attempting to attract a significant share of their foreign direct investment from US-based MNCs that are not (and are not likely to be) in an excess foreign tax credit position, or (2) countries with tax rates that are (or will become with reform) sufficiently low that they trigger current residual home country taxation under various anti-base-erosion provisions — a category that may increase over time as more countries adopt such provisions. In our base case, we assume that the fraction of firm-specific capital that is subject to residual taxation is very small ($\phi_F = 0.01$) and subject to a gross residual tax rate of 20 percent. However, we simulate a wide variety of potential residual taxation scenarios, including $0.05 \leq \tau_F/(1 + \tau_F) \leq 0.30$ and $0 \leq \phi_F \leq 0.30$, corresponding to the range of values that might arise under anti-base-erosion provisions.

[14] See IRS SOI Tax Statistics, "Table 1.1 All Returns: Selected Income and Tax Items, Tax Year 2013," https://www.irs.gov/uac/SOI-Tax-Stats---Individual-Statistical-Tables-by-Size-of-Adjusted-Gross-Income.

Finally, we assume that the effective tax haven rate is $\tau_H/(1 + \tau_H) = 0.05$, reflecting a combination of very low tax haven rates coupled with the costs of shifting income and deferring repatriation, which Grubert and Altshuler (2013) suggest range from 1–7 percent.

4.2.4. *Income shifting parameters*

There is considerable disagreement about the fraction of capital income that is currently shifted abroad. Riedel (2014) surveys the literature on international tax avoidance and reports a range of 5 percent (found in the United Kingdom by HMRC (2014)) to 30 percent (found in the United States by Clausing (2011)). In her most recent work, Clausing (2016) estimates that the amount of income shifted from the US corporate income tax base is 32–46 percent of current revenues. In our benchmark case, we adopt a fairly conservative assumption that income shifting is 15 percent of the corporate tax base ($\phi_S/(1 - \phi_S) = 0.15$ or $\phi_S = 0.13$).[15,16] Under the tax rates assumed in the model, this implies that the capital income shifting parameter is $\eta = 0.65$. However, given the uncertainty about the extent of income shifting, we simulate a wide range of values for the share of income that is shifted abroad, $0.05 \leq \phi_S/(1 - \phi_S) \leq 0.50$.

There is considerably less literature on the shifting of labor income to the corporate income tax base. However, we expect the share of labor income shifted to be modest, as relatively few individuals both have the capability to shift labor income and potentially benefit from it. The two groups most likely to engage in labor income shifting are the

[15]This aligns closely with the Dyreng and Markle (2015) estimate that income shifting the United States is roughly 13 percent of revenues — although they note that because their sample size is relatively small, their estimate is not necessarily inconsistent with larger estimates such as those found by Clausing (2011).

[16]Estimates of the tax semi-elasticity of income shifting provide another indicator of the degree of uncertainty about the extent of income shifting. For example, Clausing notes that her larger estimate implies a tax semi-elasticity of 3.3. This value, however, is relatively large in comparison to most others found in the literature; for example, Heckemeyer and Overesch (2013) argue that the consensus estimate of the tax semi-elasticity of income shifting is 0.8, although Clausing (2016) argues that most of the papers cited in this study use data that does not adequately capture income shifting to tax havens.

self-employed and individuals working in small corporations. According to The World Bank's World Development Indicators, about 35 percent of the employed population in high-FDI countries is self-employed, while in a sample of 20 OECD countries, around 24 percent of individuals work for companies with 10 or fewer employees.[17] Accordingly, in our benchmark case we set $\omega_I = 0.35$ and also consider cases where up to 50 percent of labor income can potentially be shifted. Given our assumption that 35 percent of labor income is exempt from taxation, we then assume 75 percent of remaining labor income is taxed at a rate exceeding the capital income tax rate. Additionally, we simply assume that a quarter of this potentially shiftable income is actually shifted to the corporate tax base. This calculation suggests that about 7 percent of labor income is shifted to the corporate tax base ($\phi_I/(1 - \phi_I) = 0.07$), implying $\mu = 0.16$. With 7 percent of labor income shifted to the corporate tax base, 8.7 percent of revenue raised by the capital tax reflects revenue raised from taxation of shifted labor income. This figure is slightly below the range of 10 to 17 percent labor income shifting estimated in for the EU by de Mooij and Nicodème (2006).[18]

4.2.5. *Other parameters*

Sercu and Vanpée (2007) examine a sample of 42 countries and estimate that the share of domestically-owned equity capital in total market capitalization is 80 percent. Accordingly, we assume in our benchmark case that the domestically-owned share of the location-specific capital is $\theta = 0.8$. In the simulations, we consider the full range of possibilities for this parameter, $0 \leq \theta \leq 1$.

---

[17]This calculation is based on values from OCED (2012). The 20 countries with available data include Austria, Belgium, Brazil, the Czech Republic, Denmark, Finland, Germany, Hungary, Italy, Luxembourg, Netherlands, New Zealand, Norway, Poland, Portugal, Slovak Republic, Slovenia, Spain, Sweden, and the United Kingdom.

[18]Our estimates may be conservative. Gordon and Slemrod (2000) estimate that a one percentage point decrease in the differential between the labor income and businesss tax rates leads to a fairly large 2.9 percent increase in personal income. When we simulate the effects of a small change in this tax rate differential at the initial equilibrium in our model, we obtain a smaller tax semi-elasticity of −1.36.

4.3. *Simulation results*

As mentioned above, we calibrate our model for various values of the elasticity of substitution in production, ranging from $\xi_1 = \xi_2 = 1$ to $\xi_1 = \xi_2 = 0.25$, using the Cobb–Douglas formulation as the benchmark. In Table 12.1, we present the parameters used for calibration and welfare analysis for each 0.15 increment over this range of the production substitution elasticity.

Note that as the elasticity of substitution in production declines, the optimal capital income tax rate rises, as capital income taxation is less distortionary if capital-labor substitution in production is more difficult. For example, when the elasticity of substitution in production is $\xi_1 = \xi_2 = 1$, the optimal capital income tax rate is $\tau^*/(1 + \tau^*) = 0.160$, but as the production elasticity declines to $\xi_1 = \xi_2 = 0.25$, the optimal capital income tax rate increases by nearly 18 percent to $\tau^*/(1 + \tau^*) = 0.188$.

In addition, as the optimal capital income tax rate approaches the level in our baseline, $\tau/(1 + \tau) = 0.180$, the welfare gains associated with reform — defined as the equivalent variation associated with moving from the benchmark initial equilibrium to the optimal capital income tax rate — naturally approach zero.[19] For example, at the substitution elasticity $\xi_1 = \xi_2 = 0.40$, the optimal capital income tax rate $\tau^*/(1 + \tau^*) = 0.182$ is very close to the observed rate, so that capital income tax reform produces negligible welfare gains. By comparison, moving to the optimal capital income tax rate in the Cobb–Douglas case is equivalent to receiving a transfer in the initial equilibrium equal to 0.53 percent of CIT revenues. Alternatively, consider the effects of moving from no taxation of capital income to the optimal capital income tax rate. In the Cobb–Douglas case, this results in a welfare gain equivalent to a transfer worth 4.97 percent of CIT revenues. However, at lower elasticities of substitution in production, the distortionary effects of capital income taxation are smaller, so the welfare gains associated with introducing a positive capital income tax rate are generally larger; for example, moving to the optimal capital income tax rate results in a welfare gain worth

[19] Equivalent variation is measured as the income transfer that would make the individual indifferent between receiving the transfer and remaining in the initial equilibrium and moving to the equilibrium that occurs with the move to the optimal capital income tax rate.

Table 12.1.

Optimal Capital Taxation Model, Optimal Tax Rates, and Welfare Effects, as a Function of the Elasticity of Substitution in Production

Varying the Elasticity of Substitution						
	$\xi_i = 1.00$	$\xi_i = 0.85$	$\xi_i = 0.70$	$\xi_i = 0.55$	$\xi_i = 0.40$	$\xi_i = 0.25$
G	0.198	0.2012	0.2055	0.211	0.217	0.2247
K_d	4.5	4.55	4.6	4.62	4.68	4.73
LSK	1.37	1.39	1.42	1.46	1.495	1.528
α_1	0.176	0.176	0.176	0.176	0.176	0.176
α_2	0.525	0.509	0.482	0.437	0.353	0.185
β_1	0.148	0.152	0.157	0.162	0.177	0.208
β_2	0.6	0.62	0.65	0.69	0.725	0.753
a_L	7.3	7.3	7.3	7.3	7.3	7.3
a_{C1}	6.15	6.15	6.15	6.15	6.15	6.15
a_{C2}	4.08	4.05	3.96	3.8	3.65	3.38
γ_1	0.615	0.615	0.615	0.615	0.615	0.615
γ_2	1.22	1.22	1.22	1.22	1.22	1.22
γ_L	0.413	0.412	0.415	0.417	0.418	0.421
Invariant Parameters						
$\tau_F/(1+\tau_F) = 0.20$		$p_2 = 0.9$	$\phi_{LSK} = 0$	$\theta = 0.8$	$\mu = 0.16$	$\omega_I = 0.35$
$\tau_H/(1+\tau_H) = 0.05$		$r = 0.1$	$\phi_E = 0.35$	$H = 2.85$	$\eta = 0.65$	
$\tau_{LSK}/(1+\tau_{LSK}) = 0.375$		$\rho_F = 0.35$	$\phi_F = 0.01$			
Optimal Tax Rates						
$\tau^*/(1+\tau^*)$	0.160	0.165	0.170	0.177	0.182	0.188
$\tau_L^*/(1+\tau_L^*)$	0.241	0.236	0.230	0.223	0.216	0.210
Excess Burden as a Percent of Capital Income Tax Revenue (At Initial Calibration Point)						
$\tau/(1+\tau) = 0.18$	0.53%	0.29%	0.11%	0.00%	0.00%	0.06%
$\tau/(1+\tau) = 0.00$	4.97%	5.92%	7.03%	8.08%	8.64%	8.75%
Capital Investment Changes Under Reform ($\tau = 0.00 \rightarrow \tau^*$)						
$\%\Delta(K_1 + K_2)$	−29.36%	−24.90%	−20.28%	−15.60%	−11.04%	−6.33%
$\%\Delta FSK$	−46.31%	−39.41%	−32.34%	−25.22%	−18.35%	11.08%

8.75 percent of CIT revenues in the case of an elasticity of substitution in production of 0.25.

In our benchmark calibration, 35 percent of labor income can be potentially be shifted ($\omega_I = 0.35$), only 1 percent of MNC capital income is subject to residual taxation ($\phi_F = 0.01$), there is no direct taxation of *LSK* ($\phi_{LSK} = 0$), and 20 percent of *LSK* is foreign-owned ($\theta = 0.8$). In this case, the optimal capital income tax rate is $\tau^*/(1 + \tau^*) = 0.160$ and the labor income tax rate, which is determined as a residual from the government budget constraint, is $\tau_L/(1 + \tau_L) = 0.241$.

The results of various simulations of the model are shown in Figures 12.1–12.7, where the benchmark calibration, when included, is indicated with a triangle. The basic variations on the benchmark result are illustrated in Figures 12.1a–c, which show the optimal capital income tax rates for various assumptions about the share of *LSK* owned by foreigners $(1 - \theta)$, the share of labor income that can be feasibly shifted (ω_I), and the fraction of unshifted income subject to residual taxation (ϕ_F). Note that, in contrast to our main result in the analytical model, the optimal capital income tax rate is not zero even when all location-specific capital is owned domestically and there is no residual taxation, since a portion of the capital income tax base (*LSK*) is inelastic.[20] However, the optimal capital income tax rate is small when there is no residual taxation, no potential for labor income shifting, and no foreign ownership of *LSK*, as the optimal rate is less than 3 percent, $\tau^*/(1 + \tau^*) = 0.027$ (not shown). Thus, considered in isolation, the opportunity to tax immobile location-specific rents accruing to domestic residents does not provide much of a rationale for capital income taxation in the model.

With only 1 percent of capital in the multinational sector subject to residual taxation and no labor income shifting, Figure 12.1a shows that the optimal capital income tax rate is roughly linear with respect to the share of *LSK* that is owned by foreigners, beginning at $\tau/(1 + \tau) = 0.03$ when the foreign-owned share of *LSK* is zero and reaching a maximum of $\tau/(1 + \tau) = 0.26$

[20]Tests removing *LSK* from domestic production indicate that the optimal capital tax rate is zero (with no residual taxation) as long as all capital investment is perfectly mobile, since the elasticity of labor supply is finite but non-zero. Note also that the presence of *LSK* does not produce a positive optimal capital income tax rate in our analytical model because the alternative of taxing fixed labor supply has no distortionary cost in that case.

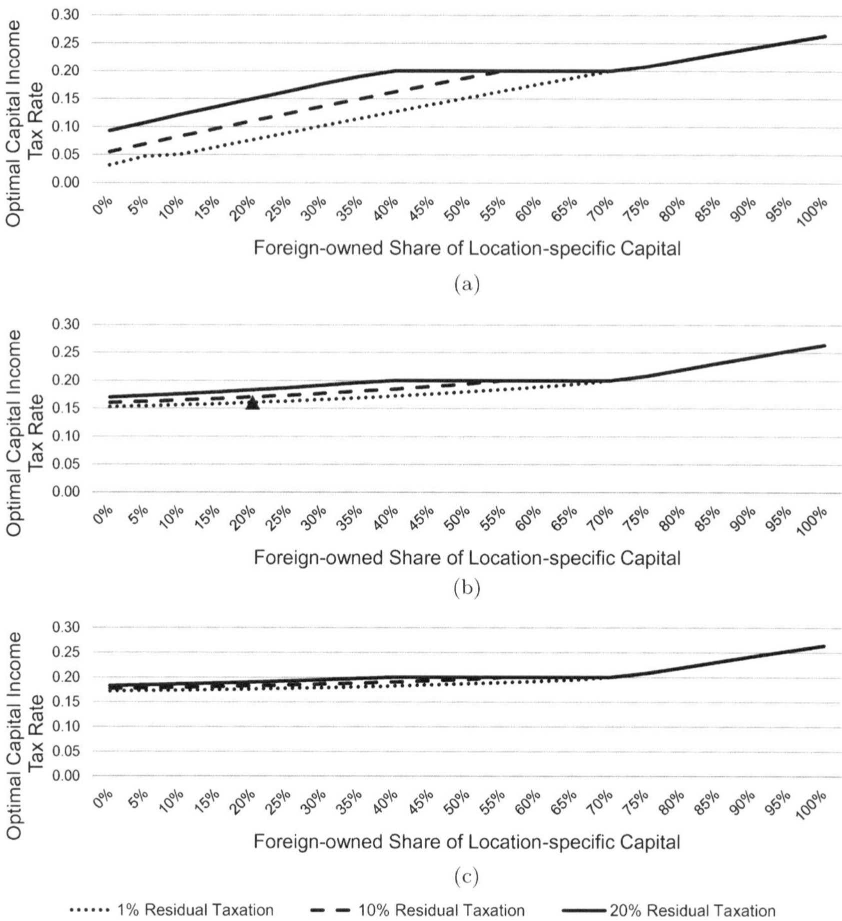

Figure 12.1.
(a) No Income Labor Income Shifting; (b) 35% of Labor Income Feasibly Shifted; (c) 50% of Labor Income Feasibly Shifted

Note: All parameters are set to base-case values unless otherwise indicated. For these figures, this implies that there is no direct taxation of *LSK*, 35% of labor income is exempt from taxation, the elasticity of substitution in production is one, the gross residual tax rate is 20%, and 1% of capital in the multinational sector is subject to residual taxation.

when all of *LSK* is foreign-owned. Thus, the opportunity to tax foreign rents may provide an important rationale for taxing capital income, as stressed by Huizinga and Nielsen (1997). At the benchmark level of foreign ownership of 20 percent (with minimal residual taxation and no income shifting), the optimal capital income tax rate is $\tau^*/(1 + \tau^*) = 0.077$, which implies a labor income tax rate of $\tau_L/(1 + \tau_L) = 0.293$.

Figure 12.1a also shows that adding the possibility of a treasury transfer effect by including residual taxation increases the optimal capital income tax rate, but only until the domestic tax rate equals the assumed residual tax rate of 20 percent. Recall that in the analytical model with full residual taxation, the optimal capital tax rate is at least as high as the foreign tax rate. By expanding the model to include ordinary capital in both sectors, we include some mobile capital that we assume is not subject to residual taxation (K_1). Although this diminishes the importance of the underlying treasury transfer effect, the presence of a residual tax still moves the optimal capital income tax rate toward the foreign tax rate. In all cases, the optimal tax rate plateaus at the assumed residual tax rate — $\tau_F/(1 + \tau_F) = 0.20$. Once this limit is reached, the optimal capital income tax rate remains constant until the foreign-owned share of *LSK* is large enough (in excess of 70 percent) to justify further increases, up to the maximum rate of 26.4 percent which occurs when all *LSK* is foreign-owned.

The same general pattern occurs in Figures 12.1b and 12.1c. However, these figures show that the sensitivity of the optimal capital income tax rate to foreign ownership of *LSK* depends heavily on the opportunity for

Figure 12.2.
Optimal Capital Income Tax Rates and Taxation of Location Specific Capital

Note: All parameters are set to base-case values unless otherwise indicated. For this figure, this implies 35% of labor income can be feasibly shifted, 35% of labor income is exempt from taxation, the elasticity of substitution in production is one, the gross residual tax rate is 20%, and 1% of capital in the multinational sector is subject to residual taxation.

labor income shifting. In all cases, the optimal capital income tax rate is 26.4 percent when all *LSK* is foreign-owned. However, at lower values of the foreign-owned share of *LSK*, the optimal capital income tax rate generally increases as labor-income shifting opportunities increase, as increased capital income taxation allows lower labor income tax rates, both of which reduce the incentive for labor income shifting, which reduces revenues and incurs costs. For example, when 35 (50) percent of labor income can be feasibly shifted to the capital income tax base, the optimal capital income tax rate rises to $\tau^*/(1 + \tau^*) = 0.153$ (0.172), even with minimal residual taxation and no foreign-ownership of *LSK*. This of course reduces the sensitivity of the optimal capital income tax rate to variation in the share of *LSK* that is foreign-owned.

Figure 12.2 illustrates that if some direct taxation of location-specific capital is available (under the assumption that direct taxes paid on location-specific rents are deductible from the capital income tax), the optimal capital income tax rate declines significantly. As discussed above, this occurs because an alternative tax instrument can be used to extract rents from the owners of location-specific rents, including foreigners, without the negative consequences on capital flight and capital income shifting associated with use of the capital income tax. For example, under our base-case assumption that 20 percent of location-specific capital is foreign-owned, the optimal capital income tax rate drops from $\tau^*/(1 + \tau^*) =$ 0.16 or 16 percent to 7.1 percent if all rents from *LSK* can be taxed directly.[21] And, if all *LSK* is foreign-owned, the optimal capital income tax rate drops from 26.4 percent to 9.4 percent. In addition, the sensitivity of the optimal capital income tax rate with respect to foreign ownership of *LSK* declines with direct taxation, since rents earned by foreigners can be taxed directly. Indeed, in the extreme case in which all location-specific capital can be taxed directly, the optimal capital income tax barely increases with the foreign-owned share of *LSK* (from $\tau^*/(1 + \tau^*) = 0.066$ with $\theta = 1$ to

[21]The optimal capital income tax rate does not drop to zero because it is still desirable to raise capital income revenue, reducing the labor income tax rate and the corresponding incentive for labor income shifting. If labor income shifting were impossible, the optimal capital income tax rate would be very near zero in this case (1.7 percent), even with variable labor supply. This small amount of capital taxation persists because *LSK* is still included in the capital income tax base (although the direct tax on *LSK* is fully deductible).

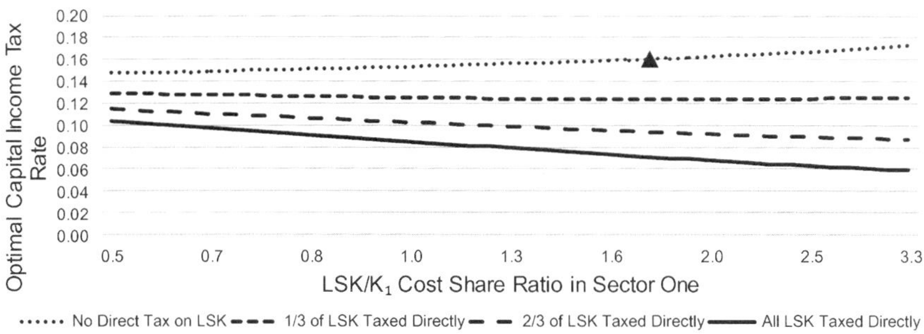

Figure 12.3.
Optimal Capital Income Tax Rates and Domestic Capital Intensity

Note: All parameters are set to base-case values unless otherwise indicated. For this figure, this implies 35% of labor income can be feasibly shifted, 20% of *LSK* is foreign-owned, 35% of labor income is exempt from taxation, the elasticity of substitution in production is one, the gross residual tax rate is 20%, and 1% of capital in the multinational sector is subject to residual taxation.

$\tau^*/(1+\tau^*) = 0.094$ with $\theta = 0$). This slight increase occurs because above-normal returns to foreign-owned *LSK* are still included in the capital income tax base, with the direct tax on *LSK* deductible.

We turn next to the sensitivity of the results to changes in firm production function parameters. Figure 12.3 examines the interaction of the relative capital shares in the production of the domestic good with the availability of a direct tax on *LSK*. Specifically, consider an increase in the production cost share of *LSK* coupled with a reduction in the production cost share of ordinary capital. When there is no direct taxation of *LSK*, this increases the optimal capital income tax rate, as *LSK* is a greater share of the capital tax base. However, when *LSK* is taxed directly, any increases in the relative cost share of *LSK* increase the revenue raised from the direct taxation of *LSK*, lowering the optimal capital income tax rate (as well as the corresponding labor income tax rate since more revenue is available). For example, in the absence of direct *LSK* taxation, increasing the cost-share ratio for *LSK* to ordinary capital from 0.5 to 3.0 (the benchmark value is 1.7) increases the optimal capital income tax rate from $\tau^*/(1+\tau^*) = 0.147$ to $\tau^*/(1+\tau^*) = 0.172$, while the labor income tax rate (not shown) declines from $\tau_L/(1+\tau_L) = 0.259$ to $\tau_L/(1+\tau_L) = 0.229$. However, if all *LSK* is taxed directly, the optimal capital income tax rate declines from $\tau^*/(1+\tau^*) = 0.103$ to

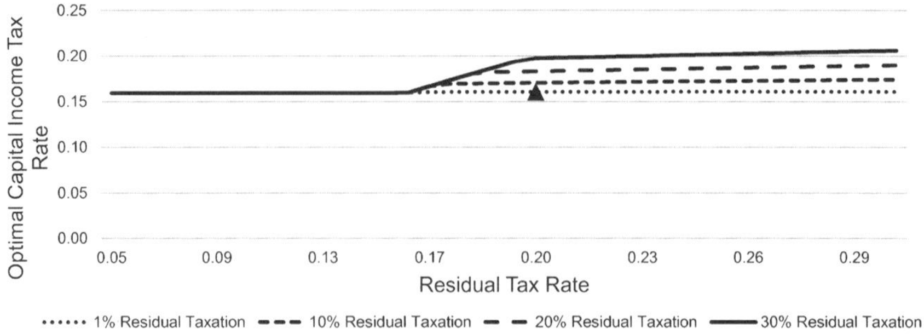

Figure 12.4.
Optimal Capital Income Tax Rates and Residual Taxation

Note: All parameters are set to base-case values unless otherwise indicated. For this figure, this implies 35% of labor income can be feasibly shifted, 35% of labor income is exempt from taxation, the elasticity of substitution in production is one, 20% of *LSK* is foreign-owned, and there is no direct taxation of *LSK*.

$\tau^*/(1 + \tau^*) = 0.059$ and the labor income tax rate declines from $\tau_L/(1 + \tau_L) = 0.224$ to $\tau_L/(1 + \tau_L) = 0.123$.

Figure 12.4 demonstrates that the amount of residual taxation is generally more influential in determining the optimal capital income tax rate than the residual tax rate. Changes in the residual tax rate have no effect on the optimal capital income tax rate so long as the residual tax rate is less than the domestic optimal capital income tax rate, which, in our base case, is as long as $\tau_F/(1 + \tau_F) \leq 0.160$. However, once the residual tax rate exceeds 16 percent, the optimal capital income tax rate equals the residual tax rate until the level of capital income taxation takes maximum advantage of the treasury transfer effect for the given amount of income subject to residual taxation (the kink point in each of the four graphs lies in the range $0.16 \leq \tau_F/(1 + \tau_F) = 0.20$). Beyond that point, the optimal capital income tax rate increases only slightly with increases in the residual tax rate.

In our benchmark calibration, 35 percent of labor income is exempt from labor taxation, producing a base-case optimal capital income tax rate of $\tau^*/(1 + \tau^*) = 0.160$ and a corresponding labor income tax rate of $\tau_L/(1 + \tau_L) = 0.241$. However, Figure 12.5 shows that as the amount of taxable labor income declines, higher marginal tax rates on labor income are needed to raise revenue, increasing the labor-leisure distortion and the amount of labor income shifting associated with labor taxation. For example,

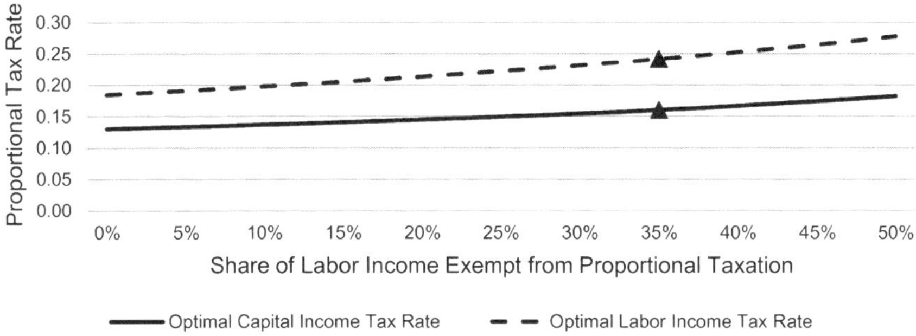

Figure 12.5.
Optimal Tax Rates and Labor Income Exemptions

Note: All parameters are set to base-case values unless otherwise indicated. For this figure, this implies 35% of labor income can be feasibly shifted, 35% of labor income is exempt from taxation, the elasticity of substitution in production is one, 20% of *LSK* is foreign-owned, there is no direct taxation of *LSK*, the gross residual tax rate is 20%, and 1% of capital in the multinational sector is subject to residual taxation.

with the 35 percent exemption, labor income shifting is calibrated to $\phi_l/(1 - \phi_l) = 0.07$ (or 7 percent), but if 25 percent of income is exempt, shifted labor income decreases to 4.8 percent of taxable unshifted income. With these decreases in the distortionary cost of labor taxation, the optimal capital income tax rate also decreases modestly (from 16 percent to 15 percent). Consequently, as the amount of exempt labor income increases, both the optimal capital income and labor income tax rates increase. However, Figure 12.5 demonstrates that the labor income tax increases more in response to labor exemptions than does the optimal capital income tax rate, which is only moderately sensitive to changes in the share of exempt labor income.

Finally, and perhaps surprisingly, differences in opportunities for international income shifting have relatively little effect on the optimal capital income tax rate in the model. The simulation results presented in Figure 12.6 examine the effects of changes in the share of capital income shifted to the tax haven — achieved by changing the international income shifting cost parameter — on the optimal capital income tax rate, for three levels of residual taxation. Holding all other parameters at their base-case values and adjusting capital income shifting costs so that the share of capital income shifted to a tax haven in the base case increases from

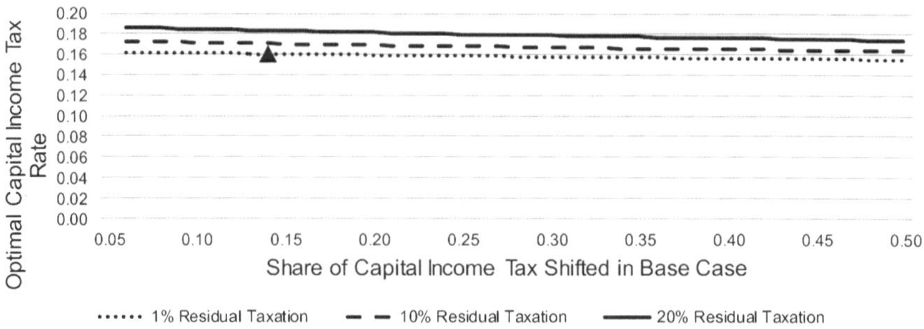

Figure 12.6.
Optimal Capital Income Tax Rates and Residual Taxation

Note: Adjustments to the share of capital income shifted in the base case are achieved by adjusting the shifting cost. All other parameters are set to base-case values unless otherwise indicated. For this figure, this implies 35% of labor income can be feasibly shifted, 35% of labor income is exempt from taxation, the elasticity of substitution in production is one, 20% of *LSK* is foreign-owned, there is no direct taxation of *LSK*, and the gross residual tax rate is 20%.

5 percent to 50 percent, the optimal capital income tax declines only from $\tau^*/(1 + \tau^*) = 0.162$ to $\tau^*/(1 + \tau^*) = 0.155$.

This relatively small effect reflects three offsetting effects of an increase in international income shifting opportunities on the optimal capital income tax rate. First, as international income shifting increases due to lower shifting costs, the size of the domestic capital income tax base decreases so that the revenue raised by the capital income tax declines; the government's desire to avoid this revenue loss puts downward pressure on the optimal capital income tax rate. Second, since location-specific capital cannot be shifted internationally, increased capital income shifting implies a larger share of the capital income tax base is immobile; this makes capital income taxation relatively more attractive and puts upward pressure on the optimal capital income tax rate. Third, as international capital income shifting increases, the negative effect on foreign direct investment of higher capital income taxes is muted, as foreign MNCs recognize that the cost of a higher domestic statutory tax rate is diminished by the potential to shift some of the income earned to a low tax jurisdiction — the cost of capital in the multinational sector is less affected by the statutory rate in the presence of income shifting, implying foreign direct investment is less sensitive to the capital income tax rate. This makes capital income taxation

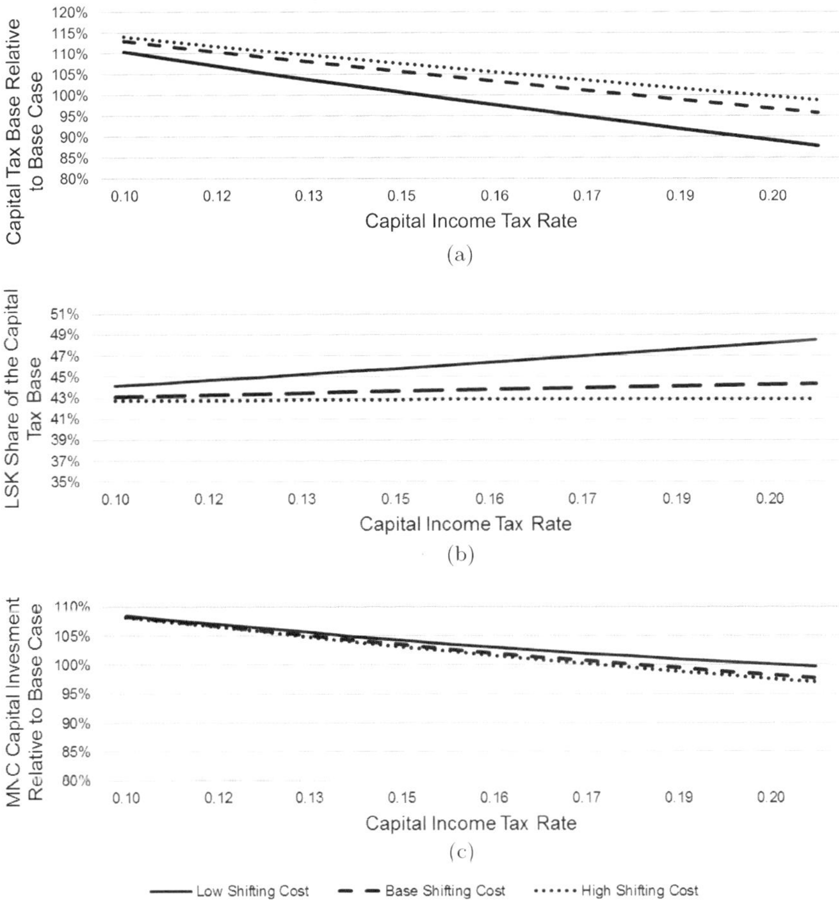

Figure 12.7.

(a) The Effects of Income Shifting on the Captial Tax Base; (b) The Effects of Income Shifting on the LSK Share of the Capital Tax Base; (c) The Effects of Income Shifting on MNC Capital Investment

Note: All parameters are set to base-case values unless otherwise indicated. For this figure, this implies 35% of labor income can be feasibly shifted, 35% of labor income is exempt from taxation, the elasticity of substitution in production is one, 20% of *LSK* is foreign-owned, there is no direct taxation of *LSK*, the gross residual tax rate is 20%, and 1% of capital in the multinational sector is subject to residual taxation. The low shifting cost is chosen so 50% of capital income is shifted internationally in the base case. The high shifting cost is chosen so 5% of capital income is shifted internationally in the base case.

less costly to the government and puts upward pressure on the optimal capital income tax rate.

These three effects are illustrated in Figures 12.7a–c. Figure 12.7a shows the capital tax base, relative to the base case, as a function of the capital income tax rate for different levels of international income shifting costs. It demonstrates that lower shifting costs, which lead to more capital income shifting, result in a smaller capital income tax base and thus revenue losses for the domestic government, putting downward pressure on the optimal capital income tax rate.

Figure 12.7b shows the *LSK* share of the capital income tax base as a function of the capital income tax rate for different levels of international income shifting costs. It demonstrates that lower shifting costs, which lead to more capital income shifting, result in a larger relative share of the capital tax base for *LSK*, making capital income taxation more attractive and thus putting upward pressure on the optimal capital income tax rate.

Finally, Figure 12.7c shows MNC investment, relative to the base case, as a function of the capital income tax rate for different levels of international income shifting costs. It demonstrates that lower shifting costs, which lead to more capital income shifting, result in slightly more investment at each value of the capital tax rate, as the potential for income shifting dampens the effect of capital income taxation on MNC investment. Figure 12.6 indicates that the last two factors are not large enough to offset the first factor described above, so that the optimal capital income tax rate declines, but only slightly, as the amount of international income shifting increases.

5. Conclusion

In this paper, we analyze the optimal taxation of capital income for a small open economy that is attempting to balance the wide variety of factors that bear on the decision to impose a source-based tax on capital. On the one hand, the standard argument — the burden of a capital income tax imposed on internationally mobile capital will be borne entirely by local factors — suggests that the optimal capital income tax rate is zero. This argument is reinforced by concerns that mobile capital may include highly productive firm-specific capital owned by MNCs that earns above-normal returns, and that high capital income tax rates may induce international income shifting by MNCs that will reduce revenues, perhaps significantly. On the other hand, some capital income taxation is desirable even in a small open economy to tax above-normal returns earned by location-specific capital, especially to the extent that capital is owned by foreigners, to limit the shifting of labor income to the capital income tax base, and to take advantage of any "treasury transfer" effects that may be available. An additional complicating factor is that the opportunity to shift income internationally may mitigate the negative effects of higher capital income tax rates on FDI (since MNCs will know that the effects of a relatively high tax rate will be dampened via income shifting) and will increase the relative capital share of location-specific capital, increasing the relative desirability of more capital income taxation.

Our base analysis confirms the standard results: if all foreign-owned capital is perfectly mobile and there is no residual taxation, the optimal capital income tax rate is zero, while with full residual taxation, the optimal capital income tax rate never falls below the foreign residual tax rate as the government takes maximum advantage of the treasury transfer effects. But in the more relevant and more general cases, the optimal capital income tax rate falls between these two extremes, and is typically below the tax rate applied to labor income.

The simulation results of course depend on the model specification and parameter values used. Subject to that caveat, the simulations provide several noteworthy results. First, although the opportunity to tax immobile location-specific rents accruing to domestic residents does not provide a significant rationale for capital income taxation in our benchmark case, the optimal capital income tax rate increases approximately linearly as the fraction of location-specific rents that accrue to foreigners increases, in some cases exceeding the tax rate on labor income. Second, an operative treasury transfer effect provides a strong rationale for capital income taxation — an effect that currently is not likely to be very important, but may become much more relevant over time, especially as domestic capital income tax rates decline, if more countries enact strict anti-base-erosion provisions. Third, the potential for labor income shifting puts upward pressure on capital income tax rates to reduce the labor-capital income tax differential, and also tends to reduce the variation in capital income tax rates. Fourth, the availability of a separate tax on the income earned by location-specific capital significantly reduces optimal capital income tax rates; for example, in the resource sector, this could be a separate income tax on *LSK* earnings or a resource rent tax (or any cash flow-based tax) that would apply tax only to the rents earned in that sector. Fifth, the optimal capital income tax rate is only moderately sensitive to wide variations in the shares of location-specific and ordinary capital. Sixth, the amount of residual taxation is generally more influential in determining the optimal capital income tax rate than the residual tax rate. Seventh, several offsetting effects of international income shifting imply that the optimal capital tax rate is only marginally sensitive to the costs of international income shifting, declining slightly as such costs decrease and the amount of income shifting increases.

These simulations suggest that determining the optimal level of source-based capital income taxation is indeed a difficult problem.[22] For many countries, various factors are likely to make the standard argument for complete exemption of capital income from source-based taxation an incomplete guide to tax policy, as some taxation of capital income is desirable under most circumstances. The primary exception is when a separate tax can be applied to much or all of the income of location-specific capital (or such capital is an insignificant factor in production); in this case, optimal capital income tax rates are quite low, and administrative concerns suggest that maintaining capital income taxation only to tax capital income at a very low rate may not be desirable.

At the same time, the optimal level of capital income taxation in our simulations is typically significantly below the tax rate applied to labor income, especially as the share of labor income exempt from taxation decreases, suggesting that the standard comprehensive income tax approach is not likely to be desirable either. Instead, more flexible tax systems, such as the dual income tax systems observed in several Nordic countries and elsewhere, may be optimal as they can achieve a balance between capital and labor income taxation that is best suited to the circumstances of a particular country — assuming that income shifting from the relatively highly taxed labor income base to the relatively lowly taxed capital income tax base can be controlled.

---

[22]There are of course numerous other factors not considered in our model that would also impact this decision (see, for example, Auerbach (2008) and Zodrow (2007)); in particular, we consider only business level taxation and ignore equity concerns. One particularly interesting factor is the extent to which capital income taxation can serve as a proxy for welfare-enhancing age-specific taxation (Erosa and Gervais, 2002; Weinzierl, 2011).

We note that the prospect of residual taxation can potentially play an important role in determining the optimal capital income tax rate. This is currently a relatively unimportant issue, since the United States is the only major country with a residence-based system and tempers its effects by allowing deferral of tax until funds are repatriated to a US parent and allowing generous cross-crediting of foreign tax credits. Nevertheless, residual taxation may become a more important factor, especially at relatively low levels of domestic capital income taxation, if more countries introduce current residual taxes as part of anti-base-erosion measures.

We close by noting that our results are generated in a static setting, and thus ignore some interesting dynamics that might affect the optimal capital income tax rate and should be the subject of further research. For example, Coates (1993) highlights the importance of imperfect capital mobility in a repeated game, arguing that the relative immobility of capital that could be attracted to a region puts further downward pressure on the capital income tax rate. However, the overall impact of dynamic considerations on capital tax competition is not obvious. Cardarelli, Taugourdeau, and Vidal (2002) acknowledge the reality that competition for mobile capital is a repeated game and consider the potential impacts of cooperation in rate setting. By employing trigger strategies, countries may be able to increase capital taxes simultaneously, raising revenue without generating capital outflows — although the gains from cooperation are limited by asymmetry between countries.

Acknowledgments

We would like to thank Alan Auerbach, the participants at the 107th Annual Conference on Taxation of the National Tax Association, Santa Fe, NM, November, 2014, and two anonymous referees for helpful comments.

References

Altig, D., Auerbach, A. J., Kotlikoff, L. J., Smetters, K. A., & Walliser, J. (2001). Simulating fundamental tax reform in the United States. *The American Economic Review*, 91(3), 574–595.

Altshuler, R., & Grubert, H. (2006). Governments and multinational corporations in the race to the bottom. *Tax Notes*, 110(February 6), 459–474.

Auerbach, A. J. (2006). The future of capital income taxation. *Fiscal Studies*, 27(4), 399–420.

Auerbach, A. J. (2008). Tax reform in the 21st century. In J. W. Diamond and G. R. Zodrow (Eds.), *Fundamental Tax Reform: Issues, Choices, and Implications* (pp. 27–74). Cambridge: MIT Press.

Becker, J., & Fuest, C. (2011). Optimal tax policy when firms are internationally mobile. *International Tax and Public Finance*, 18(5), 580–604.

Bettendorf, L., Devereux, M. P., van der Horst, A., Loretz, S., & de Mooij, R. (2009). Corporate tax harmonization in the EU. CPB Discussion Paper 133. The Hague: CPB Netherlands Bureau for Economic Policy Analysis.

Cardarelli, R., Taugourdeau, E., & Vidal, J. P. (2002). A repeated interactions model of tax competition. *Journal of Public Economic Theory*, 4(1), 19–38.

Chirinko, R. S. (2002). Corporate taxation, capital formation, and the substitution elasticity between labor and capital. *National Tax Journal*, 55(2), 339–355.

Clausing, K. A. (2011). The revenue effects of multinational firm income shifting. *Tax Notes*, 130(March 28), 1580–1586.

Clausing, K. A. (2016). The effect of profit shifting on the corporate tax base in the United States and beyond. Manuscript. Reed College, Portland, OR.

Coates, D. (1993). Property tax competition in a repeated game. *Regional Science and Urban Economics*, 23(1), 111–119.

Cronin, J. A., Yin, E. Y., Power, L., & Cooper, M. (2013). Distributing the corporate income tax: Revised U.S. treasury methodology. *National Tax Journal*, 66(1), 239–262.

de Mooij, R. A., & Devereux, M. P. (2011). An applied analysis of ACE and CBIT reforms in the EU. *International Tax and Public Finance*, 18(1), 93–120.

de Mooij, R. A., & Nicodème, G. (2006). Corporate tax policy, entrepreneurship and incorporation in the EU. Economic Papers No 269. Brussels: European Commission Directorate-General for Economic and Financial Affairs.

Deloitte (2014). Guide to controlled foreign company regimes. http://www2.deloitte.com/content/dam/Deloitte/global/Documents/Tax/dttl-tax-guide-to-cfc-regimes-210214.pdf.

Devereux, M. P., Fuest, C., & Lockwood, B. (2014). The taxation of foreign profits: A unified view. Manuscript. Centre for Business Taxation, Oxford University, Oxford, UK.

Devereux, M. P., & Loretz, S. (2013). What do we know about corporate tax competition? *National Tax Journal*, 66(3), 745–773.

Dowd, T., Landefeld, P., & Moore, A. (2016). Income shifting of U.S. multinationals. Manuscript, Joint Committee on Taxation.

Dunning, J. H. (1981). *International Production and the Multinational Enterprise.* London: Allen and Unwin.

Dyreng, S. D., & Markle, K. S. (2015). The effects of financial constraints on tax-motivated income shifting by U.S. multinationals. Manuscript. Duke University, Durham, NC.

Economic Commission for Latin America and the Caribbean (2012). *Foreign direct investment in Latin America and the Caribbean.* New York: United Nations Economic Commission for Latin America and the Caribbean.

Erosa, A., & Gervais, M. (2002). Optimal taxation in life-cycle economies. *Journal of Economic Theory,* 105(2), 338–369.

Fehr, H., Jokish, S., Kambhampati, A., & Kotlikoff, L. J. (2013). Simulating the elimination of the U.S. corporate income tax. NBER Working Paper 19757, Cambridge, MA.

Gallagher, D. R., Ignatieva, K., & McCulloch, J. (2015). Industry concentration, excess returns, and innovation in Australia. *Accounting & Finance,* 55(2), 443–466.

Gordon, R. H. (1986). Taxation of investment and savings in a world economy. *American Economic Review*, 76(5), 1086–1102.

Gordon, R. H., & Hine Jr., J. R. (2002). International taxation. In A. J. Auerbach & M. Feldstein (Eds.), *Handbook of Public Economics, Volume 4* (pp. 1935–1995). Amsterdam: North Holland/Elsevier.

Gordon, R. H., & Mackie-Mason, J. (1995). Why is there corporate taxation in a small open economy? The role of transfer pricing and income shifting. In M. Feldstein, J. R. Hines Jr., & R. G. Hubbard (Eds.), *The effects of taxation on multinational corporations* (pp. 67–91). Chicago: University of Chicago Press.

Gordon, R. H., & Slemrod, J. (2000). Are 'real' responses to taxes simply income shifting between corporate and personal income tax bases? In J. Slemrod (Ed.), *Does Atlas shrug? The Economic Consequences of Taxing the Rich* (pp. 240–280). New York: Russell Sage Foundation and Harvard University Press.

Gravelle, J. G., & Smetters, K. (2006). Does the open economy assumption really mean that labor bears the burden of a capital income tax? *The B.E. Journal of Economic Analysis & Policy*, 6(1), 1–44.

Greenhalgh, C., & Rogers, M. (2006). The value of innovation: The interaction of competition, R&D, and IP. *Research Policy*, 35(4), 562–580.

Grubert, H., & Altshuler, R. (2013). Fixing the system: An analysis of alternative proposals for the reform of international tax. *National Tax Journal*, 66(3), 671–712.

Gugl, E., & Zodrow, G. R. (2006). International tax competition and tax incentives for developing countries. In J. Alm, J. Martinez-Vazquez, & M. Rider (Eds.), *The Challenges of Tax Reform in a Global Economy* (pp. 167–192). New York: Springer.

Harberger, A. C. (1995). The ABCs of corporate tax incidence: Insights into the open-economy case. In *Tax Policy and Economic Growth*. Washington: ACCF Center for Policy Research.

Harberger, A. C. (2008). Corporate tax incidence: Reflections on what is known, unknown, and unknowable. In J. W. Diamond, & G. R. Zodrow (Eds.), *Fundamental tax reform: Issues, choices, and implications* (pp. 283–307). Cambridge: MIT Press.

Hartman, D. G. (1985). Tax policy and foreign direct investment. *Journal of Public Economics*, 26(1), 107–121.

Haufler, A., & Schjelderup, G. (2000). Corporate tax systems and cross country profit shifting. *Oxford Economic Papers*, 52(2), 306–325.

Heckemeyer, J. H., & Overesch, M. (2013). Multinationals' profit response to tax differentials: Effect size and shifting channels. Manuscript. University of Cologne, Cologne, Germany.

HM Revenue and Customs (HMRC) (2014). Tax gap estimates for 2012–23. *Measuring Tax Gaps 2014 Edition*. London, UK.

Hong, Q., & Smart, M. (2010). In praise of tax havens: International tax planning and foreign direct investment. *European Economic Review*, 54(1), 82–95.

Hou, K., & Robinson, D. T. (2006). Industry concentration and average stock returns. *The Journal of Finance*, 61(4), 1927–1956.

Huizinga, H., & Nicodème, G. (2006). Foreign ownership and corporate income taxation: An empirical evaluation. *European Economic Review*, 50(5), 1223–1244.

Huizinga, H., & Nielsen, S. B. (1997). Capital income and profit taxation with foreign ownership of firms. *Journal of International Economics*, 42(1), 149–165.

International Monetary Fund (2012). Fiscal regimes for extractive industries: Design and implementation. https://www.imf.org/external/np/pp/eng/2012/081512.pdf.

Jacobs, B. (2009). Is Prescott right? Welfare state policies and the incentives to work, learn, and retire. *International Tax and Public Finance,* 16(2), 253–280.

Karabarbounis, L., & Neiman, B. (2014). The global decline of the labor share. *Quarterly Journal of Economics*, 129(1), 61–103.

McClelland, R., & Mok, S. (2012). A review of recent research on labor supply elasticities. Working Paper 2012–12. Washington: Congressional Budget Office.

Mintz, J. M. (1995). The corporation tax: A survey. *Fiscal Studies*, 16(4), 23–68.
Nicodème, G. (2008). Corporate income tax and economic distortions. CESifo Working Paper No. 2477. CESifo, Munich, Germany.
Organisation for Economic Co-operation and Development (2012). OECD. Stat, (database). SDBS Business Demography Indicators. Accessed Sep 10, 2015.
Organisation for Economic Co-operation and Development (2013). *Addressing Base Erosion and Profit Shifting*. Paris: OECD.
PricewaterhouseCoopers (2011). Global effective tax rates. http://businessroundtable.org/sites/default/files/Effective_Tax_Rate_Study.pdf.
Razin, A., & Sadka, E. (1991). International tax competition and gains from tax harmonization. *Economics Letters*, 37(1), 69–76.
Riedel, N. (2014). Quantifying international tax avoidance: A review of the academic literature. ETPF Policy Paper 2.
Seale Jr., J. L., & Regmi, A. (2006). Modeling international consumption patterns. *Review of Income and Wealth*, 52, 603–624.
Senhadji, A. (1998). Time-series estimation of structural import demand equations: A cross-country analysis. *IMF Staff Papers*, 45(2), 236–268.
Sercu, P., & Vanpée, R. (2007). Home bias in international equity portfolios: A review. Working paper AFI 0710. Department of Accountancy, Finance, and Insurance, Katholieke Universiteit, Leuven, Belgium.
Sinn, H. (1987). *Capital Income Taxation and Resource Allocation*. Amsterdam: North Holland.
Slemrod, J. (1997). The taxation of foreign direct investment: Operational and policy perspectives. In J. M. Poterba (Ed.), *Borderline Case: International Tax Policy, Corporate Research and Development, and Investment* (pp. 11–38). Washington: National Academy Press.
Slemrod, J., & Wilson, J. D. (2009). Tax competition with parasitic tax havens. *Journal of Public Economics*, 93(11–12), 1261–1270.
Weinzierl, M. (2011). The surprising power of age-dependent taxes. *Review of Economic Studies*, 78(4), 1490–1518.
Wilson, J. D. (1986). A theory of interregional tax competition. *Journal of Urban Economics*, 19(3), 296–315.
Zodrow, G. R. (2007). Should capital income be subject to consumption-based taxation? In H. J. Aaron, L. Burman, & E. C. Steuerle (Eds.), *Taxing Capital Income* (pp. 49–81). Washington: Urban Institute Press.
Zodrow, G. R. (2010a). Capital mobility and capital tax competition. *National Tax Journal*, 63(4), 865–902.

Zodrow, G. R. (2010b). International taxation and company tax policy in small open economies. In I. Claus, N. Gemmell, M. Harding, & D. White (Eds.), *Tax Reform in Open Economies: International and Country Perspectives* (pp. 109–134). Cheltenham: Edward Elgar.

Zodrow, G. R. & Mieszkowski, P. (1983). The incidence of the property tax: The benefit view vs. the new view. In G. R. Zodrow (Ed.), *Local Provision of Public Services: The Tiebout Model After Twenty-Five Years* (pp. 109–129). New York: Academic Press.

Zodrow, G. R. & Mieszkowski, P. (1986). Pigou, Tiebout, property taxation, and the under-provision of local public goods. *Journal of Urban Economics,* 19(3), 356–370.

Part IV
State and Local Tax Policy

Chapter 13

Revenue Options for the State of Texas*

George R. Zodrow

Economics Department and Baker Institute for Public Policy
Rice University, Houston, TX, 77025, USA

1. Overview of Project

The State of Texas is contemplating sweeping changes in its revenue structure. This review is prompted to some extent by current revenue shortfalls. However, the primary impetus is clearly that the Texas Legislature is considering a variety of plans that would reform the system of K-12 school finance in the state; as discussed in Zodrow (2004), the

*This chapter is reproduced from *State Tax Notes*, **34** (12), 799–821, 2004.

In 2004, I prepared a report entitled "An Economic Evaluation of Alternative Sources of Tax Revenue for the State of Texas" for the Texas Joint Select Committee on Public School Finance. This chapter contains excerpts from a condensed version of that report that appeared in the December 20, 2004 issue of State Tax Notes, Vol. 34, No. 12, pp. 799–821. Deletions from the original text, other than minor wording changes, deleted footnotes, and deleted references, are denoted with [...] and phrases added for clarity are enclosed in brackets.

main goal is a reduction in local school property taxes coupled with increased state level funding for education.

[...]

[Following an approach commonly used by public finance specialists, I will use the criteria of efficiency, equity and simplicity to evaluate] alternative sources of state tax revenue in Texas. The analysis will first define some general directions for Texas tax policy and reform of the current system, and then evaluate a wide variety of specific tax reform options.

2. General Directions for Reform

2.1. *Expand benefit taxes*

A clear implication of [my analysis of alternative sources of state tax revenue] is that benefit and environmental taxes should be used to the maximum extent feasible. This is particularly true for benefit taxes for public services provided to businesses, especially to the extent that the state follows the recommendation, made below, to reduce non-benefit taxation of businesses.

The most obvious form of benefit taxation is user charges. Some empirical data suggest that Texas is fairly average in the extent to which it relies on user charges. Nevertheless, these data suggest some potential for increasing the extent to which the state relies on user charges. Specifically, in 1999 the ratio of a broad definition of user charges to total state and local own-source revenue in Texas was 0.297, with the state ranking 18th out of the 50 states in this category. By comparison, the state with the highest ratio is Tennessee (0.471).[1] Thus, if Texas were to raise its utilization rate to that of Tennessee, total state and local user charges would rise by roughly 59 percent; in 1999 this would have implied an increase in total state and local user charge revenue of $13.9 billion, from $23.5 billion to $37.4 billion. Although this calculation is obviously a very rough one that ignores a variety of factors, including especially differences across states in

[1] See U.S. Census Bureau, Government Finances. Table No 420, State and Local Governments: Revenues by State 1999 at http://www.census.gov/prod/2003pubs/02statab/stlocgov.pdf. This calculation follows Netzer (1992, 504).

expenditure mix, it does suggest that it would be worthwhile to investigate the extent to which reliance on user charges by the state government — as well as by local governments, which provide many of the services most amenable to the implementation of user charges — could increase.

Finally, note also that businesses receive some benefits from the provision of quality K-12 education. For example, businesses can more easily attract high-quality workers if the local education system is of high quality, and may receive other benefits from an educated local population, beyond those that are fully reflected in business costs as higher wages. However, these benefits to business would seem to be small relative to the benefits enjoyed by the direct consumers of education (Taylor 1999). Thus, the benefit principle provides only limited support for the taxation of business property to finance education expenditures, so that most school taxes applied to businesses should be viewed as non-benefit taxes applied to capital.[2]

2.2. *Limit progressivity and minimize tax burdens on the very poor*

The appropriate degree of progressivity of a tax system is always a controversial issue. This is especially true at the national level, although reforms in recent years in the U.S. and around the world suggest that social tastes for highly progressive marginal rate structures have diminished in recent years. In any case, the question of the optimal progressivity of the tax system is somewhat easier to resolve at the state level for two reasons.

First, progressive marginal tax rates at the federal level imply that significant redistribution through the tax system occurs independently of state tax policy, thus reducing any need for redistribution at the state level. [...]

[2] In addition, environmental fees provide another source of revenue that could be utilized to an increasing extent in Texas, although state governments in the U.S. typically do not rely on environmental taxes and fees to any large extent. Cordes (1992) reports that in 1989 Texas raised $10.6 million from this source, ranking 13th among the states in total revenues raised from environmental taxes and fees. See also Rabe (2003).

Second, concerns about individual mobility suggest that a highly progressive state tax structure is likely to be counterproductive, as it would tend to drive high-income individuals out of the state and perhaps attract low-income individuals. Indeed, Feldstein and Wrobel (1998) suggest that the mobility of high-income individuals is sufficiently great that changes in gross wages will completely offset any changes in state income taxes within the space of a few years, so that states have virtually no power to redistribute income. That is, Feldstein and Wrobel argue that attempts to redistribute income at the state level will lead to an inefficient out-migration of skilled labor, increasing the wages of scarcer high-skilled labor while lowering the wages of relatively plentiful low-skilled labor. The net result is that the tax burden is ultimately borne by relatively immobile low-skilled labor (or owners of land).[3] This result, which implies perfect mobility of high-skilled labor over a rather short period of time, is quite strong and has been questioned by Reschovsky (1998a) who reviews the literature and concludes that it suggests that the mobility of high-skilled labor is not sufficiently great to imply that any progressivity of a state tax structure is counterproductive. Nevertheless, the possibility that a highly progressive state tax would drive out high-skilled workers to at least some extent, coupled with the historical reluctance of Texans to utilize any form of progressive personal income tax, suggests that the state should limit consideration of alternative revenue sources to roughly proportional taxes.

There is, however, one important qualification to this suggestion. Specifically, the cost of a state income tax, taking into account federal deductibility, is lower for individuals who itemize deductions, with size of the benefit proportional to the individual's federal marginal tax rate. Both marginal tax rates and the likelihood that a taxpayer itemizes deductions

[3] Note that this argument is largely independent of the fact that most other states in the union currently have an income tax. The argument assumes that the combination of state income taxes in most other states, coupled with no income taxes in Texas and a few other states, has resulted in an equilibrium in which households are relatively indifferent among states, given their existing tax systems. If Texas were to implement a reform such as a progressive income tax that resulted in a higher net tax burden on relatively high-income individuals, the analysis of Feldstein and Wrobel (1998) implies that such individuals would move to other states until after-tax incomes were such that a new equilibrium, with individuals again relatively indifferent among alternative locations, was attained.

increase with income. Thus, a modest degree of nominal state income tax progression would be required for the actual burden of a state income tax in Texas, after federal taxes, to be proportional on average. Accordingly, consideration of potential reforms in this paper will be restricted to taxes that are "roughly" proportional, perhaps taking into account federal income tax deductibility.

Finally, longstanding practice in Texas — particularly the exemption from sales tax of commodities considered to be consumed disproportionately by the poor — suggests a desire to minimize the burden of the state tax system on very low-income individuals. That is, there seems to be little societal or political inclination to ensure that all Texans, even those at the very bottom of the income distribution, contribute to the financing of public services in proportion to their income or consumption levels. Accordingly, the analysis in the rest of the paper will assume that equity concerns imply that the state tax burden on very low-income individuals should be minimal or even zero.

2.3. *Reduce non-benefit taxation of mobile capital*

Although the case for benefit taxation of businesses is compelling, a straightforward application of the criteria presented above suggests that the rationale for additional source-based (i.e., production-based) state-level business taxes in Texas is surprisingly weak. The argument, which is based on the idea that any state can be modeled to a first approximation as a small open economy (Gordon, 1986; Razin and Sadka, 1991; Oakland, 1992), proceeds as follows.

As noted previously, any state — even one as large as Texas — is not large enough in the national or world economy to appreciably affect the rate of return to capital. Instead, since capital is in the long run highly mobile, the return to capital is determined in national and increasingly international markets. This implies that, to the extent that capital is perfectly mobile, the owners of capital invested in the state will bear none of the burden of a state-level tax on capital income. Instead, capital will leave the state until the before-tax rate of return to capital invested in the state rises by enough to entirely offset the tax. This emigration of capital lowers the productivity of the fixed factors in the state: land and labor (or at least relatively immobile labor, if relatively high-income labor is also quite mobile, as discussed above). As a result, these local factors of production ultimately bear not only the entire burden of the capital income tax but also its "excess burden" or efficiency costs. The implication of this analysis is that, solely from the viewpoint of Texas residents, it is preferable simply to tax local factors (land and relatively immobile labor) or local consumers directly, and thus avoid at least the excess burden of the tax on capital income. Note also that the analysis implies that any progressivity suggested by state level taxation of capital income is illusory, as such taxes are shifted to local factors of production and are thus borne roughly in proportion to wage income or consumption of non traded goods.

Not surprisingly, there are a variety of counterarguments to this rather stark proposition. A business income tax can serve an important function as a backstop to a state personal income tax (so that personal income retained at the business level does not escape taxation), but this argument is irrelevant in the absence of a personal income tax in Texas. More important, some businesses may have market power in national or international markets or earn above-normal economic profits (economic rents) for other reasons, which can, especially if the rents are tied to location in the state, be taxed without causing inefficient capital out-migration. Virtually all states — and indeed all countries in the international context — tax corporate income in order to capture some of these rents (Zodrow, 2003a). Note, however, that the desire to tax economic rents does not necessarily imply that a state should utilize a corporate income tax (although it is by far the most common tax instrument used to achieve this goal). In particular, economic rents are also captured by the various forms of value-added taxes (VATs), as discussed below; indeed, one of the major advantages of the consumption-based versions of these VATs is that they are relatively non-distortionary since they do not tax the normal returns to capital while taxing economic rents at the full statutory rate (Zodrow and McLure, 1991).

A separate issue is that capital may not be as responsive to tax factors as suggested by the analysis presented above. Although early empirical studies were consistent with this viewpoint, the most recent (and most carefully done) work suggests that investment is in fact relatively responsive to state and local taxes (Bartik, 1991, 1994; Wasylenko, 1997). Finally, but perhaps most important, some level of non-benefit business taxation may be indispensable politically.

These qualifications — and political realities in Texas — suggest that elimination of all non-benefit taxation of businesses is unlikely. Nevertheless, the current level of taxation of business (described above) is almost assuredly in excess of the benefits of public services received, so the balance of the report will assume that some reductions in state business taxes would be appropriate. Support for this position is provided by Taylor (2003a), who argues that Texas businesses pay considerably more in business taxes than they receive in public services, even taking into account business benefits from education, and that the relatively high tax burden imposed on business capital in Texas has played an important role in limiting the growth of the capital stock in the state.

2.4. *Avoid taxation based on gross receipts*

The final general direction for reform of the Texas tax system is that the state should avoid the introduction of any new taxes on gross receipts — including proposals for so-called "license fees" that are based on gross receipts — and reduce reliance on taxes with economic effects that are similar to those of gross receipts taxes.

On efficiency grounds, gross receipts taxes are problematic because they are primarily taxes on business inputs and such taxes are in general a relatively inefficient source of revenue.[4] Moreover, gross receipts taxes are a particularly undesirable form of taxation of business inputs, because they result in highly inefficient tax pyramiding, as multiple layers of taxation are applied to those products whose inputs happen to be transferred among firms at various stages in the production process. Under these circumstances, even a modest tax on gross receipts can compound into a high effective tax rate. The result is a haphazard pattern of effective tax rates across business inputs, which inefficiently distorts firm decisions regarding

[4] Indeed, one of the basic tenets of the branch of public finance known as optimal taxation theory is the "production efficiency theorem" which states that — under the appropriate circumstances — taxes on business inputs should be avoided entirely. For qualifications to this result, see Slemrod (1990).

input choices. The resulting increases in the effective tax rate on capital income also drive capital out of the state (as stressed above) and hamper the export prospects of Texas businesses that must compete with firms in states that have tax systems that impose lower tax burdens on business inputs. In addition, the tax pyramiding attributable to gross receipts taxes creates a tax bias toward vertical integration (organizing the production process so that multiple steps are carried out within a single firm), as firms attempt to reduce their exposure to the gross receipts tax. This reduces the efficiency of resource use in the state, especially if there are economies of scale in producing some of the inputs to the production process. Note also that a bias toward vertical integration implies a bias against small firms, especially those that might be able to provide low-cost services to larger firms but would operate at a cost disadvantage (relative to in-house production) due solely to the tax. Moreover, to the extent that tax pyramiding is shifted forward as higher consumer prices (e.g., for locally produced and consumed goods), it results in a haphazard pattern of consumer price distortions that inefficiently distort consumer decisions. Finally, it must be emphasized that the sales tax and the franchise tax in Texas have significant gross receipts components. Thus, a new gross receipts tax would exacerbate existing distortions, so that its efficiency cost would be relatively high.

Gross receipts taxes are generally undesirable in terms of other tax criteria as well. To the extent they are shifted forward as higher prices, gross receipts taxes are inequitable since they penalize those individuals who prefer to consume highly taxed goods. Since they impinge to a large extent on business inputs, the revenues of gross receipts taxes tend to be fairly cyclical (although they do tend to grow proportionately with the economy). A gross receipts tax is also a "hidden" tax, especially since the portion that is applied to business inputs is relatively high, and thus likely to promote inefficiency in political decision-making. The primary advantage of a gross receipts tax is that it is relatively simple, in terms of both compliance and administration. This simplicity is the main reason that gross receipts taxes are popular in the developing world. However, in developed countries in which most businesses have well-functioning accounting systems (and indeed must have such systems to comply with the federal income tax), this advantage is minimal and far outweighed by the costs described above. Finally, it should be noted that the relatively low nominal tax rate that obtains under a typical gross receipts tax is not an advantage. Once tax pyramiding is taken into account, the effective tax rate that occurs under even a low-rate gross receipts tax can be quite high. Moreover, a low nominal rate can be used to create the artificial perception of low-cost public services and thus create a bias toward undesirable over-expansion of the public sector. Thus, on balance, a tax on gross receipts is an unusually poor tax instrument, and Texas should avoid the introduction of new gross receipts taxes and reduce reliance on existing taxes with the characteristics of gross receipts taxes.

3. An Evaluation of Specific Tax Reform Proposals

A wide variety of specific tax reforms are evaluated in this section in terms of the tax criteria detailed above and in light of the general directions for reform specified in the previous section. The analysis begins by discussing some modest reforms of the existing system, turns next to a number of more sweeping reforms of the existing system, and concludes by examining several new forms of taxation.

3.1. *Broadening the sales tax base*

As the largest single source of state tax revenue, the general sales tax is an obvious source of additional state tax revenue. The State Comptroller estimates that an increase in the state sales tax rate of one percentage point (to 7.25 percent) on the existing base would increase annual revenues by $1.9 billion. However, such a rate increase would result in Texas having the highest sales tax rate in the nation. The evaluation of such an approach depends critically on the nature of the base broadening being envisioned, specifically on whether the goods and services that are newly included in the base are consumed by individual consumers or businesses.[5]

[5]The following discussion draws on Hendrix and Zodrow (2003); see also Fox and Murray (1988), Quick and McKee (1988), Fox (1992), and Mazerov (2003).

3.1.1. *Consumer goods and services*

In general, expanding the base of the Texas sales tax to include a wider variety of consumption goods, especially consumer services, would be desirable. The primary caveats are that base expansion should be avoided for goods or services for which administrative costs are prohibitively high (very small service providers) or for goods that are deemed to be social "merit goods" that should be exempt from tax, such as education, health care, and certain other government services. As described above, Texas is somewhat above average in the extent to which it taxes consumer services, but considerably below those states that most comprehensively tax consumer services. Thus, a wide variety of consumer services could potentially be taxed.

Estimates of the revenue gains from taxing services suggest they would be significant, although it is difficult in some cases to separate the revenues attributable to taxing consumer services from those due to taxing business services. [...] As has been observed in other states, the vast majority of currently untaxed services are either business services that should not be taxed under a consumption-based tax or services that are unlikely to be taxed for social reasons (Hendrix and Zodrow, 2003).

The case for expanding the base of the sales tax to include as many consumer goods as possible can be made on many fronts. On efficiency grounds, many — although by no means all — economists argue that taxation on the basis of consumption is inherently preferable to taxation on the basis of income. The basic arguments are that consumption taxes do not discourage individual saving, do not create tax disincentives to investment, and avoid many of the complexities associated with measuring real income accurately. By comparison, income taxes increase the price of future consumption and thus create a disincentive for saving and distort both the level and (typically) the allocation of investment, and attempts to measure income accurately, especially in the presence of inflation, account for much of the complexity of the current federal income tax.[6] Although

[6] For reviews of the advantages and disadvantages of consumption and income taxes, see Bradford (1986) and Zodrow and McLure (1991); for a recent collection of articles on this issue, see Zodrow and Mieszkowski (2002).

these arguments are most important at the national level, state taxes based on consumption avoid exacerbating the problems associated with the federal income tax. However, the advantages of using a consumption-based tax system at the state level can be obtained only if Texas is in fact administering a tax that has a broad-based measure of consumption as its base. In addition, uniform or neutral (rather than differentiated) taxation of all consumption expenditures is likely to be relatively efficient.[7] Note also that a uniform tax on consumption goods is a relatively "visible" tax (especially relative to a tax on businesses) and thus, as discussed above, tends to promote efficiency in political decision-making. Accordingly, the analysis will assume that a "neutral" tax system that taxes all consumer goods uniformly is desirable on efficiency grounds to reduce distortions of consumer decisions, and that a movement toward greater neutrality by expanding the sales tax base to include more consumer goods, including currently untaxed consumer services, will generally improve economic efficiency (Hatta, 1986). In the especially relevant case of the treatment of consumer services, some empirical support for this proposition is provided in a recent work by Merriman and Skidmore (2000), who conclude that perhaps one-eighth of the recent increase in the relative size of the service sector is attributable to sales tax differentials favoring that sector.

On horizontal equity grounds, taxing a broader base of consumer goods is also desirable because it avoids discriminating against individuals whose tastes favor taxed goods. In terms of vertical equity, expanding the tax base may reduce the regressivity of the sales tax (with respect to annual income) if the newly taxed goods tend to be disproportionately consumed by the rich. This could be the case with many consumer services, although empirical evidence on this point suggests that this effect will be small

[7]The optimal taxation literature shows that uniform taxation, which would not distort consumer decisions across consumption commodities, is desirable under certain conditions, especially if distributional concerns are addressed with the (federal) income tax. More generally, a differentiated commodity tax structure is desirable, as goods that are relatively inelastically demanded or consumed disproportionately by the rich should face relatively high tax rates. However, since these factors tend to offset one another, a uniform tax may not be far from optimal. This is especially true once one takes into account the difficulties of administering differential rates, and the likelihood that any sales tax rate differentials will be determined by political factors rather than efficiency considerations.

(Siegfried and Smith, 1991; Due and Mikesell, 1994). A more difficult issue is whether expanding the sales tax base to include items that are exempt for distributional reasons (for example, food consumed at home, prescription medicines) is desirable on vertical equity grounds. The critical point in thinking about this issue is that sales tax exemption of goods consumed disproportionately by the poor is an extremely poorly targeted means of achieving distributional goals, since the benefit of exemption accrues not only to the poor, but to the rich as well. Indeed, in absolute terms, the rich will typically benefit more from the sales tax exemption of virtually any good, even if the proportional benefit of exemption declines with income. As a result, achieving distributional goals with sales tax exemptions is very expensive in terms of revenues forgone, and thus implies significantly higher tax rates.

A preferable approach is to eliminate or significantly curtail these sales tax exemptions and couple such a reform with a means-tested sales tax rebate that would approximately offset sales tax paid up to the amount paid on some minimum level of consumption (for example, the poverty level). This approach would minimize the revenue loss (and thus the rate increases) required to achieve any particular distributional goal. Some states administer such rebates under their personal income taxes (Johnson and Lav, 1998). However, in the absence of a state personal income tax in Texas, the rebate could be administered as a stand-alone program, using information provided by (and perhaps administered in conjunction with) other state and federal programs affecting the poor, especially the Lone Star Card (used for food stamps and welfare payments), or perhaps the federal Earned Income Tax Credit, and the Social Security system. This approach obviously involves some increased administrative and compliance costs, especially with respect to identifying individuals eligible for the rebate and ensuring that they file for them, delivering the rebates, and limiting fraudulent claims (Johnson and Lav, 1998). Nevertheless, it seems likely that it would be a less expensive means of achieving distributional goals than exempting certain commodities under the sales tax. Such an approach would be especially beneficial to the poor, with the burden of the sales tax increase roughly proportional to lifetime income or regressive with respect to annual income for all other income groups.

In terms of simplicity, taxing a broader consumption base implies that some new goods, including previously untaxed services, would be brought into the tax base, which would increase administrative costs; exempting small service providers would mitigate this problem. In addition, if consumer services are taxed while business services are exempt, the owners of businesses will face an incentive to disguise the purchase of personal services as business expenditures, including tied arrangements with service providers where high-priced tax exempt business services are bundled with low-priced or free personal services. On the other hand, uniform taxation of consumption goods reduces the costs associated with differentiating between taxable and tax exempt goods, and thus lowers administrative costs.

Taxing a broad measure of consumption generally increases tax stability since demand for both consumer services as well as consumption necessities is relatively non-cyclical, especially relative to the demand for consumer durables. Stability with respect to economic growth improves because a broader sales tax base, especially one that includes more consumer services, will tend to grow proportionately with the economy (Dye and McGuire, 1992).

3.1.2. *Business goods and services*

Expanding the base of the sales tax could also include taxing additional business inputs, especially services provided to businesses. Unfortunately, the case for such an expansion of the base of the sales tax is far weaker than the case for taxing consumer services. The essence of this argument is that expanding the sales tax base to include more business inputs exacerbates the glaring weaknesses of the current sales tax. It moves the system farther away from a tax on consumption, so that the benefits of consumption-based taxation are even less likely to be realized. But more important, it increases the extent to which the sales tax assumes the characteristics of a gross receipts tax, with all of the problems noted above.

From an equity perspective, taxing business inputs results in a haphazard pattern of incidence that creates horizontal inequities to the extent that tax burdens are shifted forward as higher consumer prices, since tax burdens will vary depending on tastes for various goods. Because of this fairly random incidence, the impact of taxing business inputs on vertical equity is uncertain, although one might expect that it would be roughly proportional to consumption.

In terms of revenue stability, adding additional business inputs to the tax base, including business services, is likely to reduce stability over the business cycle, since business spending is more cyclical than consumer spending; this is especially true for certain business services, like advertising, that are highly pro-cyclical (Quick and McKee, 1988). Taxing more business inputs, especially services, might increase the stability of revenues with respect to economic growth, but this effect would likely be relatively small; in particular, the ratio of total services to GDP has not increased nearly as much as the ratio of personal services to personal consumption, and indeed has been relatively stable in recent years (Hendrix and Zodrow, 2003).

Expanding the tax base to include certain business services would also raise several thorny administrative issues. As noted above, application of sales tax to small vendors in many service sectors is relatively expensive in comparison to the revenue raised. In addition, consistent application of the sales tax to services would require taxing services purchased from out-of-state vendors. This is likely to be even more difficult than in the troublesome case of tangible goods, as most out-of-state service providers will not have a physical presence (nexus) in Texas and will thus not be legally required to collect the tax. Although Texas firms would legally be required to pay use tax on such purchases, enforcing this requirement would be difficult. To the extent that the use tax is not effectively enforced, Texas firms would face a strong incentive to purchase services from out-of-state vendors. One offsetting factor, however, is that administrative and compliance costs would fall for vendors who already sell both taxable goods and previously untaxed services, as the need to separate taxable and non-taxable items would be eliminated.

3.2. *Increasing excise taxes*

An often-mentioned source of additional revenues is increases in the excise taxes applied to goods that are perceived to cause negative externalities (such as sin taxes and taxes on motor fuels). However, excise tax rates in most states, including Texas, are in all likelihood already higher than those that could be justified on negative externality grounds. Nevertheless, increases in excise taxes may be a relatively efficient source of revenue as demands for the affected goods are likely to be relatively inelastic, and cross-border smuggling should not be too much of a problem as long as the rates in Texas are not too high relative to those in other states (although this will become more of an issue with the growth of electronic commerce in the relevant goods). Moreover, some observers advocate increases in excise taxes on alcohol and tobacco on paternalistic grounds, as they create a tax disincentive that may discourage individuals, especially youths, from engaging in unhealthy behaviors. Similarly, proponents of increases in excise taxes on motor fuels argue that they would encourage conservation and reduce traffic congestion.

Increases in excise taxes are relatively regressive; this effect is mitigated but not eliminated if a lifetime view of tax incidence is used to measure tax burdens (Poterba, 1989; Lyon and Schwab, 1995). Increases in excise taxes are relatively easy to administer, given the existing tax collection structure, unless the increases result in rates that are so high relative to other states that monitoring smuggling becomes an expensive proposition. Given relatively price and income inelastic demands for the affected goods, excise tax revenues are relatively stable with respect to the business cycle, but tend to grow less than proportionately with the economy. [...]

3.3. *Reforming the franchise tax*

The "small open economy" analysis of source-based taxes on capital income presented above, as well as the many distortions caused by the earned surplus component of the franchise tax, suggest that serious consideration should be given to reducing or indeed eliminating the franchise tax in Texas, while simultaneously increasing reliance on appropriately designed benefit taxes on businesses or introducing an alternative business tax such as the value-added tax (discussed below). However, given current revenue constraints, the enactment of such a change may be difficult. An alternative approach is to improve the existing franchise tax, and this section will examine such potential improvements.

On efficiency grounds, the effects of the franchise tax depend on the nature of the business being taxed. For a sufficiently profitable business that operates largely or exclusively in Texas, the franchise tax, to a first approximation, acts as a surcharge on the federal corporate income tax. It thus exacerbates the many distortions of that tax, including distortions of decisions regarding capital-labor ratios, capital asset mix, financing and payout (Gravelle, 1994). Increases in distortions of the choice of organization form are more modest, since the franchise tax applies to S-corporations and limited liability companies, although not to partnerships, business associations, or sole proprietorships.

The situation is much different for large firms that operate in many states. For such businesses, formula apportionment implies that the franchise tax is primarily a tax on the factors in the apportionment formula (since any change in profits in Texas has a relatively minor effect on the corporation's total profits). Since Texas uses a single-factor formula with gross receipts as the apportionment factor, this implies the franchise tax is effectively a tax on gross receipts for such firms, and shares all the problems of gross receipts taxes stressed above. Thus, the franchise tax — whether applied to predominantly Texas firms or to multi-state enterprises that generate only a small fraction of their profits in the state — is among the state's most inefficient taxes.

Another interesting efficiency aspect of the franchise tax is the effect of its net assets component. As a tax on capital, this tax shares the problems of source-based taxation stressed above and, since it is based on net assets, it exacerbates the tax bias favoring debt finance under the federal corporate income tax. In addition, the net wealth-based component of the franchise tax acts as a minimum tax. As a result, it may create a bias against risk-taking, at least for firms with earnings such that they are near the boundary that defines whether they will be subject to the income or the net assets components of the tax. In this case, firms face the prospect that if their investments are successful and the firms are profitable they must pay the income-based component of the tax, while if their investments are unprofitable, they still must pay the wealth-based component. Such asymmetric tax treatment creates a potentially important disincentive for risk-taking. One might expect that these problems would be particularly troublesome for small firms, especially those that are entirely or primarily based in the state. Although this argument creates a case for eliminating the net wealth component of the franchise tax, some alternative arguments related to revenue stability and benefit taxation (presented below) suggest that such a reform would be premature.

From an equity perspective, the "small open economy" analysis presented above suggests that, at least in the long run, the incidence of source-based taxes on capital income is roughly similar to that of a tax on wages or consumption. Thus, the long run burden of changes in the franchise tax would be roughly proportional to lifetime income and regressive with respect to annual income. However, note that since the net wealth component of the franchise tax acts as a minimum tax, it could be justified on equity grounds as an efficiency-enhancing benefit tax. Specifically, to the extent that benefits are related to the size of the capital stock (although some measure of total in-state production would seem to be preferable on these grounds), a minimum tax ensures that firms pay some tax for the public services they consume, consumption that occurs regardless of whether or not the firm is profitable.[8]

From the standpoint of administrative simplicity, the earned surplus or income component of the franchise tax is relatively simple to calculate since it is based primarily on corporate income as defined for federal tax purposes. However, since the Texas franchise tax is based on the 1996 federal law, taxable businesses in Texas face additional complexity in that they must keep a separate set of books in order to comply with the state tax law. The inclusion in the franchise tax base of the compensation of the officers and directors of the business also adds considerable complexity, as the definition of a corporate officer is unclear, resulting in frequent classification disputes. Moreover, the existence of the net asset component of the tax creates potentially significant complexity, since in making long-run investment decisions firms must predict which of the two components of the franchise tax will apply at all future times.

In addition, the structure of the tax creates opportunities for tax avoidance. Most obviously, a corporation could reorganize as a partnership and avoid the franchise tax. Alternatively, state franchise tax liability can

[8] Note, however, that businesses are also subject to local property taxes, which can also be viewed as benefit taxes.

be virtually eliminated using the so-called "Delaware sub" strategy. Under this approach, a Texas corporation enters a partnership, typically as the general partner with a one percent ownership share, with a subsidiary organized another state (e.g., Delaware) that is a limited partner with a 99 percent ownership share. The partnership entity is of course not subject to the franchise tax, and under current law the limited partner subsidiary does not have nexus in the state. Thus, virtually none of the income of the partnership is subject to the franchise tax. The income of the out-of-state subsidiary is then distributed as dividends to the Texas parent, and is not subject to tax since dividends from subsidiaries are exempt under franchise tax provisions designed to avoid double taxation.

Although the treatment of such subsidiaries is largely a legal issue, two economic perspectives deserve mention, both of which, if applied to the Texas franchise tax, would significantly limit avoidance opportunities. First, from an efficiency perspective, if a state decides to impose a tax on businesses, that is not explicitly related to benefits received from public services, it should be applied to all businesses regardless of organizational form. In the case of Texas, this would imply extending the franchise tax to partnerships, business associations, and sole proprietorships. The only exception should be for small firms (currently defined in Texas as those with gross receipts under $150,000, although this exemption level seems far too generous) on simplicity grounds with respect to both administrative and compliance costs.[9] Second, the legal rules used to determine in-state tax liability should attempt to reflect economic reality, even if only in an approximate way. This implies that Texas should consider following the lead of many other states that impose business taxes and introduce some consolidation or combination provisions under which related entities are treated as a single entity for purposes of taxing that fraction of their combined income determined to be earned in the state.[10] Similarly,

[9] Such an approach is adopted by Michigan's Single Business Tax and New Hampshire's Business Enterprise Tax, which apply to all forms of business, subject to fairly generous exemption levels. In addition, Illinois levies its income tax on partnerships and West Virginia levies its assets-based franchise tax on partnerships.

[10] Note that such rules should also eliminate opportunities to abuse small business tax exemptions by splitting up a single entity into numerous smaller entities, each of which falls below the "small business" threshold.

Texas could follow many other states in defining nexus sufficiently broadly to include out-of-state entities that are limited partners in partnerships doing business in the state (again, subject to provisions that would exclude sufficiently small limited partners and perhaps certain passive investors).

[...]

Thus, if Texas decides to keep the franchise tax, the most important reform would be to enact some or all of the provisions described above in order to close existing loopholes. The State Comptroller's office estimates that such reforms would raise $0.24 billion.

3.4. *Expanding the lottery*

[...]

Although lotteries will never become a major source of revenue, expansion of the lottery is another potential revenue source at the margin.

[...]

3.5. *Fundamental reform of the sales tax*

Fundamental reform of the sales tax would proceed in three steps. The first would be to broaden the base to include as many currently exempt consumption items as politically and administratively feasible, including most consumer services and goods that are exempt for distributional reasons. Second, the adverse distributional consequences of taxing the latter items should be offset with a means-tested rebate that would effectively exempt a level of consumption approximately equal to that associated with the poverty level, along the lines described above. Finally, all business inputs should be exempt from tax.

Such an approach would convert the Texas sales tax into a true tax on retail sales, as long recommended by tax experts specializing in the sales tax (Due and Mikesell, 1994; McLure, 2000). It would achieve the efficiency, equity, simplicity, and revenue stability advantages associated with broadening the consumption tax base, exempting the poor from sales tax in a highly targeted and inexpensive (in terms of revenues foregone) manner, and avoiding the (often multiple) taxation of business inputs. Indeed, the latter feature suggests that such a reform package would be an effective and equitable pro-growth investment tool — more so than current ad hoc economic development efforts (Zodrow, 2003).

A critical issue in effecting such a reform would be devising a means of exempting business inputs from tax. Under the current system, businesses are issued an exemption certificate that allows them to make tax-free purchases. However, many goods are not eligible for exempt purchases, partly out of concern that such purchases would be diverted to personal consumption use. This approach has the unfortunate feature of relying on vendors to determine whether or not a sale should be tax exempt, a determination that vendors are ill-equipped to make. McLure (2000) suggests that businesses be allowed to purchase all business inputs on a tax-free basis, with business inputs defined as those that are deductible under the federal income tax and firms required to substantiate claims of business use of inputs upon audit.

Gillis, Mieszkowski, and Zodrow (1996) discuss an alternative approach that would be administratively more cumbersome but arguably less subject to abuse. Under this approach, businesses would have to pay sales tax on any purchases of "dual use" goods (those that are used as both business inputs and consumption items) and then apply for monthly or quarterly rebates of sales tax paid. This approach would involve additional administrative costs, as much revenue would be collected only to be refunded. Nevertheless, it might also be much less susceptible to evasion since businesses could evade tax only by fraudulently petitioning the tax authorities for a refund on purchases of personal consumption items (rather than merely misrepresenting their intentions to the vendor). As stressed by Mikesell (1997), businesses may be much more reluctant to explicitly misrepresent their purchases to the government than to an anonymous vendor at the point of sale. In addition, on policy grounds, Texas might elect to tax certain business expenditures that are allowed as (full or partial) deductions under the federal income tax, especially meals and entertainment expenses.

The net revenue impact of such a fundamental reform of the existing sales tax is unclear. Broadening the tax base to include more consumer goods, including consumer services as well as currently exempt consumption goods (net of any rebate program), would raise revenues, while eliminating the pervasive taxation of business inputs would reduce revenues.

3.6. *Introducing a personal state income tax*

Another potential source of revenue for the state of Texas is the introduction of a personal state income tax. This reform faces formidable obstacles, as a state personal income tax is anathema to many Texans and virtually all Texas politicians, who wish to maintain the image of Texas as a low tax state with no personal income tax. This sentiment is codified in the Texas Constitution, which precludes the introduction of a state income tax without a state referendum.

Nevertheless, a state personal income tax is sometimes suggested as a revenue option, especially as an alternative to greater reliance on an unreformed sales tax (McCown and Lavine, 2004). The discussion above suggests that a state personal income tax should be roughly proportional — perhaps adjusting for the fact that the benefits of deductibility are greater for high-income households — and, like the federal income tax, should exempt the poor from tax. Despite the vehement political opposition to any form of state income tax, such a reform, like all of the other approaches analyzed in this report, has both positive and negative aspects. These can be summarized as follows.

On efficiency grounds, a personal state income tax is a residence-based tax on Texas citizens. It thus avoids the problems of a production-based or source-based tax on capital income stressed above. Note that to the considerable extent the sales tax applies to purchases of business inputs, it shares the problems of a production-based tax. Thus, if a personal income tax were used to replace lost property revenues rather than an increase in the sales tax, the taxation of business inputs would decline, as would the many problems associated with such haphazard taxation of business inputs. Nevertheless, a state income tax would distort savings decisions, adding to the distortions attributable to the federal income tax, and — like any tax on wages, income, or consumption — distort decisions regarding labor supply. However, it would distort choices across consumption goods much less than the sales tax, which results in a haphazard pattern of effective consumption tax rates, due both to differential rates on consumption products (including zero rates in many cases) and pervasive taxation of business inputs. A state income tax would also have some tendency to drive high-income high-skilled workers out of the state in the long run. However, as long as the income tax were roughly proportional and imposed at a modest rate, these effects might be fairly moderate. Finally, a personal income tax would be more visible than the sales tax, and thus would likely lead to more efficient political decision-making.

Many proponents of a state income tax argue that its primary advantage is that it is less regressive than the sales tax and thus an inherently fairer tax instrument. However, if a state personal income tax is roughly proportional and one adopts a lifetime perspective on tax incidence, the distributional differences between the two taxes are modest.[11] Nevertheless, an income tax would impose a greater tax burden than the sales tax on the very rich, which is arguably desirable on vertical equity grounds, and would reduce the overall regressivity of the Texas state tax system with respect to annual income. Perhaps more important, a state income tax would be effective at exempting the very poor from tax, while exemptions under the sales tax are both very costly in revenue terms and much less successful in reducing tax burdens on the very poor. However, the income tax has two relatively less important equity disadvantages relative to the sales tax, as the latter is more effective in taxing the elderly who are wealthy but have relatively little current taxable income, and in taxing tourists and business travelers, who receive some benefits of public services and thus should pay at least some tax.

[11] For example, Casperson and Metcalf (1994) analyze a national VAT on the assumption that it is fully shifted forward to consumers. They find that although a broad-based VAT is quite regressive with respect to annual income, it is roughly proportional with respect to annual consumption and only mildly regressive with respect to their estimates of lifetime income. They also analyze a VAT with zero ratings for food, housing, and health expenditures. In this case, the VAT is less regressive (than a comprehensive VAT) with respect to annual income, roughly proportional with respect to their estimates of lifetime income, and moderately progressive with respect to annual consumption. See also Metcalf (1994) and Fullerton and Rogers (1991, 1993).

As long as a state personal income tax were closely tied to the federal individual income tax, it would be a relatively simple tax to administer (even though the federal tax can be quite complex). In particular, if state income tax liability were simply roughly proportional to federal taxable income, then the tax would be quite simple in terms of both compliance and administration (where joint federal-state audits would be a possibility).

A state income tax should be roughly similar to the existing sales tax in terms of revenue stability over the business cycle. At first glance, one might expect that the sales tax, as a tax primarily on consumption, would be significantly more stable than the income tax, which includes a relatively unstable capital income component. However, the base of the sales tax in Texas does not include many necessities and thus foregoes the benefit of taxing a highly stable component of the tax base. In addition, nearly half of the sales tax base consists of purchases of business inputs, which are highly cyclical. Thus, much of the inherent stability of a tax on consumption is lost under the current state sales tax.

A state income tax should, however, be more stable than the sales tax with respect to economic growth, as it avoids the central problem with the sales tax — the sales tax base largely misses the relatively rapidly growing service and government sectors. Moreover, as long as the income tax were roughly proportional with respect to income, the "automatic" or unlegislated increases in revenues attributable to a progressive tax system would not be an issue.

The revenue raised by a personal income tax would depend on the specifics of the plan enactments. The simplest approach would be to apply a flat rate to the federal definition of taxable income, including all the deductions and exemptions allowed under federal law, without any state-specific modifications. The State Comptroller estimates that such a personal income tax would raise $3.0 billion per percentage point of tax, implying that a tax rate of 2.75 percent would raise annual revenues of $8.1 billion.

3.7. *Introducing statewide taxation of nonresidential property*

Another approach to obtaining additional revenues to increase state-level financing of K-12 education expenditures would be the introduction of some form of statewide property taxation (a reform that would require an amendment to the Texas Constitution). A wide variety of options might be considered. The following discussion will focus on the option most often discussed in Texas — statewide taxation of nonresidential property. In addition, the analysis will also assume that nonresidential property would be taxed at a single statewide rate.

The efficiency argument for such a reform is a backhanded one. In general, for the reasons discussed above, non-benefit property taxation of nonresidential property is undesirable because it is a source-based tax on mobile capital. This is especially true for property taxes in Texas, which apply not only to structures, land and equipment, but also to commercial and industrial personal property. Since commercial and industrial personal property is highly mobile, the arguments against source-based taxation of mobile capital are particularly relevant for this form of capital. Accordingly, consideration should be given to removing commercial and industrial personal property from the tax base regardless of what reform measures are adopted.

Nevertheless, if one assumes for political or other reasons that such a tax is to be imposed, state-level taxation of nonresidential property at a uniform rate does have important efficiency advantages over local taxation. In particular, the former approach would at least avoid distortions of business location decisions within the state, as well as the tendency for local officials to under-spend on local public services financed in part with taxes on nonresidential property that is highly mobile (at least in the long run). In addition, statewide taxation of nonresidential property would eliminate the tendency for local jurisdictions with large amounts of nonresidential property perceived to be immobile to overspend on public services, given that residents face a significantly reduced effective price for such services. Moreover, if revenue constraints permit, the effective state-level tax rate on nonresidential property could be lower than the current average rate, reducing the overall extent of non-benefit taxation of mobile capital. Finally, efficiency requires that local governments should still be free to assess some form of benefit taxes on local businesses. These could be assessed directly, but some mechanism for local taxation of nonresidential property related as closely as possible to benefits of public services received and environmental costs imposed would also be highly desirable.

Alternatively, the state could rebate some of the funds collected from state-level taxation of nonresidential property, preferably in a form tied to the levels of local public services provided to business (and perhaps environmental costs).

The primary equity rationale for statewide taxation of nonresidential property would of course be to remove one of the main causes of differences in potential tax bases across local school districts (although differences in residential property wealth would still remain). From a tax perspective, the average distributional effects of moving from the current system of local taxation to state level taxation of nonresidential property should be relatively small. However, this average tendency could mask potentially significant redistributions among property owners, from those in jurisdictions with current rates lower than the new state rate to those in jurisdictions with relatively high current rates. Note in particular that these effects would be magnified as the effects of expected change in future property tax liabilities were capitalized into current property values. On the other hand, some such redistribution is already occurring under the existing Robin Hood system, so that the changes would not be as great as they would be if the initial equilibrium were characterized purely by local property finance. In addition, any reduction in property taxation associated with greater state level K-12 education finance would also have important positive effects on property values overall and differential effects across tax jurisdictions. Thus, if a statewide property tax were ever to be adopted, transitional equity issues would be relatively smaller if such a reform were accompanied by the school finance reforms currently under consideration. The magnitude of all of these effects could be gauged only with an explicit general equilibrium analysis of a specific reform proposal, taking into account the redistribution of funds and any remaining local taxation of nonresidential property, as well as the capitalization of changes in property taxation on the values of both nonresidential and residential property. The social costs of effecting these redistributions would have to be weighed against both the efficiency gains obtained from reform as well as any equity gains that would be obtained from the associated redistribution of school expenditures. These gains would depend on the formula used to distribute education funds.

Moving from local to state level taxation of nonresidential property would have fairly limited effects on administrative and compliance costs and revenue stability. Such a substitution would have no net revenue effects if the state tax rate were the current average effective tax rate, although the state "share" of school finance would obviously increase. Nonresidential property currently accounts for slightly less than 60 percent of the total property tax base.

A move to statewide taxation of nonresidential property could also be accompanied by a structural change in the property tax such that the land component was taxed at a higher rate than the structures or capital component. Such a reform, which would move the state tax system toward increasing reliance on land value taxation, has long been advocated by some economists on both efficiency and equity grounds (Reschovsky, 1998; Netzer, 1998). In terms of economic efficiency, the basic rationale for a tax on land values is that the tax is relatively non-distortionary, since the supply of land within the taxing jurisdiction is fixed. Thus, increasing the tax rate applied to land while reducing the tax rate applied to capital, which is highly mobile in the long run, will improve efficiency (Nechyba, 1998; Oates and Schwab, 1997). On equity grounds, proponents of land value taxes argue that they approximate a benefit tax, as a significant fraction of increases in land values are attributable to the provision of government services. In addition, since land ownership is concentrated among the wealthy, a land value tax is relatively progressive. Moreover, if a land value tax were implemented as part of reform that reduced property taxation of capital, then capitalization effects would be relatively small, as the effects of the land value tax increase would be partially offset by the effects of the reduction in capital taxation. Since a differentially high tax on land value would be a relatively stable source of revenue (Reschovky, 1998), can arguably be administered reasonably well, and is deductible, it would deserve serious consideration in any move toward statewide taxation of nonresidential property.

3.8. *Introducing a value-added tax or "simplified alternative tax"*

The final revenue option to be considered is some form of state value-added tax (VAT). National VATs have often been proposed but never adopted in the U.S., although the VAT is currently used as a major revenue source by some 120 countries around the world. In the U.S., Michigan and New Hampshire utilize variants of a VAT at the state level.[12]

There are many alternative structures for a VAT (Gillis, Mieszkowski, and Zodrow, 1996). This discussion will focus on consumption-based VATs that allow full expensing of all purchases of capital equipment and inventories, but no deductions for labor costs or interest expense.[13] Such a consumption-based VAT is thus quite similar in its economic effects to a retail sales tax, except that revenues are collected at various stages of the production process rather entirely at the retail stage, and there is an automatic and effective mechanism for ensuring that business inputs are not taxed. Although most national VATs are destination-based taxes (tax is assessed in the jurisdiction of consumption, implying that exports are untaxed while imports are subject to tax), most discussions of state VATs assume an origin basis (tax is assessed in the jurisdiction of production, with exports taxed but imports exempt). Accordingly, the following discussion will focus on consumption-based, origin-based versions of the VAT. The flat rate "business activity tax" or "Flat BAT" proposed by the Texas-based Lone Star Foundation (Hartman, 2003) is a consumption-based origin-based VAT.

In addition, the discussion will consider briefly a tax system that has been described as a "Simplified Alternative Tax" or SAT (Zodrow, 1999; Zodrow and McLure, 1991), which is a variant of the Bradford (1986) X-Tax, which is in turn a multi-rate variant of the Flat Tax proposal constructed by Hall and Rabushka (1985, 1995). This approach provides for a tax that is similar to an origin-based, consumption-based VAT at the business level, except that firms get a deduction for labor compensation, which is then taxed at the individual level, subject to a standard deduction and

[12]The Michigan VAT, known as the Single Business Tax, is currently scheduled to be phased out.

[13]An alternative is an income-based VAT, under which expensing of capital purchases is replaced with deductions for depreciation, as under a standard income tax. The "Single Business Tax" utilized in Michigan is an origin-based, consumption-based VAT (Cline, 1988). The New Hampshire Business Enterprise Tax is a modified version of an origin-based, income-based VATs that does not include rents, retained earnings, or the labor earnings of sole proprietors or partners in a partnership (Kenyon, 1996).

personal exemptions.[14] All forms of business, perhaps subject to a low exemption, are subject to tax. The rate structure at the individual level can be moderately progressive, with a top rate equal to the business rate. All forms of capital income, including dividends, interest and capital gains, are not taxed at the individual level.[15]

The following discussion evaluates these two VAT derivatives.[16] Common elements are considered first, and then differences between the two alternative tax options. On efficiency grounds, the VAT has the important advantage of avoiding the problems associated with gross receipts taxes — especially haphazard, cascading, and distortionary taxation of business inputs — and can also be applied to all business sectors, including services (to the extent administratively feasible). In addition, consumption-based VATs avoid source-based taxation of mobile capital, and are thus especially well-suited tax instruments for a small open economy; they also avoid worsening the various distortions of the federal corporate income tax. VATs do not tax capital income at the individual level, and thus avoid exacerbating the bias against saving that occurs under the existing federal personal income tax. However, any VAT would distort the labor supply decisions of Texas residents and would encourage out-migration of labor, particularly high-skilled labor,

---

[14] Pensions would be treated as under current law — deductible to the firm, with earnings tax exempt but all pension payments to individuals fully taxable.

[15] The following discussion of the state SAT option is fairly cursory; for further details, see Zodrow (1999).

[16] A payroll tax is another tax reform option. Since the economic effects of a payroll tax are similar to the labor compensation component of a VAT (in particular, the individual component of a flat-rate SAT), the analysis will not also discuss the payroll tax option. Note, however, that there may be one very important difference between the VAT and payroll tax (and perhaps the SAT) options from a political standpoint. Specifically, it may be easier politically to impose a payroll tax on the non-profit and government sectors, relative to requiring these sectors to be subject to the VAT. Uniform taxation of the for-profit, non-profit, and government sectors is desirable on both efficiency and equity grounds, and such a broad base is desirable — as will be discussed in more detail below — to keep the VAT rate relatively low. Note also that a VAT differs from a payroll tax in that only the former taxes the income to old capital (depending on transition rules) as well as above-normal returns to new capital.

to some extent.[17] Note that the SAT is more visible than a standard VAT, since most of its tax burden would be assessed at the individual level; the SAT would thus be more conducive to efficient political decision-making, with the standard VAT similar to the sales tax in terms of this criterion.[18]

On equity grounds, the incidence of a consumption-based VAT would be roughly similar to that of a sales tax or a payroll tax.[19] A major advantage of the SAT is that is structured so that poor families can easily be exempted from tax and a modest degree of progressivity can easily be achieved if deemed desirable. However, distributional concerns about the effects of a VAT could, as under the sales tax, be addressed with a tax rebate program tied to an expanded version of the Lone Star Card.[20] The primary equity problem with the SAT is that the explicit exemption of ordinary returns to capital from the individual tax base is often perceived to be inequitable, given the long history of income taxation in the U.S.; however, the importance of this point may be muted in Texas, given the historical opposition to income taxation in the state. Finally, a VAT could be justified as a proxy for a benefit-related tax on businesses, assuming that business demand for public services is roughly proportional to the value-added attributable to production in the state. Of course, some businesses will always object to

[17] Note that as an origin-based tax, a state VAT is more like a tax on in-state production than a true consumption tax (McLure, 1987). Accordingly, especially for tradable goods, its burden would more likely be reflected as lower factor returns (lower wages, economic rents, and returns to old capital) than as higher prices. Note also that to any extent that a VAT were not either shifted forward as higher prices or backward as lower wages (as seems likely), it would create a tax bias against hiring labor.

[18] Note that the VAT is no more "hidden" than the sales tax, as long as retailers are required — as they should be if the VAT were to be implemented in Texas — to show the VAT separately on all invoices, calculated at the standard rate (or whatever rate applies to the commodity in the case of differential rates). Thus, concerns that the VAT is more conducive to expansion of the public sector than the sales tax are misplaced (Zodrow, 1999a).

[19] Note that although an origin-based VAT would apply to exports, the extent to which a VAT imposed by Texas could be shifted to residents of other states would be limited by the "small open economy" considerations noted previously. Thus, the VAT on tradable goods would be likely to be borne by in-state labor (Papke, 2000).

[20] Alternatively, firms could be allowed a deduction from the VAT base for some amount, such as the minimum wage, for each employee.

paying tax when they are not profitable (as can easily occur under a state VAT); indeed, this complaint was apparently the major factor in the downfall of the Michigan VAT, the "single business tax." However, it is important to note that under the benefit tax interpretation of the VAT, it is to be expected that firms in a loss position will still pay tax; that is, the payment of benefit taxes is not contingent upon profitability, any more than payments to other factors of production. Moreover, payment of tax by unprofitable firms might not be a particularly troublesome issue in Texas, where most businesses are accustomed to paying the net asset component of the franchise tax even in years in which they are not profitable.

In general, the VAT options are relatively simple taxes, especially when compared to an income tax. However, since they would be new tax instruments in Texas, (rather than taxes that can "piggyback" on existing federal taxes), they would add a new layer of complexity to administration and compliance for businesses (and for individuals under the SAT); of course, there is much VAT experience around the world on which Texas tax administrators could draw, and all of the information required for the VAT should be readily available since it is already required for federal income tax accounting.

A serious issue under the VAT options would be the treatment of multi-state firms. Since exports are included in the tax base and imported inputs are deductible (under the origin-based approach utilized), the system is subject to transfer pricing problems if tax liability is calculated on a separate entity basis (Bradford, 2003). For this reason, separate accounting is not desirable under a state VAT. In addition, since the treatment of interest income and expense differs from that under an income tax, potentially significant opportunities for tax avoidance and evasion are created that would be difficult to monitor and control (McLure and Zodrow, 1996). Of course, one potential solution to the transfer pricing problem and some of the avoidance problems would be to use formula apportionment to allocate VAT (or SAT) revenues as under the current franchise tax. The use of a single gross receipts factor would be consistent with current practice under the franchise tax. However, this would effectively convert the VAT to a levy assessed on gross receipts for such firms, negating much of its efficiency advantages; although, in contrast to formulas that use property or payroll taxes, using a single-factor (sales) formula would have the advantage of avoiding the imposition of what would effectively be a source-based tax on mobile capital and mobile high-skilled labor. Another approach, consistent with the notion of an origin-based, consumption-based tax, would be to use payroll (or total labor compensation) as the apportionment factor; the rationale for this approach is that a consumption-based tax like the VAT can be viewed primarily as a tax on labor since ordinary returns to capital are exempt from tax. Alternatively, both labor compensation and capital (or property) could be used in the apportionment formula, on the grounds that the VAT does include in its tax base above-normal returns to capital and, for a lengthy transition period, returns to old capital.[21] Finally, a separate issue is that financial institutions are not easily taxed under either of the VAT options, and a separate tax on such institutions might be required (Zodrow, 1999).[22]

To the extent that the VAT options were successful in taxing a comprehensive measure of consumption, they should be relatively stable. Note that the individual tax base of the SAT, which excludes capital income, would be more stable than the base of a personal income tax that includes relatively volatile capital income components, especially capital gains.[23]

Revenue estimates are available only for the consumption-based VAT. Significant revenues could be obtained with a comprehensive state VAT with a minimal exemption level on the order of $25,000 of gross receipts; this would be especially true if non-profit institutions were included in the tax base, presumably subject to a large exemption level, say, on the order of $100,000 of gross receipts.[24] Although application of the VAT to large non-profit institutions would be difficult from a political standpoint, it would be entirely appropriate in the context of a sweeping reform that would apply the tax system more evenly across all entities providing con-

[21] In addition, it should be noted that the use of formula apportionment creates its own efficiency problems (McLure, 1980; Gordon and Wilson, 1986).

[22] In addition, the enactment of transition rules for any of the VAT options would have to be considered, although the need for such transitional rules would be minimized to the extent that base of the VAT were extremely broad so that the rate would be low, especially if the VAT were replacing a higher-rate franchise tax (Zodrow, 2002).

[23] Taylor (2003) notes that revenues of states that utilize the income tax revenues have been highly unstable in recent years during the recent boom-and-bust cycle of the U.S. stock market.

[24] Taxing government institutions would also increase the size of the base, but is probably politically infeasible.

sumer goods and services. Since tax exempt institutions already benefit from property tax exemption and exemption from sales tax on their output as well as on most of their inputs, it would not be unreasonable for such institutions to pay a low-rate VAT to promote education and economic growth within the state. This is especially true since the VAT can be viewed to a large extent as a tax on labor compensation, and there is no particular reason to effectively exempt from tax individuals who happen to work for tax-exempt institutions. In addition, the VAT discourages labor supply and this distortion can be minimized by keeping the base as broad and the rate as low as possible.

The enactment of a state VAT would presumably be politically viable only if it were accompanied by repeal of the existing franchise tax, raising state level revenue. This could be accomplished with a truly comprehensive VAT at a rate of approximately 1.6 percent.[25] If non-profit institutions were excluded from the tax base, the required rate would increase to 2.0 percent. However, exempting non-profits would open the door to demands for exemption from other "worthy" entities, decreasing the likelihood that a broad-based, low-rate VAT would be politically attainable.

Conclusion

This paper has provided an economic evaluation of various alternative sources of additional revenues for the State of Texas that might be used to finance a greater state share of K-12 education spending and perhaps an increase in the overall level of education spending.

[…]

Acknowledgments

I would like to thank Timothy Bartik, Randall Eberts, Margaret Goertz, Harrison Keller, David Monk, Lori Taylor, and Arnold Vedlitz for helpful comments and Joyce Tung for excellent research assistance.

---

[25] As noted previously, state VATs are typically referred to as "business activity taxes" (BATs) in the U.S., and proponents of the VAT in Texas are no exception (Hartman, 2003). Note, however, that non-profit institutions might object to paying the BAT on the grounds that they are not "businesses." This issue could be avoided by following the Canadian example and referring to the tax as the "Texas Goods and Services Tax."

References

Bartik, Timothy J. 1991. *Who Benefits from State and Local Economic Development Policies?* Kalamazoo, MI: Upjohn Institute.

Bartik, Timothy J. 1994. "Jobs, Productivity, and Local Economic Development: What Implications Does Economic Research Have for the Role of Government?" *National Tax Journal* 47: 847–861.

Bradford, David F. 1986. *Untangling the Income Tax*. Cambridge, MA: Harvard University Press.

Bradford, David F., 2003. "Addressing the Transfer Pricing Problem in an Origin-Based X-Tax." *International Tax and Public Finance* 10: 591–610.

Burman, Leonard E., and Mohammed Adeel Saleem. 2004. "Income Tax Statistics for Sample Families, 2003." *Tax Notes* 102 (January 19): 413–18.

Casperson, Erik, and Gilbert Metcalf. 1994. "Is a Value Added Tax Progressive? Annual versus Lifetime Incidence Measures." *National Tax Journal* 47: 731–46.

Cline, Robert J. 1988. "Should States Adopt a Value-Added Tax?" In *The Unfinished Agenda for State Tax Reform*. Ed. Steven D. Gold. Denver, CO: National Conference of State Legislatures.

Cnossen, Sijbren, and Michael Smart. Forthcoming. "Taxation of Tobacco," In *Excise Taxes on Smoking, Drinking, Gambling, Polluting and Driving*. Ed. Sijbren Cnossen. Oxford, UK: Oxford University Press.

Cordes, Joseph J., 1992. "State Environmental Taxes and Fees." In *State Taxation of Business*. Ed. Thomas F. Pogue. London: Praeger.

Courant, Paul N., and Susanna Loeb. 1997. "Centralization of School Finance in Michigan." *Journal of Policy Analysis and Management* 16: 114–36.

Due, John F., and John L. Mikesell. 1994. *Sales Taxation: State and Local Structure and Administration*, 2nd Ed. Washington, DC: Urban Institute Press.

Dye, Richard F., and Therese J. McGuire. 1992. "Expanding the Sales Tax Base: Implications for Growth and Stability." In *Sales Taxation: Critical Issues in Policy and Administration*. Ed. William F. Fox. Westport, CT: Praeger.

Feldstein, Martin, and Marian Vaillant Wrobel. 1998. "Can States Redistribute Income?" *Journal of Public Economics* 68: 369–96.

Fischel, William A. 2001. "Homevoters, Municipal Corporate Governance, and the Benefit View of the Property Tax." *National Tax Journal* 54: 157–82.

Fox, William F. 1992. "Sales Taxation of Services: Has Its Time Come?" In *Sales Taxation: Critical Issues in Policy and Administration*. Ed. William F. Fox. Westport, CT: Praeger.

Fox, William F., and Matthew Murray. 1988. "Economic Aspects of Taxing Services." *National Tax Journal* 41:19–36.

Fritz, Randy. 1989. "Who Pays Texas Taxes." In *Rethinking Texas Taxes: Final Report of the Select Committee on Tax Equity.* Ed. Billy C. Hamilton. Austin, TX: Reproduction Division of the Texas House of Representatives.

Fullerton, Don, and Diane Lim Rogers. 1991. "Lifetime versus Annual Perspectives on Tax Incidence." *National Tax Journal* 44: 277–87.

Fullerton, Don, and Diane Lim Rogers. 1993. *Who Bears the Lifetime Tax Burden?* Washington, DC: Brookings Institution.

Gillis, Malcolm, Peter Mieszkowski, and George R. Zodrow. 1996. "Indirect Consumption Taxes: Common Issues and Differences Among the Alternative Approaches." *Tax Law Review* 51: 725–74.

Gordon, Roger H. 1986. "Taxation of Investment and Savings in a World Economy." *American Economic Review* 76: 1086–1102.

Gordon, Roger H., and John Wilson. 1986. "An Examination of Multijurisdictional Corporate Income Taxation under Formula Apportionment." *Econometrica* 54: 1357–73.

Gravelle, Jane G., 1994. *The Effects of Taxing Capital Income.* Cambridge MA: MIT Press.

Hall, Robert E., and Alvin Rabushka. 1985. *The Flat Tax.* Stanford, CA: Hoover Institution Press.

Hall, Robert E., and Alvin Rabushka. 1995. *The Flat Tax.* 2nd ed. Stanford, CA: Hoover Institution Press.

Hamilton, Billy C., ed. 1989. *Rethinking Texas Taxes: Final Report of the Select Committee on Tax Equity.* Austin, TX: Reproduction Division of the Texas House of Representatives.

Hartman, David A. 2003. *Texas Public School and Business Tax Reform Via the Flat BAT.* Austin, TX: The Lone Star Foundation.

Hatta, Tatsuo. 1986. "Welfare Effects of Changing Commodity Tax Rates Toward Uniformity." *Journal of Public Economics* 29: 99–112.

Hendrix, Michele E., and George R. Zodrow. 2003. "Sales Taxation of Services: An Economic Analysis." *Florida State Law Review* 30: 411–33.

Johnson, Nicholas, and Iris Lav. 1998. "Should States Tax Food? Examining the Policy Issues and Options." *State Tax Notes* 14 (June 1): 1785–2007.

Kenyon, Daphne A. 1996. "A New State VAT: Lessons from New Hampshire." *National Tax Journal* 49: 381–99.

Lyon, Andrew B., and Robert M. Schwab. 1995. "Consumption Taxes in A Life-Cycle Framework: Are Sin Taxes Regressive?" *Review of Economics and Statistics* 37: 389–406.

Mazerov, Michael. 2003. "Expanding Sales Taxation of Services: Options and Issues." *State Tax Notes* 29 (July 21): 183–210.

McCown, Scott, and Dick Lavine. 2004. *The Best Choice for Paying for Public Education*. Austin, TX: Center for Public Priorities.

McLure, Charles E., Jr. 1980. "The State Corporate Income Tax: Lambs in Wolves' Clothing." In *The Economics of Taxation.* Eds. Henry J. Aaron and Michael J. Boskin. Washington, DC: Brookings Institution.

McLure, Charles E., Jr. 1987. *The Value Added Tax: Key to Deficit Reduction.* Washington, DC: American Enterprise Institute.

McLure, Charles E., Jr. 2000. "Rethinking State and Local Reliance on the Retail Sales Tax: Should We Fix the State Sales Tax or Discard It?" *Brigham Young University Law Review* 2000: 77–137.

McLure, Charles E., Jr., and George R. Zodrow. 1996. "A Hybrid Consumption-Based Direct Tax Proposed for Bolivia." *International Tax and Public Finance* 3: 97–112.

Metcalf, Gilbert E. 1994. "The Lifetime Incidence of State and Local Taxes: Measuring Changes During the 1980s." In *Tax Progressivity and Income Inequality.* Ed. Joel Slemrod. Cambridge, UK: Cambridge University Press.

Merriman, David, and Mark Skidmore. 2000. "Did Distortionary Sales Taxation Contribute to the Growth of the Service Sector?" *National Tax Journal* 53: 125–42.

Mikesell, John L. 1997. "Is the Retail Sales Tax Really Inferior to the Value-Added Tax?" In *The Sales Tax in the 21st Century.* Eds. Matthew N. Murray and William F. Fox. Westport, CT: Praeger.

Nechyba, Thomas J. 1998. "Replacing Capital Taxes with Land Taxes: Efficiency and Distributional Implications with an Application to the United States Economy." In *Land Value Taxation.* Ed. Dick Netzer. Cambridge, MA: Lincoln Institute of Land Policy.

Netzer, Dick. 1992. "Differences in Reliance on User Charges by American State and Local Governments." *Public Finance Quarterly* 20: 499–511.

Netzer, Dick. 1998. *Land Value Taxation.* Cambridge, MA: Lincoln Institute of Land Policy.

Oakland, William H. 1992. "How Should Businesses Be Taxed?" In *State Taxation of Business.* Ed. Thomas F. Pogue. London: Praeger.

Oates, Wallace E., and Robert M. Schwab. 1997. "The Impact of Urban Land Taxation: The Pittsburgh Experience." *National Tax Journal* 50: 1–21.

Papke, James A. 2000. "Rethinking Local Business Taxation: Substituting a State Value Added Tax for the Local Ad Valorem Tax on Business Personal Property." *Proceedings of the Ninety-second Annual Conference on Taxation.* Washington, DC: National Tax Association.

Poterba, James M. 1989. "Lifetime Incidence and the Distributional Burden of Excise Taxes." *American Economic Review, Papers and Proceedings* 79: 325–30.

Quick, Perry D., and Michael J. McKee. 1988. "Sales Tax on Services: Revenue or Reform?" *National Tax Journal* 41: 395–409.

Rabe, Barry G. 2003. "Power to the States: The Promise and Pitfalls of Decentralization." In *Environmental Policy: New Directions for the Twenty-First Century.* Ed. Norman J. Vig and Michael E. Kraft. Washington, DC: CQ Press.

Razin, Assaf, and Efraim Sadka. 1991. "International Tax Competition and Gains from Tax Harmonization." *Economics Letters* 37: 69–76.

Reschovsky, Andrew. 1998. "Can the Land Value Tax Play an Important Role in the Financing of State and Local Governments in the United States?" In *Land Value Taxation.* Ed. Dick Netzer. Cambridge, MA: Lincoln Institute of Land Policy.

Reschovsky, Andrew. 1998a. "The Progressivity of State Tax Systems." In *The Future of State Taxation.* Ed. David Brunori. Washington, DC: Urban Institute Press.

Ring, Raymond J. Jr. 1999. "Consumer's Share and Producer's Share of the General Sales Tax." *National Tax Journal* 52: 79–90.

Siegfried, John J., and Paul A. Smith. 1991. "The Distributional Effects of a Sales Tax on Services." *National Tax Journal* 44: 41–53.

Slemrod, Joel. 1990. "Optimal Taxation and Optimal Tax Systems." *Journal of Economic Perspectives* 4: 157–78.

Smith, Stephen. Forthcoming. "Economic Issues in Alcohol Taxation," In *Excise Taxes on Smoking, Drinking, Gambling, Polluting and Driving.* Ed. Sijbren Cnossen. Oxford, UK: Oxford University Press.

Taylor, Lori L. 1999. "Government's Role in Primary and Secondary Education." *Economic Review, Federal Reserve Bank of Dallas* First Quarter: 15–24.

Taylor, Lori L. 2003. "The Sales Tax Crunch," *Southwest Economy* (May/June): 1–4.

Taylor, Lori L. 2003a. "Undue Taxes and Unintended Consequences." In *Putting the Sides Together: Twelve Perspectives on Texas Public School Finance.* Ed. Chris Patterson. Austin, TX: Texas Public Policy Foundation.

Texas Taxpayers and Research Association. 2003. *Forms of Business and the Texas Franchise Tax.* Austin, TX: Texas Taxpayers and Research Association.

Wasylenko, Michael. 1997. "Taxation and Economic Development: The State of the Economic Literature." *New England Economic Review* (March/April) 36–52.

Zodrow, George R. 1999. *State Sales and Income Taxes.* College Station, TX: Texas A&M University Press.

Zodrow, George R. 1999a. "The Sales Tax, the VAT and Taxes In Between — Or, Is the Only Good NRST a 'VAT in Drag'?" *National Tax Journal* 52: 429–42.

Zodrow, George R. 2001. "The Property Tax as a Capital Tax: A Room with Three Views." *National Tax Journal* 54: 139–156.

Zodrow, George R. 2002. "Transitional Issues in the Implementation of a Flat Tax or a Retail Sales Tax." In *United States Tax Reform in the 21st Century.* Eds. George R. Zodrow and Peter Mieszkowski. Cambridge, UK: Cambridge University Press.

Zodrow, George R. 2002a. "Streamlining the Sales Tax: Implications for Economic Growth." *State Tax Notes* 26 (October 28): 251–62.

Zodrow, George R. 2003. "Reflections on the Economic Theory of Local Tax Incentives." *State Tax Notes* 28 (June 9): 891–900.

Zodrow, George R. 2003a. "Tax Competition and Tax Coordination in the European Union." *International Tax and Public Finance* 10: 651–71.

Zodrow, George R. 2004. "An Economic Evaluation of Alternative Sources of Tax Revenue for the State of Texas," Report prepared for the Texas Joint Select Committee on Public School Finance (March 31, 2004). http://www.capitol.state.tx.us/psf/reports.htm.

Zodrow, George R., and Charles E. McLure. 1991. "Alternative Methods of Taxing Consumption in Developing Countries." *Tax Law Review* 46: 407–87.

Zodrow, George R., and Peter Mieszkowski. 2002. *United States Tax Reform in the 21st Century* Cambridge, UK: Cambridge University Press.

Chapter 14

The New View of the Property Tax: A Reformulation*

George R. Zodrow

U.S. Treasury Office of Tax Analysis, Washington, DC 20220, USA
Rice University, Houston, TX 77251, USA

Peter M. Mieszkowski

Rice University, Houston, TX 77251, USA

The 'new view' of the property tax is reformulated within the context of a model with interjurisdictional competition, endogenous local public services, individuals who are segregated into homogeneous communities according to tastes for local public services, a simple form of land use zoning, and a political or constitutional constraint on the use of head taxes by local governments. Expressions for the 'profits tax' and 'excise tax' effects of the property tax are derived. The effects of a 'consumption distortion' away from government services due to local reluctance to tax mobile capital are also examined.

*This chapter is reproduced from *Regional Science and Urban Economics*, **16**(3), 309–372, 1986.

1. Introduction

There are two popular but highly contradictory theoretical views regarding the effects of the local property tax. One is the 'benefit view', developed by Hamilton (1975), Fischel (1975) and White (1975), which holds that interjurisdictional competition and factor and consumer mobility, coupled with homogeneous local jurisdictions with the appropriate zoning restrictions,[1] ensure that the property tax is a benefit tax — a non-distortionary and non-redistributive user charge for local public services provided to individuals and businesses.

This view contrasts markedly with the 'new view' of the property tax, which holds that the primary effect of nationwide use of the local property tax is to reduce the net return to capital, while tax differentials result in relatively less important effects on consumer prices and returns to imperfectly mobile factors of production.[2] In this analysis, the property tax results in many distortions, especially in capital allocation, and has an important redistributive component as the main burden is borne by capitalists. The new view was developed by Mieszkowski (1972) who, building on the work of Brown (1924) and Thomson (1965), utilized the Harberger (1962) fixed capital stock, perfectly competitive general equilibrium model of national tax incidence to analyze the local property tax.

In an earlier article (Zodrow and Mieszkowski, 1983), we argued that the critical assumption underlying the benefit view result is that fiscal zoning is sufficiently precise that households and firms are not able to adjust their demand for capital. Interjurisdictional competition implies that benefit taxes are optimal from the viewpoint of the local government, and precise zoning converts the property tax to a benefit tax so that consumers of local public services cannot 'free ride' at the expense of nonresident or industrial capital owners. However, we noted that local head taxes are never observed while the precise zoning requirements described in the benefit view literature are seldom observed. Accordingly, we suggested that limitations on the use of precise zoning, coupled with local

[1] Hamilton (1976) has extended the benefit view result to the case of non-homogeneous communities in a model where fiscal differentials are capitalized into house prices; we limit our analysis to the case of homogeneous communities.

[2] Throughout the paper we consider only the effects of the capital portion of the property tax.

reliance on property tax finance, would imply that the effects of the property tax were accurately described by the new view.

We develop this suggestion formally in this paper. Our goal is to present a reformulation of the new view which takes into account many of the features of local use of the property tax stressed by proponents of the benefit view; these features are ignored in the Mieszkowski (1972) new-view derivation based on the Harberger general equilibrium model of national tax incidence, which abstracts from local government behavior by taking public services and taxes as exogenous. Specifically, our approach differs from the original derivation in five important respects. First, we allow for independent local jurisdictions in the economy that compete along Cournot–Nash lines, as each local jurisdiction takes the tax and expenditure policies of other jurisdictions (and the national net return to capital) as fixed; thus local government tax and expenditure policies are endogenous in the model. Second, we explicitly include local public services in individual utility functions and allow individuals to differ in their tastes. Third, we take into account the composition of individual jurisdictions and assume, as predicted by Tiebout (1956) and benefit view proponents, that individuals are segregated into communities according to their tastes for public services; as in many of the benefit view models, we assume that local jurisdictions are homogeneous. Fourth, we allow for a simple form of land use zoning in our model. Finally, we obtained explicit expressions for the 'profits tax' and 'excise tax' portions of the burden of the property tax,[3] and we also analyze the incidence effects of the endogeneity of local public service levels, emphasizing the effects of a 'consumption distortion' induced by local reluctance to subject mobile capital to property taxation.

Thus, our property tax incidence model includes many of the features of local use of the property tax stressed by proponents of the benefit view. Nevertheless, within this more general context, we demonstrate that, except for the special case of perfect fiscal zoning noted above, the results of the new view of the property tax are quite robust. In light of our belief

[3] Our paper is thus a partial response to Aaron (1975, p. 42) who notes that 'the theoretical foundations of the new view are incomplete'. The profits tax and excise tax terminology follows Mieszkowski (1972).

that the conditions required for perfect fiscal zoning are unlikely to obtain in practice, we believe that our 'reformulated new view' represents a more plausible explanation of the effects of local use of the property tax than does the 'benefit view'.

Our model is described in detail in the following section, while the incidence results are presented in Section 3. An illustrative numerical example is presented in Section 4, and the final section briefly summarizes the results.

2. The Model

We adopt the standard neoclassical assumptions of a fixed national capital stock (K_T), full employment, perfectly competitive product and factor markets, and perfect mobility of capital across all jurisdictions. The economy is divided into N jurisdictions, each of which has the same fixed land area (V_T).[4] We assume that individuals are segregated into jurisdictions which are homogeneous according to tastes for public services; there are N_1 jurisdictions composed exclusively of 'high demanders' and N_2 jurisdictions composed exclusively of 'low demanders', with $N = N_1 + N_2$. Each jurisdiction is assumed to have the same number of identical individuals — each has the same utility function, supplies the same amount of labor inelastically,[5] and owns an equal share of the jurisdiction's land. Capital ownership is shared equally among all residents in the economy; unlike land, capital need not be invested in the jurisdiction of residence. Since we are concerned primarily with the effects of the property tax on the production side of the economy, we make the simplifying assumption on the demand side that all individuals have a Cobb–Douglas utility function defined over consumption of housing, local public services and

[4] Jurisdictions of different land areas could easily be introduced into the model as multiples of our constant size jurisdictions.

[5] We make this assumption because allowing a variable labor supply would complicate the analysis considerably without changing the basic nature of the results since residents are immobile between jurisdictions in the sense that 'high demanders' do not wish to move 'low demander' jurisdictions and vice versa. For analyses of property taxation in models where labor is mobile between jurisdictions, see Brueckner (1981) and Starrett (1980).

the composite good. Public goods are modeled as equally-shared public purchases of the composite good and are treated as publicly-provided private goods [see Hamilton (1983) for a justification]. Since the Cobb–Douglas utility function is homogeneous of degree one, the aggregate utility (U_j) of a typical jurisdiction j (the sum of residents' utilities) is given by

$$U_j = \alpha \ln H_j + \beta_j \ln G_j + \gamma_j \ln C_j, \quad j = 1,2, \tag{1}$$

where $\alpha + \beta_j + \gamma_j = 1$ and H_j, G_j and C_j are aggregate housing, public good and composite good consumption in j. The indirect utility function associated with (1), neglecting constant terms, is

$$U_j' = (\alpha + \gamma_j)\ln I_j - \alpha \ln q_j - \gamma_j \ln p + \beta_j \ln G_j, \tag{1'}$$

where p is the price of the composite good which is assumed to be identical across all jurisdictions, while q_j is the price of housing and I_j is aggregate net income in jurisdiction j. Since jurisdictions of type one are those composed of high demanders, $\beta_1 > \beta_2$ and $\gamma_1 < \gamma_2$. Note that we assume for simplicity that α does not vary across jurisdictions.

The production technology is the same in both types of jurisdictions. In each jurisdiction, the composite good is produced with a constant returns to scale production function using capital, labor and land. Housing is produced with a constant returns to scale production function using capital and land. Since public services are modeled as public purchases of the composite good, there is no separate public goods technology.

Within this type of analytical framework, we have shown elsewhere [Zodrow and Mieszkowski (1983)] that if the individual local jurisdictions have head taxes at their disposal, they will use them exclusively and not rely on property tax finance; each local government fears that using the property tax will drive out mobile capital and lower land rents and so instead utilizes only head tax finance. Such a 'head tax equilibrium', where all jurisdictions of both types finance all local services exclusively with head taxes, is the benchmark for our analysis; this initial equilibrium corresponds to the case of property taxation coupled with perfect fiscal zoning which induces each household (firm) to consume (use) the efficient amount of capital.

The level of public services in the initial equilibrium is chosen by the local government to maximize (1') and is financed by head taxes Z_j, while housing and composite good demands are determined by the maximization of (1′) subject to an aggregate net income constraint. This yields

$$pG_j = Z_j = \beta_j I_j/(\alpha + \gamma_j), \tag{2}$$

$$pC_j = \gamma_j I_j/(\alpha + \gamma_j), \tag{3}$$

$$q_j H_j = \alpha I_j/(\alpha + \gamma_j) \tag{4}$$

In each jurisdiction, gross income $\left(I_j^G\right)$ is the sum of net income and head taxes paid, or

$$I_j^G = I_j + Z_j. \tag{5}$$

Substituting from (2) yields

$$I_j = (\alpha + \gamma_j)I_j^G. \tag{6}$$

Thus, in terms of gross income, government and consumer demands can be expressed as

$$pG_j = Z_j = \beta_j I_j^G, \tag{2′}$$

$$pC_j = \gamma_j I_j^G, \tag{3′}$$

$$q_j H_j = \alpha I_j^G. \tag{4′}$$

Our assumptions about factor ownership and equal-size jurisdictions with identical populations and production technologies, combined with the above demand functions, imply that composite good and housing production and all prices are identical in the two jurisdictions in the initial equilibrium. Identical factor prices imply that gross incomes are also equal. Thus jurisdictions differ only in public and private demands for the composite good. The use of head tax finance corresponds to the Tiebout paradigm where binding zoning requirements convert property tax assessments into head tax levies.

Our method of relaxing the perfect zoning assumption is to assume first that local zoning ordinances are limited to fixing residential and non-residential land use at their initial efficient levels and then introduce a constitutional or political restriction on the permitted level of head taxation. This level is determined by the value of ϕ, an exogenous parameter which specifies that only ϕZ_j can be collected as head taxes in each jurisdiction, with Z_j assumed fixed throughout the analysis. Thus a reduction in ϕ implies an equiproportionate reduction in head taxes in the two jurisdictions. Given ϕ (and Z_j, p, and r), each government sets T_j to maximize U'_j, where $T_j = 1 + \tau_j$ and τ_j is an ad-valorem tax on the return to capital in jurisdiction j. The effects of the nationwide system of property taxes are obtained as the changes in all endogenous variables in response to an exogenous change in ϕ.[6] The differential incidence expressions shown below are calculated at the initial head tax (zero property tax) equilibrium ($T_j = \phi = 1$); thus, they are only approximations for changes from finite levels of property taxation.[7]

The details of our model are as follows. For given values of Z_1, Z_2 and ϕ there are six endogenous variables in our model, the two property tax rates (T_1 and T_2), housing prices (q_1 and q_2), the composite good price (p) and the after-tax rate of return on capital (r). The development of the six-equation equilibrium system is simplified if we follow a dual approach.[8] Our zoning assumption and the assumption of inelastically supplied labor imply that, in each jurisdiction, labor and non-residential land are a fixed composite factor, hereafter referred to simply as 'labor' and denoted as L. Residential land is similarly fixed, referred to as 'land', and denoted as V.[9] Note that the quantities of the fixed factors do not vary across the two types of jurisdictions. We thus can construct restricted profit functions $\pi^{X_j}(p, rT_j, L)$ and $\pi^{H_j}(q_j, rT_j, V)$, which represent the differences between revenue and variable factor cost for each production good (X_j, H_j) in each jurisdiction. Letting subscripts denote partial differentiation, with

---

[6]This methodology follows Atkinson and Stern (1974).

[7]For the methodology of relaxing the assumption of zero initial distorting taxes, see Ballentine and Eris (1975) and Vandendorpe and Friedlaender (1976). Also, Courant (1977) addresses this question within the property tax context.

[8]See Diewert (1974, 1978) for a thorough discussion of duality theory and its application to differential incidence analysis, as well as proofs of assertions made below regarding restricted profit functions.

[9]Our identical residents are assumed to own an equal share of both types of land.

the r subscript denoting differentiation with respect to the gross price of capital rT_j, the composite good and housing supply functions and the capital demand functions are given by

$$\pi_p^{X_j} = L\pi_{Lp}^{X_j} = X_j, \tag{7}$$

$$\pi_q^{H_j} = V\pi_{Vp}^{H_j} = H_j, \tag{8}$$

$$\pi_r^{X_j} = L\pi_{Lr}^{X_j} = -K_{X_j}, \tag{9}$$

$$\pi_r^{H_j} = V\pi_{Vr}^{H_j} = -K_{H_j}. \tag{10}$$

As shown by Diewert (1978, pp. 142–143), the first set of equalities in Eqs. (7)–(10) follows from the linear homogeneity of the restricted profit functions which is implied by the constant returns to scale assumption, and the second set of equalities in Eqs. (7)–(10) follows from Hotelling's Lemma.

Also, as shown by Diewert (1974, p. 140; 1978, p. 142), the shadow prices or imputed values of a marginal unit of the two fixed factors are given by

$$\pi_L^{X_j} = w_j, \tag{11}$$

$$\pi_V^{H_j} = s_j, \tag{12}$$

where w_j and s_j are the returns to the fixed factors L and V (the division of the return to L between workers and non-residential land owners is arbitrary).

The following definitions will be useful. The own-price capital demand elasticity in the composite good sector, weighted by the amount of capital used, is

$$\mu_{X_j} = -K_{X_j}[(rT_j/K_{X_j})\partial K_{X_j}/\partial(rT_j)] = rT_j\pi_{rr}^{X_j} = -p\pi_{rp}^{X_j} = -p\pi_{pr}^{X_j} > 0, \tag{13}$$

where the third equality follows from Euler's theorem on homogeneous functions, and the direction of the inequality follows from the fact that the matrix of the second-order partial derivatives of the restricted profit function with respect to the prices p and rT_j is positive semidefinite. The analogous calculation in the housing sector yields

$$\mu_{H_j} = -K_{H_j}[(rT_j/K_{H_j})\partial K_{H_j}/\partial(rTj)] = rT_j\pi_{rr}^{H_j} = -q_j\pi_{rq}^{H_j} = -q_j\pi_{qr}^{H_j} > 0. \quad (14)$$

Similarly, the own-price supply elasticities in the two sectors are

$$\eta_{X_j} = p\pi_{pp}^{X_j}/X_j = -rT_j\pi_{rp}^{X_j}/X_j > 0, \quad (15)$$

$$\eta_{H_j} = q_j\pi_{qq}^{H_j}/H_j = -rT_j\pi_{rq}^{H_j}/H_j > 0. \quad (16)$$

Two equations of the equilibrium system are provided by Eq. (4) for $j = 1, 2$, where aggregate net income in each jurisdiction is given by

$$I_j = rK_T/N + w_jL + s_jV - \phi Z_j; \quad (17)$$

recall that K_T is the fixed national capital stock.

A third equilibrium equation is implied by the fixed national capital stock constraint which, using Eqs. (9)–(10), can be written as

$$K_T + N_1(\pi_r^{X_1} + \pi_r^{H_1}) + N_2(\pi_r^{X2} + \pi_r^{H_2}) = 0. \quad (18)$$

The derivation of the fourth and fifth equilibrium equations is more complex. The problem faced by each jurisdictional government is to choose its tax rate T_j to maximize aggregate utility (1′) subject to the budget constraint

$$pG_j = \phi Z_j + (T_j - 1)r(K_{X_j} + K_{H_j}) = \phi Z_j - (T_j - 1)r(\pi_r^{X_j} + \pi_r^{H_j}), \quad (19)$$

where the second equality follows from Eqs. (9)–(10). The solution of this problem requires calculation of the change in aggregate net income expected by the government when it changes its property tax rate. Substituting from Eqs. (11)–(12) into Eq. (17) yields

$$I_j = rK_T/N + L\pi_L^{X_j}(p, rT_j, L) + V\pi_V^{H_j}(q_j, rT_j, V) - \phi Z_j. \quad (20)$$

Each local jurisdictional government perceives p, r, ϕ and Z_j as being determined exogenously. Differentiating Eq. (20) with respect to T_j holding p, r, ϕ and Z_j constant, and then substituting from the second set of equalities in Eqs. (9)–(10), yields the perceived change in aggregate net income with respect to changes in T_j,

$$\partial I_j/\partial T_j = H_j\partial_{q_j}/\partial T_j - rK_j, \quad (21)$$

where

$$K_j = K_{X_j} + K_{H_j}, \tag{22}$$

The objective function for the local government optimization problem is obtained by substituting from Eqs. (19) and (22) into (1′) to yield

$$U' = (\alpha + \gamma_j)\ln I_j - \alpha \ln q_j - \gamma_j \ln p + \beta_j \ln\{[\phi Z_j + (T_j - 1)rK_j]/p\}. \tag{23}$$

Differentiating Eq. (23) with respect to T_j, setting the result equal to zero, and using Eq. (4) yields the first-order condition for the local government optimization problem:

$$\beta_j/pG_j - (\beta_j/pG_j)[(T_j - 1)/T_j]\eta_{K_j} - (\alpha + \gamma_j)/I_j = 0, \tag{24}$$

where η_{K_j} is the perceived elasticity of the supply of capital to the jurisdiction with respect to changes in the property tax rate; that is,

$$\eta_{K_j} = -(T_j/K_j)\partial K_j/\partial T_j, \tag{25}$$

where r, p, ϕ and Z_j are held constant. Thus, the three terms of the first-order condition Eq. (24) indicate that, for any ϕ, the government raises its property tax rate as long as the value of the marginal increase in revenue from the higher taxes [the first term in Eq. (24)] outweighs the loss in revenue from the lower tax base (the second term) and the loss in fixed factor income due to capital outmigration (the third term).

In order to solve for η_{K_j}, the perceived elasticity of housing prices with respect to property tax changes,

$$\eta_{q_j} = (T_j/q_j)\partial q_j/\partial T_j, \tag{26}$$

must be determined. Substituting from Eq. (8) into Eq. (4) and differentiating with respect to T_j, holding r, p, ϕ and Z_j constant, yields

$$(H_j + q_j\pi_{qq}^{H_j})\partial q_j/\partial T_j + q_j\pi_{qr}^{H_j} r = [\alpha/(\alpha + \gamma_j)]\partial I_j/\partial T_j. \tag{27}$$

Substituting from Eqs. (16), (21) and (26) yields

$$[\gamma_j/(\alpha + \gamma_j) + \eta_{H_j}]\eta_{q_j} = -[\alpha(\alpha + \gamma_j)]rK_jT_j/(q_jH_j) + \eta_{H_j}. \tag{28}$$

Defining

$$y_{K_j} = (rK_T/N)/I_j^G, \tag{29}$$

using Eq. (4), and solving for η_{q_j} after multiplying (28) by $(\alpha + \gamma_j)$ yields

$$\eta_{q_j} = [(\alpha + \gamma_j)\eta_{H_j} - T_j y_{K_j}]/[(\alpha + \gamma_j)\eta_{H_j} + \gamma_j]. \tag{30}$$

Turning to the perceived capital supply elasticity, substituting from Eqs. (9)–(10) into Eq. (22), differentiating with respect to T_j holding p, r, ϕ and Z_j constant, substituting from Eqs. (13)–(14), and solving for η_{K_j} as specified in Eq. (25) yields

$$\eta_{K_j} = [\mu_X + \mu_H(1 - \eta_{q_j})]/K_j. \tag{31}$$

Substituting from Eq. (30) yields

$$\eta_{K_j} = \frac{\mu_{X_j}[(\alpha + \gamma_j)\eta_{H_j} + \gamma_j] + \mu_{H_j}(\gamma_j + T_j y_{K_j})}{K_j[(\alpha + \gamma_j)\eta_{H_j} + \gamma_j]} > 0, \tag{32}$$

which is unambiguously positive, confirming that each local government expects an increase in its property tax rate to drive mobile capital out of its jurisdiction.

Finally, we choose the following price normalization:

$$Np + N_1 q_1 + N_2 q_2 = 2N, \tag{33}$$

where units are chosen so that $p = q_1 = q_2 = 1$ in the initial equilibrium. The six-equation equilibrium system is thus described by Eqs. (4) and (24) for $j = 1, 2$, Eqs. (18) and (33).

3. Differential Incidence Results

Totally differentiating the system of six equations described above yields the 'equations of change' for the model — the changes in the endogenous variables as a function of changes in the exogenous ϕ parameter. Our symmetry assumptions ensure that many quantities, including all housing market variables, gross income shares, capital stock variables and all derivatives of the profit functions, are identical in the initial equilibrium;

to simplify the notation in the discussion below, the j subscripts are dropped for all such quantities. The system of differential equations for the model, calculated at the initial equilibrium where $T_j = \phi = 1$, is obtained as follows.

It is convenient first to solve for the change in aggregate net income in a jurisdiction as a function of the changes in the six endogenous variables $(p, T_1, T_2, q_1, q_2, r)$ and the exogenous variable (ϕ). Substituting from Eqs. (11)–(12) into Eq. (17), differentiating, and collecting terms (noting that $K_T/N = K_{X_j} + K_{H_j}$ in the initial equilibrium) yields

$$\tilde{I}_j = (pX_j/I_j)\tilde{p} + (q_j H_j/I_j)\tilde{q}_j - [T_j y_{K_j}/(\alpha + \gamma_j)]\tilde{T}_j - (\phi Z_j/I_j)\tilde{\phi}, \quad (34)$$

where the tilde denotes logarithmic differentiation. Substituting from Eqs. (2)–(4) and evaluating at the initial equilibrium yields

$$\tilde{I}_j = (\alpha + \gamma_j)^{-1}[(1-\alpha)\tilde{p} + \alpha\tilde{q}_j - y_K\tilde{T}_j - \beta_j\tilde{\phi}]. \quad (35)$$

Substituting from Eq. (8) into the housing market equilibrium equation (4), differentiating, and then substituting from the definition of η_{H_j} in Eq. (16) and evaluating at the initial equilibrium yields

$$-\eta_H\tilde{T}_j + (1+\eta_H)\tilde{q}_j - \eta_H\tilde{r} - \tilde{I}_j = 0. \quad (36)$$

Substituting from Eq. (35) into Eq. (36) and collecting terms yields the first two differential equations in the model,

$$\begin{aligned}(1-\alpha)\tilde{p} + [(\alpha+\gamma_j)\eta_H - y_K]\tilde{T}_j + [(\alpha+\gamma_j)\eta_H]\tilde{r} \\ - [(\alpha+\gamma_j)\eta_H + y_j]\tilde{q}_j = \beta_j\tilde{\phi}, \quad j = 1,2. \end{aligned} \quad (37)$$

To obtain the next two differential equations in the system, note first that differentiating Eq. (19), multiplying by pG_j and evaluating at the initial equilibrium using Eqs. (2) and (25) yields

$$\tilde{G}_j + \tilde{p} = (y_{K_j}/\beta_j)\tilde{T}_j + \tilde{\phi}. \quad (38)$$

Differentiating the governmental first-order condition Eq. (24), multiplying by (pG_j/β_j), and evaluating at the initial equilibrium using Eq. (2) yields,

$$-(\tilde{G}_j + \tilde{p}) - \eta_{K_j}\tilde{T}_j + \tilde{I}_j = 0. \quad (39)$$

Substituting from Eq. (35) and (38) and multiplying by $(\alpha + \gamma_j)$ yields the third and fourth differential equations in the model,

$$(1-\alpha)\tilde{p} - [y_K/\beta_j + (\alpha+\gamma_j)\eta_{K_j}]\tilde{T}_j + \alpha\tilde{q}_j = \tilde{\phi}, \qquad j = 1,2. \tag{40}$$

Derivation of the fifth and sixth differential equations in the model is straightforward. Differentiating the capital market equilibrium Eq. (18) and substituting from Eqs. (13)–(14) yields

$$-N\mu_X\tilde{p} + \sum_{j=1}^{2}[N_j(\mu_X+\mu_H)\tilde{T}_j - N_j\mu_H\tilde{q}_j] + N(\mu_X+\mu_H)\tilde{r} = 0. \tag{41}$$

Differentiating the price normalization Eq. (33) and dividing by N yields

$$\tilde{p} + (N_1/N)\tilde{q}_1 + (N_2/N)\tilde{q}_2 = 0. \tag{42}$$

Solving this six-equation system — Eqs. (37) and (40) for $j = 1,2$, and Eqs. (41)–(42) — yields the differential incidence results for the model. These results are presented as elasticities of the endogenous variables with respect to a reduction in ϕ; thus, $\varepsilon_{T_1} = -(\phi/T_1)\mathrm{d}T_1/\mathrm{d}\phi$, etc.

The elasticities of the tax rates are

$$\varepsilon_{T_1} = \sigma_2(\alpha+\gamma_1)(2N)[\mu_X(\eta_H + 1 - \alpha) + \mu_H(1-\alpha)]/D > 0, \tag{43}$$

$$\varepsilon_{T_2} = \sigma_1(\alpha+\gamma_2)(2N)[\mu_X(\eta_H + 1 - \alpha) + \mu_H(1-\alpha)]/D > 0, \tag{44}$$

where

$$\sigma_j = (\alpha+\gamma_j)\{(\eta_{H_j} + 1 - \alpha)y_{K_j}/\beta_j + [(\alpha+\gamma_j)\eta_{H_j} + \gamma_j]\eta_{K_j} - \alpha\eta_{H_j}\} > 0, \tag{45}$$

and $D > 0$ is the determinant of the coefficient matrix of the six-equation differential system; as shown in the appendix, the second-order condition for the government optimization problem evaluated at the initial equilibrium implies $\sigma_j > 0$, while the assumption that the system is stable implies $D > 0$.

Thus, property tax rates in both jurisdictions must increase when the permitted level of head taxation (ϕ) declines.

Moreover, substituting from Eq. (45) for $j = 1, 2$ demonstrates that

$$\Omega = [\sigma_2(\alpha + \gamma_1) - \sigma_1(\alpha + \gamma_2)]/D > 0, \tag{46}$$

so that

$$\varepsilon_{T_1} - \varepsilon_{T_2} = \Omega(2N)[\mu_X(\eta_H + 1 - \alpha) + \mu_H(1 - \alpha)] > 0. \tag{47}$$

Thus, property taxes rise more in jurisdictions of type one — high-demander jurisdictions have higher property tax rates.

The price elasticity expressions presented below are each separated into two sets of terms. The first set reflects the 'new-view' effects of local use of the property tax as specified by Eqs. (43)–(44). These terms reflect the effects of the re-allocation of capital from the relatively high-tax jurisdictions of type one to the relatively low-tax jurisdictions of type two and, following the terminology in Mieszkowski (1972), are described in terms of a 'profits-tax effect' and some associated 'excise-tax effects'.

The second set reflects the effects of the 'consumption distortion' induced by the reduction in the permitted level of head taxation. This distortion arises for the following reason. In the initial head-tax equilibrium, the opportunity cost of government services is simply p, the price of the composite good. However when local governments use property tax finance, each government perceives a higher price as provision of public services has the additional cost of driving out mobile capital (as determined by η_{K_j}) and lowering local incomes.[10] Since government services are modeled simply as public purchases of the composite good, this consumption distortion has the effect of reducing total consumption of the composite good ($X_T = N_1X_1 + N_2X_2$) and increasing total consumption of housing ($H_T = N_1H_1 + N_2H_2$); specifically,[11]

$$\varepsilon_{X_T} = -2\eta_X\mu_H(N_1\theta_1 + N_2\theta_2) < 0, \tag{48}$$

[10] See Zodrow and Mieszkowski (1986) for a detailed discussion of the question of the effects of property tax finance on local public service levels.

[11] Expressions Eqs. (48)–(49) are obtained by substituting from Eqs. (7) and (8) into the definitions of X_T and H_T, differentiating, and substituting from Eqs. (43)–(44) as well as Eqs. (50), (53), and Eqs. (54)–(55) below.

$$\varepsilon_{H_T} = 2\eta_H \mu_X (N_1\theta_1 + N_2\theta_2) > 0, \tag{49}$$

where

$$\theta_1 = \sigma_2(\alpha + \gamma_1)\beta_1\eta_{K_1}/D > 0,$$
$$\theta_2 = \sigma_1(\alpha + \gamma_2)\beta_2\eta_{K_2}/D > 0.$$

The price changes induced by the reduction in ϕ are as follows. The change in the net return to capital is

$$\varepsilon_r = -[(N_1/\mathrm{N})\varepsilon_{T_1} + (N_2/N)\varepsilon_{T_2}] - (\mu_X - \mu_H)(N_1\theta_1 + N_2\theta_2). \tag{50}$$

The first term in Eq. (50) is unambiguously negative and reflects the fact that the movement of capital from the high-tax jurisdictions to the low-tax jurisdictions in response to a differential tax on capital reduces the overall net return to capital. This pure 'profits tax' effect, by itself, implies that the full burden of local use of the property tax is borne by capital owners; that is, capital bears the full burden of property taxation in the economy if

$$K_T \mathrm{d}r = -[(N_1 r K_1)\mathrm{d}T_1 + (N_2 r K_2)\mathrm{d}T_2], \tag{51}$$

or if

$$\varepsilon_r = -[(N_1/N)\varepsilon_{T_1} + (N_2/N)\varepsilon_{T_2}]. \tag{52}$$

The second term in Eq. (50) reflects the effect of the consumption distortion, as the demand for capital falls (rises) in the composite good (housing) sector which reduces (increases) the net return to capital; the net effect depends on the sign of $(\mu_X - \mu_H)$ which is theoretically ambiguous. Throughout our exposition below, we assume that either $(\mu_X - \mu_H) \geqq 0$ or, if not, the magnitude of the terms involving $(\mu_X - \mu_H)$ is sufficiently small that they do not change the signs of otherwise theoretically unambiguous expressions; this assumption is satisfied for all plausible parameter values.

For the particular price normalization Eq. (33) chosen, the change in the price of the composite good is determined solely by the effects of the consumption distortion, as

$$\varepsilon_p = -(\mu_X + \mu_H)(N_1\theta_1 + N_2\theta_2); \tag{53}$$

the reduction in composite good demand drives down its price. The changes in housing prices in the two jurisdictions are more complicated, as

$$\varepsilon_{q_1} = N_2\{\Omega\eta_H(\mu_X+\mu_H)+\lambda[(1-\alpha)(\mu_X+\mu_H)+\eta_H(\mu_X-\mu_H)]\} + N(\mu_X+\mu_H)\theta_1, \tag{54}$$

$$\varepsilon_{q_2} = -N_1\{\Omega\eta_H(\mu_X+\mu_H)+\lambda[(1-\alpha)(\mu_X+\mu_H)+\eta_H(\mu_X-\mu_H)]\} + N(\mu_X+\mu_H)\theta_2, \tag{55}$$

where λ, defined in the appendix, is positive for all plausible parameter values. The first terms in Eqs. (54) and (55) reflect one of the excise tax effects of the property tax differential. That is, the relative increase (decrease) in the gross price of capital in the high-demander, high-tax (low-demander, low-tax) jurisdictions results in an increase (decrease) in local housing prices. Note that these terms represent a pure redistribution of income between housing consumers in the two jurisdictions (multiplying the terms by N_1 and N_2, respectively, and adding yields zero) as higher housing prices in the high tax jurisdictions are offset by lower housing prices in the low tax jurisdictions. The second terms in Eqs. (54) and (55) indicate that the increased housing consumption induced by the consumption distortion drives up housing prices in both jurisdictions.

The changes in the returns to labor are calculated by differentiating Eq. (11) and substituting from the tax and price elasticities above to yield

$$y_L\varepsilon_{w_1} = -N_2\{y_{KX}(2\Omega)[\mu_X(\eta_H+1-\alpha)+\mu_H(1-\alpha)]\} - [y_L(\mu_X+\mu_H)+y_{KX}(2\mu_H)](N_1\theta_1+N_2\theta_2), \tag{56}$$

$$y_L\varepsilon_{w_2} = -N_1\{y_{KX}(2\Omega)[\mu_X(\eta_H+1-\alpha)+\mu_H(1-\alpha)]\} - [y_L(\mu_X+\mu_H)+y_{KX}(2\mu_H)](N_1\theta_1+N_2\theta_2), \tag{57}$$

where y_L is the labor share of gross income and y_{KX} is the composite good capital stock share of gross income. The first terms in Eqs. (56) and (57) again represent an 'excise tax effect' of the property tax differential as the migration of capital from (to) the high (low) tax jurisdictions lowers (raises) the marginal productivity of the fixed supplies of local labor. These terms represent pure redistribution of income as the lower wage payments made to the fixed factors in composite good production in the high tax jurisdictions are exactly offset by higher wages in the low tax jurisdictions. The second terms in Eqs. (56) and (57) indicate that the consumption distortion away from the composite good lowers the returns to labor in both jurisdictions.

The last set of price changes in the model are the changes in land prices in the two jurisdictions, which are obtained by differentiating Eq. (12) to yield

$$y_V \varepsilon_{sj} = -y_{KH}(\varepsilon_r + \varepsilon_{T_j}) + (y_{KH} + y_{VH})\varepsilon_{q_j}, \tag{58}$$

where y_V and y_{KH} are the land and housing capital shares in gross income. Substituting into Eq. (58) from the tax and price elasticities above yields expressions which are quite cumbersome; these expressions can be summarized as

$$y_V \varepsilon_{s_1} = -N_2 A + B_1(\theta_1, \theta_2), \tag{59}$$

$$y_V \varepsilon_{s_2} - N_1 A + B_2(\theta_1, \theta_2), \tag{60}$$

where A, B_1 and B_2 are defined in the appendix. The sign of A is positive if, in the high tax jurisdictions, the negative effect on land prices of higher taxes (which drive out capital and lower the marginal productivity of land) outweighs the positive effect of higher housing prices. In this case, the excise tax effects of the property tax differential, the first terms in Eqs. (59) and (60), indicate that lower land prices in the high tax jurisdictions are exactly offset by higher land prices in the low tax jurisdictions. In any case, these terms represent a pure redistribution of income between landowners in the two types of jurisdictions. Finally, since B_1 and B_2 are positive, the second terms in Eqs. (59) and (60) indicate that in both jurisdictions the price of land, the immobile factor in housing production, increases due to the consumption distortion toward greater housing consumption.

4. A Numerical Example

For purposes of illustration, we present a simple numerical example in this section. Consider our model for the case where $\beta_1 = 0.10$, $\beta_2 = 0.05$, $\gamma_1 = 0.60$,

$\gamma_2 = 0.65, N_1 = N_2 = 1$ and the composite good (housing) production function is Cobb–Douglas with a capital share parameter of 0.3 (0.7). Suppose further that in the initial equilibrium $p = q_1 = q_2 = 1$, and $K_X = K_H = 0.304, L = 1.70$, $V = 1.0$ which implies $r = 1$, $w = 0.418$ and $s = 0.131$. In this case, we have $\mu_X = \eta_X = 0.435$, $\mu_H = \eta_H = 1.015$, and $\eta_{K_1} = 1.837, \eta_{K_2} = 1.1819$.

The numerical values for the tax and price elasticities are shown below; when two numbers are listed and then added, the first corresponds to the profits tax or excise tax effects of the property tax differential and the second corresponds to the effects of the consumption distortion, as discussed in Section 3. The elasticities are:

$$\varepsilon_{T_1} = 0.194, \qquad \varepsilon_{T_2} = 0.110,$$

$$\varepsilon_p = -0.0114, \quad \varepsilon_r = -0.152 + 0.005 = -0.147,$$

$$\varepsilon_{q_1} = 0.0259 + 0.0178 = 0.0437, \quad \varepsilon_{q_2} = -0.0259 + 0.0050 = -0.0209,$$

$$y_L \varepsilon_{w_1} = -0.00881 - 0.00892 = -0.01773,$$

$$y_L \varepsilon_{w_2} = 0.00881 - 0.00892 = -0.00011,$$

$$y_V \varepsilon_{s_1} = -0.00103 + 0.00307 = 0.00204,$$

$$y_V \varepsilon_{s_2} = 0.00103 + 0.00017 = 0.00120.$$

The signs of all expressions are as described in the previous section. The return to capital falls due to the 'profits tax' portion of the tax, and the excise tax effects cause higher housing prices and lower wages and land prices in the high tax jurisdictions with exactly offsetting effects in the low tax jurisdictions. The consumption distortion results in higher housing prices and higher land prices, as well as lower composite good prices and lower wages, in both types of jurisdictions.

Note that the consumption distortion component of ε_r is quite small, so that the profits tax effect of the property tax differential on the return to capital is not mitigated to any significant extent. However, the consumption distortion effects are more important for the other price changes; in particular, the consumption distortion effects dominate the excise tax effects for ε_{w_2} and ε_{s_1}, so that wages fall in the low tax jurisdiction and land prices rise in the high tax jurisdiction.

5. Conclusion

We have analyzed the effects of nationwide use of the property tax by independent local jurisdictions within the context of a model with (i) interjurisdictional competition, (ii) endogenous local public service levels which are included in individual utility functions, (iii) individuals who differ in their tastes for public services and are segregated by taste into homogeneous communities, (iv) a simple form of land use zoning, and (v) a political or constitutional constraint on local use of head taxes. Within the context of this more general model — relative to the Mieszkowski (1972) analysis — we obtained two sets of results. First, we presented a reformulated version of the 'new view' of the incidence of the property tax; in particular, we derived expressions for the 'profits tax' effect which lowers the return to capital by the amount of the tax, and the 'excise tax' effects which cause pure redistributions of income between factor owners and consumers in the two types of local jurisdictions in the model. Second, we showed that local reluctance to impose a property tax on mobile capital results in a 'consumption distortion' away from government services and derived the effects of this phenomenon on commodity and factor prices. In our view, the perfect fiscal zoning constraints required for the validity of the alternative benefit view of the property tax are unlikely to obtain in practice, so that our 'reformulated new view' represents a more plausible explanation of the effects of local use of the property tax.

Appendix

The expressions for the σ_j, D, λ, A, B_1 and B_2 parameters used in the text are provided in this appendix. The sign of the expression σ_j Eq. (45) is obtained from the second-order condition for the local government optimization problem, evaluated at the initial equilibrium. Differentiating the governmental first-order condition Eq. (24) with respect to T_j, holding r,

p, ϕ, and Z_j constant, and evaluating at the initial equilibrium ($T_j = 1$) yields the second-order condition

$$-(\beta_j/pG_j^2)\partial G_j/\partial T_j - (\beta_j/pG_j)(1/T_j)\eta_{K_j} + [(\alpha+\gamma_j)/I_j^2]\partial I_j/\partial T_j < 0, \quad \text{(A.1)}$$

where η_{K_j} is defined in Eq. (25) as the perceived elasticity of supply of capital to the local jurisdiction with respect to changes in the jurisdiction's property tax rate. Noting from Eq. (2) that $(\beta_j/pG_j) = (\alpha+\gamma_j)I_j$ at the initial equilibrium and multiplying (A.1) by $T_jI_j/(\alpha+\gamma_j) = I_j/(\alpha+\gamma_j)$ yields

$$-\eta_{G_j} - \eta_{K_j} + \eta_{I_j} < 0. \quad \text{(A.2)}$$

where η_{G_j} (η_{I_j}) is the elasticity of government services (net income) with respect to changes in the property tax rate as perceived by the local government at the initial equilibrium.

The derivation of η_{G_j} is analogous to the derivation of Eq. (38) except that the local government perceives p and ϕ to be fixed. Thus, converting Eq. (38) to elasticity form with $\tilde{p} = \tilde{\phi} = 0$ yields

$$\eta_{G_j} = y_{K_j}/\beta_j. \quad \text{(A.3)}$$

Similarly, the derivation of η_{I_j} is analogous to the derivation of Eq. (35) with p and ϕ fixed. Converting Eq. (35) to elasticity form with $\tilde{p} = \tilde{\phi} = 0$ yields

$$\eta_{I_j} = (\alpha+\gamma_j)^{-1}(\alpha\eta_{q_j} - y_{K_j}), \quad \text{(A.4)}$$

where η_{q_j} is defined in Eq. (30) as the perceived elasticity of housing prices with respect to changes in the local property tax rate.

Substituting from Eqs. (30), (A.3) and (A.4) into (A.2), multiplying by $\{-(\alpha+\gamma_j)[(\alpha+\gamma_j)\eta_{H_j} + \gamma_j]\}$, and collecting terms noting that $(\gamma_j + \alpha\beta_j) = (1-\alpha)(\alpha+\gamma_j)$, yields

$$\sigma_j = (\alpha+\gamma_j)\{(\eta_{H_j} + 1 - \alpha)y_{K_j}/\beta_j + [(\alpha+\gamma_j)\eta_{H_j} + \gamma_j]\eta_{K_j} - \alpha\eta_{H_j}\} > 0. \quad \text{(A.5)}$$

The expression for D is obtained by evaluating the coefficient matrix of the differential Eqs. (37) and (40)–(42) at the initial equilibrium; this yields

$$D = N_1\sigma_2(\alpha+\gamma_1)\{\alpha\eta_H + (1-\alpha)(y_K/\beta_1 + \eta_{K_1})$$
$$+\eta_H[y_K/\beta_1 + \eta_{K_1}(\alpha+\gamma_1)](\mu_X - \mu_H)\}$$
$$+N_2\sigma_1(\alpha+\gamma_2)\{\alpha\eta_H + (1-\alpha)(y_K/\beta_2 + \eta_{K_2})$$
$$+\eta_H[y_K/\beta_2 + \eta_{K_2}(\alpha+\gamma_2)](\mu_X - \mu_H)\} + N\sigma_1\sigma_2(\mu_X + \mu_H). \quad \text{(A.6)}$$

We assume the system is stable, which implies $D > 0$ [see Neary (1978), or Atkinson and Stiglitz (1980)]; note that all terms other than $(\mu_X - \mu_H)$, are unambiguously positive.

The expression for λ is

$$\lambda = \{\eta_H[y_K/\beta_2 - y_K/\beta_1 + \eta_{K_2}(\alpha+\gamma_2) - \eta_{K_1}(\alpha+\gamma_1)]$$
$$+ y_K[(\beta_1/\beta_2)\eta_{K_1} - (\beta_2/\beta_1)\eta_{K_2}]$$
$$+(\beta_1-\beta_2)\eta_{K_1}\eta_{K_2}\}(\alpha+\gamma_1)(\alpha+\gamma_2)/D. \quad \text{(A.7)}$$

The sign of λ is ambiguous. However, the difference between the perceived capital supply elasticity parameters η_{K_1} and η_{K_2} is quite small for all plausible parameter values. Since, for $\eta_{K_1} = \eta_{K_2} = \eta_K$, λ becomes

$$\lambda' = \{(\eta_H y_K/\beta_1\beta_2)(\beta_1-\beta_2) + \eta_H\eta_K(\beta_1-\beta_2)$$
$$+ y_K\eta_K[(\beta_1/\beta_2) - (\beta_2/\beta_1)]$$
$$+\eta_K^2(\beta_1-\beta_2)\}(\alpha+\gamma_1)(\alpha+\gamma_2)/\mathrm{D}, \quad \text{(A.7')}$$

which is unambiguously positive, we assume that $\lambda > 0$.

The expression for A is

$$A = \Omega\, y_{KH}[2(\mu_X+\mu_H)(1-\alpha) + \eta_H(\mu_X-\mu_H)] - \Omega\, y_V\eta_H(\mu_X+\mu_H)$$
$$-\lambda(y_{KH}+y_V)[(1-\alpha)(\mu_X+\mu_H) + \eta_H(\mu_X-\mu_H)]. \quad \text{(A.8)}$$

A is positive if, in the high tax jurisdiction, the effect on land prices of higher taxes which drive out capital and lower the marginal productivity of land [the first term in (A.8)] outweighs the effect of higher housing prices which increase the demand for land [the second and third terms of (A.8)].

Finally, the expressions for B_1 and B_2 are

$$B_1(\theta_1,\theta_2) = [Ny_V(\mu_X+\mu_H) + (N+N_2)y_{KH}\mu_X]\theta_1 + N_2 y_{KH}(\mu_X-\mu_H)\theta_2. \quad \text{(A.9)}$$

$$B_2(\theta_1,\theta_2) = N_1 y_{KH}(\mu_X - \mu_H)\theta_1 + [N y_V(\mu_X + \mu_H) + (N + N_2) y_{KH}\mu_X]\theta_2. \tag{A. 10}$$

Barring implausibly large (in absolute value) negative values of $(\mu_X - \mu_H)$, both B_1 and B_2 are positive.

Acknowledgements

Financial support from the National Science Foundation (Grant SES82-09210) is gratefully acknowledged. We have benefited from the research assistance of Julie Sutterfield and from a careful reading by an anonymous referee. Opinions expressed do not reflect U.S. Treasury policy.

References

Aaron, H.J., 1975, Who pays the property tax? (Brookings Institution, Washington, DC).

Atkinson, A.B. and N.H. Stern, 1974, Pigou, taxation and public goods, Review of Economic Studies 41, 119–128.

Atkinson, A.B. and J.E. Stiglitz, 1980, Lectures on public economics (McGraw-Hill, New York).

Ballentine, J.G. and I. Eris, 1975, On the general equilibrium analysis of tax incidence, Journal of Political Economy 83, 633–644.

Brown, H.G., 1924, The economics of taxation (Holt, New York).

Brueckner, J.K., 1981, Labor mobility and the incidence of the residential property tax, Journal of Public Economics 10, 173–182.

Courant, P.N., 1977, A general equilibrium model of heterogeneous property taxes, Journal of Public Economics 8, 313–327.

Diewert, W.E., 1974, Applications of duality theory, in: M.D. Intriligator and D.A. Kendrick, eds., Frontiers of quantitative economics, Vol. II (North-Holland, Amsterdam).

Diewert, W.E., 1978, Optimal tax perturbations, Journal of Public Economics 10, 139–177.

Fischel, W.A., 1975, Fiscal and environmental considerations in the location of firms in suburban communities, in: E.S. Mills and W.E. Oates, eds., Fiscal zoning and land use controls (Lexington Books, Lexington, MA).

Hamilton, B.W., 1975, Zoning and property taxation in a system of local governments, Urban Studies 12, 205–211.

Hamilton, B.W., 1976, Capitalization of intrajurisdictional differences in local tax prices, American Economic Review 66, 743–753.

Hamilton, B.W., 1983, A review. Is the property tax a benefit tax? in: G.R. Zodrow, ed., Local provision of public services. The Tiebout model after twenty-five years (Academic Press, New York).

Harberger, A.C., 1962, The incidence of the corporate income tax, Journal of Political Economy 70, 215–240.

Mieszkowski, P.M., 1972, The property tax. An excise tax or a profits tax?, Journal of Public Economics 1, 73–96.

Neary, J.P., 1978, Dynamic stability and the theory of factor market distortions, American Economic Review 68, 671–682.

Starrett, D.A., 1980, On the method of taxation and the provision of local public goods, American Economic Review 70, 380–392.

Thomson, P., 1965, The property tax and the rate of interest, in: G.C.S. Benson, S. Benson, H. McClelland and P. Thomson, The American property tax (The Lincoln School of Public Finance, Claremont, CA).

Tiebout, C.M., 1965, A pure theory of local expenditures, Journal of Political Economy 64, 416–424.

Vandendorpe, A.L. and A.F. Friedlaender, 1976, Differential incidence in the presence of initial distorting taxes, Journal of Public Economics 6, 205–229.

White, M.J., 1975, Firm location in a zoned metropolitan area, in: E.S. Mills and W.E. Oates, eds., Fiscal zoning and land use controls (Lexington Books, Lexington, MA).

Zodrow, G.R. and P.M. Mieszkowski, 1983, The incidence of the property tax. The benefit view vs. the new view, in: G.R. Zodrow, ed., Local provision of public services. The Tiebout model after twenty-five years (Academic Press, New York).

Zodrow, G.R. and P.M. Mieszkowski, 1986, Pigou, Tiebout, property taxation and the under provision of local public goods, Journal of Urban Economics 19, 356–370.

Chapter 15

The Property Tax as a Capital Tax: A Room with Three Views*

George R. Zodrow

Economics Department, Baker Institute for Public Policy, Rice University, Houston, TX 77005

1. Introduction

The property tax has long been the major source of own-revenue at the local government level, and a huge academic literature has investigated the economic effects of this widely used tax; Mieszkowski and Zodrow (1989) and Ladd (1998) provide reviews of this literature. Nevertheless, despite all this attention, the incidence of the property tax — the critical issue of who ultimately bears the burden of the tax — is still one of the more controversial and more interesting issues in state and local public finance. Three alternative views of the incidence of the tax have appeared in the literature — the "traditional view" which argues that the property tax is

*This chapter is reproduced from *National Tax Journal*, **54**(1), 139–156, 2001.

This article draws heavily on Zodrow (forthcoming), which provides a more detailed exposition of the points made here. I have benefited from extended discussions with Peter Mieszkowski and the comments of John Yinger and Douglas Holtz-Eakin.

fully shifted forward to consumers in the form of higher housing prices, the "benefit view" which concludes that the property tax is simply a payment for local public services received, and the so-called "new view" of the property tax which argues that it is a distortionary tax on the use of capital within a local jurisdiction. This article reviews the ongoing debate regarding the incidence of the property tax, including both the theoretical underpinnings of the various views and the empirical evidence that might be used to differentiate among them.[1]

The central theme of the article is that each of the three views can — to a considerable but certainly not complete extent — be illuminated by reference to model of the property tax as a capital tax that underlies the new view. (Given that the "new" view is now approaching its thirtieth birthday, I shall — after consultation with my frequent co-author and the originator of the new view, Peter Mieszkowski — refer to it as the "capital tax" view.) In particular, as has long been understood, the traditional view can be shown to be a special case of the capital tax view. Moreover, as stressed by Zodrow (2000), when considered from the perspective of a single taxing local jurisdiction, the capital tax view implies that local use of the property tax is characterized by many of the features associated with the benefit view. However, the essential difference between the two views still remains — the capital tax view implies that the property tax is a distortionary tax on the use of capital within a jurisdiction, while the benefit view implies that the tax is a non-distortionary user charge for public services received. Nevertheless, another central theme of the article is that the two approaches are sufficiently similar that it is quite difficult to distinguish between them in empirical research.

2. The Three Views of the Property Tax

Each of the three views of the property tax has a long history. The following discussion summarizes this history and provides a brief outline of the derivations and the primary implications of the three views.

---

[1] In general, the discussion will follow the bulk of the academic literature and focus on the capital portion of the residential property tax.

2.1. *The traditional view*

The traditional view dates back to Simon (1943) and Netzer (1966), who took a partial equilibrium approach to analyzing the tax, focusing on the effects of increasing the tax in a local housing market. From this perspective, one can make the standard "open economy" assumption that the national return to capital is fixed. This in turn implies that local capital bears none of the local property tax, as capital in the long run migrates from the jurisdiction until the local after-tax return to capital equals the national value. The burden of the tax is thus borne by local factors and/or consumers, and the traditional view holds that this entire burden is borne by local housing consumers in the form of higher housing prices. The traditional view thus implies that the property tax inefficiently reduces the size of the local housing stock and that its burden is borne in proportion to housing consumption (and is thus somewhat regressive or roughly proportional with respect to lifetime income).

2.2. *The benefit view*

A second popular theory is the benefit view of the property tax. It was developed initially by Hamilton (1975, 1976a), Fischel (1975) and White (1975), and is reviewed in Hamilton (1983) and Fischel (forthcoming, and in this issue of the *NTA Forum*). This view is an important extension of the renowned Tiebout (1956) model of local government, which argues that consumer mobility ("voting with the feet" for alternative local tax and expenditure combinations) and interjurisdictional competition in the provision of local public services are, under certain conditions sufficient to ensure efficiency of resource allocation in the local public sector. Tiebout ignored local property taxation and instead assumed the existence of benefit taxes in the form of head taxes. However, in his important contributions to the literature, Hamilton developed the conditions under which the property tax can be converted into the head tax assumed by Tiebout.

Following Tiebout, Hamilton assumed that individuals are sorted into local jurisdictions according to their demands for local public services, and that there are enough local tax-expenditure packages to accommodate all tastes. In addition, Hamilton (1975) assumed that local jurisdictions are also homogeneous with respect to house values, and that there are enough jurisdictions to accommodate all desired housing/government service packages. Finally, Hamilton assumed the existence of binding zoning constraints that established a minimum house value for each community. Under these circumstances, individuals were precluded from purchasing homes with a value below the minimum and thus "free riding" on their neighbors in the sense of enjoying local public services without paying at least the taxes associated with the minimum value home. Moreover, individuals would never purchase a home with a value greater than the minimum house value established by the zoning constraint, as doing so would imply subsidizing the public service consumption of their neighbors; such individuals would instead move to a community where the demands for housing and public services exactly matched their own. Under such circumstances, all individuals in a given community pay exactly the same property tax, which functions precisely as a benefit tax.

Hamilton (1976a) extended this model to the more realistic case in which house values are heterogeneous. In this model, Hamilton assumes that all communities are fully developed, effectively precluding changes in the housing stock in response to changes in the level of property taxation. In addition, he assumed that even though some communities were heterogeneous with respect to housing consumption, communities that were homogeneous with respect to both demands for public services and housing were available as well. This assumption implies that no individuals would be willing to pay any property taxes in excess of benefits received, since the option of a fully homogeneous community is always available. Under these circumstances, Hamilton shows that "perfect capitalization" converts the property tax into a benefit tax. This result obtains because a relatively expensive home must sell at a discount equal to its "fiscal differential" or the present value of all future taxes in excess of benefits received, while a relatively inexpensive home sells at a premium reflecting its fiscal differential, which in this case is the present value of all future benefits in excess of future taxes. (In the latter case, individuals are willing to pay the premium since their only alternative is a homogeneous community with low house values and low public services.)

Hamilton's work has been extended by Fischel (1985, 1995), who argues that zoning ordinances, defined comprehensively to include a wide variety of land use regulations, are sufficiently restrictive to convert the property tax into a benefit tax in the manner envisioned by Hamilton (1975). He stresses that zoning ordinances are not limited to specifying minimum lot sizes (and one home per lot), but can encompass many other types of land use regulations. More recently, Fischel (forthcoming) has argued that a wide variety of empirical studies, especially the comprehensive work of Yinger, Bloom, Boersch-Supan and Ladd (1988), have found evidence that property taxes and local public service expenditures are capitalized into house values as predicted by the Hamilton (1976a) model. He argues that fiscal "capitalization is everywhere" and that the existence of such capitalization is sufficient to make the property tax a benefit tax at the local level.

The implications of the benefit view are striking. First, the property tax is effectively a user charge that is paid in exchange for the benefits of local public service. It is thus a non-distortionary tax. Second, as a benefit tax, the property tax has no effects on the distribution of income.

2.3. *The capital tax view*

Finally, the capital tax view (that is, the "new" view) of the property tax, first developed by Mieszkowski (1972), subsequently extended by Zodrow and Mieszkowski (1983, 1986b) and reviewed in Zodrow (forthcoming), argues that the property tax is a distortionary tax on the local use of capital, which results in a misallocation of the national capital stock across local jurisdictions. Mieszkowski (1972) stressed that the partial equilibrium analyses of the property tax that characterized the traditional view were highly misleading as they ignored the fact that the property tax was used by virtually all local jurisdictions and applied to a large fraction of the capital stock (including most non-residential capital). Adapting the Harberger (1962) general equilibrium model of tax incidence to the analysis of the property tax, he modeled the economy as having a fixed national capital stock and two types of local jurisdictions — those characterized by "high" tax rates and those characterized by "low" tax rates. In this context, Mieszkowski showed that property tax rates that exceed the national average drive capital out of the high-tax jurisdiction into a relatively low-tax jurisdiction, with opposing effects occurring in relatively low tax jurisdictions.[2] Property tax differentials thus result in an inefficient misallocation of capital across jurisdictions. In terms of incidence, the "average burden" of all of the property taxes imposed across the nation — known as the "profits tax effect" of the tax — is borne by capital owners generally. In marked contrast to the other two views, this profits tax effect implies that the property tax is relatively progressive (with respect to annual income) and is thus a relatively progressive element of the national tax structure. In addition, Mieszkowski stressed that property tax differentials about the national average result in "excise tax effects" in the form of housing and commodity price increases and wage and land price declines in relatively high tax jurisdictions; these effects are accompanied by offsetting housing and commodity price declines and wage and land price increases in relatively low tax jurisdictions. These roughly symmetric excise tax effects tend to cancel, so that from a national perspective their distributional effects are secondary; that is, the profits tax effect to and the primary factor affecting the distribution of the tax burden under the capital tax view.

This short description of the three views of the property tax obviously only provides an outline of their main tenets and derivations. Nevertheless, the analysis makes clear that the choice between the three alternative views is an important issue, as their implications for both the efficiency of resource allocation to the local public sector and the distribution of the burden of the property tax are quite different.

3. The Property Tax as a Capital Tax: A Theory (Partially) Encompassing All Three Views

As suggested in the introduction, the capital tax view can be described as being sufficiently general to encompass much, although not all, of the competing two views. In the case of the traditional view, this description is complete, as the traditional view is simply a special case of the capital

[2] In addition, local concerns about the extent to which use of the property tax may drive capital out of a jurisdiction creates a tendency for local governments to choose an inefficiently low level of public services; this point was developed Zodrow and Mieszkowski (1986b) and Wilson (1986), and the associated literature is reviewed in Wilson (1999).

tax view. Specifically, the traditional view can be interpreted as focusing exclusively on the "excise tax effects" of the capital tax view, while — as is standard for such a partial equilibrium analysis — neglecting the general equilibrium effects of the tax which in this case are its "profits tax" components. In particular, as shown by Wildasin (1986) within the context of a model that is consistent with the capital tax view, the excise tax effects of an increase in the property tax by a single jurisdiction will be fully reflected in higher housing prices only under special circumstances — specifically, when the land supply is fixed and the extent to which consumers can substitute between housing and other goods is equal to the extent to which producers can substitute between capital and land in the production of housing.[3] More generally, as described in Mieszkowski's original derivation, the excise tax effects of a property tax increase in a single jurisdiction are borne in some combination by housing consumers and the owners of labor and land in the taxing jurisdiction; in particular, backward shifting of the tax onto local landowners is more likely if individuals can move easily across competing jurisdictions.

The extent to which the capital tax view encompasses the benefit view is less complete and less transparent. The basic points can be seen by examining two alternative derivations of the capital tax view. First, Zodrow and Mieszkowski (1986a) extended the original Mieszkowski (1972) derivation to include many of the aspects of local government use of the property tax stressed by proponents of the benefit view.[4] In particular, the Zodrow-Mieszkowski model explicitly considered interjurisdictional competition, individual utility functions that include varying tastes for local public services, segregation into differing communities according to individual tastes for local public services, and a simple form of land use zoning; all of these factors were ignored in the original Mieszkowski derivation. They show that adding all of these "benefit-view-type" features

[3] More formally, the elasticity of substitution in consumption between housing and other goods in the individual utility function equals the elasticity of substitution in production between capital and land in the housing production function.

[4] This paper was partially a response to Aaron (1975, p. 42) who argued in his often-cited survey of the property tax literature that "the theoretical foundations of the new view are incomplete."

to the capital tax view model does not change its basic results, as long as (1) capital is mobile across jurisdictions in response to interjurisdictional property tax differentials, and (2) capital is fixed in total supply at the national level. Under these circumstances, the incidence of the property tax is still determined by its profits tax and excise tax effects, despite the various benefit view features that characterize the model.

The second alternative derivation of the capital tax view focuses on a general equilibrium analysis of the incidence of tax changes initiated by a single independent jurisdiction. At first glance, it might appear that the capital tax view is irrelevant for such a tax increase, as models of tax changes by such a "small open economy" typically assume that it faces an infinitely elastic supply of capital so that its policies cannot affect the after-tax return to capital. However, Zodrow and Mieszkowski (1983), following the work of Brown (1924) and Bradford (1978), demonstrate that such a view can be misleading; in particular, the capital tax view of the property tax can in fact be derived in such a context as well.[5] Specifically, even though the outflow of capital caused by an increase in the property tax by a small local jurisdiction is small, it will depress the overall return to capital very slightly. Although the taxing jurisdiction can reasonably neglect this small effect, it naturally affects a very large capital stock, and the revenue raised by the small taxing jurisdiction is also quite small. Mieszkowski and Zodrow show that under certain circumstances the overall reduction in national capital income precisely equals the amount of revenue raised by the taxing jurisdiction — that is, capital bears the full burden of the tax. This of course is simply the profits tax effect of the capital tax view, as applied to an increase in the property tax by a single small local jurisdiction.

Moreover, this analysis is entirely consistent with the standard analysis of the incidence of a tax on capital by a small taxing jurisdiction, which concludes that the tax is borne by local factors of production or local consumers.[6] This effect occurs simultaneously, as the tax-induced

---

[5] See also the excellent analysis by Lin (1986) and, in the context of state corporate tax on capital, Mieszkowski and Zodrow (1985).

[6] This is a standard "open economy" result; see for example Kotlikoff and Summers (1987). See also McLure (1977) who stresses the differences between the national effects of the property tax and its effects when imposed by a single taxing jurisdiction.

outflow of capital from the taxing jurisdiction implies lower returns to relatively immobile factors such as local land and labor and/or higher prices to local consumers. Indeed, for a sufficiently small economy — a condition which would describe virtually all local jurisdictions — Kotlikoff and Summers (1987) show that the tax burden borne by local factors is roughly equal to the total burden of the tax. The case in which the entire tax burden is shifted forward to consumers of course corresponds to the "traditional view" of the incidence of the property tax. More generally, the local burden of the tax is shared between consumers and the owners of local factors.

The critical point here is that under the capital tax view — just as under the benefit view — there is a close link between local public services and the burden of the property tax, as the burden of financing local expenditures largely falls on local factor owners and local consumers in the taxing jurisdiction. Indeed, to the extent that local landowners (in particular, homeowners) reside in the taxing jurisdiction and increases in consumer prices are limited to goods (including especially housing) that are produced and consumed locally,[7] this derivation of the capital tax view clearly has a striking benefit view flavor — the burden of increases in local government expenditures financed with increases in the local property tax tends to be borne entirely by local residents. The primary difference between this "benefit view" version of the capital tax view and the actual benefit view is that the mechanism for achieving this result under the former is different than under the latter, as the burden of the tax on local factors and consumers under the capital tax view arises due to the outflow of capital in response to the imposition of the tax.

Note also that the public choice implications of the two views may be similar. Of course, voters are unlikely to perceive the shifting mechanism underlying the "benefit view" version of the capital tax. Nevertheless, if they link property tax paid with services received and perceive that they bear the incidence of the tax, then their voting behavior — as well as the

[7] Note that in the standard small open economy model, the possibilities for forward shifting of taxes on exported goods are severely limited by national and international competition, so that local consumers tend to bear almost all of the burden of the tax that is shifted forward in the form of higher consumer prices.

incentives to "free ride" by under-consuming housing — will be similar to that under the benefit view.

Finally, Mieszkowski and Zodrow also show that the burden of the use of the property tax by a single taxing jurisdiction on local factors of production and local consumers is offset by opposing effects on the analogous factors of production and consumers in all of the non-taxing jurisdictions. That is, all of these "excise tax" effects tend to cancel in the aggregate, so that from a national perspective the main distributional effect of the use of the property tax by a single taxing jurisdiction is a reduction in the net return to capital; this result obtains despite the fact, stressed by McLure (1977), that the distributional effects of the tax increase are very different from the perspective of the local jurisdiction.[8] Thus, in an important sense there are two "burdens" of the use of the property tax by a single taxing jurisdiction — (1) the national burden, which is primarily reflected in a reduction in the overall return to capital in the economy, and (2) the local burden, which is borne by local labor and landowners as well as the consumers of locally produced goods, and accompanied by offsetting effects on factors of production and consumers in all other jurisdictions. The existence of these two simultaneous tax burdens is the key factor giving rise to the benefit tax aspect of the capital tax view.

4. Choosing Among the Three Views

A wide variety of studies have attempted to find ways to choose among the three views. One approach has been to attack the basic assumptions underlying the views. For example, the derivation of the capital tax view is suspect because it assumes a fixed national capital stock and neglects the adjustment costs involved in reallocating the capital stock in response to a tax increase, while the benefit view assumes the validity of the Tiebout

[8] More recently Ladd (1998, p. 36) has noted that, "from the perspective of the mayor of an individual city, the property tax is reasonably viewed as regressive" to the extent that the mayor focuses only on the effects of the tax in his or her jurisdiction (and consumption of housing declines with income) and ignores the effects of the use of the property tax by other jurisdictions. However, under the capital tax view, the latter factor implies that the tax is progressive from a national perspective.

model, which has been questioned by a number of authors.[9] However, most of the debate surrounding the incidence of the property tax has assumed the general validity of the underlying theoretical models and focused instead on other issues. I shall follow such an approach for the balance of the article. Moreover, since the traditional view is essentially a special case of the capital tax view, I shall focus on means of differentiating between the benefit and capital tax views. As noted above, a central message of the article is that even though there are fundamental differences between the two views, they are sufficiently similar that it is often difficult to distinguish between them empirically.

4.1. *Evidence supporting the Tiebout sorting mechanism*

Since the benefit view is essentially an extension of the Tiebout model, empirical evidence supporting the existence of the Tiebout "sorting" mechanism — under which households tend to be grouped in jurisdictions that are relatively homogeneous with respect to demands for public services — could be interpreted as providing some support for the benefit view. A number of studies provide empirical evidence that the variation in variables that might be taken as proxies for (unobservable) demands for local public services, such as income and housing consumption, is significantly less within communities than across communities.[10] However, these studies in fact provide little information on the choice between the benefit and capital tax views. For example, Oates (1994) argues that tendencies toward homogeneity are not a very strong test of the Tiebout model, as such tendencies are consistent with other models of locational behavior, especially the bidding and sorting model developed by Ellickson (1971) and Henderson (1977).[11] More fundamentally, however, Zodrow and Mieszkowski (1986a) have derived the standard capital tax view results regarding the incidence of the property tax within the context of a model that is characterized by Tiebout sorting of individuals by taste for public services; indeed, in their model, all desired public service/housing demand

[9] For example, see Zodrow (1983), Rubinfeld (1987) and Ross and Yinger (2000).

[10] See Ross and Yinger (2000) and the references cited therein.

[11] See Ross and Yinger (2000) for a recent survey.

packages are available and all communities are perfectly homogeneous with respect to both housing and public service demands. Thus, evidence supporting the existence of the Tiebout sorting mechanism does not provide compelling evidence for either the benefit view or the capital tax view.

4.2. *The elasticity of supply of communities*

The Tiebout (1956) and Hamilton (1975) models assume the existence of a sufficient number of communities to satisfy all the different individual demands for public services, while the Hamilton (1976a) model requires a sufficient number of communities to satisfy all demands for both public services and housing. Unless the number of desired taste combinations is fairly limited, these are rather strong assumptions, especially since the mechanisms for creating new communities in response to demands for particular housing, tax and services packages are costly. The reasonableness of this assumption has been debated in the literature. Fischel (1995, p. 255), drawing on earlier work (Fischel, 1981) that indicated that 80 percent of the urban population lives in areas that are highly fragmented, argues that the "choice of locality is especially wide" as most individuals live in metropolitan areas that have "scores if not hundreds of local governments." However, some observers are still skeptical that the stringent Tiebout conditions can be met even in an approximate sense; for example, Rubinfeld (1987, p. 584) stresses that in a Tiebout-Hamilton world, "The necessary number of such communities is likely to be extremely large." In any case, as above, Zodrow and Mieszkowski (1986a) show that capital tax view results can still be obtained in models that are perfectly homogeneous with respect to both housing demands and tastes for public services, so such homogeneity does not distinguish between the two views.

4.3. *Zoning requirements*

To an important extent, the choice between the benefit and capital tax views hinges on whether zoning ordinances are sufficiently restrictive to set the minimum housing level in a community, and whether such restrictions preclude the long run tax-induced changes in the capital stock predicted by the capital tax view. Fischel (1992) provides an extensive list of the types of zoning restrictions that might be encountered — and substituted for one another, depending on the circumstances. These include minimum lot sizes (and one home per lot), setbacks, height restrictions, requirements for off-street parking, restrictions to single family use, minimum square footage, and differential building code requirements, as well as designation of certain areas as off limits for environmental or other reasons and requirements for the provision of infrastructure at the expense of the developer. In addition, Fischel provides a variety of data on the quantitative significance of zoning ordinances, arguing that the practice of zoning is widespread. For example, he notes that the number of general purpose governments that could in principle enact zoning ordinances exceeds 25,000. Moreover, as detailed in Fischel (1985), there is no question that a great deal of time and effort is devoted to zoning, and that the practice of zoning has attracted a great deal of attention in the legal community. Finally, he notes (Fischel 1995, pp. 262–4) that several empirical studies have demonstrated that fiscal factors are important determinants of the nature of zoning decisions.

The admittedly widespread prevalence of zoning restrictions of various types, however, does not by itself demonstrate the validity of the benefit view. As stressed by Mieszkowski and Zodrow (1989), the Hamilton (1975) version of the benefit view obtains only if the zoning requirements are binding — it is in this sense that "perfect" zoning is required for the benefit view to be operative. Of course, as noted by Ladd (1998, p. 34) in her recent insightful review of the debate, perfect zoning in all cases would never be expected; rather the issue is whether zoning under the benefit view "sufficiently approximates reality that it becomes useful for making predictions and drawing conclusions." Unfortunately, evidence on the extent to which zoning constraints are binding is extremely difficult to obtain. Ladd notes that "no one would disagree that the property tax would distort decisions about minor expansions and repair that are beyond the purview of the zoning authority but not the tax assessor" — that is, one would not expect the benefit view to be operative at the margin for such changes in the housing capital stock. Similarly, even the most ardent proponents of the benefit view do not assert that it is operative in large and highly heterogeneous urban areas.[12] But the

---

[12] For example, Ladd (1998, p. 34–35) notes that the benefit view is also not likely to obtain in exurban or rural areas, so that under any circumstances for a "significant proportion of the U.S. population, the property tax is not appropriately viewed as a benefit tax." Fischel

extent to which zoning constraints are binding in the suburban communities that are the focus of the Tiebout-Hamilton analysis is difficult to determine. Mieszkowski and Zodrow (1989) and Fischel (1992) note the prevalence of communities that are subject to zoning that specifies minimum lot size and/or minimum square footage, but are quite heterogeneous in terms of house value — with many homes considerably larger than that specified by the zoning restrictions. Ross and Yinger (2000) note that many studies have demonstrated considerable income heterogeneity in suburban jurisdictions, which suggests that zoning constraints are typically not binding. They also argue that "zoning tools, such as lot size restrictions and set-back rules, appear far too blunt to control H (housing) precisely." Similarly, Rubinfeld (1987, p. 591) concludes that "there is reason to believe that actual zoning policies deviate substantially from the one which transforms a property tax into a head tax."

In marked contrast, Fischel argues that zoning, when defined comprehensively to include all of its many facets listed above — rather than only readily quantifiable restrictions such as minimum lot size — is in fact a binding constraint in many instances. He notes that local regulators have considerable flexibility in defining and enforcing zoning regulations, and are limited to only a relatively small extent by the legal restrictions associated with various court decisions regarding fiscal zoning.

Unfortunately, all of the arguments on the specific issue of whether zoning constraints are binding (rather than on the simpler but much less informative issue of whether a huge number of zoning restrictions exists), are quite speculative in that they are based largely on anecdotal evidence. It seems clear that communities often successfully use zoning regulations to limit or exclude a wide variety of activities that they deem undesirable, and that zoning regulations can thus have important effects on home values and should thus not be viewed as mere "window dressing." Nevertheless, these results do not demonstrate that zoning is binding in terms of establishing minimum property values. More compelling evidence, however, will be difficult to come by, as it would literally require a

(1995) agrees with this assessment and describes empirical evidence that demonstrates a variety of differences across suburban and central city communities which suggests that the assumptions underlying the benefit view are satisfied only in the suburbs.

detailed property-by-property study to determine the extent to which the combination of various zoning requirements in a jurisdiction, including variances and re-zonings in response to homeowner requests, results in binding constraints on its housing stock.

Finally, Ross and Yinger (2000) also stress that the existence of zoning is consistent not only with the benefit view, but also with several alternative models of housing and local public goods determination. Most importantly, zoning restrictions may simply ratify the nature of development that would occur in any case as a result of market forces, within the context of bidding/sorting models of community development.[13] Thus, the existence of zoning does not prove the validity of the benefit view.[14]

4.4. *Aggregate budget balance*

Another point often made in support of the benefit view is that there are powerful forces that act to prevent, in the words of Fischel (1992, p. 171) "wholesale free riding on local public goods." This point is an entirely reasonable one. It seems clear that fiscal zoning (broadly defined) can have an important influence on the nature of community development, especially in the form of precluding entry by low income households that would place high demands on local public services while providing little in the way of property tax base.[15] Similarly, Fischel is correct when he argues that the current residents of a political jurisdiction have a clear and strong incentive to insist that new developments "pay their own way" in the form of paying enough taxes to cover the costs of their public services, so as not to impose an additional property tax burden (and thus lower property values) on existing residents.

---

[13] For example, see Henderson (1977) and Wheaton (1993).

[14] In addition, Fischel (1992) argues that studies that demonstrate that zoning tends to increase the prices of existing homes are consistent with the notion of binding fiscal zoning (although he notes that other explanations could be offered as well). In any case, as stressed by Ross and Yinger (2000), the theoretical implications of zoning for existing house prices are unclear, as is the empirical evidence on this issue.

[15] Note again, however, that other models — especially the bidding and sorting models noted above — also imply income segregation.

However, once again, these phenomena are not inconsistent with the capital tax view of the property tax. Although fiscal zoning may very well change the character of the composition of a community, all that is required for the capital tax view to be operative is that the resulting communities not be zoned so precisely as to preclude the reductions in housing consumption predicted by the increase in the cost of capital attributable to the existence of, or increases in, the property tax. Moreover, capital tax view models are characterized by local government budget balance; thus, the capital tax view naturally does not imply any cross-subsidization across jurisdictions. Rather, local taxes and expenditures are equal — but at a lower than efficient level since local governments underspend on local public services in anticipation of tax-induced reduction in their property tax bases due to capital out-migration.

A similar phenomenon operates under the capital tax view for new development within an existing jurisdiction. The Tiebout-Hamilton models assume that local public services are publicly provided private goods; that is, there are no economies of scale in the provision of local public services. Facing the same property tax rate and thus the same cost of capital as existing properties, new developments will be characterized by the same less-than-efficient level of housing and public expenditures; however, the property taxes paid will be sufficient to cover the cost of providing services to the new development. Under the capital tax view, the new development is basically a replica of the existing community — characterized by the same suboptimal levels of housing consumption and public service levels, but also by "budget balance" in the sense that the increase in taxes attributable to the development equals the costs of providing it with public services.

In addition, as described above, under the "single taxing jurisdiction" version of the capital tax view, not only are statutory payments of the property tax equal to expenditures but more importantly, the economic incidence of the tax also tends to be borne by local households. That is, although an increase in property taxation by a single jurisdiction — and, by extension, a new development in an existing jurisdiction — is borne by all capital owners in the nation, the economic effects of the tax-induced outflow of capital imply that local factors and consumers bear a burden equal to the full amount of the tax as well. In this sense, as stressed above, the capital tax view of the property tax includes an important "benefit" component (even though the tax is not a non-distortionary benefit tax as viewed by Hamilton and Fischel) and new developments "pay their own way."

4.5. *Interjurisdictional capitalization*

Ever since the path-breaking article by Oates (1969), a large number of researchers have examined the capitalization into house prices of interjurisdictional differences in property taxes burdens and local expenditures. Although definitive evidence of such capitalization is difficult to establish, the current consensus seems to be that full capitalization is to a first approximation a reasonable assumption; see Dowding, John and Biggs (1994) for a recent survey, and Yinger, Bloom, Borsch-Supan and Ladd (1988) for a comprehensive study of property tax capitalization.

There is, however, no consensus about the implications of this evidence. There is general agreement that capitalization indicates that households value a relatively attractive combination of taxes and public services and will have greater demands for housing in communities in which they can obtain such a combination. Oates initially took this logic one step further and argued that capitalization was evidence for the Tiebout model and the benefit view. Similarly, as noted earlier, Fischel (forthcoming) argues that fiscal "capitalization is everywhere" and that such capitalization is sufficient to make the property tax a benefit tax at the local level.

However, as emphasized initially by Edel and Sclar (1974) and Hamilton (1976b) and more recently by Ross and Yinger (2000), capitalization does not imply the validity of the Tiebout model and the benefit view. Indeed, these authors argue that if the supply of communities is elastic in the sense that there are possibilities for new community formation (or changes in the boundaries of existing communities) or changes in the fiscal policies of existing communities, then the Tiebout model should in the long run imply zero capitalization. For example, in the context of the Hamilton (1975) model of homogeneous communities, housing prices should reflect only construction costs; property taxes paid just equal benefits received and thus have no independent effect on housing prices, just as housing prices are not affected by differences in expenditures on private goods.[16] As stressed by Ross and Yinger, empirical analyses of housing prices across jurisdictions thus should not pick up any capitalization effects whatsoever if the economy is in a Tiebout-Hamilton type of equilibrium. They stress (p. 2016) that rather than providing support for the benefit view, "Statistically significant capitalization of S (services) or t (taxes) therefore serves as a rejection of the Hamilton model." Similarly, Edel and Sclar argue that decreases over time in the extent to which capitalization is observed indicate movement toward a Tiebout equilibrium (rather than declining importance of the Tiebout mechanism), and Rubinfeld (1987, p. 593) concludes that "in the long run, capitalization is likely not to occur."

The implications of the existence of fiscal capitalization for the validity of the benefit view are thus unclear. The conditions required for the result of zero capitalization under a full Tiebout equilibrium are stringent and unlikely to be met in practice; in particular, the supply of communities to a metropolitan area is not highly elastic, jurisdictional boundaries are not flexible[17] and, as argued by Hamilton (1983), the expansion of fiscally advantaged housing will always be opposed by existing residents who fear its negative effect on the values of existing properties. Hamilton concludes that capitalization thus provides evidence of the validity of the Tiebout mechanism and that the property tax is a benefit tax. However, others have argued that the link between capitalization and the benefit is unclear, so that empirical evidence confirming the existence of capitalization does not provide definitive evidence either for or against the benefit view.[18]

More fundamentally, even if one accepts the idea that the benefit view implies fiscal capitalization, the implications of such capitalization for the choice between the benefit and capital tax views are ambiguous because some capitalization is also consistent with the capital tax view. Specifically,

[16] Hamilton (1976b) notes that this argument must be qualified by any fiscal advantages of industrial capital, differences in state or federal aid, and differential costs of providing local public services due either to differences in input costs or differences in the costs of providing services of a given quality attributable to differences in population characteristics across communities.

[17] See Epple and Romer (1989).

[18] For example, see Epple (1980), Wales and Wiens (1974), Brueckner (1979) and Epple, Zelenitz and Visscher (1978).

the "single jurisdiction" or "two burden" derivation of the capital tax view implies that any increase in local property taxes will be borne not only by capital owners nationwide, but also in a roughly equal amount by local factors of production and consumers. Thus, to the extent that this burden falls on local land owners — as is likely to occur if individuals are mobile across competing jurisdictions — the capital tax view implies that some of the burden of a local property tax increase will be capitalized into lower land prices. Similarly, the average burden of high property taxes in a jurisdiction, relative to the average national level of property taxation, may be capitalized into lower land prices. Thus, the existence of capitalization does not by itself distinguish between the benefit and capital tax views. One potential area for future research would be to construct models of the different capitalization processes and amounts capitalized under both views and then attempt to identify econometrically which view is more consistent with the resulting estimates. However, given the problems associated with estimating capitalization accurately, such an approach would be rather difficult to implement.

4.6. *Intrajurisdictional capitalization*

The extent of intrajurisdictional capitalization provides another potential test of the effects of the property tax. The capitalization of fiscal differentials — the present value of the differences between benefits received and taxes paid — is the force behind the heterogeneous community version of the benefit view derived in Hamilton (1976a). Although there is much less empirical evidence on the extent of intrajurisdictional capitalization, Yinger, Bloom, Borsch-Supan and Ladd (1988) conclude that the available studies suggest a fair degree of capitalization. Thus the relevant question is whether full capitalization allows one to distinguish between the capital tax and benefit views. However, the answer is once again largely negative.

The various derivations of the capital tax view consider only interjurisdictional tax differentials. However, in the context of heterogeneous communities, any the tax-induced changes in land values that occur due to the excise tax effects under the capital tax view would apply only to average land values within the jurisdiction — which are in fact independent of the extent of housing heterogeneity in the Hamilton (1976a) heterogeneous communities model. Given these changes in average land values within a jurisdiction, capitalization of intrajurisdictional fiscal differentials would be consistent with the capital tax view, and would indeed be expected as long as households were perfectly mobile and homogeneous communities were available, as assumed in the Hamilton derivation. That is, as argued by Mieszkowski and Zodrow (1989), under these circumstances, such intrajurisdictional "excise tax" effects of the property tax would be expected to be capitalized into property values. For example, high income housing in a heterogeneous community, which would face a high tax burden for a given level of services relative to that in a homogeneous high income housing community, would sell at a discount. Similarly, low income housing in a heterogeneous community, which would face a low tax burden for a given level of services, relative to the homogeneous low income community, would sell at a premium.[19] These effects are analogous to those occurring under the heterogeneous community version of the benefit view (although the level of the capital stock and the quantity of public services provided would be lower under the capital tax view). Thus, evidence supporting intrajurisdictional capitalization does not help distinguish between the capital tax and benefit views.

The discussion thus far suggests that, because the differences between the "benefit tax" aspects of the capital tax and benefit views are not as great as one might think, it is rather difficult to distinguish empirically between the two views of the property tax, and that several arguments often made in support of the benefit view do not provide compelling evidence in its favor. Nevertheless, several empirical tests are able to distinguish between the two views, and these are discussed in the following two sections.

4.7. *The effects of property tax differentials on capital intensity*

The different effects on capital intensity (capital-land ratios) implied by the capital tax and benefit views of the property tax provide one potentially

[19] Note, however, that such a situation, which corresponds to the case considered by Hamilton (1976a), is not a long run equilibrium, unless there is some mechanism to restrict developers from razing high income housing and replacing it with low income housing. For discussions of tbis point, see Dyer and Maher (1979) and Hamilton (1979).

effective means of distinguishing between them. The capital tax view implies that relatively high levels of property taxation should drive mobile capital out of a jurisdiction, resulting in lower capital intensity. By comparison, under the benefit view, the property tax functions as a user charge for services received so that capital intensity should be independent of the level of property taxation. In addition, under the capital tax view, capital outflow from a relatively high tax jurisdiction results in lower land and property values. In contrast, under the benefit view, a relatively high property tax rate in a community should not affect aggregate land and property values as it merely reflects a relatively high level of local public services.

Wassmer (1993) draws on these different implications of the capital tax and benefit views to conduct an intriguing empirical test of the validity of the capital tax view. Specifically, he examines a sample of 62 cities to see whether the effects of property tax differentials, relative to the average level of taxation for the sample, are consistent with the capital tax view in that a relatively high property tax rate in a city (1) depresses its property values, and (2) reduces its capital intensity. Wassmer finds evidence that supports the capital tax view; however, the effects are fairly modest as a one percent tax differential reduces property values by 0.13 percent and causes a very slight outflow of capital over a five-year period. He concludes (p. 154) that his results "provide evidence that local property taxes affect local property values in the manner predicted by the New View and are not possible under a pure Benefit View of property taxation." His results — which are consistent with the conjectures of Mieszkowski (1972) — suggest significant forward shifting of property tax differentials into higher housing prices rather than reduced property values. However, they also indicate rather little in the way of the reallocation of housing capital that is essential to the operation of the capital tax view in the long run.

Wassmer's results thus provide some support for the capital tax view, but are far from definitive. One problem with his analysis is that his measure of the capital stock in a jurisdiction — the number of homes, with some fairly imprecise controls (e.g., the number of rooms and the extent of plumbing) for the amount of capital utilized in the homes — is sufficiently imprecise that his estimates are difficult to interpret. Moreover, proponents of the benefit view typically argue that it applies primarily in suburban jurisdictions — not the sample of central cities analyzed by Wassmer. Thus, a fruitful line for future research would be to extend

Wassmer's work to a sample of suburban jurisdictions using more accurate measures of the capital stock in each jurisdiction.

4.8. *The effects of property tax differentials on housing rents*

The capital tax and benefit views of the property tax also have potentially different and thus testable implications for rental housing. In general, under the benefit view, one would expect an increase in property taxes to be reflected in an increase in housing rents, as long as the benefits received by renters equal the cost of the services being financed, as should occur in a Tiebout-Hamilton equilibrium. By comparison, under the capital tax view, the effect of property tax finance of local expenditures received by renters is unclear. As described above, an increase in property taxes on rental properties by a single jurisdiction can be reflected in either higher rents or lower returns to landlords, depending on the relative elasticities of demand and supply of rental housing. Thus, forward shifting of the tax into higher rents is consistent with both views and would be inconclusive in terms of choosing between the capital tax and benefit views, but backward shifting to landlords should occur only under the capital tax view.

In a provocative recent contribution to the literature, Carroll and Yinger (1994) use this strategy to analyze the effects of the property tax for a sample of 147 towns and cities in the Boston metropolitan area. They argue that the previous literature on the extent of forward shifting of the property tax is inconclusive, as the results obtained are very mixed. Moreover, these studies suffer from a variety of methodological problems, which Carroll and Yinger detail and address in their research. Their results are consistent with the capital tax view, as landlords bear a large fraction of a property tax increase in all of the various cases they study (with different assumptions regarding the supply and demand elasticities of rental housing and different assumptions about renter mobility); the average burden on landlords varies from 84–91 cents per dollar of increased taxes and a minimum burden over all cases and all communities of 67 cents per dollar. In addition, the authors simulate the average burden of the property tax in their initial equilibrium and find that on average landlords bear 45 percent of existing tax differentials. Carroll and Yinger (1994, p. 311) conclude that, for their sample, "the property tax on rental housing is far short of being a benefit tax."

As the most recent and most careful study of the extent of shifting of property taxes into higher rents, the Carroll and Yinger study provides strong support of the validity of the capital tax view, at least as it applies to rental housing. However, it does not preclude an equilibrium where the benefit view applies for suburban homeowners (as is most often asserted by proponents of the benefit view) even if it is invalid for renters.

More generally, although the two studies described above provide limited support for the capital tax view, considerable differences still exist regarding the extent to which the empirical literature distinguishes between the two views of the incidence of the property tax. For example, Ross and Yinger (2000, p. 2043) argue that "the evidence against the benefits view is overwhelming." By comparison, Oates (1994, p. 142) concludes that, "As things stand, it is impossible to reject either the new view or the benefits view in favor of the other."[20]

5. Conclusion

This article has reviewed the ongoing debate regarding the validity of the traditional, capital tax and benefit views of the local property tax. The capital tax view was shown to include the traditional view as a special case, and to have some important characteristics that are typically associated with the benefit view. In particular, from a local perspective, the capital tax view predicts that local residents will tend to bear the full burden of an increase in the property tax (as predicted under the benefit view). One implication of the similarity between the capital tax and

[20] Note, however, that the voluminous "tax competition" literature — mentioned above and reviewed in a recent article by Wilson (1999) — can be construed as providing evidence in support of the capital tax view. This literature examines the idea, noted above, that local jurisdictions, concerned about the outflow of capital to other jurisdictions associated with the use of a tax on mobile capital, will tend to reduce their reliance on the property tax and under-provide public services. The mere size of the this literature provides indirect support for the capital tax view; that is, if most observers subscribed to the benefit view of the property tax, the concerns of the tax competition literature regarding underprovision of services financed with property taxes on mobile capital would be largely irrelevant.

benefit views is that it is difficult to distinguish between them empirically, although several recent studies provide limited support for the capital tax view. At the same time, the differences between the two views are substantial. In particular, the capital tax view concludes that the property tax distorts the allocation of capital, including especially housing capital (and also distorts the level of local public services), while the benefit view argues that the property tax is a non-distortionary head tax. From a national perspective, the capital tax view concludes that the property tax is a tax on capital and is thus quite progressive, while the benefit view argues that the tax involves no redistribution. Thus, a resolution of this longstanding debate is critical to an understanding of the allocative and distributional effects of the local property tax. However, much further empirical investigation must be done before the validity of either view can be established definitively.

References

Aaron, Henry J., *Who Pays the Property Tax?* Washington, D.C.: Brookings Institution, 1975.

Bradford, David F., "Factor Prices May Be Constant but Factor Returns Are Not," *Economics Letters,* 1978, 1:199–203.

Brown, Harry G., *The Economics of Taxation.* New York: Holt, 1924.

Brueckner, Jan K., "Property Values, Local Public Expenditure, and Economic Efficiency," *Journal of Public Economics,* 1979, 2: 223–246.

Carroll, Robert and John Yinger, "Is the Property Tax a Benefit Tax? The Case of Rental Housing," *National Tax Journal,* 1994, 47: 295–316.

Dowding, Keith, Peter John and Stephen Biggs, "Tiebout: A Survey of the Empirical Literature," *Urban Studies,* 1994, 31:767–797.

Dyer, James C., IV, and Michael D. Maher, "Capitalization of Intrajurisdictional Differences in Local Tax Prices: Comment," *American Economic Review,* 1979, 69: 481–484.

Edel, Mathew and Sclar, Elliott. "Taxes, Spending, and Property Values: Supply Adjustment in a Tiebout-Oates Model," *Journal of Political Economy,* 1974, 82:941–954.

Ellickson, Bryan, "Jurisdictional Fragmentation and Residential Choice," *American Economic Review* 1971, 61: 334–339.

Epple, Dennis., "What Do Tests of Capitalization Show?" Working Paper, Carnegie-Mellon University Graduate School Industrial Admininstration, Sept. 1980.

Epple, Dennis and Romer Thomas, 1989, "On Flexible Municipal Boundaries," *Journal of Urban Economics*, 26: 307–319.

Epple, Dennis, Zelenitz, Allan and Visscher, Michael., "A Search for Testable Implications of the Tiebout Hypothesis," *Journal of Political Economy,* 1978, 88: 405–426.

Fischel, William A., "Fiscal and Environmental Considerations in the Location of Firms in Suburban Communities," in *Fiscal Zoning and Land Use Controls*, in Edwin S. Mills and Wallace E. Oates (eds.), Lexington, MA: Lexington Books, 1975, pp. 119–173.

Fischel, William A., "Is Local Government Structure in Large Urbanized Areas Monopolistic or Competitive?" *National Tax Journal*, 1981, 34: 95.

Fischel, William A., *The Economics of Zoning Laws: A Property Rights Approach to American Land Use Controls*, Baltimore: Johns Hopkins University Press, 1985.

Fischel, William A., *Regulatory Takings: Law, Economics, and Politics*, Cambridge, MA: Harvard University Press, 1995.

Fischel, William A., "Property Taxation and the Tiebout Model: Evidence for the Benefit View from Voting and Zoning," *Journal of Economic Literature*, 1992, 30: 171–177.

Fischel, William A., "Municipal Corporations, Homeowners, and the Benefit View of the Property Tax," in Wallace E. Oates (ed.), *Property Taxation and Local Government Finance*, Cambridge: Lincoln Institute of Land Policy, forthcoming. Appeared in *State Tax Notes,* Volume 18, No. 22 (May 22, 2000), pp. 1781–1803.

Fischel, William A., "Homevoters, Municipal Corporate Governance, and the Benefit View of the Property Tax," *National Tax Journal*, 2000, 54: 157–174.

Hamilton, Bruce W., "Zoning and Property Taxation in a System of Local Governments," *Urban Studies*, 1975, 12: 205–211.

Hamilton, Bruce W., "Capitalization of Intrajurisdictional Differences in Local Tax Prices," *American Economic Review,* 1976a, 66: 743–753.

Hamilton, Bruce W., "The Effects of Property Taxes and Local Public Spending on Property Values: A Theoretical Comment," *Journal of Political Economy,* June 1976b, 84: 205–211.

Hamilton, Bruce W., "Capitalization of Intrajurisdictional Differences in Local Tax Prices: Reply," *American Economic Review* 1979, 69: 485.

Hamilton, Bruce W., "A Review: Is the Property Tax a Benefit Tax?" in *Local Provision of Public Services: The Tiebout Model after Twenty-five Years*, in George R. Zodrow (ed.), New York: Academic Press, 1983, pp. 85–107.

Harberger, Arnold C., "The Incidence of the Corporate Income Tax," *Journal of Political Economy* 1962, 70: 215–240.

Henderson, Vernon J., *Economic Theory of the Cities,* New York: Academic Press, 1977.

Kotlikoff, Laurence J. and Summers, Lawrence H., "Tax Incidence," in *Handbook of Public Economics,* in Alan J. Auerbach and Martin S. Feldstein (eds.), Amsterdam: North Holland, 1987, pp. 1043–1092.

Ladd, Helen F., *Local Government Tax and Land Use Politics in the United States,* Northhampton MA: Edward Elgar Publishing, 1998.

Lin, Chuan. "A General Equilibrium Analysis of Property Tax Incidence," *Journal of Public Economics,* 1986, 29: 113–132.

McLure, Charles E., Jr. "The New View of the Property Tax: A Caveat," *National Tax Journal,* 1977, 30: 69–76.

Mieszkowski, Peter. "The Property Tax. An Excise Tax or a Profits Tax?" *Journal of Public Economics,* 1972, 1: 73–96.

Mieszkowski, Peter and Zodrow, George R., "The Incidence of a Partial State Corporate Income Tax," *National Tax Journal*, 1985, 38: 489–496.

Mieszkowski, Peter and Zodrow, George R., "Taxation and the Tiebout Model: The Differential Effects of Head Taxes, Taxes on Land Rents, and Property Taxes," *Journal of Economic Literature*, 1989, 27, 1098–1146.

Netzer, Dick, *Economics of the Property Tax*, Washington DC: Brookings Institution, 1966.

Oates, Wallace E. "The Effects of Property Taxes and Local Public Spending on Property Values: An Empirical Study of Tax Capitalization and the Tiebout Hypothesis," *Journal of Political Economy,* 1969, 77: 957–961.

Oates, Wallace E., "Federalism and Government Finance," in John S. Quigley and Eugene Smolensky (eds.), *Modern Public Finance*, Cambridge MA: Harvard University Press, 1994.

Ross, Stephen and John Yinger, "Sorting and Voting: A Review of the Literature on Urban Public Finance," in *Handbook of Regional and Urban Economics*, Vol. 3, Paul Cheshire and Edwin S. Mills (eds.), Amsterdam: North Holland, 2000.

Rubinfeld, Daniel L. "The Economics of the Local Public Sector," in *Handbook of Public Economics*, in Alan J. Auerbach and Martin S. Feldstein (eds.), Amsterdam: North Holland, 1987, pp. 571–645.

Simon, Herbert A., "The Incidence of a Tax on Urban Real Property," *Quarterly Journal of Economics*, 1943, 59: 398–420.

Tiebout, Charles M., "A Pure Theory of Local Expenditures," *Journal of Political. Economy*, 1956, 64: 416–424.

Wales, T. J. and Weins, E. G. "Capitalization of Residential Property Taxes: An Empirical Study," *Review of Economic Statistics,* 1974, 56: 329–333.

Wassmer, Robert W., "Property Taxation, Property Base, and Property Value: An Empirical Test of the "New View", *National Tax Journal*, 1993, 46: 135–160.

Wheaton, William C., "Land Capitalization, Tiebout Mobility, and the Role of Zoning Regulations," *Journal of Urban Economics*, 1993, 34: 102–117.

White, Michelle J. "Firm Location in a Zoned Metropolitan Area," in *Fiscal Zoning and Land Use Controls*, in Edwin S. Mills and Wallace E. Oates (eds.), Lexington, MA: Lexington Books, 1975, pp. 175–202.

Wildasin, David E. *Urban Public Finance.* New York: Harwood, 1986.

Wilson, John D. "A Theory of Inter-Regional Tax Competition," *Journal of Urban Economics,* 1986, 19: 296–315.

Wilson, John D., "Theories of Tax Competition," *National Tax Journal*, 1999, 52: 269–304.

Yinger, John, Bloom, Howard S., Boersch-Supan, Axel, and Ladd, Helen F. *Property Taxes and House Values: The Theory and Estimation of Intrajurisdictional Property Tax Capitalization*, San Diego, CA.: Academic Press, 1988.

Zodrow, George R., "The Tiebout Model After Twenty-Five Years: An Overview," in *Local Provision of Public Services: The Tiebout Model After Twenty-Five Years,* in George R. Zodrow (ed.), New York: Academic Press, 1983, pp. 1–16.

Zodrow, George R., "Reflections on the New View and the Benefit View of the Property Tax," in Wallace E. Oates (ed.), *Property Taxation and Local Government Finance*, Cambridge: Lincoln Institute of Land Policy, forthcoming. Appeared in *State Tax Notes,* Volume 18, No. 22 (May 22, 2000), pp. 1805–1821.

Zodrow, George R. and Mieszkowski, Peter, "The Incidence of the Property Tax. The Benefit View vs. the New View," in *Local Provision of Public Services: The Tiebout Model after Twenty-five Years,* in George R. Zodrow (ed.), New York: Academic Press, 1983, pp. 109–129.

Zodrow, George R. and Mieszkowski, Peter, "The New View of the Property Tax: A Reformulation," *Regional Science and Urban Economics,* 1986a, 16: 309–327.

Zodrow, George R. and Mieszkowski, Peter, "Pigou, Tiebout, Property Taxation and the Under-provision of Local Public Goods," *Journal of Urban Economics*, 1986b, 19: 356–370.

Chapter 16

Intrajurisdictional Capitalization and the Incidence of the Property Tax*

George R. Zodrow

Cline Professor of Economics and Rice Scholar, Baker Institute for Public Policy, Rice University, Houston TX, USA, International Research Fellow, Centre for Business Taxation, Oxford University, Oxford UK
zodrow@rice.edu

Two views dominate the debate about property tax incidence — the "capital tax" or "new" view, under which the tax distorts capital allocation and is borne primarily by capital owners, and the "benefit tax" view, under which the tax is an efficient user charge. Evidence of both interjurisdictional and intrajurisdictional capitalization of property taxes and public services has been argued to provide compelling evidence for the benefit tax view. This paper focuses on the latter — the *intra*-jurisdictional capitalization effects that underlie what is arguably the most plausible

*This Chapter is reproduced from *Regional Science and Urban Economics*, **45**, 57–66, 2014.

derivation of the benefit tax view of the property tax. The analysis provides a model in which the capital reallocations that characterize the capital tax view induce intrajurisdictional capitalization effects that are generally similar — indeed, in the benchmark case, identical — to those that arise under the benefit tax view, suggesting that empirical evidence supporting such capitalization effects cannot distinguish between the two views. In addition, the analysis shows that these capitalization effects imply that even under the stringent assumptions of the benefit view, the property tax is *not* a benefit tax for a property-tax-financed increase in local public services; rather, it only becomes a benefit tax for future home purchasers — after the modeled intrajurisdictional capitalization effects occur.

Keywords: property tax incidence; intrajurisdictional capitalization; capital tax view; new view; benefit tax view

1. Introduction

The debate surrounding the incidence of the property tax has raged for nearly 50 years, dating to the classic contributions of Netzer (1966), Mieszkowski (1972), and Oates (1969). Two opposing views — the "benefit tax" view and the "capital tax" or "new" view — dominate the debate. Under the benefit tax view, the property tax functions as an efficient user charge, an indirect payment for the benefits of local public services received by the residents of the taxing jurisdiction. In marked contrast, under the capital tax view, the property tax inefficiently distorts the allocation of capital, and its incidence is reflected primarily in a reduction in the national return to capital, coupled with increases in housing prices and reductions in the returns to labor and land in relatively high tax jurisdictions that are largely offset by decreases in housing prices and increases in the returns to labor and land in relatively low tax jurisdictions.[1]

[1]This analysis focuses solely on the residential property tax; for recent discussions of non-residential property taxes, see Muthitacharoen and Zodrow (2006, 2012). In addition, a third "traditional" view, under which residential property taxes are shifted forward as higher housing prices, is a special case of the capital tax view (Zodrow, 2001a, b).

Many observers have noted that a resolution of the debate is among the more pressing issues in state and local public finance (Youngman, 2002; Fisher, 2009), especially since property taxes account for roughly three-fourths of total local tax revenues and nearly half of local own-source revenues (Alm, Buschman, and Sjoquist, 2011). The differences in the economic effects of the property tax under the two views is striking, as are the policy implications of pervasive use of the tax by local governments.

Under the benefit view, the property tax — as a user charge that is paid in exchange for the benefits of local public service received — corresponds closely to the head tax originally envisaged in the celebrated Tiebout (1956) model, under which interjurisdictional competition and perfectly mobile consumers result in efficient provision of local public goods. The property tax is thus the rare example of a purely non-distortionary tax; in particular, it does not distort housing consumption, the allocation of housing capital (or other forms of capital), or the provision of local public services. Second, as a benefit tax, the property tax has no effects on the distribution of income. Instead, given the existing distribution of income, the incidence of the property tax simply corresponds to the benefits of local public services received. From a policy perspective, the property tax is the efficient user charge often recommended for local government by experts in local public finance (see Mills (2008) for a recent discussion). At the same time, however, its use is subject to the standard criticism of user charges and benefit taxes, and more generally the Tiebout model — although allocative efficiency is an important criterion in evaluating the performance of the local public sector, an efficient user charge system may be viewed as highly inequitable, as access to essential local public services such as primary and secondary education and police and fire protection will be largely determined by income. Indeed, numerous court cases have successfully challenged local use of the property tax on such equity grounds.

In marked contrast, under the capital tax view, the property tax is an inefficient tax instrument, as it reduces housing consumption and distorts resource allocation, driving capital out of high tax jurisdictions and into low tax jurisdictions. Moreover, the efficiency costs of the capital misallocations due to the property tax may be significant under the capital tax view. For example, the central estimates of Muthitachareon and Zodrow (2010) — whose analysis focuses on interjurisdictional property tax differentials when the tax applies to both residential and non-residential property and thus does not include the intrajurisdictional misallocations analyzed in this paper — suggest average efficiency costs of roughly 6–16 percent of property tax revenues (0.24–0.65 percent of total consumption expenditures) and marginal efficiency costs of roughly twice that magnitude.[2] In addition, the use of the local property tax can lead to inefficient underprovision of local public services, as government officials, concerned about tax-induced outflows of mobile capital, reduce the level of public services provided (Zodrow and Mieszkowski, 1986a; Wilson, 1986, 1999). Wildasin (1989) suggests that such underprovision may also lead to significant inefficiencies. The distributional effects of the property tax are also markedly different under the capital tax view. The central tenets of this view (described in more detail below) is that the average burden of the tax is borne by all owners of capital, both housing and nonhousing, with additional effects across jurisdictions that tend to cancel in terms of their effects on the distribution of income. Given the concentration of capital income among higher income groups, this capital tax aspect of the property tax implies that it is progressive (at least with respect to annual income) and represents a relatively progressive element of the national tax structure. That is, in marked contrast to the benefit view, which implies the property tax is an efficient tax that has no effects on the distribution of income but may result in an inequitable distribution of public services, the capital tax view implies that the property tax is a relatively progressive tax that results in several potentially significant inefficiencies in the allocation of capital and the determination of local public service levels.

Despite the importance of a resolution of the debate on the economic effects and incidence of the property tax, the literature is far from arriving

[2] For purposes of a rough comparison, Cho and Francis (2011) estimate that eliminating the home mortgage interest deduction would result in an increase in aggregate welfare of 0.16 percent, while eliminating the deductibility of property taxes would result in an increase in aggregate welfare of 1.36 percent.

at a consensus on this issue. The depth of the lack of consensus is illustrated by two surveys of this literature. Fischel, Oates, and Youngman (2011, p. 1) begin their recent review by observing that, "Our understanding of the incidence of local property taxes is in a sad state." They conclude (pp. 19–21) that the benefit view applies in urbanized areas, so that "the vast majority (70 to 80 percent) of the U.S. population would be candidates for the benefit view of property taxes" and that the "Tiebout model, and the associated benefit view, have long been taken by scholars in local public finance to provide a description of the working of the local public sector in metropolitan areas." In marked contrast, in a widely cited review of the urban public finance literature, Ross and Yinger (1999, p. 2043) argue that the property tax does in fact distort the allocation of capital and arrive at the unequivocal conclusion that "the evidence against the benefits view is overwhelming."[3]

A central issue in the debate, dating back to the work of Oates (1969), has been whether econometric evidence of fiscal capitalization — the capitalization of property taxes and local expenditure levels into land values — provides empirical support for the benefit view. Most of this discussion has focused on *inter*-jurisdictional capitalization. However, *intra*-jurisdictional capitalization is certainly highly relevant as well, especially since it is the key element in the most plausible theoretical exposition of the benefit view, originally developed by Hamilton (1976), under which perfect capitalization of intrajurisdictional fiscal differentials is required to convert the property tax into a benefit tax in communities with heterogeneous housing.[4] By comparison, the role of intrajurisdictional capitalization in the capital tax view of the property tax has not been fully developed (Mieszkowski and Zodrow, 1989; Zodrow, 2001a, b). Accordingly, this paper focuses solely on intrajurisdictional

[3] One element of such evidence, discussed further below, is wide disparities in property taxes paid and local public services received. For example, Kurban, Gallagher, and Persky (2012) estimate that two-thirds of property tax payments used for education finance in Chicago suburbs reflect payments in excess of education benefits received.

[4] An alternative view, developed by Hamilton (1975) and discussed below, assumes homogeneous housing.

capitalization. It does so within the context of a highly simplified model that adopts most of the (admittedly rather stringent) assumptions of the models used to derive the benefit tax view, and is used to capture the essence of both the capital tax and benefit tax views. The main conclusion of the analysis is that the amounts of intrajurisdictional capitalization that would be expected to occur under the two views are remarkably similar, and indeed are identical in one fairly standard benchmark case. Thus, empirical evidence that is consistent with full capitalization of property taxes and local expenditure levels into land values is of little if any help in distinguishing between the two alternative views of the incidence of the property tax. In addition, the analysis shows that these capitalization effects imply that even under the stringent assumptions of the benefit view, the property tax is *not* a benefit tax when its rate increases to finance new public expenditures, as the associated tax-induced capitalization effects imply that the prices paid by different residents for the expanded public services (the combination of actual taxes paid and capitalization effects) differ significantly from the value of services received. Instead, the property tax only becomes a benefit tax for future home purchasers — after the modeled intrajurisdictional capitalization effects occur and are borne by homeowners at the time of the tax change.

The paper is organized as follows. The following section provides a brief overview of the property tax incidence debate. Section 3 reconstructs the benefit tax view within the context of a partial equilibrium version of the standard differential tax incidence model, including a derivation of the intrajurisdictional capitalization effects that would be expected under the benefit view. Section 4 then alters the model to make it broadly consistent with those used to generate the capital tax view, and shows that, under the appropriate circumstances, intrajurisdictional capitalization effects are identical under the two views. More generally, in Section 5, the results of a simple simulation suggest that the amount of intrajurisdictional capitalization that occurs under the two views is broadly similar, consistent with the central thesis of the paper that empirical evidence regarding such capitalization is of limited help in distinguishing between the two views. The final section concludes.

2. Overview of the Property Tax Incidence Debate

The voluminous literature on the incidence of the property tax can only be summarized briefly here; for additional details, see Ross and Yinger (1999), Nechyba (2001), Netzer (2001), Zodrow (2001a), Youngman (2002), Fisher (2009), and Fischel, Oates and Youngman (2011).

Theoretical Results. The benefit tax view is closely linked to the classic Tiebout (1956) model in which interjurisdictional competition in local public service provision coupled with perfect household mobility results in an efficient local public goods equilibrium, as consumers reveal their public goods preferences by "voting with their feet" and sorting themselves into jurisdictions that are completely homogeneous with respect to local public service demands. Although Tiebout assumed head tax finance (as do Oates and Schwab (1988) in a more recent reconstruction of the argument), other researchers have extended the model to include property tax finance.

In the earliest of these contributions, Hamilton (1975) constructed a model in which local jurisdictions were also homogeneous with respect to house values, there were enough jurisdictions to accommodate all desired combinations of housing and government services, and binding zoning constraints establish a minimum house value for each community. Under these circumstances, all individuals in a given community pay exactly the same property tax, which then functions precisely as a benefit tax. This work was extended by Fischel (1985, 1998), who argues that zoning, defined comprehensively to include a wide variety of land use regulations, is sufficiently restrictive to convert the property tax into the uniform payment for local public services envisioned by Hamilton. The assumptions of this model, however, are difficult to reconcile with the considerable heterogeneity of home values observed in virtually all communities — heterogeneity that Rhode and Strumpf (2003) estimate is significant and does not appear to be decreasing over time.

Thus, a key development in the evolution of the benefit tax view was the extension of the model to the more realistic case in which house values within a community are heterogeneous (Hamilton, 1976). In this version, Hamilton constructed a model in which all communities were fully developed (precluding any tax-induced changes in the housing stock, which effectively was supplied perfectly inelastically) and perfectly mobile consumers had the option of living in communities that were homogeneous with respect to both demands for public services and housing. Under these circumstances, Hamilton showed that "perfect capitalization" of fiscal differentials — the difference in present values of future taxes and the value of benefits received — again converts the property tax into a benefit tax as, for example, any excess property taxes paid by the owners of high-value homes is exactly offset by lower home values due to capitalization. More recently, Fischel (2001a, b) has noted that a wide variety of empirical studies have found evidence that intrajurisdictional differences in property taxes are capitalized into house values as predicted by Hamilton's model of heterogeneous communities. He argues that the existence of such capitalization is sufficient to convert the property tax a benefit tax.

In marked contrast, under the capital tax view formulated by Mieszkowski (1972) and extended by Zodrow and Mieszkowski (1983, 1986b), capital is mobile so that the property tax inefficiently reduces housing consumption and distorts resource allocation, driving capital out of high tax jurisdictions and into low tax jurisdictions.[5] Under the capital tax view, the property tax causes (1) a "profits tax effect" that reflects the average burden of all property taxes imposed across the nation and is borne by capital owners, and (2) "excise tax effects" that capture the effects of local tax differentials around the national average. These excise tax effects are reflected as housing and commodity price increases and wage and land price declines in relatively high tax jurisdictions, with offsetting effects in relatively low tax jurisdictions. Because these roughly symmetric effects tend to cancel in the aggregate, from a national perspective, the relatively progressive profits tax effect is the primary factor affecting the distribution of the property tax burden.[6]

[5] In addition, local use of the property tax can lead to inefficient under-provision of local public services, as government officials, concerned about tax-induced outflows of mobile capital, reduce the level of public services provided (Zodrow and Mieszkowski, 1986a; Wilson, 1986, 1999; Zodrow, 2003).

[6] See Muthitacharoen and Zodrow (2012) for a recent analysis of the excise tax effects of the property tax.

In addition, by examining the tax from the perspective of a single local taxing jurisdiction, Zodrow and Mieszkowski (1983) show that the excise tax effects imply that the local property tax has some important "benefit tax" aspects, as the tax-induced outflow of capital from the taxing jurisdiction implies lower returns to relatively immobile factors such as local land and labor and/or higher prices to local consumers. Thus, there is a loose link between increases in local public services and the burden of the property tax under the capital tax view, as the burden of financing local expenditures largely falls — in the aggregate — on local factor owners and local consumers.

Empirical Results. A complete review of the empirical research on the property tax is far beyond the scope of this paper; see Ross and Yinger (1999), Fischel (2001a), Zodrow (2001a), and Lutz (2009) for discussions of this literature. Instead, the analysis will focus on the area of greatest relevance to this paper — the extent to which evidence of capitalization of property tax differentials into land values demonstrates the validity of the benefit tax view of the property tax.

Most of the property tax capitalization literature, dating to Oates (1969), has focused on *inter*-jurisdictional capitalization. Although the current consensus seems to be that full capitalization of interjurisdictional property tax differentials is a reasonable assumption (Dowding, John and Biggs, 1994; Fischel, 2001a, b), there is no consensus about the implications of this evidence. Oates (1969) and Hamilton (1983) conclude that capitalization provides evidence for the Tiebout model and the benefit tax view, and Fischel (2001a, b) argues that capitalization is sufficient to make the local property tax a benefit tax. However, Ross and Yinger (1999), among others, argue that if the supply of communities is elastic — with possibilities for new community formation, changes in existing community boundaries, or changes in the fiscal policies of existing communities — then the Tiebout model should in the long run imply zero capitalization; that is, as land is reallocated in the long run to eliminate all land price differentials, local economies will move toward a Tiebout equilibrium and capitalization will disappear.

In any case, this paper focuses instead on the implications of *intra*-jurisdictional capitalization of the property tax. As described above, intra-jurisdictional capitalization is the critical element of what will hereafter be called the Tiebout-Hamilton-Fischel (THF) model of the benefit tax view, which is characterized by communities with heterogeneous houses that are supplied perfectly inelastically. In such a setting, high-value homes sell at a discount and low-value homes sell at a premium, each reflecting the differences in present values of future taxes paid and the value of public services received, converting the property tax to a user charge or benefit tax.

Before proceeding further, however, it should be emphasized that the THF formulation of the benefit view is a long run result based on an analysis of the total prices for public goods — property taxes plus fiscal capitalization effects — faced by new purchasers of homes *after* home prices have adjusted to a property tax change. However, upon implementation of any change in property taxes, such capitalization effects significantly impact current landowners in a way that is *not* related to benefits received, with owners of large homes suffering capital losses and owners of small homes experiencing capital gains. These effects are pure redistributions[7] and, if unanticipated, should not create inefficiencies in housing consumption decisions. But they are very likely to create inefficiencies in decisions regarding local public service provision, as residents contemplating an increase in public services will face implicit costs that differ greatly from the benefits of public services received; for example, owners of large homes will anticipate suffering a capital loss that might be 10–20 times the excess of the increase in their property tax payments over the value of benefits received from the service expansion, while the owners of small homes will anticipate analogous gains. This scenario is far removed from the efficient operation of the local public sector in a Tiebout (1956) world, where all residents of a jurisdiction contemplating an increase in local public services, regardless of the value of their homes, would face an equal increase in head taxes. Thus, although these intrajurisdictional capitalization effects in the THF model set the stage for the property tax to be a benefit tax for future purchasers as described by Hamilton (1976, 1983), the tax is by no means a benefit tax at the time that it is imposed or at any subsequent time that it is changed.

---

[7] Indeed, they could be likened to the local government "regulatory takings" analyzed by Fischel (1998).

The most recent example of arguments linking intrajurisdictional capitalization and the benefit tax view are due to Fischel (1985, 1992, 2001a, b). For example, Fischel (2001a, b) argues that the empirical evidence supporting intrajurisdictional fiscal capitalization is conclusive (for example, see Palmon and Smith (1998) and Gallagher, Kurban, and Persky (2013)), suggesting that fiscal "capitalization is everywhere" (Fischel, 2001a, p. 56). He further argues that this provides compelling evidence that the benefit tax view as developed in the THF model accurately describes the effects of the property tax in suburban jurisdictions.[8]

This contention is examined in this paper, which focuses on the intrajurisdictional capitalization that is the linchpin of the THF model and underlies Fischel's arguments. Specifically, I construct a model, similar to those used to generate the benefit tax view, which shows that a broadly similar pattern of *intra*-jurisdictional land value fiscal capitalization occurs under both views. Moreover, numerous papers, dating back to Kotlikoff and Summers (1987) have shown that under the capital tax view, differentially high property taxes drive mobile capital out of the taxing jurisdiction and thus reduce the productivity of, and returns to, immobile local factors including land — that is, they cause *inter*-jurisdictional capitalization. Together, these results imply that the widely observed phenomenon of property tax capitalization (of either kind) provides little if any evidence that distinguishes between the capital tax and benefit tax views of the property tax.

3. A Differential Tax Incidence Model of Capitalization under the Benefit Tax View

The derivations of the benefit tax and capital tax views of the property tax are based on rather different theoretical approaches that must be reconciled for this analysis. The THF benefit tax view model characterizes the

[8] Similarly, Oates (2006, p. 27) notes that "many studies now take full capitalization as a premise" and stresses that intrajurisdictional capitalization is the essential feature of the benefit view of the property tax described here as the THF model, which is more plausible than the homogeneous housing version, which "doesn't seem to characterize the real world very well" (p. 28).

properties of a local economy in equilibrium, with local public services in communities with heterogeneous housing financed by residential property taxes. In contrast, the derivations of the capital tax view use differential tax incidence analysis in which the effects of the property tax are analyzed by first constructing an initial equilibrium with either no taxes or only non-distortionary lump-sum taxes, and then introducing property tax finance on a revenue-neutral basis and analyzing its differential effects. In the following analysis, all of the intrajurisdictional fiscal capitalization results obtained in the THF equilibrium model of the benefit tax view are derived in a differential tax incidence model that is typical of the capital tax view, but includes the basic assumptions characteristic of derivations of the benefit tax view. Although these assumptions are widely recognized as rather stringent (Rubinfeld, 1987; Ross and Yinger, 1999), they are nevertheless adopted in the analysis below — not because they are necessarily plausible but because they must be made in order to replicate the benefit tax view capitalization results.

The details of the model are as follows.[9] The model follows the THF model in assuming that households are perfectly mobile across local jurisdictions. Local public services per household G are common to all households in a jurisdiction,[10] and, following most of the literature, are modeled as publicly provided private goods. There are a sufficient number of jurisdictions to satisfy all tastes for local public services. Households are assumed to have an exogenous source of income, y, which is identical across all households. Note that, as in the THF model, a fixed y implies the analysis ignores the income effects associated with fiscal capitalization of property tax differentials in land values. Although this strong assumption might be justified in several ways (e.g., absentee landlords, small income shares for land rents, roughly offsetting land value capitalization

[9] A list of all variables used in the model is provided in Table A1 in the appendix.

[10] Although this assumption is consistent with virtually all of the Tiebout literature, one could argue that larger homes might typically be associated with greater demands for local public services — e.g., more demand for public education due to a larger number of children — which would tend to reduce the magnitudes of the distortions caused by the property tax under the capital tax view. Nevertheless, the same issues analyzed in this paper would still arise as long as there was heterogeneity in housing demands among both the high and low demanders for local public services.

effects), it is made primarily to be consistent with the THF approach, dating back to the Tiebout (1956) assumption that all households have only fixed levels of dividend income.

To introduce the intrajurisdictional heterogeneity with respect to housing demands characteristic of the THF approach, the model has two types of households, indexed by superscripts $i = h, l$, with N^h high demanders of housing who each consume H^h units of housing, and N^l low demanders who each consume $H^l < H^h$ units of housing. The total population in the jurisdiction is $N = N^h + N^l$. Initially, the local economy is assumed to be in an efficient Tiebout equilibrium, with an optimal level of local public services financed with uniform head taxes of Z per household. All other goods in the economy are treated as a single composite numeraire good. Note that the assumption that all households have the same exogenous income y implies that high (low) demanders of housing must be low (high) demanders of the composite good. Household utility is defined over consumption of housing with price q_j, the composite good, which is chosen as the numeraire good, and the common level of local public services G. Since both types of households are perfectly mobile across jurisdictions, household utility for each must equal an exogenously specified level $\bar{U}^i$; that is, with indirect utility functions W^i, perfect mobility implies $W^i(q_j, y - Z, G) = \bar{U}^i$ for each of the two types of households.

In this initial "head tax" equilibrium, the supply of land V within each jurisdiction is assumed to be fixed, and is used either for large houses for high demanders V^h or small houses for low demanders V^l. The total amount of land used for each type of house is thus $V_L = N^l V^l$ and $V_H = N^h V^h$, where the subscripts $j = H, L$ indicate the two house types. Both types of housing are produced with capital (K_H, K_L) and land using a constant returns to scale production function. In the initial equilibrium, the prices of both types of housing are equal as they reflect only resource costs and both capital and land costs are initially identical.

Zoning is introduced into the model by assuming that the amounts of land used for large and small houses are fixed at their initial efficient equilibrium values (where the prices of the two types of land are assumed to be equal). This is a weak form of the assumption made by Hamilton, who assumes fully developed communities and thus precludes any change in either the land or the capital allocated for the two types of housing. Note that some form of land use zoning must be assumed for any capitalization to occur; otherwise, as discussed previously, land would be reallocated until it all sold for the same price and there would be no capitalization. However, Fischel (2001a, b) and Oates (2006) argue that the supply of housing land is inelastic and indeed that fixed supplies are a reasonable assumption, at least for a lengthy "intermediate run" period. Moreover, the empirical results of Stadelmann and Billion (2008) generally support the importance of examining the incidence of the property tax within the context of such an intermediate view, as they find that fiscal capitalization is roughly constant or may even increase over time. Accordingly, the model allows for capitalization effects by assuming fixed quantities of land used for large and small houses[11]; it thus clearly focuses solely on an "intermediate run" view of the effects of the property tax.[12]

Property taxation is introduced by assuming an exogenous uniform reduction in head taxes, with the resulting reduction in revenues offset with an increase in residential property taxes, holding the level of public services per capita fixed.[13] Specifically, in response to the uniform per household reduction in head taxes, property taxes are applied at the same rate t to all capital income $rK_H + rK_L$ and land rents $s_H V_H + s_L V_L$ earned in both types of residential housing within the jurisdiction, where r is the net return to capital, which is fixed under the assumption that the taxing jurisdiction can be modeled as a small open economy, and s_j is the return

[11] Indeed, as pointed out by an anonymous referee, such an assumption also has an intuitively plausible rationale: although households can easily make marginal changes in the levels of their consumption of housing capital by making (or not making) home improvements or by allowing a property to depreciate, it is considerably more difficult to "tear down" a home and thus convert land used for small homes to land used for large homes or vice versa.

[12] By comparison, in a long run equilibrium in which land was reallocated until land prices were equalized, there could be no capitalization effects and the property tax could not be a benefit tax, as individuals with relatively high demands for housing would bear a disproportionate share of the burden of the tax.

[13] Although the latter assumption ignores the tendency toward property-tax-induced under-provision of local public services that is the focus of the tax competition literature noted above, it is consistent with the THF approach, under which fiscal capitalization effects are due to a mismatch between property tax payments and services received, rather than due to any tax-induced under-provision of local public services.

to land used in the production of housing of type j. (Alternatively, since capital and land are the only inputs into housing, the property tax could be modeled as an excise tax on housing at the same rate.) Thus, the gross price of capital is rT, where $T = 1 + t$, and gross land rents are $s_j V_j T$.

Finally, as stressed by Mieszkowski and Zodrow (1989), Nechyba (2001), and Fischel, Oates, and Youngman (2011), a key factor distinguishing the existing models of the benefit tax and capital tax views is that the supply of housing capital is typically assumed to be inelastic under the benefit tax view (especially in THF-type models in which perfect fiscal capitalization is required to convert the property tax to a benefit tax), but highly elastic under the capital tax view (in order to get the capital reallocations that drive its results). Accordingly, in the benefit tax version of the model, the capital stocks of both types of housing (and thus both the aggregate and individual consumption levels of housing) are fixed, while in the capital tax version of the model, capital is perfectly mobile across jurisdictions.[14]

From this initial equilibrium, the calculations under the benefit tax view of the intrajurisdictional capitalization effects associated with a uniform reduction in head taxes and an offsetting increase in the property tax are straightforward.[15] The local government budget constraint requires that $(N^h + N^l)G = (N^h + N^l)Z + (T - 1)[r(K_H + K_L) + s_H V_H + s_L V_L]$. Differentiating and evaluating at the initial equilibrium $(T - 1)$ with fixed government services and capital and land stocks implies $(N^h + N^l)(-dZ) = [r(K_H + K_L) + s_H V_H + s_L V_L]dT$. Letting a tilde reflect logarithmic differentiation, defining population shares as $n^i = N^i/(N^h + N^l)$, housing expenditure shares in net income for each type of household as $\alpha^i = q_j \bar{H}^i / (y - Z)$, and the ratio of government services to net income (for both types of households) as $\beta = G/(y - Z)$, while recalling that for constant returns to scale production functions $q_j H_j = T(rK_j + s_j V_j)$, the percentage increase in

[14] Indeed, one could argue that the analysis suggests that the benefit tax view could be viewed as a special case of the capital tax view in which housing supply and demand elasticities are zero.

[15] To keep the notation simple, all variables in the remainder of this section refer to values under the benefit view, while all variables in the following section refer to the analogous values under the capital tax view. All expressions in both sections reflect the effects of an increase in the property tax from the same initial efficient head tax equilibrium.

the property tax required for budget balance in response to a given percentage reduction in the head tax is

$$\tilde{T} = [\beta / (n^h\alpha^h + n^l\alpha^l)](-\tilde{Z}). \tag{1}$$

Differentiating the indirect utility functions of both types of households (with fixed incomes and service levels) yields $(\partial W^i/\partial q_j)dq_j + [\partial W^i/\partial(y - Z)](-dZ) = 0$. Using Roy's identity, this implies $\bar{H}^i dq_j = -dZ$. Thus, with perfectly mobile households, the price of each type of housing must rise by just enough to offset the value of the decline in head taxes, so that the net cost of living in the taxing community yields the fixed utility level available in other communities for each type of household; this decline in head taxes equals the cost of the public services that are now financed with property taxes. Rearranging yields

$$\tilde{q}_j = [\beta/\alpha^i]\,(-\tilde{Z}), \quad \text{or}$$

$$\tilde{q}_H = [\beta/\alpha^h]\,(-\tilde{Z}) > 0; \quad \tilde{q}_L = [\beta/\alpha^l]\,(-\tilde{Z}) > 0; \tag{2}$$

the percentage increase in house prices is of course larger for smaller homes ($\tilde{q}_L = (\alpha^h/\alpha^l)\tilde{q}_H$).

Consider next the key issue of the extent of capitalization in the benefit view version of the model, that is, under the assumption that housing capital stocks are fixed. Note that since both housing land and capital are fixed, any capitalization effects are effectively borne by the entire property, so that the division of this burden between land and capital is arbitrary. To facilitate the comparison with the capital tax view, the analysis assumes that all of the capitalization is reflected in land values; however, one could just as easily assign some of this burden to capital — although the key issue for purposes of comparing the two views is the total amount of capitalization. Under this assumption, the change in the price of land used for high-value homes is obtained by differentiating the zero profit condition, $q_H H_H = T(rK_H + s_H V_H)$, and substituting from Eqs. (1) and (2) to yield

$$\tilde{s}_H = -\frac{1}{f_{VH}}\frac{\beta n^l(\alpha^h - \alpha^l)}{\alpha^h(n^h\alpha^h + n^l\alpha^l)}(-\tilde{Z}) < 0, \tag{3}$$

where $f_{VH} = S_H V_H/(rK_H + S_H V_H)$ is the land share in production costs for high-value homes. Since $\alpha^h > \alpha^l$ by assumption, high-value home prices unambiguously decline in response to the head tax reduction financed with a property tax increase, and the decline is proportional to the difference in relative demands for housing $(\alpha^h - \alpha^l)$. Moreover, this decline corresponds exactly to the discount for high-value homes envisioned in the THF model. To see this, note that full capitalization occurs if annual land rents for large homes — and thus the capitalized value of future land rents in the current prices of land used for such homes — fall by the high-value home fiscal differential, defined as the difference between the cost of the increase in total property taxes on high-value homes and the associated benefit of the reduction in head taxes for their owners. In the aggregate, this requires $V_H ds_H = -[(rK_H + s_H V_H)d^T - N^h(-dZ)]$. Dividing by $q_H H_H$ and substituting from Eq. (1) shows that this expression is equivalent to (3). Thus, for high-value homes, the negative fiscal differential arising from a property tax increase that exceeds the benefit of a uniform reduction in head taxes is fully capitalized, and high-value homes sell at the discount predicted by the THF model.

An analogous calculation yields the change in the price of land used for low-value homes, which in this case is unambiguously positive

$$\tilde{s}_L = \frac{1}{f_{VL}} \frac{\beta n^h(\alpha^h - \alpha^l)}{\alpha^l(n^h\alpha^h + n^l\alpha^l)}(-\tilde{Z}) > 0, \tag{4}$$

where f_{VL} is the land share in production costs for low-value homes. Again, this increase corresponds exactly to the premium for low-value homes in the THF model, since it equals the (negative) difference between the increase in property taxes paid on such homes and the associated benefit of the reduction in head taxes for their residents, or

$$V_L ds_L = -[(rK_L + s_L V_L)\, dT - N^l(-dZ)].$$

Both of the capitalization effects obtained in the model thus correspond to those predicted under the benefit view. In addition, as stressed above, the differences between property taxes paid and benefits received (the reduction in the head tax) for both types of households make it clear that the property tax is *not* a benefit tax for the combined property tax rate increase and head tax reduction; rather, the property tax only becomes a benefit tax for future purchasers — after the calculated intrajurisdictional capitalization effects occur.

Finally, a property of the THF benefit tax view model is that the net change in land values due to intrajurisdictional capitalization is zero, as the aggregate discount for larger homes equals the aggregate premium for smaller homes. The capitalization effects Eqs. (3–4) satisfy this property, as

$$V_H ds_H + V_L ds_L = [N^h q_H \bar{H}^h] f_{VH} \tilde{s}_H + [N^l q_L \bar{H}^l] f_{VL} \tilde{s}_L = 0.$$

4. Intrajurisdictional Capitalization under the Capital Tax View

Generating the capital tax view within the context of the model constructed above requires only that the capital stock be allowed to vary (while, as discussed above, the total amount of land used for high and low value houses is fixed in this intermediate run incidence analysis).[16] That is, under the capital tax view of the incidence of the property tax, households can reduce their housing consumption in response to an increase in the property tax. In addition, allowing variable housing implies that the numbers of high and low income households living within the taxing jurisdiction are no longer fixed. Instead, consistent with the assumption of perfect household mobility that characterizes the THF approach, the populations N^h and N^l are assumed to adjust so that the exogenously specified utility levels for each type of household are attained in the new equilibrium.

Specifically, the capital tax view is obtained in the model as follows. As above, the government budget constraint implies (1) and perfect mobility of households implies (2). Housing demands for each type of household are obtained by using Roy's identity to yield $H^i(q_j, y-Z, G) = -W_q^i(q_j, y-Z, G) / W_y^i(q_j, y-Z, G)$. With fixed supplies of land of each type and a uniform property tax, housing production can

[16]The partial equilibrium model utilized of course cannot capture the effect of nationwide use of the property tax on the return to capital, which is assumed to be exogenous. However, it is possible to capture this effect by examining the incidence of the use of a capital tax in a small taxing jurisdiction in a general equilibrium context (Zodrow, 2001a, b). In addition, the model assumes that the supply of any perfectly homogeneous communities is limited so that some households must live in communities that use the distortionary property tax.

be modeled using the restricted profit function approach, with before-tax profits (total gross land rents) for each type of housing represented as $\Pi^j(q_j, rT, V_j)$, and housing supply, housing capital demand, and the gross price of land equal to the partial derivatives of the three arguments of the restricted profit function, respectively. Equality of supply and demand in the two housing markets requires $\Pi^j_q(q_j, rT, V_j) = N^i H^i(q_j, y-Z, G), (i,j) = (h,H); (l,L)$.

In contrast to the benefit tax view analysis, under the capital tax view the changes in the property tax cause a reallocation of housing capital that is the key factor in determining the incidence of the tax. Specifically, differentiating the factor demands for housing capital $K_j = -\Pi^j_r(q_j, rT, V_j)$ yields $\tilde{K}_j = -[(\Pi^j_{rq} q_j)/K_j]\tilde{q}_j - [(\Pi^j_{rr} rT)/K_j]\tilde{T}$. Denoting the own-price factor demand elasticity for housing capital of type j (defined to be positive) as $\mu_j = (rT/K_j)\Pi^j_{rr} = -(q_j/K_j)\Pi^j_{rq} = -(q_j/K_j)\Pi^j_{qr} > 0$, and the own-price supply elasticity for housing of type j as $\varepsilon_j = q_j \Pi^j_{qq}/H_j = -rT\Pi^j_{rq}/H_j > 0$, implies that $\tilde{K}_j = (\varepsilon_j/f_{Kj})\tilde{q}_j - \mu_j \tilde{T}$, where the capital share in housing costs is $f_{Kj} = rTK_j/q_jH_j$. Moreover, since $\varepsilon_j = f_j \mu_j$, this simplifies to $\tilde{K}_j = \mu_j(\tilde{q}_j - \tilde{T})$, which, substituting from Eqs. (1) and (2) yields

$$\tilde{K}_H = -\frac{\beta\mu_H n^l(\alpha^h - \alpha^l)}{\alpha^h(n^h\alpha^h + n^l\alpha^l)}(-\tilde{Z}) < 0; \quad \tilde{K}_L = \frac{\beta\mu_L n^h(\alpha^h - \alpha^l)}{\alpha^l(n^h\alpha^h + n^l\alpha^l)}(-\tilde{Z}) > 0. \quad (5)$$

This is the central result of the capital tax view, expressed in terms of the effects of the use of the property tax within a single heterogeneous taxing jurisdiction. The tax is distortionary, as it causes capital to flow out of the production of large houses where property taxes are high relative to benefits received, and into production of smaller homes where the property tax bill is low relative to benefits received.

Differentiating the expressions for the gross prices of the two types of land $s_jT = \Pi^j_V(q_j, rT, V_j)$ yields the price effects of this property-tax-induced reallocation of capital, or

$$\begin{aligned}\tilde{s}_j + \tilde{T} &= [(\Pi^j_{Vq} q_j)/(s_jT)]\tilde{q}_j + [\Pi^j_{Vr} rT/(s_jT)]\tilde{T} \\ &= [q_jH_j/(s_jTV_j)]\tilde{q}_j - [rTK_j/(s_jTV_j)]\tilde{T}.\end{aligned}$$

Substituting from Eqs. (1) and (2) yields the changes in net land prices under the capital tax view

$$\tilde{s}_H = -\frac{1}{f_{VH}} \frac{\beta n^l (\alpha^h - \alpha^l)}{\alpha^h (n^h \alpha^h + n^l \alpha^l)} (-\tilde{Z}) < 0, \tag{6}$$

$$\tilde{s}_L = \frac{1}{f_{VL}} \frac{\beta n^h (\alpha^h - \alpha^l)}{\alpha^l (n^h \alpha^h + n^l \alpha^l)} (-\tilde{Z}) > 0. \tag{7}$$

Thus, the capital outflow from production of large houses unambiguously reduces the productivity of, and thus the net rents earned by, land used for such houses, while the capital inflow into production of small houses increases the net rents earned by land used for small houses.

It is these changes in land rents — caused by the tax-induced reallocation of housing capital described above but precluded under the benefit tax view — that are capitalized into land prices under the capital tax view of the property tax. However, a comparison of Eqs. (6–7) with (3–4) reveals immediately that the changes in land prices — and thus the predicted land value capitalization effects — under the capital tax and benefit tax views of the property tax, in the context of the partial equilibrium models utilized in this paper (when evaluated at the undistorted initial equilibrium, with $T = 1$ and the consumption of both types of housing at their initial efficient levels in the head tax equilibrium), are identical. The analysis thus suggests that the existence of capitalization of intrajurisdictional property tax differentials into land values is of little help in distinguishing between the two competing views of the property tax.

The model generates several additional results. Since the land price changes under the capital tax view are identical to those calculated under the benefit tax view, the aggregate value of land in the taxing jurisdiction is again unchanged, as the two capitalization effects exactly offset. Somewhat surprisingly, the aggregate capital stock is also unchanged, as the capital outflow from the production of large homes is exactly offset by the increase in capital used in the production of small homes. To see this, note that in the initial equilibrium (with equal capital-land ratios, housing prices, and land rents per unit of land), $K_H/K = q_H H_H/(q_H H_H + q_L H_L) = n^h \alpha^h/(n^h \alpha^h + n^l \alpha^l)$ and $K_L/K = n^l \alpha^l/(n^h \alpha^h + n^l \alpha^l)$. Substituting from Eq. (5) yields the change in the total capital stock

$$\tilde{K} = (K_H/K)\tilde{K}_H + (K_L/K)\tilde{K}_L = \frac{\beta n^l n^h (\alpha^h - \alpha^l)}{(n^h \alpha^h + n^l \alpha^l)^2} (\mu_L - \mu_H)(-\tilde{Z}) = 0. \tag{8}$$

That is, since the restricted profit function is linear in the fixed factor (land zoned for housing of each type) for a constant returns to scale production function, and the prices q_j and $rT = r$ and thus the capital-land ratios are identical in the initial equilibrium, the two own-price capital factor demand elasticities are identical ($\mu_H = \mu_L$). Thus, despite the fact that the local economy is open to capital flows (with a fixed after-tax rate of return), the net effect on the total capital stock in the taxing jurisdiction is zero — housing capital is reallocated but the total stock is unchanged.

The changes in the total amounts of the two types of housing are obtained by differentiating the supply equation $H_j = \Pi_q^j(q_j, rT, V_j)$ to yield

$$\tilde{H}_j = \varepsilon_j(\tilde{q}_j - \tilde{T}) = f_{Kj}\mu_j(\tilde{q}_j - \tilde{T}) = f_{Kj}\tilde{K}_j,$$

so that

$$\tilde{H}_H = -f_{KH}\mu_H \frac{\beta n^l(\alpha^h - \alpha^l)}{\alpha^h(n^h\alpha^h + n^l\alpha^l)}(-\tilde{Z}) < 0;$$

$$\tilde{H}_L = f_{KL}\mu_L \frac{\beta n^h(\alpha^h - \alpha^l)}{\alpha^l(n^h\alpha^h + n^l\alpha^l)}(-\tilde{Z}) > 0. \qquad (9)$$

Thus, as expected under the capital tax view, the total amount of high-value housing unambiguously decreases, while the total amount of low-value housing unambiguously increases.

Nevertheless, despite the distortion of the allocation of housing capital under the capital tax view, local use of the property tax, as noted above, still has some features that are characteristic of a benefit tax, at least after all capitalization effects occur. Specifically, in the post-tax equilibrium, residents pay for net local public services received (those not financed with head taxes) in the form of higher housing prices. Simultaneously, since fiscal differentials have been capitalized into land values, the net effect of the property tax burden and land value capitalization of the fiscal differential is that purchasers of both types of homes effectively pay only for services received. Thus, in the context of this partial equilibrium model of heterogeneous communities with the net national return to capital fixed, the essential difference between the two views of the property tax is not that residents "pay for what they get" as stressed by proponents of the benefit tax view — as that occurs under both views — but that, under the capital tax view, land value capitalization occurs due to capital reallocations across housing types, implying inefficiency in the housing market. By comparison, under the benefit tax view, capitalization occurs with respect to fixed housing capital stocks, so there can be no distortion of the allocation of housing capital. And, to repeat, existing landowners suffer property-tax-induced capital gains and losses at the time of the imposition of the tax that are unrelated to the benefits received at the time of the increase in the property tax.

Consider next the changes in per capita housing consumption and the population changes induced by the tax change. Totally differentiating the housing market equilibrium equations and substituting from Eq. (1) yields $\tilde{H}_j - \tilde{N}^i = -\eta^i_q \tilde{q}_j + \beta\eta^i_y(-\tilde{Z}) = -(\omega^i_q + \alpha^i\eta^i_y)\tilde{q}_j + \beta\eta^i_y(-\tilde{Z})$, where η^i_q are the uncompensated elasticities of housing demand, η^i_y are the income elasticities of housing demand, and $\omega^i_q = \eta^i_q - \alpha^i\eta^i_y$ are the compensated elasticities of demand. Substituting from Eq. (2) yields

$$\tilde{H}_j - \tilde{N}^i = -(\omega^i_q\beta/\alpha^i)(-\tilde{Z}) < 0. \tag{10}$$

Thus, per capita housing consumption declines unambiguously for both types of households — the standard capital tax view result that the property tax inefficiently reduces housing consumption.

Finally, substituting into Eq. (10) from (9), the changes in population are

$$\tilde{N}^l = \left[\frac{\omega^l_q\beta}{\alpha^l} + f_{KL}\mu_L \frac{\beta\eta^h(\alpha^h - \alpha^l)}{\alpha^l(\eta^h\alpha^h + \eta^l\alpha^l)}\right](-\tilde{Z}) > 0;$$
$$\tilde{N}^h = \left[\frac{\omega^h_q\beta}{\alpha^h} - f_{KH}\mu_H \frac{\beta\eta^l(\alpha^h - \alpha^l)}{\alpha^h(\eta^h\alpha^h + \eta^l\alpha^l)}\right](-\tilde{Z}). \tag{11}$$

Thus, in this partial equilibrium model, if the total amounts of housing were fixed (the second terms above were zero), the total number of both types of households would have to increase to attain an equilibrium, given the declines in per capita housing consumption and the fixed amount of land of each type in the jurisdiction. However, the second terms in Eq. (11) capture the effects of the tax-induced reallocation of housing capital, as the amount of low-value housing increases but the amount of high-value housing decreases. Thus, the number of households who purchase small houses must unambiguously increase for an equilibrium to obtain. However, the net effect on the number of households who purchase large houses is theoretically ambiguous, since the decline in per capita consumption is accompanied by a decrease in the total amount of large housing.

This implies that the change in total population, expressed in percentage terms, is

$$\eta^h \tilde{N}^h + \eta^l \tilde{N}^l = \left\{ \begin{matrix} \dfrac{\eta^h \omega_q^h \beta}{\alpha^h} + \dfrac{\eta^l \omega_q^l \beta}{\alpha^l} + \dfrac{\beta \eta^h \eta^l (\alpha^h - \alpha^l)}{(\eta^h \alpha^h + \eta^l \alpha^l)} \\ \left[\dfrac{f_{KL} \mu_L}{\alpha^l} - \dfrac{f_{KH} \mu_H}{\alpha^h} \right] \end{matrix} \right\} (-\tilde{Z}) > 0. \qquad (12)$$

Since the capital shares and the own-price capital demand elasticities are identical in the initial equilibrium and $\alpha^h > \alpha^l$, this expression is unambiguously positive. Thus, the total population in the jurisdiction unambiguously increases, as the increase in population attributable to the increase in consumption of small houses outweighs the reduction in population due to the decrease in consumption of large houses. Note that these results obtain only because the supply of land in each jurisdiction is fixed and population is perfectly mobile in the partial equilibrium context utilized in this paper. If instead land were variable and population were fixed, the use of property tax finance would cause the community to shrink in size (e.g., land at the perimeter would be converted to agricultural use). This in turn explains why the total capital stock and aggregate land values do not decrease with use of the property tax but instead remain constant, at least for the first increase in the property tax from the initial Tiebout equilibrium. That is, these results obtain only because the total population of the taxing jurisdiction increases, which increases aggregate demand for housing and housing capital as well as land prices. These immigration-related effects precisely offset the reduction in the demand for housing capital and the associated reduction in aggregate land values that typically arise under the capital tax view of the property tax.

5. Some Simulation Results

The analysis above obtains the strong result that intrajurisdictional capitalization effects are identical under the capital tax and benefits tax views. Since the reduction in the use of the head tax is identical in the two models and both are characterized by perfectly mobile individuals and assume that land (and capital in the case of the benefit view) used for both types of housing is fixed, it is plausible that the differential effects of local use of the property tax under both views are captured as capitalization effects. However, these capitalization effects under the two views are precisely identical only because all of these differential effects, including those involving capitalization, are calculated at the same efficient initial (head tax) equilibrium, so that all of the excess burden effects associated with property tax increase are second-order effects and drop out of the differential analysis.[17] Accordingly, the two capitalization effects would not be expected to be identical when evaluated at a distorted initial equilibrium that included a positive level of property taxation. A natural question is the robustness of the finding of equal capitalization effects to a finite reduction in the head tax coupled with a finite property tax increase. Similarly, the finding of the differential incidence analysis that the total capital stock in the taxing jurisdiction is unchanged despite an increase in the property tax rate depends on the absence of property-tax induced inefficiencies in the initial efficient head tax equilibrium. One would expect that the inefficiencies that would arise for a finite tax increase would drive capital out of the taxing jurisdiction, as in the traditional analyses of the capital tax view (Mieszkowski, 1972; Zodrow and Mieszkowski, 1986). This section describes a simulation exercise that explores these questions.

Specifically, consider the models described above, assuming the utility function is Cobb–Douglas; to allow for large potential capitalization effects, suppose that the housing expenditure shares are relatively large, 35 percent for high demanders and 15 percent for low demanders, who are present in equal numbers in the initial equilibrium. Suppose further that the housing production function is also Cobb–Douglas, with a capital share in production costs of 75 percent (Albuoy, 2008). Local government expenditures (including those financed with external

[17]The analysis is thus strictly accurate only for an infinitesimally small change from the initial efficient equilibrium (Fullerton and Metcalf, 2002).

funds such as intergovernmental grants) are assumed to be 9.2 percent of income ($\beta = 0.092$).[18] Within this context, consider the effects of a finite reduction in head taxes, coupled with a balanced-budget increase in property taxes. Using Texas, a relatively high property tax state, as an example, the share of local expenditures financed with local property taxes in 2010 was 30.1 percent[19] and the share of total property taxes attributable to residential property in 2010 was 44.8 percent,[20] which implies that 13.5 percent of local expenditures are financed with residential property tax revenues. Within the context of the model utilized in this paper, I assume that all public services are initially financed with head taxes; this assumption is of course unrealistic to the extent that other taxes (e.g., sales or income taxes) cause their own distortions and because in reality all residents within a jurisdiction will not have the identical incomes assumed in the model. To approximate the introduction of the property tax from such an initial equilibrium, the simulation examines the effects of incremental reductions in head taxes from an initial equilibrium in which all public services are financed with head taxes until $-\Delta Z/Z = 0.15$.

Table 16.1 provides the simulation results. Columns (3) and (6) of the first panel show the capitalization effects that would occur under the benefit tax view, with land rents falling for V_H and increasing for V_L as predicted. Columns (4) and (7) show the analogous effects under the capital tax view, and columns (5) and (8) calculate the differences between the two views. As expected, the changes in land rents under the two views are virtually identical for the first increase in the property tax rate ($-\Delta Z/Z =$ 0.1 percent). This relationship is no longer exact for finite property tax increases, as each incremental increase in the property tax creates two types of first-order efficiency costs under the capital tax view: (1) it further distorts the intrajurisdictional allocation of housing capital, and (2) it

[18] This figure reflects total local expenditures as a fraction of national income in 2010; see U.S. Bureau of Economic Analysis, National Income and Product Accounts, Tables 1.7.5 and 3.21.

[19] See U.S. Census Bureau, 2010 State and Local Government Finances, Table 1.

[20] See Texas Comptroller of Public Accounts (2012), Biennial Property Tax Report: Tax Years 2010 and 2011, Exhibit 4.

drives capital out of the taxing jurisdiction — in contrast to the analysis above where the total capital stock was unchanged for the first increase in the property tax from the initial efficient head tax equilibrium. Note that in the latter case, the property-tax-induced outflow of capital is zero only for the first incremental increase in the property tax, and ranges up to nearly 0.75 percent (column 9).

Nevertheless, the differences between the capitalization effects in the two cases (columns 5 and 8) are relatively small: roughly 5 percent for V_H and 12.5 percent for V_L for the full increase in the property tax (from zero to the current level in a fairly high residential property tax state), and roughly 1–2.5 percent for each incremental property tax increase (for each increase in $(-\Delta Z/Z)$ of 3 percentage points, which corresponds to an increase in $(\Delta T/T)$ of roughly one percentage point). Such differences seem small enough to be broadly consistent with the main thesis of this paper — that the benefit tax and capital tax views generate rather similar intrajurisdictional capitalization effects so that tests of capitalization are of little help in distinguishing between the two views. In particular, although admittedly speculative, it seems unlikely that most empirical estimates of the extent of capitalization — which would typically examine incremental changes in the property tax — would be precise enough to identify such small differences. For example, the results of Palmon and Smith (1998), which they and Fischel (2001a) characterize as roughly consistent with complete intrajurisdictional capitalization of property tax differentials, range from nearly 40 percent under-capitalization to slight over-capitalization. Similarly, the work of Lutz (2009), cited by Fischel, Oates, and Youngman (2011) as consistent with full interjurisdictional capitalization, finds 75–95 percent capitalization. Thus, in my view, the results of this admittedly simple simulation do not undermine the basic implication of the theoretical model — it is difficult if not impossible to use empirical results on intrajurisdictional capitalization to distinguish between the benefit tax and capital tax views of the property tax.

Finally, the remaining results shown in the second panel of Table 16.1 are consistent with various other results presented above. For example, for the case of a 15 percent drop in head taxes, (1) the amount of H_H declines by nearly 5 percent (column 10), while the amount of H_L increases by over 9 percent (column 11), with total H declining slightly (column 12), (2) the

Table 16.1.
Simulation Results for Capital Tax (CT) View, Relative to Benefit Tax (BT) View
(All variables are expressed as changes in percentage terms)

(1) $\frac{\Delta Z}{Z}$	(2) $\frac{\Delta T}{T}$	(3) $\frac{\Delta s_H V_H}{s_H V_H}(BT)$	(4) $\frac{\Delta s_H V_H}{s_H V_H}(CT)$	(5) $\frac{C-B}{B}(s_H V_H)$	(6) $\frac{\Delta s_L V_L}{s_L V_L}(BT)$	(7) $\frac{\Delta s_L V_L}{s_L V_L}(CT)$	(8) $\frac{C-B}{B}(s_L V_L)$	(9) $\frac{\Delta K}{K}$
0.1	0.032	−0.04	−0.04	−0.031	0.085	0.085	−0.088	0.000
1.0	1.003	−0.370	−0.375	−0.318	0.861	0.853	−0.883	−0.003
3.0	1.010	−1.145	−1.156	−0.956	2.575	2.508	−2.629	−0.028
6.0	1.977	−2.365	−2.410	−1.922	5.130	4.866	−5.197	−0.114
9.0	3.009	−3.627	−3.731	−2.901	7.663	7.008	−7.632	−0.260
12.0	4.074	−4.994	−5.238	−3.898	10.174	9.150	−10.068	−0.463
15.0	5.171	−6.444	−6.758	−4.868	12.539	10.977	−12.580	−0.739

(1) $\frac{\Delta Z}{Z}$	(10) $\frac{\Delta H_H}{H_H}$	(11) $\frac{\Delta H_L}{H_L}$	(12) $\frac{\Delta H}{H}$	(13) $\frac{\Delta N_H}{N_H}$	(14) $\frac{\Delta N_L}{N_L}$	(15) $\frac{\Delta N}{N}$	(16) $\frac{\Delta(H_H/N_H)}{H_H/N_H}$	(17) $\frac{\Delta(H_L/N_L)}{H_L/N_L}$
0.1	−0.027	0.065	0.000	−0.013	0.110	0.048	−0.014	−0.045
1.0	−0.28	0.64	0.00	−0.14	1.10	0.48	−0.14	−0.45
3.0	−0.86	1.92	−0.02	−0.43	3.28	1.42	−0.43	−1.34
6.0	−1.77	3.81	−0.10	−0.93	6.65	2.86	−0.85	−2.66
9.0	−2.74	5.66	−0.22	−1.48	10.01	4.26	−1.27	−3.96
12.0	−3.72	7.46	−0.39	−2.10	13.39	5.65	−1.69	−5.24
15.0	−4.83	9.20	−0.62	−2.76	16.78	6.93	−2.09	−6.50

population of households with high-value homes declines by nearly 3 percent (column 13) while the population of households with low-value homes increases by nearly 17 percent (column 14), with an overall population increase of nearly 7 percent (column 15), and (3) per capita housing consumption declines for both groups, by 2.1 percent for households with high-value homes (column 16), and by 6.5 percent for households with low-value homes (column 17).

6. Conclusion

The analysis in this paper suggests that, at least in the context of the "benefit tax-type" partial equilibrium model analyzed in this paper, *intra*-jurisdictional capitalization into land values of fiscal differentials — the differences between property taxes paid and the benefits of public services received in communities that are heterogeneous with respect to house value — is entirely consistent with, and indeed predicted by, the capital tax view of the property tax. Coupled with earlier similar findings on *inter*-jurisdictional capitalization, these results suggest that empirical evidence supporting full capitalization of property taxes does not provide compelling evidence that allows researchers to distinguish between the capital tax and benefit tax views of the property tax. Instead, other empirical tests must be utilized to choose between the two views.[21] In addition, the analysis shows that these intrajurisdictional capitalization effects imply that even under the stringent assumptions of the benefit view, it is clear that the property tax is *not* a benefit tax when its rate increases to finance an expansion of local public services; rather, the property tax only becomes a benefit tax for future home purchasers — after all of the various intrajurisdictional capitalization effects, which do not correspond to benefits

[21] For example, Wassmer (1993), Carroll and Yinger (1994), and Lutz (2009) provide empirical evidence that they conclude is consistent with the capital tax view of the property tax. However, the property-tax-induced reallocations of capital found by Wassmer are fairly small, Carroll and Yinger focus solely on rental housing, and, as noted above, Fischel, Oates, and Youngman (2011) interpret Lutz's results as supportive of the benefit view. More generally, Lutz (2009) concludes that existing empirical work has largely failed at distinguishing between the two views; see also Nechyba (2001) and Zodrow (2001a). Clearly new studies providing more definitive empirical evidence would be extremely helpful in choosing between the two competing views of the effects of the property tax.

received, are borne by the owners of high- and low-value homes existing at the time of enactment of the tax change.

Finally, it should be again stressed that the results presented in this paper, while using a modeling approach consistent with the THF literature, are limited by the partial equilibrium nature of the analysis. In particular, the model utilized (1) does not specify the effects of the property tax increase in the jurisdiction analyzed on housing and land prices, per capita housing consumption, capital stocks, population, etc., in other jurisdictions, or (2) calculate the economy-wide efficiency effects of the property tax increase in the taxing jurisdiction (recall that the assumption that residents are perfectly mobile implies that their utility levels are fixed). In addition, the analysis focuses solely on the residential property tax and thus ignores non-residential property taxation, and does not consider the roles of other taxes on housing decisions, especially the favorable treatment of owner-occupied housing under the personal income tax, which provides deductions for home mortgage interest and property taxes while exempting imputed rents from tax and taxing housing capital gains very lightly. A full-scale general equilibrium analysis of both the interjurisdictional and the intrajurisdictional effects of the property tax, coupled with a comprehensive calculation of the excess burdens associated with its use that would include consideration of the special treatment of housing under the personal income tax — for example merging the model constructed in this paper with an expanded version of the general equilibrium modeling approaches used in Muthitachareon and Zodrow (2010, 2012) — is left to future research.

Appendix Table A1. Variable Definitions

N	Total number of households in the taxing jurisdiction
N^h, N^l	Number of households with high and low demand for housing
n^h, n^l	Population shares of high and low housing demanders
y	Fixed level of income per household
Z	Head taxes per household
G	Fixed level of public services per household
β	Ratio of government services to net income (both types of households)
H^h, H^l	Housing consumption for high and low housing demanders

$\bar{H}^h, \bar{H}^l$	Fixed housing demands under the benefit tax view
q_H, q_L	Price of high-value and low-value housing
α^h, α^l	Housing expenditure shares for high and low housing demanders
η_q^h, η_q^l	Uncompensated elasticities of housing demand, high and low demanders
ω_q^h, ω_q^l	Compensated elasticities of housing demand, high and low demanders
η_y^h, η_y^l	Income elasticities of housing demand, high and low demanders
$\bar{U}^h, \bar{U}^l$	Fixed level of utility for high and low housing demand households
W^h, W^l	Indirect utility function for high and low housing demand households
V^h, V^l	Amount of land used for a high-value and a low-value house
V_H, V_L	Fixed total amounts of land used for high-value and low-value houses
f_{VH}, f_{VL}	Land share of production costs for high-value and low-value homes
K_H, K_L	Total amount of capital used for high-value and low-value houses
f_{KH}, f_{KL}	Capital share of production costs for high-value and low-value homes
t	Property tax rate ($T = 1 + t$)
r	After-tax return to capital
s_H, s_L	After-tax return to land used in high-value and low-value housing
Π^H, Π^L	Restricted profit function for high-value and low-value homes
μ_H, μ_L	Own-price capital demand elasticity, high-value and low-value housing
$\varepsilon_H, \varepsilon_L$	Own-price supply elasticity, high-value and low-value housing

Acknowledgements

I have benefited from the comments of Peter Mieszkowski, Wally Oates, and two anonymous referees, and from the research assistance of Elisabeth Gugl and Athiphat Muthitacharoen. This research was supported with a grant from the Lincoln Institute of Land Policy.

References

Albouy, David, 2008. "What are Cities Worth? Land Rents, Local Productivity and the Value of Amenities." Unpublished manuscript, University of Michigan.

Alm, James, Robert D. Buschman, and David L. Sjoquist, 2011. "Rethinking Local Government Reliance on the Property Tax." *Regional Science and Urban Economics* 41 (4), 320–331.

Carroll, Robert and John Yinger, 1994. "Is the Property Tax a Benefit Tax? The Case of Rental Housing." *National Tax Journal* 47 (2), 295–316.

Cho, Sang-Wook (Stanley), and Johanna L. Francis, 2011. "Tax Treatment of Owner Occupied Housing and Wealth Inequality." *Journal of Macroeconomics* 33 (1), 42–60.

Dowding, Keith, Peter John and Stephen Biggs, 1994. "Tiebout: A Survey of the Empirical Literature." *Urban Studies* 31, 767–797.

Fischel, William A., 1985. *The Economics of Zoning Laws: A Property Rights Approach to American Land Use Controls.* Baltimore: Johns Hopkins University Press.

Fischel, William A., 1992. "Property Taxation and the Tiebout Model: Evidence for the Benefit View from Voting and Zoning." *Journal of Economic Literature* 30 (1): 171–177.

Fischel, William A., 1998. *Regulatory Takings: Law, Economics, and Politics*, Cambridge, MA: Harvard University Press.

Fischel, William A., 2001a. "Municipal Corporations, Homeowners and the Benefit View of the Property Tax," in Wallace E. Oates, ed., *Property Taxation and Local Government Finance*. Cambridge, MA: Lincoln Institute of Land Policy, 33–77.

Fischel, William A., 2001b. "Homevoters, Municipal Corporate Governance, and the Benefit View of the Property Tax," *National Tax Journal* 54 (1), 157–173.

Fischel, William A., Wallace E. Oates, and Joan Youngman, 2011. "Are Local Property Taxes Regressive, Progressive, or What?" Unpublished manuscript.

Fisher, Ronald, 2009. "Property Taxes for Local Finance: Research Results and Policy Perspectives," Lincoln Institute of Land Policy Working Paper WP09RF1. Cambridge, MA: Lincoln Institute of Land Policy.

Gallagher, Ryan M., Haydar Kurban, and Joseph J. Persky, 2013. "Small Homes, Public Schools, and Property Tax Capitalization." *Regional Science and Urban Economics* 43 (2), 422–428.

Hamilton, Bruce W. 1975. "Zoning and Property Taxation in a System of Local Governments." *Urban Studies* 12 (2), 205–211.

Hamilton, Bruce W. 1976. "Capitalization of Intrajurisdictional Differences in Local Tax Prices." *American Economic Review* 66 (5), 743–753.

Hamilton, Bruce W., 1983. "A Review: Is the Property Tax a Benefit Tax?" in George R. Zodrow, ed., *Local Provision of Public Services: The Tiebout Model after Twenty-five Years*. New York: Academic Press, 85–107.

Kotlikoff, Laurence J. and Lawrence H. Summers, 1987. "Tax Incidence," in Alan J. Auerbach and Martin S. Feldstein, eds., *Handbook of Public Economics, Volume I.* Amsterdam: North Holland, 1043–1092.

Kurban, Haydar, Ryan M. Gallagher, and Joseph J. Persky, 2012. "Estimating Local Redistribution through Property-Tax-Funded Public School Systems." *National Tax Journal* 65 (3), 629–652.

Lutz, Byron F., 2009. "Fiscal Amenities, School Finance Reform, and the Supply Side of the Tiebout Market." Federal Reserve Board Working Paper.

Mieszkowski, Peter, 1972. "The Property Tax: An Excise Tax or a Profits Tax?" *Journal of Public Economics* 1 (1), 73–96.

Mieszkowski, Peter and Zodrow, George R., 1989. "Taxation and the Tiebout Model: The Differential Effects of Head Taxes, Taxes on Land Rents, and Property Taxes." *Journal of Economic Literature* 27 (3), 1098–1146.

Mills, Edwin S., 2008. "User Fees." In *The New Palgrave Dictionary of Economics*, edited by Steven N. Durlauf and Lawrence E. Blume. Hampshire, UK: Palgrave Macmillan.

Muthitacharoen, Athiphat and Zodrow, George R., 2006. "State and Local Taxation of Business Property: A Small Open Economy Perspective," *Proceedings of the Ninety-Eighth Annual Conference on Taxation*. Washington, DC: National Tax Association, 434–440.

Muthitacharoen, Athiphat and Zodrow, George R., 2010. "The Efficiency Costs of a Local Property Tax." In *Challenging the Conventional Wisdom on the Property Tax*, edited by Roy Bahl, Jorge Martinez-Vazquez and Joan Youngman, pp. 15–42. Lincoln Institute of Land Policy, Cambridge MA.

Muthitacharoen, Athiphat and George R. Zodrow, 2012. "Revisiting the Excise Tax Effects of the Property Tax." *Public Finance Review* 40 (5), 555–583.

Nechyba, Thomas J., 2001. "The Benefit View and the New View: Where Do We Stand, Twenty-Five Years into the Debate?" in Wallace E. Oates, ed., *Property Taxation and Local Government Finance.* Cambridge MA: Lincoln Institute of Land Policy, 113–121.

Netzer, Dick, 1966. *Economics of the Property Tax.* Washington DC: Brookings Institution.

Netzer, Dick, 2001. "Local Property Taxation in Theory and Practice: Some Reflections," in Wallace E. Oates, ed., *Property Taxation and Local Government Finance.* Cambridge MA: Lincoln Institute of Land Policy, 321–338.

Oates, Wallace E., 1969. "The Effects of Property Taxes and Local Public Spending on Property Values: An Empirical Study of Tax Capitalization and the Tiebout Hypothesis." *Journal of Political Economy* 77 (6), 957–961.

Oates, Wallace E., 2006. "The Many Faces of the Tiebout Model," in William A. Fischel (ed.), *The Tiebout Model at Fifty*. Cambridge MA, Lincoln Institute of Land Policy, 21–45.

Oates, Wallace E. and Robert M. Schwab, 1988. "Economic Competition Among Jurisdictions: Efficiency-Enhancing or Distortion-Inducing?" *Journal of Public Economics* 35 (3), 333–354.

Palmon, Oded and Barton A. Smith, 1998. "New Evidence on Property Tax Capitalization," *Journal of Political Economy* 106 (5), 1099–1111.

Ross, Stephen and John Yinger, 1999. "Sorting and Voting: A Review of the Literature on Urban Public Finance," in Paul Cheshire and Edwin S. Mills, eds., *Handbook of Regional and Urban Economics, Volume 3.* Amsterdam: North Holland, 2001–2060.

Rhode, Paul W., and Koleman S. Strumpf, 2003. "Assessing the Importance of Tiebout Sorting: Local Heterogeneity from 1850 to 1990." *American Economic Review* 93 (5), 1648–1677.

Rubinfeld, Daniel L., 1987. "The Economics of the Local Public Sector," in Alan J. Auerbach and Martin S. Feldstein, eds. *Handbook of Public Economics, Volume 1.* Amsterdam: North Holland, 571–645.

Stadelmann, David, and Steve Billon, 2008. "Does Capitalization of Fiscal Variables Decrease over Time?" Unpublished manuscript.

Tiebout, Charles M., 1959. "A Pure Theory of Local Expenditures." *Journal of Political Economy* 1956, 64 (5), 416–424.

Wassmer, Robert W., 1983. "Property Taxation, Property Base, and Property Value: An Empirical Test of the 'New View'." *National Tax Journal* 46 (2), 135–160.

Wildasin, David, 1989. "Interjurisdictional Capital Mobility: Fiscal Externality and a Corrective Subsidy." *Journal of Urban Economics* 25 (2), 193–212.

Wilson, John D., 1986. "A Theory of Inter-Regional Tax Competition." *Journal of Urban Economics* 19 (3), 296–315.

Wilson, John D., 1999. "Theories of Tax Competition," *National Tax Journal* 52, 269–304.

Youngman, Joan, 2002. "Enlarging the Property Tax Debate: Regressivity and Fairness," *State Tax Notes* 26 (October 3), 45–52.

Zodrow, George R., 2001a. "Reflections on the New View and the Benefit View of the Property Tax," in Wallace E. Oates, ed., *Property Taxation and Local Government Finance.* Cambridge MA: Lincoln Institute of Land Policy, 79–111.

Zodrow, George R., 2001b. "The Property Tax as a Capital Tax: A Room with Three Views," *National Tax Journal* 54 (1), 139–156.

Zodrow, George R., 2003. "Tax Competition and Tax Coordination in the European Union," *International Tax and Public Finance* 10 (6), 651–671.

Zodrow, George R., and Peter Mieszkowski, 1983. "The Incidence of the Property Tax. The Benefit View vs. the New View," in George R. Zodrow, ed., *Local Provision of Public Services: The Tiebout Model after Twenty-Five Years*. New York: Academic Press, 109–129.

Zodrow, George R., and Peter Mieszkowski, 1986a. "Pigou, Tiebout, Property Taxation and the Under-Provision of Local Public Goods." *Journal of Urban Economics* 19 (3), 356–370.

Zodrow, George R., and Peter Mieszkowski, 1986b. "The New View of the Property Tax: A Reformulation." *Regional Science and Urban Economics* 16 (3), 309–327.

Part V

Tax Competition

Chapter 17

Pigou, Tiebout, Property Taxation, and the Underprovision of Local Public Goods*

George R. Zodrow and Peter Mieszkowski

Department of Economics, Rice University, Houston, Texas 77251

Pigou's proposition that the use of distorting taxes rather than neutral head taxes reduces public service levels is examined in this paper. A simple model with a national system of competing local governments is utilized to demonstrate that the use of a distorting property tax on mobile capital decreases the level of residential public services. The case where public services are an intermediate producer good is also considered.

1. Introduction

A large literature on the efficiency properties of a system of competing local governments has concluded that global equilibria in a federal system are generally inefficient.

*This chapter is reproduced from *Journal of Urban of Economics*, **19**(3), 356–370, 1986.

At least three strands of this literature can be distinguished. The first, emphasized by Williams (1966) and Brainard and Dolbear (1967), is that for some public services benefits provided by one community spillover to other communities. Since communities do not consider the benefits of spillover effects, there is a tendency for underprovision of local expenditures relative to the optimum.

The second strand focuses on the fiscal externality or fiscal migration effects of multigovernment systems. Buchanan and Goetz (1972), Flatters *et al.* (1974) and Stiglitz (1977, 1983) all argue that, in general, migration of population between a limited number of communities results in an inefficient equilibrium, as migrants do not take into account the fiscal externalities they create in migrating. Starrett (1980) and Boadway (1982) investigate how the tendency for underprovision or overprovision of local public goods in such models depends on the method of local taxation.

The third strand is the focus of our inquiry. It is the proposition, first advanced by Pigou (1947), that the supply of public services is lower in situations where distortionary taxes are used relative to a first-best optimum where lump sum finance is used.[1]

Our work is most closely related to the analysis of Atkinson and Stem (1974) on the validity of Pigou's proposition that public services are undersupplied when financed by distorting taxes. We adopt their methodology of varying exogenously the level of nondistorting head taxes which is "permitted" and observing the consequences for the optimal level of public service provision. Our focus is the effect of property tax finance in a national system of independent local governments.

Interestingly, for the case of distorting commodity taxes (when leisure is not directly subject to taxation) and a single public good, Atkinson and

---

[1]The head tax local public goods equilibrium, which serves as a benchmark in our analysis, has been analyzed frequently in the local public finance literature. Primary proponents are Hamilton (1975), Fischel (1975), and White (1975) who argue that the stratification of households and firms in homogeneous communities coupled with precise zoning requirements on the amount of housing or industrial capital used in a particular community transforms local property taxes into a set of nondistorting user charges. For the purposes of this paper, we explicitly reject this proposition on the grounds that zoning is not so precise that marginal capital use decisions are not distorted by the local property tax. Instead, we focus on the effects of the local property tax in a model without zoning.

Stem (1974) show that a marginal reduction in the possibilities for lump sum taxation from the first-best head tax optimum leads to a fall in the optimal quantity of the public good. But they find the establishment of global results to be more difficult and are able to demonstrate that the level of public good provision is lower in the commodity tax case relative to the lump-sum tax case only for the special case of the Cobb–Douglas utility function. Similarly, Atkinson and Stiglitz (1980) point out that while marginal analysis suggests that " there may be a presumption that expenditure will be reduced," in general "global results cannot be deduced." Thus it appears the Pigou proposition is of limited validity for a national public good financed with distorting commodity taxes. In contrast, we are able to show for a model of a national system of independent local governments that the presumption of undersupply of local public goods with distorting property taxation is more general.

The "optimal property taxation" problem facing a jurisdictional government is similar to that examined at the national level by Atkinson and Stern (1974). We consider two types of local public goods. First, when local public goods are provided as public services to residents, we obtain unambiguous results without restrictions on individual utility functions — increased use of the distortionary property tax coupled with less reliance on a nondistortionary head tax always reduces local public expenditure, both globally and at the margin, regardless of the level of property taxation. Second, when local public goods are an input into the production process, we derive the conditions under which the same result obtains. Note that our analysis has a slightly different emphasis than that of Atkinson and Stem. They conduct a normative analysis of the optimal level of public services provided by an optimizing national government, while we assume that all local governments optimize in a similar fashion and conduct a positive analysis of the effects of such behavior in a national system of independent local governments.

2. Underprovision of Residential Public Services

Consider a national economy composed of N identical jurisdictions (indexed by $i = 1,\ldots, N$). Each jurisdiction has an identical supply of a fixed factor, hereafter referred to as land. The national capital stock $(\bar{K})$ is fixed, and capital is perfectly mobile across jurisdictions so that all capital earns the same net return (r). Land and capital are the only factors of production in the economy.

Output is produced in each jurisdiction by perfectly competitive firms who use a twice differentiable constant returns to scale production function

$$F(K), \quad F_K > 0, \quad F_{KK} < 0,$$

where K is the capital stock in a representative jurisdiction $i(NK = \bar{K})$ and the fixed land argument is suppressed.

Each community has the same number of identical residents.[2] Each resident owns an equal share of the land in the jurisdiction in which he resides and an equal share of the national capital stock, which is not necessarily invested in the jurisdiction of residence. There is no other source of individual income. Since all individuals in each jurisdiction are identical, we normalize the population in each community to be equal to one; all quantities thus are defined on a per capita basis.

Local public services (P) in representative jurisdiction i are modeled as public purchases of output which are financed either by a specific unit property tax on capital (T) or by a head tax assessed against all local residents (H); government budget balance requires

$$P = TK + H. \tag{1}$$

The "permitted" amount of lump sum taxation is assumed to be fixed exogenously at the same level for all communities. Local public services are treated as publicly provided private goods with no spillover effects (see Hamilton (1983) for a justification) and are shared equally by all residents.

Note that our assumptions eliminate the spillover and fiscal externality problems frequently encountered in Tiebout-type models and discussed in the Introduction. Instead, we have a model of identical jurisdictions where the effects of reductions in the exogenous level of head taxation[3] on the amount of property taxation and on the level of local

[2] We are obviously considering only allocative rather than distributive issues.

[3] Our approach of determining the effects of an exogenous change in the level of head taxation on the level of public services follows Atkinson and Stem (1974).

public services can be easily analyzed by examining a single representative jurisdiction.[4]

Interjurisdictional competition is modeled along Cournot–Nash lines, and each jurisdiction is assumed to be small relative to the national economy. The local government in each jurisdiction acts on the assumptions that all other jurisdictions do not respond to changes in its property tax rate and that its actions cannot affect the national net return to capital r.

Each local government acts to maximize the utility of a representative resident, where the utility function $U(C, P)$, identical for all individuals in the economy, is a strictly quasiconcave, twice differentiable function defined over consumption of private goods (C) and public goods; both goods are assumed to be normal. The level of private goods is determined from the private budget constraint

$$C = [F(K) - (r + T)K] + r(\bar{K} / N) - H, \tag{2}$$

where the first term is the return to land, the second is the return to capital, and the third reflects head taxes paid.

Substituting from Eqs. (1) and (2), the optimization problem facing each local government is

$$\max_{T} U\{[F(K) - (r + T)K + r\bar{K}/N - H], TK + H\}, \tag{3}$$

where each government perceives r and H to be fixed and the first-order conditions for firm optimization require that

$$r + T = F_K(K). \tag{4}$$

Differentiating Eq. (4) yields the change in the local capital stock expected by the local jurisdiction when it uses the property tax:

$$\phi = -dK/dT = -1/F_{KK} > 0. \tag{5}$$

[4]Note also that our assumptions of identical communities with publicly provided private goods permits us to avoid potential inefficiencies where Tiebout-type communities are inefficiently organized or inappropriately stratified by taste class. The work of Pestieu (1977), Bewley (1981), Stiglitz (1983), and Brueckner (1983) has shown that utility maximization or Cournot–Nash-type property value maximization can lead to a local optimum where each community is internally Pareto efficient but where coordinated rearrangement of the population could lead to a Pareto-superior outcome.

This term represents the distortionary effect of the property tax; each community, acting in isolation, is concerned that higher property taxes will drive out capital and decrease its income from land rents.

Note first that if H were a local government choice variable (along with T) the first-order conditions would be

$$U_P/U_C = 1, \tag{6}$$

$$U_P/U_C = 1/[1-(T\phi/K)] \tag{7}$$

where the subscripts denote partial derivatives of the utility function. Thus, the optimal property tax would be zero and head tax financed public services would be provided up to the point where the marginal rate of substitution equaled the marginal rate of transformation (equal to unity); the local government would prefer the head tax to the distortionary property tax which lowers land values.[5]

However, when the head tax is exogenously constrained to less than this level, the representative jurisdictional government's first-order condition for T is

$$U_P/U_C = 1/[1-T\phi/K] > 1. \tag{8}$$

Thus, since the marginal rate of transformation between private and public goods is greater than one, Eq. (8) indicates underprovision of local services at the margin.

The next step in our argument is to determine the national effects which occur when each jurisdiction sets its property tax rates as specified by (8). The fixed national capital stock requirement implies that

$$NdK = 0 \tag{9}$$

so that, in the Cournot–Nash equilibrium when all jurisdictions act identically in response to an exogenous change in H, substituting from the result of differentiating Eq. (4) yields

$$dr = -dT. \tag{10}$$

Thus, we obtain a typical new view result — when all jurisdictions increase the rate of property taxation of capital and the national capital stock is fixed, capital bears the full burden of the tax as the gross price of capital

[5] See Zodrow and Mieszkowski (1983) for further discussion of the local choice between head tax and property tax finance.

$(r + T)$ is unchanged in each jurisdiction. Accordingly, the capital stocks K, land prices, and the individual jurisdictional governments' perception of $\phi = -dK/dT$ are all unchanged in the Cournot–Nash equilibrium.

These results permit us to establish unambiguously the effect of a change in H — the "permitted" level of lump sum taxation — on local public service levels. Totally differentiating Eq. (8) for $dH > 0$ and substituting from (10) when $dK = d\phi = 0$ yields

$$[\alpha K - U_P/(KF_{KK})]\, dT = -\alpha\, dH, \tag{11}$$

where

$$\alpha = \alpha_1 + \alpha_2(1 - U_C/U_P) > 0,$$

$$\alpha_1 = -[U_{CC} - 2(U_C/U_P) + U_{PP}(U_C/U_P)] > 0,$$

$$\alpha_2 = -\,[U_{PP}(U_C/U_P) - U_{PC}] > 0,$$

and strict quasiconcavity of the utility function ensures $\alpha_1 > 0$, the normal goods assumption ensures that $\alpha_2 > 0$, and Eq. (8) ensures that $\alpha > 0$. Thus, dT/dH is unambiguously negative — reduced reliance on lump-sum taxation implies increased reliance on property taxation. Substituting from Eq. (11) into the result of differentiating Eq. (1) yields

$$\frac{dP}{dH} = \frac{U_P/(-F_{KK}K)}{\alpha K + U_P/(-F_{KK}K)} > 0. \tag{12}$$

Thus, reduction in the permitted head taxation in the economy causes a reduction in the level of local public services. Note that the derivation does not assume a zero initial property tax — it is valid for all values of T between $T = 0$ and the value of T when $H = 0$.

This situation is depicted in Fig. 17.1 The slope of the production possibilities frontier (AB) for a jurisdiction is negative one. With sole reliance on head tax finance, the slope of the indifference curve at utility U^H is negative one and P^H local public goods are provided. With sole reliance on property tax finance, the model is constructed so that simultaneous use of the property tax by all jurisdictions implies that the production possibilities frontier is unchanged (the tax has no "income effects" on the jurisdiction's " budget constraint") since each jurisdiction's capital stock is unchanged in the Cournot-Nash equilibrium and the

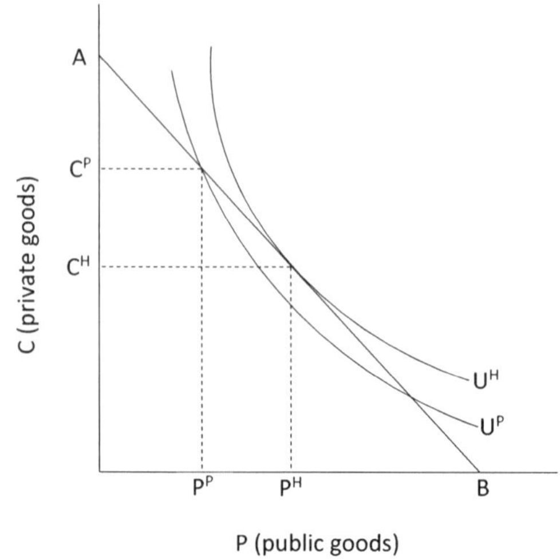

Figure 17.1. Public Goods Equilibria with Head Taxes and Property Taxes

marginal rate of transformation is still negative one. However, in the property tax equilibrium, the slope of the indifference curve is greater (in absolute value) than one [as shown in Eq. (8)] due to the perceived distortionary effect of the property tax. Due to the consumption distortion, the property tax equilibrium requires the intersection of *AB* and an indifference curve with slope greater than one in absolute value which can occur only at a lower level of public services ($P^P < P^H$) and at a lower level of utility ($U^P < U^H$).

3. Underprovision of Business Public Services

In this section, we consider a model similar to the one discussed in the previous section, but where all local public services go to business as an input into the production process.

In this case, the firm production function in each jurisdiction is

$$F(K,B), \quad F_{KB} > 0, \quad F_B > 0, \quad F_{BB} < 0,$$

where *B* is the level of publicly provided services to business. The local government budget constraint in a representative jurisdiction is

$$TK + H = B, \tag{13}$$

while the first-order condition for firm optimization is

$$r + T = F_K(K, B). \tag{14}$$

The change in the capital stock in response to a change in the property tax perceived by each jurisdiction is obtained by combining the results of differentiating Eqs. (13) and (14) to yield

$$\phi = \frac{-dK}{dT} = -\frac{1 - KF_{KB}}{F_{KK} + TF_{KB}} \tag{15}$$

which can be viewed as a function of K, B, and H. We assume that the model is stable in the sense that the marginal cost of diverting a unit of output to public services for firms (which is equal to unity) is greater than the associated increase in output due to the increased marginal productivity of capital (KF_{KB}); that is,

$$1 - KF_{KB} > 0. \tag{16}$$

We also assume the model is stable in the sense that each jurisdiction perceives that raising taxes will drive out capital ($\phi > 0$); otherwise, taxes would always be raised. This implies that

$$\mathrm{T} < -F_{KK}/F_{KB}. \tag{17}$$

The optimization problem facing the government is simply

$$\max_T F(K, TK + H) - (r + T)K + r\bar{K}/N - H \tag{18}$$

since there is only one consumption good in this model. If the head tax were a choice variable, the first-order conditions would prescribe $T = 0$ and

$$F_B = 1; \tag{19}$$

thus, local governments would use only head tax finance and would purchase public services up to the point where the marginal product of services was equal to the marginal cost of unity. If the use of the head tax is constrained below this level, the first-order condition for T is

$$F_B = 1/[1 + (T/K)(dK/dT)] = 1/(1 - T\phi/K); \tag{20}$$

thus, $F_B > 1$ for $T > 0$, production is inefficient and, in contrast to the case analyzed in the previous section, there is an inward shift in the jurisdiction's production possibilities frontier (the tax has an "income effect" on each jurisdiction's "budget constraint"). Two propositions follow. First, if the local governments must rely solely on property tax finance ($H = 0$), there is an undersupply of public goods. This follows because the capital stock is fixed in each jurisdiction in the Cournot–Nash equilibrium and $F_B(K, B) > 1$ implies that B must be less in the property tax case than in the head tax equilibrium (where $F_B = 1$). Second, a marginal reduction in the permitted level of head taxation at the head tax optimum ($T = 0, F_B = 1$) reduces public services. To see this, differentiate Eq. (20) and evaluate at $T = 0, F_B = 1$ to yield

$$\frac{dT}{dH} = \frac{F_{BB}}{\phi / K - F_{BB} K} < 0. \tag{21}$$

Thus, a reduction in the head tax implies an increase in the property tax. Substituting into the result of differentiating Eq. (13) yields

$$\frac{dB}{dH} = \frac{\phi / K}{\phi / K - K F_{BB}} > 0. \tag{22}$$

Thus, a marginal reduction in the opportunities for head taxation at the head tax optimum unambiguously decreases public services provided to firms.

However, a theoretical ambiguity arises for reductions in H when $T > 0$ (i.e., along the path from the zero property tax equilibrium to the zero head tax equilibrium). The first-order condition Eq. (20) can be rewritten as

$$F_B T \phi = K(F_B - 1). \tag{23}$$

That is, the perceived marginal cost of raising the property tax — the erosion of the tax base which implies a reduction in output $F_B T \phi$ — must equal the marginal gain — increased output due to higher services less the increase in the supply price of capital $[K(F_B - 1)]$. Thus, in deciding its tax policy, the community must balance the tax base erosion effect against the value of the additional revenues.

The theoretical ambiguity arises because the perceived deleterious effect of raising T on the tax base ($\phi = -dK/dT$) is a function of B which changes as H changes [see Eq. (15)]. The change in ϕ depends on the third derivatives of the production function which are theoretically ambiguous in sign. However, the possible outcomes can be classified as follows.

Dividing Eq. (23) by F_B yields

$$T\phi = K(F_B - 1)/F_B = \psi.$$

In the Cournot-Nash equilibrium, $dK = 0$ for all jurisdictions. Thus, ψ can be viewed as a function only of B, where

$$\frac{d\psi}{dB} = \frac{KF_{BB}}{(F_B)^2} < 0 \tag{24}$$

while $T\phi$ can be viewed as a function of B and H where

$$\left.\frac{\partial(T\phi)}{\partial H}\right|_B = \frac{F_{KK}(1 - KF_{KB})}{K(-F_{KK} - TF_{KB})^2} < 0 \tag{25}$$

and, although we know $\partial T/\partial B$ (holding H constant) is positive, $\partial(T\phi)/\partial B$ (holding H constant) is theoretically ambiguous.[6] The three possible outcomes are shown in Figs. 17.2 a–c.

First, suppose $\partial\phi/\partial B$ is positive so that $\partial(T\phi)/B$ is positive — the perceived tax base erosion effect increases as the level of public services increases. In this case a decrease in the head tax H will lead to an unambiguous *decrease* in B, the level of expenditures on the publicly provided good. The intuition behind this result is as follows. In Fig. 17.2a, a decrease in H leads to an upward shift in the $T\phi$ curve, shown as $(T\phi)'$. Consequently, the tax base erosion effect is increased holding the value of B fixed, and the disequilibrium between $T\phi$ and ψ can be eliminated only by a decrease in B. A decrease in B increases the marginal product F_B (increasing ψ) and decreases $T\phi$ until equilibrium is reached.

In Fig. 17.2b, we illustrate a second case where the relationship between ϕ and B is negative and the slope of $T\phi$ is negative but less (in absolute value) than the slope of ψ. For this case, a decrease in H also leads to a decrease in B. The intuition is that while a decrease in B does not generate a decrease in the tax base erosion term $T\phi$, the increase in the

[6]The second-order conditions for each jurisdiction's optimal tax rate specify a (negative) lower bound for $\partial(T\phi)/\partial B$ which is smaller than $d\psi/dB$; thus, $\partial(T\phi)/\partial B < d\psi/dB$ cannot be ruled out (see Fig. 17.2c).

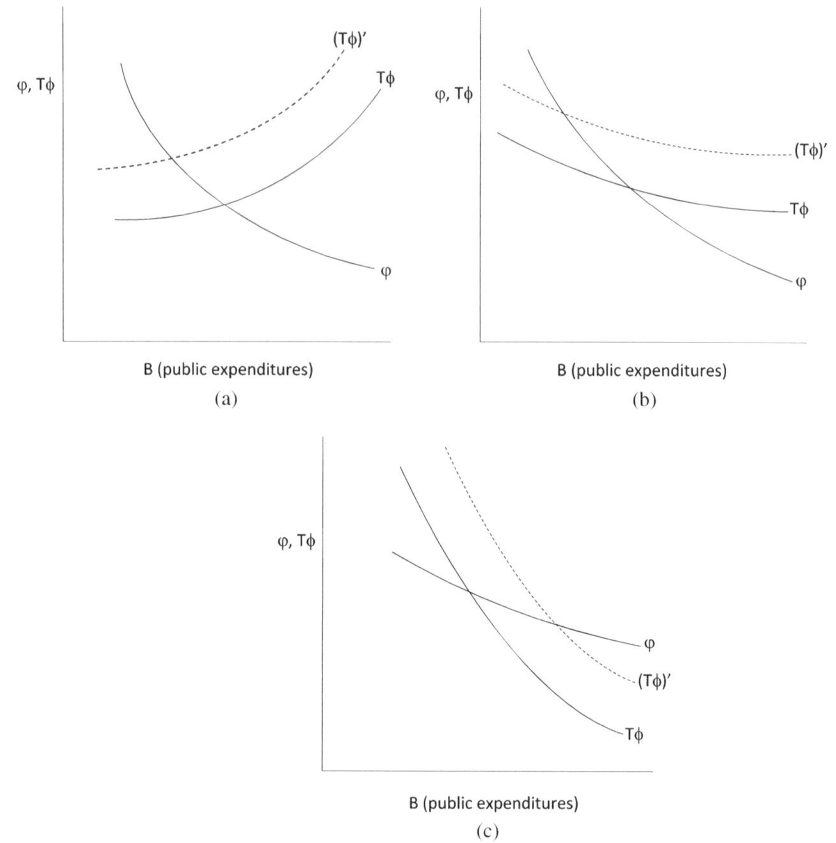

Figure 17.2. Tax Effects on Business Public Expenditures

marginal product F_B with respect to a decrease in B is sufficient to offset the increase in $T\phi$.

The third case is the counterintuitive possibility that a marginal decrease in H leads to a marginal increase in public expenditure; this case is presented in Fig. 17.2c. Here the decline in the perceived outflow of capital with respect to changes in the tax rate that follows from an increase in B is large enough that the slope of $T\phi$ is negative and larger in absolute value than the slope of ψ. Consequently, the disequilibrium between the value of ψ and the tax base erosion effect $T\phi$ that follows a decrease in the head tax cannot be eliminated through a decrease in B. A decrease in public expenditures will increase the marginal product of the producers' good and thus ψ; however, the increase in $T\phi$ for a unit decrease in B is even larger thus widening the difference between ψ and $T\phi$; hence an increase in B is required.

The case described in Fig. 17.2c is analogous to market situations where a downward sloping demand curve interacts with a more steeply declining supply curve (a decreasing cost industry) so that increases in quantity supplied at every price (an upward shift in the supply schedule) lead to decreases in equilibrium price. As this is a curiosum, it is tempting, by analogy, to characterize similarly the case depicted in Fig. 17.2c where an increase in the head tax leads to a decrease in public expenditure; nevertheless it can theoretically occur (locally) for small change in the head tax.

4. Combining the Two Models

Although a full analysis of the case where local governments simultaneously provide public services to individuals and firms would be rather cumbersome and not offer much additional insight, the basic elements of the story are outlined briefly in this section. Using the previous notation, the government faces a budget constraint of

$$TK + H = B + P. \tag{26}$$

The optimization problem facing the representative jurisdictional government is

$$\max_{T,B} U\{[F(K,B) - (r+T)K + r\bar{K}/N - H], (TK + H - B)\}. \tag{27}$$

First-order conditions for T and B (when the government is constrained to use less head taxation than at the first-best optimum where $T = 0$, $U_P/U_C = 1$, $F_B = 1$) are

$$U_P/U_C = 1/(1 - T\phi/K) > 1, \tag{28}$$

$$F_B = \frac{1 + T_{KB}F_{BB}}{1 - (T\phi/K)}. \tag{29}$$

$F_B > 1$ is implied by Eq. (29) as long as the stability condition Eq. (16) is satisfied. This again implies that, in the property tax equilibrium ($H = 0$), public services to firms are underprovided relative to the head tax case.

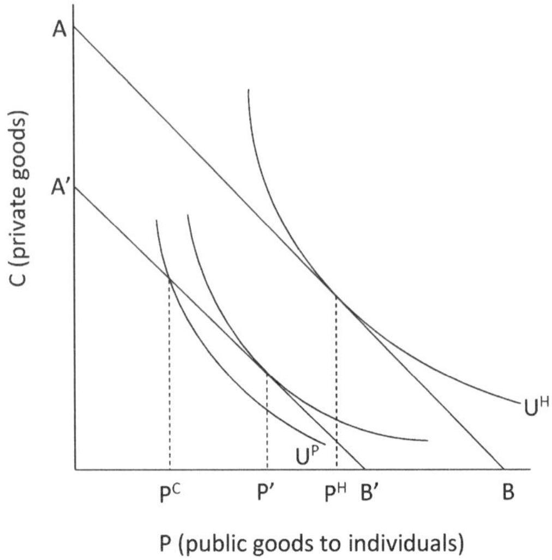

Figure 17.3. Effects on Public Goods to Individuals with Business and Individual Public Services

Moreover, public services to individuals are also underprovided in the property tax equilibrium, as shown in Fig. 17.3.

The level of individual public services in the head tax equilibrium is shown as P^H, where the slope of the indifference curve is equal to negative one, the slope of the production possibilities frontier AB. A shift to the property tax equilibrium ($H = 0$) implies an inward shift of the production possibilities frontier to $A'B'$ — production is inefficient since $F_B > 1$, but given B, the marginal rate of transformation between C and P is still negative one. The inward shift of the production possibilities frontier implies a lower P ($P' < P^H$ is implied by the normal goods assumption), while the consumption distortion implies a further reduction in P ($P^C < P'$ as in Section 2). Thus, the property tax equilibrium is characterized by a lower level of both public services than the head tax equilibrium.

Also, a marginal reduction in the permitted level of head taxation from the head tax equilibrium implies a reduction in the levels of both public services. To see this, differentiate Eqs. (26), (28), and (29) and evaluate at $T = 0$, $F_B = 1$, $U_P/U_C = 1$ which yields

$$\frac{dB}{dH} = \frac{\alpha U_P(1 - KF_{KB})/(-KF_{KK})}{D} > 0, \tag{30}$$

$$\frac{dT}{dH} = \frac{\alpha U_C F_{BB}}{D} < 0, \tag{31}$$

$$\frac{dP}{dH} = \frac{U_P U_C F_{BB}/(KF_{KK})}{D} > 0, \tag{32}$$

where

$$D = \alpha U_P(1 - KF_{KB})/(-KF_{KK}) - \alpha U_C KF_{BB} + U_P U_C F_{BB}/(KF_{KK}) > 0. \tag{33}$$

However, the effect of changes in the permitted level of head taxation on public services provided to firms is theoretically ambiguous when $T > 0$ for the same reasons discussed at length in Section 3. Accordingly, the effect of changes in H on the level of public service provision to individuals is also theoretically ambiguous when $T > 0$ (since the direction of the change in the production possibilities frontier is ambiguous).

5. Conclusion

In this paper, we have examined the level of public service provision in a simple fixed national capital stock, one production good model of a national system of independent local governments, without any strong restrictions on individual preferences. We have shown that, although the optimal property tax problem facing a single local government is similar to those studied earlier, calculating the national effects of property tax finance by all local jurisdictions provides sufficient information to obtain more general results.[7] In a model with all local public services provided to individuals, all marginal reductions in lump sum taxation (and thus any finite change) result in lower levels of public service

[7] Note that it is the interaction between optimizing behavior by local governments and the national effects of universal use of the property tax that yields our results rather than just the fact that the actual capital supply elasticity to each jurisdiction is zero under the Cournot–Nash assumption — in the Atkinson and Stem (1974) model, a zero factor supply elasticity implies that the public expenditure level is independent of the permitted level of head taxation.

provision.[8] When local public services are instead provided to firms, the same result obtains as long as the perceived capital response to changes in property taxation does not fall too drastically as the level of public services increases.

Acknowledgements

Research support from the National Science Foundation (Grant SES82-09210) is gratefully acknowledged. We would like to thank John D. Wilson for helpful comments on an earlier draft.

References

Aaron, H. J., 1969. Local public expenditures and the "migration effect," *West Econom. J.,* **7**, 385–390.

Arnott R. and Grieson, R. E. 1981. Optimal fiscal policy for a state or local government, *J. Urban Econom.*, **9**, 23–48.

Atkinson A. B. and Stern, Pigou, N. H. 1974. taxation and public goods, *Rev. Econom. Stud.,* **41**, 119–128.

Atkinson A. B. and Stiglitz, J. E. 1980 "Lectures on Public Economics," McGraw-Hill, New York.

Beck, J. H. 1983. Tax competition, uniform assessment, and the benefit principle, *J. Urban Econom.,* **13**, 127–146.

Bewley, T. 1981. A critique of Tiebout's theory of local public expenditures, *Econometrica,* **49**, 713–740.

Boadway, R. 1982. On the method of taxation and the provision of local public goods: Comment, *Amer. Econom. Rev.,* **72**, 846–851.

Boskin, M. J. 1973. Local government tax and product competition and the optimal provision of public goods, *J. Pol. Econom.,* **81**, 203–210.

[8] As described above, this occurs due to the negative "fiscal externality" perceived by the government as raising property taxes drives out mobile capital. Note that a similar analysis could be applied in a very different model. Suppose that labor is mobile, communities use head taxes, and there are economies of scale in the provision of local public services. Then competing local governments would perceive a positive "fiscal externality" to using head tax finance (attracting residents and lowering per capita public service costs) and tend to oversupply local public services as in Starrett (1980).

Brainard W. C. and Dolbear, T. 1967. The possibility of oversupply of local public goods, *J. Pol. Econom.*, **75**, 86–92.

Brueckner, J. K. 1983. Property value maximization and public sector efficiency, *J. Urban Econom.*, **14**, 1–15.

Buchanan J. M. and Goetz, C. J. 1972. Efficiency limits of fiscal mobility: An assessment of the Tiebout model, *J. Publ. Econom.*, 1, 25–44.

Epple D. and Zelenitz, A. 1981. The implications of competition among jurisdictions: Does Tiebout need politics? *J. Pol. Econom.*, **89**, 1197–1217.

Fischel, W. A. 1975. Fiscal and environmental considerations in the location of firms in suburban communities, in "Fiscal Zoning and Land Use Controls" (E. S. Mills and W. E. Oates, Eds.), Lexington Books, Lexington, Mass.

Flatters, F. Henderson, J. V. and Mieszkowski, P. M. 1974. Public goods, efficiency, and regional equalization, *J. Publ. Econom.*, **3**, 99–112.

Hamilton, B. W. 1975. Zoning and property taxation in a system of local governments. *Urban Stud.*, **12**, 205–211.

Hamilton, B. W. 1983. A review: Is the property tax a benefit tax?, in "Local Provision of Public Services: The Tiebout Model after Twenty-Five Years" (G. R. Zodrow, Ed.), Academic Press, New York.

Ladd, H. F. 1975. Local education expenditures, fiscal capacity, and the composition of the property tax base, *Nat. Tax. J.*, **28**, 145–158.

Mieszkowski, P. M. 1972. The property tax: An excise tax or a profits tax?, *J. Publ. Econom.*, **1**, 73–96.

Pestieu, P. 1977. The optimality limits of the Tiebout model, in "The Political Economy of Fiscal Federalism" (W. E. Oates, Ed.), Lexington Books, Lexington, Mass.

Pigou, A. C. 1947. "A Study in Public Finance," Macmillan, London.

Sonstelie J. C. and Portney, P. R. 1978. Profit maximizing communities and the theory of local public expenditure, *J. Urban Econom.*, **5**, 263–277.

Starrett, D. 1980. On the method of local finance and the provision of local public goods, *Amer. Econom. Rev.*, **70**, 380–392.

Stiglitz, J. E. 1977. The theory of local public goods, in "The Economics of Public Services" (M. S. Feldstein and R. F. Inman, Eds.), Macmillan, London.

Stiglitz, J. E. 1983. The theory of local public goods twenty-five years after Tiebout: A perspective, in "Local Provision of Public Services: The Tiebout Model after Twenty-Five Years" (G. R. Zodrow, Ed.), Academic Press, New York.

Tiebout, C. M. 1956. A pure theory of local expenditures, *J. Pol. Econom.*, **64**, 416–424.

White, M. J. 1975. Firm location in a zoned metropolitan area, in "Fiscal Zoning and Land Use Controls" (E. S. Mills and W. E. Oates, Eds.), Lexington Books, Lexington, Mass.

Williams, A. 1966. The optimal provision of public goods in a system of local governments, *J. Pol. Econom.*, **74**, 18–33.

Zodrow G. R. and Mieszkowski, P. M. 1983. The incidence of the property tax: The benefit view versus the new view, in "Local provision of Public Services: The Tiebout Model after Twenty-Five Years" (G. R. Zodrow, Ed.), Academic Press, New York.

Chapter 18

Capital Mobility and Capital Tax Competition*

George R. Zodrow

Economics Department and Baker Institute for Public Policy
Rice University, Houston, TX, 77025, USA

1. Introduction

The topic of this special issue of the *NTJ* — the implications for tax policy of increasing mobility of factors of production and goods in the modern global economy — is certainly an important one, underlying many debates on tax reform at all levels. Critical to these debates are the extent to which the mobility of capital has increased and, if it has, the extent to which it has resulted in interjurisdictional tax competition designed to attract such mobile capital and the effects of such competition. This paper examines several strands of the literature that shed light on these questions.

[...]

*This chapter is reproduced from *National Tax Journal*, **63**(4), 865–902, 2010. It contains excerpts from a paper that appeared in a December 2010 special issue of the *National Tax Journal*; deletions from the original text, other than deleted footnotes and references, are denoted with [...]. The special issue included papers presented at a conference on "Mobility and Tax Policy: Do Yesterday's Taxes Fit Tomorrow's Economy?" held at the Center for Business and Economic Research, University of Tennessee, Knoxville, TN on October 2–3, 2008.

2. Capital Mobility

This section examines three different ways that economists have attempted to discern the extent of capital mobility: (1) estimating the effects of taxation on foreign direct investment, (2) estimating the incidence of taxes on capital, especially corporate income taxes, to see if the results are consistent with a high degree of capital mobility, and (3) examining saving and investment correlations and identifying their implications for capital mobility.

[...]

2.1. *Tax sensitivity of foreign direct investment*

A natural way to measure the mobility of capital is to estimate the sensitivity of capital flows to changes in after-tax rates of return, including those caused by changes in tax variables. [...]

There is a general consensus that this empirical evidence demonstrates that FDI is in fact sensitive to tax factors, and suggests that this sensitivity may be increasing over time. For example, Gordon and Hines (2002, 49) conclude that the "econometric work of the last fifteen years provides ample evidence of the sensitivity of the level and location of FDI to its tax treatment." A similar conclusion is reached by de Mooij and Ederveen (2003, 2005), who perform "meta analyses" of the literature, in which they correlate the results of a wide range of empirical studies of the effects of taxes on FDI to the characteristics of the underlying studies. Several econometric approaches have been utilized in this literature. The early studies were primarily time series analyses that estimated the effects of variations in host country tax rates on aggregate FDI (Hartman, 1984; Boskin and Gale, 1987; Young, 1988; Slemrod, 1990). Gordon and Hines (2002) conclude that these studies suggest an elasticity of FDI with respect to after-tax returns of approximately 1.0, which is roughly equivalent to an investment elasticity with respect to effective tax rates of about –0.6, for both FDI by U.S. multinationals and for FDI in the U.S. by multinationals based in other countries. Cross-section studies of the effects of variations of host country tax rates across countries on multinational investments in property, plant and equipment

(PPE) suggest somewhat greater sensitivity of investment to tax rates, with elasticities around –1.0 (Hines and Rice, 1994; Grubert and Mutti, 2000). Perhaps more importantly, the most recent and most careful studies — especially Altshuler, Grubert and Newlon (2001) and Grubert and Mutti (2001), as well as de Mooij and Ederveen (2003) — tend to obtain the largest estimates. For example, Altshuler, Grubert and Newlon estimate that the elasticity of investment with respect to after-tax host country rates of return for U.S. multinationals increased from 1.5 in 1984 to 2.8 in 1992. Grubert and Mutti (2001) estimate an investment elasticity of roughly 3 for countries with relatively open trade regimes. Finally, for the sample of studies they analyze, de Mooij and Ederveen calculate a median estimate of the investment elasticity of 3.3; they also note that the more recent studies tend to obtain the largest elasticities.

These studies are limited to data from the early 1990s. An interesting complication is that increasing tax avoidance activity on the part of U.S. multinationals suggests that foreign direct investment may become less sensitive to taxes, since the burden of high host country rates can be more easily avoided. Nevertheless, more recent research suggests that, at least through 2000, the tax sensitivity of FDI is not declining and may even still be increasing. For example, Altshuler and Grubert (2006) examine data for 1992, 1998 and 2000, and find that their estimated investment tax elasticities are increasing over the period (with some estimates in the range of –4), although this result is quite tentative as the differences in the elasticities over time are not statistically significant (see also de Mooij and Everdeen (2005). However, Overesch (2009) provides some contrasting evidence. He examines investment in relatively high-tax Germany by multinationals based in lower tax countries, and finds that a one percentage point increase in the tax differentials between the two countries increases investment in Germany by nearly one percent — a result that he attributes to greater potential for income shifting to ameliorate the effects of the high German statutory tax rate.

To sum up, the empirical literature as a whole suggests that international capital is quite mobile and in particular is significantly affected by tax factors. However, there is some preliminary evidence which suggests that the tax sensitivity of FDI may be reduced by possibilities to shift income to lower tax countries and thus ameliorate the effects of relatively high statutory tax rates.

2.2. *The incidence of corporate taxes*

Another interesting approach infers the mobility of capital from results on the incidence of taxes on capital income, most often the corporate income tax. The theoretical models that have appeared in the literature have strong implications for the incidence of a source-based tax on capital if such capital is mobile. Indeed, in the simplest models in which the taxing jurisdiction is a small open economy, capital bears none of the burden of the tax which, with the assumption of perfectly mobile capital, is borne by local factors, land and relatively immobile labor, and consumers of nontradable goods. By comparison, if the taxing jurisdiction is large but capital is mobile among all jurisdictions, the share of the burden of the tax borne by capital is roughly equal to its share of the world capital stock. Indeed, in more complicated general equilibrium models with perfectly mobile capital, a tax on capital income may be shifted more than 100 percent to labor. For example, Harberger (1995, 2008) constructs a four-sector general equilibrium model in which labor must bear all the burden of the corporate income tax since capital is perfectly mobile and the price of the output of the corporate sector is fixed on world markets. But since labor is mobile across production sectors, the price of labor in other sectors declines as well. As a result, labor bears more than 100 percent of the burden of the tax — 130 percent in the central case analyzed by Harberger (2008). These models suggest that a test of capital mobility is whether taxes on capital income are in fact shifted to labor, especially in small open economies.

This reasoning has been questioned by Gravelle and Smetters (2006), who argue that, even if capital is perfectly mobile internationally, capital in the US will bear more of the burden of the corporate income tax than the US share of world output if domestic goods and imports are not perfect substitutes. In a model similar to that constructed by Harberger, they show that the capital share of the tax burden increases dramatically as the substitutability between domestic goods and imports falls. For example, if the elasticity of substitution in consumption between traded corporate domestic goods and imports is reduced from infinity to 3.0 (a value that Gravelle and Smetters argue is consistent with the empirical literature), the share of the tax burden on domestic capital increases from roughly 30 percent to 62 percent.

However, the Gravelle and Smetters result has been challenged on two grounds. First, McDaniel and Balistreri (2002) note that many trade economists are skeptical of the relatively low estimates of import substitution elasticities found in the literature. Similarly, Harberger (2008) argues that relatively low elasticities of substitution imply an implausibly large degree of market power for domestic producers. Moreover, several studies have obtained significantly higher estimates of the import substitution elasticity. For example, Erkel-Rousse and Mirza (2002) estimate an overall import substitution elasticity of 3.8, with many industries characterized by elasticities between 6.5–7.0 and some as high as 13.0, and Hertel, *et al.* (2004) obtain an estimated import substitution elasticity for 40 different products of 7.0, with estimates that exceed 10 in some cases.

Second, Randolph (2006) argues that a plausible extension of the model constructed by Gravelle and Smetters dramatically alters its results. Specifically, he extends the Gravelle-Smetters model to allow a domestic corporate sector that produces two types of traded goods — some that are perfect substitutes for imports and others that are imperfectly substitutable. In this case, if the capital intensities in the two corporate tradable goods sectors are identical, the incidence of the corporate income tax is independent of the degree of import substitutability in the second sector and, if capital is perfectly mobile, capital bears slightly less than 30 percent of the corporate tax burden in the U.S., as predicted in the simplest tax incidence models noted above.

Taken together, these results suggest that empirical estimates of the incidence of a tax on capital income would provide some useful information on the extent of capital mobility. Estimating the incidence of corporate income taxes is notoriously difficult, especially in country cross-section analyses that face the daunting task of controlling for a multitude of factors other than the corporate income tax that might affect wages and the process of wage determination within each country. Nevertheless, three recent studies have attempted to do so and thus indirectly shed light on the question of the mobility of capital.

Each of these studies examines various samples of OECD countries and estimates that differences in corporate income taxes across countries are to a large extent reflected in differences in wages. Arulampalam, Devereux and Maffini (2008) analyze micro data on wages from France,

Italy, Spain and the UK over the period 1993–2003 in the context of a wage bargaining model that determines how firm owners and labor divide economic rents, including how the corporate income tax affects this division of rents. (They thus do not consider explicitly the tax-induced capital emigration stressed above.) Their central estimates suggest that 62 percent of the corporate income tax is borne by labor in the short run, and labor fully bears the burden of the tax in the long run.

Hassett and Mathur (2006) examine a large sample of 72 countries using data from 1981–2002, looking at the relationship between five-year averages of hourly wages in manufacturing and corporate income taxes, measured using either statutory tax rates, effective marginal tax rates, or average effective tax rates. They estimate extremely large elasticities of the labor tax burden with respect to the various measures of the corporate tax rate that range between 0.5–1.0. Indeed, Gravelle and Hungerford (2007) argue that the results are highly implausible, as a wage elasticity of 1.0 would imply that a one percent increase in corporate revenues would be accompanied by a fall in wages that would be roughly 26 times as large. They replicate the Hassett–Mathur analysis under different assumptions and obtain much smaller effects of the corporate tax on wages.

Finally, Felix (2007) examines a sample of 19 OECD countries over the period 1979–2002. She uses the statutory tax rate as a measure of the corporate tax burden and analyzes labor compensation for workers at three skill levels as measured by education level. In her central case, which controls for the extent to which the economy is open, she obtains estimates that imply that a one percentage point increase in the average corporate tax rate would reduce labor compensation by roughly four times the amount of revenue collected, with little variation across the skill groups. These results also imply a significant amount of overshifting of the burden of the corporate income tax to labor, although considerably less than that reported by Hassett and Mathur.

Because these studies are new and in light of the inherent difficulties of measuring the incidence of corporate tax burdens across countries, the results of these studies must be viewed as quite tentative. Nevertheless, they are generally suggestive of considerable international mobility of capital, and further research examining the robustness of their conclusions is no doubt in the offing.

2.3. *Saving and investment correlations*

Although most of the literature discussed thus far suggests substantial international mobility of capital, an important line of research provides a significant cautionary note. Specifically, this alternative approach to examining the extent of capital mobility, pioneered by Feldstein and Horioka (1980) with subsequent papers by Feldstein (1983), Feldstein and Bacchetta (1991) and Feldstein (1994), focuses on measuring the correlation between domestic saving and domestic investment as an indicator of international capital mobility. Feldstein and Horioka (1980), hereafter FH, note that the fraction of an increase in domestic saving reflected in an increase in domestic investment (termed the "saving retention coefficient" in subsequent work) should be approximately one if economies are largely closed. By comparison, if capital is highly mobile internationally, domestic saving and investment should be nearly uncorrelated, as any increase in domestic saving is distributed across the world economy to maximize after-tax returns and increases in domestic investment are financed from the world supply of capital rather than from domestic saving.

[...]

Not surprisingly, synthesizing and interpreting all of these conflicting results is exceedingly difficult. In particular, Feldstein's arguments that high savings and investment correlations imply that international capital is relatively immobile certainly suggest that caution is appropriate in simply assuming capital mobility, and that it is inappropriate to model large economies as facing a perfectly elastic supply of capital. Nevertheless, even researchers who have followed in the FH tradition have found savings investment correlations that have declined considerably over time, and that are smaller in more highly integrated economies and in smaller and developing economies, and in one case (Coakley, Fuertes and Spagnolo, 2004), alternative estimation techniques have resulted in a savings retention coefficient that is virtually zero. In addition, the various alternative explanations of the FH result have some plausibility, and the results and interpretations of the empirical macroeconomics literature raise some troublesome issues with the traditional interpretation of high savings-investment correlations, although the practical relevance of the long run solvency constraint is unclear. On balance, a reasonable interpretation may be the now somewhat dated but still highly relevant view of Harberger (1980), who argues that while international capital may not be perfectly mobile, the mobility of capital is relatively high, especially among smaller economies and the developing emerging countries and in the long run, and that with the inexorable march of globalization the level of capital mobility is likely to continue increasing over time — a development that deserves serious consideration in the formulation of tax and other economic policies.

3. Evidence on Tax Competition

Assuming that capital is either partially or fully mobile across taxing jurisdictions, a large literature has examined whether countries and indeed subnational governments engage in tax competition designed to attract that capital. This section first examines the predictions of theoretical tax competition models, and then turns to various empirical approaches that have been utilized in an attempt to discern the extent of tax competition.

3.1. *Theoretical models of tax competition*

The early models of tax competition were relatively simple, with an economy consisting of many small identical jurisdictions engaged in Cournot-Nash competition in capital income tax rates to attract perfectly mobile capital. In this context, if a tax on immobile local factors is available, then a source-based tax on mobile capital is undesirable — the now-standard "zero tax result" indicative of a "race to the bottom" in capital income tax rates (Zodrow-Mieszkowski, 1983; Gordon, 1986; Razin-Sadka, 1991). The logic underlying this result is that, even purely from the perspective of local residents, a source-based tax on capital income is counterproductive; specifically, such a tax would drive out perfectly mobile capital until the nationally or internationally determined after-tax rate of return to capital was achieved, with the burden of the tax borne entirely by local residents in the form of lower wages and land rents or higher prices for non-tradable goods. As a result, it is preferable simply to tax local residents directly and at least avoid the efficiency costs of the tax, including the effects of capital emigration, lower capital intensities in production, and a tax bias against consumption of capital-intensive goods. If instead the government is for political or other reasons constrained to utilize a source-based tax on capital income, it is likely to under-provide public services due to concern about driving mobile capital out of the jurisdiction (Zodrow and Mieszkowski, 1986; Wilson, 1986; Bucovetsky and Wilson, 1991; Brueckner, 2000).[1] In addition, independent of tax competition considerations, these arguments for low levels of capital income taxation may be bolstered by the traditional rationales for consumption-based rather than income-based taxation (Zodrow, 2007). Moreover, several models suggest not only that capital income should not be taxed, but that it should be subsidized. For example, subsidies to capital income may be desirable to attract foreign investment by companies who have relatively poor information on the host countries investment prospects, market conditions, accounting rules, likelihood of expropriation, etc. (Gordon and Bovenberg, 1996), or to offset the effects of imperfect competition in the markets for capital goods (Judd, 1997, 2001).

However, these rather stark predictions have been tempered by numerous models that elaborate in various ways upon the structure of the basic tax competition models. For example, recent extensions have examined the role played by imperfect competition and economic rents, especially rents earned by multinational enterprises (MNEs). Although the basic tax competition results obtain if firm-specific economic rents are added (Gordon and Hines, 2002), this is not the case if the economic rents are location-specific, in which case taxation of capital income as a means of capturing some of these rents becomes highly desirable, especially if they accrue to foreign residents. Moreover, the distinction between statutory/average effective tax rates and effective marginal tax rates, which is not an issue in the basic model, becomes very important in this context, as the level of taxation of economic rents is largely determined by the

[1] On the other hand, tax competition may restrain "Leviathan" tendencies for overconsumption of public services and encourage governments to use desirable user charges and benefit taxes (McLure, 1986; Edwards and Keen, 1996; Huber and Runkel, 2004). See Wilson (1999), Fuest, Huber and Mintz (2003), Wildasin and Wilson (2004) and Zodrow (2003) for discussions of the negative and positive aspects of tax competition.

statutory tax rate. Thus, one would also expect tax competition in statutory tax rates as countries attempt to attract highly mobile capital that generates firm-specific economic rents, tempered by the desire to tax location-specific rents, especially if a significant fraction of such rents accrue to foreigners (Devereux and Hubbard, 2003; Huizinga and Neilsen, 1997; Sorensen, 2006). Note that this reasoning suggests that tax competition will be more severe for small economies with little potential for location-specific economic rents. For example, Bucovetsky and Wilson (1991) construct models of asymmetric tax competition where only large countries with market power in capital markets have positive taxes on capital income, and the "new economic geography" models implies that larger "core" countries with agglomeration economies have relatively high tax rates on capital income, which are avoided by relatively smaller and less developed "peripheral" economies (Baldwin and Krugman, 2004).

The difference between statutory and marginal tax rates is also critical when the basic tax competition model is extended to include the potential for income shifting across jurisdictions. Much empirical evidence suggests that multinational enterprises and multistate corporations (in the absence of unitary combination) have considerable latitude in reallocating profits across jurisdictions in response to tax differentials through the use of various financial accounting manipulations, including the use of transfer prices, loans and other intercompany transactions, and judicious allocation of general expenses (Hines, 1999; Altshuler and Grubert, 2002, 2004; Grubert, 1998, 2003; Bartlesman and Beetsma, 2003; Buettner and Wamser, 2007; Desai, Foley and Hines, 2004, 2006) and that such income shifting is increasing over time (Altshuler and Grubert, 2006). The benefits of income shifting are determined primarily by the statutory tax rate, as firms face obvious incentives to shift revenues to jurisdictions with relatively low statutory tax rates and deductions to jurisdictions with relatively high statutory tax rates. The implication again is that tax competition extends to statutory tax rates.

Indeed, several recent studies suggest that if income shifting is sufficiently important, competition in statutory tax rates may be more important than competition in effective marginal tax rates in attracting mobile capital. For example, Haufler and Schjelderup (2000) and Devereux, Lockwood and Redoano (2008) construct tax competition models with income shifting in the form of transfer pricing and show that lowering the statutory tax rate while increasing effective marginal tax rates can be desirable, especially if a local firm is partially owned by foreigners. Similar results were obtained in models in which firms can easily reallocate debt (Fuest and Hemmelgarn, 2005), and in models in which firms are differentially mobile with the more mobile firm generating higher profits (Becker and Fuest, 2005). Thus, because reductions in statutory tax rates simultaneously attract corporations that generate firm-specific rents, reduce the incentives for revenue-decreasing income shifting, and lower the tax burden on marginal investments (as long as this effect is not offset by other measures), tax competition in statutory tax rates may be even more intense than competition in effective marginal tax rates, and Devereux, Lockwood and Redoano (2008) provide some empirical evidence supporting this proposition. In addition, consistent with the standard argument that tax competition may lead to under-provision of public services, Gomes and Pouget (2008) provide evidence that such tax competition has led to a significant decline in spending on public infrastructure; they estimate that the decline of roughly 15 percentage points in the statutory corporate income tax rate that has occurred in their sample of 21 OECD countries has led to a reduction in public investment of between 0.6–1.1 percent of GDP.

On the other hand, several factors act to temper tax competition. For example, low taxes on capital income create incentives for income shifting from the personal income tax base, that is, for disguising labor income as relatively lowly taxed capital income (Gordon and Slemrod, 2000). In an international context, host countries that import capital from countries such as the US and the UK that allow foreign tax credits will face an incentive to keep their taxes high to the extent that they will be offset currently by such tax credits; however, as discussed above, this effect is tempered by the facts that such credits are deferred until the funds are repatriated to the parent, many multinationals have excess foreign tax credits, some foreign tax credit countries allow tax sparing, and the use of tax avoidance techniques by some US multinationals to eliminate home country tax liability. Also, if public goods generate significant positive spillover benefits across jurisdictions, the incentive for a government to lower its capital income taxes to attract mobile capital declines to the extent that such a capital reallocation results in lower public services being produced in other jurisdictions and thus lower spillover benefits. Indeed, if local goods are pure public goods and all jurisdictions use capital income taxes, there is no incentive for underprovision of public services (Bjorvatn and Schjelderup, 2002). In addition, numerous policy initiatives have attempted to place constraints on the extent of international tax competition, including the OECD's Initiative on Harmful Tax Competition, the European Commission's Code of Conduct (McLure, 2006), and ongoing discussions about EU corporate income tax harmonization, and several decisions by the European Court of Justice have also had the effect of tempering tax competition within the EU.

Finally, the implications for tax competition of corporate tax avoidance are complex. As noted above, the potential for income shifting creates another dimension of tax competition, especially in statutory tax rates. However, the existence of the potential to avoid the negative effects of higher tax rates suggests that their deleterious effects on investment may be significantly smaller than suggested by the standard tax competition literature (Hong and Smart, 2010). For example, Altshuler and Grubert (2006) argue that tax competition is increasingly taking the form of allowing tax avoidance by multinational enterprises. In particular, they stress that the "check the box" rules in the US greatly facilitated tax avoidance by US multinationals by allowing the creation of hybrid entities that allow the shifting of interest and other forms of income to tax havens without triggering current taxation under the US controlled foreign corporation rules.

To sum up, the basic tax competition model as well as several of its extensions suggest that if capital is mobile tax rates on capital income should be relatively low and indeed in some cases should be zero or even negative. Moreover, tax competition extends to statutory rates, especially to the extent such rents are firm specific and firms have the potential to shift income. However, the rather stark results obtained with these models are tempered by a variety of additional considerations, including the desire to tax location specific economic rents, especially if such rents are earned by foreigners. Thus, the extent of tax competition is ultimately an empirical issue. Various strands of the empirical evidence on this question are examined in the following sections.

3.2. *Corporate tax rates*

It is clear that statutory corporate tax rates have declined significantly in recent years. For example, Devereux, Griffith and Klemm (2002) note that average statutory corporate income tax rates in the EU and U.S. fell dramatically from 48% in 1982 to 35% in 2001. Similarly, Devereux (2007) shows that the average statutory tax rate in the OECD was roughly 40 percent over the period from 1965 to the early 1990s, but dropped from 41 percent in 1988 to 33 percent in 1993, and was roughly constant at that level through 2004 (when it was 32 percent). At the same time, however, these rate reductions have often been accompanied by base-broadening efforts, so that overall corporate tax revenues as well as average and especially marginal effective tax rates have declined considerably less (Devereux, Griffith and Klemm, 2002; Gorter and de Mooij, 2001; Becker and Fuest, 2005); indeed, corporate tax revenues as a share of total revenues have risen over the past two decades in the U.S. (Auerbach, 2006). Similarly, corporate tax revenues as a fraction of GDP in the OECD have been roughly constant over the past 40 years, and indeed have increased in recent years (Devereux, 2007). This evidence is suggestive of tax competition in statutory rates, but also implies that tax competition has not yet had as significant an impact in these countries on the effective tax rates that were the focus of the earlier theoretical tax competition models.

More generally, although the data are now somewhat dated, Grubert (2001) examines a sample of 60 countries and shows that average effective tax rates, defined as foreign taxes paid relative to net income as reported by US multinationals, fell by almost ten percentage points between 1984–1992, with statutory rates falling by a somewhat smaller amount (and rates in the EU falling by less than this average). This result is more consistent with the existence of tax competition in effective tax rates, as is Grubert's finding that average effective tax rates fell much more in the small, open and relatively poor countries that are more susceptible to the effects of tax competition. Altshuler and Grubert (2006) find that the rate of decline in average effective tax rates continued but moderated over the 1992–2000 period, and that although the declines were more pronounced in smaller countries through 1997, this result vanishes for 1998–2000. (As will be discussed below, they attribute this result to the increased importance of tax planning and tax avoidance activities.) Similarly, Slemrod (2004) finds that statutory tax rates are negatively associated with measures of openness (although he does not find evidence of such a link for revenues as a fraction of GDP), Winner (2005) finds that decreasing capital tax burdens and increasing labor tax burdens over time are especially pronounced for smaller countries, and Bretschger and Hettich (2002) obtain similar results for statutory corporate income tax rates.

Garretson and Peeters (2006) examine the impact of increasing capital mobility (measured as either increases in FDI flows relative to gross capital formation or using an index of the extent of the legal restriction placed on international capital mobility) on corporate tax rates for a sample of 19 OECD countries. They base their model on the theory of tax competition with agglomeration economies noted above, which posits that tax competition should be less intense among "core countries" that are characterized by significant economies of agglomeration, relative to smaller less developed "peripheral" countries (Baldwin and Krugman, 2004). They find that increased capital mobility does lead to tax competition in the form of lower corporate tax rates, but that this effect is considerably less pronounced for countries with significant agglomeration economies (estimated using several measures of market potential); they conclude (Garretson and Peeters, 2006, p. 1) that, "If there is a race to the bottom, it seems that it is more real for some countries than others."

Similarly, Keen and Simone (2004) argue that tax competition has been more pronounced in developing countries, where competition has not been limited to statutory tax rates, but also to average and marginal effective tax rates as well as revenues, primarily due to generous tax holidays and tax incentives designed to attract foreign direct investment. For example, in a sample of developing countries using data from the early 1990s to the early 2000s, average statutory rates declined by six percentage points or 16%, and corporate tax revenues relative to GDP declined by 20%. This result is confirmed by Huizinga, Laeven and Nicodéme (2006) who find that corporate tax revenues relative to GDP decline with size (measured as GDP). However, this result has been questioned by Hines (2007) who examines a longer time period and a different sample of non-OECD countries and finds the corporate tax revenues relative to GDP are roughly constant over the period 1972–2004; even in this case, however, corporate tax revenues relative to GDP decline if one assumes that tax competition was not an important force until the early 1980s. Hines also finds that tax competition has significantly reduced foreign taxes on U.S. multinationals, as their average effective foreign tax rates fell from 43% in 1982 to 26% in 1999.

3.3. *Reaction functions*

Another strand of the empirical literature tests for tax competition by looking for evidence of strategic interactions among governments in setting tax rates on capital, as predicted in models of tax competition in which governments take into account the tax policies of neighboring jurisdictions (rather than assuming them to be fixed). Brueckner (2003) surveys the literature that examines this issue in the subnational context, including important contributions by Heyndels and Vuchelen (1998), Brett and Pinkse (2000), Buettner (2001), Hayashi and Boadway (2001) and Brueckner and Saavedra (2001). He notes that the slope of a local government's tax reaction function is theoretically ambiguous in sign. For example, if neighboring jurisdictions lower their tax rates, the standard tax competition argument implies that the local government should react by lowering its own tax rate (a positively sloped reaction function); however, the capital outflow induced by the rate reduction of other jurisdictions implies a reduction in revenues and, if local tastes for public services are sufficiently strong, the local tax rate can increase. Nevertheless, Brueckner (2003) notes that in virtually all of the empirical studies he analyzes, the estimated tax reaction function confirms strategic interaction and is upward sloping, indicating that the traditional tax competition factors dominate.[2] Devereux, Lockwood and Redoano (2008) utilize a similar approach in an international context. Following Devereux and Griffith

[2] Note that tax competition among the states in the US, where the allocation of corporate profits across states is determined by formula apportionment with formulas that vary across states, can also take the form of changing a state's formula to increase the weight on sales while reducing the weights on payroll and property, or facilitating tax avoidance in the form of income shifting across states by allowing firms to use separate rather than combined accounting (Edmiston, 2002; Mazerov 2005, 2009). Mintz and Smart (2004) discuss similar issues in the Canadian context.

(1998, 2003), they construct a model in which multinationals choose their investment locations in response to differences in statutory tax rates and choose their level of investment, given location, in response to the marginal effective tax rate. In addition, firms are assumed to be able to use transfer pricing, limited by the threat of audit, to shift profits across jurisdictions. Devereux, Lockwood and Redoano analyze multinational investment decisions in a sample of 21 OECD countries over the period 1982–1999. They find strong evidence of international tax competition over statutory corporate tax rates; specifically, they estimate that a one percentage point reduction in the weighted average statutory tax rate in other countries results in a 0.7 percentage point reduction in the home country tax rate. They also find evidence of competition in marginal effective tax rates, but the magnitudes of the effects are much smaller. Finally, they note that their estimated government tax reaction functions suggest that equilibrium statutory tax rates should have fallen substantially over the time period considered, consistent with the data described above.

Heinemann, Overesch and Rincke (2008) also provide a recent test for the existence of tax competition. They examine a series of discrete tax reform events involving reductions in statutory tax rates in a sample of 32 European countries to test for interactions among neighboring countries. They estimate that a country reduces its own statutory tax rate by 1.5–3.2 percentage points in response to a reduction in statutory tax rates of one percentage point in neighboring countries. Similarly, Altshuler and Goodspeed (2002) estimate that the EU has a positive tax reaction function to tax changes in the US (which they model as a Stackelberg leader) and the tax competition between the EU and US has become increasingly intense, and Besley, Griffith and Klemm (2001) show that corporate income tax rates are positively related to tax rates in other countries, especially within the EU, but such a strategic relationship does not hold for other taxes. All of these studies suggest that international tax competition is an important ongoing phenomenon.

3.4. *Competition in allowing tax avoidance*

As discussed above, the potential for tax avoidance and income shifting in general provides another explanation for why tax competition in statutory corporate income tax rates might be observed, as lower statutory rates reduce incentives for multinational enterprises (MNEs) to shift revenues out of, and deductions into, a country. However, possibilities for tax avoidance by MNEs also may temper tax competition. Specifically, tax avoidance opportunities may imply that the negative impact of relatively high statutory and effective tax rates on foreign direct investment may be muted if MNEs are easily able to mitigate their effects on the cost of capital with tax planning.

This creates an interesting dilemma for tax policy makers. On the one hand, governments in the industrialized world have for many years engaged in a wide variety of efforts to protect tax revenues by limiting opportunities for tax avoidance and tax evasion by domestic- and foreign-based multinationals; these include extensive transfer pricing rules, controlled foreign corporation limits on earning passive income abroad, thin capitalization and earnings stripping rules, limits on interest deductibility, withholding taxes, etc., as well as treaties designed to limit opportunities for avoidance and evasion. Moreover, the OECD is currently engaged in several long-standing efforts to coordinate policies to limit what it deems to be harmful tax competition (European Commission, 1997; Organisation for Economic Cooperation and Development, 1998, 2000; Nicodème, 2009).

On the other hand, the availability of strategies for tax planning that are available only to MNEs suggests an interesting "optimal capital income tax" strategy that might be pursued by countries attempting to attract FDI at minimal revenue cost. Specifically, to the extent that MNEs are more mobile than purely domestic firms (and neglecting the higher administrative and compliance costs of differential taxation), optimal tax theory suggests that the former should be taxed at relatively lower rates — indeed, as described above, at a zero rate if they are perfectly mobile (Gugl and Zodrow, 2006). Several studies have examined the revenue effects of preferential tax regimes for mobile capital, reaching different conclusions depending on assumptions regarding the relative mobility of the different tax bases (Janeba and Peters, 1999; Keen, 2001; Janeba and Smart, 2003). In practice, political considerations generally preclude the taxation of foreign firms at rates that are explicitly lower than those applied to domestic firms. However, the same result can be achieved if host countries allow MNEs access to tax avoidance devices — e.g., through explicit regulations or lax enforcement — that are legally or effectively not available to domestic firms.

Indeed, Peralta, Wauthy and van Ypersele (2006) and Hong and Smart (2007) conclude that such practices may be desirable as a means of allowing host countries to approach the "zero tax result" for mobile international capital while still applying a high corporate tax rate to relatively immobile domestic capital. In addition, readily accessible possibilities for tax avoidance imply that real foreign direct investment will be less sensitive to tax rate differentials, thus allowing higher corporate tax rates in host countries to be welfare-increasing for their citizens.[3,4]

Altshuler and Grubert (2006) argue that this phenomenon provides an important explanation of the recent behavior of host countries, as tax competition among countries increasingly takes the form of allowing tax avoidance rather than explicit tax rate reductions. Furthermore, they argue that home countries face an incentive to allow or even facilitate tax avoidance by MNEs if they believe that the gains from increased competitiveness of their MNEs outweigh the associated revenue losses. As noted above, the prime example of such behavior is the adoption of the "check-the-box" regulations in the U.S. in 1997, which allowed affiliated firms to choose their tax status as a subsidiary, subject to separate taxation, or a branch, taxed on a pass-through basis to the parent firm, and greatly facilitated various tax avoidance schemes.

Altshuler and Grubert provide several examples of tax avoidance activity made easier by the "check-the-box" rules. In general, these strategies

---

[3] Similarly, Grubert and Mutti (2001) argue that because taxes due on repatriation can be easily avoided (e.g., through arbitrage transactions involving a conduit company in a third country), their distortionary (and revenue) impacts are relatively small. Altshuler and Grubert (2006), however, acknowledge that the six-fold increase in inflows of repatriated funds into the U.S. in response to the recent temporary rate reduction for repatriated funds calls this view into question.

[4] Bucovetsky and Haufler (2008) make similar points in a model in which mobile multinational firms can change their organizational structures. In contrast, Slemrod and Wilson (2006) argue that the impact of facilitating avoidance is negative once one considers the costs of labor income shifting and the costs of enforcement and administration.

involve circumvention of the "controlled foreign corporation" (CFC) rules that require current taxation of income transferred to tax havens. For example, the new rules allow U.S. firms to use tax haven finance subsidiaries, under which the U.S. parent can inject equity funds to an affiliated company in a low-tax haven that in turn loans the funds to another affiliated company in a high-tax country. Under the former regulations, the payment of interest to the company in the tax haven would have been taxable currently under the CFC rules. However, with the new regulations, the company in the high tax host country can be a "hybrid entity" — one that is treated as a corporation by the host country, but as an unincorporated branch of the company in the tax haven by the U.S. — so that transfers between them are intercompany transfers and thus not subject to the CFC rules. As a result, the company in the high tax country gets a deduction for interest at a relatively high rate, but the associated interest income is taxed at a very low rate in the tax haven, with U.S. tax deferred, perhaps indefinitely.

Altshuler and Grubert provide empirical evidence to support their view that international tax competition increasingly takes the form of allowing tax avoidance, examining various phenomena before and after the 1997 tax change. First, they examine changes in average effective tax rates, which continued to decline over the period 1992–2002, although at a slower rate than the decline documented in the studies cited above. They conclude that after 1998 tax avoidance behavior was much more important in explaining these declines in host country effective tax rates than the declines in statutory tax rates that occurred over the same period, as the correlation between effective and statutory tax rates declined significantly. Second, the extent to which the reported profitability of subsidiaries in low-tax countries exceeded that in high-tax countries grew considerably after 1997, suggesting profit shifting to low-tax jurisdictions. Third, Altshuler and Grubert show that intercompany tax payments and holding company income grew considerably after 1997, as would occur if the various strategies described above were used to shift income to lower-tax countries. They estimate that in 2002 U.S. multinationals saved 15 percent of their total foreign tax burden by using these techniques.

4. Conclusion

This paper has examined the literatures on two questions that are essential to any discussion of mobility and taxation — the extent to which capital is mobile internationally and the extent to which the mobility of capital has resulted in interjurisdictional capital tax competition.

[...]

Acknowledgments

I have benefited greatly from the comments of Charles McLure and an anonymous referee, and from suggestions from the participants at a conference on "Mobility and Tax Policy: Do Yesterday's Taxes Fit Tomorrow's Economy?" held at the Center for Business and Economic Research, University of Tennessee, Knoxville, TN on October 2–3, 2008. I would like to thank Leslie Countryman for research assistance.

References

Ahearne, Alan G., William L. Griever, and Frank E. Warnock, 2004. "Information Costs and Home Bias: An Analysis of U.S. Holdings of Foreign Equities." *Journal of International Economics* 62 (2): 313–336.

Altshuler, Rosanne and Timothy Goodspeed, 2002. "Follow the Leader? Evidence on European and U.S. Tax Competition," *Rutgers University Economics Department Working Paper No. 200226.*

Altshuler, Rosanne and Harry Grubert, 2002. "Repatriation Taxes, Repatriation Strategies, and Multinational Financial Policy." *Journal of Public Economics* 87: 73–107.

Altshuler, Rosanne and Harry Grubert, 2004. "Taxpayer Responses to Competitive Tax Policies and Tax Policy Responses to Competitive Taxpayers: Recent Evidence." *Tax Notes International* (June 28) 34 (13): 1349–1362.

Altshuler, Rosanne and Harry Grubert, 2006. "Governments and Multinational Corporations in the Race to the Bottom." *Tax Notes* (February 6) 110: 459–474.

Altshuler, Rosanne, Harry Grubert and T. Scott Newlon, 2001. "Has U.S. Investment Abroad Become More Sensitive to Tax Rates?" In *International Taxation and Multinational Activity,* by James R. Hines, Jr. Chicago: University of Chicago Press, pp. 9–32.

Arulampalam, Wiji, Michael P, Devereux and Giorgia Maffini, 2008. "The Direct Incidence of Corporate Income Tax on Wages," manuscript, University of Warwick.

Auerbach, Alan J., 2006. "Why Have Corporate Tax Revenues Declined? Another Look." National Bureau of Economic Research Working Paper 12463. Cambridge MA: NBER.

Baldwin, Richard and Paul Krugman, 2004. "Agglomeration, Integration and Tax Harmonization." *European Economic Review* 48: 1–23.

Becker, Johannes and Clemens Fuest, 2005. "Optimal Tax Policy when Firms are Internationally Mobile." Working Paper No. 1592, CESifo, Munich.

Besley, Timothy, Rachel Griffith and Alexander Klemm, 2001. "Empirical Evidence on Fiscal Interdependence in OECD Countries," *Institute for Fiscal Studies Working Paper*.

Bjorvatn, Kjetil and Guttorm Schjelderup, 2002. "Tax Competition and International Public Goods," *International Tax and Public Finance* 8(2): 111–120.

Boskin, Michael J., and William G. Gale, 1987. "New Results on the Effects of Tax Policy on the International Location of Investment," in *The Effects of Taxation on Capital Accumulation*, edited by Martin S. Feldstein. Chicago: University of Chicago Press, pp. 201–219.

Bretschger, Lucas and Frank Hettich, 2002. "Globalization, Capital Mobility and Tax Competition: The Theory and Evidence for OECD Countries," *European Journal of Political Economy* 18 (4): 695–716.

Brett, C. and J. Pinske, 2000. "The Determinants of Municipal Tax Rates in British Columbia," *Canadian Journal of Economics* 33: 695–714.

Brueckner, Jan K., 2000. "A Tiebout/Tax Competition Model." *Journal of Public Economics* 77, 285–306.

Brueckner, Jan K., 2003. "Strategic Interaction Among Governments: An Overview of Empirical Studies," *International Regional Science Review* 26 (2): 175–188.

Brueckner, Jan K. and Luc A. Saavedra, 2001. "Do Local Governments Engage in Strategic Tax Competition?" *National Tax Journal* 54: 203–229.

Bucovetsky, Sam and John D. Wilson, 1991. "Tax Competition with Two Tax Instruments." *Regional Science and Urban Economics* 21, 333–350.

Bucovetsky, Sam and Andreas Haufler, 2008. "Tax Competition when Firms Choose their Organizational Form: Should Tax Loopholes for Multinationals be Closed?" *Journal of International Economics* 74: 188–201.

Buettner, Theiss, 2001. "Local Business Taxation and Competition for Capital: the Choice of the Tax Rate," *Regional Science and Urban Economics* 31: 215–245.

Buettner, Theiss and Georg Wamser, 2007. "Intercompany Loans and Profit Shifting — Evidence from Company-Level Data," *International Tax and Public Finance.*

de Mooij, Ruud A., and Gaëtan Nicodème, 2008. "Corporate Tax Policy and Incorporation in the EU," *International Tax and Public Finance* 15: 478–498.

de Mooij, Ruud A. and Sjef Ederveen, 2003. "Taxation and Foreign Direct Investment: A Synthesis of Empirical Research." *International Tax and Public Finance* 11: 673–693.

de Mooij, Ruud and Sjef Ederveen, 2005. "Explaining the Variation in Empirical Estimates of Tax Elasticities of Foreign Investment." Tinbergen Institute Discussion Paper TI 2005–108/3. Rotterdam: Tinbergen Institute.

Desai, Mihir, C. Fritz Foley and James R. Hines Jr., 2004. "Foreign Direct Investment in a World of Multiple Taxes," *Journal of Public Economics* 88 (12): 2727–2744.

Desai, Mihir, C. Fritz Foley and James R. Hines Jr., 2006. "The Demand for Tax Havens," *Journal of Public Economics* 90 (3): 513–531.

Devereux, Michael P., 2007. "Developments in the Taxation of Corporate Profit in the OECD since 1965: Rates, Bases and Revenues." Oxford University Centre for Business Taxation WP 07/04. Oxford: Oxford University Centre for Business Taxation.

Devereux, Michael P. and Rachel Griffith, 1998. "Taxes and the Location of Production: Evidence from a Panel of U.S. Multinationals." *Journal of Public Economics* 68: 335–367.

Devereux, Michael P. and Rachel Griffith, 2003. "The Impact of Corporate Taxation on the Location of Capital: A Review." *Economic Analysis and Policy* 33: 275–292.

Devereux, Michael P., Rachel Griffith and Alexander Klemm, 2002. "Corporate Income Tax Reforms and International Tax Competition." *Economic Policy* 35: 451–495.

Devereux, Michael P. and R. Glenn Hubbard, 2003. "Taxing Multinationals." *International Tax and Public Finance* 10: 469–487.

Devereux, Michael P., Ben Lockwood and Michela Redoano, 2008. "Do Countries Compete over Corporate Tax Rates?" *Journal of Public Economics* 92 (5–6): 1210–1235.

Edwards, Jeremy and Michael Keen, 1996. "Tax Competition and Leviathan." *European Economic Review* 40, 113–134.

Edmiston, Kelly D., 2002. "Strategic Apportionment of the State Corporate Income Tax," *National Tax Journal* 55: 239–262.

Erkel-Rousse, Helene and Daniel Mirza, 2002. "Import Price Elasticities: Reconsidering the Evidence." *Canadian Journal of Economics* 35: 282–306.

European Commission. (1997). "Towards Tax Co-Ordination in the European Union: A Package to Tackle Harmful Tax Competition." COM(97) 495 final.

Feldstein, Martin, 1983. "Domestic Saving and International Capital Movements in the Long Run and the Short Run," *European Economic Review* 21: 129–151.

Feldstein, Martin, 1994. "Tax Policy and International Capital Flows." *National Bureau of Economic Research Working Paper No. 4851* (September).

Feldstein, Martin and Phillipe Bacchetta, 1991. "National Saving and International Investment," in *National Saving and Economic Performance*, edited by B. Douglas Bernheim and John B. Shoven. Chicago: University of Chicago Press.

Feldstein, Martin S. and Charles Horioka, 1980. "Domestic Savings and Capital Flows," *Economic Journal* 90(2): 314–329.

Felix, R. Alison, 2007. "Passing the Burden: Corporate Tax Incidence in Open Economies," manuscript, Federal Reserve Bank of Kansas City.

Fuest, Clemens and Bernd Huber, 2004. "Why Do Countries Combine the Exemption System for the Taxation of Foreign Profits with Domestic Double Taxation Relief?" *Journal of International Economics* 62: 219–231.

French, Kenneth R. and James M. Poterba, 1991. "Investor Diversification and International Equity Markets," *American Economic Review* 81(1): 222–226.

Fuest, Clemens and Thomas Hemmelgarn, 2005. "Corporate Tax Policy, Foreign Firm Ownership and Thin Capitalization." *Regional Science and Urban Economics* 35: 508–526.

Fuest, Clemens, Bernd Huber and Jack Mintz, 2003. "Capital Mobility and Tax Competition: A Survey." In *Foundations and Trends in Microeconomics* 1:1–62.

Garretson, Harry and Jolanda Peeters, 2006. "Capital Mobility, Agglomeration and Corporate Tax Rates: Is the Race to the Bottom for Real?" De Nederlandsche Bank Working Paper No. 113.

Gomes, Pedro and Francois Pouget, 2008. "Corporate Tax Competition and the Decline of Public Investment," *European Central Bank Working Paper No. 928.*

Gordon, Roger H. and A. Lans Bovenberg, 1996. "Why is Capital so Immobile Internationally? Possible Explanations and Implications for Capital Income Taxation." *American Economic Review* 86: 1057–1075.

Gordon, Roger H. and James R. Hines, Jr., 2002. "*International Taxation.*" In *Handbook of Public Economics, Volume 4,* edited by Alan J. Auerbach and Martin Feldstein. Amsterdam: North Holland/Elsevier.

Gordon, Roger H. and Joel Slemrod, 2000. "Are 'Real' Responses to Taxes Simply Income Shifting Between Corporate and Personal Income Tax Bases?" In Joel Slemrod (ed.), *Does Atlas Shrug? The Economic Consequences of Taxing the Rich.* New York and Cambridge MA: Russell Sage Foundation and Harvard University Press.

Gordon, Roger H., 1986. "Taxation of Investment and Savings in the World Economy." *American Economic Review* 76: 1086–1102.

Gorter, Joeri and Ruud de Mooij, 2001. *Capital Income Taxation in Europe: Trends and Tradeoffs.* The Hague: CPB Netherlands Bureau for Economic Policy Analysis.

Gravelle, Jane G. and Thomas L. Hungerford, 2007. "Corporate Tax Reform: Issues for Congress," *Congressional Research Service Report RL34229.*

Gravelle, Jane G., and Kent A. Smetters, 2006. "Does the Open Economy Assumption Really Mean that Labor Bears the Burden of a Capital Income Tax? *Advances in Economic Analysis and Policy* 6: 1–42.

Grubert, Harry, 1998. "Taxes and the Division of Foreign Operating Income among Royalties, Interest, Dividends and Retained Earnings." *Journal of Public Economics* 68: 269–290.

Grubert, Harry, 2001. "Tax Planning by Companies and Tax Competition by Governments: Is There Evidence of Changes in Behavior?" In James R. Hines, Jr., *International Taxation and Multinational Activity.* Chicago: University of Chicago Press, pp. 113–139.

Grubert, Harry, 2003. "Intangible Income, Intercompany Transactions, Income Shifting, and the Choice of Location." *National Tax Journal* 56: 211–242.

Grubert, Harry and Rosanne Altshuler, 2008. "Corporate Taxes in the World Economy: Reforming the Taxation of Cross-Border Income." In *Fundamental Tax Reform: Issues, Choices and Implications,* edited by John W. Diamond and George R. Zodrow. Cambridge MA: MIT Press.

Grubert, Harry and John Mutti, 2000. "The Influence of Taxation on Industrial Location," *National Tax Journal* 53(4): 825–839.

Grubert, Harry and John Mutti, 2001. "Taxing International Business Income: Dividend Exemption Versus the Current System." Washington DC: AEI Press.

Gugl, Elisabeth and George R. Zodrow, 2006. "International Tax Competition and Tax Incentives for Developing Countries." In *The Challenges of Tax Reform in a Global Economy,* edited by James Alm, Jorge Martinez-Vasquez and Mark Rider. New York: Springer, pp. 167–191.

Harberger, Arnold C., 1980. "Vignettes on the World Capital Market," *American Economic Review* 70 (2): 331–337.

Harberger, Arnold C., 1995. "The ABCs of Corporate Tax Incidence: Insights into the Open-economy Case." In *Tax Policy and Economic Growth*. Washington D.C.: ACCF Center for Policy Research.

Harberger, Arnold C., 2008. "Corporate Tax Incidence: Reflections on What is Known, Unknown, and Unknowable." In *Fundamental Tax Reform: Issues, Choices and Implications*, edited by John W. Diamond and George R. Zodrow. Cambridge MA: MIT Press.

Hartman, David G., 1984. "Tax Policy and Foreign Direct Investment in the United States." *National Tax Journal* 37: 475–487.

Hassett, Kevin A. and Aparna Mathur, 2006. "Taxes on Wages," *American Enterprise Institute Working Paper No. 128.*

Hassett, Kevin A. and Kathryn Newmark, 2008. "Taxation and Business Behavior: A Review of the Recent Literature." In *Fundamental Tax Reform: Issues, Choices and Implications,* edited by John W. Diamond and George R. Zodrow. Cambridge MA: MIT Press.

Haufler, Andreas and Guttorm Schjelderup, 2000. "Corporate Tax Systems and Cross Country Profit Shifting." *Oxford Economic Papers* 52: 306–325.

Hayashi, Masayoshi and Robin Boadway, 2001. "An Empirical Analysis of Intergovernmental Tax Interaction: The Case of Business Income Taxes in Canada," *Canadian Journal of Economics* 34: 481–503.

Heinemann, Friedrich, Michael Overesch and Johannes Rincke, 2008. "Rate Cutting Tax Reforms and Corporate Tax Competition in Europe," *Center for European Economic Research (ZEW) Discussion Paper No. 08–20.*

Hertel, Thomas, David Hummels, Maros Ivanic and Roman Keeney, 2004. "How Confident Can We Be in CGE-Based Assessments of Free Trade Agreements?" Center for Global Trade Analysis Working Paper 26. West Lafayette IN: Purdue University.

Heyndels, Bruno and Jef Vuchelen, 1998. "Tax Mimicking among Belgian Municipalities," *National Tax Journal* 51: 89–101.

Hines, James R., Jr., 1999. "Lessons From Behavioral Responses to International Taxation." *National Tax Journal*, June, 305–322.

Hines, James R., 2007. "Corporate Taxation and International Competition," in *Taxing Corporate Income*, edited by Alan J. Auerbach, James R. Hines and Joel Slemrod. Cambridge UK: Cambridge University Press, pp. 268–295.

Hines James R., Jr., and Eric M. Rice, 1994. "Fiscal Paradise: Foreign Tax Havens and American Business." *Quarterly Journal of Economics* 109: 149–182.

Hong, Quing, and Michael Smart, 2010. "In Praise of Tax Havens: International Tax Planning and Foreign Direct Investment." *European Economic Review* 54 (1): 82–95.

Huber, Bernd and Marco Runkel, 2004. "Tax Competition, Excludable Public Goods and User Charges," *CESifo Working Paper Series No. 1172.*

Huizinga, Harry and Soren Bo Nielsen, 1997. "Capital Income and Profit Taxation with Foreign Ownership of Firms." *Journal of International Economics* 42: 149–165.

Huizinga, Harry, Luc Laeven and Gaetan Nicodème, 2006. "Capital Structure and International Debt Shifting." European Economy Economic Paper No. 263. Brussels: European Commission.

Janeba, Eckhard and W. Peters, 1999. "Tax Evasion, Tax Competition and the Gains from Nondiscrimination: The Case of Interest Taxation in Europe." *Economic Journal* 109: 93–101.

Janeba, Eckhard and Michael Smart, 2003. "Is Targeted Tax Competition Less Harmful Than Its Remedies?" *International Tax and Public Finance* 10: 259–280.

Judd, Kenneth L., 1997. "The Optimal Tax Rate for Capital Income Is Negative." National Bureau of Economic Research Working Paper 6004. Cambridge MA: NBER.

Judd, Kenneth L., 2001. "The Impact of Tax Reform in Modern Dynamic Economies." In *Transition Costs of Fundamental Tax Reform,* edited by Kevin A. Hassett and R. Glenn Hubbard. Washington, DC: AEI Press.

Keen, Michael, 2001. "Preferential Regimes Can Make Tax Competition Less Harmful." *National Tax Journal* 54: 757–762.

Keen, Michael and Alejandro Simone, 2004. "Is Tax Competition Harming Developing Countries More Than Developed?" *Tax Notes International* 34(13) (June 28): 1317–1325.

Mazerov, Michael, 2005. "The 'Single Sales Factor' Formula for State Corporate Taxes A Boon To Economic Development or a Costly Giveaway?" Center on Budget and Policy Priorities. http://www.cbpp.org/cms/index.cfm?fa=view&id=1754

Mazerov, Michael, 2009. "A Majority of States Have Now Adopted a Key Corporate Tax Reform — Combined Reporting." Center on Budget and Policy Priorities. http://www.cbpp.org/4-5-07sfp.pdf.

McDaniel, Christine A. and Edward J. Balistreri, 2002. "A Discussion on Armington Trade Substitution Elasticities." U.S. International Trade Commission Office of Economics Working Paper.

McLure, Charles E., Jr., 1986. "Tax Competition: Is What's Good for the Private Goose Also Good for the Public Gander?" *National Tax Journal* 39: 341–348.

McLure, Charles E., Jr., 2006. "Transfer Pricing and Tax Havens: Mending the Revenue Nets of Developing and Transition Countries," in *The Challenges of*

Tax Reform in a Global Economy, edited by James Alm, Jorge Martinez-Vasquez and Mark Rider. New York: Springer.

Mintz, Jack M. and Michael Smart, 2004. "Income Shifting, Investment, and Tax Competition: Theory and Evidence from Provincial Taxation in Canada," *Journal of Public Economics* 88: 1149–1168.

Nicodème, Gaëtan, 2009. "On Recent Developments in Fighting Harmful Tax Practices, " *National Tax Journal* 62 (4), 755–771.

Organisation for Economic Cooperation and Development, 1998. *Harmful Tax Competition: An Emerging Global Issue*, Paris: Organization for Economic Co-operation and Development.

Organisation for Economic Cooperation and Development, 2000. *Towards Global Tax Co-operation: Progress in Identifying and Eliminating Harmful Tax Practices.* Report to the 2000 Ministerial Council Meeting and Recommendations by the Committee on Fiscal Affairs. Paris: Organization for Economic Co-operation and Development.

Overesch, Michael, 2009. "The Effects of Multinationals' Profit Shifting Activities on Real Investments," *National Tax Journal* 62: 5–23.

Randolph, William C., 2006. "International Burdens of the Corporate Income Tax." CBO Working Paper. Washington DC: Congressional Budget Office.

Razin, Assaf and Efraim Sadka, 1991. "International Tax Competition and Gains from Tax Harmonization." *Economics Letters* 37: 69–76.

Slemrod, Joel and John D. Wilson, 2006. "Tax Competition with Parasitic Tax Havens," *National Bureau of Economic Research Working Paper No. W12225.*

Slemrod, Joel, 1990. "Tax Effects on Foreign Direct Investment in the United States: Evidence from a Cross-Country Comparison." In *Taxation in the Global Economy,* edited by Assaf Razin and Joel Slemrod. Chicago: University of Chicago Press.

Slemrod, Joel, 2004. "Are Corporate Tax Rates, or Countries, Converging?" *Journal of Public Economics* 88: 1169–1186.

Sorensen, Peter Birch, 2006. "Can Capital Income Taxes Survive? And Should They? *CES-ifo Working Paper No. 1793.*

Wildasin, David E. and John D. Wilson, 2004. "Capital Tax Competition: Bane or Boon?" *Journal of Public Economics* 88: 1065–1091.

Wilson, John D., 1986. "A Theory of Interregional Tax Competition." *Journal of Urban Economics* 19: 296–315.

Wilson, John D., 1991. "Tax Competition with Interregional Differences in Factor Endowments." *Regional Science and Urban Economics* 21, 423–452.

Wilson, John D., 1999. "Theories of Tax Competition." *National Tax Journal* 52: 269–304.

Winner, Hannes, 2005. "Has Tax Competition Emerged? *International Tax and Public Finance* 12 (5): 667–687.

Young, K.H., 1988. "The Effects of Taxes and Rates of Return on Foreign Direct Investment in the United States." *National Tax Journal* 41: 109–121.

Zodrow, George R., 2003. "Tax Competition and Tax Coordination in the European Union." *International Tax and Public Finance* 10: 651–671.

Zodrow, George R. 2006. "Capital Mobility and Source-Based Taxation of Capital Income in Small Open Economies." *International Tax and Public Finance* 13: 269–294.

Zodrow, George R. and Charles E. McLure, Jr., 1987. "Treasury I and the Tax Reform Act of 1986: The Economics and Politics of Tax Reform," *Journal of Economic Perspectives* 1: 37–58.

Zodrow, George R. and Peter Mieszkowski, 1983. "The Incidence of the Property Tax: The Benefit View versus the New View." In *Local Provision of Public Services: The Tiebout Model after Twenty-Five Years,* edited by George R. Zodrow. New York: Academic Press.

Zodrow, George R. and Peter Mieszkowski, 1986. "Pigou, Tiebout, Property Taxation, and the Underprovision of Local Public Goods." *Journal of Urban Economics* 19: 356–370.

Zodrow, George R., 2007. "Should Capital Income be Subject to Consumption-Based Taxation?" In *Taxing Capital Income*, edited by Henry Aaron, Leonard Burman and C. Eugene Steuerle. Washington DC: The Urban Institute.

Zodrow, George R., 2008. "Corporate Income Taxation in Canada," *Canadian Tax Journal* 56: 392–468.

Chapter 19

Tax Competition and the Efficiency of "Benefit-related" Business Taxes*

Elisabeth Gugl

Department of Economics University of Victoria, P.O. Box 1700 STN-CSC Canada – Victoria, BC, V8W 2Y2
egugl@uvic.ca,
https://orcid.org/0000-0003-2140-0989

George R. Zodrow

Rice University Department of Economics, 6100 Main Street, MS-22, Houston TX 77005, USA,
zodrow@rice.edu

We construct a tax competition model in which local governments finance business public services with either a source-based tax on mobile capital, such as a property tax, or a tax on production, such as an origin-based Value Added Tax, and then assess which of the two tax instruments is more efficient. Many taxes on business apply to mobile inputs or outputs, such as property taxes, retail sales taxes, and destination-based VATs, and their

*This chapter is reproduced from *International Tax and Public Finance*, **26**(3), 486–505, 2019.

inefficiency has been examined in the literature; however, proposals from several prominent tax experts to utilize a local origin-based VAT have not been analyzed theoretically. Our primary finding is that the production tax is less inefficient than the capital tax under many — but not all — conditions. The intuition underlying this result is that the efficiency of a user fee on the public business input is roughly approximated by a production tax, which applies to both the public input and immobile labor (in addition to mobile capital). In marked contrast, the capital tax applies only to mobile capital and is thus likely to be relatively inefficient.

Keywords: Tax competition, Business taxes, Business public services, Production tax, Capital tax

1. Introduction

At the state and local levels in the United States and at the provincial level in Canada, retail sales taxes often apply tax to business inputs, even though in principle they should be limited to final consumer goods. However, eliminating such taxes on business can provoke strong opposition from the electorate. For example, in 2010 British Columbia moved from a retail sales tax that was known to tax business inputs due to problems in its administration to a "pure" consumption tax — the Harmonized Sales Tax (HST), which combined the provincial retail sales tax and the federal Goods and Services Tax into a single value-added tax. This reform was projected to decrease tax payments from business by Canadian $730 million (The Independent Panel, 2011), prompting critics of the HST to decry its shift away from taxing business (CBC News, 2011). Premier Gordon Campbell introduced the HST shortly after winning office, despite denying any intent to do so during his campaign; as a result, the way the provincial government introduced the change also sparked strong opposition to the replacement of the provincial sales tax with the HST. The opposition was so fierce that continuation of the HST was the subject of a mail-in referendum, in which 55% of voters opposed the HST. As a result, British Columbia abandoned the HST and had to make the costly transition to re-establishing its provincial retail sales tax.

Motivated partly by the political argument that business should pay its "fair share" of taxes and partly by the economic argument that efficiency requires that businesses pay for the public services they consume (e.g., by paying user charges or being assessed "benefit taxes"), we analyze the impacts of imposing a production tax or a capital tax on local business in order to finance a public service that serves as an input in firms' production functions. Because our model is characterized by a single consumption good and fixed labor supply, a consumption tax such as a destination-based VAT would result in an efficient equilibrium. Nevertheless, we analyze production and capital taxes on business within the context of this model because we are interested in the impact of such narrower (capital tax) and broader (production tax) levies on business and government, including their effects on the level of public services. These issues are especially relevant in light of common political perceptions that firms should pay their "fair share" for public services they utilize as well as the economic efficiency argument for requiring firms to pay benefit taxes or user charges, and in light of the widespread use of subnational taxes on business in practice.

Indeed, in addition to taxing retail sales of business inputs, subnational taxes in the United States and Canada and in many other countries often include property taxes on business capital as well. Both forms of business input taxation may distort a wide variety of decisions, including those regarding production, capital accumulation and allocation, and, as stressed in the tax competition literature, the level of public services.

In light of this situation, several prominent public finance experts have argued that, in the absence of the assessment of explicit benefit taxes or user charges on business, broad-based taxes on local production, such as an origin-based value-added tax (VAT), are an attractive option (Bird, 2000; Hines, 2003). Their primary rationale is that such taxes serve as a proxy for the user charges that are desirable on economic efficiency grounds — that is, they are relatively efficient "benefit-related" taxes.

In this paper, we provide what we believe is the first attempt to analyze systematically the assertion that a production-based tax can be viewed as a proxy for a benefit tax, and is thus preferable to the often-used alternative of direct or indirect taxes on business inputs, especially capital. Our paper provides the theoretical basis underlying the simulation results presented in the context of CES production functions in Gugl and Zodrow (2015).

Many papers analyze the efficiency of capital taxation when firms receive public services and jurisdictions compete with each other for mobile capital; a partial list includes Zodrow and Mieszkowski (henceforth ZM) (1986), Oates and Schwab (1988, 1991), Noiset (1995), Sinn (1997), Keen and Marchand (1997), Bayindir-Upmann (1998), Richter (1994), Matsumoto (1998, 2000), and Dhillon, Wooders and Zissimos (2007). However, these papers focus on the inefficiency of capital taxation alone and do not consider a tax on local production or compare such a production tax to a capital tax.

Our results provide some support for the idea that a production-based tax may be viewed as a "benefit-related" tax, although only under special circumstances does a production tax substitute perfectly for an explicit user charge. The characteristics of the firm's production function — specifically, its log modularity properties (discussed at length below) — play a major role in determining the relative efficiency properties of production-based taxes and capital taxes, an issue that has thus far not been examined in models of interjurisdictional tax competition.

In our analysis, we assume that output is produced with a constant returns to scale (CRS) production function using labor, capital, and business public services as inputs. The log modularity properties of the production function with respect to capital and business public services indicate how the elasticity of output with respect to increases in business public services varies at different levels of the amount of capital employed in production. Specifically, if the production function is log modular (log submodular, log supermodular) in capital and business public services, then the elasticity of output with respect to business public services is constant (decreases, increases) as the capital employed in production increases. Note that all three possibilities are consistent with a CRS production function; in particular, a linearly homogenous Cobb–Douglas production function is log modular, while a constant elasticity of substitution (CES) production function is log submodular (log supermodular) if the elasticity of substitution is greater than (less than) one.

In the special case of a production function that is log modular in capital and the public service, a production tax is effectively a benefit tax and is thus analogous to a user charge for public services that ensures an efficient level of public service provision. In the same vein, if the production function is log submodular in capital and public services (e.g., a CES production function with an elasticity of substitution greater than one), a production tax is inefficient and leads to underprovision of the public service, but it results in less underprovision and thus is less inefficient than a capital tax. However, although we can show that the production tax leads to overprovision of public services in the case of a log supermodular production function (e.g., a CES production function with an elasticity of substitution smaller than 1), the ambiguity of the effect of a capital tax on public services in this case implies that a ranking of the relative efficiency properties of the two taxes is impossible without further restrictions on the production technology. In our companion paper (Gugl and Zodrow, 2015), we provide a wide variety of simulations using the CES production function and find only modest efficiency gains in the instances in which capital taxes are more efficient than the production tax.

There is also a vast literature analyzing the relative efficiency of destination-based and origin-based value-added taxes (VATs). In a closed economy, there is no difference between a uniform tax on all consumption and a similar tax on production. In contrast, as economies become increasingly more open, the distinction between a tax on local production and a tax on local consumption becomes important in terms of efficiency (Mintz and Tulkens, 1986; Kanbur and Keen, 1993; Lockwood, 2001; Haufler and Pflueger, 2007). In tax competition models in which firms are perfectly competitive, a tax on local consumption such as a destination-based VAT is efficient when countries are too small to affect world prices (Lockwood, 2001). Haufler and Pflueger (2007) investigate the difference between a destination-based and an origin-based VAT in several settings of international duopoly and find that only the former is efficient when competition between countries is imperfect. In contrast, McLure (2003) notes that the growing importance of electronic commerce implies that a destination-based VAT is increasingly difficult to administer, providing an argument in favor of an origin-based VAT.[1]

[1]This problem has been mitigated recently in the United States by the decision of the U.S. Supreme Court in South Dakota v. Wayfair Inc., which specifies that remote sellers can under certain circumstances be required to collect sales taxes even in states in which they have no physical presence.

In practice, most existing value-added taxes and retail sales taxes are destination-based taxes. However, there are numerous exceptions to this general rule, that is, cases in which these taxes are assessed on an origin basis and are thus similar to the origin-based production tax analyzed in this paper (Bird, 2003). For example, 11 U.S. states tax intrastate sales on an origin basis (a business selling a good or service to a consumer in a different taxing jurisdiction in the same state is taxed in the home jurisdiction of the business), while California has a mixed system in which state, county, and municipal taxes are assessed on an origin basis but special districts use a destination-based approach.[2] Similarly, the subnational VATs in Brazil and Argentina and the regional business tax in Italy (imposta regionala sulle attività produttive or IRAP) are origin-based VAT, as is the VAT in Japan (Bird and Gendron, 2007; Crawford, Keen and Smith, 2010). Finally, note that the Hall and Rabushka (2007) flat tax proposal in the United States, as well as most of its many progeny which are still attracting the interest of some proponents of tax reform, is essentially a "two-part" origin-based VAT.[3]

Despite the vast literature on different forms of VATs, an origin-based VAT has not been analyzed in a model of tax competition in which public services are provided to firms. To the best of our knowledge, this paper, along with Gugl and Zodrow (2015), is the first to examine this issue.

In the next two sections, we present the model and discuss our results on the production tax. We then contrast these results with the well-known properties of capital taxation in Section 4. Section 5 compares the efficiency properties of a capital tax and a production tax, and Section 6 concludes. We provide a detailed discussion of log modularity in production in the Appendix.

---

[2]The 11 states with origin-based treatment of intrastate sales are Arizona, Illinois, Mississippi, Missouri, New Mexico, Ohio, Pennsylvania, Tennessee, Texas, Utah, and Virginia (Faggiano, 2017).

[3]The Hall-Rabushka flat tax uses the "subtraction" method rather than the almost universally used "invoice-credit" VAT method. Under the subtraction method wages are deductible from the tax base at the business level but taxed, subject to a standard deduction and personal exemptions, at the individual level.

2. The Model

Our model follows the ZM (1986) framework.[4,5] A federation or union consists of N jurisdictions, each with the same number of residents who are immobile across jurisdictions. All residents have identical preferences and endowments. Individuals work where they live, provide a fixed amount of labor, L, and obtain utility from consumption of an aggregate composite good, X. The labor supply of each jurisdiction is therefore fixed.[6] People own an equal share of the union's capital stock, $\bar{K}$ which is fixed in total supply at $N\bar{K}$.

Labor and capital are the private inputs in the production of the consumption good. In addition, the local government provides a fully congestible business public service, denoted by B_i, that is used directly in the production of the consumption good. Each jurisdiction produces with a technology characterized by constant returns to scale (CRS) in the two private inputs and the public input. We assume throughout the paper that the production function is strictly concave in capital and the business public service. The consumption good is assumed to be tradable and is taken as the numeraire. We assume that the number of firms is fixed in each jurisdiction (or equivalently, given CRS, that there is a single representative firm) and focus therefore on the aggregate production function in each jurisdiction, given by $F(B_i, K_i, L)$. The marginal product of each input is positive and strictly decreasing and cross derivatives are positive.[7] That is, $F_B, F_K, F_L > 0$, $F_{BB}, F_{KK}, F_{LL} < 0$, and $F_{BK}, F_{BL}, F_{KL} > 0$. The consumption good can be transformed into the public service at a constant marginal rate of transformation of 1, so the unit cost of B is also equal to one,[8] i.e., for the economy as a whole

---

[4] Gugl and Zodrow (2015) provide further discussion of the assumptions of the model.

[5] See also Wilson (1986). For reviews of the tax competition literature, see Wilson (1999), Wilson and Wildasin (2004), and Zodrow (2003, 2010).

[6] The fixed factor can also be thought of as a combination of labor and land, as assumed by ZM.

[7] See, e.g., ZM, Bayindir-Upmann (1998), Keen and Marchand (1997), Dhillon *et al.* (2007) for the same assumptions.

[8] We follow most of the literature in assuming constant marginal costs for business public services (Oates and Schwab, 1988 and 1991; Sinn, 1997, Bayindir-Upmann, 1998; Keen and Marchand, 1997; Richter, 1994; and Matsumoto, 2000). Two alternative approaches, which Matsomoto (2000) points out are equivalent, would be to assume either an imperfectly congestible public input and a constant marginal cost of producing that public input,

$$\sum_{i=1}^{N} F(B_i, K_i, L) = \sum_{i=1}^{N} X_i + B_i. \tag{1}$$

Before we analyze the decisions of the governments of the local jurisdictions, we derive the efficient amount of business public services in this economy, denoted by B and state the conditions that lead to efficient local production of business public services, B, in each jurisdiction.

To create a benchmark, we begin by calculating the efficient amount of business public services if all inputs can move freely across jurisdictions. Given CRS,

$$F(B, N\bar{K}, NL) = NF(B/N, \bar{K}, L) \tag{2}$$

This function implies that production is independent of where labor is located. Although we assume labor is fixed and identically distributed across jurisdictions, for now we neglect this constraint to determine the allocation of labor, capital, and business public services that is efficient without jurisdiction-specific constraints. Since the total amounts of capital and labor are fixed in the whole economy, and consumers care only about the consumption good, the sole choice variable in determining efficiency is how much business public services should be produced to maximize consumption, that is,

$$\max_{B} F(B, N\bar{K}, NL) - B. \tag{3}$$

The first order condition is

$$F_B - 1 = 0, \tag{4}$$

which simply indicates that the efficient aggregate amount of business public services occurs where the marginal product of such services equals the marginal rate of transformation of 1. Given our assumption of identical jurisdictions and fixed labor, the efficient amount of capital in each jurisdiction is equal to $\bar{K}$ and the efficiency condition for public services in each jurisdiction is

$$F_B(B, \bar{K}, L) - 1 = 0. \tag{5}$$

---

or a perfectly congestible public input (i.e., our publicly provided private service) and decreasing marginal costs of producing the public service.

In analyzing the impact of financing business public services either with a capital tax or a tax on production, we compare the marginal productivity of business public services in a jurisdiction under either of the two taxes with the efficient marginal productivity of one. If the marginal productivity of business public services is smaller (larger) than one, there is overprovision (underprovision) as, in equilibrium, the amount of public services that each jurisdiction provides is larger (smaller) than the efficient amount. Next, we turn to the financing of business public services with a production tax.

3. Production Tax

Suppose that local jurisdictions tax local production to finance the provision of public services to firms. The amount of capital a local jurisdiction might attract depends on the level of business public services and the production tax rate t_i; hence, K is a function of the policy mix B_i, t_i. We derive below the perceived change in capital in a jurisdiction as it increases its production tax to finance an increase in its level of business public services. For now, we simply note that capital is perceived to change with changes in the policy mix, i.e., $K_i(B_i, t_i)$.

The local government's budget constraint is given by

$$B_i = t_i F(B_i, K_i(B_i, t_i), L) + H, \tag{6}$$

where H is a fixed amount of public services that is financed externally. We will focus on the jurisdiction's problem when $H = 0$, but it is useful to consider the case of $H > 0$ when interpreting the Lagrange multiplier λ below.

Firms maximize profits, given factor prices, the tax on production, and the level of local business public services provided. They demand both labor and capital, but since labor is fixed in each jurisdiction, the local labor market will clear at L. Since capital is perfectly mobile across jurisdictions, the after-tax rate of return to capital, r, is the same in every jurisdiction. The jurisdiction takes as given the firm's profit maximization condition

$$(1 - t)\, F_K(B_i, K_i(B_i, t_i), L) = r. \tag{7}$$

We assume the local government acts to maximize the welfare of its representative resident, who owns all of the fixed labor input, and that any profits earned from production due to the provision of business public services will accrue to that resident as well. Thus, the profits in any given jurisdiction enter the local government's social welfare function together with locally earned wages and the capital income earned by its resident. To simplify the notation below, we suppress the subscript i in analyzing a single local government's optimization problem, which is to choose the production tax rate and the level of business public services to

$$\max_{B,t}\left[(1-t)F(B,K(B,t),L)-rK(B,t)\right]+r\bar{K}, \tag{8}$$

subject to Eqs. (6) and (7).

The term in square brackets of Eq. (8) is the sum of wage income and profits generated in the jurisdiction. The Lagrange function for the government's optimization problem is

$$\max_{B,t}\left[(1-t)F(B,K(B,t),L)-rK(B,t)\right] \\ +r\bar{K}+\lambda[H+tF(B,K(B,t),L)-B]. \tag{9}$$

The first order conditions with respect to B, t taking Eq. (7) into account are

$$(1-t)F_B+\lambda\left(tF_B+tF_K\frac{\partial K}{\partial B}-1\right)=0 \tag{10}$$

$$-F+\lambda\left(F+tF_K\frac{\partial K}{\partial t}\right)=0. \tag{11}$$

Note that at the optimal production tax and level of business public services, an increase in H and hence less reliance on self-financing of business public services leads to an increase in residents' income/consumption equal to λ.

Consider first the hypothetical case in which capital is fixed in a jurisdiction, i.e., $\partial K/\partial B$ and $\partial K/\partial t$ are zero. In this case, the first order conditions imply that the local jurisdiction provides business public services such that $F_B = 1$ and that $\lambda = 1$. By the Envelope Theorem, the Lagrange multiplier measures how much residents' income would increase if local jurisdictions faced a "soft" budget constraint and were given one unit of public services for free. Given that the Lagrange multiplier is 1 when local jurisdictions do not perceive a change in the capital in their jurisdiction, residents' income would go up by 1, which is equal to the marginal rate of transformation between the consumption good and business public services; as local governments receive a unit of the business public service for free, they save the marginal cost of business public services.

By comparison, if capital reacts to changes in the level of business public services and the production tax, then $\partial K/\partial B$ and $\partial K/\partial t$ are derived as follows. Differentiating Eq. (7) with respect to the production tax and capital and solving for $\partial K/\partial B$ yields

$$\frac{\partial K}{\partial B} = \frac{-F_{KB}}{F_{KK}} > 0. \tag{12}$$

Differentiating Eq. (7) with respect to business public services and capital and solving for *dK*/*dt* yields

$$\frac{\partial K}{\partial t} = \frac{F_K}{(1-t)F_{KK}} < 0. \tag{13}$$

Thus, from the local government's perspective, an increase in the production tax without an increase in public services would drive out capital, and an increase in public services without an increase in the production tax would attract capital to the jurisdiction. These two perceived distortions created by mobile capital need to be considered in setting the optimal production tax rate and the associated level of business public services. Note that the two distortions are characterized as perceived in the sense that, in equilibrium, each jurisdiction follows the same policies and thus adopts the same production tax rate, so that each jurisdiction receives an equal share of the total (mobile) national capital stock.

If we were to impose a consumption tax, c, instead of the production tax, this would be equivalent to imposing an income tax on residents on all sources of income and thus would yield a budget balance condition of

$$B = c[F(B, K, L) - rK + r\bar{K}] + H,$$

and a profit maximization constraint

$$F_K = r.$$

With these changes to our model, a consumption tax, i.e., a destination-based VAT, would lead to efficiency as all sources of distortion would be removed. However, as discussed in our introduction, we focus on taxes that are levied on business to examine the extent to which they can be viewed as benefit-related taxes.

Returning to our analysis of a production tax, substituting from Eqs. (12) and (13) into the first order conditions (10–11) yields the optimal tax rate

$$t = \frac{(1-F_B)F_{KK}F}{F_K(F_BF_K - FF_{KB})}. \tag{14}$$

Note that by Young's Theorem, $F_{KB} = F_{BK}$. The elasticity of the marginal productivity of capital with respect to an increase in capital is $\varepsilon_{F_K,K} = -F_{KK}K/F_K$, the elasticity of the marginal productivity of public services with respect to an increase in capital is $\varepsilon_{F_B,K} = F_{BK}K/F_B$, and the output elasticity of capital is $\varepsilon_k = F_KK/F$. Using these elasticities, Eq. (14) becomes

$$t = \frac{(1-F_B)\varepsilon_{F_K,K}}{F_B(\varepsilon_{F_B,K} - \varepsilon_K)}. \tag{15}$$

Whether the production tax rate leads to overprovision or underprovision of business public services therefore depends on the difference between $\varepsilon_{F_B,K}$ and ε_K. The numerator of Eq. (15) is positive if there is overprovision of public services, i.e., if $F_B < 1$ and an interior solution for the production tax rate must thus be characterized by a positive difference between $\varepsilon_{F_B,K}$ and ε_K. We summarize our finding below.

Proposition 1: *With a positive production tax rate, overprovision of business public services occurs if at* $F_B < 1, \varepsilon_{F_B,K} > \varepsilon_K$. *Underprovision occurs if at* $F_B > 1, \varepsilon_{F_B,K} < \varepsilon_K$.

In the case in which production functions are log submodular or log supermodular, $\varepsilon_{F_B,K}$ and ε_K exhibit the same relationship to each other, regardless of the amounts of *B*, *K*, and *L*.

Lemma 1: *A production function is log sub (super) modular if and only if* $\varepsilon_{F_B,K} < \varepsilon_K (\varepsilon_{F_B,K} > \varepsilon_K)$.

The proof of Lemma 1 is provided in the Appendix, which includes a detailed discussion of log sub (super) modularity.

In the simulations performed in Gugl and Zodrow (2015), we use the CES production function with an elasticity of substitution less than 1 as an example of a log supermodular production function and the CES production function with an elasticity of substitution greater than 1 as an example of a log submodular production function. We provide more examples of log sub (super) modular production functions in the Appendix.

Our next result follows immediately from Lemma 1 and Proposition 1.

Corollary 1: *A production tax is inefficient whenever the production function is log submodular or log supermodular in capital and business public services. Log submodularity (supermodularity) leads to underprovision (overprovision) of business public services.*

Note that Eq. (15) cannot be used to assess the interior solution if the difference between $\varepsilon_{F_B,K}$ and ε_K is zero. Instead, we take a different approach to assess this case and ask what would happen when a budget-balanced increase in the tax rate and public services is considered, in which case both budget balance and the firm's profit maximization condition, that is, Eqs. (6) and (7), must hold. Totally differentiating both equations with respect to the production tax, capital, and the public service, yields

$$\frac{dK}{dt} = \frac{(1-tF_B)F_K - (1-t)F_{KB}F}{(1-t)(F_{KB}tF_K + (1-tF_B)F_{KK})}. \tag{16}$$

Suppose jurisdictions choose the efficient amount of business public services, i.e. $F_B = 1$. In this case Eq. (16) becomes

$$\frac{dK}{dt} = \frac{F_K - F_{KB}F}{(F_{KB}tF_K + (1-t)F_{KK})}. \tag{17}$$

Governments will set the level of business public services efficiently only if they are assured that no capital flows in or out of their jurisdiction at the tax rate that leads to $F_B = 1$. Put differently, $dK/dt = 0$, if at $F_B = 1$ the numerator of Eq. (17) is zero and hence $F_B F_K = F_{KB} F$ at $F_B = 1$. In terms of elasticities, we need the difference between $\varepsilon_{F_B,K}$ and ε_K to be zero at $F_B = 1$.

We summarize our result in the next proposition.

Proposition 2: *With a positive production tax rate, efficient provision of business public services occurs if at* $F_B = 1$, $\varepsilon_{F_B,K} = \varepsilon_K$.

Lemma 2: *The equality $\varepsilon_{F_B,K} = \varepsilon_K$ is always satisfied when the production function is log modular in B and K.*

The proof is in the Appendix, where we provide examples of log modular production functions. As noted previously, a prominent example of the log modular case is the Cobb–Douglas function.

Corollary 2: *If a production function is log modular, a production tax is efficient.*

The intuition underlying these results is as follows. The government of the jurisdiction considering an increase in the production tax balances two factors. First, an increase in the tax will reduce profits, and thus tends to drive capital out of the jurisdiction. Second, the increase in business public services financed with the tax will increase the productivity of capital (generating more output at any given level of capital), and thus attract capital to the jurisdiction, which will in turn increase the productivity of local business public services. The case of log modularity corresponds to a production function for which these two effects are exactly offsetting. In this case, the increase in the capital stock attracted by the increase in public services generates an "average" increase in the productivity of public services, that is, one equal to the increase in output due to the same increase in capital.

By comparison, in the case of a log supermodular production function, the production tax increase has an additional benefit: the production function is such that, as the capital stock increases in response to the provision of additional public services, the productivity of public services increases more than proportionately. This additional benefit implies that the total marginal benefit to capital of the additional production-tax-financed public services outweighs the cost of paying the additional tax, and the production tax attracts capital to the jurisdiction. This ability to attract capital is sufficient to cause the government of the jurisdiction to overprovide business public services in order to attract additional capital. (It does not take into account the cost to other jurisdictions that are losing capital as a result of their policy.)

These results are reversed in the case of a log submodular production function, as the productivity of public services increases less than proportionately (relative to the increase in output) as additional capital is attracted to the jurisdiction with production-tax-financed public services, in which case the tax effect outweighs the productivity effect, and capital is driven out of the jurisdiction. As noted above, these two distortions attributable to the mobility of capital are only perceived distortions in the sense that, in equilibrium, each jurisdiction follows the same policies and thus adopts the same production tax rate, so that each jurisdiction receives an equal share of the total (mobile) national capital stock.

4. Capital Tax

Many authors have analyzed capital taxes using the original ZM framework.[9] Our analysis of capital taxation follows the approach used above to analyze the production tax in order to facilitate comparisons of the effects of the capital tax to those of the production tax.

Suppose that local governments impose a tax on capital at rate τ to finance business public services. The firm's condition for profit maximization under the capital tax is

$$F_K(B, K(B, \tau), L) = r + \tau. \tag{18}$$

Analogous to the production tax case, the jurisdiction solves the problem

$$\max_{B,\tau}[F(B,K(B,\tau),L)-(r+\tau)K]+r\bar{K}+\mu[H+\tau K-B], \tag{19}$$

subject to Eq. (18), where the first term in square brackets is the sum of wage income and profits generated in the jurisdiction and the second term in square brackets reflects the jurisdiction's budget constraint. The first order conditions for the government's optimization problem are

$$F_B + \mu\left(\tau\frac{\partial K}{\partial B}-1\right)=0 \tag{20}$$

$$-K + \mu\left(K+\tau\frac{\partial K}{\partial \tau}\right)=0. \tag{21}$$

As in the previous section, if the capital stock is unchanged in the jurisdiction, $F_B = \mu = 1$.

[9] For a detailed literature review, see Gugl and Zodrow (2015).

The jurisdiction takes the firm's profit maximization condition as given when deriving its perceived change in capital due to changes in the capital tax rate and the level of business public services. Differentiating Eq. (19) with respect to the capital tax and capital and solving for $\partial K/\partial \tau$ yields

$$\frac{\partial K}{\partial \tau} = \frac{1}{F_{KK}} < 0. \tag{22}$$

The reaction of capital to an increase in the level of public services is the same under both taxes and is given by Eq. (12).

From Eqs. (12), (20), (21) and (22) we find the optimal capital tax

$$\tau = \frac{-F_{KK} K(1 - F_B)}{F_{KK} K - F_B}. \tag{23}$$

Expressing the optimal capital tax Eq. (23) in terms of the elasticity of the marginal productivity of business public services with respect to an increase in capital,

$$\tau = \frac{F_K (1 - F_B)\varepsilon_{F_K, K}}{F_B(\varepsilon_{F_B} K^{-1})}, \tag{24}$$

which implies our next result.

Proposition 3: *With a positive capital tax, underprovision of business public services occurs if at* $F_B > 1, \varepsilon_{F_B,K} < 1$. *Overprovision of business public services occurs if at* $F_B < 1, \varepsilon_{F_B,K} > 1$.

Proposition 3 states that if we deal with production functions that exhibit $\varepsilon_{F_B,K} < 1$ for any B and K, we will always have underprovision of public services under a capital tax.[10]

Note that Eq. (24) cannot be used to assess the interior solution if $\varepsilon_{F_B,K} = 1$. In order to examine this case, consider again the perceived outflow of capital after taking into account budget balance, following the approach we utilized for the production tax in Section 3, or

$$\frac{dK}{d\tau} = \frac{1 - F_{KB} K}{F_{KK} + \tau F_{KB}} = \frac{F_B(1 - \varepsilon_{F_B, K})}{F_{KK} + \tau F_{KB}}. \tag{25}$$

[10] Such is the case for a Cobb-Douglas production function and any CES production function with substitution elasticity greater than 1; see, e.g., Gugl and Zodrow (2015).

Local jurisdictions do not perceive an outflow of capital if $\varepsilon_{F_B,K} = 1$. This implies

Proposition 4: *With a positive capital tax, efficient provision of business public services occurs if and only if at* $F_B = 1$, $\varepsilon_{F_B,K} = 1$.

Propositions 3 and 4 relate to the existing literature on the efficient provision of business public services with a capital tax. Matsumoto (1998, p. 471) notes: "If the number of firms is constant in each jurisdiction (normalized to one), [...] [F_B] may be below one because the sign of [$F_{KB}K - F_B$]is indeterminate under linear homogeneity with respect to all inputs. This argument corresponds to the Noiset (1995) result of potential overprovision in the [ZM] model where the variability of the number of firms is not explicitly considered." Dhillon *et al.* (2007) construct a model with two production inputs (capital and public services only) and then show that overprovision, efficient provision, or underprovision of business public services can occur depending on whether the production function is only locally or globally strictly concave in capital and the public service. In Gugl and Zodrow (2015), we use a CES production function with a substitution elasticity less than one to provide numerical examples in which the capital tax is efficient.

5. Efficiency Properties of the Production and Capital Taxes

The various equilibrium outcomes under the production tax and capital tax regimes can be summarized as follows (Table 19.1).

We turn next to an evaluation of the relative efficiency properties of the two taxes.

Corollaries 1 and 2 identify the properties of the production function that guarantee efficient provision, overprovision, or underprovision under the

Table 19.1.
Comparison of Production Tax and Capital Tax Equilibria

	Efficient provision $F_B = 1$	Under provision $F_B > 1$	Over provision $F_B < 1$
Production tax	$\varepsilon_{F_B,K} = \varepsilon_K$	$\varepsilon_{F_B,K} < \varepsilon_K$	$\varepsilon_{F_B,K} > \varepsilon_K$
Capital tax	$\varepsilon_{F_B,K} = 1$	$\varepsilon_{F_B,K} < 1$	$\varepsilon_{F_B,K} > 1$

production tax. We first consider production functions for which log modularity (with $\varepsilon_{F_B,K} = \varepsilon_K$) or log submodularity (with $\varepsilon_{F_B,K} < \varepsilon_K$) holds and investigate the relative efficiency properties of the production tax and the capital tax under the same technologies. In order to do this, it is important to note how these properties relate to the question of whether $\varepsilon_{F_B,K} < 1$.

Proposition 5: *If $F(B, K, L)$ is log submodular or log modular and strictly concave in (B, K), then $\varepsilon_{F_B,K} < 1$.*

***Proof*:** For a strictly concave function in K, $F_K K < F$ and hence $\varepsilon_K < 1$. By Lemmas 1 and 2, a log (sub) modular production function in (B, K) exhibits $\varepsilon_{F_B,K} \leq \varepsilon_K$. Together, these two properties imply the stated result. Note, however, that even if $\varepsilon_K < 1$ holds, there is no restriction on the log modularity property of $F(B, K, L)$ in (B, K).

Proposition 5 in turn implies

Proposition 6: *If $F(B, K, L)$ is log modular, then the production tax leads to efficient provision while the capital tax leads to underprovision of business public services; hence the production tax is more efficient than the capital tax.*

By comparison, in the case of log submodular production functions, underprovision occurs under both tax regimes. Nevertheless, it is possible to rank the efficiency properties of the two taxes, as shown in

Proposition 7: *Suppose that the production function is log submodular in (B, K) and that interior solutions to both the optimal capital tax and the optimal production tax problems exist. Under these conditions, the production tax is unambiguously more efficient than the capital tax.*

***Proof*:** We first provide an outline of the proof. Suppose that under the capital tax each jurisdiction chooses the tax rate optimally and the economy is in equilibrium so that $B^{\tau} = \tau \bar{K}$. Total output is the same in all jurisdictions (given symmetry and a fixed national aggregate capital stock), and thus all derivatives of the production function with respect to B and K are also identical across jurisdictions. Using the optimality condition for the capital tax Eq. (24) we can calculate the production tax equivalent that would result at the same level of business public services as under the optimal capital tax equilibrium if all jurisdictions assumed that capital reacts to their provision of public services and to a tax increase exactly as under the equilibrium capital tax. We then show that the optimality condition for the production tax Eq. (15) does not hold simultaneously at this production tax rate. In particular, the level of the production tax given the calculated elasticities at B^{τ} and $\bar{K}$ is higher, which implies a larger B; this in turn implies that, for a given increase in business public services B, the jurisdiction perceives a smaller capital outflow under a production tax than under the capital tax, which implies a higher level of B under the optimal production tax than under the optimal capital tax. Since both tax regimes lead to underprovision, the production tax must thus result in less underprovision than the capital tax.

More formally, the production tax equivalent of the capital tax rate under the optimal capital tax equilibrium is given by

$$t^{\tau} = \frac{B^{\tau}}{F\left(B^{\tau},\bar{K},L\right)} = \frac{F_K^{\tau}\left(1-F_B^{\tau}\right)\varepsilon_{F_K,K}^{\tau}\bar{K}}{F_B^{\tau}\left(\varepsilon_{F_B,K}^{\tau}-1\right)F^{\tau}}. \tag{26}$$

The optimal production tax, however, at the elasticities evaluated at B^{τ} and $\bar{K}$ is

$$t\left(B^{\tau},\bar{K}\right) = \frac{\left(1-F_B^{\tau}\right)\varepsilon_{F_K,K}^{\tau}}{F_B^{\tau}\left(\varepsilon_{F_B,K}^{\tau}\quad \varepsilon_K^{\tau}\right)}. \tag{27}$$

Thus, if $t^{\tau} < t(B^{\tau},\bar{K})$, then the capital tax results in more underprovision of business public services than the production tax and hence is less efficient. Note that

$$\frac{F_K^{\tau}\left(1-F_B^{\tau}\right)\varepsilon_{F_K,K}^{\tau}\bar{K}}{F_B^{\tau}\left(\varepsilon_{F_B,K}^{\tau}-1\right)F^{\tau}} < \frac{\left(1-F_B^{\tau}\right)\varepsilon_{F_K,K}^{\tau}}{F_B^{\tau}\left(\varepsilon_{F_B,K}^{\tau}-\varepsilon_K^{\tau}\right)} \tag{28}$$

if and only if

$$-\frac{1}{\varepsilon_K^{\tau}}\left(\varepsilon_{F_B,K}^{\tau}-1\right) > -\left(\varepsilon_{F_B,K}^{\tau}-\varepsilon_K^{\tau}\right), \tag{29}$$

which is unambiguously true, as both sides are positive and strict concavity of the production function in K implies that the left-hand side is greater than the right-hand side.

Our results in the cases of log modular and log submodular production functions validate the conjecture that a broad-based tax on local production is more efficient than a tax on capital. However, there is no analog to Proposition 7 in the case of log supermodular production functions, as either the production tax or the capital tax can be the more efficient business tax option. Moreover, there are prominent examples of such functions. As noted previously, the family of CES production functions includes examples of all three log modularity properties — log submodularity, log modularity, and log supermodularity — depending on whether the elasticity of substitution between capital and public services/labor is greater than, equal to, or less than one. In Gugl and Zodrow (2015), we examine more closely CES production functions characterized by log supermodularity in the context of tax competition in the provision of business public services. We show that both the production tax and the capital tax can be the more efficient tax option, but in the latter case, the efficiency gain from utilizing the capital tax instead of the production tax is relatively small. By comparison, relatively large efficiency gains can sometimes be obtained by using the production tax rather than the capital tax in those cases in which the production tax is the more efficient tax option.

6. Conclusion

Can a production tax, such as an origin-based value-added tax, approximate a benefit tax for public services provided to businesses, as suggested by Bird (2000) and Hines (2003)? How does a source-based capital tax such as the property tax compare to a production tax as a proxy for a benefit tax? Using the ZM model of interjurisdictional tax competition, we find that a production tax more closely approximates a benefit tax than does a capital tax in many instances. In particular, although a production tax is efficient only when the production function is log modular in business public services and capital, it is always *less* inefficient than a capital tax in the case of log submodular production technologies.

The basic intuition underlying the result that the production tax is often more efficient than the capital tax is that the capital tax applies to a narrower and relatively mobile tax base, while the production tax applies to a broader base that includes both relatively immobile labor and local business public services. However, if there is very strong complementarity between capital and business public services (as assumed by Sinn, 1997 and Oates and Schwab, 1988, 1991), then the capital tax is more likely to approximate a benefit tax than when capital and business public services are more substitutable. By comparison, in the presence of significant substitution opportunities between capital and business public services, a broader tax base that includes both immobile labor and the contribution of public services to output mimics more closely efficient user charges on public services.[11]

Our results have some interesting implications for potential reforms of state/provincial tax systems, as they suggest that a production tax may be a viable business tax alternative to the state/provincial retail sales tax, which is typically characterized by significant taxation of business inputs similar to that which occurs under a capital tax. By comparison, at least under certain circumstances in our admittedly highly stylized model, a production tax is less distortionary than the capital tax portion of a retail sales tax.

Appendix: Log (Sub/Super) Modularity

Before discussing log (sub/super) modularity, we first review (sub/super) modularity and then point out the differences between these two related concepts.

A.1 *Definition and examples*

To define (sub/super) modularity of B and K, consider any two input vectors with the same amount of labor but different amounts of B and K, with one input vector containing strictly less of both $(\underline{B}, \underline{K}, L)$ than the other

[11] In an earlier version of this paper (Gugl and Zodrow, cesifo1_wp5555.pdf), we also compared the production tax to a uniform tax on only private inputs, under the assumption of Cobb-Douglas production functions. The latter tax is efficient in Matsumoto and Sugahara (2017) where the production function is CRS in private inputs only, but we show that it is inefficient in the case of many Cobb-Douglas production functions if the function is CRS in all inputs including public services even though such technology implies that the production tax is efficient.

$(\bar{B},\bar{K},L)$. Since we keep labor the same in all our analysis, L is suppressed in our analysis. By definition, modularity holds if and only if

$$F(\underline{B},\underline{K})+F(\bar{B},\bar{K})=F(\underline{B},\bar{K})+F(\bar{B},\underline{K}). \tag{A1}$$

Under modularity, a given increase in one input results in the same increase of output regardless of how much output is being produced. Another way of thinking about the implications of modularity is by choosing the input combinations on the RHS of Eq. (A1) such that

$$F(\underline{B},\bar{K})=F(\bar{B},\underline{K})=Y^0. \tag{A2}$$

With modularity, the arithmetic mean of $F(\underline{B},\underline{K})$ and $F(\bar{B},\bar{K})$ must equal Y^0. For super (sub) modularity, the arithmetic mean of $F(\underline{B},\underline{K})$ and $F(\bar{B},\bar{K})$ must be greater (less) than Y^0. For example, in the case of submodularity, total output of Y^0 can be produced with the arithmetic mean of $F(\underline{B},\underline{K})$ and some other output level generated with larger amounts of both inputs, but the output level $F(\bar{B},\bar{K})$ is not large enough to achieve this; instead, inputs larger than $(\bar{B},\bar{K})$ are necessary to achieve an arithmetic mean of Y^0.

An example of a production function that is modular in B and K is one for which the functions involving inputs B and K enter additively, i.e.,

$$F(B,K,L)=g(B)h(L)+i(K)j(L)+m(B)+o(K)+p(L),$$

where all the individual functions are increasing in their inputs. By comparison, a function of the form

$$F(B,K,L)=g(B)h(L)i(K)j(L)+m(B)+o(K)+p(L)$$

is supermodular.

Log modularity, in contrast, compares relative marginal products rather than the absolute marginal products of inputs. That is, log modularity in B and K holds if and only if

$$F(\underline{B},\underline{K})F(\bar{B},\bar{K})=F(\underline{B},\bar{K})F(\bar{B},\underline{K}). \tag{A3}$$

As in the discussion of (sub/super) modularity, another way to think about the implications of log modularity is by choosing the input combinations on the RHS of Eq. (A3) so that (A2) holds. For log modularity, the *geometric* mean of $F(\underline{B},\underline{K})$ and $F(\bar{B},\bar{K})$ must equal Y^0. For log super (sub) modularity, the geometric mean of $F(\underline{B},\underline{K})$ and $F(\bar{B},\bar{K})$ must be greater (less) than Y^0. For example, in the case of log submodularity, total output of Y^0 can be produced with the geometric mean of $F(\underline{B},\underline{K})$ and some other output level generated with higher amounts of both inputs, but the output level $F(\overline{B},\overline{K})$ is not large enough to achieve this; instead, inputs larger than $(\overline{B},\overline{K})$ are necessary to achieve a geometric mean of Y^0.

An example of a production function that is log modular in B and K is one for which the inputs enter multiplicatively, e.g.,

$$F(B, K, L) = g(B)\, h(K)\, i(L),$$

where all the individual functions are increasing in their inputs. Note that such functions are simultaneously supermodular in B and K. An example of a log supermodular function is

$$F(B, K, L) = g(B)\, h(K)\, i(L) + j(L),$$

which is simultaneously super modular in B and K.

An example of a log submodular function is

$$F(B, K, L) = g(B) + h(K) + i(L),$$

which is simultaneously modular in B and K. However, log submodular functions can also be simultaneously supermodular; an example is

$$F(B, K, L) = [g(B) + h(K) + i(L)]^{\alpha},$$

where $\alpha > 0$.

A.2. *Proof of Lemma 1: Expressing log (sub/super) modularity in terms of elasticities*

Note that log modularity can be expressed as

$$\frac{F(\underline{B},\overline{K})}{F(\underline{B},\underline{K})} = \frac{F(\overline{B},\overline{K})}{F(\overline{B},\underline{K})}. \tag{A4}$$

Hence a log modular production function must exhibit the same percentage change in output due to a given increase in K, regardless of the level of B, or

$$\frac{\partial \varepsilon_K}{\partial B} = 0, \tag{A5}$$

where $\varepsilon K = F_K K/F$, which holds if and only if

$$K\frac{F_{KB}F - F_B F_K}{F^2} = 0. \tag{A6}$$

Since by Young's Theorem $F_{KB} = F_{BK}$, and $\varepsilon_{F_B,K} = F_{BK}K / F_B$, (A6) can be expressed as

$$\varepsilon_{F_B,K} = \varepsilon_K . \tag{A7}$$

Similarly, log submodularity requires $\varepsilon_{F_B,K} < \varepsilon_K$ and log supermodularity requires $\varepsilon_{F_B,K} > \varepsilon_K$.

Acknowledgements

We thank an anonymous referee, Steve Billon, Jed Brewer, Alexander Ebertz, Bill Fox, Timothy Goodspeed, Brad Hackinen, Andreas Haufler, James Hines, Margaret McKeehan, Matt Krzepkowski, David Wildasin, and John Wilson for helpful comments on earlier versions of this paper.

References

Bird, R. M. (2000). Subnational VATs: Experience and prospects. *Proceedings. Annual Conference on Taxation and Minutes of the Annual Meeting of the National Tax Association,* 93, 223–228.

Bird, R. M. (2003). A new look at business taxes. *Tax Notes International,* 30(7), 695–711.

Bird, R. M., & Gendron, P-P. (2007). *The VAT in developing and transitional countries.* Cambridge, UK: Cambridge University Press.

Bayindir-Upmann, T. (1998). Two games of interjurisdictional competition when local governments provide industrial public goods. *International Tax and Public Finance,* 5, 471–487.

CBC News (2011). B.C. promises HST cut to 10% by 2014: Tax hike for corporations and cheques for families also promised. http://www.cbc.ca/news/canada/britishcolumbia/story/2011/05/25/bc-hst-changes.html. Accessed 15 August 2018.

Crawford, I., Keen, M., & Smith, S. (2010). Value-added tax and excises. In Institute for Fiscal Studies (Ed.), *Dimensions of Tax Design: The Mirrlees Review* (pp. 275–362). London, UK: Oxford University Press.

Dhillon, A., Wooders, M., & Zissimos, B. (2007). Tax competition reconsidered. *Journal of Public Economic Theory,* 9(3), 391–423.

Faggiano, M. (2017). Origin-based and destination-based sales tax collection 101. https://blog.taxjar.com/charging-sales-tax-rates/. Accessed 31 August 2018.

Gugl, E., & Zodrow, G. R. (2015). Competition in business taxes and public services: Are production-based taxes superior to capital taxes? *National Tax Journal,* 68(3S), 767–802.

Hall, R., & Rabushka, A. (2007). *The flat tax.* Stanford, CA: Hoover Institution Press.

Haufler, A., & Pflueger, M. (2007). International oligopoly and the taxation of commerce with revenue-constrained governments. *Economica,* 74(295), 451–473.

Hines, J. R. Jr. (2003). Michigan's Flirtation with the Single Business Tax. In C. L. Ballard, P.N. Courant, D. C. Drake, R. C. Fischer, & E. R. Gerber (Eds.), *Michigan at the Millennium: A Benchmark and analysis of its fiscal and economic structure* (pp. 603–628). East Lansing: Michigan State University Press.

Kanbur, R., & Keen, M. (1993). Jeux sans frontiers: Tax competition and tax coordination when countries differ in size. *American Economic Review,* 83(4), 877–892.

Keen, M., & Marchand, M. (1997). Fiscal competition and the pattern of public spending. *Journal of Public Economics,* 66(1), 33–53.

Lockwood, B. (2001). Tax competition and tax co-ordination under destination and origin principles: A synthesis. *Journal of Public Economics,* 81(2), 279 319.

Matsumoto, M. (1998). A note on tax competition and public input provision. *Regional Science and Urban Economics,* 28(4), 465–473.

Matsumoto, M. (2000). A tax competition analysis of congestible public inputs. *Journal of Urban Economics,* 48(2), 242–259.

Matsumoto, M. & Sugahara, K. (2017). A note on production taxation and public-input provision. *The Annals of Regional Sciences,* 59(2), 419–426.

McLure, C. E., Jr. (2003). The value added tax on electronic commerce in the European Union. *International Tax and Public Finance,* 10(6), 753–762.

Mintz, J. M., & Tulkens, H. (1986). Commodity tax competition between member states of a federation, equilibrium and efficiency. *Journal of Public Economics,* 29(2), 133–372.

Noiset, L. (1995). Pigou, Tiebout, property taxation, and the underprovision of local public goods: A comment. *Journal of Urban Economics,* 38(3), 312–316.

Oates, W. E., & Schwab, R. M. (1988). Economic competition among jurisdictions: Efficiency enhancing or distortion inducing? *Journal of Public Economics,* 35(3), 333–354.

Oates, W. E., & Schwab, R. M. (1991). The allocative and distributive implications of local fiscal competition. In D. A. Kenyon & J. Kincaid (Eds.), *Competition among states and local governments: Efficiency and equity in American federalism* (127–146). Washington, DC: The Urban Institute Press.

Richter, W. F. (1994). The efficient allocation of local public factors in Tiebout's tradition. *Regional Science and Urban Economics*, 24(3), 323–340.

Sinn, H-W. (1997). The selection principle and market failure in systems of competition. *Journal of Public Economics,* 66(2), 247–274.

The Independent Panel (2011). HST or PST/GST: It's your decision. http://www.slideshare.net/hstinbc/its-your-decisionhstgstpst. Accessed 15 August 15 2018.

Wilson, J. D. (1986). A theory of interregional tax competition. *Journal of Urban Economics,* 19(3), 296–315.

Wilson, J. D. (1999). Theories of tax competition. *National Tax Journal,* 52(2), 269–304.

Wilson, J. D., & Wildasin, D. E. (2004). Tax competition: Bane or boon?" *Journal of Public Economics,* 88(6), 1065–1091.

Zodrow, G. R. (2003). Tax competition and tax coordination in the European Union. *International Tax and Public Finance,* 10, 651–671.

Zodrow, G. R. (2010). Capital mobility and capital tax competition. *National Tax Journal,* 63(4), 865–901.

Zodrow, G. R., & Mieszkowski, P. (1986). Pigou, Tiebout, property taxation and the underprovision of local public goods. *Journal of Urban Economics,* 19(3), 356–370.

Index